THE LEGAL STATUS OF INTERSEX PERSONS

AF775744

The publication of this book was supported by

UNIVERSITY OF CAMBRIDGE

CFL | CAMBRIDGE FAMILY LAW

LMU LUDWIG-MAXIMILIANS-UNIVERSITÄT MÜNCHEN

Philipps Universität Marburg

DAAD Cambridge

THE LEGAL STATUS OF INTERSEX PERSONS

Edited by
Jens M. Scherpe
Anatol Dutta
Tobias Helms

intersentia
Cambridge – Antwerp – Chicago

Intersentia Ltd
Sheraton House | Castle Park
Cambridge | CB3 0AX | United Kingdom
Tel.: +44 1223 370 170 | Fax: +44 1223 370 169
Email: mail@intersentia.co.uk
www.intersentia.com | www.intersentia.co.uk

Distribution for the UK and Ireland:
NBN International
Airport Business Centre, 10 Thornbury Road
Plymouth, PL6 7PP
United Kingdom
Tel.: +44 1752 202 301 | Fax: +44 1752 202 331
Email: orders@nbninternational.com

Distribution for Europe and all other countries:
Intersentia Publishing nv
Groenstraat 31
2640 Mortsel
Belgium
Tel.: +32 3 680 15 50 | Fax: +32 3 658 71 21
Email: mail@intersentia.be

Distribution for the USA and Canada:
Independent Publishers Group
Order Department
814 North Franklin Street
Chicago, IL 60610
USA
Tel.: +1 800 888 4741 (toll free) | Fax: + 1312 337 5985
Email: orders@ipgbook.com

The Legal Status of Intersex Persons
© The editors and contributors severally 2018

The editors and contributors have asserted the right under the Copyright, Designs and Patents Act 1988, to be identified as authors of this work.

No part of this book may be reproduced, stored in a retrieval system, or transmitted, in any form, or by any means, without prior written permission from Intersentia, or as expressly permitted by law or under the terms agreed with the appropriate reprographic rights organisation. Enquiries concerning reproduction which may not be covered by the above should be addressed to Intersentia at the address above.

Artwork on cover: M.C. Escher's 'Eight Heads' © 2018 The M.C. Escher Company B.V. – Baarn – Holland. All rights reserved. www.mcescher.com

ISBN 978-1-78068-475-8
D/2018/7849/68
NUR 822

British Library Cataloguing in Publication Data. A catalogue record for this book is available from the British Library.

PREFACE

The idea for this book began as a workshop supported by the DAAD Cambridge Research Hub with funds from the German Federal Foreign Office (FFO), the University of Regensburg and Cambridge Family Law.

The workshop was held at the University of Cambridge/Gonville and Caius College on 21–22 July 2016, jointly organised by the editors of this book. The workshop was attended not only by academics from Australia, Germany, the UK, Ireland, New Zealand, Spain and Italy, but also by representatives of the Law Commission of England and Wales, the German Federal Ministry of Justice and Consumer Protection (Berlin), the German Institute for Human Rights (Berlin) and the Ministry for Social Dialogue, Consumer Affairs and Civil Liberties (Malta). While the focus was on legal developments and regulation, there also were contributions from theology, medicine and psychology. There was an intense and productive interdisciplinary and interjurisdictional debate over the two days, and much of this is now reflected in this book. After the workshop, and indeed as a result of it, the research project leading to this book was started, and many additional chapters were commissioned in order to present an even broader discussion of the issues.

However, all major research projects face difficulties of varying kinds, and this one certainly was no exception. Several people who had promised to participate dropped out or failed to deliver. Houses were flooded, illnesses overcome, jobs changed, and children born during the period it took to put this book together. But in the end things came together, and we are pleased with the outcome and the broad range of contributions. We truly hope that this book will contribute to the national and international debates and lead to a focus on the autonomy of the people concerned.

We also are very grateful to many institutions and persons supporting the research project and publication of the book: the Ludwig Maximilian University of Munich for supporting the significant editorial work that needed to be undertaken, and which was handled expertly by Intersentia Publishing; Dafni Lima for her help with the initial editorial work; the Gonville and Caius Conference Office, and particularly Laura Webb, for ensuring that the workshop could take place in such a pleasant and well-organised environment; Ingrid Hobbis of the Cambridge Research Hub for her administrative support; Prof. Chris Young, the Co-Director of the Cambridge Research Hub, for his continuous support of this project; and Intersentia Publishing and particularly Rebecca Moffat, for their work to get this book published. Finally, we would like to thank the contributors to the workshop and particularly the contributors of this volume for their patience and understanding. It has been a long road …

The editors
Cambridge/Munich/Marburg, March 2018

CONTENTS

LIST OF CONTRIBUTORS

Nina Althoff
German Institute for Human Rights, Berlin, Germany

Marjolein van den Brink
School of Law, University of Utrecht, The Netherlands

Morgan Carpenter
Sydney Health Ethics, University of Sydney, Australia; Co-executive Director of Intersex Human Rights Australia (IHRA); GATE, New York, USA

Milton Diamond
John A. Burns School of Medicine, University of Hawai'i, United States of America

Duncan Dormor
United Society Partners in the Gospel, London, England, United Kingdom

Peter Dunne
Faculty of Law, University of Bristol, England, United Kingdom

Anatol Dutta
Faculty of Law, Ludwig Maximilians University of Munich, Germany

Claire Fenton-Glynn
Faculty of Law, University of Cambridge, England, United Kingdom

Jameson Garland
Faculty of Law, Uppsala University, Sweden

Dan Christian Ghattas
Executive Director of Organisation Intersex International Europe (OII Europe), Berlin, Germany

Julie Greenberg
Emeritus Faculty, Thomas Jefferson School of Law, San Diego, California, United States of America

Tobias Helms
Faculty of Law, Philipps University Marburg, Germany

Joe Herbert
John van Geest Centre for Brain Repair, Department of Clinical Neurosciences, University of Cambridge, England, United Kingdom

Ieuan Hughes
Department of Paediatrics, University of Cambridge, England, United Kingdom

Moshe Lavee
Department of Jewish History and Thought, University of Haifa, Israel

Thomas Meyer
Federal Ministry of Justice and Consumer Protection, Berlin, Germany

Tanya Ní Mhuirthile
School of Law and Government, Dublin City University, Ireland

Benjamin Moron-Puech
Faculty of Law, Pantheon-Assas University Paris (Paris II), France

Stefano Osella
Department of Law, European University Institute, Florence, Italy

Ruth Rubio-Marín
Faculty of Law, University of Sevilla, Spain; School of Transnational Governance, European University Institute, Florence, Italy

Tali Artman Partock
Faculty of Divinity, University of Cambridge, England, United Kingdom

Vickie Pasterski
Department of Psychology, University of Cambridge, England, United Kingdom

Walter Pintens
Faculty of Law, Catholic University of Leuven, Belgium; Faculty of Law, Saarland University, Germany

Kirsten Sandberg
Faculty of Law, University of Oslo, Norway

Jens M. Scherpe
Faculty of Law, University of Cambridge, England, United Kingdom; University of Hong Kong; Aalborg University, Denmark

Smita Shah
Department of Law, European University Institute, Florence, Italy

Alain Wijffels
Faculty of Law, Catholic University of Leuven and Catholic University of Louvain, Belgium; Faculty of Law, University of Leiden, The Netherlands; Centre d'Histoire Judiciaire (CNRS), France

THE LEGAL STATUS OF INTERSEX PERSONS: AN INTRODUCTION

Jens M. Scherpe

1. AIM AND PURPOSE OF THIS BOOK

Issues surrounding legal gender have been the subject of much debate in the last decades, at least in the Western jurisdictions. However, much of this debate was focused on recognition of the preferred gender, i.e. the legal issues surround the legal status of transsexual and transgender persons.[1] The legal issues concerning intersex persons, which are distinct and must be considered as such,[2] have received much less attention, particularly in national jurisdictions. From a legal perspective, the key issues are (1) the designation of a legal gender and the right to a gender identity, and (2) the legitimacy of surgical and other medical interventions, as well as injuries caused by them, particularly on new-borns without the capacity to consent. Particularly the latter is of grave concern, and there is a wide debate about the soundness of judicial deference to the clinical management of these conditions as primarily medical matters, as it has become apparent that irreversible surgical interventions and hormonal therapies have been carried out on infants and very young children without long-term data confirming their necessity, safety and efficacy.[3]

---

1 On this, see J.M. Scherpe (ed.), *The Legal Status of Transsexual and Transgender Persons* (2015).

2 On this particular issue, see the chapters by P. Dunne and J.M. Scherpe in this volume.

3 On this, see the chapter by J. Garland and M. Diamond in this chapter, as well as J.M. Scherpe and J. Garland, 'Ethical and Legal Aspects of DSD/Intersex', in *Encyclopedia of Endocrine Diseases*, 2nd ed. (forthcoming in 2018).

The aim of this book is to highlight the need and urgency to deal with these crucial issues, and by providing a wide range of accessible material to make these issues more visible to the general public and thus to further and broaden the debate. To this end, this book not only comprises purely legal views (Parts III–IV), but also medical and psychological (Part I) as well as theological and historical ones (Part II).

2. TERMINOLOGY

But in order to engage in any debate, it is necessary to deal with matters of terminology first, which can be very controversial. It is important to acknowledge at the outset that experiences of gender and sexed bodies are deeply personal and therefore inevitable vary from person to person. Hence, it is impossible to choose a terminology that would reflect everyone's experience of self, and any term chosen therefore may be perceived as inappropriate and even as hurtful. Therefore, it is important to state clearly that the intention of all authors of this volume is to be respectful, and that no offence or disrespect is intended. But in order to have a basis for debate and writing, terminological choices had to be made; and, as can be seen, the authors of the contributions in this volume have made different choices, in line with their own preferences and perceptions. But it is worth stating expressly that while the authors (and indeed the editors) of this book may hold different views on terminology and substance, they are united in the view that the legal issues of intersex must be addressed as a matter of urgency and in accordance with international human rights standards.

In the biomedical debates, the term 'disorder/difference in sex development' (DSD) currently seems to be most widely accepted term.[4] But it needs to be said that the term 'disorder' is highly problematic in this context. While it may be correct from a medical point to say that the physical condition of the persons concerned deviates from the medical norm and therefore is 'disordered', this can be (and indeed is) perceived as discriminating and degrading by the persons concerned.[5] 'Disorder' also implies a pathology and a need to 'bring order', i.e. that there is a need to 'normalise' as far as possible by making the bodies

4 On this, see e.g. I. Hughes, in this volume and I. Hughes, C. Houk, S.F. Ahmed et al., 'Consensus statement on management of intersex disorders' (2006) 91 *Archives of Disease in Childhood* 554–563, as well as P.A. Lee, A Nordenström, C.P. Houk et al., 'Global disorders of sex development update since 2006: perceptions, approach and care' (2016) 85 *Hormone Research in Paediatrics* 158–180.

5 See e.g. E. Reis, 'Divergence or Disorder? The politics of naming intersex' (2007) 50(4) *Perspectives in Biology and Medicine* 535–543 and G. Davis, *Contesting Intersex: The Dubious Diagnosis* (2015). In 2016, a broad group of experts formally recognised that the term 'disorder' is considered stigmatic and unacceptable by some patent groups and support groups, see Lee, Nordenström, Houk et al., above n. 4.

of those concerned fit what the medical perception of 'normal' is. Therefore if 'DSD' is to be used, the first 'D' should be understood to mean 'difference' rather than 'disorder'. This is not merely a semantic change. 'Disorder' implies 'wrongness' and the need to 'order' and to 'normalise', thus encouraging surgical and other medical intervention. By contrast, difference merely means that the person concerned is not the same as the comparator, in principle without any value judgement or implications for any need of action.[6] Another, and arguably better way, would be to use the term 'variance' instead of 'difference'.

However, for the title of this book the term 'intersex' was chosen. As Dan Christian Ghattas explains under the heading 'Who are intersex people?':[7]

> Intersex individuals are born with sex characteristics (such as chromosomes, genitals, and/or hormonal structure) that do not belong strictly to male or female categories, or that belong to both at the same time. Doctors often advise parents to perform surgical and other medical interventions on intersex new-borns and children, to make their body (seemingly) conform to male or female characteristics. In most cases, such interventions are not medically necessary and can have extremely negative consequences on intersex children as they grow older.
>
> 'Intersex' stands for the spectrum of variations of sex characteristics that naturally occur within the human species. It also stands for the acceptance of the physical fact that sex is a spectrum and that people with variations of sex characteristics other than male or female do exist.
>
> Historically, the term 'intersex' was used as if it was as a disorder that needed medical intervention to 'fix it'. In the past two decades, the term has been reframed and established by intersex human rights defenders and their organisations as the human rights-based umbrella term.
>
> Our sex characteristics are set out from birth, whether we are intersex or not. However, the fact that someone has an intersex body can become apparent at different times in their life: at birth, during childhood, in puberty or even in adulthood. Depending on the specific life circumstances and the degree of taboo in their environment, a person might learn that they have an intersex body at a very early age or later in life. Some intersex people never find out at all.

So, while the term 'intersex' may have had negative connotations in the past, it best captures what the legal debates are about. As Ghattas has rightly stated, 'intersex' today has a different connotation, being very prominent in the human rights discourse and should be understood as identifying and empowering.

---

6 Although admittedly being declared 'different' of course also has the potential to be used in a pejorative and degrading way, but certainly less so than being 'disordered'.

7 D.C. Ghattas, *Standing up for the human rights of intersex people – how can you help* (2015), p. 9; available at <https://oiigermany.org/toolkit-standing-up-human-rights-intersex-people/> (last accessed 09.03.2018). Excerpts of this publication can be found in the chapter by D.C. Ghattas in this volume.

It also is being used by human rights-based advocacy groups as well as international human rights authorities. It is for these reasons that it was chosen for the title of this book.

3. CORE LEGAL ISSUES AND THE CONTRIBUTIONS IN THIS BOOK

As mentioned at the beginning, intersex persons face many legal and social problems in society today, but the two core legal issues concern (1) being subjected to surgical and other medical interventions at a time when the person concerned (very often a new-born) does not have the capacity to consent, so the decisions about 'normalising' surgery are taken for them; and (2) the designation of a legal gender at birth or at a later stage in life. The contributions to this book were, inter alia, chosen because of the specific way they address these issues.

To hear directly the voices of the people concerned is absolutely essential for this. Therefore, the decision was taken to begin the book with the Malta Declaration (Statement of the Third International Intersex Forum) of 1 December 2013, the Darlington Statement (Joint Consensus Statement from the Intersex Community Retreat in Darlington) of March 2017 and the Vienna Statement (Statement of the First European Intersex Community Event), also of March 2017. These represent the views and demands of intersex persons and therefore should be considered throughout the book when reading the various contributions (and beyond). For the same reasons, it is also worth highlighting at this stage, in particular, the contributions of Dan Christian Ghattas, the Executive Director of Organisation Intersex International Europe (OII Europe) and Morgan Carpenter, Co-executive Director of Intersex Human Rights Australia (IHRA, formerly Organisation Intersex International Australia).

As already mentioned above, the book is divided into parts. In Part I there are four contributions on the *medical and psychological* views on intersex, including a critical evaluation of the *clinical practice and existing guidelines*.

Part II contains *theological views* from Christian and a rabbinic perspective, as well as some *historical legal background*. Intersex persons have been around since the beginning of humanity, and there is a long and rich history of both religious and legal debates. As these to a certain extent shape the current discourse, or at least can help explain it, it is important to include such contributions.

Part III is the first of the 'legal' parts and contains two contributions on the *intersection of transgender/transsexuality and intersex*. While the former has received much legal and social attention, intersex issues often have been subsumed (and even appropriated) into a broader LBGTI rights discussion. But being intersex is not about sexual orientation and not, at least not primarily, about gender identity. It is about sexed bodies and sex characteristics. Therefore, the legal and other issues of intersex are distinct and must be heard separately and independently. That said, this does not preclude that intersex rights and activism can benefit from the advances and achievements of other minorities, and this is what the contributions in this part deal with.

Part IV canvasses the legal developments in some jurisdictions that are of particular interest, namely *Australia, Sweden, India, the Netherlands, France, Colombia, the USA, Malta* and *Germany*. The latter is of particular interest, first, because of the controversial 2013 legislation which for the first time allowed leaving the gender entry on the birth certificate of a person blank ('indeterminate'), and, second, because of a seminal decision of the *Bundesverfassungsgericht* (German Constitutional Court) in 2017 which mandated the introduction of a legal gender option (or options) other than male or female by the end of 2018, spelling the end for the legal gender binary in Germany.[8] Therefore, three contributions look at the developments in German law. Malta is also of particular importance because the Maltese Gender Identity, Gender Expression and Sex Characteristics Act 2015 made unlawful any sex assignment treatment or surgical intervention on the sex characteristics of a minor if those treatments or interventions could be postponed until the person treated can provide informed consent.

Since designation and recognition of legal gender in one country does not necessarily guarantee that the same legal gender will be recognised/attributed in another, Part V deals with the *private international law* (so cross-border) aspects of intersex.

The book in Part VI concludes with three contributions on the *human rights* aspects of intersex. While these of course have been discussed in the other contributions on individual jurisdictions as well, in this Part they are looked at detached from national jurisdictions and make powerful statements about the general human rights standards to which all jurisdictions ought to adhere.

4. THE BOOK COVER

The artwork chosen for the cover of this book is 'Metamorphosis II' by Maurits Cornelis Escher. Some may note that the same picture was chosen for a book on 'The Legal Status of Transsexual and Transgender Persons'.[9] This of course is no coincidence. In the introduction to that book the following explanation for using this artwork was given:

> The notion of 'male' or 'female', i.e. the gender binary, is often used to impose 'normative' standards and behaviour patterns on people in general, but particularly

8 Bundesverfassungsgericht 10.10.2017, *Zeitschrift für das gesamte Familienrecht (FamRZ)* 2017, 2046. On this, see also the chapters by T. Helms, T. Meyer and N. Althoff in this volume.

9 See above n. 1.

> on transsexual and transgender persons. All this is based on the patently absurd idea that there is something like 'the real male' and 'the real female', and that there are certain behaviours and physical characteristics which precisely define gender. (...)
>
> So while the artwork used is entitled 'Metamorphosis', which generally implies a change of physical appearance and which certainly is not apt in this context, the depictions of the 'male' and 'female' persons in the artwork, almost caricatures, are intended to make a mockery of harmful ideas about rigid 'gender'; also, the 'male' and the 'female' invariably are parts of each other and 'flowing into one another', rendering any clear-cut distinctions between them meaningless. So for the purposes of this book the artwork should be understood to ask questions about, and indeed challenge, strict societal and legal perceptions about gender, as well as the pre-conceptions on which they are based. Moreover, the picture (and this book) can also be understood as a challenge to the binary legal gender system and the very notion of a 'legal gender' itself, suggesting that it is the individual person who matters and not their appearance.[10]

These observations of course hold true and apply equally to the legal and social issues faced by intersex persons. The fact that some physical sex characteristics are not classified by medical standards as strictly male or female (or as belonging to both categories) is not 'the problem'. The problem is how societies and laws currently deal with this, based on preconceived notions of 'normality' and maleness and femaleness instead of being open-minded, embracing difference and respecting the autonomy of the individual.

10 pp. 6–7.

MALTA DECLARATION[1]

Statement of the Third International Intersex Forum[2] of 1 December 2013

Preamble

We affirm that intersex people are real, and we exist in all regions and all countries around the world. Thus, intersex people must be supported to be the drivers of social, political and legislative changes that concern them.

We reaffirm the principles of the First and Second International Intersex Fora and extend the demands aiming to end discrimination against intersex people and to ensure the right of bodily integrity, physical autonomy and self-determination.

Demands

- To put an end to mutilating and "normalizing" practices such as genital surgeries, psychological and other medical treatments through legislative and other means. Intersex people must be empowered to make their own decisions affecting own bodily integrity, physical autonomy and self-determination.
- To put an end to preimplantation genetic diagnosis, pre-natal screening and treatment, and selective abortion of intersex foetuses.
- To put an end to infanticide and killings of intersex people.
- To put an end to non-consensual sterilisation of intersex people.
- To depathologise variations in sex characteristics in medical guidelines, protocols and classifications, such as the World Health Organization's International Classification of Diseases.
- To register intersex children as females or males, with the awareness that, like all people, they may grow up to identify with a different sex or gender.

---

1 Also available at https://oiieurope.org/malta-declaration/ (last accessed 26.2.2018).

2 Between 29 November and 1 December 2013, the Third International Intersex Forum, supported by ILGA and ILGA-Europe, took place in Valletta, Malta. This event brought together 34 activists representing 30 intersex organisations from all continents.

- To ensure that sex or gender classifications are amendable through a simple administrative procedure at the request of the individuals concerned. All adults and capable minors should be able to choose between female (F), male (M), non-binary or multiple options. In the future, as with race or religion, sex or gender should not be a category on birth certificates or identification documents for anybody.
- To raise awareness around intersex issues and the rights of intersex people in society at large.
- To create and facilitate supportive, safe and celebratory environments for intersex people, their families and surroundings.
- To ensure that intersex people have the right to full information and access to their own medical records and history.
- To ensure that all professionals and healthcare providers that have a specific role to play in intersex people's wellbeing are adequately trained to provide quality services.
- To provide adequate acknowledgement of the suffering and injustice caused to intersex people in the past, and provide adequate redress, reparation, access to justice and the right to truth.
- To build intersex anti-discrimination legislation in addition to other grounds, and to ensure protection against intersectional discrimination.
- To ensure the provision of all human rights and citizenship rights to intersex people, including the right to marry and form a family.
- To ensure that intersex people are able to participate in competitive sport, at all levels, in accordance with their legal sex. Intersex athletes who have been humiliated or stripped of their titles should receive reparation and reinstatement.
- Recognition that medicalization and stigmatisation of intersex people result in significant trauma and mental health concerns.
- In view of ensuring the bodily integrity and well-being of intersex people, autonomous non-pathologising psychosocial and peer support be available to intersex people throughout their life (as self-required), as well as to parents and/or care providers.

In view of the above the Forum calls on:

1. International, regional and national human rights institutions to take on board, and provide visibility to intersex issues in their work.
2. National governments to address the concerns raised by the Intersex Forum and draw adequate solutions in direct collaboration with intersex representatives and organisations.
3. Media agencies and sources to ensure intersex people's right to privacy, dignity, accurate and ethical representation.

4. Funders to engage with intersex organisations and support them in the struggle for visibility, increase their capacity, the building of knowledge and the affirmation of their human rights.
5. Human rights organisations to contribute to build bridges with intersex organisations and build a basis for mutual support. This should be done in a spirit of collaboration and no one should instrumentalise intersex issues as a means for other ends.

DARLINGTON STATEMENT: JOINT CONSENSUS STATEMENT FROM THE INTERSEX COMMUNITY RETREAT IN DARLINGTON, MARCH 2017

Joint statement by Australia and Aotearoa/New Zealand intersex community organisations and independent advocates, including the Androgen Insensitivity Support Syndrome Support Group Australia (AISSGA),[1] Intersex Trust Aotearoa New Zealand (ITANZ),[2] Organisation Intersex International Australia (OIIAU),[3] Eve Black, Kylie Bond (AISSGA), Tony Briffa (OIIAU/AISSGA), Morgan Carpenter (OIIAU/Intersex Day Project[4]), Candice Cody (OIIAU), Alex David (OIIAU), Betsy Driver (Bodies Like Ours), Carolyn Hannaford (AISSGA), Eileen Harlow, Bonnie Hart (AISSGA), Phoebe Hart (AISSGA), Delia Leckey (ITANZ), Steph Lum (OIIAU), Mani Bruce Mitchell (ITANZ), Elise Nyhuis (AISSGA), Bronwyn O'Callaghan, Sandra Perrin (AISSGA), Cody Smith (Tranz Australia), Trace Williams (AISSGA), Imogen Yang (Bladder Exstrophy Epispadias Cloacal Exstrophy Hypospadias Australian Community – BEECHAC[5]), Georgie Yovanovic.

Preamble

A. Intersex people are born with physical or biological sex characteristics (such as sexual anatomy, reproductive organs, hormonal patterns and/or chromosomal patterns) that are more diverse than stereotypical definitions for male or female bodies. For some people these traits are apparent prenatally or at birth, while for others they emerge later in life, often at puberty (see UN definition[6]). We recognise our diverse histories and use the word intersex inclusively, and acknowledging our right to self-determination.

---

1 http://aissga.org.au.
2 http://ianz.org.nz.
3 http://oii.org.au.
4 http://intersexday.org.
5 http://beechac.com.
6 http://www.ohchr.org/EN/NewsEvents/Pages/DisplayNews.aspx?NewsID=20739&amp%3BLangID=E.

B. We observe that, despite the best efforts of intersex human rights defenders, discrimination, stigmatisation and human rights violations, including harmful practices in medical settings, continue to occur in Australia and Aotearoa/New Zealand.
C. We observe the 2013 Senate Community Affairs References Committee report, *Involuntary or coerced sterilisation of intersex people in Australia,*[7] and the 2016 Family Court of Australia case, *Re Carla (Medical procedure).*[8] We observe the *Concluding observations on the fifth periodic report of New Zealand* by the UN Committee on the Rights of the Child in 2016.[9]
D. We recognise the international obligations of our countries, having signed the *Convention against Torture*, the *Convention on the Rights of the Child*, the **Convention on the Elimination of Discrimination against Women**, and the **Convention on the Rights of Persons with Disabilities**.
E. We note that intersex peer support remains largely unfunded, advocacy funding remains precarious and limited, and intersex-led organisations rely on volunteers to address the many gaps in services left by other, well-resourced health, social services and human rights institutions.
F. We acknowledge the kind support for this event from the National LGBTI Health Alliance,[10] Twenty10,[11] Astraea Lesbian Foundation for Justice,[12] and an anonymous donor.
G. Recognising these issues, this gathering of Australian and Aotearoa/New Zealand intersex community organisations and individuals in March 2017, meeting on Gadigal Land in Darlington, Australia, acknowledges and respects the work of support organisations and human rights advocates over past years and acknowledges –
   1. The ***Malta Declaration*** of the Third International Intersex Forum in 2013.[13]
   2. That intersex people **exist in all cultures and societies**, throughout history, and that the existence of intersex people is worthy of celebration.
   3. The **diversity of our sex characteristics** and bodies, our identities, sexes, genders, and lived experiences. We also acknowledge **intersectionalities** with other populations, including same-sex attracted people, trans and gender diverse people, people with disabilities, women, men, and Indigenous – Aboriginal and Torres Strait Islander, Tangata Whenua – and racialised, migrant and refugee populations.

---

7 http://www.aph.gov.au/Parliamentary_Business/Committees/Senate/Community_Affairs/Involuntary_Sterilisation/Sec_Report/index.
8 *Re Carla (Medical procedure) [2016] FamCA 7.*
9 http://tbinternet.ohchr.org/Treaties/CRC/Shared%20Documents/NZL/INT_CRC_COC_NZL_25459_E.pdf.
10 http://lgbtihealth.org.au.
11 http://twenty10.org.au.
12 http://astraeafoundation.org.
13 https://oii.org.au/24241/public-statement-by-the-third-international-intersex-forum/.

4. That the word 'intersex', and the intersex human rights movement, **belong equally to all people born with variations of sex characteristics**, irrespective of our gender identities, genders, legal sex classifications and sexual orientations.
5. Our rights to **bodily integrity, physical autonomy and self determination**.
6. Our opposition to **pathologising terminology** such as "disorders of sex development", not only because such labels are inherently disordering, but also because this promotes the belief that intersex characteristics need to be "fixed".

Human rights and legal reform

7. We call for the immediate **prohibition as a criminal act** of deferrable medical interventions, including surgical and hormonal interventions, that alter the sex characteristics of infants and children without personal consent. We call for freely-given and fully informed consent by individuals, with individuals and families having mandatory independent access to funded counselling and peer support.
8. Regarding **sex/gender classifications**, sex and gender binaries are upheld by structural violence. Additionally, attempts to classify intersex people as a third sex/gender do not respect our diversity or right to self determination. These can inflict wide-ranging harm regardless of whether an intersex person identifies with binary legal sex assigned at birth or not.

   Undue emphasis on how to classify intersex people rather than how we are treated is also a form of structural violence. The larger goal is not to seek new classifications but to **end legal classification systems** and the hierarchies that lie behind them. Therefore:
   a. As with race or religion, sex/gender should not be a legal category on birth certificates or identification documents for anybody.
   b. While sex/gender classifications remain legally required, sex/gender assignments must be regarded as provisional. Given existing social conditions, we do not support the imposition of a third sex classification when births are initially registered.
   c. Recognising that any child may grow up to identify with a different sex/gender, and that the decision about the sex of rearing of an intersex child may have been incorrect, sex/gender classifications must be legally correctable through a simple administrative procedure at the request of the individual concerned.
   d. Individuals able to consent should be able to choose between female (F), male (M), non-binary, alternative gender markers, or multiple options.

9. We call for **effective legislative protection** from discrimination and harmful practices on grounds of **sex characteristics**.
10. We call on governments and institutions to **acknowledge** and **apologise** for the treatment of people born with variations of sex characteristics, and provide **redress and reparation** for people born with variations of sex characteristics who have experienced involuntary or coercive medical interventions. There must be no time limit on access to redress and reparation.
11. We call for an end to **genetic discrimination**, including in insurance and employment.
12. We call for all adults to have the **right to marry and form a family** irrespective of their sex characteristics.
13. We note the difficulty that many intersex people have when **travelling**, including experiences of discrimination and harassment due to their bodily diversity, through the requirements of gendered documents, gendered screening and restrictions on travel with pharmaceutical prescription documents. We call on our governments to work with states, countries and international regulators to resolve these issues.
14. We call for meaningful **participation** by, and **consultation** with, intersex people and community organisations in all issues and policies affecting us.

Health and wellbeing

15. We acknowledge the **long-term physical and psychological implications of harmful and continuing medical practices**, and limited access to support and peers.
16. Current forms of **oversight of medical interventions** affecting people born with variations of sex characteristics have proven to be inadequate.
    a. We note a lack of transparency about diverse standards of care and practices across Australia and New Zealand for all age groups.
    b. We note that the Family Court system in Australia has failed to adequately consider the human rights and autonomy of children born with variations of sex characteristics, and the repercussions of medical interventions on individuals and their families. The role of the Family Court is itself unclear. Distinctions between "therapeutic" and "non-therapeutic" interventions have failed our population.
17. We call for the implementation of advisory bodies to develop appropriate **human rights-based, lifetime, intersex standards of care** with full and meaningful participation by intersex community representatives and human rights institutions.

18. We call on the Australasian Paediatric Endocrine Group[14] and other medical/health bodies to stand alongside intersex-led community organisations to develop **human rights-based lifetime standards of care**.
19. We recognise that **intersex people have health and medical needs**, sometimes related to having an intersex variation, and sometimes not. We recognise that for people with an intersex variation, misconceptions and associated stigma can act as barriers to treatment. Current practices are often based on the needs of other populations.
20. We recognise access limitations in **rural, regional and remote** settings.
21. We call for **resourced access to necessary and appropriate health, medical and allied services and treatment**, including surgeries and hormone treatment, psychosocial, psychosexual and psychological support, and including reparative treatments. **Standards of care** must support reparative treatments, and must not require conformity with stereotypical and clinical norms for female or male bodies, women and men, nor impose inappropriate psychiatric eligibility assessments.
22. We call for the provision of alternative, independent, effective **human rights-based oversight mechanism(s)** to determine individual cases involving persons born with intersex variations who are unable to consent to treatment, bringing together human rights experts, clinicians and intersex-led community organisations. The pros and cons for and against medical treatment must be properly ventilated and considered, including the **lifetime health, legal, ethical, sexual and human rights implications.**
23. Multi-disciplinary teams must operate in line with **transparent, human rights-based standards of care** for the treatment of intersex people and bodies. Multi-disciplinary teams in hospitals must include human rights specialists, child advocates, and independent intersex community representatives.
24. Some people need pap smears, some people need prostate examinations or mammograms, and some people need a combination of these. **National screening programs and computerised systems** must recognise the needs of people born with intersex variations.
25. We call for an end to the use of IVF and other forms of **genetic selection** to de-select variations of sex characteristics.
26. We call for **access to reproductive services** and fertility counselling for all intersex people, with protection of our reproductive autonomy, regardless of whether or not our capacity for fertility is considered to be in line with our legal sex.

---

[14] http://apeg.org.au.

27. Intersex-led organisations must be resourced to develop **patient rights and human rights toolkits** for intersex people and our families to improve access to healthcare, and ensure enjoyment of the highest attainable standard of physical and mental health.
28. Children with intersex variations require clear, **age-appropriate disclosure** of their intersex variations, and affirmative support, including peer support.
29. We call for regular **public disclosure of accurate summary data** on all medical interventions to modify the sex characteristics of children, and disclosure of historical data.
30. We call for more research, including **clinical, sociological and psychological research, led by community input.** Clinical research, including longitudinal research, requires true, non-medicalised controls.
31. We call for improved and ongoing **education of health, welfare and allied professionals** in issues relating to intersex bodies, including human rights issues.
32. Children with intersex variations should never be subjected to **medical photography** and display.
33. We call for respect for the **privacy, integrity, and security of our medical records.**
34. Recognising the difficulty that some intersex people have in accessing childhood medical records, we call for **full access to medical records**. Paediatric hospital records should be kept indefinitely. The medical records of people with whole-of-life medical issues should also be kept indefinitely.
35. We call for **access to sport** at all levels of competition by all intersex persons, including for all intersex women to be permitted to compete as women, without restrictions or discriminatory medical investigations.
36. Hormone treatment is required for a lifetime after sterilisation or in cases where gonads do not produce adequate hormones. However, people with intersex variations face **unnecessary costs and challenges in accessing and managing appropriate hormone treatment**. These include access to sex hormones, the unfair and undisclosed cost of treatment required as a consequence of unwanted medical interventions, accessing testosterone and estrogen at the same time, changing from one sex hormone to the other, accessing screening, and travel restrictions, including travelling with medication and physical screening. We call for national and clinical standards to address these issues.
37. We call for the implementation of **adequate clinical transition pathways** from paediatric to adult services.

38. We call for equitable access to social and welfare services for people with intersex variations. The needs of people with intersex variations in **aged care, home care, state care, and disability services** require further investigation, with full and meaningful participation by intersex-led organisations.

Peer support

39. We recognise the **trauma and mental health concerns** caused by the unnecessary medicalisation of intersex people, as well as stigmatisation of intersex characteristics that has resulted in a legacy of isolation, secrecy and shame.
40. We recognise the fundamental importance and benefits of **affirmative peer support** for people born with variations of sex characteristics.
41. Our peer support organisations and other peer communities need resourcing and support to **build communities and networks** inclusive of all intersex people. No intersex person or parent of an intersex child should feel they are alone, irrespective of their bodily variation or the language they use.
42. We recognise the needs and lived experience of **youth**, and of people coming from varied **cultural and faith backgrounds**. We recognise these experiences as valid and legitimate.
43. We recognise the fundamental importance and benefits of **peer support for parents, caregivers, and families** of people with variations of sex characteristics. We recognise the importance and benefits of **peer support for friends, partners, and others** who support intersex people in their day-to-day lives.
44. **Peer support must be integrated** into human rights-based multi-disciplinary medical approaches, teams and services.
45. We call for **public, governmental, and philanthropic support** for funded, affirmative peer support.
46. We acknowledge that intersex people are the **experts** on our own lives and lived experience. Intersex people are experts in understanding the long term effects of medicalisation and medical interventions.

Allies

47. Intersex is distinct from other issues. We call on allies to actively **acknowledge** our distinctiveness and the diversity within our community, to **support** our human rights claims and **respect** the intersex human rights movement, **without tokenism**, or instrumentalising, or co-opting intersex issues as a means for other ends. "Nothing about us without us."

48. We encourage all organisations and bodies that support the intersex movement to **recognise this Darlington statement**.
49. We call for intersex people, and the intersex human rights movement, **to be allies** to the LGBTQ, disability, Indigenous, anti-racist, and women's movements.
50. We call on intersex people to recognise our own diversity, and call for **intra-community dialogue and mutual support**.

Education, awareness and employment

51. We acknowledge that **stigma is often the result of misconceptions** about intersex which is compounded by a lack of education and awareness.
52. We recognise that the stigmatisation and pathologisation of people born with variations of sex characteristics **hinders self-acceptance, access to community, help-seeking, and accessing of services** including healthcare.
53. We acknowledge the impacts of stigma, trauma and unwanted medical interventions on access to **education** and on **employment**, and consequences that include high rates of **early school leaving, poverty, self-harm and suicidality.**
54. We call for the inclusion of accurate and affirmative material on bodily diversity, including intersex variations, in **school curricula**, including in health and sex education.
55. We call on education and awareness providers to develop content with intersex-led organisations, and promote delivery by intersex people.
56. We call on **employer groups, governments, institutions and trade unions to develop affirmative policies and practices** to support employees with intersex variations.
57. We call for policies in **educational institutions and employment** to recognise that some people born with intersex variations may benefit from **accommodations and reasonable adjustments**, including special needs requirements, workplace adjustments, job access assistance, and provisions for medical leave.
58. We acknowledge the **vital importance of positive stories and role models** and the existence of some positive media coverage of intersex people. We acknowledge that much media work unfortunately perpetuates the stigmatisation of intersex people and bodies. We call on the **media to work with intersex-led organisations** to improve their understanding of intersex people and our human rights issues.
59. We call for an **end to the stigmatisation and unnecessary pathologisation** of intersex bodies.

VIENNA STATEMENT (STATEMENT OF THE FIRST EUROPEAN INTERSEX COMMUNITY EVENT, VIENNA, 30TH–31ST OF MARCH 2017)[1]

On the 30th – 31st of March 2017 in Vienna, Austria the first OII Europe community event took place. During the community event 28 Intersex people from 16 Council of Europe member states, some activists and some not, came together to share their experiences, and their varied objectives and strategies for the full implementation of human rights, bodily integrity, self-determination and societal acceptance of intersex people within Europe.

We affirm that intersex people are real, and we exist in all regions and all countries around the world.

We reaffirm the Malta Declaration and its demands, formulated at the 3rd International Intersex Forum (2013),[2] as well as the objectives formulated by the 1st European Intersex Meeting in the Riga Statement (2014).[3]

We also stress the fact, that until this day more than 50 times UN bodies, regional and national human rights bodies have called on governments, policy makers and stakeholders to put an end to human rights violations faced by intersex people – including taking the necessary legislative, administrative and other measures to guarantee respect for the physical integrity and autonomy of intersex persons and to ensure that no one is subjected during infancy or childhood to non-urgent medical or surgical procedures intended to decide the sex of the child.

Ensuring the right of intersex people of bodily integrity, physical autonomy and self-determination must be a priority in all action taken. Intersex people must be supported to be the drivers of social, political and legislative changes that concern them.

1 Also available at : https://oiieurope.org/statement-1st-european-intersex-community-event-vienna-30st-31st-march-2017/ (last accessed 26.2.2018).

2 https://oiieurope.org/malta-declaration/; reprinted in this volume (last accessed 26.2.2018).

3 https://oiieurope.org/statement-of-riga/ (last accessed 26.2.2018).

We therefore call on governments to:

- Recognise intersex people as a community that has specific and vital needs and that their human rights need protection.

To this aim governments should take decisive action to:

- Install legislative protections that ban medical interventions on children with variations of sex characteristics, on social, psychosocial, cultural or cosmetic grounds. A ban on Intersex genital mutilation is necessary as IGM is equatable with female genital mutilation that takes place within hospital settings. This may include installing legislative measures that penalise medical professionals that commit or assist in IGM.
- Ensure that medical practitioners or other professionals do not conduct any treatment to the purpose of modifying sex characteristics which can be deferred until the person to be treated can provide full, free and informed consent. Medical and psychological treatment that is performed without the intersex person's free, personal and fully informed consent, unless life-saving, should be made unlawful. Informed consent requires being informed of different options, including, but not limited to, medical, sociological and human rights based information. Peer-counselling should be mandatorily included in the decision process.
- Ensure that intersex people are protected from discrimination. To this aim governments should install constitutional protection, anti-discrimination and hate crime and hate speech legislation on the grounds of sex characteristics. If adding a new ground is not an option "sex characteristics" should be included explicitly in the ground of "sex". Intersex people must benefit from the same rights and protections given to other citizens.
- Provide intersex people who endured medically unnecessary or degrading treatment with reparations.

In the field of education we call on governments, universities and schools to take action to:

- Include intersex realities as a mandatory part of school curriculums, especially in biology and sex education.
- Inform professionals that play a role in intersex people's lives, including but not limited to future physicians, surgeons, midwives, nurses, healthcare assistants, teachers and administrative officers about the existence of people with variations of sex characteristics and intersex realities. All training should be provided from a depathologizing and human rights perspective.

- Install intersex inclusive anti-bullying policies in schools. Schools should take into account that gendered activities may be difficult and exclusionary for some intersex youth.

In the field of healthcare we call on governments, doctors associations, health insurances and other decision and policy makers working in the area of healthcare, to

- Ensure intersex people's full access to medical records.
- Educate all healthcare professionals and providers about respectful behaviour towards intersex people and ensuring their privacy.
- Cover all health related needs of intersex people, including those that were created by previous medical and psychological interventions.

In regards to support for intersex people and their families we call on governments to

- Ensure that peer counselling, which approaches intersex issues in a depathologizing and human rights affirming manner, led by intersex adults is easily available for parents, families, intersex children and intersex adults.
- Ensure that professional counselling services that approach intersex issues in a depathologizing and human rights affirming manner are easily available for parents, families, intersex children and intersex adults.

In the field of media we call on all professionals working in this field as well as media ethic bodies to

- Increase positive representation in all fields of media, whether that be in films, tv shows, books, magazine articles and other areas.
- Discuss intersex issues without bias and without reproducing prejudices, stereotypes or assumptions.
- Ensure that people with variations of sex characteristics and intersex issues are not exoticised or "othered" by any means. Press councils and other media related ethic bodies should take action to ensure that intersex people are not discriminated against in the media and that their human rights are respected.

In regards to gender markers and gendered facilities we call on governments to

- Install an easy administrative process to facilitate gender/sex marker change on the basis of self-determination and self-declaration. A neutral marker should be made available.

- Make non-gendered facilities available for all people.
- Not permit educational institutions and businesses to require gendered dress codes. While sex and gender are two distinct facets of a person, the gender binary is harmful, especially for intersex people.

Allies should be aware that

- They must not instrumentalise intersex realities for their own purposes.
- Intersex activists need their support.
- They should under no circumstances exoticise intersex people, use intersex people in a tokenistic way or appropriate intersex issues or intersex funding.
- They must avoid exclusionary or pathologizing language.
- Safe spaces for intersex people need to be created.
- They must learn about intersex issues from intersex people, without pressuring intersex people to provide input unless they themselves want to. Seek out local or regional intersex organisations and the resources that they provide.
- They must promote intersex rights as human rights.
- Allyship manifests itself in actions, not identities, i.e., identifying as an ally is not enough to be an ally, you must act like one.

PART I

MEDICINE AND PSYCHOLOGY

BIOLOGY OF FETAL SEX DEVELOPMENT

Ieuan HUGHES*

1. INTRODUCTION

Mammalian sex development is a binary process established before birth so that the expectation at birth is that the sex of the baby is instantly recognisable as

* Studies referred to in this chapter and undertaken by the author were supported by the NIHR Cambridge Biomedical Research Centre.

being female or male. When that is not the case, the term intersex has historically been used to describe an infant in whom the external genitalia are ambiguous in appearance and could be consistent with either a male or a female. Such a degree of ambiguity in humans is estimated to occur in 1 in 4,500 to 5,500 births.[1] If less severe forms of atypical genital development are also included, the problem affects as many as 1 in 300 births.[2]

In order to understand the origins of intersex development, this chapter reviews how the outcome of the biological process of sex development is binary in the human fetus yet the embryological structures are present for that outcome to be bipotential. For that to happen, the bipotential structures must develop in response to biological drivers. These are genes and hormones which are produced during a critical period of fetal life and expressed in optimal concentrations.

2. THE EMBRYOLOGY

The development of the reproductive tract is sub-divided into formation of the internal and external genitalia. In both categories, the structures are bipotential with the capacity to form either male or female genitalia. Which it is, depends on genes and hormones.[3]

2.1. THE GONADS

The structure which forms the gonads is termed the genital ridge, a region where the kidneys and adrenal glands also form. Until about five to six weeks of human gestation, the tissue forming the gonad is indeterminate on histological examination as being neither a testis or an ovary. The gonad is bipotential at this stage. A key gene which is present only on the Y (male) chromosome becomes expressed in the gonad if the egg at conception has been fertilised by a male bearing sperm (see Figure 1 and later in the text). Thereafter, the gonad becomes histologically distinguishable as a testis by cells that make testosterone (the male hormone) and other specialised cells that in later postnatal life make sperm. The bipotential gonad develops as an ovary when a female bearing sperm fertilises the egg and the Y chromosome-related key gene is absent.

---

1 L. Sax, 'How common is intersex? A response to Anne Fausto-Sterling' (2002) 39 *J Sex Res* 174–178.

2 A.S. Nordenvall, L. Frisen, A. Nordenstrom et al., 'Population based nationwide study of hypospadias in Sweden, 1973–2009: incidence and risk factors' (2014) 191 *J Urol* 753–789.

3 J. Brennan, B. Capel, 'One tissue, two fates: the molecular genetic events that underlie testis versus ovary development' (2004) 3 *Nat Rev Genet* 502–521.

Figure 1. Mammalian reproduction

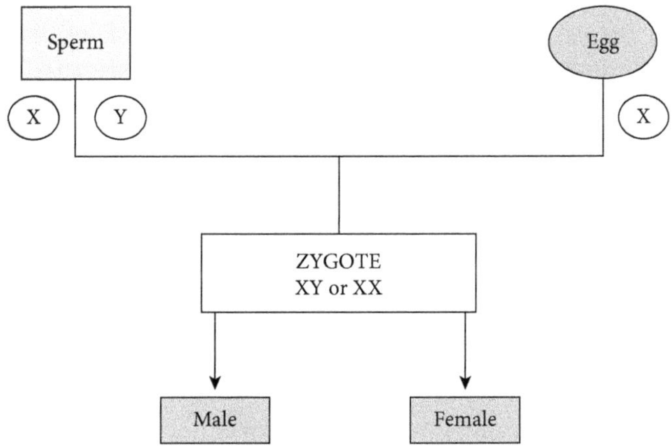

Fertilisation of the egg by an X- or Y-bearing sperm to form a zygote determines the sex of the fetus.
Source: Produced by the author.

2.2. THE INTERNAL GENITAL DUCTS

The reproductive system requires a plumbing system to transport sperm produced in the testis to the penis for ejaculation. In the female, the eggs produced by the ovary need to be transported to the uterus at the optimum time ready for fertilisation after sexual intercourse. Both sets of plumbing develop in early fetal life and hence there is again a bipotential system in place. In the male, the embryological precursor is the Wolffian ducts which, under the influence of testosterone, develop into the vas deferens and epididymis (to transport sperm from the testis) and the seminal vesicles (the structure which stores the sperm for ejaculation). In the female, the equivalent embryological structures are the Mullerian ducts which form the Fallopian tubes that capture the eggs released from the ovary, the uterus that receives the eggs transported via the Fallopian tubes and the upper part of the vagina. The early male and female fetus has both Wolffian and Mullerian ducts. The bipotential system changes to a single system under the influence of hormones, dependent on either male or female development (see below).

2.3. THE EXTERNAL GENITALIA

These structures develop from a common genital anlagen (embryological structure) which later in gestation develops into the penis and scrotum in the male and the clitoris and labia in the female. Again, the genital anlagen is bipotential for development and the early external genitalia are indistinguishable between male and female appearance on direct examination of an early fetus. This is also the case when using ultrasound examination to sex a baby in pregnancy, the distinguishing sex dimorphic features only being reliably evident by around 16 weeks of pregnancy. The development of the external genitalia is again hormone dependent.

3. CONTROL OF FETAL SEX DEVELOPMENT: GENES AND HORMONES

3.1. THE GENES

The key gene which determines the development of the indifferent or bipotential gonad as a testis is *SRY*, the acronym standing for sex-related gene on the Y chromosome. The SRY protein is a transcription factor which upregulates the expression of other genes required for testis development. It was identified in humans by studying individuals with XY chromosomes who were female and others with XX chromosomes who were male. The latter phenomenon occurs due to inadvertent transfer of the SRY gene from a segment of the Y chromosome to the X chromosome during pairing of these two sex chromosomes in paternal meiosis, a process of reductive cell division in sperm which produces cells with half the number of chromosomes before fertilisation restores the normal number of chromosomes in the zygote (the product of the fused sperm and egg).

Once the SRY and other testis-determining genes are expressed, the structure of the gonad differentiates into specialised cells such as the Leydig cells, which make testosterone, and the Sertoli cells, which support the development of tubules where the sperm is subsequently produced. It used to be thought that the ovary would form only when the SRY gene and its partners were not expressed in the bipotential gonad making female sex development in the fetus a passive process. However, ovarian-determining genes also occur, leading to the concept that testis and ovary-determining genes antagonise each other in a yin-yang fashion to result in sex determination. These sex-specific genes can be manipulated in mouse embryos through over-or under-expression at critical time windows that alter the sex of the fetus. This illustrates how sensitive the early developing organism is to alterations in gene expression which has profound relevance for understanding the causes of atypical sex development in the human.

3.2. THE HORMONES

Once the gonad has formed as either a testis or an ovary, its hormonal products control the subsequent development of the internal genitalia (Wolffian and

Mullerian ducts) and the external genitalia.[4] This is an active and passive process in the male and female, respectively. Two hormones are critical for differentiation of the male genitalia. Testicular Leydig cells start secreting testosterone at around eight to ten weeks of pregnancy under the control of a hormone produced by the placenta (Figure 2). The concentration of this steroid hormone approaches values within the adult range, a massive fetal androgen exposure to initiate programming of male reproductive development. Such exposure is also relevant to sex dimorphic brain development (as discussed in the contribution by Herbert in Chapter 4 of this volume). The aforementioned Wolffian ducts are maintained in order to differentiate as the internal male genital ducts (vas deferens, epididymis) and the seminal vesicles. But what about the Mullerian ducts, the forerunner of the internal female genital ducts? It is the testis that also control these structures by the Sertoli cells secreting an anti-Mullerian hormone (AMH) which causes regression of the Mullerian ducts and thus suppressing the development of the Fallopian tubes, uterus and the vagina in the fetal male.

Figure 2. Pattern of testosterone secretion in the male

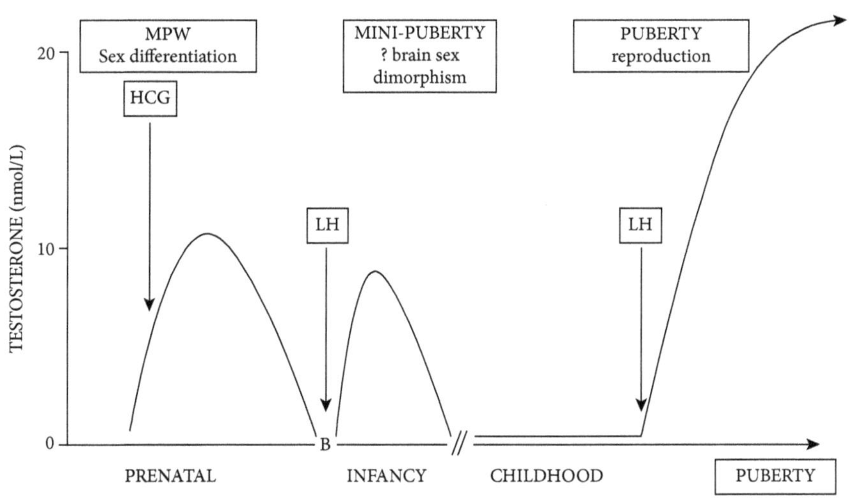

Concentrations of testosterone (nmol/L) shown on the vertical axis are depicted in relation on the horizontal axis to fetal, infant and childhood/pubertal periods in the male. The arrows indicate the hormones that stimulate the peaks of testosterone required for male sex differentiation. The rise in infancy is labelled as 'mini'-puberty, perhaps influencing brain sex dimorphism. MPW, male programming window; HCG, human chorionic gonadotrophin; LH, luteinising hormone.

Source: Produced by the author.

---

4 O. Hiort, 'The differential role of androgen in early human sex development' (2013) 11 *BMC Med* 152; D.J. Macleod, R.M. Sharpe, M. Welsh et al., 'Androgen action in the masculinisation programming window and development of male reproductive organs' (2010) 33 *Int J Androl* 279–289.

The fetal ovary does not produce AMH, but does so in postnatal life. Hence the Mullerian structures are stabilised in the female fetus to enable development of the Fallopian tubes and uterus. The female hormone, estrogen, is not required for this process to occur.

The forerunner of the development of the external genitalia is the genital anlagen in both sexes. In the presence of testosterone, the anlagen masculinises in the male to form the penis and scrotum. The urethra, the opening at the tip of the penis through which urine and sperm passes, is initially sited on the perineum (the region between the base of scrotum and anus). This is similar to the situation in the female where there are separate openings for the urethra and vagina on the perineum. The opening of the urethra has to 'migrate' to the tip of the penis and this is controlled by testosterone being converted to a far more potent androgen, dihydrotestosterone (DHT). Failure of this conversion results in a condition called hypospadias in which the opening of the urethra is at the under-surface of the penis. The genital anlagen in the female fetus is not exposed to androgens during normal development so the clitoris, the equivalent derivative of the genital tubercle as the penis, does not enlarge and the labial folds do not fuse to form a scrotum. However, if the female fetus is exposed to androgens, as in a condition called congenital adrenal hyperplasia, the clitoris can enlarge considerably to resemble a penis (see below). Again, the female hormone estrogen plays no role in development of the external genitalia in the female fetus.

4. INTERSEX: TERMINOLOGY

The term 'intersex' is a composite one to embrace a variety of conditions that can lead to confusion with the sex of an individual as defined in the binary sense of male or female. This reflects a biological perspective on sex development. While this term is the one used in the title of this book, it is important to note that some persons with intersex express disquiet about a term which can be perceived as pejorative. This is particularly the case amongst parents of affected children. Consequently, health professionals involved with the care of intersex persons responded to these concerns by convening an interdisciplinary meeting of experts to discuss alternative terminology and, *pari passu*, a modus operandum as to how to simplify the classification of the causes of intersex.

A Consensus document was published in 2006 which proposed the use of alternative terminology to replace terms such as 'intersex' (see above) and old diagnostic nomenclature which was confusing not only to affected persons but also to healthcare professionals.[5] These included the terms male and female

[5] I.A. Hughes, C. Houk, S.F. Ahmed et al., 'Consensus statement on management of intersex disorders' (2006) 91 *Arch Dis Child* 554–563.

pseudohermaphroditism and dated eponyms. The acronym, DSD, standing for disorders (or differences) of sex development, is defined as a congenital condition in which the chromosomal, gonadal or phenotypic (physical) sex is atypical. Figure 3 illustrates how a simpler classification of the myriad causes of intersex was derived from the DSD definition by using knowledge of the sex chromosomes (karyotype) as the starting point. Thus, based on knowledge of the biology of normal fetal sex development previously outlined, the type of DSD could be at three levels of development: sex chromosomes (an abnormal Y or X chromosome); gonadal (a mutation in a gonad-determining gene); hormonal (a deficiency of hormone production or action). Illustrative examples from each category are described below.

Figure 3. Causes of disorders of sex development (DSD)

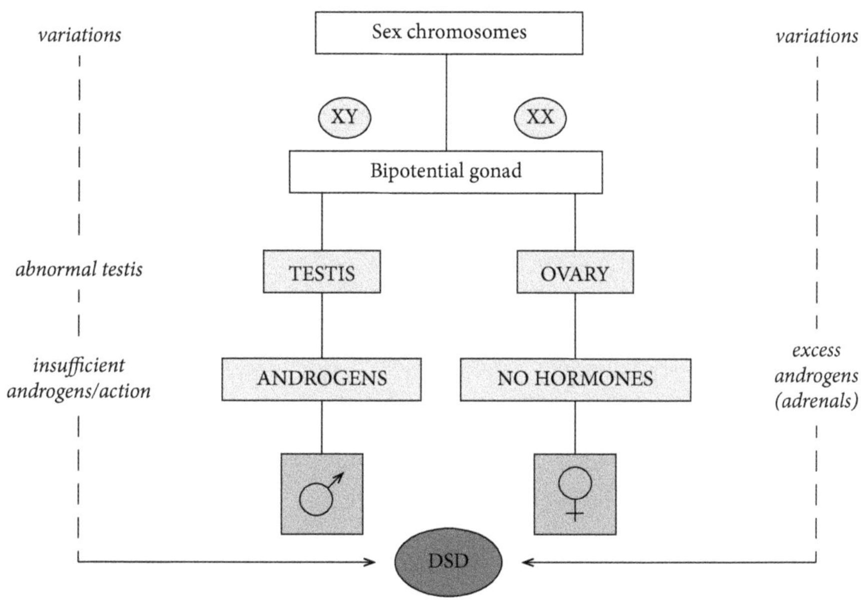

The three main categories are shown: variations in sex chromosomes, abnormal gonad development, deficient androgen production and action. In the female pathway, excess production of androgens from the adrenal glands is the primary cause of DSD.

Source: Produced by the author.

The new terminology comprising the acronym DSD has generally been accepted amongst the biomedical profession and is used widely in the medical literature and at scientific conferences. Not all persons with intersex favour the use of DSD, particularly the word, *disorder*, which is perceived as pathologising the individual.[6] But pathology is what medicine defines as disease, albeit from more

[6] E.K. Johnson, I. Rosoklija, C. Finlayson et al., 'Attitudes towards "disorders of sex development" nomenclature among affected individuals' (2017) 13 *J Pediatr Urol* 608.e1–608.e8.

of a laboratory than a clinical perspective. The word, *difference*, is suggested as an alternative. Such a neutral term is non-threatening, retains the DSD acronym but can be used as appropriate. Some individuals with atypical genitalia have advocated using the word, *variation*, to reflect a spectrum of sex development that is not abnormal. This is unrealistic from a medical standpoint.[7] A condition such as congenital adrenal hyperplasia which causes not only markedly atypical genitalia in an affected female but also life-threatening salt loss in the majority is not a variation of normal physiology. Neither can a type of gonad determination resulting in gonadal dysgenesis with a high risk of gonadal malignancy be construed as a variation of sex development. For the purpose of this chapter, the terminology 'intersex' and 'DSD' (disorder/difference in sex development) are used interchangeably. A recent re-evaluation of the original Consensus document endorses the continued use of the DSD terminology but with added input from a wider spectrum of stakeholders, including patient advocacy and support groups.[8]

5. CAUSES OF INTERSEX/DSD: ILLUSTRATIVE EXAMPLES

This is a vast topic and readers can refer to *Williams Textbook of Endocrinology*, the 'bible' of the subject, where there is a comprehensive chapter which describes all the causes of DSD.[9]

5.1. MALE AFFECTED

5.1.1. Sex Chromosome Anomalies

A chromosome complement of X/XY instead of either XX or XY leads to the formation of a formed gonad on one side (usually a testis) and an abnormal or 'streak' gonad on the other side which resembles an incompletely developed ovary. The condition is often referred to as mixed gonadal dysgenesis. The external genitalia can vary from a male appearance through ambiguity to a female appearance with some enlargement of the clitoris. Indeed, most individuals with

---

7 I.A. Hughes, 'Consequences of the Chicago DSD Consensus: a personal perspective' (2015) 47 *HormMetabRes* 394–400.

8 P.A. Lee, A. Nordenstrom, C.P. Houk et al., 'Global disorders of sex development update since 2006; perceptions, approach and care' (2016) 85 *Horm Res Paediatr* 158–180.

9 J.C. Achermann, I.A. Hughes, 'Pediatric disorders of sex development' in S. Melmed, K.S. Polonsky, P.R. Larsen, H.M. Kronenberg (eds.), *Williams Textbook of Endocrinology*, 13th ed., Elsevier, Philadelphia 2016, pp. 893–963.

this chromosome make-up are normally developed males and may not know they have the condition. Sometimes it is discovered during investigation for male factor infertility. Short stature may be present as a result of the loss of one X chromosome.

A condition related to mixed gonadal dysgenesis is true hermaphroditism. Hermaphroditos was the son of Aphrodite and Hermes in Greek mythology. Hermaphrodite is the clinical term applied to an intersex condition where an affected individual possesses both ovarian and testicular tissue. The prefix, true, was used to ensure the hermaphroditic state was indeed the case by demonstrating on histological examination the presence of ovarian tissue with follicles (eggs). This was to distinguish the condition from other forms of intersex in genetic males (classified as male pseudohermaphroditism) and in genetic females (female pseudohermaphroditism). This confusing nomenclature was the catalyst to the aforementioned Consensus; the clinical terminology now used for hermaphroditism is ovotesticular DSD. The chromosome pattern can be XX, XY, XX/XY; the commonest form is XX ovotesticular DSD.

The external genitalia are often ambiguous and the internal genitalia are likewise a mixture of Wolffian and Mullerian duct remnants. Sex assignment can either be male or female dependent on the reproductive tract anatomy and sex hormone production. There is fertility potential for either sex assignment;[10] often the gonads develop as ovotestes in which case it would be necessary to dissect away the ovarian or testicular component depending on the sex assignment.

5.1.2. XY Gonadal Dysgenesis

The problem in this category of DSD is abnormal formation of the testis in early fetal life when sex determination occurs. A large number of testis-determining genes are required to process the bipotential gonad as a testis. The clearest example of the genetic control of this process is exemplified by a mutation in the SRY gene. This results in complete gonadal dysgenesis, a condition also referred to as Swyer's syndrome. The phenotype is female; puberty fails to develop normally and there is a high risk of gonadal malignancy. The gonads need to be removed and hormone replacement with estrogens provided at puberty.

Partial forms of gonadal dysgenesis also occur where the phenotype is characterised by varying degrees of abnormal development of the external genitalia. Thus, the list of other possible causes to exclude is longer than for the complete form. Furthermore, the precise genetic cause often remains unknown. There are some forms of gonadal dysgenesis which are associated with abnormal

---

10 E.K. Johnson, C. Finlayson, E.E. Rowell et al., 'Fertility preservation for pediatric patients; current state and future possibilities' (2017) 198 *J Urol* 186–194.

development of other organs. One such example arises from a mutation in a gene called WT-1 (Wilms' tumour suppression gene) which is expressed very early in a region of the developing fetus called the urogenital ridge. This gives rise to development of both the gonads and kidneys. So a WT-1 mutation presents with features of partial gonadal dysgenesis, abnormal kidney structure and function and development of a tumour. It is important with presentations of DSD to ensure a thorough examination of other systems to exclude the presence of additional organ abnormalities.

5.1.3. Disorders of Androgen Production and Action

Once the bipotential gonad has developed as a testis, this organ becomes the source of hormones that control the development of the internal genitalia and the external genitalia from their respective precursor structures, the Wolffian ducts and the genital anlagen, respectively. This process is called sex differentiation. Androgens, particularly testosterone, are the key hormones required for sex differentiation. The production of androgens takes place via a series of chemical steps controlled by enzymes, starting with cholesterol. This substrate is essential for the production of all steroid hormones. There are many steps in the pathway, with each enzyme under the control of a specific gene. Consequently, a mutation in any one of these genes will reduce the production of androgens to a varying degree during the critical period of masculinisation in the early fetus and result in a DSD.

The final step in testosterone production and the subsequent conversion of testosterone to a more potent androgen, dihydrotestosterone (DHT), is critical for sex differentiation in the male. Mutations in the cognate genes result in a wide spectrum of abnormality of the external genitalia. The natural history of this form of DSD is that virilisation will spontaneously occur at puberty if the infant had been sex assigned female initially. Indeed, 5alpha-reductase deficiency, the enzyme which converts testosterone to DHT, is prevalent in isolated communities in the Dominican Republic, New Guinea and Turkey.[11] The Samibian tribe in New Guinea has traditionally had pubertal male initiation rites and some affected infants raised female have undergone 'turim-man' (Melanesian pidgin) in the belief of an innate and biological drive to masculinise at puberty in 5alpha-reductase deficiency. This change in gender role and subsequent recognition of male gender identity is relevant to the question of the appropriate management of an infant with this form of DSD and taking decisions (such as gonadectomy) that have irreversible consequences. The enzyme deficiency also occurs sporadically and in Western populations. When the diagnosis is made

---

11 H.J. Kang, J. Imperato-McGinley, Y.S. Zhu, Z. Rosenwaks, '5alpa-reductase-2 deficiency's effect on human fertility' (2014) 101 *Fertil Steril* 310–316.

early, sex assignment is now increasingly male in the knowledge of the profound virilisation at puberty and the oft reassignment to male in those who have been raised female. These phenomena are surely apposite to any consideration about the legal aspects of intersex.

The entire pathway of male development can be intact; an XY zygote at fertilisation, formation of normal testes with an intact SRY gene, the production of normal concentrations of testosterone and DHT. ... yet an entirely normal external female phenotype. How could this occur? The answer lies within the nucleus of target cells which contain receptors for the androgen to bind and in turn, switch on genes that mediate the signs of masculinisation. In fetal life, these signs are elicited as male sex differentiation and thereafter at puberty and into adulthood, growth of the genitalia and sexual hair, muscle development and voice changes and sperm production. All these processes require an androgen receptor (AR) that responds to androgenic hormones such as testosterone and DHT. The aforementioned scenario of a female phenotype associated with an otherwise normal male pathway defines a condition called complete androgen insensitivity syndrome (CAIS). It was previously named the testicular feminisation syndrome. The gene that codes for the AR protein is located on the X chromosome; CAIS is inherited in a sex-linked recessive fashion, meaning that the mother is a carrier of an AR mutation which can be passed on to 50 per cent of her male offspring. The inheritance pattern for CAIS is similar to that associated with the bleeding disorder, haemophilia. CAIS may present in infant girls with swellings in the groins or labia that are due to the presence of testes. More commonly, the presentation is not until adolescence when a girl is investigated for not having started her periods. In other respects, her breast development is normal as the testosterone produced by the testes is converted to estrogen, the female sex hormone. However, there is no or scanty pubic and axillary hair because of a dysfunctional AR. There is a risk of a tumour forming in the testis for which removal of both testes is advised sometime after puberty.[12] Some women opt not to have the testes removed as the risk is quite low (2–5 per cent) and they report a better quality of life compared with the use of hormone replacement therapy. The uterus is absent and the vagina shortened from the inhibiting effects of AMH produced by the fetal testes. This may create difficulty with sexual intercourse; the use of vaginal dilators is generally helpful but occasionally surgery is required to fashion a vagina.

CAIS is caused by a mutation in the AR gene which renders the AR protein incapable of binding androgens. It is akin to a faulty key incapable of unlocking

---

12 S. Chaudhry, R. Tadokoro-Cuccaro, S.E. Hannema, C.L. Acerini, IA Hughes, 'Frequency of gonadal tumours in complete androgen insensitivity syndrome (CAIS): a retrospective case-series analysis' (2017) 13 *J Pediatr Urol* 498.e1–498.e6.

a door. This is a relatively straightforward explanation of an example of a DSD, which strictly is not an intersex as the external genitalia are normal female. A more complex scenario arises with other types of AR mutation where the genitalia are atypical and range from a slightly virilised female appearance to a mildly under-masculinised male. This defines a partial form of androgen insensitivity, PAIS. Now the clinical signs may fit with any number of XY DSD causes. Consequently, it can be quite challenging to reach a firm diagnosis and thence, come to an agreement with the family about an appropriate sex assignment for the infant. Laboratory studies of the mutant AR identified in PAIS show that the reduced efficiency of the receptor in regulating androgen-responsive genes can be overcome by exposing the cells to higher levels of androgens. How that knowledge can be applied clinically in order to predict whether infants with PAIS assigned male develop at puberty, is the subject of ongoing longer-term outcome studies. There is also evidence that quantitative analysis of the degree of under-masculinisation of the external genitalia at birth is a reasonable predictor of the likelihood of the boy entering puberty spontaneously without the need for extra testosterone treatment. Spermatogenesis requires an intact AR functioning within the sperm-producing cells of the testis. Consequently, males with PAIS are rarely fertile although there are examples of fatherhood through the use of artificial reproductive techniques. Overall, infants with XY forms of DSD where the external genitalia are under-masculinised to varying degrees are now more likely to be sex assigned male than in previous generations.[13] Factors which have probably influenced this change include improvements in the techniques of male genital reconstructive surgery, a reluctance to perform irreversible gonadectomy (particularly before the child can consent), an improved understanding of the effects of prenatal androgen exposure on gender identity and perhaps the practice in some countries of legal constraints on genital surgery in minors.

5.1.4. *Other XY DSD Examples*

The development of the testis in the fetus takes place within the abdomen, close to where the kidneys develop. The testes later migrate down the abdomen to enter the inguinal canal in the groin to emerge in the scrotum just before birth. This ensures that the testes are positioned 'outside' the body so that it is at a lower ambient temperature. This is essential for normal sperm production. When this migration fails to occur, there is an undescended testis which can occur on both sides or just unilaterally on one side. The condition is called cryptorchidism.

---

13 Z. Kolesinksa, S.F. Ahmed, M. Niedziela et al., 'Changes over time in sex assignment of disorders of sex development' (2014) 134 *Pediatrics* 710–715.

It is common, affecting 2–9 per cent of male infants at birth. Furthermore, there is evidence that the prevalence of cryptorchidism has increased in recent years. This has been attributed to chemicals in the environment (more than 80,000) many of which act as endocrine disrupters. These interfere with endocrine pathways, especially during critical and sensitive periods of development such as the masculinising programming window in the male fetus. There has also been an increase in testicular cancer which may be linked to environmental effects. Treatment for cryptorchidism requires early surgery to bring the testes down in to the scrotum which reduces the risk of testis cancer and optimises sperm production at puberty. Rarely, the testes are absent at birth (anorchia) in an otherwise normally developed boy. Hence the fetal testes must have developed initially to induce normal sex differentiation; the cause of anorchia is probably due to intra-uterine torsion of the testes in late pregnancy which obliterates the blood supply. When surgeons explore the abdomen to search for the testes, only remnants of fibrous tissue are found. Boys with anorchia start treatment with testosterone at around 11 years of age to induce puberty and later have testis prostheses inserted in the empty scrotal sac.

Hypospadias, where the opening of the urethra is at the under surface of the penis rather than at its tip, is also quite common affecting about 0.8 per cent of boys. It is also a component of more severe forms of XY DSD which have been discussed. The isolated form has increased in prevalence, also thought to be related to environmental effects. Single gene defects are identified in a small minority of cases. Treatment is surgical to re-site the urethral opening to the tip of the penis to enable a normal urinary stream and subsequent ejaculation of semen.

Another form of XY DSD is the Persistent Mullerian Duct Syndrome (PMDS). This is characterised by normal male development apart from perhaps an undescended testis on one side or occasionally where both testes have migrated to one side of the scrotum, leaving the other side empty. When the surgeon performs an exploration to identify the testes in order to place them in the correct position, a Fallopian tube and/or part of a uterus is found. These are remnants of Mullerian ducts which normally regress in the developing male fetus under the influence of AMH, the anti-Mullerian hormone produced by the fetal testis. However, in PMDS there is a mutation in the AMH gene which leads to failure of AMH production and hence lack of Mullerian duct regression. In other cases of PMDS, the production of AMH is normal and the defect lies at the level of its cell receptor so there is resistance to the action of AMH in target tissues. Either way, the clinical findings are similar. Treatment aims to re-site the testes in the correct position but this may not be possible if the blood supply to the testis is at risk of being damaged in the procedure. The same caution applies to any attempt at removing the Mullerian remnants which can usually be left in place.

5.2. FEMALE AFFECTED

5.2.1. *Congenital Adrenal Hyperplasia (CAH)*

CAH is the dominant form of XX DSD affecting females. It is the commonest cause of ambiguous genitalia in the new-born.[14] The adrenal glands lie adjacent to the kidneys and produce steroid hormones which maintain normal metabolic homeostasis. A key hormone produced by the adrenals is cortisol which is essential for life. Other hormones control salt balance and the adrenals also produce a small amount of androgens. This complex production line of steroid hormones is controlled by a series of enzymatic steps. It is one of these steps which is disrupted in CAH owing to a gene mutation. The net result is failure of cortisol production and also salt retention in the majority of affected cases. Because of the deficiency of cortisol, the adrenals try to compensate by increasing the action of the enzymes in the pathway of cortisol production. However, the block in cortisol is towards the end of the pathway so that every steroid above the block is over-produced. This includes the pathway leading to androgens which is normally insignificant compared with androgens produced elsewhere in the body, such as by the testes.

The consequence of increased adrenal androgen production in a girl is to virilise the external genitalia. Since the adrenals start producing steroids in early fetal life, a female fetus affected by CAH is born with ambiguous genitalia from the effects of the excess androgens. There is a range of severity such that the genitalia may resemble a normal male: the clitoris enlarged to form a penis with the urethra opening at the tip, and the labia fused with pigmented and rugose skin to resemble a scrotum. Not surprisingly in this situation, the new-born infant may be declared male at birth. However, the scrotum is empty of palpable gonads and this should raise alarm bells about questioning the correct sex of the baby. So the routine examination of all new-borns when undertaken competently should avoid a mistaken sex assignment and an inappropriate sex of rearing. If a mistake is made and it is realised later that the 'boy' is in fact a girl, the question of sex reassignment must be addressed. The concept of gender identity and how soon it becomes established in childhood is discussed in detail in the contribution by Pasterski in this volume. Generally, sex reassignment to female in a case like this example of CAH would be undertaken in infancy up to about 18 months to two years of age. Later, the decision to maintain male assignment would usually prevail because of the likely cementing of a male gender identity. This is despite the knowledge of the presence of ovaries, a uterus and the potential for fertility. If male assignment is maintained, appropriate measures need to be taken by

---

14 A.A. Pasa, M.I. New, 'Steroid 21-hydroxylase deficiency in congenital adrenal hyperplasia' (2017) 165 (Pt A) *J Steroid Biochem Mol Biol* 2–11.

the age of puberty to prevent the onset of menstruation which, in this instance, would result in blood flow via the 'penile' urethra. Such management raises matters of consent and perhaps legal ones and the surety of full understanding by the child and his carers of what the future holds in adulthood.

The presentation of CAH in infancy with ambiguous genitalia will prompt early investigation and a diagnosis, often within a few days of birth. It is also important to establish whether the infant has the salt-losing form of CAH which can be life-threatening. Boys with CAH have normal genitalia so that the early signs of salt loss (failure to gain weight with feeding) may not be specific enough to warrant investigation. Later, there is weight loss, vomiting and dehydration which can result in collapse if not promptly treated. This led to CAH being added in most Western countries to the list of conditions which are screened for at birth. However, this is not the case in the UK mainly because of the practice of the blood spot specimen for screening not being collected until five to seven days after birth by the visiting nurse at home. By the time the blood results become available, the infant will have already presented with signs of salt loss. Recent studies in the UK have not shown an increased mortality rate in new-born males not screened for CAH.[15]

Treatment for CAH from a medical perspective is relatively straightforward. Cortisol is replaced in doses appropriate for body size as well as using a salt-retaining hormone for those who are also salt-losers. The doses of steroids are carefully titrated to ensure normal growth through childhood and subsequent pubertal development. If control is inadequate, the potential for fertility can be seriously compromised in both females and males with CAH. Surgical management of the female with CAH is a more complex issue. Typically, there is enlargement of the clitoris and partial fusion of the labial folds which results in a single opening on the perineum, rather than two separate openings for the urethra and vagina. It was routine practice to perform surgery in infancy to reduce the size of the clitoris and to bring the opening of the vagina to the outside by a vaginoplasty procedure. The cosmetic results were generally excellent owing not only to the technical expertise of the surgeon but also because of the rapid healing properties of the delicate infant tissues. It then became apparent from longer-term outcome studies of adult females with CAH that all was not well. There were major problems with sexual intercourse and an inability to form satisfactory relationships. This was due to reduced sensitivity of the clitoris remnant caused by damage during surgery to the rich network of nerves which supplies the clitoris. Repeated surgery to the vagina was often required around puberty because of narrowing of the vagina from scarring. This has led to a re-evaluation of the place and timing of genital surgery in females with CAH.

---

15 B.E. Hird, L. Tetlow, S. Tobi, L. Patel, P.E. Clayton, 'No evidence of an increase in early infant mortality from congenital adrenal hyperplasia in the absence of screening' (2014) 99 *Arch Dis Child* 158–164.

Some have advocated a moratorium on any genital surgery in DSD, but for CAH in particular, until 16 years of age unless there is a medical indication for surgery.[16] How such proposals may impact on DSD management from a medical perspective is untested but the legal issues are discussed in detail in several chapters in this book.

One aspect of CAH management which needs highlighting in the context of consent and the concept of, 'first do no harm' embedded in the Hippocratic oath, is prenatal treatment for CAH. The fetal adrenal gland in CAH starts producing excess amounts of androgens as early as six to seven weeks of pregnancy, hence the outcome of a virilised female with CAH at birth. Postnatal treatment with hydrocortisone (the name of the manufactured form of cortisol) is given to replenish cortisol deficiency but also to suppress the excess production of androgens. In pregnancy, most of the cortisol produced by the mother is metabolised as it crosses the placenta and so is not sufficient to suppress the androgens produced by the fetal adrenal gland. However, another synthetic steroid, dexamethasone, is a potent form of cortisol which crosses the placenta from the mother and is not metabolised. Giving dexamethasone to a mother who is at risk of having another child with CAH (one in four chance) early in pregnancy was tried more than 30 years ago and does prevent virilisation of an affected female fetus. However, treatment was instituted in 'blind' fashion without knowing the sex of the fetus (males do not need to be treated) and whether a female fetus was indeed affected by CAH. Based on the inheritance pattern of the one in four risk (for an autosomal recessive genetic condition) and males, affected or not, who do not need treatment, the calculation leads to the result that seven out of eight fetuses are exposed unnecessarily to a potent steroid. Tests in later pregnancy can confirm if the fetus does have CAH so that dexamethasone can be discontinued in the non-affected pregnancies. Nevertheless, outcome studies show some adverse neurodevelopmental effects in children who were exposed to dexamethasone during pregnancy, including those whose exposure was short. So what relevance does this history have when considering the legal question of intersex persons? Sweden, a country which undertook pioneering, well-conducted and comprehensive clinical trials of CAH prenatal treatment, has banned the practice. This may change now that it is possible to target only the affected female fetus for treatment using analysis of fetal DNA in the mother's blood very early in pregnancy. This enables the sex to be established and, if female, whether a mutation is found in the CAH gene. Nevertheless, this still raises a question of how a fetus can give consent and, while the ambiguity of the external genitalia can be prevented by dexamethasone

16 J.A. Greenberg, 'Legal, ethical, and human rights considerations for physicians treating children with atypical or ambiguous genitalia' (2017) 41 *Semin Perinatol* 252–255.

exposure, what is the longer-term outcome in adolescence and adulthood from the toxic effects of such a potent steroid?[17]

5.2.2. Other XX DSD Examples

A number of genes are required for development of the ovary. A mutation results in ovarian dysgenesis, which is usually not manifest until puberty with failure of breast development, lack of menses and subsequent infertility. As with CAH, there are much rarer forms of increased androgen production affecting an XX fetus. Some may arise from a maternal source of androgens such as an ovarian tumour. Another cause is aromatase deficiency, the enzyme which converts androgens to estrogens. The enzyme is also produced in the placenta so when deficient, both a female fetus and her pregnant mother become virilised. The virilisation resolves in the mother after delivery, only to recur in subsequent pregnancies.

There are rare syndromes that can affect the reproductive tract of females. One example is the Mayer-Rokitansky-Kuster-Hauser (MRKH) syndrome whereby the Mullerian ducts fail to develop resulting in the absence of both the uterus and vagina. There may also be associated kidney abnormalities. The ovaries develop normally.

6. MANAGEMENT OF INTERSEX

It is evident that a team of health professionals is required to care for children and their families with intersex problems. The team should comprise a paediatric endocrinologist, clinical psychologist, a paediatric surgeon (usually a specialist in urology), a gynaecologist specialising in children and adolescents and a clinical geneticist. Other experts in social care, medical ethics and legal matters should be available to the team for additional advice where necessary. The management of intersex persons should be undertaken in specialist centres which see sufficient numbers of cases to acquire the expertise to deal with often complex issues. This is particularly important when genital surgery needs to be considered.

6.1. INTERSEX IN THE NEW-BORN

Whether a pregnancy produces a boy or a girl is instantaneously known at birth. Indeed, that information is often known before birth from the results

---

17 M.I. New, Y.K. Toni, T. Yuen et al., 'Noninvasive prenatal diagnosis of congenital adrenal hyperplasia using cell-free fetal DNA in maternal plasma' (2014) 99 *J Clin Endocrinol Metab* E1022–1030.

of ultrasound tests and, increasingly, the use of analysis of fetal DNA in the mother's blood to determine the sex. Several websites now advertise services for parents who wish to know whether they are expecting a girl or a boy. So when a baby is born whose sex is indeterminate, this can understandably cause considerable distress for the parents. Health professionals should resist the temptation to opine on what they think the sex is likely to be. That is unhelpful and may lead to further distress when the prediction is false. The first conversation with the parents and the words chosen are critical to determining how well the family will cope with the stress. Studies indicate that parents, years later, may still harbour feelings akin to a post-traumatic stress disorder.[18] It is important from the outset to be honest with the parents by accepting that currently, the sex of the baby is not known, explain simply how that may occur, and then describe the tests to be performed to determine the cause. These will be done as quickly as possible but not at the expense of having an inadequate investigation which may lead to a wrong diagnosis. Frustrating though delays can be, better to take the time to get the correct answer. This in turn will lead to a position of knowledge to help guide the health professionals *and* the family to reach a decision on the appropriate sex assignment. The time taken to complete the investigations will vary according to the cause. In the case of ambiguous genitalia due to CAH, a combination of an ultrasound that shows a uterus, an increase in an adrenal steroid marker in the blood and evidence of XX chromosomes clinches the diagnosis within three to five days of birth. The baby will also be tested for salt loss. Treatment starts early and discussions can take place later about whether and when surgery may be necessary on the genitalia. The causes of XY DSD are more complex and it may take a number of weeks before the results of tests become available. This is a trying time for the family who need appropriate counselling and regular updates on progress with the investigation.

There is a legal requirement to register a birth within a certain time-frame. For England, Wales and Northern Ireland this is 42 days. Parents need to be advised to delay birth registration until all the investigations are complete and enough time is taken to fully discuss the options for sex assignment. As long as the office of the Registrar for Births, Marriages and Deaths is contacted to request a delay in registration, the interval can be as long as it takes to make a decision on sex assignment. Once sex assignment is made this decision is complemented by the sex of rearing. Of course, the biological sex may not be congruent as with the example of CAIS where the sex assignment and sex of rearing, despite the presence of a Y chromosome and testes, are unequivocally congruent as female. In other causes of DSD, there are occasions where sex reassignment may occur and especially at the time of puberty.

---

18 V. Pasterski, K. Mastroyannopoulou, D. Wright, K.J. Zucker, I.A. Hughes, 'Predictors of posttraumatic stress in parents of children diagnosed with disorders of sex development' (2014) 43*Arch Sex Behav* 369–375.

6.2. INTERSEX AT PUBERTY

Illustrative examples of intersex due to disorders of androgen production in XY DSD have been described whereby the sex assignment and rearing have been female, but profound virilisation occurs at puberty. This is obviously also distressing and particularly so for the intersex person. In this situation options involve retaining the sex of rearing (female) or reassigning to a male sex, with both options requiring appropriate hormonal manipulation and possibly genital surgery. Here, the assessment by a clinical psychologist of the person's gender identity is of paramount importance. If a female sex is to be retained, the excess production of androgens can be switched off by hormone blockers pending planned surgery to remove the testes, perhaps to reduce the size of the clitoris and undertake a vaginoplasty. Thereafter, hormone replacement treatment with estrogens is needed. A decision to reassign as male is aided by the effects of endogenous androgens which cause an increase in the size of the phallus, deepening of the voice, increased muscle mass and descent of the testes in to an enlarged labioscrotal sac. Normal sperm production can occur and fertility rarely.

6.3. PSYCHOLOGICAL ASPECTS

This is discussed in detail in the contribution by Pasterski in this volume. However, members of the health professional team providing a clinical service for persons with intersex need to be familiar with the concepts of gender role and gender identity that are relevant to the biology of fetal sex development. So in girls with CAH, they often display a behaviour pattern more akin to boys than girls and hence changes in gender role. In contrast, gender identity has been deemed to be female in most instances although some girls demonstrate traits that would border on the criteria for gender dysphoria in the non-CAH population.[19] Overall, it appears that the prevalence of gender dysphoria is not markedly increased in persons with intersex, despite what intuitively one would expect based on severity of the atypical sex development.

It is now recognised that gender identity is non-binary and can be fluid, unlike what has been described in this chapter for the biological aspects of sex determination and sex differentiation. While it may be useful to add the 'I' of Intersex to LGBT from the social and perhaps legal perspective, this is not

---

19 V. Pasterski, K.J. Zucker, P.C. Hindmarsh et al., 'Increased cross-gender identification independent of gender role behaviour in girls with congenital adrenal hyperplasia: results from a standardized assessment of 4- to 11-year old children' (2015) 44 *Arch Sex Behav* 1363–1375.

appropriate for the management of intersex or DSD.[20] Nor do persons in general with DSD want to be badged as LGBTI. Certainly, there are convincing studies undertaken on male twin pairs that sexual orientation has a genetic component with chromosomal regions, including the X chromosome, showing increased associations amongst homosexuals.[21]

However, a 'gay' gene *per se*, has not been identified. Prenatal factors may be relevant as illustrated by some women with CAH demonstrating non-heterosexual behaviour. In addition, there are social factors to be considered when explaining the complex interplay which determines sexual orientation. As far as one can determine, the binary process of sex determination (formation of a testis or an ovary) and sex differentiation (the anatomy of the internal and external genitalia, consequent upon sex determination) is the same in LGBT persons. Hence the need to distinguish intersex/DSD from LGBT, at least with respect to medical management.

7. CONCLUSIONS

The biology of sex development in the fetus describes a binary process characterised by the bipotential of embryonic tissue to develop as either male or female reproductive organs. Control of the definitive sex dimorphic pathway is mediated by key genes and hormones which operate in a time and concentration-dependent manner during a critical window of fetal programming. Knowledge of this pathway provides a logical approach to classifying causes of intersex and DSD. This allows a rational approach to investigation and management. Only a team of health professionals working in specialised centres should undertake this work and to provide support for persons with intersex and their families. The misuse of terminology in the field of intersex is unhelpful; clarity is needed to focus on what are primarily biomedical factors versus those that are more relevant from a social perspective. The aim of this chapter has been to explain in the context of a book on legal issues how a male and a female develops from a common structure, why that process may deviate from a binary biological pathway and how the management of intersex/DSD conditions which then arise may have relevance to the law.

---

20 M. Cools, M. Simmonds, S. Elford et al., 'Response to the Council of Europe Human Rights Commission's issue paper on Human Rights and Intersex people' (2016) 70 *Eur Urol* 407–409.

21 T.C. Ngun, E. Vilain, 'The biological basis of human sexual orientation: is there a role for epigenetics?' (2014) 86 *Adv Genet* 167–184.

INTERSEX IN THE BRAIN: WHAT NEUROSCIENCE CAN TELL THE LAW ABOUT GENDER IDENTITY

Joe HERBERT*

1. SCIENCE AND THE LAW

Science has had a huge impact on the law.[1] No contemporary crime scene would be complete without a corps of white-coated technicians taking samples or making measurements. But this extra information has no influence on the legal process. The rules of evidence are not altered, the methods of arriving at a verdict are the same, the sentencing policy is untouched. Psychiatrists may be asked to assess a perpetrator's mental state, but the court decides whether this alters its view of responsibility, and the psychological consequences of an action may influence

* I am most grateful to John Bancroft, Richard Green, Ken Zucker and Jens Scherpe for their helpful comments which greatly improved an earlier version.

1 R. GREEN, *Sexual science and the law*, Harvard University Press, Massachusetts, USA 1992.

how a court assesses injury. But there are circumstances in which science can influence the composition of the law, or the process by which it is operated. This is one way in which changing cultural or social conditions are – eventually – reflected in the law. The issues surrounding gender identity are a prime example. It is thus essential that lawyers know what science can tell them and, equally, where its limits are: what is not known, or uncertain, as well as what is known.

The term 'intersex' originally referred to those with genitalia that were indeterminate, so complicating or confusing gender assignment at birth. In extreme cases, this meant that the individual's genitalia did not correspond with his/her gender identity. However, a similar disassociation occurs if the person's gender identity does not correspond with his/her genitalia, the latter being the form expected on the basis of chromosomal constitution (XY – male, XX – female). The appearance of an individual's genitals can have profound effects on self-image. So, aberrations in gender identity are also part of 'intersex' (i.e. a dissociation between the brain and the genitals).[2] The brain and the genitals are intertwined and the term 'intersex' incorporates them both. Gender identity raises many of the same legal questions as disturbances in the development of the genitalia. Current legal debates surrounding gender identity, a relatively new problem for the law, come up against the long-standing and copious body of information on the science of sexuality.

What does neuroscience tell us about gender? Does gender identity lie in the brain: does the brain have a 'gender'? If it does, what does this tell us about the definition of gender? Does any of this knowledge assist the legal profession? Does it have implications for social attitudes towards transgender, and will this, in turn, affect how the law deals with transgender? The latter is likely to vary considerably in different cultures: for example, in Western countries and Muslim communities. The science of transgender has had little impact on such differences, but history shows that this may change with wider education and a more inclusive social structure. Science, it is presumed, offers unbiased and validated information on gender and its variants. It is the responsibility of the law to make good and appropriate use of this information, recognising that cultural or religious elements may intervene. But this connection also depends on how accurate, complete and relevant is the scientific information that is provided. This is what is considered in this chapter.

2. THE PARTICULAR CASE OF GENDER DYSPHORIA

Whatever the legal concerns about gender identity, from a medical standpoint there is only one objective: to reconcile a person's view of themselves (identity)

---

2 D. Frimberger and J.P. Gearhart, 'Ambiguous genitalia and intersex' (2005) 75(4) *Urol Int* 291–297.

with the body – particularly their genitalia. It is a medical concern because gender dysphoria can be a highly distressing condition, which has markedly adverse consequences for a satisfactory lifestyle with psychological, or often psychiatric, consequences,[3] and to resolve or lessen these may need treatment. The use of surgical or hormonal procedures to help such a reconciliation is therefore a matter for medicine, but not only medicine. Young people who transition socially reduce their risk of later mental disorder.[4] Gender has social, financial and political consequences as well. This is one reason for involving the law. A second legal interest concerns medical intervention: since this is life-changing, and may be irreversible,[5] there have to be legal constraints and supervision of its application, and penalties for those appearing to contravene accepted procedures. But these procedures need to be guided by the scientific evidence. This depends, essentially, on knowing the best course of action for each individual, whether this varies according to circumstance and what the social and health consequences for that person might be. Gender identity, and thus its disorders (dysphoria), arise in the brain;[6] the way this comes about and whether it can be moderated is a scientific issue. How this alters a person's legal status or entitlements remains a legal issue. Can neuroscience tell lawyers anything useful or relevant about gender identity?

3. THE NATURE OF GENDER DYSPHORIA

Before we consider gender identity further, we should recognise that both gender identity (a neural event) and the formation of the genitalia (a developmental event), although commonly classed into two categories (male, female), in fact lie on a continuum. This continuum has several dimensions: for example, the external genitalia may resemble the usual male, female configuration or lie somewhere intermediate – or even resemble neither.[7] This may, or may not, apply to the internal genitalia (e.g. the presence of a womb, seminal vesicles etc.). The gonads themselves may be sex typical, or contain elements of both sexes (formerly called true hermaphroditism, now ovotesticular disorder of sexual development).[8] This is equally true for the neural mechanisms underlying

---

3 J. Bancroft, *Human sexuality and its problems*, 3rd ed., Churchill Livingstone Elsevier, Edinburgh 2008.

4 R. Green, *New Oxford Textbook of Psychiatry*, M. Gelder (ed.), Oxford University Press, Oxford 2009.

5 J.U. Berli et al., 'What Surgeons Need to Know About Gender Confirmation Surgery when Providing Care for Transgender Individuals: A Review' (2017) 152 *JAMA Surg.* 394–400.

6 M. Hines, *Brain gender*, Oxford University Press, Oxford 2005, p. 336.

7 Frimberger, Gearhart, above n. 2.

8 The term that has replaced older ones, such as intersex. See I.A. Hughes, C. Houk, S.F. Ahmed, P.A. Lee and LWPES/ESPE Consensus Group, 'Consensus statement on management of intersex disorders' (2006) 2 *J Pediatr Urol* 148–162.

gender identity. This has a direct bearing on how the law views or classifies a person's gender.

Gender identity is thus not uni-dimensional or binary. This is despite the fact that society (and the law) in most countries attribute distinct characteristics and allowances to males and females. (Note, however, the existence of 'third' genders in some societies: e.g. the Indian Hijras.) Furthermore, the distinction between gender identity (considering oneself either male or female) and gender role (social expectations or allowances influenced by perceived gender) is not always clear. Nevertheless, most individuals classify themselves as either one or the other. However, the evidence shows that there is a continuum between 'typical' (usually classed as 'normal') male and 'typical' female in both the brain mechanisms responsible for gender identity and the developmental processes that give rise to the adult form of the genitalia.[9] So, mismatches between

Figure 1. The brain and gender identity

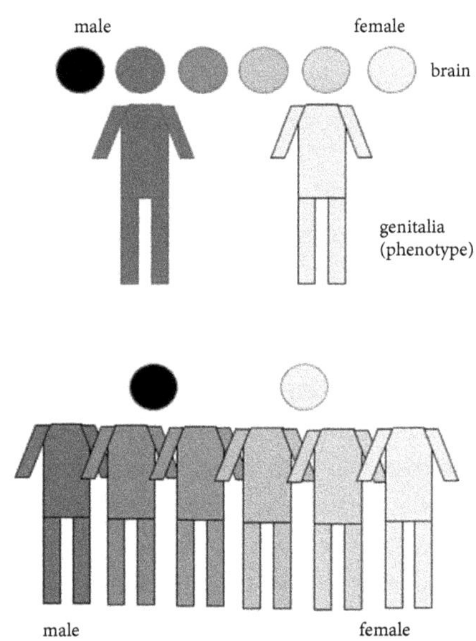

The contributions of either the brain or the genitalia to gender dysphoria. Each can be represented as a continuum from 'male' to 'female'; a mismatch between either can underlie gender dysphoria. Above: a range of possible brain states of gender identity, ranging from 'male' to 'female' through a series of intermediate stages associated with either a male or female body (phenotype); below, one of two possible brain states (male, female) associated with a range of genitals, ranging from typical male through intermediate stages to typical female. Although these are shown as independent variables, intermediate variations in both may occur together.

Source: Produced by the author.

9 S.M. Rosenthal, 'Transgender youth: current concepts' (2016) 21(4) *Ann Pediatr Endocrinol Metab* 185–192.

the two can arise in the brain, genitalia, or both, and are not a binary quantity in either (Figure 1). The simplest form of gender dysphoria is when self-assignment does not match the person's genitalia (and, by extension, usually their chromosomal – XY, XX – constitution). So, the evident solution is equally simple: reconcile the two, so that the person now functions at both levels (brain and genitals) in one of the two usual configurations.[10] This is where the problems begin.

4. NATURE VERSUS NURTURE: A FUTILE DEBATE

The way that gender identity is determined has been fiercely disputed by those proposing 'nature' (e.g. biological factors) vs. 'nurture' (the predominance of social factors). This debate is both tendentious and irrelevant. It is now very clear that all developmental processes involve both, and that the two are not separable, that they interact, and are therefore different facets of a single process. For example: genes (e.g. on the Y chromosome) determine the formation of testes, which then secrete testosterone during early embryonic life.[11] Experiments in animals show that this has long-lasting effects on the brain and sex-typical behaviour. In humans, inability to respond to testosterone (the androgen insensitivity syndrome: AIS) in a ('male') embryo results in a child (and adult) that is female both in appearance and gender identity, despite male levels of testosterone.[12] There are no measurable differences in such features as psychological well-being, self-esteem, core gender identity, sexual orientation and gender role behaviour between these individuals and 'normal' XX women, though all differ between them and 'normal' XY men.

However, we also know that the experience of that child in early life can influence how it sees itself, including its gender attribution. So, in the case of AIS (genes), the child's appearance (phenotype) will influence the way others, particularly its parents, treat it. This may also influence its gender identity.

---

10 M.D. Connolly et al., 'The Mental Health of Transgender Youth: Advances in Understanding' (2016) 59(5) *J Adolesc Health* 489–495.

11 J. Herbert, *Testosterone: sex, power and the will to win*, Oxford University Press, Oxford 2015.

12 J. Balthazart, 'Minireview: Hormones and human sexual orientation' (2011) 152(8) *Endocrinology* 2937–2947; B. Gottlieb et al., 'The androgen receptor gene mutations database: 2012 update' (2012) 35(3) *Hum Mutat* 887–894; M. Hines, 'Prenatal endocrine influences on sexual orientation and on sexually differentiated childhood behavior' (2011) 32(2) *Front Neuroendocrinol* 170–182.

5. THE ROLE OF TESTOSTERONE IN GENDER IDENTITY

Nevertheless, there is justified suspicion that early exposure of the infantile brain to testosterone may play a very significant role in the development of gender identity.[13] We lack comprehensive data on exposure to testosterone during pregnancy in a large number of cases, as well as measures of sensitivity to testosterone (this depends on another molecule, the testosterone receptor, which is individually genetically variable), together with an equally comprehensive follow-up of subsequent individual and social behaviour during infancy, childhood and adulthood. Such a study is technically and ethically impossible at present. Firm evidence on the role of testosterone would allow us to determine if variations in this exposure were responsible, in some cases at least, for subsequent gender dysphoria (e.g. subnormal testosterone in phenotypic boys, supranormal in girls).

So how does gender dysphoria happen? Ultimately, it is a neural event. What the law would like is a clear and objective definition of gender identity at the level of the brain (Figure 2).

Figure 2. Imaginary diagram of defining 'true' gender identity

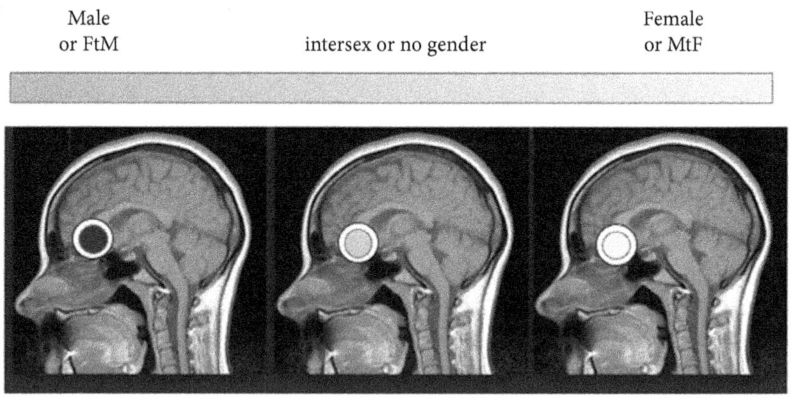

An entirely imaginative representation of the quality of information about brain gender that might help the law. It is supposed that there is a scanning method that reveals the 'true' gender identity of the individual, which would lie on a continuum from entirely 'male' through intermediate stages to entirely 'female'. It is assumed that gender identity has only one dimension. The subject in the middle represents someone who would be categorised as 'bigender'. This technique does not exist at present.

Source: Produced by the author.

The problem here is that we do not know the nature of this event – that is, what condition in the brain represents gender identity (even supposing this is

13 M. Hines, 'Gender development and the human brain' (2011) 34 *Annu Rev Neurosci* 69–88.

binary). There are known sex differences in the brain, including those in the hypothalamus, the part of the brain established as being essential for sexual behaviour in both animals and humans (see below).[14] However, since it has proved impossible so far to study gender identity in animals (see below), we do not know whether these differences, some of which are regulated by early testosterone, represent the neural expression of gender identity. They could equally easily underlie other aspects of sexuality, including sexual preference.[15] This means that any experimental attempt to develop treatments that might alter or reinforce gender identity cannot be made (assuming these to be ethically acceptable). Neither do we have an objective way of assessing the 'true' gender identity of a given individual (e.g. by a scan) (see Figure 2). Since gender identity can be fluid in early life, this would be valuable. There is fierce debate over the age at which gender identity becomes explicit and fixed.[16] This has huge influence over decisions about when, how or if to treat gender dysphoria. Most clinicians, for example, say that about three-quarters of those children expressing dysphoria when very young never ask for or require gender transition.[17] The problem is to separate these from the other quarter: an objective test would be game-changing. As it is, there is an equally fierce debate over whether to delay puberty in such cases so as to allow for more mature decisions, and avoid the child going through a puberty that accentuates the distress of the dysphoric state. It would be highly useful if neuroscience could advise the law about when or if there should be medical intervention in cases of gender dysphoria. But these disputed areas mean that neuroscience cannot give clear and unambiguous directions or precise information on how to assess individual factors when considering the timing or nature of such interventions.[18]

---

14 E. Maccoby and C.N. Jacklin, *The psychology of sex differences*, Stanford University Press, Stanford 1974; A.N. Ruigrok et al., 'A meta-analysis of sex differences in human brain structure' (2014) 39 *Neurosci Biobehav Rev* 34–50.

15 Balthazart, above n. 12; S.M. Breedlove, 'Prenatal Influences on Human Sexual Orientation: Expectations versus Data' (2017) 46 *Arch Sex Behav* 1583–1592.

16 K.J. Zucker and D.P. Vanderlaan, 'The self in gender dysphoria: a developmental perspective', in M. Kyrios, R. Moulding, G. Doron, S. Bhar and M. Nedeljkovic (eds.), *The self in understanding and treating psychological disorders*, Cambridge University Press, Cambridge 2016, pp. 222–232.

17 L. Mizock, 'Transgender and Gender Diverse Clients with Mental Disorders: Treatment Issues and Challenges' (2017) 40(1) *Psychiatr Clin North Am* 29–39; K.J. Zucker, A.A. Lawrence and B.P. Kreukels, 'Gender Dysphoria in Adults' (2016) 12 *Annual Rev Clin Psychol* 217–247.

18 J. Bancroft, *Human sexuality and its problems*, 3rd ed., Churchill Livingstone Elsevier, Edinburgh 2008; B. Gibson, 'Care of the child with the desire to change genders--Part II: Female-to-male transition' (2011) 31(4) *Urol Nurs* 230–235; B. Gibson and A.J. Catlin, 'Care of the child with the desire to change genders--Part III: Male-to-female transition' (2011) 31(4) *Urol Nurs* 236–241.

6. EVIDENCE FROM EXPERIMENTAL STUDIES

Much of what we know about sexuality comes from experiments and observations on animals. We can study sexual behaviour and see how it is altered by hormones or which parts of the brain seem to be involved. We can investigate the relative contributions of early (developmental) events in the animal's life, and those occurring later (e.g. puberty, or the effects of the cyclic secretions of hormones). We can study sexual preference: both within and between sexes: this has particular relevance to understanding hetero- and homosexuality.[19] How far experimental studies on animals will apply to the more complex human brain is always a question, but at least there is a biological foundation for our understanding of sexuality. This is not the case for gender identity. Though there have been some attempts to model this experimentally, none are convincing. So we rely for our knowledge of the foundations of gender identity entirely on observations on humans (Figure 3). The only 'experimental' data is that which can be gained from aberrations or variations in human sexuality – so-called 'experiments of nature'. Studying the basis of such variants may shed light on their underlying cause, but this will always be limited by the degree to which they occur or are recognised, and technical or ethical issues over the means of studying them.

Figure 3. Methods of investigating sexual behaviour

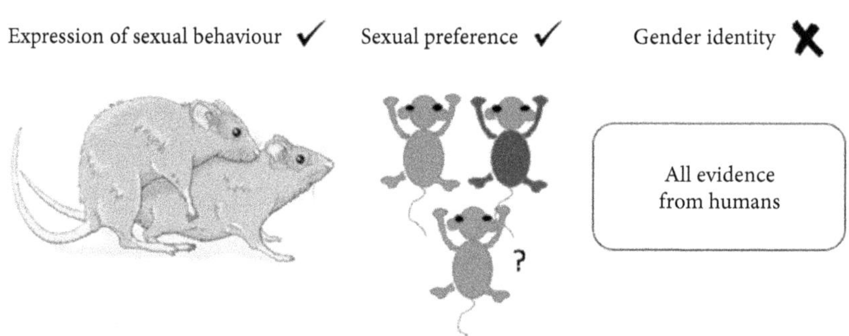

This demonstrates the contribution and limitations of experimental studies on sexual behaviour to our understanding of human sexuality. Gender-specific patterns of sexual behaviour and factors influencing sexual preference can be investigated, but gender identity cannot.

Source: Produced by the author.

---

19 A. Agmo, 'Animal models of female sexual dysfunction: basic considerations on drugs, arousal, motivation and behavior' (2014) 121 *Pharmacol Biochem Behav* 3–15; M.M. McCarthy and B.M. Nugent, 'Epigenetic contributions to hormonally-mediated sexual differentiation of the brain' (2013) 25(11) *J Neuroendocrinol* 1133–1140; M.M. McCarthy et al., 'Surprising origins of sex differences in the brain' (2015) 76 *Horm Behav* 3–10; A. Petrulis, 'Chemosignals, hormones and mammalian reproduction' (2013) 63(5) *Horm Behav* 723–741; C.F. Yang and N.M. Shah, 'Representing sex in the brain, one module at a time' (2014) 82(2) *Neuron* 261–278.

7. NEURAL SEPARATION OF GENDER IDENTITY AND SEXUAL ORIENTATION

Clinical experience tells us that sexual preference (i.e. hetero- and homosexuality, themselves part of a continuum) is independent of gender identity.[20] Thus, there are those who are transgender but find their original sex attractive, and those who prefer the other sex. This clearly demonstrates that there are similarly separable neural mechanisms for gender identity and sexual preference, though exactly how this is represented in the brain, and how these different aspects of sexuality are formed, remain unknown.

From what we know of other aspects of sexuality, largely from experiments on animals, it is unlikely that there would be a single 'gender identity centre' in the brain. Sexual interaction involves several areas of the brain, including those concerned with recognising a conspecific, its gender, its attractiveness and the activation of particular motivational states (e.g. arousal). So it is likely that there is a neural system that underlies the various components of gender identity, and that these may well differ between individuals. Furthermore, each of these neural components will not necessarily fall easily into 'male' or 'female'. Should we identify a crucial neural construction or system that underlies gender identity, it is likely that this would lie on a range from 'very male' to 'very female' but with intermediate states, including those that do not specify either gender, reflecting the variable expression of gender identity at the psychological level.

8. THE LIMITS OF NEUROSCIENCE

Why is our knowledge of the neural basis of gender identity so incomplete? This is one example of a more general problem. Neuroscience is a highly active area of research: it is said that there are now more neuroscientists alive than have ever lived. But much of the advances – and there have been many – lie at the level of the cell. We now know a great deal more than we did about how a nerve cell (neuron) is constructed, how it develops, how it makes connections with other neurons (an essential property of the brain), how it changes its properties with time and circumstance and how it responds to injury. We also have more precise information about the function of different parts of the brain. But we also know that the brain works as an assembly of neurons, both in local parts of the brain and as connected networks. What is lacking is understanding of how these assemblies actually produce the functions of the brain. We do not

---

20 Balthazart, above n. 12; M.K. Auer et al., 'Transgender transitioning and change of self-reported sexual orientation' (2014) 9(10) *PLoS One* e110016; S.L. Katz-Wise et al., 'Differences in Sexual Orientation Diversity and Sexual Fluidity in Attractions Among Gender Minority Adults in Massachusetts' (2016) 53(1) *J Sex Res* 74–84.

know how they form a memory, compile a perception, learn a skilled movement, generate an emotion or a motivational state (e.g. hunger) and so on – let alone consciousness. Computer simulations of neuronal assemblies show that they can have properties that are difficult or impossible to predict from looking at the behaviour of the single neurons that make up such assemblies. There is not even a plausible theoretical framework to account, for example, why a particular part of the brain (in this case, the amygdala) at one time generates a psychological state we call 'fear' but, on another occasion, 'happiness', 'liking' or 'sexual interest'. Understanding the neural basis of gender identity falls into the same category: the difficulty of extrapolating neural activity to a functional (psychological) state.[21] Incidentally, this is not the case for other organs, such as the liver or heart: we have a good basic understanding of how they do what they do. The complexity of the brain limits our understanding of how it works.

Even when we detect gender differences in the brain, we may not be able to ascribe meaning to them. For example, it has been known for many years that there is a collection of nerve cells in the hypothalamus of rats which is larger in males than females (Figure 4). Furthermore, this size difference can be reversed by giving new-born female rats doses of testosterone, or castrating new-born males (thus depriving them of testosterone). But how this contributes to the different patterns of sexual behaviour or preference in rats has never been established, so the biological significance of this marked gender difference remains mysterious. The same applies to the many sex differences that both anatomical and scanning methods have shown in the human brain, including areas in the hypothalamus similar to those in the rat (Figure 4), though many are small, inconsistent and disputed.[22] Contemporary scanning methods (e.g. MRI) do not have enough resolution to determine whether there are small anatomical features in the brains of living transgender persons that distinguish them from others, and might assist diagnosis or classification. Even if this were possible, such information would have very limited usefulness: we need to know about detailed differences in connections, arrangements of neurons and their neurochemistry: all beyond current techniques. Such studies would also be complicated by possible confusion between brain mechanisms underlying transgender, sexual orientation or those responsive to hormonal treatment.[23]

---

21 A. Safron et al., 'Neural Correlates of Sexual Orientation in Heterosexual, Bisexual, and Homosexual Women' (2018) 8 *Sci Rep* 673; A. Safron et al., 'Neural Correlates of Sexual Orientation in Heterosexual, Bisexual, and Homosexual Men' (2017) 7 *Sci Rep* 41314.

22 A.N. Ruigrok et al., 'A meta-analysis of sex differences in human brain structure' (2014) 39 *Neurosci Biobehav Rev* 34–50; A. Guillamon, C. Junque, E. Gomez-Gil, 'A Review of the Status of Brain Structure Research in Transsexualism' (2016) 45(7) *Arch Sex Behav* 1615–1648.

23 S.C. Mueller et al., 'A Structural MRI Study in Transgender Persons on Cross-Sex Hormone Therapy' (2017) 105 *Neuroendocrinology* 123–130.

Figure 4. Gender differences in the brain

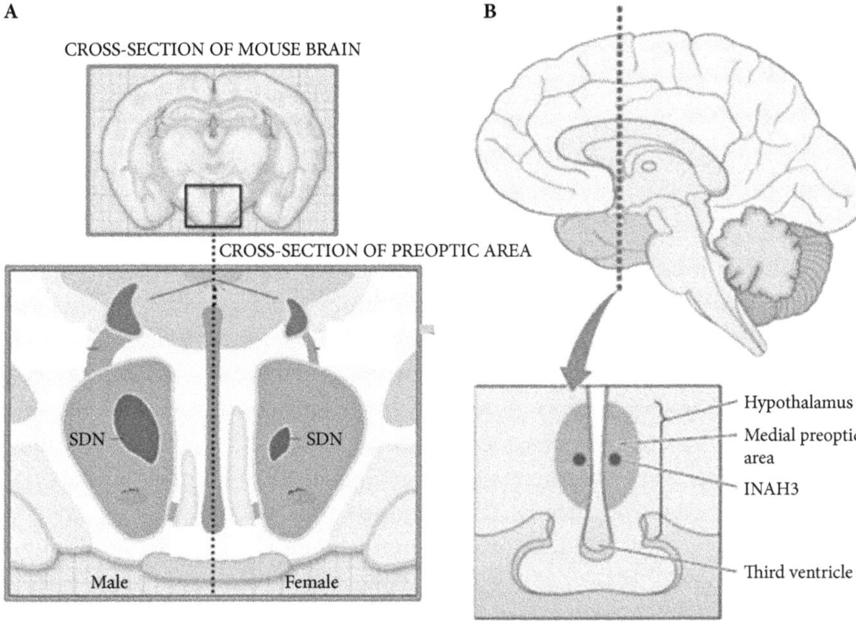

(A) A cross-section through the base of the rat's brain to show the area in the hypothalamus (SDN: sexually dimorphic nucleus) that is larger in males (left) than females (right).

(B) A corresponding section though the human brain to show an apparently homologous structure (INAH3: interstitial nucleus of the anterior hypothalamus) that is also larger in males than females. In neither case is the function of these structures known with certainty. A smaller INAH has been associated with male homosexuality. Redrawn from McCarthy (2015) and Swaab (2008)

Source: (A) M.M. McCarthy et al., *Surprising origins of sex differences in the brain* (2015) 76 *Horm Behav* 3–10.

(B) D.F. Swaab, *Sexual orientation and its basis in brain structure and function* (2008) 105(3) *Proc Natl Acad Sci U S A* 10273–4.

9. TREATING GENDER DYSPHORIA

The lack of knowledge of the neural basis of gender identity means that current attempts to reconcile gender dysphoria with the body (phenotype) are limited either to psychological methods (reinforcing gender identity etc.) directed towards the brain or medical interventions directed towards the genitalia (hormones and surgery, though hormones will also alter brain function).[24]

24 Berli et al., above n. 5; J.D. Frey et al., 'An Update on Genital Reconstruction Options for the Female-to-Male Transgender Patient: A Review of the Literature' (2017) 139(3) *Plast Reconstr Surg* 728–737; R.N. Gorton and L. Erickson-Schroth, 'Hormonal and Surgical

The fluidity of gender identity in early life has already been mentioned: this signals caution about premature, irreversible or possibly damaging interventions. The whole issue has become highly politicised.[25] There are those who suggest that any child expressing doubts about their gender should be treated as a transgender person. Any attempt to investigate the child, or to see if their evident identity is really the true one, is labelled as 'conversion therapy'. This has malignant connotations from a time when there were attempts to 'cure' or 'convert' homosexuals to heterosexuality by a variety of often crude, but always unsuccessful, means. This view, often almost fanatically held, attempts to criminalise those who attempt a more nuanced approach, recognising the complex nature of identity, the fact that it can be fluid, and that the majority of children expressing doubts about their gender do not become transgender. Reinforcing a child's view of itself, or clarifying that view, or waiting until a more accurate diagnosis can be more easily recognised, or the child can take informed and mature decisions, are not attempts to 'cure' or 'convert' anything, but prudent measures to deal with a complicated and poorly-understood situation.[26] Uncertainty breeds disagreements, but the considerable degree of uncertainty in this field behoves a more modest approach by all those concerned.

10. THE ROLE OF HORMONES IN THE TREATMENT OF GENDER IDENTITY DISORDERS

Hormones play a central part both in the development and expression of sexuality, as well as the treatment of transgender persons (see above). It is important to know what they do and their limitations, since this will have a direct impact on legal, as well as medical, considerations. The role of testosterone in the development of gender identity has already been mentioned. However, there are two caveats. The first is that variations in embryonic exposure, if they can be assessed, are likely to affect the way an adult responds to hormones. So measures of, say, mutations in the androgen receptor, responsible for individual differences in sensitivity to testosterone, may become relevant to legal assessments in the

Treatment Options for Transgender Men (Female-to-Male)' (2017) 40(1) *Psychiatr Clin North Am* 79–97; C.A. Unger, 'Hormone therapy for transgender patients' (2016) 5(6) *Transl Androl Urol* 877–884.

25 J. Herbert, 'Prejudice, Not Science, Wins the Day in Toronto' (2016) *Psychology Today*, available at <https://www.psychologytoday.com/gb/blog/hormones-and-the-brain/201602/prejudice-not-science-wins-the-day-in-toronto>.

26 K.J. Zucker et al., 'A developmental, biopsychosocial model for the treatment of children with gender identity disorder' (2012) 59(3) *J Homosex* 369–397; R. Green, 'Banning Therapy to Change Sexual Orientation or Gender Identity in Patients Under 18' (2017) 45(1) *J Am Acad Psychiatry Law* 7–11.

future. Secondly, some pregnant women are given steroids, usually progesterone or compounds related to it, to reduce the risk of miscarriage.[27] There might be legal questions over whether such treatment has any effect on the sexuality, including gender identity, though there is no certain evidence on this point at present.[28]

11. MASCULINISED OR INDETERMINATE GENITALIA: A LEGAL AS WELL AS A MEDICAL PROBLEM

Although this chapter is concerned principally with the brain, we need to consider, briefly, the impact of indeterminate or gender-atypical genitalia on gender identity. The presence of anomalous genitals may itself contribute to gender dysphoria. It may also may give rise to incorrect assignment at birth and influence subsequent treatment or even legal status.

There are several enzyme mutations that result, in both sexes, in the adrenal gland producing excessive amount of testosterone during embryonic life. This condition, called congenital adrenal hyperplasia (CAH), also causes deficiency in another hormone, cortisol, which is essential for life.[29] During pregnancy, the baby's cortisol will be supplied by the mother. After birth, the baby may need urgent supplementation. In males, CAH has little effect on gender or sexual orientation (they are not 'super-males'). In females, however, the external genitalia are often highly masculinised, such that gender assignment at birth may be uncertain or mistaken. When this is discovered, the question is then whether to try to restore more normal female genitalia by surgery. The crux is that the baby cannot give consent; but delaying restorative surgery until later not only means that the girl grows up with male-like genitals – with the accompanying psychological and social implications – but that later surgery is sometime less effective, since very young tissue has remarkable healing ability. Moreover, if some females with CAH were subsequently to develop a male gender identity, such procedures might not be in their best interest. There has been much debate on this as a human rights issue versus the welfare of the child. But what

---

27 C.E. Lim et al., 'Combined oestrogen and progesterone for preventing miscarriage' (2013) 9 *Cochrane Database Syst Rev* CD009278.

28 J.M. Reinisch, E.L. Mortensen and S.A. Sanders, 'Prenatal Exposure to Progesterone Affects Sexual Orientation in Humans' (2017) 46 *Arch Sex Behav* 1239–1249.

29 M. Hines, 'Prenatal endocrine influences on sexual orientation and on sexually differentiated childhood behavior' (2011) 32(2) *Front Neuroendocrinol* 170–182; M.L. Butovskaya et al., 'Aggression, digit ratio, and variation in the androgen receptor, serotonin transporter, and dopamine D4 receptor genes in African foragers: the Hadza' (2012) 42(4) *Behav Genet* 647–662; G.A. Mathews et al., 'Personality and congenital adrenal hyperplasia: possible effects of prenatal androgen exposure' (2009) 55(2) *Horm Behav* 285–291; D.A. Puts et al., 'Spatial ability and prenatal androgens: meta-analyses of congenital adrenal hyperplasia and digit ratio (2D:4D) studies' (2008) 37(1) *Arch Sex Behav* 100–111.

also concerns us here is whether this excessive exposure to testosterone has any effect on the brain, particularly gender identity.

A number of studies show evidence for some masculinisation of the brain in female cases of CAH. This expresses itself as increased levels of male-like play behaviour (so-called 'rough and tumble') during infancy and somewhat greater autistic traits (more common in males)[30] but there are conflicting reports.[31] Later in life, as puberty occurs, there is an increased incidence of homosexuality (but this is also not a universal finding), or same-sex fantasies and some dissatisfaction with gender identity or role. However, gender dysphoria or transition, though it does occur somewhat more frequently than in control populations, is not a consistent feature of CAH.[32] If testosterone is such a potent determinant of gender identity (and, maybe, sexual orientation) why is dysphoria not more common in female CAH? There is no certain answer to this question, though the fact that exposure to excess testosterone may occur during the later stages of pregnancy may be important. The influence of their upbringing as a female should also be considered. The effect of testosterone on later gender identity may depend more on an earlier, more sensitive period in the development of the brain. The principal concern for lawyers in cases of CAH is with their genitals rather than their brain.

Cloacal exstrophy is a rare condition that involves a range of developmental abnormalities including the genitalia, which are unformed and resemble neither male nor female. Since constructing an adequate penis is much more difficult than making a vagina, males (XY) with this condition were historically reassigned as females, with the appropriate corrective surgery.[33] Follow-up showed that this was successful in about half these children; that is, their new gender was accepted.[34] This might be taken to indicate the power of parental and social upbringing on the development of gender identity. However, this view is tempered by the fact that we do not know the cause of cloacal exstrophy, which might also include defects in the brain that could make gender identity more fluid or malleable. More recently, in the light of more adequate surgery,

---

30 R. Knickmeyer et al., 'Androgens and autistic traits: A study of individuals with congenital adrenal hyperplasia' (2016) 50(1) *Horm Behav* 148–153.

31 K.T. Kung et al., 'No relationship between prenatal androgen exposure and autistic traits: convergent evidence from studies of children with congenital adrenal hyperplasia and of amniotic testosterone concentrations in typically developing children' (2016) 57(12) *J Child Psychol Psychiatry* 1455–1462.

32 V. Pasterski et al., 'Increased Cross-Gender Identification Independent of Gender Role Behavior in Girls with Congenital Adrenal Hyperplasia: Results from a Standardized Assessment of 4- to 11-Year-Old Children' (2015) 44(5) *Arch Sex Behav* 1363–1375.

33 J. Gordetsky and D.B. Joseph, 'Cloacal Exstrophy: A History of Gender Reassignment' (2015) 86(6) *Urology* 1087–1089.

34 W.G. Reiner, 'Gender identity and sex-of-rearing in children with disorders of sexual differentiation' (2015) 18(6) *J Pediatr Endocrinol Metab* 549–553.

there is an increasing tendency to allow XY babies with this condition to remain as males.[35]

Testosterone is converted to dihyrotestosterone (DHT) by an enzyme, 5-alpha-reductase (5αR). DHT is more potent that testosterone and seems particularly important for the development of the genitalia. Male babies with mutations in 5αR that prevent or reduce the formation of DHT are born with genitals that either look female or are indeterminate (depending on the particular mutation of the gene for 5αR). They are often raised as girls, but at puberty the increasing amount of testosterone from their testes (which may be hidden in the abdomen) causes their undeveloped penis to enlarge – though not to a normal size. About 50–60 per cent of these individuals then change their gender identity to male.[36] This raises several interesting questions. If testosterone exposure during early life regulates gender identity, is conversion of DHT in the brain necessary? Does the fact that children raised as girls then transition their gender mean that parental upbringing and attitudes have no role, or a variable one? The fact that only about two-thirds of 5αR mutants make the transition to a male gender clouds either conclusion. There seems no relation between the degree of genital masculinisation at birth and subsequent gender transition, suggesting that the two processes are not inter-dependent. Access to available or affordable medical care may contribute. There is also a potentially interesting legal question: suppose that an effective way were to be developed of diagnosing these cases at birth, together with an equally effective way of restoring their genitals to the usual male format. Would this prevent any subsequent gender dysphoria, and, if not, would the fact that around a third opt for a female gender complicate early treatment of the remainder?

The apparent division between biological events during development and early social experience in determining gender identity is blurred even further by the recent realisation that such experience may alter the way that genes function (epigenetics), thus closing the loop.[37] So arguments over whether biology (e.g. testosterone) or upbringing (e.g. parents) is more important for gender identity are irrelevant in the light of contemporary knowledge. It is the interaction that matters for this as for many other qualities.[38]

---

35 D.A. Diamond et al., 'Gender assignment for newborns with 46XY cloacal exstrophy: a 6-year followup survey of pediatric urologists' (2011) 186 (4 Suppl.) *J Urol* 1642–1648.

36 P.T. Cohen-Kettenis, 'Gender change in 46,XY persons with 5alpha-reductase-2 deficiency and 17beta-hydroxysteroid dehydrogenase-3 deficiency' (2005) 34(4) *Arch Sex Behav* 399–410.

37 M.K. Skinner, 'Environmental Epigenetics and a Unified Theory of the Molecular Aspects of Evolution: A Neo-Lamarckian Concept that Facilitates Neo-Darwinian Evolution' (2015) 7(5) *Genome Biol Evol* 1296–1302.

38 J. Bancroft, 'The behavioral actions of testosterone', in N. Nieschlag, H.M. Behre and S. Nieschlag (eds.) *Testosterone: action, deficiency, substitution*, Cambridge University Press, New York 2012, pp. 87–122; Herbert, above n. 11.

12. WHAT HORMONES DO IN THE BRAIN: 'MALE' AND 'FEMALE' HORMONES

An equally pertinent issue concerns the action of steroids on a pre-pubertal child, or a post-pubertal adult. Giving either testosterone or oestrogens to a pre-pubertal child will initiate an artificially early puberty, and so has no place in the treatment of gender dysphoria. In the adult, the notion that oestrogens are 'female' hormones whereas testosterone is a 'male' one has no scientific support. Some testosterone in the male is converted, particularly by the brain, to oestrogen, though there is still some uncertainty about how much of its action depends on this conversion, or on a more direct action or even conversion to other compounds. But there is no doubt about the essential role of testosterone in adult male sexuality. Castration, or compounds that antagonise testosterone, will reduce the ability of males to have sex (impotence) as well as their sexual 'drive' or motivation, though the degree to which this happens varies individually. But testosterone is also important for women's sexuality: this is shown by the negative effects on sexual desire of removal of the ovaries or oral contraceptives; both lower testosterone levels.[39] Giving it commonly increases sexual drive ('libido') in women and it is used for this purpose in the clinic. So testosterone is important for levels of sexuality in both men and women.[40]

13. HORMONES AND THE DETERMINATION OF GENDER IDENTITY

What testosterone in the adult does not do is alter either gender identity or sexual orientation. So treating gender dysphoric persons with testosterone (or oestrogens) will have no effect on either of these qualities. Transgender males are given testosterone to maintain their sexual drive, but equally importantly so that they develop secondary male-like sexual characteristics such as facial hair, increased muscle mass and a deepening voice. It is not effective for growing a functional penis (though the clitoris may enlarge): this requires surgery. The somatic response will occur irrespective of whether they have their ovaries or wombs removed, or their breasts amputated. Whether this has any long-term health implications is disputed: men have more heart attacks than women, and the prostate, which is residual in females, responds to testosterone and is a frequent site for cancer. Female (MtF) transgenders often have their testes

---

39 Bancroft, above n. 38.

40 J. Bancroft, 'The endocrinology of sexual arousal' (2005) 186(3) 411–427; S.R. Davis, 'Androgen therapy in women, beyond libido' (2013) 16 *Climacteric*, Suppl. 1: pp. 18–24; J.S. Peper et al., 'Sex steroids and connectivity in the human brain: a review of neuroimaging studies' (2011) 36(8) *Psychoneuroendocrinology* 1101–1113.

removed, to eliminate endogenous testosterone, and are then given oestrogen or oestrogen and progesterone (in the correct sequence). This has the desired effect on breast development but does not raise the pitch of the voice. The longer-term effects of hormonal treatment of MtF transgender persons deserves more attention, as for FtM.[41] Depression and anorexia are more common in women than men: whether this risk also applies to hormone-treated MtF individuals is still uncertain, but well worth investigation. A recent study found increases in depression and anxiety in both classes of transgender subjects.[42] Corrective surgery on their genitalia varies according to individual choice or opportunity. It is a surgical fact that constructing a vagina is more successful than making a penis.[43] However, it has to be said that in overall appearance of their body, FtM transitions often seem more successful than MtF, since hormone treatment of the latter does not always enable all aspects of physique to become female-like. Social anxiety is a prominent feature of transgender persons. Whether or not those with gender dysphoria need to undergo hormonal treatment or genital surgery as a necessary prerequisite for establishing their legal status as male or female varies in different jurisdictions.

14. NEUROSCIENCE, TRANSGENDER AND THE LAW: MATCHES AND MISMATCHES

A simple view of science would state that it is objective, accurate and not influenced by culture, politics or nationality. Thus, the structure of DNA is the same everywhere, and the second law of thermodynamics has universal application. Of course, it is not really like that: there are fashions in science, and constant disagreements, as there are in other human activities as well as misconceptions, changes of mind and political forces.[44] For example, the notion that alterations in the body in response to the environment are not inherited (contrary to the view of Lamarck), a long-standing central tenet in biology, is being questioned by recent advances in epigenetics.[45] Dissidents in the Soviet Union were assumed to be mentally ill, and so sent to secure mental hospitals. The science of sexuality is not immune from cultural or political influence. There was a proposal in the former East German Republic, then part of the Soviet

41 Y. Ortiz-Martinez and CM Rios-Gonzalez, 'Need for more research on and health interventions for transgender people' (2017) 14 *Sex Health* 196–197.

42 S.L. Budge, J.L. Adelson and K.A. Howard, 'Anxiety and depression in transgender individuals: the roles of transition status, loss, social support, and coping' (2013) 81(3) *J Consult Clin Psychol* 545–557.

43 Berli et al., above n. 5.

44 J. Bentham, *Offences against one's self: paederasty*, 1785.

45 W.W. Tang et al., 'A Unique Gene Regulatory Network Resets the Human Germline Epigenome for Development' (2015) 161(6) *Cell* 1453–1467.

Union, that homosexuality was 'caused' by low levels of testosterone during the prenatal life of male babies: thus, all mothers should be tested, and those with lower levels required to have an abortion, thereby eliminating homosexuality.[46] This policy, strongly advocated by certain scientists who were influenced by moral concerns, was not actually adopted. However, science can alter the law. The notion that same-sex parents (e.g. lesbian couples) were disadvantageous for a child (though not necessarily similar in all respects to heterosexual upbringing) was refuted by careful studies, and the law (in some countries) changed.[47] But science was not responsible for more liberal attitudes towards homosexuality and its elimination as a criminal act. That was a cultural event, not a scientific one. Although science has a great deal to say about homosexuality, none of this had much impact on social or legal attitudes.[48] Medical attitudes reflected social change, rather than initiating it.

Though philosophers debate whether there is such a thing as universal justice, or a common basis for ethics, there is little to suggest that the law is universal: there are marked differences across cultures, and within cultures over time. So, when we try to relate the law to science, we are not comparing like with like, though both are changeable. In matters concerning sexuality, there will always be strong social and religious pressures on the form and application of the law, and these will differ between cultures and along the trajectory of history. As already pointed out, science – and particularly neuroscience – always incomplete and to a degree provisional, will have only a limited impact. Nevertheless, in the case of transgender, this impact might be expected to be greater than in some other instances. This is because some of the decisions that need to be made by lawyers and the law will depend on some understanding of the facts that surround the phenomenon of transgender, a matter for neuroscience, but also for developmental biology, psychology and sociology.

Even given all these uncertainties, there is one glaring disparity between the legal and neuroscientific view of transgender. In most countries, the law still recognises two genders, male or female, though there are signs that this is changing in some jurisdictions. Neuroscience, on the other hand, is clear that gender identity is not a binary event, neither is it a one-dimensional property of a given individual. It may even be absent, a condition rather clumsily called 'gender-queer' or (better) 'a-gender'. Furthermore, there are distinctions to be made on developmental, neural and psychological grounds on mismatches

---

46 G. Dorner and G. Hinz, 'Induction and prevention of male homosexuality by androgen' (1968) 40(3) *J Endocrinol* 387–388.

47 M. Regnerus, 'How different are the adult children of parents who have same-sex relationships? Findings from the New Family Structures Study' (2012) 41(4) *Soc Sci Res* 752–770; C.H. Van Nijnatten, 'Sexual orientation of parents and Dutch family law' (1995) 14(5–6) *Med Law* 359–368.

48 J.M. Bailey et al., 'Sexual Orientation, Controversy, and Science' (2016) 17(2) *Psychol Sci Public Interest* 45–101.

between a person's psychological state (how he/she views him/herself) and the appearance or functioning of his/her genitalia. The medical concern is reconciling the function of brain and genitalia so that both operate in the best interest of that person. That best interest may be influenced by individual, social and cultural factors, as well as reproductive biology. The legal concern is how that person is classified in the society to which he/she belongs. Both medicine and the law have concerns about the best way to treat or classify transgender persons. Neither profession has a definite or established view. Science cannot tell the rest of the world why some people are transgender or have no gender. Neither has it yet undisputed views of how or when to treat such people. The law is therefore handicapped over deciding which treatment regimen is acceptable, or which is malpractice. Whether gender should be declared under specific contexts (for example, on a birth certificate or a passport) is a legal matter, but this needs to reflect the nuanced view from neuroscience (which includes, for this purpose, psychology and sociology) on the nature of gender identity. The law has much to say about sexual behaviour, but what it says is rarely influenced by the findings of social or biological science research over recent decades. The wider question of how society treats transgender people is a matter for that society, a social and political process, but may well be reflected in the laws relating to transgender. It should not have any impact on scientific understanding of transgender, but history shows us that we need constantly to be on our guard against that possibility. We should not forget that it was the medical profession that once labelled homosexuality as a 'perversion', reflecting the social and legal views of that time. Facebook currently has 50 options for defining gender in the USA, and no less than 71 in the UK. Whilst many of these may be disputed, spurious or irrelevant, it does seem that, not for the first time, social views on gender have outstripped neuroscience, medicine and the law.

GENDER IDENTITY AND INTERSEX CONDITIONS

Vickie Pasterski

1. INTRODUCTION

Gender identity refers to the core sense of the self as male, female or somewhere on the spectrum outside the binary. Though Facebook users can now choose from (at least) 71 gender identities, a number of them are distinct by virtue of variation in other domains, such as gender role behaviour and sexual preferences. For example, the identity 'Femme' is usually interpreted as a feminine-identifying gay woman. Though there tends to be a high degree of covariance among gender identity, gender role and sexual preferences, they are independent constructs. Indeed, the vast array of gender identities colouring the current social landscape appears to have spawned from conscious appreciation of independent variance of domain-specific characteristics.

The recent expansion of gender expression in the form of varied identities highlights the complexity of any one person's gendered experience. While only a minority of these identities represent distress on the level felt by those who eventually seek medical intervention, they represent factors which may contribute to such outcomes. For example, the identity label 'Butch' represents a lesbian who sees herself as more masculine than other women, or in comparison to a lesbian who identifies as 'Femme'. Nevertheless, the Butch-identified person does not seek to change her identity label or physical status to male in alignment with a masculine gender role and sexual orientation. From a clinical perspective, the difficulty lies in distinguishing subtle differences between the two conditions. Potential influential factors include self-perceptions of gender typicality, felt pressure with respect to typicality and gender contentedness.[1] The degree to which one feels out of place among same-gender peers, while feeling pressure to conform and low levels of contentedness may prompt one to seek physical gender change. But how do we explain the variance in self-perceived gender typicality, felt pressure and gender contentedness? Upbringing, cultural norms and religious beliefs are likely to play a role. From a completely pragmatic perspective, sexual orientation may play a significant role for individuals living in cultures where homosexuality is a crime on religious grounds.

Further complexities lie in individual differences in experiences of the gendered body. Even among individuals who seek clinical support for self-reported gender dysphoria, some will suggest that the primary source of distress is living with secondary sex characteristics that are at odds with their sense of self, while others will express indifference about physical traits. They simply want to live and be treated as the other gender. Without a doubt, physical sex characteristics and outward social appearances play into self-perceptions of gender-typicality and gender contentedness.

Complexities (and Facebook's constructions) notwithstanding, the starting point from a scientific and clinical perspective, is understanding mechanisms that influence the differentiation of core gender constructs. *Gender identity* refers to the core sense of the self as male, female or somewhere outside the binary. *Gender role* refers to behaviours, preferences and characteristics that differ, on average, between males and females. *Sexual orientation* refers to physiological arousal patterns, and to preferences for partners in terms of sexual engagement, sexual fantasies and/or romantic attractions. Differences in gender role are greatest during childhood, beginning as early as 12 months of age.[2] Hundreds of studies across cultures and time have shown that boys and girls differ in preferences for toys, play styles and playmates.[3] While girls tend to prefer dolls and dishes, low levels of rough-and-tumble play, and girls as primary playmates, boys tend to prefer toy vehicles and weapons, higher levels of rough-and-tumble play, and boys as primary playmates.[4] Though such differences diminish with

---

1 S.K. Egan and D.G. Perry, 'Gender identity: a multidimensional analysis with implications for psychosocial adjustment' (2001) 37 *Developmental psychology* 451.

2 V. Jadva, M. Hines and S. Golombok, 'Infants' preferences for toys, colors, and shapes: sex differences and similarities' (2010) 39 *Archives of Sexual Behaviour* 1261–1273.

3 M. Hines, 'Sex-related variation in human behavior and the brain' (2010) 14 *Trends in Cognitive Sciences* 448–456.

4 V. Pasterski, M.E. Geffner, C. Brain, P. Hindmarsh, C. Brook and M. Hines, 'Prenatal hormones and postnatal socialization by parents as determinants of male-typical toy play in girls with congenital adrenal hyperplasia' (2005) 76 *Child Development* 264–278; V. Pasterski,

age, differences in sexual preferences,[5] and cognitive abilities to a lesser extent,[6] emerge in their place. The sex difference in sexual orientation is large, though not as large as the sex difference in gender identity.

Within and between sex variance on these dimensions further distinguishes them as independent. While there is a great deal of overlap in gender role behaviour between adult men and women, for example, there is much less overlap in sexual orientation or in gender identity.[7] In the general population, the majority of individuals assigned male at birth report sexual attractions to females and identify as male. Conversely, the majority of individuals assigned female at birth report sexual attractions to males and identify as female. The relatively high degree of covariance on these constructs, though they are distinct, is also suggestive of shared underlying causal factors. Research which informs the development in one domain, may shed light on development in the others.[8] As this relates to individuals with intersex conditions, consideration of relative influences, such as prenatal hormone exposure and postnatal gender-related experiences, is critically important. While the incidence of gender dysphoria and gender change is higher among individuals with intersex conditions than in the general population,[9] it is still relatively low. That said, a low rate of gender change in no way demarcates a successful outcome. Lesser degrees of gender variance may cause distress. Optimal clinical care should include social and psychological support, in part based on clarity about gender-related development.

P. Hindmarsh, M. Geffner, C. Brook, C. Brain and M. Hines, 'Increased aggression and activity level in 3- to 11-year-old girls with congenital adrenal hyperplasia (CAH)' (2007) 52 *Hormones and Behavior* 368–374; V. Pasterski, M.E. Geffner, C. Brain, P. Hindmarsh, C. Brook and M. Hines, 'Prenatal hormones and childhood sex segregation: playmate and play style preferences in girls with congenital adrenal hyperplasia' (2011) 59 *Hormones and Behavior* 549–555; V. Pasterski, S. Golombok, and M. Hines, 'Sex Differences in Social Behavior', in P.K. Smith and C.H. Hart (eds.), *The Wiley-Blackwell Handbook of Childhood Social Development*, 2nd ed., Blackwell Publishing Ltd, 2011, pp. 281–298.

5 M. Hines, 'Prenatal endocrine influences on sexual orientation and on sexually differentiated childhood behavior' (2011) 32 *Frontiers in Neuroendocrinology* 170–182.

6 M. Hines, *Brain gender*, Oxford University Press, 2004.

7 M. Hines, 'Gender development and the human brain' (2011) 34 *Annual Review of Neuroscience* 69–88.

8 Hines, above n. 5.

9 V. Pasterski, K.J. Zucker, P.C. Hindmarsh, I.A. Hughes, C. Acerini, D. Spencer, S. Neufeld and M. Hines, 'Increased cross-gender identification independent of gender role behavior in girls with congenital adrenal hyperplasia: Results from a standardized assessment of 4- to 11-year-old children' (2015) 44 *Archives of Sexual Behavior* 1363–1375; N. Callens, M. van Kuyk, J.H. van Kuppenveld, S.L. Drop, P.T. Cohen-Kettenis, A.B. Dessens and DSGo DSD, 'Recalled and current gender role behavior, gender identity and sexual orientation in adults with Disorders/Differences of Sex Development' (2016) 86 *Hormones and Behavior* 8–20.

2. CLINICAL CONCEPTUALISATION OF GENDER IDENTITY AND DYSPHORIA

Gender dysphoria, also referred to as *Transsexualism*, arises when there is incongruence between gender assigned at birth and gender identity experienced by the individual. The incongruence manifests as distress around an intense and persistent wish to live as the sex opposite to that assigned at birth. According to prevalence data, gender dysphoria is considered rare, with rates approximated at 0.005–0.014 per cent for adult natal males and 0.002–0.003 per cent for adult natal females.[10] While some may suggest that the numbers are higher, the exact prevalence is difficult to ascertain. Discrepancies are likely due to changes in diagnostic conceptualisation and changes in social acceptance of gender-non-conforming presentation. Paradoxically, the wider acceptance of gender variance seems to have resulted in greater numbers of referrals to gender identity clinics.[11] Though greater freedom to express gender variance could have the effect of attenuating feelings of incongruence between assigned gender and gender expression, it seems that a more fundamental incongruence related to physical sex characteristics underlies the diagnosis for many individuals. It seems that greater social acceptance has translated to less stigma associated with seeking clinical intervention.

The most recent revision of diagnostic criteria as they are defined in the *Diagnostic and Statistical Manual for Mental Disorders* (DSM) from DSM-IV-TR (the Text Revision version of the IV edition) to DSM-5[12] has incorporated two fundamental changes essential to clinical management. These changes reflect the distinction between (non-pathological) gender-non-conforming behaviour and gender dysphoria in childhood/early adolescence, and an allowance for the diagnosis to be applied to individuals with an intersex condition (in children, adolescents and adults). Regarding the first change, inclusion criteria for establishing the presence of 'a wish to be the other sex' (criterion A; See Table 1) now require that sub-criterion A1 is met in addition to a combination of other manifestations. In previous versions, a combination of gender-non-conforming behavioural traits did not necessarily include the strong desire to be the other gender, or the insistence that s/he is the other gender. This change was instated to differentiate between children who simply presented with gender-non-conforming behaviour from those who stated the wish to change.[13]

---

10 A P Association, *Diagnostic and statistical manual of mental disorders*, 5th ed., American Psychiatric Publishing, 2013.

11 K.J. Zucker and A.A. Lawrence, 'Epidemiology of gender identity disorder: Recommendations for the standards of care of The World Professional Association for Transgender Health' (2009) 11 *International Journal of Transgenderism* 8–18.

12 A P Association, above n. 10.

13 K.J. Zucker, P.T. Cohen-Kettenis, J. Drescher, H.F. Meyer-Bahlburg, F. Pfäfflin and W.M. Womack, 'Memo outlining evidence for change for gender identity disorder in the DSM-5' (2013) 42 *Archives of Sexual Behavior* 901–914.

In adolescents and adults, this distinction is not necessary as the manifestations in older ages directly reflect gender identity in terms of features which distinguish adult males and females.

With respect to the change incorporating intersex conditions, which can be seen as a 'specifier' following criterion B, the implications are somewhat evident. Though the reasoning for the inclusion was not based on new information about mechanisms underlying the development of gender identity, the recognition that chances of gender dysphoria may be increased is considered relevant. This added inclusion criterion allows for greater access to gender-identity specialist clinical services where protocols for diagnosis and treatment may be incorporated with existing intersex-related healthcare.

Another key feature of the diagnostic criteria for gender dysphoria incorporates a dislike of one's sex-related physical characteristics in addition to the wish to be the other gender. In children, this is manifested by stated dislike of genitalia and/or wish to have the genitalia of the other gender. This is often accompanied by distress at the (prospect of) development of unwanted secondary sex characteristics. In adolescents and adults, there is often the expressed desire to be rid of unwanted secondary sex characteristics and to receive treatment with sex hormone replacement therapy and/or gender reassignment procedures to align the body with the inner gender experience.

Once a diagnosis of gender dysphoria has been established, clinical management depends to a large extent on the age of the individual. Current wisdom dictates that resolution of the conflict lies with alignment of the body with the mind, rather than the reverse, and treatment with hormones or surgery is usually initiated post-puberty. For younger patients, the first step may involve puberty-blocking hormone therapy to arrest the development of unwanted secondary sex characteristics. However, this treatment, and subsequent treatment with cross-sex hormones and/or surgical intervention is controversial. This is because longitudinal data following individuals from childhood into and past puberty suggest that the rate of persistence of the dysphoria is only about 50 per cent at best. That is, many individuals who present in childhood do not continue with the wish to change. Studies have shown that some percentage will eventually differentiate a homosexual sexual identity, but that others will experience a complete resolution of the distress without intervention. Age at presentation varies to some extent between countries. For example, in cultures where a wider range of gender expression is accepted, presentation tends to be later; while in more traditional cultures, where cross-sex behaviour is not well tolerated, a child may be referred for clinical assessment very early on. Though a later onset, at or after puberty, may present unique challenges, concerns about persistence are less relevant. The greatest clinical concern overall is administering partially or fully irreversible treatment to an individual who will eventually wish to live in the gender assigned at birth. In recent years, the debate about likelihood of persistence versus desistence of gender dysphoria has extended to include

Figure 1. DSM-5 diagnostic criteria for gender dysphoria in children

GENDER DYSPHORIA:
CHILDREN

A. Marked incongruence between one's experienced gender and one's assigned gender, of at least six months' duration (must meet at least six, including A I):
   1. A strong desire to be the other gender, or insistence that one is the other gender.
   2. In boys, a preference for cross-dressing or simulating female attire; in girls, a preference for wearing only typical masculine clothing.
   3. A strong preference for cross-gender roles in make-believe play.
   4. A strong preference for the toys, games, or activities stereotypically preferred by the other gender.
   5. A strong preference for playmates of the other gender.
   6. In boys, a strong rejection of typically masculine toys, games and activities.
   7. A strong dislike of one's sexual anatomy.
   8. A strong desire for the primary and/or secondary sex characteristics that match one's experienced gender.

B. The condition is associated with clinically significant distress or impairment in social, school, or other important areas of functioning.

   Specify if: With a disorder of sex development (DSD; e.g., congenital adrenal hyperplasia or androgen insensitivity syndrome)

Source: Produced by the author.

Figure 2. DSM-5 diagnostic criteria for gender dysphoria in adolescents and adults

GENDER DYSPHORIA:
ADOLESCENTS & ADULTS

A. Marked incongruence between one's experienced gender and one's assigned gender, of at least six months' duration (must meet at least two):
   1. A marked incongruence between one's experienced gender and primary and/or secondary sex characteristics (or in young adolescents, the anticipated secondary sex characteristics).
   2. A strong desire to be rid of one's primary and/or secondary sex characteristics because of a marked incongruence).
   3. A strong desire for the primary and/or secondary sex characteristics of the other gender.
   4. A strong desire to be of the other (or some alternative gender).
   5. A strong desire to be treated as the other (or some alternative) gender.
   6. A strong conviction that one has the typical feelings and reactions of the other (or some alternative) gender.

B. The condition is associated with clinically significant distress or impairment in social, occupational, or other important areas of functioning, or with a significantly increased risk of suffering, such as distress or disability.

   Specify if: With/out a DSD; Specify if: Post-transition.

Source: Produced by the author.

the merits of sociological intervention, namely the facilitation of social gender transition by parents of children in the pre-pubertal developmental period. Given that some number of individuals may express cross-gender ideation as part of an eventual homosexual identity, social transition is seen as potentially problematic. A significant body of retrospective research, and a new longitudinal study, provide robust evidence of childhood gender-non-conforming behaviour among homosexual men and women. More than 60 studies have consistently shown that homosexual men and women report significantly more gender-non-conforming behaviour than their heterosexual counterparts.[14] Further evidence comes from a prospective, population-based, longitudinal study of 2,428 girls and 2,169 boys who have been followed from the prenatal period through to adolescence.[15] Li et al. found that levels of gender-typed behaviour at ages 3.5 and 4.75 years significantly and consistently predicted sexual orientation at age 15 years. The finding held true even when sexual orientation was conceptualised as a spectrum.

The implications of this natural history of sexual orientation is that gender-non-conforming behaviour in childhood may eventually differentiate as part of a homosexual orientation rather a cross-gender identity in adulthood. Anecdotally, I have encountered a great many individuals presenting in gender identity clinics who reported having experienced some degree of confusion between sexual and gender identities as their sexuality emerged during puberty, with many having identified as gay at some point. Though social transition does not entail irreversible physical changes, reversal of the social gender identity is not without consequences. In addition to the potential for social stigma associated with a public reversal, a child whose parents (and family) have invested in the initial social gender change may feel compelled to maintain the changed identity for fear of letting others down. The developmental literature is clear about children's desire for parental approval and acceptance.

3. DIFFERENTIATION OF GENDER IDENTITY

Theories attempting to explain the development of human behaviour may be broadly classified as biological or psychological, though such distinctions can be misleading. We now know that biology and psychological factors continue to influence one another throughout the lifespan. And while studies of human development may describe phenomena from one theoretical perspective at

14 J.M. Bailey and K.J. Zucker, 'Childhood sex-typed behavior and sexual orientation: A conceptual analysis and quantitative review' (1995) 31 *Developmental Psychology* 43; K.J. Zucker, 'Reflections on the relation between sex-typed behavior in childhood and sexual orientation in adulthood' (2008) 12 *Journal of Gay & Lesbian Mental Health* 29–59.

15 G. Li, K.T. Kung and M. Hines, 'Childhood gender-typed behavior and adolescent sexual orientation: A longitudinal population-based study' (2017) 53 *Child Development* 764–777.

a time, findings should be integrated wherever possible. Knowledge about the development of sexually dimorphic behaviour in humans has been primarily considered from three theoretical perspectives: perinatal hormonal exposure, postnatal socialisation by parents and peers, and postnatal cognitive developmental processes. With respect to gender identity specifically, it is difficult to build a clear picture without also considering other gender-related behaviours. For example, clinical presentation of gender dysphoria in childhood is largely characterised by gender-nonconforming preferences. While we know that core gender identity may not always align with a particular gender-specific profile of behaviour, the degree of covariance is high, suggesting a role for a similar underlying causal mechanism. Furthermore, as mentioned earlier, the degree of self-perceived gender typicality may contribute to contentedness with one's gender (assignment).

With respect to individuals with intersex conditions, studies investigating the development of gender-related behaviour, including gender identity, are of critical importance. In addition to increasing scientific understanding of such processing, the potential to ascertain relative influences of fetal hormone exposure and later socialisation and cognitive developmental experiences informs clinical management, including decisions about gender assignment. Though surgical intervention aimed at cosmetic correction of ambiguous genitalia in line with gender assignment has been widely condemned in recent years, the practical necessity of social gender assignment remains. The majority of parents are not equipped to raise a child without a gender under current societal conditions. Confusion about a child's gender can be stigmatising for both parents and the child. As such, increasing clarity about factors likely to influence a child's eventual gender identity and gender-related contentedness is crucial. In the section below, we will first consider hormonal influences on gender-related development, followed by evidence for influences of socialisation and cognitive developmental processes. The latter two will be further considered in the context of variance in hormone exposure characteristic of intersex conditions.

3.1. HORMONE INFLUENCES ON GENDER DEVELOPMENT

Based on observations that physical sex differentiation occurs under the control of testicular hormones, the *organisational hypothesis*[16] posited that similar action may be responsible for sexually differentiated behaviour. Since the hypothesis was developed in 1959, hundreds of experimental studies in non-human vertebrates have established the link between fetal hormone

[16] C.H. Phoenix, R.W. Goy, A.A. Gerall and W.C. Young, 'Organizing action of prenatally administered testosterone propionate on the tissues mediating mating behavior in the female guinea pig 1' (1959) 65 *Endocrinology* 369–382.

exposure and behavioural outcomes. For example, female animals treated with testosterone during critical periods of brain development show increased male-typical, and decreased female-typical sexual and non-sexual behaviours. Likewise, removal of testosterone in male animals by castration reverses the pattern. Furthermore, investigations of sex differences in brain structures have shown that manipulation of fetal hormones produces concomitant structural changes. Over time, findings have extended to multiple brain structures and have been shown in a wide range of species.

In humans, experimentation with fetal hormone exposure is unethical, though similar mechanisms are assumed to underlie neurobehavioural sex differences. At the same time, studies of outcomes in individuals with intersex conditions have shown a great deal of variance gender-related behaviour, both systematically and in accordance with predictions of the organisational hypothesis. The bulk of evidence comes from studies of congenital adrenal hyperplasia (CAH)[17] and androgen insensitivity syndrome (AIS).[18] Girls with CAH who have been exposed to excess testosterone, beginning prenatally, show increased male-typical and decreased female-typical childhood play behaviour.[19] Specifically, studies have reliably shown that, compared to unaffected girls, girls with CAH are more likely to prefer boys' toys,[20] to engage in higher levels of rough-and-tumble play,[21] and to prefer boys as playmates;[22] and comparisons between groups of girls with varying degrees of disease severity (and increased androgen exposure) suggest a dose-response relationship.[23] In addition, girls and women with CAH show

17 V. Pasterski and I.A. Hughes, 'Hypothalamic pituitary adrenal axis: Congenital adrenal hyperplasia', in D.W. Pfaff and M. Joels (eds.), *Hormones, brain and behaviour*, Academic Press, 2016.

18 I.A. Hughes, J.D. Davies, T.I. Bunch, V. Pasterski, K. Mastroyannopoulou and J. MacDougall, 'Androgen insensitivity syndrome' (2012) 380 *The Lancet* 1419–1428.

19 Pasterski, Geffner, Brain, Hindmarsh, Brook and Hines, above n. 4; Pasterski, Hindmarsh, Geffner, Brook, Brain and Hines, above n. 4; Pasterski, Geffner, Brain, Hindmarsh, Brook and Hines, above n. 4.

20 Pasterski, Geffner, Brain, Hindmarsh, Brook and Hines, 'Prenatal hormones and postnatal socialization by parents as determinants of male-typical toy play in girls with congenital adrenal hyperplasia', above n. 4; S.A. Berenbaum and M. Hines, 'Early androgens are related to childhood sex-typed toy preferences' (1992) 3 *Psychological Science* 203–206; M. Hines, 'Sex steroids and human behavior: prenatal androgen exposure and sex-typical play behavior in children' (2004) 1007 *Annals of the New York Academy of Sciences* 272–282.

21 Pasterski, Hindmarsh, Geffner, Brook, Brain and Hines, above n. 4; Pasterski, Geffner, Brain, Hindmarsh, Brook and Hines, 'Prenatal hormones and childhood sex segregation: playmate and play style preferences in girls with congenital adrenal hyperplasia', above n. 4.

22 Pasterski, Geffner, Brain, Hindmarsh, Brook and Hines, 'Prenatal hormones and childhood sex segregation: playmate and play style preferences in girls with congenital adrenal hyperplasia', above n. 4.

23 A. Nordenstrom, A. Servin, G. Bohlin, A. Larsson and A. Wedell, 'Sex-typed toy play behavior correlates with the degree of prenatal androgen exposure assessed by CYP21 genotype in girls with congenital adrenal hyperplasia' (2002) 87 *The Journal of Clinical Endocrinology & Metabolism* 5119–5124.

alterations in gender identity[24] and sexual orientation.[25] Conversely, girls and women with AIS, who are insensitive to the effects of androgens despite having a male-typical karyotype and functional testes, show female-typical patterns of childhood play behaviour, sexual orientation and gender identity.[26]

Studies of normative populations, though fewer in number due to logistical difficulties, provide convergent evidence for the role of fetal hormones. In contrast to studies of CAH and AIS, where variance in hormone exposure is quite dramatic, within-sex variability in typically developing children can be difficult to ascertain. Nevertheless, hormone assays can be performed with maternal blood serum, cord blood or amniotic fluid and compared to later behavioural outcomes in offspring. In a study of 342 boys and 337 girls, sex hormone binding globulin (SHBG), a proxy for testosterone exposure, measured in maternal blood samples during pregnancy related to preschool sex-typed behaviour in girls at 3.5 years old. Taken together with studies of CAH and AIS, convergent evidence suggests that prenatal androgen exposure alters gender-related behavioural outcomes in humans in line with experimental evidence in non-humans.

More recent research has also suggested that effects of androgens on brain development may not be limited to the prenatal period. Though levels of sex hormones are negligible until the onset of puberty, there is a brief surge of testosterone between birth and about three months of age. The testosterone surge, also called *mini-puberty*, is larger in male infants that in female infants and has been reliably linked to further development of genitalia[27] in boys. Utilising change measurements of penile length during mini-puberty as a proxy for hormone exposure, a study of 81 boys demonstrated a link to later

---

24 Pasterski, Zucker, Hindmarsh, Hughes, Acerini, Spencer, Neufeld and Hines, above n. 9.

25 M. Hines, C. Brook and G.S. Conway, 'Androgen and Psychosexual Development: Core Gender Identity, Sexual Orientation, and Recalled Childhood Gender Role Behavior in Women and Men with Congenital Adrenal Hyperplasia (CAH)' (2004) 41 *The Journal of Sex Research* 75–82; H.F. Meyer-Bahlburg, 'Male gender identity in an XX individual with congenital adrenal hyperplasia' 2008 *Journal of Sexual Medicine* 6 297–8; author reply 298–299; H.F. Meyer-Bahlburg, C. Dolezal, S.W. Baker and M.I. New, 'Sexual orientation in women with classical or non-classical congenital adrenal hyperplasia as a function of degree of prenatal androgen excess' (2008) 37 *Archives of Sexual Behavior* 85–99.

26 Hughes, Davies, Bunch, Pasterski, Mastroyannopoulou and MacDougall, above n. 18; M. Hines, S.F. Ahmed and I.A. Hughes, 'Psychological outcomes and gender-related development in complete androgen insensitivity syndrome' (2003) 32 *Archives of Sexual Behaviour* 93–101.

27 M. Boas, K.A. Boisen, H.E. Virtanen, M. Kaleva, A.M. Suomi, I.M. Schmidt, I.N. Damgaard, C.M. Kai, M. Chellakooty and N.E. Skakkebæk, 'Postnatal penile length and growth rate correlate to serum testosterone levels: A longitudinal study of 1962 normal boys' (2006) 154 *European Journal of Endocrinology* 125–129.

sex-typed behaviour.[28] Furthermore, researchers in this study controlled for penile length at birth and overall body growth during the study period. Regression analysis suggested that penile growth during mini-puberty, independent of penile length birth, predicted later masculine behaviour. The implication is that hormonal influences on neurobehavioural development continue into the perinatal period.

3.2. SOCIALISATION AND GENDER DEVELOPMENT

According to the social learning theory of gender development, gender-related behaviour is learned through interactions with the social environment. Processes involving reward and punishment for sex-appropriate behaviour, imitation of same-sex models and learned responses to explicit gender-based labelling of objects and activities, are posited as primary drivers of gender-specific development. Hundreds of studies have provided support for such perspectives by showing that social influences exist alongside gendered behavioural outcomes, and that outcomes can be manipulated experimentally. For example, it has been reliably shown adults treat male and female infants differently and that parents often establish gendered environments and provide sex-typed opportunities for play (e.g., colouring a baby's room in pink or blue, or buying sex-typed toys as gifts).

In keeping with this perspective of gender development, some have suggested that masculine behaviour observed in girls with CAH cannot automatically be attributed to hormonal influences, given that many of these girls are born with virilised genitalia. Parents could be subtly reinforcing male-typical behaviour in response to their daughters' appearance at birth. To test this theory, researchers have observed parental reinforcement of sex-typed behaviour in daughters with CAH compared to unaffected daughters.[29] This study revealed, however, that parents were not reinforcing male-typical behaviour. In fact, parents were more strongly rewarding feminine play in daughters with CAH. A significant and positive correlation suggested that increased male-typical behaviour was met with greater reinforcement of female-typical behaviour. Though these findings suggest that parental reinforcement is likely not responsible for

---

28 V. Pasterski, C.L. Acerini, D.B. Dunger, K.K. Ong, I.A. Hughes, A. Thankamony and M. Hines, 'Postnatal penile growth concurrent with mini-puberty predicts later sex-typed play behavior: evidence for neurobehavioral effects of the postnatal androgen surge in typically developing boys' (2015) 69 *Hormones and behavior* 98–105.

29 Pasterski, Geffner, Brain, Hindmarsh, Brook and Hines, 'Prenatal hormones and postnatal socialization by parents as determinants of male-typical toy play in girls with congenital adrenal hyperplasia', above n. 4.

masculine behaviour in girls with CAH, they do not negate social learning influences altogether. Increases in masculine behaviour are often in comparison to other girls. Behavioural comparisons to both genders often show that girls with CAH fall between typical girls and typical boys. In this case, it could be that reinforcement of female-typical play has had an attenuating effect on a predisposition toward a more masculine profile.

3.3. COGNITIVE DEVELOPMENTAL INFLUENCES ON GENDER DEVELOPMENT

While social learning theories position the developing child as a somewhat passive agent, responding to reinforcements in the process of gender development, cognitive theories suggest that adoption of gender-typed behaviours results from a conscious integration of information in the environment. Accordingly, children learn by watching and imitating models in their environment and by taking in information about sex-appropriate behaviour. Studies using experimental methods have shown that children can be influenced to express gender-related preferences for otherwise gender-neutral objects that have modelled by same-sex adults or explicitly labelled by adults as 'for girls' or 'for boys'. For example, in a modelling paradigm, children may be shown a video in which male and female adults systematically state preferences for one or the other item in a pair, e.g., a pencil versus a pen. After seeing the video, experimenters ask the children which object they prefer. In a rather reliable fashion, girls prefer the item chosen by female models and boys prefer items chosen by male models. Likewise, in a labelling paradigm, children are told that a green balloon, for example is 'for boys', while a silver balloon is 'for girls', or the reverse. This can be done with other neutral objects as well. When the children are given the opportunity to play with the toys, they generally follow the 'rules' that were established according to gender.

To better understand the interaction of hormonal and cognitive factors, a study was conducted using these two experimental paradigms in a cohort of boys and girls with CAH. They found the expected pattern of behaviour among unaffected boys and girls, as well as boys with CAH. By contrast, girls with CAH did not show any influence of the modelling or the labelling. That is, they chose the objects modelled by males and females roughly equally, and they played with both the green and silver balloons. These findings are quite significant as the implication is that not only does prenatal androgen exposure influence a more masculine pattern of sex-typed behaviour, but it appears to reduce their responsiveness to effects of modelling and labelling in the environment. Crucially, these findings should be considered in light of the fact that all of the girls in the study lived and identified as female.

4. GENDER DYSPHORIA AND GENDER CHANGE IN INTERSEX CONDITIONS

Factors contributing to gender dysphoria and/or gender change in intersex conditions are incredibly complex. The brief review above, highlighting factors shown to influence gender-related development suggests a critical role for perinatal hormone exposure in sex differentiated childhood behaviour. However, there appears to be less of an influence on sexual orientation and still less on gender identity. Further considerations in the case of intersex conditions include differences between diagnoses, differences in severity within diagnoses, the presence of genital ambiguity, potential iatrogenic effects of hormone treatments and surgical interventions, complications around initial gender assignment, and psycho-social factors, such as family dynamics and peer relations. Furthermore, reports of gender dysphoria and gender change are not ideally reliable. While instances of gender change may be noted from medical records, instances of gender dysphoria may only be picked up with participation in follow-up or outcome studies, which have notably low participation rates. Nevertheless, efforts are continually made to improve continuity of clinical care from childhood into adulthood and major specialist centres have come together to establish large-scale follow-up protocols. This last point is critically important as outcomes relevant to specific diagnoses are difficult to ascertain given the rarity of many conditions. To date, most studies reporting on psycho-sexual outcomes combine groups of individuals with different conditions, making interpretation of condition-specific influences difficult.

The clearest reporting of gender identity, dysphoria and gender change comes from studies of girls with CAH and those with the complete form of 46,XYAIS (CAIS). Studies suggest that gender-related distress is exceptionally low in girls and women with CAIS. This is likely due to several factors. First, individuals with this condition are assigned female in nearly 100 per cent of cases given the female-typical appearance at birth. In this complete form of AIS, the androgen receptor is completely unresponsive, resulting in no signs of virilisation, including in neural regions believed to underpin behavioural outcomes. Girls and women with CAIS generally show female-typical gender role, sexual orientation and gender identity. Though there are fewer data, cases of 46,XY complete gonadal dysgenesis (GD), show similar outcomes, such as a female gender identity, female-typical gender role behaviour and preferences and sexual attractions to males. Outcomes in both cases have been interpreted to result from lack of neurobehavioural masculinisation, either due to a faulty androgen receptor or the lack of androgen production.[30]

---

[30] Hines, Ahmed and Hughes, above n. 26; A.L. de Vries, T.A. Doreleijers, and P.T. Cohen-Kettenis, 'Disorders of sex development and gender identity outcome in adolescence and

In girls and women with CAH, physical and neurobehavioural masculinisation does not often extend to gender identity. Though rates of gender dissatisfaction or dysphoria have been consistently reported as higher than in the general population (~5.0 per cent compared to 0.01 per cent),[31] actual gender change is rare. Interestingly, and as stated previously, girls and women with CAH show significantly increased masculine, and decreased feminine, behaviour compared to unaffected controls.[32] However, further findings that girls with this condition were less responsive to self-socialisation influences,[33] e.g., modelling and labelling of sex-appropriate behaviour, could be interpreted as reduced sensitivity to concerns about gender-typicality. Reports of gender-related outcomes in 46,XX CAH raised as male are rare as assignment is usually as female. However, in a study reporting on 33 male-raised 46,XX CAH, four of them changed gender to female. This is remarkable given that a male assignment in 46,XX CAH is usually only made where prenatal virilisation is very high (some cases may have been mistaken for genetic males). It could be assumed that in such cases, neurobehavioural masculinisation would also be high. This high rate of gender change supports the argument for a female assignment even in cases of male-appearing genitalia at birth and suggests that other postnatal factors likely contribute to satisfaction with assigned gender.

Across other intersex conditions, many of which are quite rare, the picture is less consistent, though outcomes reported in earlier studies have provided valuable insight and clinical guidance. For example, reports of gender change in cases of partial AIS (PAIS), 17ß-Hydroxysteroid dehydrogenase deficiency (17ßHSD), 5α-reductase-2 deficiency (5ARD2) and partial GD, who share the 46,XY karyotype status, but only partial virilisation, have shown high rates of gender change. This has primarily been the case for individuals assigned female

adulthood: understanding gender identity development and its clinical implications' (2007) 4 *Pediatric Endocrinology Review* 343–351; A.B. Wisniewski, C.J. Migeon, H.F. Meyer-Bahlburg, J.P. Gearhart, G.D. Berkovitz, T.R. Brown and J. Money, 'Complete androgen insensitivity syndrome: long-term medical, surgical, and psychosexual outcome' (2000) 85 *Journal of Clinical Endocrinology and Metabolism* 2664–2669.

31 Pasterski, Zucker, Hindmarsh, Hughes, Acerini, Spencer, Neufeld and Hines, above n. 9; A.B. Dessens, F.M. Slijper and S.L. Drop, 'Gender dysphoria and gender change in chromosomal females with congenital adrenal hyperplasia' (2005) 34 *Archives of Sexual Behavior* 389–397.

32 Pasterski, Geffner, Brain, Hindmarsh, Brook and Hines, 'Prenatal hormones and postnatal socialization by parents as determinants of male-typical toy play in girls with congenital adrenal hyperplasia', above n. 4; Pasterski, Hindmarsh, Geffner, Brook, Brain and Hines, above n. 4; Pasterski, Geffner, Brain, Hindmarsh, Brook and Hines, 'Prenatal hormones and childhood sex segregation: playmate and play style preferences in girls with congenital adrenal hyperplasia', above n. 4.

33 M. Hines, V. Pasterski, D. Spencer, S. Neufeld, P. Patalay, P.C. Hindmarsh, I.A. Hughes and C.L. Acerini, 'Prenatal androgen exposure alters girls' responses to information indicating gender-appropriate behaviour' (2016) 371 *Philosophical Transactions of the Royal Society B* 2015.0125.

at birth. For example, rates have been reported as 9.1 per cent for PAIS,[34] between 39–64 per cent in cases of 17ßHSD[35] and 56–63 per cent in cases of 5ARD2.[36] Gender change was attributed, at least in part, to effects of prenatal androgen exposure. Other studies of 46,XY individuals presenting with genital anomalies due to a midline defect, cloacal exstrophy or penile agenesis, showed similarly high rates of gender change from female to male.[37] In recent years, there has been a trend toward male assignment in 46,XY infants born with ambiguous genitalia, evidence of testicular function, of androgen exposure in utero (i.e., 68 per cent of children born after 1999 versus 35 per cent born before 1990).[38]

The most recent comprehensive report on gender role, sexual orientation and gender identity in range of intersex conditions has provided further insight with respect to gender-related distress and gender change.[39] Out of 123 individuals, four were diagnosed with gender dysphoria, and a further four had changed gender by the time of follow-up. Interestingly, however, of the four who changed gender, all of whom had 46,XY intersex conditions with evidence of partial androgen effects, two changed from male to female, and the other changed from female to male. Analysis of factors contributing to (dis)satisfaction with gender assignment, including diagnosis, initial gender assignment, karyotype, disease severity, evidence of prenatal androgen exposure, gender role behaviour and sexual orientation, revealed that initial gender assignment was the best predictor of later gender assignment. The authors noted, however, that gender assignment at birth was not random. That is, children with greater degrees of genital virilisation were assigned male and those will lesser genital virilisation were assigned female. With respect to conclusions regarding gender role and sexual orientation, their findings were in line with what has been previously reported. That is, prenatal androgen exposure related most strongly to gender role, and to a lesser extent to sexual orientation. Gender identity showed the least effects of androgen.

---

34 T. Mazur, 'Gender dysphoria and gender change in androgen insensitivity or micropenis' (2005) 34 *Archives of Sexual Behavior* 411–421.

35 P.T. Cohen-Kettenis, 'Gender change in 46, XY persons with 5α-reductase-2 deficiency and 17β-hydroxysteroid dehydrogenase-3 deficiency' (2005) 34 *Archives of Sexual Behavior* 399–410.

36 Ibid.

37 H.F. Meyer-Bahlburg, 'Gender identity outcome in female-raised 46, XY persons with penile agenesis, cloacal exstrophy of the bladder, or penile ablation' (2005) 34 *Archives of sexual behavior* 423–438.

38 Z. Kolesinska, S.F. Ahmed, M. Niedziela, J. Bryce, M. Molinska-Glura, M. Rodie, J. Jiang, R.O. Sinnott, I.A. Hughes and F. Darendeliler, 'Changes over time in sex assignment for disorders of sex development' (2014) 134 *Pediatrics* e710-e715.

39 Callens, van Kuyk, van Kuppenveld, Drop, Cohen-Kettenis, Dessens and DSGo DSD, above n. 9.

5. SUMMARY

The current chapter has provided a conceptual framework for considering gender identity, gender dysphoria and gender change in the context of gender development and in relation to other gender constructs. Though gender identity is generally highly correlated with gender role behaviour and preferences, and sexual orientation, underlying mechanisms are not the same. For example, while prenatal androgen exposure has been shown reliably to relate to neurobehavioural masculinisation, effects are less evident for sexual orientation and gender identity compared to gender role. Nevertheless, it is possible that while effects may not be direct, they could be moderated by other factors, such as self-perceived gender typicality and gender contentedness. Influences, such as socialisation and cognitive developmental processes appear to have only moderate effects on gender-related development in comparison to prenatal androgen exposure, as demonstrated in studies of children with CAH. Finally, though gender dysphoria and gender change is rare in cases of intersex conditions, it is higher than expected based on rates in the general population. Multiple factors associated with specific intersex conditions and subsequent condition-related experiences likely contribute to (dis)satisfaction with gender assignment. At this point, however, initial gender assignment appears to be the best predictor of future gender identity.

EVIDENCE-BASED REVIEWS OF MEDICAL INTERVENTIONS RELATIVE TO THE GENDER STATUS OF CHILDREN WITH INTERSEX CONDITIONS AND DIFFERENCES OF SEX DEVELOPMENT

Jameson GARLAND and Milton DIAMOND

1. INTRODUCTION

Twenty years ago, standard clinical practice regarding the treatment of infants with intersex conditions and differences of sex development reached a critical turning point, particularly on the question of what gender to assign the affected children and whether their gender assignments should be reinforced with surgical interventions.[1] Prior to this period, prominent clinicians tended to minimise as anomalous the statements of aggrieved adults whose bodies had been surgically modified in childhood and who suffered physical pain, genital dysfunction, loss of fertility, and sexual sensitivity, as well as those who considered the interventions a violation of their identity and personal integrity. By 1997, however, case studies had been published confirming rejections of

[1] This chapter uses the terms 'intersex condition' and 'differences of sex development' together to respect the diversity of viewpoints among persons for whom diagnoses of medical conditions that do not respect their diverse gender identities. P.A. LEE ET AL., 'Global Disorders of Sex Development Update since 2006: Perceptions, approach and care' (2016) 85 *Hormone Research in Paediatrics* 158, 159.

gender assignments by older minors and adults who had been subjected to medical gender-conforming procedures in childhood.[2] These disclosures led to the first reform guidelines proposing that while a social gender assignment for infants could be expected to continue, clinical practice should be more open to recognition of diverse gender identities and resistant to surgical interventions designed to reinforce an assigned gender.[3] On the whole, however, clinical practitioners did not appear to embrace these guidelines. Rather, while the calls for practice changes were expected to 'accelerate the re-examination of the clinical care of the intersex patient',[4] they instead marked the start of a period of a 'crisis in clinical management', one in which many clinicians found it difficult to change their practices without scientific evidence conclusively proving that all gender-conforming medical interventions are too risk-laden or unnecessary to support gender assignment on infants and young children.[5]

Concerned about the quality of evidence supporting clinical practice, a group of prominent expert-clinicians organised several invitational gatherings of their colleagues to review gender-assignment practices and the medical interventions used to reinforce them. The first of these gatherings took place in Chicago in 2005 and was dubbed the Chicago Consensus, which led to the publication of a Consensus Statement the following year.[6] This Consensus Statement recommended caution for a limited number of interventions but acknowledged that the lack of long-term outcome data was a 'major shortfall' of clinical practice, including gender assignment in infancy.[7] In the years that followed, the Consensus co-chairs retrospectively elaborated that the findings of the Consensus were at best 'tentative' because of the 'low level of scientific

---

2 W.G. Reiner, 'Case Study: Sex Reassignment in a Teenage Girl' (1996) 35 *Journal of American Academy of Child and Adolescent Psychiatry* 799; W.G. Reiner, 'Sex Assignment in the Neonate with Intersex or Inadequate Genitalia' (1997) 151 *Archives of Pediatrics & Adolescent Medicine* 1044; M. Diamond and K.H. Sigmundson, 'Sex Reassignment at Birth: Long-Term Review and Clinical Implications' (1997) 151 *Archives of Pediatrics & Adolescent Medicine* 298.

3 M. Diamond and K.H. Sigmundson, 'Management of intersexuality: guidelines for dealing with individuals with ambiguous genitalia' (1997) 151 *Archives of Pediatric Adolescent Medicine* 1046.

4 M. Grumbach, I.A. Hughes and F.A. Conte, 'Disorders of sex differentiation', in J.D. Wilson (ed.) *Williams' Textbook of Endocrinology*, 9th ed., WB Saunders, Philadelphia 2003, pp. 962–963.

5 National Institutes of Health/National Institute of Diabetes and Digestive and Kidney Diseases Research (NDDKR), *Strategic Plan for Pediatric Urology*, U.S. National Institutes of Health, Bethesda 2006, pp. 53–54. For recent surveys of how practice may not have changed, see L. Michala et al., 'Practice changes in childhood surgery for ambiguous genitalia?' (2014) 10 *Journal of Pediatric Urology* 934–939; F. Yankovic et al., 'Current practice in feminizing surgery for congenital adrenal hyperplasia; A specialist survey' (2013) 9 *Journal of Pediatric Urology* 1103–1107.

6 I.A. Hughes et al., 'Consensus Statement on Management of Intersex Disorders' (2006) 2 *Journal of Pediatric Urology* 148.

7 Ibid, 158.

support that underpins them',[8] with significant 'ignorance of how little is known about so many aspects' of being born with differences of sex development, including 'how sex assignment at birth square[s] with outcome[s] at puberty and beyond'.[9] In addition to encouraging multidisciplinary teams and the use of support groups for parents and patients, the most widespread achievement of the Consensus was the establishment of an umbrella nomenclature for all diagnoses of 'atypical' sex development as a '*disorder of sex development*'.[10] Controversial from the start, the nomenclature remains contested, criticised for labelling a variant physical condition as a pathological one, rather than reflecting the natural diversity of human gender development.[11]

Since the Chicago Consensus, two expert-led reviews of evidence have taken place, both reaching critical conclusions about the quality of evidence supporting clinical practices and gender assignment. The first of these was a gathering of fifty of the world's leading practitioners in Annecy, France ('the Annecy Working Party'), which concluded that even the best studies on current treatments 'lack the necessary detail to base further recommendations' on care for individual children.[12] The Annecy Working Party warned that the quality of life of surgically altered children was a poorly researched area, whereas the sexual quality of life of these patients in adulthood was overall 'impaired'.[13] The Working Party also advised that gender identity could not be predicted in infancy and that the claim of necessity or benefit of gender-reinforcing surgeries was a commonly-held perception unsubstantiated by data.[14] The second review, from an American Psychiatric Association (APA) Task Force, similarly reported that gender assignment for children with differences of sex development is 'complex and fraught with uncertainties'.[15] On the question of the quality of evidence supporting clinical practice, the Task Force concluded that it is

---

8 C.P. Houk and P.A. Lee, 'Approach to Assigning Gender in 46,XX Congenital Adrenal Hyperplasia with Male External Genitalia: Replacing Dogmatism with Pragmatism' (2010) 95 *The Journal of Clinical Endocrinology & Metabolism* 4501, 4504.

9 I.A. Hughes, 'Consequences of the Chicago DSD Consensus: A Personal Perspective' (2015) *Hormone and Metabolic Research* 394, 398.

10 Hughes et al., above n. 6, p. 149.

11 G. Davis, 'The power in a name: Diagnostic terminology and diverse experiences' (2014) 5 *Psychology & Sexuality* 15–27; M. Holmes 'The Intersex enchiridion: Naming and knowledge' (2011) 1 *Somatechnics* 388–411.

12 P.A. Lee et al., 'Review of recent outcome data of disorders of sex development (DSD): Emphasis on surgical and sexual outcomes' (2012) 8 *Journal of Pediatric Urology* 611, 14.

13 J. Schober et al., 'Disorders of Sex Development: Summaries of Long-Term Outcome Studies' (2012) 8 *Journal of Pediatric Urology* 616, 619 and 621.

14 See L.M. Liao et al., 'Determinant Factors of Gender Identity: A Commentary' (2012) 8 *Journal of Pediatric Urology* 597, 599. S. Creighton et al., 'Timing and Nature of Reconstructive Surgery for Disorders of Sex Development – Introduction' (2012) 8 *Journal of Pediatric Urology* 602.

15 W. Byne et al., 'Report of the American Psychiatric Association Task Force on Treatment of Gender Identity Disorder' (2012) 41 *Archives of Sexual Behavior* 759, 767.

'difficult to draw conclusions sufficient for evidence-based recommendations' and that the available guidelines are 'uncomfortably nonspecific'.[16] In the wake of these reviews, a broad coalition of experts from different disciplines, known as the Global DSD (Update) Consortium, revisited the Chicago Consensus recommendations in 2016 and concluded that 'data remain inadequate' to address both 'the assignment of male or female sex' and 'predictors of gender identity development', with no consensus on 'unresolved questions and dilemmas regarding indications, timing and procedures' related to each child's gender development.[17]

Despite the candour of these reviews regarding the evidentiary deficit behind clinical practice, an important question remains as to what these reviews have *not* stated about the implications of assigning a male or female gender to a child in a state of scientific uncertainty – whether or not they are reinforced with medical interventions – as well as in regard to what *criteria* are used to determine a child's gender assignment.[18] Of equal importance, these expert reviews and statements have not fully addressed the legal implications of using non-consensual medical interventions to reinforce such a gender assignment, which in many countries may be difficult to change once registered.[19] For this reason, it is essential to scrutinise what leading experts have concluded about the quality of evidence supporting gender assignment and medical interventions to reinforce them, as well as the historical medical context in which they arose. The text that follows, therefore, is a detailed parsing of expert-led position statements and reviews of evidence on their own terms, to assess how they have analysed the unpredictability of gender identity and what the resulting uncertainty signifies for clinical authority in establishing the juridical gender of children with intersex conditions or differences of sex development.

2. THE CLINICAL BASES FOR ESTABLISHING GENDER STATUS

2.1. THE HISTORICAL CONTEXT

Much critical commentary on clinical practices in the care of children with differences of sex development traces these practices to research and

16 Ibid, 789.

17 Lee et al, above n. 1, 159, 170–173.

18 J. Garland, *On Science, Law, and Medicine, The case of gender-'normalizing' interventions on children diagnosed as 'different in sex development'*, Uppsala University Press, Uppsala 2016, pp. 94–125.

19 See e.g. European Union Agency for Fundamental Rights, *The fundamental rights situation of intersex people*, EU FRA 2015, pp. 4–5 (describing that in almost all EU nations, the primary responsibility falls to clinicians to assign gender despite the problems associated with initial juridical gender assignment and the mechanisms to change it).

experimentation at Johns Hopkins University Hospital.[20] In reality, the practice of reinforcing gender assignment with hormonal treatment and surgery in infancy arose more broadly from the evolution of surgical gender-conforming practices on older children that became more frequent in the 1940s, including but not limited to practices in the United States. As leading experts have noted, prior to the 1950s, 'patients were largely managed by surgeons and urologists' for whom 'the sex of the gonad was a cardinal criterion for determination of assigned sex. The mantra was "It's an anatomical anomaly, fix it or cut it out"'.[21] Because of concerns about the implications of these practices for gender assignment and the overall psychological health of the children involved, leading clinicians from three prominent medical institutions in the US – namely, the University of California at San Francisco Hospital (1951), Harvard Medical School (1954) and Johns Hopkins University (1955) – publicly advocated for a surgical model that would attempt to resolve questions about the gender of children with differences of sex development in infancy.[22] The goal of these proposals was in part to spare children surgery later in childhood and avert the risk of severe psychological harm, but also to take a stand on what was perceived as an appropriate gender and to prevent what clinicians perceived as 'humiliation' and 'shyness' among children whose bodies were not deemed typical for their assigned gender.[23] Leading proponents of infant surgery also expressed concerns about rejection of the children by parents and peers, as well as anxiety about the risk that the children might engage in 'perversions' of an 'ambisexual' or 'bisexual' nature relative to their gender assignment.[24]

Because surgery alone could not prevent further physical and hormonal changes to a child or development of a non-conforming gender identity, researchers at Johns Hopkins University played a critical role in developing new

---

20 Garland, above n. 18, pp. 54–79.

21 Grumbach et al, above n. 4, p. 962.

22 Garland, above n. 18, pp. 74–79. Lawson Wilkins of Johns Hopkins University announced and generally endorsed the trend in his treatise in 1950; L. Wilkins, *The Diagnosis and Treatment of Endocrine Disorders in Childhood and Adolescence*, Thomas, Springfield 1950. Clinicians affiliated with the University of California advocated infant surgery broadly in 1951; F.S. Howard, 'The Surgery of Intersexuals' (1951) 65 *Journal of Urology* 636 and F. Hinman, 'Advisability of Surgical Reversal of Sex in Female Pseudohermaphroditism' (1951) 146 *Journal of the American Medical Association* 423; F. Hinman, 'Sexual Trends in Female Pseudohermaphrodism' (1951) 11 *Journal of Clinical Endocrinology & Metabolism* 477. Clinicians affiliated with Harvard University presented their proposal to the American Academy of Pediatrics in 1954 and submitted it for publication but it was not published until the next year; R.E. Gross and I.A. Meeker, 'Abnormalities of Sexual Development' (1955) 16 *Pediatrics* 303; A multidisciplinary team, led by Wilkins, formally endorsed its comprehensive policy in 1955; L. Wilkins et al., 'Hermaphroditism: Classification, Diagnosis, Selection of Sex and Treatment' (1955) 16 *Pediatrics* 287.

23 Gross and Meeker, above n. 22, pp. 314–319, and Wilkins et al., above n. 22, 296.

24 Gross and Meeker, above n. 22, p. 303, and Wilkins et al., above n. 22, 287 and 296.

theories to justify medical interventions in infancy. First, a series of experiments led by Lawson Wilkins confirmed that endocrine interventions begun in infancy could deter virilisation in 46,XX infants who often appeared more masculine in childhood, leading to the theory that these interventions could be adapted to support gender assignments of other children when coupled with surgery.[25] Under Wilkins' direction, researchers John Money and John and Joan Hampson also conducted what are now known to be the last comprehensive psychological studies of individuals with differences of sex development who were raised without surgical intervention. In these studies, Money et al. confirmed that nearly all of the individuals studied formed a stable gender even without surgical intervention, even if genital anomalies gave them appearances incongruous with their assigned gender.[26] Emphasising the 'surprising adaptability' of children, the researchers found that only in rare cases was there even 'any question of psychologic non-healthiness on grounds of a demonstrably ambiguous gender role and orientation'.[27] Thus, Money et al. concluded that even if surgery were delayed, children would 'accommodate to the impositions and embarrassments of a genital anomaly' and could undergo gender-conforming interventions in their teenage years, but then only with their consent.[28] Nevertheless, without evidence, they hypothesised that this adaptability would not preclude complications from gender assignment, especially if gender-conforming surgeries could reinforce an 'optimal' gender for infants and young children.[29]

For reasons that have yet to be fully explained, practitioners worldwide adopted a version of this '*optimal gender*' policy, despite a lack of careful research and follow-up to validate its theoretical foundations.[30] Under this policy, gender assignment and conforming medical interventions were believed to be capable of serving three interwoven ambitions, namely to (1) 'bring the genital appearance in line with the assigned gender' in order to 'facilitate the acceptance of the child … in the social environment'; (2) 'minimize the occurrence of later body image problems and gender doubts' of the child through 'gender-appropriate rearing'; and

---

25 S. Eder, 'From "following the Push of Nature" to "restoring One's Proper Sex" – Cortisone and Sex at Johns Hopkins's Pediatric Endocrinology Clinic' (2012) *Endeavour* 69; Garland, above n. 18, pp. 76–78.

26 J.G. Hampson, 'Hermaphroditic Genital Appearance, Rearing and Eroticism in Hyperadrenocorticism' (1955) 96 *Bulletin of the Johns Hopkins Hospital* 265, 266; J. Money, J.G. Hampson and J.L. Hampson, 'Sexual Incongruities and Psychopathology: The Evidence of Human Hermaphroditism' (1956) 98 *Bulletin of the Johns Hopkins Hospital* 43.

27 Ibid.

28 J. Money, J.G. Hampson and J.L. Hampson, 'Hermaphroditism: Recommendations Concerning Assignment of Sex, Change of Sex and Psychologic Management' (1955a) 97 *Bulletin of the Johns Hopkins Hospital* 284, 290 and 295.

29 Ibid, 288.

30 W.G. Reiner, 'Prenatal Gender Imprinting and Medical Decision-Making: Genetic Male Neonates with Severely Inadequate Penises', in S Preves (ed.), *Ethics and Intersex*, Springer, Dordrecht 2005, pp. 153–163.

(3) 'provide the capacity for penile-vaginal intercourse in adulthood'.[31] These considerations were also apparently thought to minimise anxiety about the child's sexual orientation, albeit in peculiarly gendered ways. For example, to preserve fertility in children with female reproductive organs, a female gender assignment – often combined with feminising surgery – was preferred for 46,XX infants. And yet, because of the difficulty of masculinising surgery and a belief in a notion that sexuality could be steered by gender assignment, 46,XY infants deemed 'inadequate males' were also routinely feminised, followed by stages of vaginoplasty, to make them suitable for penile penetration. Clinicians at Harvard Medical School and Johns Hopkins University Hospital proffered that these children would be 'reasonably happy' having sexual intercourse with men and that the 'the whispered talk, fantasies, and rumination about sex matters in the group of girls or of boys of which she or he is a part' would lead children away from 'sexual perversions and bisexual or ambisexual behavior'.[32]

These practices reflected what has been dubbed a 'bias for female assignment',[33] one that was eventually undermined by the rejection of gender assignment by surgically feminised children. Though some evidence exists of practice changes relative to traditional gender assignment, the lack of a comprehensive audit makes these claims difficult to substantiate.[34] As a result, clinicians today face many scientifically unresolved questions in practice regarding gender assignment – namely, how to assign a male or female gender to a child whose sex development does not conform to gendered expectations. As the reviews of evidence summarised in this chapter indicate, a particular clinical challenge arises from the lack of any expert consensus as to whether assignment can be based on (1) projected gender identity; (2) presumed sexual desires and functions; and (3) social, cultural and legal factors. While some clinicians have openly urged more cautious and holistic care in making key decisions, including with regard to gender assignment and delayed surgical intervention, the expert-led reviews analysed in this chapter have cautioned that many clinicians may still be making these decisions on a case-by-case basis, together with parents, despite considerable scientific uncertainty.[35] At this stage, therefore,

---

31 Byne et al, above n. 15, 789.

32 Gross and Meeker, above n. 22, p. 315; Wilkins et al., above n. 22, 297.

33 Byne et al., above n. 15, 789.

34 A. Kyriakaou et al., Current models of care for disorders of sex development – results from an international survey of specialist centres (2016) 11 *Orphanet Journal of Rare Diseases* 155(1), 10. For example, a common claim is that a trend now exists to assign 46,XY children as male. See e.g. P.D.E. Mouriquand et al., 'Surgery in disorders of sex development (DSD) with a gender issue: If (why), when, and how?' (2016) 12 *Journal of Pediatric Urology* 139, 145. The only source for this claim, however, is self-reported outcomes by some care centres, not a comprehensive thorough audit. Z. Kolesinska et al, 'Changes over time in sex assignment for disorders of sex development' (2014) 134 *Pediatrics* 2014, e710, e5.

35 Schober et al., above n. 13, 621; Creighton et al., above n. 14, 608–609.

the expert-led reviews have posed important questions as to what the clinical criteria are for assigning gender to children, recognising a potential for 'bias in gender decisions' and an 'urgent need' for consensus based on evidence.[36]

2.2. GENDER ASSIGNMENT BASED ON PROJECTED GENDER IDENTITY

With recognition of the tragic consequences of surgically assigning a child a gender that the child might later reject, a better understanding of the future gender identity of a child with differences of sex development would seem to play a significant role in gender assignment. Indeed, since the Chicago Consensus, the expert reviews and statements have consistently acknowledged that unknown biological factors may affect the gender identity of a child in unpredictable ways, such as androgen exposure to the central nervous system (CNS) *in utero*.[37] As the Global DSD Consortium explained, however, a 'biomarker of gender identity is not (yet) available' and

> [e]ven if at some point in the future such an interpretation of [brain imaging] should become possible for individuals at later stages of cognitive development, it is questionable that the brain of a newborn is developed enough for the prediction of gender identity years later.[38]

The consensus among these reviews and statements, therefore, appears to be that any current theoretical projection of gender identity cannot guarantee that a gender assignment for a specific child will be 'correct' as a long-term reflection of the gender identity of the child into adulthood. The lingering question, therefore, is how that unpredictability of gender identity affects gender assignment.

A survey of the expert recommendations indicates that the experts themselves have struggled with the low quality of available data to guide clinicians in what weight to give to an estimated likelihood of how children will develop identities and feelings related to their gender when they are born with differences of sex development. Beginning with the Chicago Consensus, the reviewers have identified several of the most common conditions associated with differences of sex development, conceding rates of gender assignment dissatisfaction from 5 per cent to more than 60 per cent among these groups of individuals, with the highest rates of gender assignment dissatisfaction reported among persons with 46,XY genetic configurations, even when feminised.[39]

---

36 Lee et al., above n. 1, 169.

37 Byne et al., above n. 15, 786–788; Lee et al., above n. 1, 168; Liao et al., above n. 14, 599.

38 Lee et al., above n. 1, 168.

39 Hughes et al., above n. 6, 152; Garland, above n. 18, pp. 108–110.

Despite such data, a lack of consensus on the factors determining gender assignment has left an indeterminate threshold as to when a rate of reported gender assignment rejection or dissatisfaction is sufficiently high to discourage any particular assignment or surgical intervention supporting it. Thus, the Global DSD Consortium implicitly, if not formally, endorsed continued assignment of female for many children – despite a reported 5 per cent gender rejection (1 in 20 children) identified for 46,XX infants with congenital adrenal hyperplasia (CAH), as well as for a reported 25 per cent gender rejection (1 in 4) among 46,XY infants with partial androgen insensitivity syndrome (PAIS).[40] These statements have also been made without taking any position on whether these assignments should be reinforced surgically.

The limitations of the use of available empirical data can further be illustrated for children with the highest reported rates of gender assignment dissatisfaction – starting with children with 46,XY genetic configurations diagnosed with 5-α-reductase deficiency and 17-β-hydroxysteroid dehydrogenase deficiency. Children diagnosed with these conditions are considered 'undermasculinised' in infancy, though they are expected to masculinise to varying degrees over time, especially in puberty. The conditions were discovered in the 1970s through research in areas of the world where medical intervention was uncommon and the children, left to their own natural development, masculinised physically. Almost all of the children studied identified as male.[41] Since then, both the Chicago Consensus and the Global DSD Consortium have reported a 50 per cent or greater chance of gender assignment dissatisfaction for persons who are born with these conditions and subjected to feminising interventions in infancy.[42] And yet, none of the evidence-based reviews have categorically rejected a female assignment with feminising surgery for these children. Indeed, in 2016, the Global DSD Consortium formally endorsed a male assignment for these children but then equivocated on that same recommendation as follows:

> Male assignment is recommended for those with 5α-reductase deficiency, since 60% later identify themselves as male, and for 17β-HSD3 deficiency, since >50% later switch to male .... While there has been a trend to assign most 46,XY patients with DSDs as male, individualized caution must be taken with male assignment based on evidence of androgen responsiveness and CNS androgen exposure during fetal life. Although 60% of all 46,XY patients with 5α-reductase deficiency develop a male gender identity, there are reports of those assigned female with satisfactory sexual activity. Hence, individual male or female assignment should be based of [sic] physical development, hormonal secretion, the presence/absence of genetic mutation and the response to hormonal therapy .... For those with 46,XY with 17β-HSD3 deficiency, care must be

40 Lee et al., above n. 1, 168–169.
41 Garland, above n. 18, p. 238.
42 Lee et al., above n. 1, 168–169.

> taken to assess all aspects, since there is evidence of satisfactory sexual function both among those raised male and those raised female. Among those raised male, there is considerable penis length dissatisfaction, and among those raised female, there is clinical distress. … It is clear that the same care plan cannot be applied to all individuals with a given diagnosis/syndrome and severity; each must be carefully individualized with specific assessment of each aspect.[43]

In short, while these recommendations purport to favour individualised clinical assessments of each child, it is clear that the infant's actual gender assignment may, in some cases, be based on determinations by parents and clinicians in individual cases of what is believed best for the child, perhaps even regardless of the statistical evidence of high risks of dissatisfaction with the gender assignment given to that child.

For 46,XX infants, similar problems attend the use of data without careful regard for the interests of the individual child, particularly, for example, children with congenital adrenal hyperplasia (CAH), for whom consensus recommendations appear largely closed to any assignment other than female. Considerable clinical reliance in this regard has been placed on a single retrospective review of the medical literature by Dessens et al. (2005), with both the Chicago Consensus and Global DSD Consortium appearing to rely heavily on that review for the claim that 95 per cent of 46,XX infants with CAH are reported to identify with a female gender.[44] Dessens and her colleagues actually reported that they reviewed 250 patient histories summarised in the medical literature, with most of the patients raised female with genitoplasty.[45] The authors claimed that only 5 per cent or fewer (13 of 217) rejected a surgically assigned female gender while 12 per cent (4 of 33) of those raised male had gender difficulties. Thus, on the basis of clinical definitions of gender dysphoria, the authors concluded, there was a greater risk of gender dissatisfaction among those assigned male. But examination of the underlying data casts serious doubt on those claims.[46] For those raised female and classified as having gender problems, the outcome data relied upon by the study reflected numerous children who were never examined as adults – some of whom were last examined before age ten and as young as age two. The authors also included individuals as successfully assigned females even if they questioned their gender identity and felt more male at some times in their lives, with last reported results for some patients reaching back to the 1960s and 1970s. In contrast, for those raised male and alleged by the authors to have not fully accepted their gender assignment,

43 Ibid.

44 Hughes et al., above n. 6, 152 and Lee et al., above n. 1, 168.

45 A.B. Dessens et al., 'Gender Dysphoria and Gender Change in Chromosomal Females with Congenital Adrenal Hyperplasia' (2005) 34 *Archives of Sexual Behavior* 389.

46 For the actual underlying data, see Garland, above n. 18, pp. 119–120.

only one (3 per cent of 33) had actually identified for a period as female, and none – or 0 per cent – had actually lived as a female.[47] Neither Dessens et al. nor any reviews of evidence since have provided additional statistical data to reinforce a female assignment for all 46,XX infants with CAH – the class of which comprises a wide range of conditions and other characteristics that indicate that many children may have identities far more complex than simply female.

The expert-led reviews' use of statistics, thus, raises a central question: What role does empirical data play in determining not only gender assignment for a child but whether gender-conforming surgery should be done early to reinforce that assignment?[48] Indeed, despite a presumed risk of a catastrophic error of 1 in 20 cases or even 1 in every 4 children for a particular diagnosis, none of the reviews has noted a consensus as to whether gender assignments should be tentative, cautioning against surgically reinforced assignments. This lack of consensus is made even more problematic because the reviews uniformly acknowledge that these estimates are not based on continuous and comprehensive long-term data on sufficient numbers of children followed over long periods into adulthood, but rather on sparse data in the available medical literature. Indeed, the studies relied upon by the Global DSD Consortium in 2016 for statistics of gender acceptance and rejection are virtually identical to those invoked by the Chicago Consensus in 2006. Apart from addressing the logistical difficulties of such research and follow-up, the reviews have not addressed the limitations of data and conservative estimates to capture the diversities of gender feelings and gender identities that may be felt by persons who consider themselves as intersexed, intergender, or non-binary, much less whether what is accepted by *some* children will be healthy for *all*.[49]

Consequently, it appears that expert-led reviews of practice demonstrate a lack of consensus as to how resolve or address the use of limited evidence on probable gender identity for children with differences of sex development. On this point, the Annecy Working Party has only cautioned that even acceptance of assigned gender does not translate to 'gender wellness' and that for persons with differences of sex development, the 'clinical need to understand the issues of sex-of-rearing versus gender identity, gender dysphoria, genital surgery, and related psychosexual development is profound'.[50] The APA Task Force similarly

---

47 In fact, of the 3 included as gender dysphoric or not accepting their male identity, 1 was reported as homosexual, 1 reported as 'not adjusting' and 1 as having a 'reportedly disturbed gender identity' without further data. Ibid.

48 A. Tamar-Mattis, 'Patient advocate responds to DSD surgery debate' (2014) 10 *Journal of Pediatric Urology* 788.

49 K. Schweizer et al., 'Gender experience and satisfaction with gender allocation in adults with diverse intersex conditions (divergences of sex development, DSD)' (2014) 5 *Psychology & Sexuality* 56–82; P.S. Furtado et al., 'Gender dysphoria associated with disorders of sex development' (2012) 9 *Nature Reviews Urology* 620–627.

50 Liao et al., above n. 14, 600; Schober et al., above n. 13, 620.

acknowledged that systematic studies are lacking regarding gender evaluation of children with differences of sex development, while the spectrum of gender identities has increasingly become more flexible and diversified and needs to be better understood.[51] And yet, the Global DSD Update Consortium affirms that clinicians may be expected to still consider a multitude of factors in gender assignment *beyond* 'probable adult gender identity (considered most important, but only tentatively predictable)' – instead with such data counterbalanced by assessments of 'anticipated quality of sexual function', 'surgical options/indications/risks' and 'psychosocial factors (familial, social and cultural)'.[52]

2.3. GENDER ASSIGNMENT BASED ON SEXUAL PRESUMPTIONS

Because anticipated 'sexual function' is considered a factor in gender assignment for a child, it is essential to understand how sexual function is conceptualised and measured to be used for gender assignment for children as future adults. Since the Chicago Consensus, the evidence-based reviews and position statements have all conceded that expectations regarding penile-vaginal intercourse frame both gender assignment and considerations for gender-conforming surgeries to reinforce such an assignment.[53] Nevertheless, apart from assessing the risks that surgery will cause physical harm and undermine sexual satisfaction, the expert statements and reviews offer little detail as to how a future adult's *desired sexual function*, whatever it may be, can be projected in infancy. As the Annecy Working Party explained, the matter is not simply that sexual quality of life is 'impaired', but that clinicians 'generally concentrate on aspects that they can easily influence by treatment, such as hormonal control and anatomical alteration of the external genitalia' but as children grow they 'may be more concerned with criteria that are much more difficult to quantify and are often ignored in the medical literature'.[54] Similarly, the Global DSD Consortium concluded, although 'anticipated quality of sexual function is a key factor' in gender assignment, it is also 'most difficult to predict' – as 'neither the anatomy nor a consult with sexual medicine can predict the quality of sexual function, since it depends upon interpersonal dynamics and the individual's abilities to participate and respond during sexual situations'.[55]

To the extent that anticipated sexual function is not related to penile-vaginal intercourse, only the APA Task Force has directly addressed the implications

---

51 Byne et al., above n. 15, 787–788.

52 Lee et al., above n. 1, 168.

53 Creighton et al., above n. 14, 603; Byne et al., above n. 15, 789; Lee et al., above n. 1, 167.

54 Schober et al., above n. 13, 619–620.

55 Lee et al., above n. 1, 169.

associated with presumptions about sexual orientation that steer traditional practice, writing that

> [c]onsiderations of the implications of a patient's present or emerging sexual orientation are ... typically missing in existing discussions regarding the indications for genital surgery. The capacity for penile-vaginal intercourse may be valued differently depending on the sexual orientation of the individual, especially relative to all the difficulties that the required surgeries sometimes entail.[56]

In contrast, the Chicago Consensus concluded that '[h]omosexual orientation (relative to sex of rearing) or strong cross-sex interest in an individual with DSD is not an indication of incorrect gender assignment'.[57] The Annecy Working Party similarly asserted that 'the terms homosexual (meaning the same sex) and heterosexual (meaning the different sex) are largely irrelevant'.[58] The Global DSD Consortium has merely acknowledged this criticism, noting an unusual 'preoccupation with heterosexual intercourse' among clinicians given the 'higher incidence of nonheterosexual orientation' among some surgically altered children.[59]

Each of these position statements raises more questions than they answer regarding how a gender assignment will affect the sexual identity imposed on a child (and future adult) and how such considerations, in turn, currently affect gender assignment. In one sense, the reviews may be interpreted as a progressive indication that a 'homosexual' identity is considered clinically neutral – certainly not harmful to the child – perhaps because of increased social and medical acceptance of homosexuality. None of the reviews, however, explain their conclusions in this way, nor do they reference any studies reflecting any well-considered calculus that a child will be better off if, because of gender assignment, the child and future adult might be socially and legally classified as gay, lesbian or bisexual – rather than intersex, intergender or transgender – especially if the identity is effectively imposed through gender assignment and reinforced with surgery. Thus, to the extent that the expert reviews presume that anticipated sexual function is relevant to gender assignment, the question remains why sexual orientation is 'irrelevant' to that assignment, or whether the failure to consider it may be relevant to each affected child and future adult.

Closer reading of the reviews indicates that clinical views about an infant's future sexual satisfaction as a 'male' or 'female' may bias their views on gender assignment. For 46,XY patients with 'micropenis', for example, both the

---

56 Byne et al., above n. 15, 789.
57 Hughes et al., above n. 6, 150.
58 Schober et al., above n. 13, 617.
59 Lee et al., above n. 1, 167 and 169.

Chicago Consensus and Global DSD Update Consortium confirmed a high-rate of male identification of those patients, but neither firmly recommended against feminisation of these children or addressed the consequences of such an assignment for their sexual identity and orientation, in part based on presumed sexual function and satisfaction.[60] The Annecy Working Party, more curiously, equivocated on this matter as follows:

> [I]n males with micropenis, the limited data available suggest that sexual function as a male is acceptable, at least to the patients themselves. There are no data to tell us the views of their female sexual partners. Should such men, therefore, be encouraged to accept the small size of their phallus, or have it enlarged for the greater satisfaction of their partner or transgender [sic] to female on the grounds that they are inadequate males?[61]

The first claim – that available data indicate that sexual function is 'acceptable to the patients' – would appear to stand on its own from a scientific point of view, favouring a male sex assignment and settling the issue. The qualification 'at least to the patients themselves' is more perplexing, if it is intended to suggest that a patient should change gender because others think so. Indeed, the Working Party's interest in the views of the patients' 'female sex partners' is particularly problematic, even apart from its heterosexual presumption. If the patients have found relationships in which they themselves are sexually satisfied, the clinical significance of their sex partners' views should be nil – given that some female sex partners' dissatisfaction should not mean that all male infants with 'micropenis' should be surgically feminised and would grow up healthy and sexually satisfied as females. The final commentary – even as a hypothetical question – is profoundly contrary to medical science: no known standard of care indicates that clinicians should 'encourage' a patient to transition to any gender, much less question an individual's gender on the basis of theoretical partners' (heterosexual) sexual satisfaction.

To date, the expert-led reviews and position statements have not addressed the aetiology of sexual orientation, which is neither predictable nor fully understood, either in medical science or other disciplines, but is presumed to have at least some biological if not genetic-endocrine influence.[62] Since the 1980s,

---

60 See Hughes et al., above n. 6, 152 and Lee et al, above n. 1, 169.

61 Schober et al., above n. 13, 621.

62 A.R. Sanders et al., 'Genome-wide scan demonstrates significant linkage for male sexual orientation' (2015) 47 *Psychological Medicine* 1379–1388; J.M. Bailey, M.P. Dunne and N.G. Martin, 'Genetic and environmental influences on sexual orientation and its correlates in an Australian Twin Sample' (2000) 78 *Journal of Personality and Social Psychology* 524–536; F. Whitam, M. Diamond and J. Martin 'Homosexual orientation in twins: A report on 61 pairs and three triplet sets' (1993) 22 *Archives of Sexual Behavior* 187–206.

researchers have reported findings of 'homosexuality' in persons diagnosed with differences of sex development and subjected to gender-conforming surgery.[63] For 46,XX patients with CAH, for example, studies have confirmed that significant percentages of these persons may identify as lesbian after surgical assignment as female – even though no expert-led review has formally challenged a female assignment for these patients.[64] While comprehensive studies have not been performed on all diagnostic groups regarding their sexual orientation relative to their gender, reports of gender assignment rejection and homosexuality among even small percentages of these children diagnosed with different conditions would seem to undermine any simple presumption that they will identify as heterosexual relative to their assigned gender. Indeed, the best available evidence indicates that sexual orientation in heterosexual, gay, lesbian, bisexual, and transgender persons does not predictably correlate with a gender identity or role.[65] In short, while the medical literature contains evidence that sexual orientation classification may be affected by or become a cause for dissatisfaction with gender assignment, it remains unclear, from expert-led reviews and position statements, how clinicians are expected to assess such data in assigning a gender to a child.

The question, thus, remains open as to what medical-scientific data clinicians are expected to utilise in assigning a gender to children based on anticipated sexual function, especially given the potentially diverse individual interests in sexual function that a child might have as an adult. For example, a 46,XX child without medical intervention might grow to appear more 'male' to others, including with a 'phallic' appearance of the genitals, but might still identify as a female and prefer to keep what she considers to be her clitoris intact, in order to preserve

---

63 J. Money, H. Devore and B.F. Norman, 'Gender Identity and Gender Transposition: Longitudinal Outcome Study of 32 Male Hermaphrodites Assigned as Girls' (1986) 12 *Journal of Sex and Marital Therapy* 165–81; J. Money, M. Schwartz and V.G. Lewis, 'Adult Erotosexual Status and Fetal Hormonal Masculinization and Demasculinization: 46,XX Congenital Virilizing Adrenal Hyperplasia and 46,XY Androgen-Insensitivity Syndrome Compared' (1984) 9 *Psychoneuroendocrinology* 405–414.

64 L. Frisén et al., 'Gender role behavior, sexuality, and psychosocial adaptation in women with congenital adrenal hyperplasia due to CYP21A2 deficiency' (2010) 95 *Journal of Clinical Endocrinology and Metabolism* 3633–3640; M.F.L. Meyer-Bahlburg, C. Dolezal, S.W. Baker and M.I. New, 'Sexual orientation in women with classical or non-classical congenital adrenal hyperplasia as a function or degree of prenatal androgen excess' (2008) 37 *Archives of Sex Behavior* 85–99; F. Gastaud et al., 'Impaired Sexual and Reproductive Outcomes in Women with Classical Forms of Congenital Adrenal Hyperplasia' (2007) 92 *Journal of Clinical Endocrinology and Metabolism* 1391–1396; M. Hines, C. Brook and C.S. Conway, 'Androgen and psychosocial development: Core gender identity, sexual orientation and recalled childhood gender role behavior in women and men with congenital adrenal hyperplasia (CAH)' (2004) 41 *Journal of Sex Research* 75–81.

65 This has been well-established since the 1940s, including in the key studies on which the optimal gender policy relied. See A. Ellis, 'The Sexual Psychology of Human Hermaphrodites' (1945) 7 *Psychosomatic Medicine* 108.

her sexual sensitivity and her overall uniqueness and integrity.[66] Another 46,XX person with similar development might identify as male and might also prefer to keep to what he considers his penis from being removed and feminised, perhaps even considering his phallus essential to his male identity, regardless of whether he identifies as a heterosexual, gay or bisexual male. Still other persons with that development might not wish to identify as 'male' nor 'female' and might also not describe their genitals in traditional gendered terms.[67] Though some prominent expert-clinicians have raised these possibilities, the expert-led reviews and statements suggest that these questions are not fully addressed because they are matters on which no scientific or clinical consensus exists.

2.4. GENDER ASSIGNMENT BASED ON SOCIAL, CULTURAL AND LEGAL FACTORS

Since the Chicago Consensus, the expert reviews and position statements have acknowledged that gender assignment of an infant is based in part, or may be affected by, 'the views of the family and sometimes, circumstances relating to cultural practices'.[68] None of the four expert-led reviews and statements analysed here, however, set forth any detail as to how familial and culture views are factored into gender assignment relative to other data. The Annecy Working Party summarised that gender expression and development may be 'multi-dimensional' relative to how typical a child feels relative to social and cultural pressures, so much so that what is perceived as gendered behaviour and expression may appear individualised even though 'the cultural scaffolding buttressing these expressions is dimly visible'.[69] The Chicago Consensus indicated only that 'social and cultural factors, as well as hormonal effects, appear to influence a gender role' only for children with 5α-reductase deficiency (with no comment on other groups), otherwise explaining categorically that differences of sex development may result in 'stigma' and that 'social factors' can affect 'gender role change', whereas 'female infertility precludes marriage, which also affects employment prospects and creates economic dependence'.[70] The APA Task Force limited its consideration of social and cultural factors to gender change as well, noting that 'different cultures and even subcultures within a given country may differ in the prevailing gender categories and the salience and weight of criteria used in decision-making on gender assignment'.[71] The Global DSD Consortium

66 Diamond and Sigmundson, above n. 3, 1050.

67 I. Morland, 'Between critique and reform: Ways of Reading the Intersex Controversy', in M. Holmes (ed.), *Critical Intersex*, Routledge, London 2016, p. 196.

68 Hughes et al., above n. 6, 152.

69 Liao et al., above n. 14, 598–600.

70 Hughes et al., above n. 6, 155.

71 Byne et al., above n. 15, 787.

concluded broadly that 'only a proportion' of children with differences of sex development 'present a major challenge regarding male or female assignment', apparently limited to cases where 'external genitalia are sufficiently ambiguous to hamper' the assignment, but conceded that 'data remain inadequate' regarding gender assignment and did not elaborate as to which persons would find the genitals 'ambiguous' and from which perspective.[72]

These statements all leave unanswered what *weight* might be given to social and cultural considerations in gender assignment, relative to other factors, such as predictions of probable gender identity and sexual function or orientation. Only the Global DSD Consortium offered a specific example of such weighing, recommending possible consideration of raising a 46,XX child with a virilised appearance as a male, but then only when the 'social and cultural environment[s] are supportive'.[73] The remaining expert-led commentaries provide little information as to whether parental choice may prove decisive over all other factors. In this regard, the lack of consensus reflected in the Global DSD Consortium may be most revealing, as other position statements from different groups of clinicians have described parents' 'expectations' as a critical factor in gender assignment in general.[74] Several experts who have led and participated in the reviews assessed in this chapter have also issued their own recommendations for practice – indicating that 'the cultural environment of the child is of utmost importance in the decision process' for gender assignment for 46,XX children and that '[f]amily dynamics and sensitivity play an essential role in the decision process' for children with mosaic genetic configurations.[75] Notably, this subgroup of experts framed these conclusion with two observations: (1) that 'evidence-based medicine meets major hurdles' in the care of children with differences of sex development, such that clinical management is itself 'mostly subjective, examiner-dependent, and culturally influenced'; and (2) that for infants the 'only identity that can be defined is the "social identity" … how the "society" mirrors the individual … with social visibility or gender assignment recommended by most to make the child socially visible'.[76]

Recommendations such as these sharply conflict with the expert-led reviews of evidence and research of other expert group members overall. As the Annecy Working Party explained, one of the most 'difficult aspects' of gender assignment on infants and related treatment is getting 'parents and medical staff to realise that responsibility for all decisions must transfer to the patient', as 'it will often become apparent that the desires of the patient are not the same as those of

72 Lee et al., above n. 1, 159.
73 Ibid, 169.
74 Mouriquand et al., 'Editorial: The ESPU/SPU standpoint on the surgical management of Disorders of Sex Development (DSD)' (2014) 10 *Journal of Pediatric Urology* 8–10.
75 Mouriquand et al., above n. 34, 144–145.
76 Ibid, 140.

the parents and may often appear unconventional'.[77] As the Chicago Consensus noted, the traditional justification for surgical gender assignment was often that it 'relieves parental distress and improves attachment between the child and the parents', even though 'the systematic evidence for this belief is lacking'.[78] Indeed, the Global DSD Consortium has acknowledged that children in families that do not support atypical gender behaviour may even be more likely to conceal discomfort with their gender assignment,[79] whereas the APA Task Force warned that supporting older children with differences of sex development in these situations requires 'cautious shielding of the young patient from family and peer pressures'.[80] All of these concerns are supported by extensive research by social psychologists that indicates that parents of children with differences of sex development often worry about their children's atypical gender behaviour, feel pressured to impose gender norms on their children, and may have difficulties parenting their children in the process.[81] As a recent statement from other members of these expert-led reviews has noted, 'parents need help' – as do patients themselves – because 'coping' with differences of sex development 'at any stage in life, remains challenging', requiring clinical support in addressing the insensitivity, criticism and stigmatisation of outsiders for individuals' differences of genital appearance, infertility, subfertility and gender-atypical behaviour.[82]

Given the clinical weight that may be given to the views of parents and a hostile social setting in assessing social and cultural factors, it is noteworthy that most of the expert reviews and statements were issued before human rights recommendations began to coalesce around the precept that decisions regarding gender identity belong to each person born with intersex conditions and differences of sex development, not to parents or society as a whole. So far, only the Global DSD Consortium's statement has been issued in the wake of the surge of these recommendations. As the Consortium accordingly explained:

> Although parents are responsible for consenting to interventions believed on the basis of available evidence to be in the best interests of their child, their right to consent

77 Schober et al., above n. 13, 617.

78 Hughes et al., above n. 6, 153.

79 Lee et al., above n. 1, 168.

80 Byne et al., above n. 15, 787.

81 T. Lundberg et al., 'From Knowing Nothing to Knowing What, How and Now: Parents' Experiences of Caring for Their Children with Congenital Adrenal Hyperplasia' (2017) 42 *Journal of Pediatric Psychology* 250–259; C. Wolfe-Christensen et al., 'Caregivers of children with a disorder of sex development: associations between parenting capacities and psychological distress' (2014) 10 *Journal of Pediartic Urology* 538–543; H.P. Crissman et al., 'Children with disorders of sex development: a qualitative study of early parental experience' (2011) *International Journal of Pediatric Endocrinology* 10.

82 A. Dessens et al., 'Understanding the needs of professionals who provide psychosocial care for children and adults with disorders of sex development' (2017) 1 *BMJ Paediatrics Open* 1, 2.

> to non-medically necessary irreversible procedures that may adversely affect the child's future sexual function and/or reproductive capacity has been questioned [by human rights authorities], particularly when such parental decisions preclude the child's ability to be involved in decision making. In addition, many guidelines deem children's participation and input indispensable to decisions, especially those that will have a life-long deeply personal impact on their lives, with heightened awareness that young children, in particular, may not be able to vocalize adverse reactions to many interventions .... Physicians working with these families should be aware that the trend in recent years has been for legal and human rights bodies to increasingly emphasize preserving patient autonomy.[83]

It remains to be seen whether this 'trend' will be reflected in clinical practice changes or whether it will only complicate the weight given to parents' desires and social and cultural considerations for gender assignment in the future.

3. FINAL REFLECTIONS

Twenty years ago, the first guidelines calling for changes to current clinical practice focused on two categorical reforms – *first*, that any socio-legal gender to a child should be assigned without any non-consensual gender-normalising medical interventions and *second*, that any such reconstructive surgery, in particular, should be delayed until the individual undergoing those procedures can choose them and be involved in how they are carried out.[84] The thread that united both of these recommendations was the importance of consent on matters central to personhood. Since 2006, only one set of clinical guidelines, devised by intersex advocates in collaboration with a small number of clinicians, has integrated this recommendation into a model of care for children.[85] While an increasing number of clinicians appear to be striving to provide holistic care with as much possible deference to the wishes of children with differences of sex development, the diversity of clinical practice indicates that any consensus among experts on the evidentiary bases by gender assignment, among other aspects of clinical management, is so lacking that it is difficult to generalise about what current practice is. As one recent poignant commentary has noted, many clinical practices will continue to 'result from a combination of traditional

---

83 Lee et al., above n. 1, 176–177.

84 Diamond and Sigmundson, above n. 3, 1046–1050.

85 Consortium on the Management of Disorders of Sex Development, Clinical guidelines for management of intersex disorders in childhood (2006) <http://www.dsdguidelines.org/files/clinical.pdf> (last accessed 19.08.2017).

beliefs, folk remedies and prejudices, fed by rumour and discrimination and available healthcare resources and expertise'.[86] Nevertheless:

> [I]t should be appreciated that people with [differences of sex development (DSD)] have the same desires as everyone else: to find a peer who will love them; to be a valuable part of society; to be comfortable with their body; to be able to have satisfactory sexual relations; to integrate into the community; and to trust their medical caregivers. More clinical studies as well as academic and public debate are needed to support people with DSD with sex assignment, gender identity development, atypical gender role behavior, sexual orientation and satisfaction with their own sexuality. ... People with DSD who are discontent may simply be showing an evolving discrepancy between the gender identity they experience and the sex of rearing which, in most cases was chosen by their carers at birth. All carers, parents and professionals, should be aware that possibility of dissatisfaction with the assigned sex, however small, does exist and centres that provide expert care should be prepared to support the patient and the family, if required.[87]

The expert-reviews of evidence regarding current gender assignment practices indicate not only that clinicians are attempting to base their decisions on medical science, but on social and cultural factors as well – all of which should raise questions as to whether the clinical role should be advisory, rather than dispositive, in juridical gender-assignment decisions. As gender identity is increasingly considered to be an individual right, more and more individuals should be expected to embrace an array of gender identities,[88] with children needing to discuss their feelings of being accepted and supported to express their gender and parents needing counselling, peer support, and parenting strategies.[89] Thus, as the 1997 guidelines urged, clinicians must change their focus to supporting children in their gender, all the while helping parents in understanding that their children may behave in non-stereotypical ways or identify with an unconventional gender, relative to the gender assigned to them at birth. This includes supporting children and adults who prefer 'the designation of intersex ... as an optional identity along with male and female'.[90] In this light, it bears noting that the uncertainty in the bases for gender assignment raises concerns still today, as in 1997, as to whether such

---

86 R. Markosyan and S.F. Ahmed, 'Sex Assignment in Conditions Affecting Sex Development' (2017 suppl. 1) 9 *Journal of Clinical Research in Pediatric Endocrinology* 106, 111.

87 Ibid.

88 Diamond and Sigmundson, above n. 3, 1046.

89 E.A. Riley, G. Sitharthan, L. Clemson and M. Diamond, 'The Needs of Gender-Variant Children and Their Parents According to Health Professionals' (2011) 13 *International Journal of Transgenderism* 54.

90 Diamond and Sigmundson, above n. 3, 1048 (Guideline 19).

an assignment should be reinforced medically. Indeed, as Diamond and Sigmundson elaborated:

> We are often asked about those intersexed individuals that have had early surgery of one sort or another, or even sex reassignment, and gone on to be happy and lead successful lives. Doesn't that demonstrate the wisdom of past practices? Our response: Humans can be immensely strong and adaptable. Certainly some intersexed individuals can, in dignity, maintain themselves in a manner that they neither would have chosen nor in which they feel comfortable – as have others with a life condition from birth that cannot be changed ....
>
> Many can adjust to surgery and reassignment for which they were not consulted and many have learned to accept secrecy, misrepresentations, white and black lies and loneliness. People make life accommodations every day and try to better their lot for tomorrow.
>
> We are aware of individuals that have come to terms with their life regardless of how stressed or painful. To them we offer our praise and admiration for their fortitude, strength and courage. Similarly we do the same for those that have rebelled against their circumstances and changed their lives with elective sex reassignment, surgery or whatever. However, unlike individuals who have been given neonatal surgery for cleft palate or myelomeningocele, many of those who have had genital surgery or been sex reassigned neonatally have complained bitterly of the treatment. Some have sex reassigned themselves. Others treated similarly have reasons not to make an issue of the matter but are living in silent despair but coping.[91]

As the first reform guidelines concluded decades ago, all individuals 'must be involved in any decision ... so crucial to their lives' as gender assignment, including the 'last word' in any genital modification to reinforce it.[92] Sexual orientation, sensitivity, and desire are deeply personal concerns to every human being, not mere scientific factors that can be projected in infancy and calculated to assign a gender for a person, particularly if reinforced by surgery in infancy. Currently, only a minority of clinicians appear to have endorsed this view, awaiting support from consensus-based, expert-led organisations, with the future of children with differences of sex development remaining largely at stake.

91 Ibid, 1050.
92 Ibid, 1046 and 1050.

PART II

THEOLOGY AND LEGAL HISTORY

INTERSEX IN THE CHRISTIAN TRADITION: PERSONHOOD AND EMBODIMENT

Duncan Dormor

1. INTRODUCTION

Like everyone else, individuals whose bodies are different from the majority of the population on account of variations in their sexed development[1] seek to live a fulfilling life: to be happy; to experience good health and mental well-being; to have agency and the freedom to choose how they live their life; and to be treated justly, equitably within society and not be subjected to harm by others. Like everyone else, their well-being is caught up with their sense of self, identity and narrative, 'their story'; and, this is shaped by language, by the ways in which they are recognised by others, by their actions in the world and the actions of the world upon them. Clearly people with variations in sex development are likely to have to negotiate particular challenges in making sense of their embodiment and in realising certain common human aspirations – including intimate relationships and parenthood. So, alongside the usual cast list of those who play a key role in the shared and fundamentally human task of making sense of the self – parents, siblings or friends – or the key institutional settings of socialisation (education, employment), contemporary individuals with variations in sex development are also very likely to be shaped by extensive experience of clinical medical settings.

This chapter seeks to set the experience of people with unusual sexed embodiment within the larger narrative of Christianity, the cornerstone of Western culture and thought, especially of its morality.[2] The first substantial section will therefore consider theological and ethical reflections within early Christianity through a focus on two surprisingly pertinent passages within authoritative writings – *The Gospel according to Matthew* and Saint Augustine's *City of God*.[3] It will be argued that in both, the authors challenge inherited cultural categories in ways that rehabilitate and promote the well-being of

1 The issue of language and terminology is especially complex in relation to intersex persons. It ranges from that which denotes an identity (intersex), to that which references a range of medical conditions (disorders of sex development). An alternative to the latter – variations in sex development – is, perhaps, less normative in its construal and draws attention to the fact of natural human variation. This chapter will also use a range of terms and expressions, including 'variantly sexed', 'embodied difference' or 'unusually-sexed bodies'. It is important to remember that, however designated, we are speaking of people within a range of subgroups with different diagnoses and concerns who have been aggregated into an umbrella category.

2 This chapter can usefully be seen as a companion piece to D.J. Dormor, 'Transgenderism and the Christian Church: An Overview' in J.M. Scherpe (ed.), *The Legal Status of Transsexual and Transgender Persons*, Intersentia, Cambridge 2015, pp. 27–76.

3 Augustine's magnus opus, *De civitate Dei contra paganos*, was written between 413–427 AD. For an English translation, see Saint Augustine, *Concerning the City of God against the*

individuals with variations in sex development. This section is followed by a consideration of the contemporary situation. Here, particular attention is drawn to the dissensus that exists between the medical sphere that focuses on 'disorders of sex development' and the more identitarian orientation of some intersex activism and human rights advocacy. This impasse is understood primarily as a consequence of the conflict between the nature of the respective spheres and their characteristic discourses, and how they relate to different aspects or conceptions of the human person. Finally, it is argued in the last section that, whilst official documents from contemporary Christian denominations on intersex issues have been disappointing, an approach from theological anthropology has significant potential to help resolve this contemporary dissensus and provide pointers to the future treatment of intersex persons.

In preparation for the substantial content of this chapter, this introduction will begin by considering the ways in which human cultures categorise and recognise people who are different, and then, seek to provide an ethical account of what might be expected of the good life by drawing on the work of the philosopher of religion, Paul Ricoeur.[4]

1.1. PERSONHOOD: INDIVIDUALS, CATEGORIES AND CONTEXTS

This book is concerned with the well-being of individuals who are grouped together, classified and subsequently designated *at some level* as constituting a type of person on the basis of their embodied difference. The contemporary approach to that grouping and classification is 'objective', and determined, primarily, by scientifically-based medical criteria. Within this broad understanding two such designations have particular currency in contemporary society. That is, they are dominant; but they are also divergent: one, associated with the political sphere, broadly conceived, and patterned on that of contemporary sexual and gender minorities (LGBT), in effect creates a 'personage ... a type of life, a life form,

Pagans, H. Bettenson (transl.), Penguin Books, London 1972; and also Saint Augustine, *The City of God against the Pagans*, R.W. Dyson (ed. and transl.), Cambridge University Press, Cambridge 1998.

4 Paul Ricoeur (1913–2005) was a French philosopher who made major contributions to the field of hermeneutics, in particular through his exploration of the phenomenology of religion. This chapter draws on his work on ethics, which is firmly grounded in the Western philosophical tradition, most evidently in the thinking of Aristotle, Spinoza and Kant. See P. Ricoeur, 'Approaching the Human Person' (1999) 1 *Ethical Perspectives* 45–54; P. Ricoeur, *The Just*, D. Pellauer (transl)., University of Chicago Press, Chicago 2000; and P. Ricoeur, *Reflections on the Just*, D. Pellauer (transl.), University of Chicago Press, Chicago 2007. See also J. Carter, *Ricoeur on Moral Religion: A Hermeneutics of Ethical Life*, Oxford University Press, Oxford 2014.

and a morphology'.[5] That person, the intersex individual, is thus located within an 'identitarian regime';[6] as, at some level, an alternative or third gender. The other, weaker designation addresses a person who, as a member of a group, *suffers* from a quite particular kind of impairment, disorder or disability – hence they are a person with a *disorder of sex development* (DSD).[7] Both designations are normative in character, although they are not always recognised as such.

In principle, at least, a person with a DSD could simply be considered as someone with a medical condition or disorder in the same sort of way as others living with a form of disability that brings specific limitations, the negative consequences of which can be treated or ameliorated.[8] Whilst such an approach might be desirable, what makes this construal problematic is that this particular class of disorder is widely perceived to bring into question an individual's ability to successfully develop a gender and personal identity, and, thus, to be fully recognised as a person. In short, notwithstanding the efforts of policy-makers, activists, advocacy and support groups and the medical profession, such persons are at significant risk of being pathologised.

One of the fundamental aspects of personhood is that it is historically contingent and culturally located; that is, the sense of self is deeply shaped by the society in which individuals are nurtured and socialised, and the assumptions, categories and classifications which constitute its symbolic universe. As social animals and cultural beings, humans are thus embedded in particular ways of seeing the world through epistemological framings or discourses; that is, sets of regulated practices and unwritten rules and statements that bring a certain coherence, a 'normality' to the social world.[9] The 'common and collective ethical ethos'[10] created by such discourses render to social life a sense of reality, that something is true and sane; acceptable and obvious. Conversely, to contradict

---

5 As Foucault famously describes the 'invention' of the 'homosexual': M. Foucault, *The Will to Knowledge the History of Sexuality volume 1*, R Hurley (transl.), Penguin, London 1978, p. 43.

6 M. Holmes (ed.), *Critical Intersex*, Ashgate, Farnham 2009, p. ix.

7 The nomenclature and umbrella classification, 'Disorders of Sex Development' (DSD), was introduced as a consequence of the Consensus Statement on Management of Intersex Disorders produced with the support and authority of the Lawson Wilkins Pediatric Endocrine Society and the European Society for Paediatric Endocrinology. See P.A. Lee, C.P. Houk, S.F. Ahmed and I.A. Hughes, 'Consensus Statement on Management of Intersex Disorders' (2006) 118(2) *Pediatrics* e488–500; and IA Hughes et al., 'Consensus Statement on Management of Intersex Disorders' (2006) 2(3) *Journal of Pediatric Urology* 148–162.

8 This argument is advanced in E.K. Feder, 'Normalizing Medicine: Between "Intersexuals" and Individuals with "Disorders of Sex Development"' (2009) 17(2) *Health Care Analysis* 134–143. Feder's own position has developed subsequently: see E.K. Feder, *Making Sense of Intersex: Changing Ethical Perspectives in Biomedicine*, Indiana University Press, Indiana 2014.

9 The concept of the discourse was developed and elaborated by the French philosopher, Michel Foucault (1926–1984). For an account, see S. Mills, *Michel Foucault*, Routledge, London 2003, pp. 53–66.

10 J. Butler, *Giving an Account of Oneself*, Fordham University Press, New York 2005, p. 3.

the central tenets of a discourse is to break a taboo, to seem mad, eccentric, immoral or just plain wrong. Sex/gender provides a very good example: until recently within Western society, it was 'common sense' that gender was equal and opposite, fixed and binary, male and female; it was thus understood that every person had a 'true sex', a real essence. Discourses are also therefore simultaneously claims to authority. So, whilst such embeddedness is unavoidable; renders the world familiar; and anchors a person's sense of who they are and might become, it comes at a price. For social order can only be imposed on the world through the enactment of forms of sanctioned violence, rhetorical or physical, which frequently result in psychological or embodied harm being perpetrated against particular individuals, intentionally or otherwise.

The recognition and flourishing of persons who are visibly different presents significant challenges to all human societies, to their social and symbolic forms of classification and to the ways in which they generate solidarity: for the creation of a sense of identity, of 'us', simultaneously creates various forms of 'them', or the 'other'. All sorts of difference and anomaly thus have the potential to threaten social order leading some individuals to be construed as less than fully human in one way or another. Thus, in the many human societies where distinct gender roles play a fundamental part in social ordering, ambiguity of sex can be perceived as threatening[11] exposing intersex individuals to a range of potential harms from stigma or exclusion to death.[12]

The possibility of sanctioned violence, that is violence that is habitually not perceived as such, is thus written into the ordinary, 'normal' language and everyday practices of the social order and can bring wounds, damage and harm trailing in their wake, at least for some: 'norms are not so much thrown up intellectually as written in blood and carried by autonomous interpretative communities'.[13] The individual thus comes into the world inheriting ways of seeing, and inhabiting language and practices that may, in some cases, threaten their own physical, psychological or social well-being.

From the point of view of the ordinary, everyday perspective, as well as that of the hermeneutic, cultural disciplines, be they historical, sociological or theological, it is not then the 'objective' scientific criteria that are primarily determinative of personhood. Rather it is the culturally dominant norms and narratives which appropriate and co-opt scientific ideas to cultural and social projects. So, as the historian, Thomas Laqueur, points out, in understanding our

---

11 K. Long, *Hermaphrodites in Renaissance Europe*, Ashgate, Aldershot 2006, pp. 40–41.

12 The traditional Roman attitude to hermaphrodites was one of fear and superstition. The births of such infants were seen as indicative of divine displeasure and many accounts, by Livy and others, suggest such infants were killed, at least prior to the first century BC; see J.M. Beagon, *The Elder Pliny on the Human Animal, Natural History Book 7*, Clarendon Press, Oxford 2005, p. 167.

13 D. Martin, *Ruin and Restoration: On Violence, Liturgy and Reconciliation*, Routledge, Abingdon 2016, p. 17.

sexed nature in the construal of gender it is the governing narrative or ideology that really counts:

> The history of the representation of the anatomical differences between men and women is extraordinarily independent of the actual structures of these organs or of what was known about them. Ideology, not accuracy of observation, determined how they were seen and which difference would matter.[14]

Clearly in identifying anomalies, in recognising departures from the social norm, the key factor is visible difference. For the individual, all manner of social consequences, historically and culturally contingent, flow from the apprehension of visible difference. That is abundantly clear if we consider ethnicity. But it is equally true for albinism or the occurrence of identical twins. So, whilst the scientific classification of various medical conditions with implications for sexed difference has populated the umbrella category of 'intersex' in the last hundred years, in reality it has been the existence of individuals with ambiguous external genitalia which has been the primary focus for social concern and cultural anxiety. And, indeed, this remains the case today. So, for example, the XY person with Complete Androgen Insensitivity Syndrome (CAIS); that is, a genetic male who develops to look like a female person (albeit without internal reproductive organs) and has a female gender identity, has tended, historically, to fall, outside the parameters of close cultural scrutiny.[15]

Many of those individuals, who might now be designated intersex, have as historical subjects been assigned to a range of alternative or 'third' gender categories, most evidently 'eunuch' and 'hermaphrodite'. However, in their scope, these categories only partially overlap with the modern designation of intersex. For both eunuchs and hermaphrodites, ambiguous genitalia were an important factor in establishing that an individual belonged to such a category, but only amongst other visible criteria also judged to be important (e.g. the ability to grow a beard or the display of masculine or feminine behaviours).[16] In historic settings where, broadly speaking, there is a greater emphasis on social status and role than individual identity, concern was also more clearly focused on the 'social goods' of marriage and procreation. Indeed, it has been argued

---

14 T. Laqueur, *Making Sex: Body and Gender from the Greeks to Freud*, Harvard University Press, Cambridge Mass. 1990, p. 88.

15 Female gender identity is entirely typical for CAIS individuals. See e.g. M. Hines, S.F. Ahmed and I.A. Hughes, 'Psychological outcomes and gender-related development in complete androgen insensitivity syndrome' (2003) 32 *Archives of Sexual Behavior* 93–101; and M. Jürgensen, O. Hiort, P.M. Holterhus and U. Thyen, 'Gender role behavior in children with XY karyotype and disorders of sex development' (2007) 51 *Hormones and Behavior* 443–453.

16 C. Rolker, 'The two laws and the three sexes: ambiguous bodies in canon law and Roman law' (2014) 100 *Zeitschrift der Savigny-Stiftung für Rechtsgeschichte: Kanonistische Abteilung* 178–222.

that the sex/gender of an individual could be most clearly established by the act of getting married.[17] Likewise, some individuals, who today would be formally classified as intersex (e.g. CAIS women), would not have been 'read' historically as hermaphrodites, but rather as barren or childless women.

The classification and understanding of gender difference itself also shows great variation historically and cross-culturally.[18] In the West, historians note a significant shift at the point of the Enlightenment, such that from the eighteenth century onwards gender is perhaps best understood in terms of the 'two-sex' model identified by Thomas Laqueur.[19] Prior to this development, Laqueur argues, women and men were seen as two different forms of the one sex rather than, as they were subsequently perceived, as essentially different. Thus, it became 'common sense' to see gender as equal and opposite; fixed and binary; male and female. Unsurprisingly, this naturalising rhetoric of a belief in the two-sex system and 'the commitment to "one-body, one-sex"' has had a major impact on the way in which intersex, and indeed trans, people are understood or 'read' within the characteristic discourses and sets of institutional practices that dominate the various spheres of society, including the medical, legal and religious. One powerful example from the second half of the twentieth century can be found in the protocols developed by John Money (1921–2006) for the treatment of intersexed infants,[20] another in the doctrine of 'true sex' that lay at the heart of the *Corbett* case.[21]

Throughout, this chapter places a degree of emphasis on the importance of the historical and cultural shaping of our understanding of gender and the implications of its classification for those whose embodiment is different from the majority. As a corollary the chapter will also argue for a perspective in which there is understood to be a close interweaving of ideas and practices of secular and sacred provenance. In the accompanying task of ethical reflection, the chapter

---

17 Ibid, 210: 'People with ambiguous genitalia not only had the possibility to marry – they may also have been under pressure to marry once their gender was under discussion. Society may have expected them to marry simply to fix their gender.'

18 See e.g. G Herdt (ed.), *Third Sex, Third Gender: Beyond Sexual Dimorphism in Culture and History*, Zone Books, New York 1996 and M. Peletz, *Gender Pluralism: Southeast Asia since Early Modern Times*, Routledge, New York 2009.

19 Laqueur, above n. 14.

20 For a critical account of the legacy of John Money's pioneering work, see L. Downing, I. Morland and N. Sullivan, *Fuckology: Critical Essays on John Money's Diagnostic Concepts*, University of Chicago Press, Chicago 2015, especially chapters by N. Sullivan, 'The Matter of Gender', pp. 19–40, and I. Morland, 'Gender, Genitals, and the meaning of Being Human', pp. 69–98.

21 *Corbett v. Corbett (otherwise Ashley)* [1971]. See S. Gilmore, 'The Legal Status of Transgender and Transsexual Persons in England and Wales', in J.M. Scherpe (ed.), *The Legal Status of Transsexual and Transgender Persons*, Intersentia, Cambridge 2015, pp. 183–206 and S. Gilmore, '*Corbett v Corbett (Otherwise Ashley)* – Once a man, always a man?', in S. Gilmore, J. Herring and R. Probert (eds.), *Landmark Cases in Family Law*, Hart Publishing, Oxford 2011, pp. 47–72.

therefore eschews abstraction, but rather seeks to engage in 'a hermeneutics of the lived context'[22] that assumes that each and every human being is fully embedded in the complexities and ambiguities of quotidian existence. Such an account takes seriously what I regard to be the facts of the human condition, namely that our personhood entails the biological, the existential and the social. Our bodies, our self-consciousness and our relationship with others are all crucial and constitutive of our personhood and there is no clear sense of priority or hierarchy at work between these aspects of personhood. Conversely, to deny or relegate one of these is to distort what it means to be a human being. In this, I must acknowledge my debt to the thinking and in particular the *religious* ethics of the philosopher Paul Ricoeur and his hermeneutics of the ethical life.

1.2. DESIRING AN ACCOMPLISHED LIFE, WITH OTHERS, IN JUST INSTITUTIONS

Paul Ricoeur's approach to the ethical life is marked by a number of key features that I believe make him a helpful companion to 'think with' in exploring some of the issues associated with intersex. The first lies in the way in which he draws close connections between his account of the human condition, i.e. anthropology, and his ethical formulations. This can be seen from his formulaic summary of the ethical life as being constituted by: 'the desire for an accomplished life – with and for others – in just institutions'.[23] In this statement, Ricoeur simultaneously embeds assumptions about our humanity (that we need others and we need to live for others) whilst also pointing to the fundamental necessity of justice as a condition for the flourishing of the individual. This sense of the embeddedness of the self, of a vision for individual human capability that demands recognition of our shared status as human subjects is grounded in what human beings universally share and what binds them together. Ricoeur thus provides a 'broad and inclusive conception' of what might be called 'a common or civil religion'. Hence his project has been construed as one with a 'distinctly religious dimension' and described as an exercise in 'moral religion'.[24] As such it is an account that is capable of reconciling tensions between different sectors or regions of society, as well as operating in a pluralistic world, independently of any particular religious tradition. In the context of this chapter therefore Ricoeur provides an approach to ethics that, whilst not theocentric in character, is entirely compatible with

22 H. Ulrich, 'The Ways of Discernment', in R. Song and B. Waters (eds.), *The Authority of the Gospel: Explorations in Moral and Political Theology in Honor of Oliver O'Donovan*, Eerdmans, Grand Rapids 2015, p. 183.

23 Ricoeur (1999), above n. 4, p. 45.

24 Carter, above n. 4, pp. vi, v, 20.

a Christian understanding of the human condition.[25] In particular, with the powerful notion that lies at the root of Christian theological anthropology, namely that *all* human beings are made in the image of God, *imago Dei*, that a person's being, value, destiny and identity finds their ultimate, grounding in the transcendent.

So what is Ricoeur driving at with his formulation of 'the desire for an accomplished life – with and for others – in just institutions'?

The starting point is desire: ethics for Ricoeur has to be rooted in the desire of the individual person, the ethical aspect of which he describes as *self-esteem*. Self-esteem entails intentionality and initiative: The person with self-esteem is then someone who has the ability to act on their own intentions and to be effective in the world. It is then 'as an agent that we enjoy our own self-esteem'.[26] An essential aspect of such self-esteem is the idea of *narrative identity*; that is 'the cohesion of a person within the sequence of a human life'.[27] Clearly then capacity for self-designation is an essential component of a narrative identity, but to recognise oneself as a person it is also critical to be able to address another and be recognised by them in terms which cohere with one's own sense of identity. The self-esteem and narrative identity of the individual is then inextricably tied to the life of others. Nothing in our human experience can arrive at meaning unless 'it is borne by language' hence the speaking person is of primary consideration in thinking about personhood.[28] Personal names and other designations that speak to our individuality are thus crucial to our singularity as persons; speech renders identification. To be a self we need to be capable of self-designation, yet even in this self-designation we know that we are a person among other persons. However, all sorts of experiences, life events and circumstances can significantly damage an individual's ability to render themselves intelligible to themselves or others. So, for example, if important information about a person's body has been kept from them or they have developed a sense of shame about their embodiment or uncertainty concerning their gender identity, then their ability to develop a narrative identity, and to speak or act in the world on the basis of it, can be impeded to the detriment of their self-esteem and flourishing.

Thus, for Ricoeur, the 'other' is essential, indeed integral to the development of the self. But that 'other' is encountered in two quite distinct ways.

The first 'other' is encountered in person through another's face or voice: for the individual exists in dynamic relation to others; exists in a state of reciprocity that Ricoeur identifies as *solicitude*. That solicitude is established by recognition. Recognition takes place within a number of different types of

---

25 Richard Kearney argues that: 'For Ricouer, the philosopher as responsible thinker remains suspended between the secular and the sacred', quoted in Carter, above n. 4, p. 149.
26 Ricoeur (1999), above n. 4, p. 51.
27 Ibid, p. 53.
28 Ibid, p. 48.

relationship of varying degrees of equality (family, friends and neighbours) but, ultimately, the relationship between self and other is understood by Ricoeur to have at its heart the 'search for moral equality'.[29] Friendship is thus the virtue associated with solicitude. The narrative identity of the individual person is then deeply 'entangled', shaped and influenced by the life stories of others. Given the centrality of sex and gender in the recognition of another, the sharing of stories and the establishment of moral equality can be particularly challenging for intersex individuals.[30]

The first entanglement with others begins, of course, with the story of an individual's parents. Parenting is always a challenging task, but parents of intersex children face quite specific demands in the provision of care and nurture. In those cases where decisions about surgery become a source of deep regret on the part of the intersex person or their parents, these primary human relationships may also be damaged. In addition, 'collateral damage', usually invisible, may also be suffered by siblings.[31]

The second 'other' is an institutionally mediated 'distanced other', an 'anonymous anyone'. Whereas friendship is emblematic of interpersonal relations, justice is that virtue which pertains to institutions, for the task of justice requires 'a relation of distance from the other'.[32] Institutions are, among other things, schemes of distribution for 'rights and duties, obligations, advantages, responsibilities and honours' as well as goods and merchandise.[33] Thus, individuals have institutionally mediated relationships with agencies of education and socialisation, like schools, or are subject to the protections (or otherwise) of the processes and rules that govern employment. Within these institutions and indeed as citizens within a state, individuals are subject to the structures of distribution. The good life for a person involves living in just institutions that are fair and equitable in their treatment of different groups of individuals, who may have different needs and requirements.

It is crucial to note that for Ricoeur, these three dimensions are not sequential but of a piece in the constitution of the human person, and their desire to live well: 'the wish to live in just institutions arises from the same level of morality as do the desire for personal fulfilment and the reciprocity of friendship'.[34]

---

29 Ibid, p. 47.

30 Fiction provides one of the most effective genres for conveying such information. Many of the challenges involved in what I describe as 'recognition', and its relation to self-esteem, can be noted in the novel by J. Eugenides, *Middlesex*, Picador, New York 2002, which tells the story of Cal who has 5-alpha-reductase deficiency and is raised as a girl before embracing a male identity as a teenager. On the importance of literature for moral reflection, see B. Williams, *Morality*, Canto, Cambridge University Press 1993, p. xix.

31 Feder (2014), above n. 8, pp. 91–92, 103–107.

32 Carter, above n. 4, p. xiii.

33 Ricoeur (1999), above n. 4, p. 47.

34 Carter, above n. 4, p. xv.

Our desire to live in *just institutions* is thus an essential aspect of our striving as a person for the good life. Thus, it is not simply amongst friends or family, but also 'as citizens that we become human'.[35]

Similarly, for Ricoeur there is no sense of priority between what might be described as the three essential characteristics of our human nature – our embodiment, our sense of self and our social existence. The three are deeply and inextricably intertwined. Thus he firmly rejects 'the myth of the solitary subject living "inside" the visible body',[36] or indeed other reductive or truncated accounts of the human (for example, those that place too much or too little significance on the body).[37] As a consequence his description of the human subject goes well beyond that of the autonomous rational actor, who exercises choice or expresses preference in the world, to note the constitutional fragility and vulnerability of the self alongside the relational character of human autonomy. Ricoeur thus 'attends to, and seeks to ameliorate, the lived experience of human beings as capable, acting and suffering subjects'.[38]

Finally, we should note that Ricoeur places a clear emphasis on the teleological, in the wish for the fulfilled life.[39] Thus the sphere of obligation, of the deontological, of duty and norm, and the obligation of agents to exercise power over others in pursuit of justice and impartiality, whilst essential, is a subsequent concern: for the sense of justice entailed is clearly rooted in this originating desire for a good life. Finally, Ricoeur notes there has to be a move into the sphere of practical reason: judgements have to be made in 'real life'; in the concrete everyday in pursuit of that which is equitable.

To provide an account of the ethical life that aspires to be universal, to transcend history and culture, to reconcile religious and secular accounts is highly ambitious. Nevertheless, throughout, this chapter shall seek to consider the challenges faced by intersex people from the perspective of Ricoeur's account of the ethical life and, in particular, his benchmark formula of 'the desire for an accomplished life – with and for others – in just institutions'.

The vision for the accomplished life that has dominated Western civilisation is that shaped or seeded by Christianity. Alongside the Greco-Roman inheritance, it has been, both, the crucible of Western civilisation, but also the dominant intellectual tradition that has shaped European philosophy as well as generating a rich vein of theological reflection. Most of our moral instincts, values and practices, and indeed our root metaphors and paradigms for thinking about the

---

35 Ibid, p. xvi.

36 R. Williams, 'The Suspicion of Suspicion: Wittgenstein and Bonhoeffer', in M. Higton (ed.), *Wrestling with Angels: Conversations in Modern Theology*, SCM, London 2007, p. 186.

37 Morland, above n. 20.

38 Carter, above n. 4, p. 144.

39 For Ricoeur, human subjects 'pursue the *telos* of *eudaimonia* or the good life as acting and suffering subjects vulnerable to factors beyond their control'. Carter, above n. 4, p. 144.

human situation – even when they conflict – have their origins in Christianity. So it is to a brief sketch of this tradition that we now turn.

2. IN THE IMAGE OF GOD? INTERSEX IN HISTORIC CHRISTIANITY

In this section we will consider how historic Christianity, through its ideas and practices, has shaped wider culture and thus the experience of the lives of those with variations in sex development, affecting their ability to live accomplished lives alongside others in society. In doing so we will draw attention to the fundamental tension within Christendom between the radical idealism of the vision of the Kingdom of God and the exercise of power, especially hegemonic power, within society with all its attendant implications for the ordering of gender. In particular we will consider the ancient gender categorisations of the eunuch and the hermaphrodite and the way in which two foundational Christian texts have influenced how individuals with variations of sex development have been recognised and treated within these historic personages.

2.1. THE KINGDOM AND THE WORLD

2.1.1. An Inclusive Vision

In the person, ministry and teaching of Jesus as conveyed especially by the four Gospels of the New Testament we have a radical vision of a world ordered by the principles of non-violence, universalism, self-sacrifice and service.[40] That new social ordering, the 'Kingdom of God', envisages the inclusion of all those groups of people on the margins of society, those who are despised, shunned, feared, hated; among others, the mentally ill, the unclean leper, the notorious sinner, those in league with the occupying military force and the Samaritan – the impure ethnic neighbour: in short, all those outside the circles of religious and social privilege that prevailed within the Judaism of Jesus' day.[41]

In transcending the boundaries of religious purity, ethnic identity and the allegiance owed to family and kin, the inclusive vision of the New Testament provides a radical template that challenges all manifestations of human power and the 'cruel exclusions'[42] generated by the pursuit of social solidarity and

---

40 In different ways, these principles can be found throughout the 27 books of the New Testament.

41 The paradigmatic examples within the teaching of Jesus are probably the parables of the Good Samaritan (Luke 10:25–37) and the Prodigal Son (Luke 15:11–32).

42 MARTIN, above n. 13, p. viii.

allegiance. Developing the tradition of social justice found within the Hebrew prophets of the eighth century BC, most notably Isaiah, the exemplary acts and parables of Jesus, intended to illustrate the nature of the Kingdom of God, provide a particularly dramatic substantiation of the idea that *all* human beings are made *imago Dei*. The radical nature of this shift can be seen most clearly in the rite of incorporation into the community, with the Jewish rite of circumcision, an affirmation of a chosen people on the grounds of ethnicity, being replaced with Christian baptism, in which the stranger is joined to a new family of sisters and brothers, a spiritual kinship, amongst whom there is 'no longer Jew or Greek, there is no longer slave or free, there is no longer male and female', rather all are children of God.[43]

This universalist and inclusive teaching at the heart of the Gospels is thus substantial 'good news' for any and every stigmatised group. The moral imperative is simple, direct, powerful and clear. And indeed the fact that intersex infants have been routinely baptised, and thereby fully incorporated as persons within the moral community throughout Christian history provides a clear, unequivocal ritual affirmation of this teaching.[44]

So far, so clear: however, the vision of the kingdom of God as expressed in the person of Jesus Christ is exactly that, an eschatological vision; a picture of a utopian social order – that is unrealistic and unrealisable at the level of whole societies. It envisages a perfected time when, 'the wolf will live with the lamb' and 'the nursing child shall play over the hole of the asp'.[45] Likewise, the realisation of a radically inclusive, non-violent human society is also impossible as the work of historians, and social and political scientists readily testify. In a world that Christians describe as 'fallen' and 'sinful', where violence and power are unavoidable realities, the powerful pull of family, ethnicity and other sources of social solidarity sit in profound tension with the radical call of the Kingdom vision.

Down the centuries, but especially in the post-Constantinian world with the establishment of Christendom, the Church has been deeply and inevitably implicated in the secular world and compromised by the exercise of power, the exigencies of elites and the imperatives of peoples and nations.[46] As a consequence, the Church has been deeply invested in establishing and maintaining the attendant norms of behaviour in terms of gender roles and sexuality. The experience and treatment of intersex individuals within Christendom has

---

43 Galatians 3:28.

44 The duty to baptise hermaphrodites is explicitly stated in medieval canon law. ROLKER, above n. 16, 184.

45 Isaiah 11:6–9.

46 There is a rich vein of sociological reflection on this instigated by the church historian, Ernst Troeltsch (1865–1923), and the sociologist Max Weber (1864–1920). See especially, E. TROELTSCH, *The Social Teaching of the Christian Churches*, vol. I, O. WYON (transl.), Harper and Row, New York 1960 and E. TROELTSCH, The Social Teaching of the Christian Churches,

therefore been primarily framed by the prevailing hegemonic constructions of gender and their implications for the historic, overlapping categories of eunuch, hermaphrodite and intersexual.

2.1.2. *Theological Anthropology in the Twentieth Century*

These hegemonic constructions have evolved over time with significant implications for intersex individuals. For much of the twentieth century, commensurate with the cultural framing of the 'two-sex theory',[47] gender ideology has been strongly essentialist and fixed in its approach to male and female bodies. This can be seen, for example, very clearly in the dominant medical and legal discourses.[48] Such thinking is equally evident within theology with influential mid-twentieth-century theologians, such as Karl Barth, John Paul II and Hans Urs von Balthasar, weaving a deeply ontological understanding of gender difference into traditional Christian understanding, essentially rendering maleness and femaleness as theological categories.[49] In a striking passage, von Balthasar stated:

> The male body is male throughout, right down to each cell of which it consists, and the female body is utterly female; and this is also true of their whole empirical experience and ego-consciousness ...[50]

Grounded in a theology of creation, which finds its *locus classicus* in Genesis 1:27,[51] it has therefore become commonplace for theologians to argue that humanity exists in two clearly anatomically distinct forms, male and female; that this sexed identity is an essential human characteristic; that to be a properly human being one is either a male or a female; and, finally that anatomical sex and gender identity are indivisible. Thus gender is also 'destiny'; that is, we are all designed to be attracted to the 'opposite' sex, and thus for procreation.[52]

---

vol. II, O. Wyon (transl.), Harper and Row, New York 1960; and H.H. Gerth and C.W. Mills (eds.), *From Max Weber: Essays in Sociology*, Routledge, London 1991.

47 Laqueur, above n. 14.

48 See above nn. 20 and 21.

49 Karl Barth (1886–1968) was the most influential Protestant theologian of the 20th century, Pope John Paul II (1920–2005) and Hans Urs von Balthasar (1905–1988), 2 of the most important Catholic theologians. For a more detailed discussion, see Dormor, above n. 2; and D. Dormor, 'Rebellious Bodies and Disordered Desires: The Challenge of Transsexuality to influential Christian Theologies of Creation', in N. Reilly and S. Scriver (eds.), *Religion, Gender, and the Public Sphere*, Routledge, London 2014, pp. 120–130.

50 H.U. von Balthasar, *Theo-Drama: Theological Dramatic Theory. Vol. 2: The Dramatis Personae: Man in God*, G. Harrison (transl)., San Francisco, Ignatius Press 1990, pp. 365–366.

51 'So God created humankind in his image, in the image of God he created them; male and female he created them.'

52 Dormor, above n. 2, pp. 36–39.

This account of theological anthropology, which has been described as the 'male-and-female' model[53] or the 'Order of Creation' argument,[54] clearly does not create 'space' for any sustained discussion of intersex persons.

Such cosmic assertions, simultaneously grounded and evoking 'obvious' natural observations, have been made to bear a great deal of theological signification within the official teaching of the Catholic Church.[55] Yet these are without secure anchorage in the historical record of the Christian tradition, being built on '... the exhausted sexual essentialisms of modernity';[56] theological appropriations from modern biology and nineteenth-century romanticism. Whilst such ideas are 'thoroughly modern', they are, nevertheless, 'claimed to be a legitimate development of scripture and tradition' and have proved highly influential in shaping ecclesial responses to the challenges posed by feminism and the 'sexual revolution' of the 1960s.[57] Believing themselves to be the guardians of a timeless tradition that is scrupulously faithful to the witness of scripture, advocates of this normative, and thus authoritative, account have deployed it to argue for traditional gender roles; to limit women's reproductive rights; and, to oppose the legitimation of same-sex relationships.[58]

Such ideas have not, of course, gone unchallenged: There has been an emergent awareness amongst theologians of the ways in which the construction of gender is historically contingent and reflective of hegemonic interests and therefore a growing wariness of essentialised identities, whether they are construed as liberal and emancipatory or conservative and traditional. As a consequence, many theologians writing about the theological significance of gender,

---

53 See S. Cornwall, *Sex and Uncertainty in the Body of Christ Intersex Conditions and Christian Theology*, Equinox, London 2010.

54 See Dormor, above n. 49.

55 The most remarkable of these assertions being the view that the complementarity of the sexes reflects the very nature of God: Catholic Church (CC) and Congregation for the Doctrine of the Faith (CDF), *On the pastoral care of homosexual persons, Homosexualitatis Problema, Letter to the Bishops of the Catholic Church*, 01.10.1986, <http://www.ewtn.com/library/curia/cdfhomop.htm> (last accessed 21.05.2018), para. 2. For discussion, see Dormor, above n. 49, pp. 127–128; and G. Moore, *A Question of Truth: Christianity and Homosexuality*, Continuum, London 2003.

56 T. Beattie, 'The Theological Study of Gender', in A. Thatcher (ed.), *The Oxford Handbook of Theology, Sexuality and Gender*, Oxford University Press, Oxford 2015, pp. 32–52.

57 E. Stuart, 'The Theological Study of Sexuality', in Thatcher, above n. 56, pp. 20–21.

58 See CC and CDF, above n. 55; and, John Paul II, *Ordinantio Sacerdotalis*, (Apostolic letter 'On reserving priestly ordination to men alone'), 22.05.1994, <http://w2.vatican.va/content/john-paul-ii/en/apost_letters/1994/documents/hf_jp-ii_apl_22051994_ordinatio-sacerdotalis.html> (last accessed 21.05.2017). See also Dormor, above n. 2, especially pp. 36–52: An emphasis on the complementarity of the sexes has also come to the fore in a wide range of documents produced by the Church of England. See e.g. Church of England, *A Response to the Government's Equalities Office Consultation – 'Equal Civil Marriage'*, <https://www.churchofengland.org/media/1475149/s-s%20marriage.pdf> (last accessed 21.05.2017), para. 13, 10, where reference is made to 'the fundamental complementarity' of men and women, and its 'underlying, objective, distinctiveness'. For a discussion of this recent

sexuality and the body have embraced the perspective of *queer theology*,[59] a reframing of theological concerns that is deeply indebted to the work of critical theorists like Judith Butler[60] and Michel Foucault.[61] Whilst queer theology can be described very simply as 'a critical and constructive rereading of established categories of sex and gender from a Christian theological perspective',[62] it is important to note that, being primarily concerned with power and legitimation, queer theology is best characterised as a perspective and approach rather than a concern with a certain subject area. Queer theologians are therefore also interested in questions of race, ethnicity and class and engage in fruitful dialogue with, amongst others, liberationist and postcolonial theologians.[63]

2.1.3. *Sacred and Secular: Debts and Influences*[64]

As we have seen from this brief consideration of contemporary Christian theological anthropology there is a dynamic relationship between those patterns of thought that originate in a sacred context and those which emerge from more secular sources. This is unsurprising as the development of Western society is inextricably tied to the history of Christianity; its ideas, images and practices underpin, frame and permeate much that we habitually describe as 'secular' – and vice versa. So, whilst the radical founding vision of the New Testament is inevitably compromised in much Christian thinking and practice, it is also the case that its commitments to social justice and compassion have enshrined

---

development, see M. Higton, 'Marriage, Gender and Doctrine', in J. Bradbury and S. Cornwall (eds.), *Theological Questions*, SCM, London 2016, pp. 14–28.

59 Introductory accounts of queer theology can be found in P.S. Cheng, *Radical Love: An Introduction to Queer Theology*, Seabury Books, London 2011; P.S. Cheng, 'Contributions from Queer Theory' in Thatcher, above n. 56, pp. 151–169; S. Cornwall, *Theology and Sexuality*, SCM, London 2013; and R. Muers, 'Feminism, Gender and Theology', in D. Ford and R. Muers (eds.), *The Modern Theologians: An Introduction to Christian Theology since 1918*, Blackwell, Oxford 2005. Key works would include M. Althaus-Reid, *Indecent Theology: Theological Perversions in Sex, Gender and Politics*, Routledge, London 2000; M. Althaus-Reid, *The Queer God*, Routledge, London 2004; M.D. Jordan, *The Invention of Sodomy in Christian Theology*, University of Chicago Press, Chicago 1997; and E.F. Rogers, *Sexuality and the Christian Body*, Blackwell, Oxford 1999. See also the edited collections by Thatcher, above n. 56, and G. Loughlin (ed.), *Queer Theology: Rethinking the Western Body*, Blackwell, Oxford 2007 and also S. Cornwall, *Controversies in Queer Theology*, SCM, London, 2011.

60 See especially J. Butler, *Gender Trouble*, Routledge, New York 1992; and J. Butler, *Undoing Gender*, Routledge, New York 2004.

61 See especially, Foucault, above n. 5. Foucault also directed the publication, in English and French, of the memoirs of Alexina/Alex Barbin (1838–1868): see H. Barbin, *Hercule Berbin: Being the Recently Discovered Memoirs of a Nineteenth Century French Hermaphrodite*, R. McDougall (transl.), Pantheon, New York 1980. See also the discussion in A.D. Dreger, *Hermaphrodites and the Medical Invention of Sex*, Harvard University Press, Cambridge Mass. p. 199.

62 R. Muers, 'A Queer Theology: Hans Urs von Balthasar' in Loughlin, above n. 59, p. 200.

63 Cornwall (2013), above n. 59, p. 138.

64 In this section I am particularly indebted to Martin, above n. 13.

themselves in institutions and practices, many of which we would now describe as secular. Ideas with clear Christian provenance can be found within the codifications and obligations that prevail within the legal sphere, in the continued influence of Just War theory in military thinking and practice,[65] or in the development of medical care in the West from the origin and evolution of the hospital to contemporary physician's professional and bioethical guidelines.[66] It is also the case that 'seeds' from the Kingdom vision often 'fructify' far 'from their point of origin',[67] for example in the indignation of the radical activist standing in solidarity with those whose dignity and well-being is poorly served by their host society. Or indeed in the more aspirational proclamations of liberalism,[68] most notably the Universal Declaration of Human Rights strongly shaped by mainstream Protestantism[69] and the Anglo-American legal tradition.[70] In light of this last observation, it is worth reiterating here that when it comes to articulating a response to the contemporary ethical issues at stake for intersex people, we need to look to theological thinking that is generously, rather than narrowly, religious in its scope.

We have sought in this section to highlight the tension that exists between the ideals and values of the Kingdom and the secular exigencies of Christendom. Before coming to a consideration of the lived context of contemporary intersex persons, we turn first to a more detailed consideration of the way in which Christian ideas affected historic intersex subjects within two ancient gender categories.

2.2. ANCIENT PEOPLES: EUNUCHS AND HERMAPHRODITES

To understand how the intersex person might have been recognised or understood within the early, formative centuries of Christianity we must enter the world of ancient gender systems and consider their hegemonic constructions. In this section, then, we will explore two key Christian texts, both of which have left a deep imprint on the development of European culture. This chapter will argue

---

65 See e.g. C. Reed and D. Ryall (eds.), *The Price of Peace: Just War in the Twenty-First Century*, Cambridge University Press, Cambridge 2007.

66 See T.L. Beauchamp and J.F. Childress, *Principles of Biomedical Ethics*, 7th ed., Oxford University Press, Oxford 2012. The standard reference work in biomedical ethics, both of its authors originally studied theology.

67 Martin, above n. 13, p. 4.

68 Ibid, p. 79.

69 See G. Newlands, *Christ and Human Rights*, Ashgate, Aldershot 2006; and J. Nurser, *For All Peoples and All Nations – The Ecumenical Church and Human Rights*, Georgetown University Press, Washington DC 2005.

70 Inevitably the UDHR embeds key cultural assumptions that betray this provenance; see T. Asad, *Formations of the Secular: Christianity, Islam, Modernity*, Stanford University Press, Stanford 2003.

that both texts, in their treatment of eunuchs and hermaphrodites respectively, promote values associated with the eschatological vision of the Kingdom against the excluding characteristic dynamics of social solidarity.

In the first case, the eunuch, a diminished male, will be explored through the lens of the Gospel of Matthew against the backdrop of first-century Jewish understanding and practice; in the second, the hermaphrodite, a dual-sexed person as understood within the context of traditional pagan Graeco-Roman culture of the fourth century AD, will be considered with the aid of St. Augustine, and his treatment of the issue in his magnus opus, the *City of God*. In the case of both gender categories, but especially the hermaphrodite, there have been a rich and variegated set of cultural readings across the centuries ranging from those that focus on practical reflections (e.g. medical, legal) generated by embodied sexual indeterminacy to those which shade into philosophical or mythic speculation.[71] Thus both hermaphrodites and eunuchs stimulate wider cultural, and often political, imaginings (and anxieties) around gender and sexuality, and indeed the nature of the social order. Many of these recur throughout history. For example, the hermaphrodite has been cast as a threatening 'monstrous being' in political contexts as diverse as the Roman Republic and early-modern Europe.[72] Yet in approaching our texts, we should also note the widespread importance of the androgynous ideal in shaping both pagan and Christian imaginings of *both* the origin *and* the destiny of human beings.

2.2.1. The Androgynous Ideal

The idea that human beings, males and females, were generated from primal androgynous beings was widespread in the ancient world. The most influential of such mythological accounts was that of Aristophanes' tale in Plato's *Symposium*.[73] Here the androgynous state was seen as one of a primal

71 See, e.g., Long, above n. 11; R. Gilbert, *Early Modern Hermaphrodites: Sex and Other Stories*, Palgrave, Basingstoke 2002. For a fascinating discussion of the relationship with the 'science' of alchemy, see L. DeVun, 'The Jesus Hermaphrodite: Science and Sex Difference in Premodern Europe' (2008) 69(2) *Journal of the History of Ideas* 193–218.

72 Long, above n. 11; Gilbert, above n. 71.

73 Written between 385–370 BC, great caution should be exercised in the interpretation of this passage concerned with the origin and nature of sexuality in Plato, given that it issues from the lips of the comic playwright, Aristophanes. For an English translation, see Plato, *Collected Works of Plato*, 4th ed., B. Jowett (transl.), Oxford University Press, Oxford 1953, 189c–193e, pp. 520–525. By contrast, Aristotle (384–322 BC) only mentions hermaphrodites in passing; see J. Barnes, *The Complete Works of Aristotle*, vol. 1, Princeton University Press, Princeton 1984, Generation of Animals Book IV, pp. 1195–1196. See also the account of Ovid (43 BC–17 AD), which tells of the beautiful son of Aphrodite and Hermes with whom the water nymph Salmacis fell in love. Imploring the gods that she might be united with him forever, they were melded together into a chimeric, androgynous form. For Ovid's account of Hermaphroditus see, Ovid, *Metamorphoses I–IV*; D. Hill (ed. and transl.), Aris & Phillips Publishers, Warminster 1985, Book IV 4.285-388, pp. 139–145.

undifferentiated unity in which original eight-limbed beings suffered division at the hands of the gods; the human desire for sexual union a manifestation of a yearning for return to such primal unity. But, the creation of humanity in the Jewish scriptures at least in the first of the two accounts in the book of Genesis,[74] also appears to depict an androgynous progenitor: for humanity is here described as *ha-'adam*', a description that is collective and makes no sexual differentiation. This was certainly a common Jewish reading of the text.[75] Such mythic accounts of androgynes cannot be seen in isolation from one another. So, for example, early Rabbinic interpretation of the Adam-Androgyne myth took place against background knowledge of the Platonic myth, which early Jewish Rabbis co-opted in their interpretation of Genesis 1–2, though to specific ends, namely to stress the naturalness of monogamy and heterosexuality.[76] Similarly these various accounts continued to influence writers of theological, medical, legal and other forms of literature down the Christian centuries.[77]

Implied within such accounts is the idea that the destiny of humanity also lies in a return to an original unity through the reconciliation of opposites: the implication being that sexed difference is ultimately temporary, a feature of this fallen, imperfect world. Here, the New Testament scholar, Wayne Meeks, has made a convincing case for the *symbolic* importance of the reconciliation of the sexes as a manifestation of the 'new creation' that comes with being 'in Christ'.[78] In particular, he suggests the Adam-Androgyne myth was influential within Pauline circles, and was adapted to the eschatological sacrament of baptism. For in that act of incorporation the Christian becomes a new person; rejecting the 'old self' and becoming clothed 'with the new self created according to the likeness of God'.[79] This 'new self' is 'in Christ', who is a 'second Adam', and enters upon a life within a community of restored humanity in which there is 'no longer Jew or Greek ... slave or free ... male and female'.[80]

---

74 Genesis 1:26–28; 2:4–7, 18–23.

75 W.A. Meeks, 'The Image of the Androgyne: Some Uses of a Symbol in Earliest Christianity' (1974) 13(3) *History of Religions*, 165–208,. See also Gilbert, above n. 71 p. 15.

76 Meeks (1974), above n. 75, 165, 186.

77 See e.g. the discussion of Ovid's *Metamorphoses*, in R. Mills, *Seeing Sodomy in the Middle Ages*, University of Chicago Press, Chicago 2015, especially pp. 98–106.

78 The idea of the 'new creation' is a common theme in the writings of St. Paul, but is stated most succinctly in 2 Corinthians 5:17: 'So if anyone is in Christ, there is a new creation: everything old has passed away; see, everything has become new.' The underlying androgynous nature of humanity is asserted by a number of Christian theologians The most prominent of these was St. Gregory of Nyssa (335–394 AD), who not only is clear that in the resurrected life, the Christian returns to the prelapsarian state, but perceived in the life of his sister, St. Macrina, a person who, through *ascesis*, was already moving beyond gender; see Stuart, above n. 57, p. 27. See also V. Burrus, 'Queer Father: Gregory of Nyssa and the Subversion of Identity', in Loughlin, above n. 59, pp. 147–162; and S. Coakley, *God, Sexuality and the Self: An Essay 'On the Trinity'*, Cambridge University Press, Cambridge, 2013. See Meeks, above n. 75.

79 Ephesians 4:22, 24.

80 Galatians 3:28.

Fairly swiftly, however, Meeks argues, ideas of such 'cosmic audacity' lose their 'ultimate significance' within early Christianity and are not realised in radical social practices that abolish the distinction between the sexes:[81] although some within early Christianity clearly did think of themselves as restoring an original, paradisiac humanity, and traces of such ideas and related practices can clearly be seen within the Corinthian church.[82] Nevertheless the Christian imagination was seeded with this powerful symbolism and it continued to influence certain strands of Christian practice over the coming centuries: from the female saints who dressed and acted as men[83] to those men who saw themselves as 'brides of Christ'.[84] Such 'queer' practices also extended to the language of hymnology and spirituality and to the representation of Jesus, most evidently as a mother 'birthing' the Church through his pierced side represented as a vagina.[85]

Let us now turn from the ideal and symbolic to the somatic and social; and, consider in more concrete terms, the two categories of the eunuch and the hermaphrodite within which an intersex persons might be identified within historical Christianity through two key texts: The Gospel of Matthew and St. Augustine's *City of God*.

2.2.2. The Gospel of Matthew: Eunuchs amongst the Jews and Christians

The primary reference of the eunuch is, of course, to the castrated male. However the category was a broad one with a great number of symbolic and imaginative associations that evolved significantly during the early Christian centuries.[86] The inability to procreate was clearly the defining aspect, but this aspect rendered the very existence of such unmanned men a 'lightening rod for male anxiety'.[87] In a pervasively patriarchal world, masculinity was perceived to

---

81 Meeks (1974), above n. 75, 165, 208.

82 Some within the Corinthian church seemed to possess an 'overrealised eschatology', that is they saw themselves perfected, 'like angels' and therefore transcending the constraints of their distinctiveness as sexed persons. See e.g. G. Fee, *The First Epistle to the Corinthians*, NICNT, William D. Eerdmans, Grand Rapids 1987, pp. 10–15, 16–20. Divine androgyny played a very important part within Gnosticism, a widespread pattern of religious thinking of the first two centuries AD, whose ideas overlapped with those of Jewish and Christian groups. See B. Layton, *The Gnostic Scriptures*, SCM, London 1987, see also S.G. Hall, *Doctrine and Practice in the Early Church*, SPCK, London 1991, pp. 39–45.

83 M. Kuefler, 'Desire and the Body in the Patristic Period', in Thatcher, above n. 56, p. 250.

84 Ibid, p. 246.

85 G. D'Costa, *Sexing the Trinity: Gender, Culture and the Divine*, SCM, London 2000, pp. 40–97.

86 See M. Kuefler, *The Manly Eunuch: Masculinity, Gender Ambiguity, and Christian Ideology in Late Antiquity*, University of Chicago Press, Chicago 2001; and K.M. Ringrose, *The Perfect Servant: Eunuchs and the Social Construction of Gender in Byzantium*, University of Chicago Press, Chicago 2003.

87 J.D. Hester, 'Eunuchs and the Postgender Jesus: Matthew 19.12 and Transgressive Sexualities' (2005) 28(1) *Journal for the Study of the New Testament* 13, 21.

have a precarious quality; it needed to be continually asserted and established. Contemporary 'science' understood male and female to be essentially extreme developments of a single sex, and masculine privilege could be lost in all sorts of ways through unmanly activity: eating the wrong food, bathing too frequently, etc.[88] Eunuchs, as gender-liminal figures, were therefore subjects of tremendous suspicion, a *locus* of projected fears and anxieties for much of this period; characters to whom a wide range of attributes were ascribed – moral and upright not being among them. In such a world, according to the limited evidence we have, male persons of ambiguous sex were perceived to be a type of eunuch.

We know this primarily from a rather remarkable reference in the Gospel of Matthew,[89] that includes a saying from Jesus about a group of people understood to be congenital eunuchs. The saying comes in the context of a discussion of marriage and divorce, in which Jesus argues against the traditional Jewish practice in which a man could divorce his wife with relative ease.[90] The disciples who seem perturbed at the prospect of lifelong monogamy in such circumstances suggest that it is therefore not expedient to marry. At this point the ethical discussion takes an eschatological turn and Jesus outlines a typology of three sorts of men (eunuchs) who should not marry:

> For there are eunuchs who have been so from birth, and there are eunuchs who have been made eunuchs by others, and there are eunuchs who have made themselves eunuchs for the sake of the kingdom of heaven.[91]

It is impossible to say definitively whether these are the authentic words of Jesus rather than those of the evangelist Matthew, though this is widely believed to be the case.[92] It is, however, no coincidence that they are found in Matthew's gospel,

---

88 Ibid, 18–20.

89 The Gospel of Matthew is generally dated c. 85–100 AD. The author is usually believed to be of a Jewish Christian background writing from a Christian community which may have been located in Syria or Palestine; see e.g. D. Harrington, *The Gospel of Matthew*, Liturgical Press, Minnesota 1991.

90 J. Collins, 'Appropriation and Development of Castration as Symbol and Practice in Early Christianity', in L. Tracy (ed.), *Castration and Culture in the Middle Ages*, DS Brewer, Woodridge 2013, p. 75.

91 Matthew 19:12.

92 In reading the direct words of Jesus within the New Testament, scholars seek to judge between traditional logion, those which originate with Jesus, and those of redactional genesis, originating from the community or pen of the respective evangelist. Although this logion is only found in Matthew, there is a general consensus that Matthew 19:12 is a traditional logion. See e.g. U. Luz, *Matthew 8-20: A Commentary*, Hermeneia, Augsburg Fortress, Minneapolis 2001, p. 501. See also the detailed arguments of W.D. Davies and D.C. Allison, *The Gospel According to Saint Matthew*, vol. III, ICC, T & T Clark, Edinburgh 1997, p. 24; and R.W. Funk and R.W. Hoover (eds.), *The Five Gospels, the Search for the Authentic Words of Jesus*, Macmillan, New York 1993, pp. 221–222.

widely regarded as the most 'Jewish' of the gospels, and it is highly likely that in elaborating his threefold typology, Matthew's Jesus draws on a well-established, pre-existing Jewish understanding that distinguished between the congenital eunuch and the castrated male. Indeed, the elaboration of a 'third type' ('for the Kingdom') is rhetorically dependent on the existence of just such a pre-existent distinction. This interpretation is further supported by the existence of a tradition of debate and commentary on the matter of castration found within the Jewish Mishnah and Talmud and in particular a discussion attributed to the first century between Rabbi Aquiba and Rabbi Eliezer[93] that makes a distinction between *sĕrîs ḥammâ* (literally a 'sun eunuch', i.e. clear at first sight on the day of birth) and *sĕrîs 'ādām* (a eunuch made by man).

Given the rarity of intersexed persons, the identification of a 'congenital eunuch' in such a text is very striking. It suggests an established cultural awareness of intersex significantly greater than exists today. There may be a number of reasons for this, but it is unsurprising given that one of the distinctive features of Judaism is the very high religious value it places on fertility and marriage: for the first commandment of God is to 'be fruitful and multiply'.[94] Judaism is thus marked by a persistent horror of sterility and barrenness.[95] The Law of Moses explicitly excludes the man-made eunuch from the 'assembly of the Lord'[96] and the focus of dispute between Rabbis Aquila and Eliezer was whether a *sĕrîs ḥammâ* could be cured and become capable of procreation. It is the conviction that this is at least possible sometimes that leads to the establishment of a more tolerant approach, for in later Jewish writings the congenital eunuch is in fact permitted to marry and be part of the worshipping community. The topic remains a persistent concern within Judaism and leads subsequently to the elaboration of a typology of variantly sexed individuals, and how they might be diagnosed and treated within the community.[97]

Thus, Jewish concern is clearly focused on the issue of reproduction. The *sĕrîs 'ādām* is traditionally excluded from the 'assembly of the Lord', because of his

---

93 Mishnah Yevamot 8:4–6 || BavliYevamot 79b. Also, 'the dates of these traditions are notoriously difficult to fix, so even sayings attributed to first-century rabbis cannot be taken as *prima facie* evidence of a prevailing Jewish standards in Jesus' time'. Collins, above n. 90, p. 75.

94 Genesis 1:28.

95 Within the Talmud, 'one who does not marry is like a person who sheds blood' and 'a man who has no wife is no man'. See: J. Kodell, 'The Celibacy Logion in Matthew 19:12' (1978) 8(1) *Biblical Theology Bulletin: Journal of Bible and Culture* 19–23.

96 Deuteronomy 23:1.

97 See S.L. Lev, 'They Treat Him As a Man and See Him as a Woman: The Tannaitic Understanding of the Congenital Eunuch' (2010) 17 *Jewish Studies Quarterly* 213–243; S.L. Lev, 'How the *'Aylonit* Got Her Sex' (2007) 31(2) *AJS Review* 297–316; J.H. Barth and M. Zemer, 'The Congenital Eunuch: A Medical-Halachic Study', <https://www.jewishvirtuallibrary.org/jsource/Judaism/Eunuch.pdf> (last accessed 03.04.2017); F. Retief, J. Cilliers and S. Riekert, 'Eunuchs in the Bible' (2005) 7 *Acta Theologica Supplementum* 247–258; and Collins, above n. 90.

inability, by definition, to procreate. In questioning this foundational premise in the case of the *sĕrîs ḥammâ* a Jewish discourse develops in which the 'congenital eunuch' is included without compromising the fundamental commitment to procreation. In short, the *sĕrîs ḥammâ* ceases to be recognised as a eunuch.

Let us turn now to the broader argument.

Christian exegesis of Matthew 19:12 has been dominated by a concern with the meaning and implications of 'eunuchs for the sake of the kingdom' in light of the subsequent development of widespread celibacy with the Christian Church. Consonant with the arguments above, the rejection of procreation implied by this verse should be seen in the context of eschatology and of a religious identity that seeks to transcend allegiances to family and (Jewish) ethnicity. The obvious, overlooked point here is that Jesus (very unusually an unmarried Jewish teacher), makes a clear identification between being a eunuch and being a highly committed Christian disciple. This identification strikes at the very heart of the canons of both Jewish and Graeco-Roman ideals of masculinity. Perhaps the unmarried Jesus, and his disciples, were the subject of name-calling, branded eunuchs rather than 'real' men.[98] It is certainly a possibility. In which case, parallel to the contemporary term 'queer', Jesus turns the insult into an identification. Such a move is entirely consistent with a number of reversals that lie at the heart of Jesus' teaching about the nature of the Kingdom of God. More particularly, it forms part of a broader weave that subverts the hegemonic masculine model with its emphasis on mastery, control and virtue: for, in Jesus, a crucified saviour, we have a story of failed masculinity.

This text from Matthew is not simply an isolated curiosity. It has a clear precursor in the eschatological vision of Isaiah that envisages a time when, contrary to the Mosaic injunction, the eunuch will be included in the community of the beloved.[99] This hoped-for, idealised social order is indeed brought at least to partial fulfilment in the story of the conversion and baptism of the Ethiopian eunuch in the New Testament book of Acts.[100] Indeed, it is difficult to imagine a more transgressive individual than a foreign eunuch to underline the radical difference between entry into the old Mosaic covenant through circumcision and the radical inclusion envisaged by the Christians baptising believers seeking the 'Kingdom of God'. The story of the Ethiopian eunuch thus marks a pivotal

---

98 Whether this is the case or not, there is, 'an inherent ambiguity in the gendered portrayal of Jesus'; C.M. Conway, 'The Construction of Gender in the New Testament' in Thatcher, above n. 56, p. 230. See also A.E. Harvey, 'Eunuchs for the Sake of the Kingdom' (1995) <www.biblicalstudies.org.uk/pdf/eunuchs_harvey.pdf> (last accessed 21.05.2017).

99 Isaiah 56:3c–5: 'Do not let the eunuch say, "I am just a dry tree." For thus says the Lord: To the eunuchs who keep my sabbaths, who choose the things that please me and hold fast my covenant, I will give, in my house and within my walls, a monument and a name better than sons and daughters; I will give them an everlasting name that shall not be cut off.' See also Wisdom 3:13–14.

100 Acts 8: 26–40. For a fuller account, see Dormor, above n. 2, pp. 54–56.

moment signalling the arrival of the messianic age and a turn away from Jerusalem to that other city, Rome, and outwards to the rest of the world. In the choice of a eunuch the text also provides, simultaneously, an extraordinary affirmation of an alternative category of person, that includes those who would today be designated as intersexed individuals, as well as a de-throning of values (the importance of procreation) and institutions (marriage) central to the physical and symbolic reproduction of society.

The passing reference to the congenital eunuch in Matthew 19:12 is set in a context that challenges fundamentally the traditional Jewish emphasis on marriage and procreation. This challenge is an inevitable corollary of its radical advocacy of a new universalist social order in which brothers and sisters are united as 'spiritual kin' through baptism. In this context, the divergence between traditional Judaism and its younger rival is at maximum stretch, with the former looking back to the creation ordinance to 'be fruitful and multiply' and the latter looking forward to the coming messianic age for which some might choose as religious virtuosi to be 'eunuchs for the kingdom of heaven'.[101]

This intriguing text brings into sharp focus a point of radical disjuncture between the emerging Christian worldview and the Judaism of its day – namely the importance of procreation. It highlights pre-existing Jewish knowledge of the congenital eunuch within the context of an eschatologically-oriented discourse that challenges hegemonic masculinity. We turn now to another major Christian text in which an awareness of those born with intersexed conditions can be found in the context of a theological argument. Here the focus is more explicitly on theological anthropology, and the cultural issues and the epistemological framing are also quite different, indeed, more fundamental: namely whether such individuals should properly be counted amongst the children of Adam; that is as fully human.

2.2.3. Augustine on Hermaphrodites: From Monster to Marvel

In his magisterial *City of God*,[102] the most influential theologian within Western Christianity after Paul, Augustine of Hippo (354–430 AD) produced a theological reading of history that sought to address the claim that the newly enshrined imperial religion, Christianity, was to blame for the decline of Roman power. A diverse and wide-ranging work, it includes, in an account of the history of humanity,[103] a section devoted to explaining 'the origin of recorded

---

101 A number of studies also suggest significant continuity between the 2 developing faith traditions across many areas in terms of practical ethics, which may well have had implications for the way in which intersex individuals were treated. See e.g. D. Horrell, *Solidarity and Difference: A Contemporary Reading of Paul's Ethics*, T & T Clark, London 2005, p. 16.

102 Quotations in this section are drawn from the translation by Bettenson, see above n. 3, pp. 661–664.

103 Ibid, Book XVI, ch. 8.

monstrosities', which Augustine sets within a natural theology that rests on the fundamental goodness of God's creation.

Drawing heavily on Pliny's *Historia Naturalis,*[104] Augustine begins by providing an account of 'certain monstrous races of men' that are believed to exist. There follows a list that includes some recognisable ('pygmies') and some mythic human morphological variations, and it includes those individuals who 'have the characteristics of both sexes, the right breast being male and the left female, and in their intercourse they alternate between begetting and conceiving'.[105] Augustine does not dwell on the exoticisation of the categories of person listed although he is clearly sceptical of the existence of some of them.[106] However he is remarkably clear about their common humanity:

> But no faithful Christian should doubt that anyone who is born anyway as a man – that is, a rational and mortal being – derives from that one first-created human being. And this is true, however extraordinary such a creature may appear to our sense in bodily shape, in colour, or motion, or utterance, or in any natural endowment, or part of quality.[107]

All such persons, whatever their morphology, are for Augustine, children of Adam – like his readers. Furthermore Augustine argues, although it is 'clear what constitutes the persistent norm of nature in the majority' each such individual by virtue of their 'very rarity, constitutes a marvel'.[108]

By way of explanation he then proceeds to draw a clear distinction between divine knowledge and insight and the more limited assessment of mere human beings:

> For God is the creator of all, and he himself knows where and when any creature should be created or should have been created. He has the wisdom to weave the beauty of the whole design out of the constituent parts, in their likeness and diversity. The observer who cannot view the whole is offended by what seems the deformity of a part, since he does not know how it fits in, or how it is related to the rest.[109]

What Augustine presents then is an argument of natural theology that moves from observations about human diversity to an affirmation of all humans,

---

104 The *Historia Naturalis* is a wide-ranging encyclopaedia that runs to 37 volumes. Written by Pliny the Elder (23–79 AD) between 70–77 AD, Book 7 focuses on anthropology and human physiology, Augustine is especially indebted to 7.2. For a translation and commentary on the text, see Beagon, above n. 12.

105 Augustine, above n. 3, p. 661.

106 'Now we are not bound to believe in the existence of all of the types of men which are described'. Ibid, p. 662.

107 Ibid.

108 Ibid.

109 Ibid.

however divergent from the 'persistent norm of nature in the majority'. In so doing he provides a clear assertion of the goodness of creation and the benevolent, if mysterious, intentions its creator: 'he whose operations no one has the right to criticise knows what he is about'.[110] The ethical consequences, implied rather than spelt out, are very clear: that such 'monsters' are not, in fact, monsters, that is threatening entities outside of the natural order which should be eliminated, but rather forms of marvellous variation within the human fold who should be accorded the full dignity of moral persons. The significance of this tolerance and assertion of a universal humanity grounded in the rational nature of the human being is highlighted when one considers the fate of hermaphrodites and others in traditional pagan Rome, before 90 BC. Then, the birth of a hermaphrodite was regarded as a portent, a sign of divine anger and of a fundamental disturbance of the social order: a source of fear; such anomalous individuals were killed in an effort to purify the city state.[111]

Following this clear statement of theological anthropology, Augustine adds a further specific reference to those of 'doubtful sex':

> As for *Androgynes*, also called Hermaphrodites, they are certainly very rare, and yet it is difficult to find periods when there are no examples of human beings possessing the characteristics of both sexes, in such a way that it is a matter of doubt how they should be classified. However, the prevalent usage has called them masculine, assigning them to the superior sex; for no one ever used the feminine names, *androgynaecae* or called them *hermaphroditae*.[112]

Three points are worth noting here: the first is the confidence that Augustine expresses that the occurrence of such individuals constitute a permanent feature of human populations. The second is the clear apprehension, that unlike the 'congenital eunuch' of Matthew 19, the individual under scrutiny is not a 'diminished' male, but someone who displays 'characteristics of both sexes'. As with the earlier, more explicit, characterisation of a person with a breast of each biological sex and the capacity to both beget and conceive, the 'person' being envisaged is clearly a genuine hermaphrodite. Thirdly, we are still firmly within the unquestioned bounds of a clear gender hierarchy: for Augustine, keen to show 'charity' to such individuals, to give them the benefit of the doubt, seeks to assign hermaphrodites to the culturally privileged, and therefore more fortunate, male sex.[113]

---

110 Ibid.

111 See Beagon, above n. 12, p. 167. See also Rolker, above n. 16, 178, 187, and Gilbert, above n. 71, pp. 21–22.

112 Augustine, above n. 3, p. 663.

113 This is echoed in the treatment of individuals with CAH in contemporary Saudi Arabia. See S. Taha, 'Male Pseudohermaphroditism: Factors determining the Gender of Rearing in Saudi Arabia' (1994) 43(3) *Urology* 370–374.

In his discussion of hermaphrodites, Augustine is simply employing the category known to him within which persons with variations of sex development are culturally located,[114] a category that dominates Western thinking down to the nineteenth century. However, just as the category of the eunuch undergoes a counter-cultural rehabilitation as a consequence of Matthew 19:12, so Augustine 'redeems' the hermaphrodite from the realm of the monstrous. In so doing he was in the company of many classical writers. However, what is distinctive and significant is Augustine's provision of a robust theological anchorage for the moral equality of the hermaphrodite, made *imago Dei*.

The writings of major theologians are not, however, the only, or even the most natural, place to find substantive and detailed discussion of hermaphroditism in the centuries that follow. Here, the writings of canon lawyers, anchored in the Roman law 'doctrine of the prevailing sex' focused on making everyday practical judgements, are more pertinent.[115] Building on the foundations of Roman law, but undoubtedly informed by Augustine's views, medieval canon law understood hermaphrodites as a 'third sex', bodily distinct from 'normal' men and women, in both theory and practice. Canon lawyers thus adopted and developed the Roman 'doctrine of the prevailing sex' and sort to assign individuals as male or female on the basis of various criteria.[116] Debates were oriented to the making of everyday practical judgements: most obviously whether, and to whom, an individual could marry, but also who, being judged a male, could exercise the privileged task of witnessing testaments or being ordained.[117] In his wide-ranging review Christian Rolker argues that the medieval courts were largely pragmatic and humane in their assessments, unfazed by unusual genital anatomy or the possibility of sex/gender change, and that in practice they seem 'to have given hermaphrodites considerable individual freedom, including a limited choice of gender'.[118]

As the most influential Christian writer since St. Paul, Augustine's views on hermaphrodites continued to shape European thinking, secular and sacred, over subsequent centuries. His text provided a 'compelling precedent' for a tolerant approach to the anomalous case of 'monsters' like the hermaphrodite, in sharp contrast to the Aristotelian view.[119] His was thus an authoritative voice of moderation to which others could turn, not least in the early-modern period,

114 See above n. 73. The saliency of the myth of Hermaphroditus was doubtless reinforced by cultic practices; see Beagon, above n. 12, p. 166.
115 See the chapter by Wijffels in this volume.
116 These included: the capacity to grow a beard, the inspection of genitals and the behaviour of the individual concerned and whether they were drawn to male or female habits, tasks and roles. Unsurprisingly, canon lawyers came to different judgements about which factors were most decisive. See Rolker, above n. 16, 178, 189–203.
117 Ibid, 201.
118 Ibid, 211.
119 Long, above n. 11, p. 19.

when life became more precarious for hermaphrodites and other marginal groups, as a consequence of stricter access to marriage; greater anxiety around masculinity; and increased persecution for crimes against nature.[120]

2.3. THE MODERN ERA: THE INTERSEXUAL[121]

As we step forward into our more immediate past, the power of the Church and the influence of theology and its associated disciplines recede, giving way to a dominant medico-scientific paradigm. Against the backcloth of an emergent gender ideology associated with the Enlightenment and its privileging of a 'biologically-based' gender binary, hermaphrodites, as historical subjects, became increasing seen, as the nineteenth century advanced, through the gaze and the writings of medical and scientific men.[122] Their pursuit of a clearer demarcation between the sexes went hand-in-hand with the consolidation of a biomedical approach to the study of hermaphrodites that sought, in contrast to the wisdom of medieval canon lawyers, to locate *the* 'single reliable marker of "true" sex'.[123] In this enterprise, the foundational text was that produced in 1876 by Theodor Klebs, who introduced an influential categorisation that distinguished between 'true' and 'pseudo' hermaphrodites on the basis of the distribution of gonads.[124] Within this text the seeds were sown for the demise of the dual-sexed 'hermaphrodite' and our final umbrella category, the 'intersexual', conceived primarily in biomedical terms, begins to come into sight.[125]

Despite being a rather vague, umbrella term with no substantive content or direct scientific reference, except to the existence of the presumed gender binary to which it denotes exception, 'intersexual' became progressively the term of choice within the medical sphere. The term was used almost exclusively within the medical sphere until circa 1993, when, rather abruptly, it was also widely adopted by activists as an identity.[126] Scientific understanding of the various medical conditions, making up the category of the 'intersexual', advanced rapidly in the 1950s as a result of the work of the pioneering pediatric endocrinologist

---

120 Rolker, above n. 16, 178, 218–219; See Long, above n. 11.

121 The term 'Intersexual' was coined in 1917 by the biologist Richard Goldschmidt.

122 Indeed, as Dreger clearly documents, increased access to medical care and elevated levels of reporting medical findings led to the perception of 'a virtual explosion of human hermaphroditism' in the second half of the 20th century. Dreger, above n. 61, pp. 24–26. See also F. Dabhoiwala, *The Origins of Sex: A History of the First Sexual Revolution*, Penguin, London 2012; and Laqueur, above n. 14.

123 Dreger, above n. 61, p. 29.

124 Hence, what Dreger has labelled the 'Age of Gonads' (1870–1915), ibid, pp. 139–166.

125 'True hermaphroditism started to disappear because medical and scientific authorities cooperatively revised the criteria for this condition such that it became almost impossible by the end of the century for any body to satisfy those guidelines.' Ibid, p. 139.

126 For a succinct but useful account, see Holmes, above n. 6, p. 4.

Lawson Wilkins (1894–1963) and his team at Johns Hopkins Medical School.[127] However, alongside this advance in physiological understanding, a set of protocols were also developed by John Money for the treatment of those born with ambiguous genitalia. Most problematically such protocols sought to establish or determine the 'true sex' of an individual.[128] This in turn legitimated radical, but often cosmetic, surgery that was perceived to 'establish' the gender of the infant – a claim we shall consider further in the next section of this chapter.

2.4. TRANSCENDING CATEGORIES: AN INTERIM SUMMARY

In this section we have sought to explore some of the historic resources within the Christian tradition that have the potential to cast light on the current debate. Noting the inevitable tension between the radical call to inclusivity that lies at the heart of teaching about the Kingdom of God and the 'natural' dynamics of social solidarity which privilege family and ethnicity, we have drawn attention to the way in which Christian baptism bears witness to an account of the origin and destiny of human beings that transcends sexual difference; that carries the potential to dissolve gender, and other forms of social distinction, 'in Christ'.

More specifically, we have considered two important texts that relegate inherited cultural values and raise fundamental questions about the nature of the categories within which intersex individuals might be situated, drawing them back towards an understanding of their shared humanity. In the first example, from the Gospel of Matthew, we have the clear identification of an intersex historical personage (the 'congenital eunuch') alongside the rehabilitation of the despised, umbrella category – the eunuch – within a strongly eschatological narrative with its implicit critique of hegemonic masculinity. In the second, we have with Augustine's discussion of the dual-sexed hermaphrodite, an interesting companion piece: for Augustine's arguments are rooted in natural theology rather than eschatology. Here, grounded in an account of God as the creator, we have a robust theological legitimation for human morphological diversity that can be appropriated by mainstream society and even cited by lawyers.

In their engagement with those with variations in sex difference and their willingness to challenge inherited cultural categories, these historic examples from the earlier formative period of Christianity provide something of a challenge to the preoccupation of much twentieth-century theological writing. Exemplified by Barth and John Paul II, this writing has sought to essentialise the difference between men and women, and thus reinforce a gender ideology

[127] So e.g. in 1950 Wilkins was responsible for unravelling the pathophysiology of both AIS and CAH and developing the use of adrenal cortical extracts to treat children with CAH in 1950.

[128] 'The import of the work by Money and the Hampsons in shaping protocols for intersex treatment cannot be overstated'; Downing, Morland and Sullivan above n. 20, p. 4.

that has rendered intersex more marginal and muted. It is certainly striking to consider the possibility that those who listened to Jesus recognised the *sĕrîs ḥammâ* more readily than members of our society would recognise intersex. In a similar vein, as we turn in the next section to consider the implications of the 'optimal gender policy' and its pursuit of 'true sex' we may note the parallel with Augustine and his 'charitable' desire (on the pretext of grammar), to assign hermaphrodites to the more favoured (male) gender. However, the disconcerting aspect of the 'gender optimal' paradigm is that personhood appears to be contingent on the clear ascription of gender established, if and when necessary, by surgical alteration of genitalia, rather than on being a given, anchored in the inalienable *Imago Dei*.

3. MINDING THE GAP: MEDICAL CARE AND POLITICAL REPRESENTATION

What constitutes 'the good' for individuals with variations of sex development is heavily contested within contemporary society. Indeed, as I shall argue, a significant dissensus exists between different spheres or regions in society, in particular between the medical and the political: that dissensus is far-reaching and extends even to disagreement about names and basic terminology, though given the importance of self-designation for the development of the narrative identity of individuals this is unsurprising.

As institutional spheres, both medicine and politics seek to promote the well-being of those with variantly sexed bodies and, in particular, to remove associations between intersex and pathology. Yet in both cases their associated practices raise significant ethical issues about the possibilities for embodied and psychological harms. These arise because of the nature of their engagement with the issues that inevitably prioritise particular aspects of the person (bodies, self-consciousness and our relationships with others) to the neglect or detriment of the whole. So, the institutional practices of medicine naturally focus on the functioning of the body yet they also express concerns about the capacity of patients to be recognised and thrive in the 'real world' free of stigma. By contrast, many activists and potential legislators prioritise the agency and autonomy of the individual and the need for just institutions that serve the well-being of all citizens. With respect to the former, concerns have been expressed about the damaging consequences that 'normalising surgery' performed on infants can bring – secrecy, shame and surgery. In the latter, concerns have been raised about representation, of who speaks for whom, and of the appropriateness of 'intersex' as a type of person.

This section will consider how individuals might achieve 'an accomplished life – with and for others – in just institutions' in light of the issues raised by the recent Consensus Statement of 2006 and the underlying substantive disputes of how to make sense of intersex/DSD. Disputes that at many points seem to echo historic debates.

3.1. A CONTEMPORARY DISSENSUS

3.1.1. Altercations and Exchanges

In 2015, the Council of Europe published *Human Rights and Intersex People* (HRIP).[129] Noting that intersex people lacked recognition it sought to highlight and address the 'human rights issues at stake' through two courses of action: First, by helping to end the 'medically unnecessary "normalising" treatment of intersex persons' that took place without the consent of the individual affected; second, by finding ways to protect intersex people from discrimination, including the 'recognition of their sex on official documents'.[130]

Swiftly, HRIP generated a concise, courteous, but far-reaching critical response from a group of leading medical practitioners.[131] Their concerns, focusing on issues of representation, were as follows: that the authors of the report had not engaged sufficiently with some of the important stakeholders, in particular support and advocacy groups; that in advancing intersex as an identity the Council of Europe was enacting political agendas rooted in the LGBT movement rather than speaking on behalf of those with intersex conditions and their families;[132] that the portrayal of contemporary medical practice in the field was a misrepresentation; and, finally, the authors expressed significant reservations about the term 'intersex'.[133]

---

129 Council of Europe Commissioner for Human Rights, *Human Rights and Intersex People*,(2015) Issue paper <https://rm.coe.int/16806da5d4> (last accessed 23.05.2017).

130 Ibid, p. 8. HRIP warns against lumping 'all intersex people into a new collective category, such as a "third sex", perhaps running parallel to female and male', and notes that intersex is an umbrella term including people with '"variations in sex characteristics", rather than a type *per se*'; it is not clear how legal provision recognising sex on official documents can be achieved without *de facto* creating another gender. Ibid, p. 15.

131 M. Cools et al., 'Response to the Council of Europe Human Rights Commissioner's Issue Paper on Human Rights and Intersex People' (2016) 70 *European Urology* 407–409. This response was issued on behalf of the Management Committee of the European Cooperation in Science and Technology Action BM1303.

132 Though by implication, there is a criticism of several intersex advocacy groups including: ILGA-Europe, '... a driving force for political, legal and social change at European level'; see <http://www.ilga-europe.org/who-we-are/what-ilga-europe> (last accessed 28.03.2017). Also, Organization Intersex International Europe, which understands itself to be 'the umbrella organisation of European human rights-based intersex organisations'; see <https://oiieurope.org/about/>, and the respective global networks <https://oiiinternational.com/> and <http://ilga.org/> (all last accessed 28.03.2017).

133 'Some of us think the term intersex people is not widely recognized as appropriate among adults and children having atypical sex development'; Cools et al., above n. 131, 407.

A year later; another exchange: this time, however, the stimulus was an article authored by leading medical experts reviewing the management of the five main groups of DSD patients with atypical genitalia.[134] The response came from philosopher, Ellen Feder, and historian of medicine, Alice Dreger.[135] They argued that, 'damningly', at no point did the medical specialists engage with any of the 'conspicuous ethical questions … raised by countless critics':[136] So there was no discussion of the rights of patients' to decide whether healthy sexual tissue could be removed; a lack of provision of psycho-social support for infants or children affected, or their families in a scenario in which tolerance might be fostered towards genital diversity; and, apparently no awareness that prevailing standards of care are increasing perceived to be violations of human rights. To Feder and Dreger the review reads 'like it was written 20 years ago'.[137]

3.1.2. *Contesting Language*

Within this dissensus, even the basic terms are heavily contested: So, in 2006, those medical professionals with expertise in the area sought to review their approach producing a new 'Consensus Statement on Management of Intersex Disorders'.[138] An important aspect of this radical change was an overhaul of the repertoire of nomenclature for the various conditions under consideration. In particular, they sought to replace all terms 'perceived as potentially pejorative by patients' and 'confusing to practitioners and parents alike'.[139] In an article intended to disseminate knowledge of this radical development, one member of the group described it as a 'silent revolution', in which 'the key and revolutionary step was to banish to antiquity the term, *intersex*' and replace it with 'an all-embracing Disorders of Sex Developments (acronym, DSD) terminology'.[140] This change also saw the final removal of a suite of terms with anachronistic resonance like hermaphroditism and pseudo-hermaphroditism. This new consensus and its associated repertoire of language was regarded as something of a triumph.[141] Significantly the new terminology came with the endorsement

---

134 P.D. Mouriquand et al., 'Surgery in disorders of sex development (DSD) with a gender issue: if (why), when, and how?' (2016) 12 *Journal of Pediatric Urology* 139–149.

135 E.K. Feder and A. Dreger, 'Still ignoring human rights in intersex care' (2016) 12(6) *Journal of Pediatric Urology* 436–437. Both are authors of significant texts on intersex, see above n. 8 and n. 61.

136 Ibid, 436.

137 Ibid, 437.

138 Lee, Houk, Ahmed and Hughes, above n. 7 ; and Hughes et al., above n. 7.

139 Lee et al., above n. 7, 488.

140 I.A. Hughes, 'The Quiet Revolution' (2010) 24 *Best Practice & Research Clinical Endocrinology & Metabolism* 159–160.

141 'What other branch of medicine can provide an example of such fundamental change in nomenclature that is incorporated in to practice overnight?' Indeed, 'the DSD nomenclature and its spin-offs have arrived at *the high altar of medical practice*' (emphasis added). Ibid, 160.

of a leading advocacy and support organisation, the Intersex Society of North America (ISNA), which decided in 2008 to set up a successor non-profit organisation, Accord Alliance, to help ensure the promulgation of appropriate care for people with DSD.[142]

For many, the significant advance made with the 2006 Consensus lies precisely in the move away from an identification of the individual person with one aspect of their embodiment. As the Accord Alliance puts it: 'By contrast to these older terms, the term DSD refers to a condition that a person *has*, not who a person *is*. It seeks to put the person first'.[143]

It seems curious then that ten years on from this 'triumph' banishing the pejorative term 'to antiquity', the Council of Europe should produce a document that not only deploys 'intersex' in the title, but also advances proposals for legal provision in the name of the 'intersex' person. And the Council is not alone; for in 2012 an umbrella organisation for European human rights intersex organisations was formed – Organization Intersex International Europe – clearly demonstrating that not all advocacy groups speak the same language.

The 2006 Consensus has not garnered universal support; indeed, in the perception of many, the new language, specifically *disorder*, far from removing the pathological, in fact *re*-stigmatises.[144] Just such an argument is advanced by Morgan Holmes who argues that it is 'too soon to accept the language of *disorder* wholesale' or to dispense with intersex entirely. Instead she advocates the adoption of a 'critical stance toward the use … of intersex'.[145]

So, like intersex, *disorder* also divides: for those within the medical profession, the language of disorder is understood as both neutral and ultimately, non-negotiable, as it relates to the 'normal' functioning of the body.[146] For the medical practitioner, the language of disorder is seen as self-evidently appropriate, indeed essential, as it identifies abnormal physiology. It is thus perceived to be

---

See also V. Pasterski, P. Prentice and I.A. Hughes, 'Impact of the consensus statement and the new DSD classification system' (2010) 24 *Best Practice & Research Clinical Endocrinology & Metabolism* 187, 193.

142 See <http://www.isna.org/> and <http://www.accordalliance.org/> (last accessed 03.08.2017). The unequivocal endorsement of the 2006 Consensus and its associated terminology is exemplified by 2 publications promoted by Accord Alliance and available on its website: Consortium on the Management of Disorders of Sex Development, *Clinical Guidelines for the Management of Disorders of Sex Development in Childhood*, Intersex Society of North America, Rohnert Park 2006a, and Consortium on the Management of Disorders of Sex Development, *Handbook for Parents*, Intersex Society of North America, Palo Alto 2006b.

143 See <http://www.accordalliance.org/learn-about-dsd/faqs/> (last accessed 23.05.2017) (original italics).

144 The shift in language 'reinstitutionalises clinical power to delineate and silence those marked by the diagnosis'; M. Holmes, 'The Intersex Enchiridion: Naming and Knowledge' (2011) 1(2) *Somatechnics* 388.

145 Holmes, above n. 6, pp. 1, 5.

146 Pasterski, Prentice and Hughes, above n. 141, 187, 189.

descriptive, accurate and 'true'. However, that is only the case within a certain limited epistemological framework (i.e. in relation to the physical body), for in relation to persons, disorder is normative language connecting as it does to the language of health and concepts of dis-ease and dis-ability.[147] Thus, for many others, the use of disorder conjures a different field of associations and exemplifies some of the problems that exist with the medical treatment of those with intersex conditions.

How then are we to understand or bridge this gap in language and understanding?

3.1.3. Conflicting Discourses

These interactions take us into the heart of some of the dilemmas and paradoxes involved in this arena. In contemplating the 'gap' between those with relevant medical expertise and experience and a political institution like the Council of Europe, we are primarily considering the difference between two very different institutional spheres within society: the political and the medical, and their associated discourses. These spheres have very different goals and entail different paradigms, protocols and practices. And they raise the spectre of ethical violations in each other's arenas. So, the political discourse of human rights focuses on a person's agency and autonomy; on the person as citizen in an institutional sphere that prioritises justice over other values. Thus, it comes to conceive of intersex persons as constituting a minority 'community of interest' who, at least potentially, require various forms of protection. Whereas the medical discourse is concerned with the care and well-being of the individual person, embedded as they are in a web of relationships of family and friends. However, it is also firmly anchored in an empirically-grounded approach to understanding the body and its proper functioning. The contemporary dissensus is then a direct consequence of the challenges involved in relating these discourses to each other.

These two discourses map onto different regions of human experience and therefore represent incomplete or truncated views of personhood. From the human rights perspective, the fundamental issue at stake is the autonomy of the individual. So, the right of a person not to have their body altered or 'corrected' through surgery without their consent is fundamental and non-negotiable – except under those circumstances where a failure to take action would be life-threatening or very clearly detrimental to the individual's long-term well-being. However, this leads us swiftly into deeply contested territory, for surgery undertaken on intersex infants has been justified historically on the assumption that being ambiguously sexed *per se* brings harm to the development of the psycho-social development of the person. Political advocacy for the creation of

[147] See Ricoeur (2007), above n. 4, pp. 187–197.

a new space that goes beyond the binary distinction of male and female and provides for intersex people 'an adequate recognition of their sex'[148] can thus be seen as an ameliorative response given this dominant cultural assumption. Such provision is thus intended to set individuals free from the coercive power of normative social forces, which are embedded, among many other sites, in medical protocols and practices. Such a move is simultaneously a return to the public acknowledgement of a 'third sex' in European law and a manifestation of the liberal progress narrative; a pattern of thinking deeply embedded in institutions like the Council of Europe. If enacted, such a political initiative could provide, potentially, a powerful and public statement of affirmation of persons with unusual embodiment.

By contrast, the physician operates in a much more immediate and concrete context: it is not their task to advocate the social project of identity creation; to 'correct' society. Rather, medical care focuses on the particular patient as an individual person who *suffers* from a complex condition, one among others within a heterogeneous grouping, which has been assigned the shorthand 'intersex'. The physician thus approaches the person as a patient; a subject of diagnosis and treatment. Yet, like the human rights activist, the medic is also, intentionally or otherwise, engaged in an idealist project, in the making of normative judgements: for radical but 'normalising', cosmetic surgery, involving the removal of healthy tissue, is very frequently performed upon intersex infants. Such practices have been central to the medical management regime in which intersex infants and children were assigned to an 'optimal gender' of rearing following surgery since the 1950s. However, since the mid-1990s this 'optimal gender' policy,[149] has been subject to much criticism. Nevertheless, many of its assumptions continue to shape current medical practice, albeit in a modified form.

3.2. THE MEDICAL DISCOURSE, 'OPTIMAL GENDER' AND 'NORMALISING SURGERY'

Whilst the individual patient is a unique person, they are also a medical case, and as such, subject to a regime of knowledge and practice concerning diagnosis, treatment and prognosis. As a consequence, Paul Ricoeur argues, there is a sense in which: 'the whole medical institution' is inserted 'into the intimate relation between the patient and his or her physician'.[150] Not only that, Ricoeur continues, but the institutional structures that make up the sphere of

148 Council of Europe Commissioner for Human Rights, above n. 129, p. 8.
149 See e.g. J.D. Hester, 'Intersex(es) and informed consent: How Physicians' rhetoric constrains choice' (2004) 25 *Theoretical Medicine* 21, 25.
150 Ricoeur (2007), above n. 4, p. 193.

medicine are connected to the whole complex of other structures within society (administrative, juridical etc.) that shape the politics of health. The potential power that medicine can wield over the individual is thus immense as is clear from the standard medical management of intersex infants within the paradigm of the 'optimal gender' policy.

3.2.1. *The Optimal Gender Policy*

The 'optimal gender' policy was constituted by a widely accepted set of guidelines that involved the ascription of gender; early surgical intervention; and, an acceptance by all those involved of the 'real sex' of the individual infant. Adopted by pediatricians within the ambit of Western medicine the guidelines were proposed and developed in 1955 by John Money and his colleagues. As a consequence, so-called 'normalising' surgery was undertaken on a great many individuals over the decades from the 1950s and, indeed, continues today within new guidelines, despite overt condemnation in some, and significant reservations in other quarters.

In outline the guidelines were as follows:

> (1) Gender assignment should go to the gender most likely to maintain reproductivity, good sexual function, normal-looking external genitalia and stable gender identity; (2) the decision should be made as early as possible, within the newborn period, but no later than 18–24 months, with initial genital reconstruction surgeries performed within this timeframe; (3) parents and professionals should be fully committed to the final decision about gender assignment and the subsequent gender of rearing, should inform the child with age-appropriate explanations of their situation, and should follow-up with the administration of gender-appropriate hormones at the onset of puberty.[151]

In procedural terms, within this framework, when a child is born whose biological sex is ambiguous, a 'social emergency' is declared and following a diagnosis of the underlying medical condition, a gender is assigned. For the case of genetic females the guidelines proscribe that the assigned gender should be female, irrespective of the degree of virilisation, as this best preserves the individual's reproductive potential. For genetic males, assignment is more precarious, depending on the anatomy, predominantly the size of the phallus, with those with a very small penis and underdeveloped male genitalia being assigned as females. Such 'normalising' genital surgery has thus been predominantly 'feminising' reducing 'oversized' female genitalia in virilised females and surgically altering the genitalia of some genetic males to resemble more closely that of a female, by 'changing' the micropenis into a clitoris and

[151] Hester, above n. 149, 21, 25.

creating or extending a vaginal opening. Clearly the grounds for this approach are, in part, a testament to the limitations of the surgeon's power to construct a functioning, 'normal'-sized penis. However it is equally clear that this approach embeds a number of cultural values and empirical assumptions.

The optimal gender paradigm rests on a number of beliefs: That to flourish as a person each individual needs a clear sense of gender identity within a binary frame, whether as male or female. Second, that the appearance of their external genitalia and certain aspects of sexual or reproductive functioning are an important component in the development of gender identity. And third, that infants (up to 24 months) have a psycho-sexual neutrality, that they are tabula rasa upon which gender can be imprinted by upbringing and socialisation; that with consistent reinforcement the child in question will grow up within their assigned gender identity as a 'normal' and 'healthy' girl or boy. The third of these assumptions was thoroughly and rather dramatically overturned in the late 1990s by exactly the case study that Money used to help establish his theory, that of David Reimer.[152] This, in combination with the intersex activism from the 1990s onwards has led to some significant re-evaluation, *partly* reflected in the 2006 Consensus. Nevertheless, cosmetic surgery with the stated aim of reinforcing gender identification remains surprisingly common, even if the 'blame' is laid more clearly today at the feet of parents than physicians.[153]

3.2.2. Embodying Harm: Secrecy, Shame and Surgery

Before turning to consider in more detail why it is that cosmetic surgery continues to be practised on intersex infants, it is worth noting the physical and psychological harms that individuals have experienced. Feder identifies six, which she suggests are 'surprising for their consistency, literally across generations of individuals':

> Intrusive and embarrassing examinations as young children and teens without being informed of the rationale …; experiences of a gender identity being 'forced' upon them that felt contrary to their own inclinations; having one's diagnosis withheld; prevention of access to medical records; assured that treatment decisions were made in their best interests even as they were made to feel that their treatment was not for their own benefit; told there was 'no one else like them.'[154]

---

152 See M. Diamond and K. Sigmundsen, 'Sex Reassignment at Birth: A Long Term Review and Clinical Implications' (1997) 151 *Archives of Pediatrics and Adolescent Medicine* 298–304; Butler (2004), above n. 60, pp. 57–74.

153 E.K. Feder, 'Beyond Good Intentions' (2015) 5(2) *Narrative Inquiry in Bioethics* 133, 134; L.M. Liao, D. Wood and S.M. Creighton, 'Parental Choice on normalizing cosmetic genital surgery: Between a rock and a hard place' (2015) 351 *BMJ* h5124.

154 Feder, above n. 153, 133.

These are not abstractions, but experiences with a profound bearing on real lives. So, for example, Michelle O'Brien's autobiographical account of discovering, (and perhaps recovering) herself as intersex captures something of this in personal narrative:

> Through snippets of information from doctors, supplemented with my own research, I began to unravel things about my childhood that turned my world upside down. I realize that I was not the person that I thought I was. The more I learned, the more I felt torn in two. I am not sure how I survived that time. What I came to understand was that I was born with intersex characteristics, and had at least two gender-reinforcement surgeries to make me appear more masculine, as well as psycho-social gender-reinforcement.[155]

Thus, as O'Brien makes clear, the consequences of secrecy and the violation of one's body without consent can almost 'undo' a person's sense of self, their narrative identity.[156] And, again and again, in accounts of the experience of those operated on as infants and children it is this trio of – secrecy, shame and surgery – that emerges as the key legacy with which the adult has to grapple in order to establish a secure personal identity.[157]

The practice of 'normalising' surgery does not just violate human rights, which might be construed as aspirational, but also – arguably – some of the key principles of medical ethics, most evidently *primum non nocere* and patient autonomy. This can be seen through a closer consideration of that critical context for the fate of those born with ambiguous genitalia, namely, the medical consultation between the physician and the parents, or guardians, of the infant. At the heart of a medical consultation lie three elements: the sharing of a medical secret; the patient's right to know the truth about their situation and the proposal for care and treatment based on the diagnosis, as well as the likely outcome; and, finally, the right to informed consent.[158] How then are we to understand not just the embodied harms[159] inflicted on individuals, but also the apparent breaches of standard medical convention and protocol?

3.2.3. *Rhetoric and the Establishment of 'True Sex'*

Parents discover that there is 'something wrong' with their child in a clinical context through a conversation initiated by a medical professional and framed by

---

155 M. O'Brien, 'Intersex, Medicine, Diversity, Identity', in C. Beardsley and M. O'Brien (eds.), *This is my body: Hearing the theology of transgender Christians*, DLT, London 2016, pp. 46–47.

156 Butler (2004), above n. 60, pp. 57–74.

157 See e.g. O'Brien, above n. 155, p. 51.

158 Ricoeur, above n. 4, p. 194.

159 Such harm was clearly not intentional, but rather might be considered the consequence of a form of medical error; see Feder (2015), above n. 153.

a discipline that seeks to identify, diagnose and provide treatment for individuals who are dis-eased. Yet, in his analysis of the historic 'optimal gender' paradigm, Hester argues that this consultation takes place within a rhetorical framework that embeds and reinforces certain assumptions.[160] Central to this framework is the 'naturalising rhetoric' of a belief in the two-sex system and 'the commitment to "one-body, one-sex"'. Thus, he argues, a culturally mediated gender system is 'the constraining hegemony over the medical field'.[161]

Within this constraining hegemony Hester suggests that the body of the intersex child undergoes a 'profound evidential shift'.[162] Critically it is viewed not on the basis of the underlying condition that results in the 'ambiguous' genitalia, but on the grounds of external genital markers. Thus, the rationale for radical surgical intervention lies with the maintenance of 'a culturally and historically derived gender ideology' rather than a consideration of how to address 'any physiological issue detrimental to the safety of the child'.[163] It is then 'the *rhetoric* employed by the physician that pathologises the genitalia, not the condition behind the ambiguity'.[164]

It could be argued that as decisions are effectively made on the grounds of that which is visible, this is no different, in principle, from a judgement being made on the grounds of skin colour. However, evaluation is not simply skin-deep as the potential for certain biological functionality is also integral to the paradigm, namely female reproductive capacity and male sexual function. Clearly reproductive and sexual functioning are both important considerations within a pursuit of the good for a human life. However, the difficulty lies with the fact that such priorities reflect a clear hierarchy of social values.[165] Why is it that these particular biological functions are considered *the* crucial factors in the development of surgical protocols and gender assignment? And why are the 'two' genders treated so differently with the respective value of male fertility and female sexual pleasure downgraded?

One remarkable corollary of this commitment to an idealised binary is that it overrides a basic ethical imperative, namely truth-telling. As Hester observes, the protocol requires a commitment by all those involved to be 'discrete' and not to send 'confusing messages'. In practice then, it is explained to parents that their child 'really does have a gendered identity', but that the genitals or gonads being incomplete the 'true sex' of the child has to be more fully investigated before

---

160 Much of the following section draws on HESTER, above n. 149. Though see also M. HOLMES, 'Mind the Gaps: Intersex and (Re-productive) Spaces in Disability Studies and Bioethics' (2008) 5 *Bioethical Inquiry* 169–181.

161 HESTER, above n. 149, 21, 27.

162 Ibid, 36.

163 Ibid, 37.

164 Ibid, 38.

165 This is especially concerning given the dominance of a single individual, i.e. John Money. See DOWNING, MORLAND AND SULLIVAN, above n. 20, especially pp. 1–16.

procedures which will 'correct' or 'complete' the process.[166] Thus it would seem, at least historically, parents may not have been fully informed, and crucially it was felt that the patient, the intersexed person should not know about their own condition.[167] This is a truly extraordinary state of affairs and involves physicians setting aside what they know of the complexity of human sexual formation to become gate-keepers for a cultural understanding of gender thereby flouting the fundamental principles of the medical consultation: the sharing of medical knowledge and the giving of informed consent.

In Hester's analysis of the medico-rhetorical context, a 'truth' is discovered about the intersex body that renders the body itself, rather than any particular aspect of it, pathological: thus, the patient becomes a 'pathological object'.[168] Their personhood can only be reclaimed when their 'true sex' has been identified and steps taken to more firmly establish that sexed body and identity. In short, to reach back to our earlier discussion, before this point of revelation, the infant exists in a liminal space and is rendered a kind of 'monster'. The infant only becomes fully human, is only made 'intelligible' to society as a consequence of medical intervention; their personhood is thus conditional on the ascription of gender/sex. Prior to this, they are, in effect, unrecognisable as persons. As a corollary, before the discovery of the individual's 'true sex' it would seem then that the 'usual rules' of medicine simply do not apply.[169]

In failing to acknowledge that intersex conditions are part of the natural range of human variation and to provide medical assistance to individuals on a case-by-case basis as, and only when necessity arises, Hester argues that medical practice, as manifest in the 'gender optimal' paradigm, slips into an 'idealist enterprise':[170] that is it endorses cultural norms and provides solutions to the 'problem' of anomalous individuals who sit outside the binary gender classification system of contemporary Western society.

3.2.4. The Normal and the Normative: An Easy Slippage

It is easy to see how medicine as a discourse slips into becoming an idealist enterprise – indeed it is probably inevitable. But in the case of the 'optimal gender policy' such slippage contributes significantly to the dissensus outlined above. At its heart lies an elision between two quite different readings of the norm and the normal: first, there is the statistical; that which relates to frequency and deviation in relation to an average. St. Augustine, above, provides a particularly clear reference in pointing to the 'very rarity' of certain human morphologies in

166 Hester, above n. 149, 21, 26.
167 Ibid, 38–39. See also O'Brien, above n. 155.
168 Ibid, 38.
169 See Feder, above n. 153, 133, 137.
170 Hester, above n. 149, 21, 37.

relation to 'the persistent norm of nature in the majority'.[171] And then, there is the ideal: that relating to some model which manifests ideas of success, happiness, well-being, etc.[172] Whilst this distinction is easily drawn in the abstract, within the field of medicine, both understandings are simultaneously in operation within notions of health and disease. For on the one hand, that which is 'not normal' relates to a deficit or disorder (i.e. the pathological), yet on the other it simply relates to difference – to an alternative form of organisation. This is the distinction that inheres then between describing intersex in terms of *disorders of sex development* and *variations of sex difference* respectively. In the first, a medical classification seeks to identify physiology and anatomy that 'falls short' of an ideal and is understood as dysfunctional. The second recognises a fundamental reality of the human condition and indeed biological life, namely extensive individual variation; that at the biological level no fundamental distinctions can be identified, for we are all 'roughly hewn'. Thus, whether we have the genetic 'defect' of blue eyes; are non-neurotypical; have an intersex condition; or, any of a range of more modestly limiting variations there is no perfect model – from which only a few of us have fallen: hence, the critique of DSD which argues that the medical profession has interpreted 'morphological variation as disease'.[173]

There is then a fundamental ambiguity within the idea of health, and an inescapable elision of different understandings of the normal that therein lie. Neither health nor disease can have an objective, uncontestable meaning. Rather, they can only be properly understood or discerned within the life of an individual. This is especially well-understood by those who work in the field of disability studies, where in addition to the dominant medical model, academics and activists have identified a range of supplementary models and understandings.[174] The most influential of these, the 'social' model, developed out of sociological theorising (labelling theory and social deviance), argues that the 'problem' of disability is not primarily located in an individual's body, but rather with society's response to certain kinds of human embodied experiences, that 'disability' is very substantially a social construct.[175] This model suggests that what constitutes disability will change over time and across context depending on the categories with which society operates. Such an approach doesn't ignore notions of suffering or of limitation, but simply sets them alongside other considerations.

---

171 Augustine, above n. 3, p. 662.

172 Ricoeur (2007), above n. 4, pp. 189–190.

173 Holmes, above n. 144, 388.

174 D.B. Creamer, 'Disabled People', in A. Thatcher (ed.), *The Oxford Handbook of Theology, Sexuality and Gender*, Oxford University Press, Oxford 2015, pp. 676–678.

175 The social model of disability was first described in M. Oliver, *Social Work with Disabled People*, Macmillan, Basingstoke 1983. See also M. Oliver and C. Barnes, *The New Politics of Disablement*, Palgrave, Basingstoke 2012.

In his interrogation of the language of pathology, Paul Ricoeur, echoing our earlier anthropological reflections upon societies' intolerance of anomaly, argues that:

> society would like to ignore, hide, even eliminate its handicapped ... because they constitute a silent menace, a disturbing reminder of our fragility, our precariousness, our mortality. They constitute an unbearable *memento mori*.[176]

In more provocative vein, Ricoeur goes onto argue that inferiority and depreciation is *required* of the pathologised to maintain what he labels the 'insolent aspect of health'.[177] Here Ricoeur draws our attention to the tendency of the dominant majority to glorify in their good health and power to act in the world. Yet such buoyancy is parasitic and rests on comparison, for it demands the negative evaluation of others, which is 'ratified, consolidated, and turned into confidence and assurance by social success'. Biological difference 'thus find itself dramatically consolidated by social distinction'.[178] In this sense the pathologisation of the intersex person bolsters and affirms societal gender norms and the individual's sense of being a man or a woman, quelling uncertainty and anxiety through the act of comparison. When cultural anxieties about gender or sexuality are especially aroused, this routine, unacknowledged, everyday, pathologisation is ratcheted up to include scapegoating, persecution and other manifestations of harm or cruel exclusion.

3.2.5. Moving Forward: The 2006 Consensus

I have presented the 'optimal gender' policy as historic in character because much has changed since the mid-1990s. The 2006 Consensus consolidated a break with the paradigm and introduced a number of changes in medical care.[179] Perhaps the most significant of these was the welcome demise of the notion of the 'social emergency'. A corollary has been a clear shift towards parental autonomy at the expense of medical paternalism. Whilst this is to be welcomed, as many physicians acknowledge, there is very little evidence that parents are well-equipped to make effective decisions in such circumstances.[180] This is

---

176 Ricoeur, above n. 4, p. 192.

177 Ibid, p. 191.

178 Ibid, p. 192.

179 e.g., there was recommendation against surgery and gender reassignment for XY males with 'micropenis'.

180 'Furthermore their emotional states may not be optimal ... There is no evidence that parents are given sufficient time to appreciate their child, effective psycho-social support to manage their emotional reactions, or help to slowly digest the highly complex medical information and implications.' Liao, Wood and Creighton, above n. 153, p. 1. See also Pasterski, Prentice and Hughes, above n. 141, 187, 190: 'Parents are extremely vulnerable at this stage with heightened anxieties and desperation for solutions.'

unsurprising, given that surgical intervention has long been the established practice. Further, as the status quo is anchored in the axioms of a dominant gender ideology, few parents are aware that in pursuing that course 'they are *de facto* opting for experimental surgery on their children'[181] rather than choosing the option best supported by evidence-based medical research. For, in reality, one of the difficulties is that 'little is known about the physical, psychological, social, and sexual effects untreated atypical genitalia associated with different diagnoses'.[182] This makes it very difficult for medics to fulfil what many perceive to be part of the physician's remit, namely to consider: 'the impact of non-treated DSD during childhood for the individual development, the parents, society and the risk of stigmatization'.[183] In essence, it would seem, the physician is required to 'play sociologist' extrapolating from the present and making predictions about the future social norms and character of society – an extremely precarious activity.

It is quite clear that in many cases there is significant parental distress at the birth of a child with ambiguous genitalia, and under these circumstances, 'normalising surgery', especially to reduce 'clitoromegaly', appears an attractive option. Indeed, it would seem that the number of such surgeries has increased.[184] Yet such invasive surgery is routinely undertaken despite significant ethical reservations: a lack of evidence-based research; concern from adults who have experienced surgery in childhood; and, increasingly expressions of regret from parents.[185] *If* unnecessary psychological and embodied harm is being inflicted on some infants – and a case can certainly be made – it is then the consequence of two factors: a medical praxis that is more indebted to a taken-for-granted set of assumptions about gender than is acknowledged; and too narrow a focus on the somatic to the detriment of the existential and social aspects that make up the individual person.

3.3. IDENTITY CLAIMS AND REPRESENTATIONAL COLONISATION

Returning to the dissensus with which this section opened, we noted that the critical response to HRIP[186] raised the question of representation, of what we might identify as an inappropriate ventriloquism: that is an over-zealous advocacy. Such activity touches on issues of power-over-others, and potentially of restrictions on the ability of people to 'tell their own story'. As the critics point

181 Liao, Wood and Creighton, above n. 153, 1.
182 Ibid, 1.
183 Mouriquand et al., above n. 134, 139, 140.
184 Feder, above n. 153, 133, 134.
185 Liao, Wood and Creighton, above n. 153.
186 Cools et al., above n. 131.

out the creation of a new sexed identity, 'intersex', seeks to 'normalise' a new 'kind of person', and to create from such persons a 'community of interest'. The generation of such new norms creates the conditions in which individuals may feel pressure to conform and narrate their identity within certain parameters. Indeed, it has been argued that such a process of normalisation, involves the re-creation, or perhaps the recycling, of what is, at root, a medicalised or pathological identity.[187]

In his ethnographic investigation of transgender, the anthropologist, David Valentine[188] makes a number of interesting observations about the relationship between violence and the emergence of transgender as a category. One of these is relatively unsurprising: namely, that the threat or reality of physical violence stimulated the development of the identity category by prompting individuals to mobilise and form communities agitating for greater protection: thus, he argues '"transgender" is institutionally, narratively, and biographically linked to the experience of violence'.[189] There are clear parallels here with the development of an intersex identity in the 1990s[190] linked to the embodied harms entailed in infant surgeries. A second, more challenging observation is that the category of 'transgender' itself inflicts 'unintended representational violence'.[191] Again, there are implications here for intersex as an identity, though this observation requires a little further parsing.

Like transgender, intersex is a collective term that incorporates a wide variety of sexed embodiment, of experiences and identifications. But, from the perspective of the activist, umbrella terms such as 'intersex' are essential to the formation of a constituency, they are 'the path to *being* represented',[192] within contemporary liberal democracies. So, increasingly people are recognised as being transgender or being intersex. Such identities are thus the vehicles 'for activist practices'.[193] One difficulty with this identitarian move is that it can lead to homogenisation, to a levelling out of the complexities of people's experiences which erodes the richness of their lived experience and seeks to locate them simply within an identity template. In his ethnographic account of the 'transgender community' in Manhattan, Valentine discovered that most of its 'members' did not in fact identify with the term, which he argues is actually

---

187 Feder (2009), above n. 8.

188 D. Valentine, '"The calculus of pain": Violence, anthropological ethics, and the category transgender' (2003) 68:1 *Ethnos* 27–48. See also D. Valentine, *Imagining Transgender: An Ethnography of a Category*, Duke University Press, London 2007, pp. 204–230.

189 Valentine (2003), above n. 188, 27, 43.

190 'The establishment of something called a transgender community was facilitated by the explosion of internet technologies'; ibid, 28. A very similar assertion could be made about the intersex 'community'.

191 Ibid, 32.

192 Ibid, 35.

193 Ibid, 32.

based on '... an implicitly white, implicitly middle-class model of identity-based claims'.[194] As such, 'transgender' particularly excluded those whose lives were are at some social distance from activist and academic circles, ironically, often those in greatest need of support. So, whilst political reality might demand an engagement with identity categories,[195] it can also constitute a 'representational colonisation' of people's lives.[196]

The logic of 'transgender' and by analogy, 'intersex' as collective modes of political identity is thus only intelligible if differences and alternative identifications are excluded or erased.[197] Thus, 'intersex' could potentially lead to the representational colonisation of individual persons in several ways.

First, through homogenisation of the various subgroups within the category 'intersex', as if their experiences and concerns were identical: so, for example, some but not all DSDs lead to ambiguous genitalia, some but not all lead to infertility. So, notwithstanding the heterogeneity of experiences within subgroups, the characteristic experiences of those persons, for example, with AIS or 5-alpha-reductase deficiency or CAH are quite distinct.

Second, there is the problem of priority; that intersex could operate 'to the exclusion of other social identities and other ways of conceptualizing gender and sexual identity';[198] quite simply, individuals may not wish to identify with 'intersex' or think that the nature of their sexed embodiment is more important than, say their ethnicity, religion or class.

Third, there is the danger that the category 'intersex' itself, as a politicised identity, is simply derivative; that it is a mere extension of an LGBT activist agenda. Cools et al. suggest this in their criticisms of HRIP, where they note their serious concerns about the involvement of the 'powerful campaigning voice of LGBT groups ... in representing people with variant sex development'. Involvement, which they argue works from 'the assumption that intersex is *per se* related to sexual orientation and gender dysphoria or confusion'.[199] Inclusion under the LGBT umbrella, the urologists argue, also has a detrimental impact on the public understanding of variations in sex development and may have a negative impact on those working for the best outcomes.

Whilst some individuals may identify with or 'learn' to become intersex, finding this conducive to self-narration, the categories remain irreducibly those of political action tied to powerful social institutions and thus have the potential

---

194 As Valentine further observes the idea of the 'transgender community' grew out of 'the contexts of activism and social service provision ... to create a coherent polity as the basis for political recognition and the achievement of social justice'; ibid, 44.

195 An imperative that also leads to the reification of ethnicity and religious categories, e.g. *the* Muslim community, *the* Black community.

196 Valentine (2003), above n. 188, 27, 45.

197 Ibid, 44.

198 Ibid, 32.

199 Cools et al., above n. 131, 407–408.

for representational colonisation of the individual. It is difficult to assess the existential harms that might flow from this and, of course, they must be evaluated in the context of the continued dominance of the medical discourse. However, we should note that many of those who might be assigned an intersex identity do not recognise or embrace that identification.[200]

3.4. THE PROBLEM OF PARTIALITY: AN INTERIM SUMMARY

In this section we have explored aspects of the current discussion around intersex/DSD through a consideration of the significant dissensus that exists between, broadly speaking, the fields of medicine and political action. It has been argued that the profound differences of opinion, which extend even to disagreement about basic nomenclature, are primarily a consequence of the shape and character of the discourses that operate within these two spheres. Both discourses, inevitably, are partial in both senses of that word: that is, they are committed; they are oriented towards specific ends; and, they represent a part, rather than the whole of the human experience. These differing perspectives on personhood, which emphasise respectively the physical body and the idea of health; and, the citizen and human rights generate, in effect, a regional ethics which map to different parts of the human condition and experience.

The consequence of such partiality is that both discourses raise significant ethical issues for the other. Even where there is strong agreement about the desired outcome, namely that personhood should not be pathologised, conflict remains. For the medic the move from 'the intersexual' to 'a person with a DSD' is a significant development, shifting the focus from a pathological identity to the dysfunction of the body. Thus, the person with a DSD is simply classed amongst a group of people with a particular range of disorders in a world where many individuals suffer from this or that disorder. For the critic, this is naïve: for our sexed nature is such a significant part of our personal identity that it cannot be treated with such dispassionate objectivity. Persistent and widespread beliefs concerning the benefits of 'normality' undermine the credibility of the narrow construal of 'the problem of intersex as a problem of abnormal individual bodies'.[201]

Those who see in the introduction of 'disorder' a re-pathologisation can easily point to the historical paradigm of the 'gender optimal policy' within which the intersex infant is implicitly pathological; their personhood conditional on a

---

200 'Intersex people *usually* identify as male or female, remain in their assigned gender from birth, but quite a few transition as adults, or identify as intersex per se' (emphasis added); O'Brien, above n. 155, p. 49.

201 Feder, above n. 153, 133, 135.

medical diagnosis. The testimony of intersex adults to the ways in which legacies of shame, secrecy and surgery have impeded their ability to develop a coherent personal narrative provides further weight to such arguments. Here, we might add a footnote to the account of the dissensus between discourses: namely, their orientation to history and the past. For medicine, as a scientifically-based, empirically grounded discipline, the past is to be moved on from, the orientation is to the future; medicine is about improvement, the past is only relevant in so far as it helps to determine the right course for the patients of the future. There is little desire to 'dwell on the past'. By contrast, the political involves the active contemplation of human nature, individual and collective, and the continual re-emergence of familiar patterns. Here, the present is very much about the past, and impatience with past mistakes or their consequences can so easily appear unwise, even arrogant.

For many intersex individuals, it is difficult to underestimate the influence of the medical context, both for the development of their internal sense of self and their engagement with society, alongside their physical embodiment. The claim that medical practice has breached fundamental principles of medical ethics, as a consequence of physicians acting (unwittingly) as gatekeepers for a cultural understanding of gender, needs to be addressed. Nevertheless we must also bear in mind the potential for representational colonisation, of the inherent dangers in some organisations and groups speaking on behalf of others and generating, in the name of emancipation, new social norms with the potential to cause harm.[202]

In this section we have sketched the dissensus that exists between two 'secular' discourses within contemporary society that present the individual, who is variantly sexed, with two powerful, persuasive, but different understandings of their situation: a medical discourse focused on their body that designates them as someone with a 'disorder', which without 'correction' and a clear gender ascription could render them, at least potentially, 'unrecognisable' as a person within society; and, a human rights discourse which identifies them as a particular 'kind of person', as intersex, and thus a member of a community with shared concerns akin to sexual or gender identity minority groups. These two discourses mediate quite different understandings, advocate different practices and prompt different pathways for the way in which an individual might make sense of their story.

In the next section we will return to more explicitly theological concerns. We will begin by noting the limited nature of the churches' engagement with intersex people and their concerns, and argue that discussion has been framed

---

202 For a dramatic example of the negative aspects of identity politics, see A. Dreger, 'The Controversy Surrounding *The Man Who Would Be Queen*: A Case History of the Politics of Science, Identity, and Sex in the Internet Age' (2008) 37(3) *Archives of Sexual Behaviour* 366–421.

largely by a powerful commitment to defending a binary understanding of gender. Furthermore, that a preoccupation with issues of sexuality and gender in recent decades has dominated the internal dynamics of many Christian denominations, and that the noise of such debates has made it difficult to hear the voice of intersex persons. However, I will also make the case that theology has an important role to play in transcending the regional ethics associated with the divergent discourses we have identified and in drawing attention to a more holistic account of the human condition with the potential to support the flourishing of intersex persons, that they, alongside others, 'may have life, and have it abundantly'.[203]

4. CONTEMPORARY CHRISTIAN THEOLOGY AND INTERSEX

Christianity makes a number of claims about the nature of reality, and the character and destiny of human beings. In this last substantive section, we will consider the ways these claims have been, or might be, realised for individuals with variations of sex development. We will begin by considering the ways in which intersex persons have been treated by the churches, before turning to look at the work of the one theologian, Susannah Cornwall, who has written extensively and engagingly with intersex drawing on the perspectives of disability theology and queer theology, and has sought to resist both the essentialisation of gender difference, but also the identitarian turn.[204] Finally, we will consider how a focus on some of the fundamental characteristics of a Christian theological anthropology could enrich the consideration of intersex issues.

4.1. SOMEWHERE IN THE FOOTNOTES

As a focus for contemporary ecclesial attention on its own terms, intersex has barely broken surface, with explicit discussion of intersex persons within contemporary Church documents and policies being very limited indeed. In this section we will not attempt a wide-ranging survey of the various Christian denominations,[205] but instead briefly provide evidence for a simple

203 John 10:10.

204 Dormor, above n. 2, pp. 56–57.

205 Though were such a review to be conducted particular mention should be made of Sally Gross (1953–2014). Raised as a male person, she was ordained a Dominican priest in 1987. She received a formal intersex diagnosis in 1993 and subsequently adopted a female gender identity. As a consequence, she was no longer permitted to continue in ordained ministry. Sally Gross became the founder of Intersex South Africa and a prominent intersex activist

thesis: namely that, within official Church documents, intersex is framed by wider ecclesial preoccupations with gender and sexuality; specifically, that intersex is put to rhetorical use as 'the exception that proves the rule' by those seeking to withhold or deny legitimacy to advocates of from those who espouse a transgender identity. Let me provide two examples.

The first comes from what is perhaps the only publicly endorsed theological statement on intersex, namely a recent resolution of the Southern Baptist Convention (SBC): 'On Transgender Identity'.[206] As the title suggests, the resolution is primarily concerned with gender identity and an opposition to 'all cultural efforts to validate claims to transgender identity'.[207] In so doing, it affirms 'God's good design' as the 'creation of two distinct and complementary sexes, male and female', a distinction 'embedded in the very biology of the human race'.[208] It also affirms distinctions in 'masculine and feminine roles' to be part of the created order which 'should find expression in every human heart'.[209] Furthermore that gender identity is 'determined by biological sex and not by one's self-perception'.[210] In firmly grounding a clear understanding of biological sex in God's intentions as Creator, the existence of intersex persons, as 'deviations from the binary norm',[211] needs addressing. Having clearly distinguished transgenderism ('psychologically ambiguous') from 'hermaphroditism or intersexualism' ('biologically ambiguous') the SBC further resolves that:

> We grieve the reality of human fallenness which can result in such biological manifestations as intersexuality or psychological manifestations as gender identity confusion and point all to the hope of the redemption of our bodies in Christ.

Given that the creation of male and female is part of God's original 'good design', it would seem that intersex, alongside transgender identity, is thus firmly designated as a *specific* consequence of 'the Fall'; that is of the rebellion of the

---

and speaker. Her story is related in 3 articles by the journalist Stephen Coan in *The Natal Witness:* 'The Journey from Selwyn to Sally', 21.02.2000, <http://www.isna.org/pdf/gross1.pdf>; 'Shunned by the Church', 22.02.2000, <http://www.isna.org/pdf/gross2.pdf>; 'The Struggle to be Sally', 25.02.2000, <http://www.isna.org/pdf/gross3.pdf>, (all last accessed 12.03.2017). See also Cornwall, above n. 53, pp. 10–12; M.K. DeFranza, *Sex Difference in Christian Theology: Male, Female, and Intersex in the Image of God*, Eerdmans, Grand Rapids, Michigan 2015, pp. 13–17; and S. Gross, 'Intersexuality and Scripture' (1999) 11 *Theology and Sexuality* 65–74.

206 SBC, *On Transgender Identity - Baltimore md - 2014*, Resolution 2250, <www.sbc.net/resolutions/2250/on-transgender-identity> (last accessed 20.03.2017). Further discussion can be found in Dormor, above n. 2, pp. 37–38.

207 SBC, ibid, statement 9.

208 Ibid, statement 2.

209 Ibid, statement 3.

210 Ibid, statement 16.

211 A.T. Walker and D. Burk, *National Geographic's 'Gender Revolution': Bad Argument and Biased Ideology*, Public Discourse, 06.01.2017, The Witherspoon Institute, <http://www.thepublicdiscourse.com/2017/01/18491/> (last accessed 02.04.2017).

created human being against the Creator, described in the foundational account of Adam and Eve. It should be noted here that biological sexual dimorphism is being specifically privileged as part of God's design distinct from all other human characteristics, including those variations in human morphology with aetiologies parallel to those of many intersex conditions.

The second example is from a Protestant state church, the Church of England, which has a long tradition of serious engagement with scientific and medical issues. And yet, it is extremely difficult to locate discussion of intersex in any of its official documents. There is, however, the briefest acknowledgement in *Some Issues in Human Sexuality* (SIHS),[212] a document intended to be a wide-ranging consideration of issues of sexuality and gender. The brief reference, which takes the form of a secondary quotation, comes in a chapter given over to a discussion of transsexuality, with which it is contrasted. Here intersex conditions are described as follows: 'hermaphroditism … a congenital disorder in which both male and female gonads are present and the external genitalia are not clearly male or female'.[213] As this brief quotation indicates, the account of intersex within SIHS is remarkably ill-informed, muddled and anachronistic in its reference.[214]

Such dismissive brevity itself is odd given the relative prevalence of intersex and transsexual persons.[215] It is entirely unsurprising however, as the reference comes in the context of arguments about transsexuality: Here, intersex operates as a foil, with a contrast being draw between the indisputable 'concrete set of facts' of biology and the delusional 'state of mind'[216] of the transsexual person

212 The Archbishop's Council, *Some Issues in Human Sexuality: a guide to the debate*, Church House Publishing, London 2003. See also C. Beardsley, 'Nudging towards Serendipity: The Church of England and Transsexual People' (July–September 2013) *Crucible* 17–24.

213 This quotation comes from a longer quotation of R. Holder, 'The Ethics of Transsexualism, Part 1: The Transsexual Condition and the Biblical Background to an Ethical Response' (1998) 37 *Crucible* 89, 90.

214 The shortcomings of this definition, its source in Holder, above n. 213, and similar misunderstandings in another important source for SIHS, namely, Evangelical Alliance Policy Commission, *Transsexuality*, Evangelical Alliance, London 2000, are clearly documented in S. Cornwall, '"State of Mind" versus "Concrete Set of Facts": The Contrasting of Transgender and Intersex in Church Documents on Sexuality' (2009a) 15(1) *Theology and Sexuality* 7–28. The account in SIHS is in stark contrast to the brief reference to intersex and trans experience in Methodist Church of Great Britain, *Report of the Conference Commission on Human Sexuality*, <http://www.methodist.org.uk/who-we-are/views-of-the-church/human-sexuality> (last accessed 01.04.2017), paras. 137, 138. Cornwall comments that this report is 'strikingly well-researched, generous and forward-looking', 16.

215 The omission of a substantial discussion of intersex, 'speaks powerfully of an agenda dominated by the particular dynamics of an internal church debate rather than one that seeks to speak to the diversity of actual human experience and the challenges individuals face'; J. Hare, '"Neither male nor female": the case of intersexuality', in D. Dormor and J. Morris (eds.), *An Acceptable Sacrifice? Homosexuality and the Church*, SPCK, London p. 99. See also Beardsley, above n. 212.

216 Cornwall, above n. 214.

(even when the 'facts' presented are woefully inaccurate). The example of intersex is thus deployed tactically to render transgender less legitimate.[217]

If intersexuality plays the role of a tactical footnote, which helps to advance a claim about transsexuality, then the latter itself constitutes a strategic argument nested within a much wider cultural war in the arena of gender and sexuality.[218] This finds its ecclesial frontline in the controversies around women's ordination and the marriage or blessing of same-sex relationships – but it also reflects a wider conflict focused on gender and sexuality arising in the wake of the increased emancipation of women in the twentieth century, and their greater reproductive and sexual autonomy. This framing set of priorities and concerns has thus reduced intersex to a mere 'adjunct to reflection on transsexualism or homosexuality'.[219] Such erasure further renders the voices of intersex persons marginal and mute within wider society.

4.2. INTERSEX, IDENTITY AND DISABILITY: SUSANNAH CORNWALL

In terms of the theological engagement with issues of intersex, one theologian, Susannah Cornwall, stands out, in terms of the extent, depth and quality of her engagement.[220] An Anglican theologian, she has advanced the case for a proper consideration of intersex in relation to many of the major categories of theology – including Christology, eschatology and anthropology.[221] In seeking to 'resist oppressive ideologies'[222] that, through their privileging of 'discrete and stable sex-gender identities',[223] erase and marginalise the voices and experience of intersex people, Cornwall draws primarily on queer and disability theologies. In so doing, and in seeking to 'render intersex/DSD theologically meaningful', it is then inevitable that 'the strands within theology which have

217 Ibid, 14–16.

218 The relatively pragmatic approach taken by the Church of England bishops in the House of Lords during the debate on the Gender Recognition Act, 2006 suggests that transsexuality *per se* is not an issue of fundamental principle; see Dormor, above n. 2, pp. 67–73.

219 S. Cornwall, 'Theologies of Resistance: Intersex/DSD, Disability and Queering the Real World', in M. Holmes (ed.), *Critical Intersex*, Ashgate, Farnham, 2009b, p. 215.

220 Though see also Defranza, above n. 205.

221 See S. Cornwall, 'Intersex, Christology, and the Maleness of Jesus' (2014) 30(2) *Journal of Feminist Studies in Religion* 23–39; S. Cornwall, 'Asking About What Is Better: Intersex, Disability, and Inaugurated Eschatology' (2013)b 17(4) *Journal of Religion, Disability & Health* 369–392; and S. Cornwall, 'Intersex and the Rhetorics of Disability and Disorder: Multiple and Provisional Significance in Sexed, Gender, and Disabled Bodies' (2015)b 19(2) *Journal of Disability and Religion* 106–118.

222 Cornwall, above n. 219, p. 223.

223 Cornwall, above n. 214, 7, 8.

privileged heteronormativity and unambiguous sex' are themselves called into question and found wanting.[224]

In this, Cornwall's theological analysis resonates with the work of historians and historical theologians whose work draws attention to the plurality of gender constructions within Christian history.[225] Taking the 'existence of bodies which differ from the expected physiological norms' seriously[226] inevitably prompts theological reflection that challenges the two-sex model and the theological writings of apologists for the 'male-and-female' account of gender. However, Cornwall goes further, and in her robust criticism of this dominant view, she turns to the central theological category of idolatry: thus, she writes of the challenge intersex makes to the 'cult of all-encompassing male-and-female' that seeks to 'protect and fetishize a non-existent truth'; of 'resistance to the twin idols of male-and-female and heteronormativity'; and, of the apotheosis of heterosexual intercourse and 'patriarchal social and familial structures'. In so doing, Cornwall seeks to bring into sharper focus the 'anti-imperial, anti-idolatrous and anti-monolithic'[227] strands of Christian theology; and, to value the 'marginal and polyphonic voices in theology'.[228]

This theological exposure of the dominant model of man-and-woman as idolatrous and as a 'socially limiting construct'[229] brings in its wake, for Cornwall, clear implications for both theological anthropology and ethics. In articulating resistance to theologies that sacralise gender roles and procreative capacity at the expense of marginalised human groups, Cornwall's account resonates strongly with the challenge to hegemonic masculinity laid down by Jesus as recorded in the *Gospel of Matthew* (19:12). Similarly, in emphasising the theological importance of human diversity Cornwall echoes St. Augustine's firm affirmation in the *City of God* through her statement that 'the image of God is not reflected more perfectly in some ... human bodies than in others'.[230] This flows immediately into practical ethical application: 'human bodies need not be altered to "fit"', and as a corollary 'the Church must speak *with* those whose bodies and souls are written out of legitimacy'. Thus, in rejecting the dominant model operating within the Church as a 'system of privilege', Cornwall envisages:

> The end of exclusivity, heteronormativity, and a model of complementarity which erodes difference even as it prescribes it. This also means no more taxonomies of

---

224 Cornwall, above n. 53, p. 231.

225 See, e.g. nn. 60 and 77 above. See also e.g., C.W. Bynum, *Jesus as Mother: Studies in the Spirituality of the High Middle Ages*, University of California Press, Berkeley 1982, and L. Gowing, M. Hunter and M. Rubin, *Love, Friendship and Faith in Europe, 1300–1800*, Palgrave, Basingstoke 2005.

226 Cornwall, above n. 53, p. 231.

227 Ibid, pp. 231–236.

228 Cornwall, above n. 219, p. 222.

229 Cornwall, above n. 53, p. 232.

230 Ibid, p. 234.

> goodness of perfection attached to how a body meets heteronormative criteria for maleness or femaleness, and no more annexations of bodies by misplaced moralistic pronouncements about how a small decent clitoris or a large, powerful penis should look.[231]

Cornwall's approach to the subject starts from an understanding that there is a basic affinity between intersex and impairment or disability, rather than locating intersex concerns within an identitarian discourse about gender and sexuality. Thus, Cornwall seeks to construe or reconfigure intersex conditions:

> as physical variations akin to impairments – which may preclude particular, limited physical activity, or may simply appear as physiological difference, but in no way compromise the personhood or predetermine the gender identity of the individuals involved.[232]

Whilst this approach echoes the logic of the medics who seek to portray DSD as simply 'one disorder' among others, Cornwall's sympathies lie firmly with those theologians who construe intersex as a 'nonpathological variation' in contrast to those theologians who perceive something which is disordered and falls 'short of a divinely instituted plan'.[233] Indeed she draws attention to the fact that the Christian intersex persons she interviewed frequently interpreted their condition as 'intended'; as a 'gift' from God.[234] Such ideas are clearly highly problematic within the medical discourse, yet in terms of the narrative of an individual's identity, such an understanding, and crucially the associated self-acceptance, makes a great deal of existential sense.

Thus, as Cornwall points out, many of the concerns around authority and subjectivity faced by people with intersex conditions, or their parents on their behalf, are very similar to those that disability activists have sought to address over many years. Most intersex persons are not, she argues, looking for a politicised identity, a third gender or seeking to identify as queer. Rather, drawing on reflections from theologies of disability, Cornwall seeks to call mainstream theology to account where it makes 'pronouncements about the cosmic significance of different types of bodies in the first place'.[235] As a natural corollary, Cornwall poses the hypothetical question: Was Jesus Christ an intersex person? Whilst statistically unlikely and impossible to establish, her point is to argue that theologies that are dependent on the maleness of Jesus need to

---

231 Ibid, pp. 232–233.
232 Cornwall, above n. 219, p. 217.
233 Cornwall (2014), above n. 221, 23, 30.
234 Ibid, 30–31; see also O'Brien, above n. 155.
235 Cornwall, above n. 219, pp. 218–219.

be interrogated, in the light of the existence of the unusually-sexed bodies of intersex persons.[236]

In articulating a range of theological responses that explicitly address the lives of those of embodied difference, Cornwall has made a wide-ranging and uniquely important contribution and has laid down a clear challenge to the Christian community to rethink its approach. In drawing this chapter to a conclusion I offer some final reflections on some closely related dimensions of theological anthropology – the transcendent, teleological, holistic, relational and particular – which may enhance our collective aspirations for those with unusually sexed bodies to help realise more fully the accomplished life with others in just institutions.

4.3. TOWARDS A CHRISTIAN ANTHROPOLOGY FOR INTERSEX

For the theologian, the existence of intersex persons is primarily an issue of theological anthropology: the way in which Christians have thought about the human person; the grounding of personhood and personal identity, and in this instance the significance of variantly sexed bodies in relation to the fields of gender and sexuality. As we have noted above there are some deep and persistent tensions within society and its constituent spheres that frustrate the ways in which intersex persons might pursue the 'accomplished life, with and for others in just institutions'.[237]

The foundation is clear: namely that all human beings are made in the image of God, *imago Dei*, and that a human person's being, value, identity and destiny find their ultimate grounding in the divine. Augustine's discussion in the *City of God* provides a clear illustration of this, as does the consistent inclusivity of the practice of Christian baptism. This transcendent grounding for anthropology is unapologetically *ec-static;* that is, in such an account, the human being cannot be truly comprehended by human investigation: personhood exceeds and 'goes beyond'; this conception stands against all culturally particular, reductive, instrumental or narrow conceptions of the *conditio humana* rooted in human ideologies or particular epistemological frameworks, that by design or default, often lead to the stigmatisation and the 'othering' of particular groups. In its

236 Cornwall (2014), above n. 221, 23, 24–27. The articulation of such ideas can generate powerful responses in conservative Christian circles. Over 13,000 people signed a petition, *STOP Blasphemous Speaker at Santa Clara University. Defend Our Lord*, to try to ensure that an invitation extended to Dr. Cornwall to speak at the Jesuit University of Santa Clara University was withdrawn. See <https://www.tfpstudentaction.org/news/public-blasphemer-invited-to-speak-at-jesuit-santa-clara-university> (last accessed 06.05.2017). See also, the blog of Lutheran pastor, Clint Schnekloth, at <http://lutheranconfessions.blogspot.co.uk/2016/04/was-jesus-intersex.html> (last accessed 06.05.2017).

237 Ricoeur (1999), above n. 4, p. 45.

affirmation that all individuals have an inherent and inalienable dignity, this universalistic vision thus relativises all human distinctions and categories. As a consequence, persons can never be reduced simply to political actors or legal personae or medical cases. We are all – all these – and so much more. So, notwithstanding the necessity in particular situations for certain aspects of a person to be foregrounded (and others hidden), in say the courtroom or when under medical examination, each and every individual person exceeds such designations. Similarly, accounts of personhood that place too much emphasis on one aspect of our condition or reify a particular identification, say as female or gay or intersex, also misconstrue our nature: the danger here lies in the misrepresentation, the non-recognition, even the erasure of persons who do not 'fit' or conform to a dominant, or frequently, coercive categorisation. Efforts to provide a sufficient account of personhood will thus continue to engage and elude philosophers and theologians and poets – resolution being endlessly deferred. For as St. Augustine, among others, observed we are mysteries to ourselves.[238]

The assertion of a transcendent, ecstatic grounding of human nature is simultaneously a statement about our nature and value. For in addition to seeking an understanding of the human condition, the *imago Dei* also testifies to an inalienable quality and value, such that no human beings should ever be considered instrumentally, as a means to an end. The claim that we are all made *imago Dei* thus has concrete implications providing an important intellectual counterpoint or corrective to culturally dominant patterns of thinking that shape assumptions and thinking, and ultimately policies and practices, and puts us on guard against truncated and reductive accounts of the human person.

Equally, Christian anthropology is *teleological* in character, that is, it recognises that human persons, being temporal, are oriented to the future. As human beings, we hope, and therefore strive for particular goods and goals (to be married, have children, a rewarding occupation, etc.); we have a sense of purpose, of living towards, and thus invest our activities and projects with meaning. This in turn shapes who we become. Thoroughly embedded in historical and cultural contexts, an individual's investment in meaning cannot be detached from dominant regimes of understanding. In terms of the larger narrative of Christianity we have therefore noted above a tension between one account of gender, which draws a sharp line between the sexes and sees gender as destiny; and, a second view, which understands a paradisiac humanity to transcend gender – that 'in Christ' there is 'no longer male and female'.[239] The first of these views makes for a discourse that is inhospitable to the intersex person, providing little space for bodies that are variantly sexed: A straitjacket, the freedom of

[238] Saint Augustine, *Confessions*, H. Chadwick (ed.), Oxford University Press, Oxford 1998, especially Book X, pp. 179–220.

[239] Galatians 3:28.

the individual is significantly restrained and embodied and psychological harms may well be inflicted. As individuals cannot but partake of wider cultural narratives to construct their own worlds of meaning, a strong argument can be advanced that this theological version of the 'true sex' discourse is damaging to the well-being of many individuals, inhibiting their ability to realise moral equality with others. By contrast, without endorsing his patriarchal assumptions, Augustine's robust theological legitimation of morphological variation grounded in God's creative purposes seems positively liberating, and it is noteworthy that, at least in some assessments, hermaphrodites in the medieval world enjoyed 'considerable individual freedom' extending on occasion to a choice of gender.[240] Similarly, the eschatological critique of kinship and of the traditional commandment to 'go forth and multiply' alongside the rehabilitation of the eunuch in Matthew's Gospel created new spaces within early Christianity where individuals could be recognised and fully accepted without producing offspring: procreation was thus no longer an essential requirement of the accomplished life.

Turning to the individual seeking to making sense of their own story, it is striking that at least some intersex people feel able to affirm their embodied condition as a 'gift', even 'God-given'.[241] More broadly, it is important to facilitate individuals' capacity to narrate their own story in light of the dominant discourse of modern medicine, which has unwittingly acted as a cultural gatekeeper to acceptable personhood, and more recently that of activists and political institutions with their identitarian advocacy. Both have impaired the capacity of individuals to narrate their own story: however, this is most serious and concrete in the approach that perceives the intersex infant to be a 'problem to be fixed'. Here contemporary medical practice, lacking a teleological orientation, has failed 'the eventual adult' by denying them the choice to make their own decision about their body, in addition to the imposition of frequent additional harms in the form of secrecy and shame.[242] The argument that physicians have no particular obligation to diverge from the dominant values of society and that an uncritical continuance of cosmetic or 'normalising' surgery misses the key point: namely that the patient is not being given full consideration as a person. It is an undue focus on the somatic and the neglect of the teleological dimension of personhood that is crucial here.

A third characteristic of Christian anthropology then is its *holistic* orientation: that is, it recognises that a number of different aspects constitute our deep core – the organic, that is the body; the psychological, our consciousness and emotions; and, the social. Further, that our nature as persons cannot be simply reduced to one of these elements. It is perhaps particularly important to note in this

240 Rolker, above n. 16, 178, 221.

241 O'Brien, above n. 155; Cornwall (2014), above n. 221, 23, 31–32.

242 Holmes, above n. 160, 169, 179.

context that Christian anthropology takes the body seriously; that we *are* bodies rather than merely *have* bodies. This emphasis is underlined by the centrality that the doctrine of the incarnation plays within mainstream Christian theology that insists that in addition to being divine, Jesus Christ must be understood to be fully and truly human.

Both of the contemporary discourses under discussion above, in their different ways, have the potential to marginalise the self-consciousness and agency of the intersex person: within the medical discourse, there is a risk that the intersex person is rendered a 'pathological object';[243] whereas within the political discourse there is a danger that the individuality of a person is eroded in favour of a collective identity. Both have a clear interest and concern with the 'intelligibility' of the individual within wider society, yet in both cases the recognition of the individual person is to some degree contingent – either on the normal appearance of their genitalia or their adoption of an identity.

A deeper appreciation of the holistic character of the human condition can also draw our attention to deeper cultural patterns. So, for example, the philosopher, Ludwig Wittgenstein, a person of significant religious sensibility, observed a number of general tendencies deeply embedded within the weave of Enlightenment thinking: namely, that it was deeply dualistic; averse to the reality of human finitude and mortality; and, showed a disinclination to engage with particularity.[244] The existence of such tendencies helps to explain how the infant surgery protocols of John Money became so influential, so swiftly, in the early 1960s.[245] So, in his analysis, Morland argues that a utopian humanist strain of thought, which emphasised the plasticity of human nature and prioritised the educative nature of the social over the material nature of the human body, played a key role in the appropriation of Money's ideas through its shaping of background assumptions.[246] Articulating an understanding of the human that fully embraces materiality, finitude and limits, including our mortality is thus an important corrective to such culturally dominant understandings. Similarly it is crucial to appreciate that we are not simply, or always, autonomous subjects exercising our choices and expressing our preferences, but are also suffering and uncertain persons caught up in a web of reciprocity and obligation with others.

---

243 Hester, above n. 149, 21, 38.

244 See e.g. the discussion of Wittgenstein in Williams, above n. 36, p. 189: 'the bondage of European thought to an epistemological problematic that remains obstinately dualist and so obstinately discontented with finitude.'

245 Morland, above n. 20.

246 Money's publications were 'singularly influential in shaping medical theory and practice' and deemed 'self-evidently right' because: '... humanism has been fundamental to the establishment of surgery as a medical protocol. Specifically ... the notion of human genitals and gender as surgically and socially plastic depends on the conceptualization in twentieth century science of plasticity as a quintessential human attribute'; Morland, above n. 20, p. 69.

Christian anthropology is thus also deeply *relational*. It conceives of the individual human discovering who they are and finding fulfilment in relationship 'with, and for others', summarised in the command 'to love God, and your neighbour as yourself'.[247] Again, it is not simply that there is an ethical imperative placed upon individuals to reach out to others in compassion, but rather that to be human is to be implicated in webs of obligation and reciprocity.[248] For the Christian we are 'made' for relationship and it is in relationship with others that we become more fully ourselves; good relationships have a demonstrably positive impact upon our physical and mental well-being; they constitute armour against *anomie*. The intersex person needs to be fully accepted and welcomed on their own terms within their families, amongst peers and neighbours, and treated equitably by the institutions of society. Anything that does not lead to full inclusion in the social contract, but to an unequal access to the goods and services of society, infringes on the ability of the individual to achieve moral equality with their peers and to live the most accomplished life of which they are capable.

Finally, Christian anthropology recognises the significance of our *particularity*, that there is an irreducible uniqueness to each individual person: That we are, in the words of the Psalmist, 'fearfully and wonderfully made'.[249] This affirmation is crucial in light of societies' intolerance of anomaly borne of the dynamics that establish social solidarity and of notions of idealised or Platonic forms of the human that seem to haunt our various discourses. Similarly, we are all 'roughly hewn' or in Augustine's language 'marvels' and his theological legitimation of human difference and plurality should be understood as axiomatic.

5. CONCLUSION

As Judith Butler observes:

> There is no 'I' that can fully stand apart from the social conditions of its emergence, no 'I' that is not implicated in a set of conditioning moral norms, which, being norms, have a social character that exceeds a purely personal or idiosyncratic meaning.[250]

This is perhaps especially clear when the 'I' in question is a person of unusual sexed embodiment. For such individuals have found themselves within the arc

---

247 Known as the Great Commandment, Jesus is recorded as citing it in Mark 12:28–31; Matthew 22:35–40 and Luke 10:25–28.

248 e.g. Feder also notes the 'collateral damage' experienced by siblings of intersex infants who have undergone surgery; Feder (2014), above n. 8, pp. 91–92, 103–106.

249 Psalm 139:14.

250 Butler, above n. 10, p. 7.

of history encompassed within distinctive historic personages – like the eunuch, hermaphrodite or intersexual – and been constantly subjected to the powerful effects of hegemonic gender. As a consequence, the history of intersex has been characterised by 'a kind of cyclic movement'[251] in which such individuals have been periodically perceived as a threat to society, and as a consequence subjected to forms of sanctioned violence.

For such individuals today, seeking to make sense of their embodiment, their own life stories and their place in society, two powerful but conflicting discourses anchored in different regions of society confront them offering to frame their experience in terms of either an identity or a disorder. I have argued that these, the discourses of human rights and medicine respectively, conflict primarily because of the character of their core activities and their associated paradigms. As a consequence, such discourses tend to relate to the individual person in a selective and truncated fashion (e.g. as a patient or citizen), which can hinder an individual's capacity to generate a coherent self-narrative. So, for example, as Holmes points out, within the medical framework, clinicians can 'easily conflate disease and difference, suffering and impairment'.[252]

Nevertheless, this dissensus also reflects a wider realignment in society as the dominant social model of (binary) gender has itself become 'a site of contest, a theme and an object of democratic debate'.[253]

In this chapter I have sought to set the issues facing contemporary individuals with unusual sexed embodiment in a theological frame that grounds moral reflection in theological anthropology: in particular, in the claim that all humans share a fundamental moral equality, being made *imago Dei* and desiring an accomplished life of moral equality with others in which they are treated equitably by human institutions. In my account, I have suggested that theological anthropology through its emphasis on a number of aspects of the human condition – teleological, relational, holistic and particularistic – gives us a better handle on the complexity and mystery of being mortal; of living 'in the constraints of a finite and material world without resentment',[254] as well as operating as a helpful corrective to more selective or totalising interpretations of personhood.

---

251 Feder (2014), above n. 8, p. 22.
252 Holmes, above n. 160, 169, 178.
253 Butler, above n. 10, p. 6.
254 Williams, above n. 36, p. 186.

FOUR SEXES, TWO GENDERS: THE RABBINIC MOVE FROM LEGAL TO ESSENTIALIST POLARISATION OF IDENTITIES

Moshe LAVEE and Tali ARTMAN PARTOCK*

Early Rabbinic Judaism is the name given to the group of people who produced, from the first to approximately the seventh century CE, the post Biblical canonic texts of Judaism. This 'new' Judaism, which grew in parallel to early Christianity, was highly invested in the concept of law. This is reflected not only in interpreting the Hebrew Bible which is considered to be a book of laws, but also in the production of a legal codex of their own time (the Mishnah, edited in the early third century),[1] and its interpretations (the Palestinian Talmud, edited in the fifth century, and the Babylonian Talmud, which had several layers of editing, the latest of which is in the seventh century). These legal codices still serve as the basis for any ruling on questions relating to intersex people in Jewish law, and often in Israeli law.[2]

---

* The authors are aware that some of the language and terminology used in this chapter may be offensive. This is a result of the source language of the texts discussed. The authors wish to emphasise that these are the terms and conceptualisations of texts from the first half of the first millennium, not their own.

1 A. TROPPER, *Wisdom, Politics, and Historiography: Tractate Avot in the Context of the Graeco-Roman Near East*, Oxford University Press, Oxford 2004, pp. 190–207.

2 See H. GREY, 'Not Judging by Appearances: The Role of Genotype in Jewish Law on Intersex Conditions' (2012) 30(4) *Shofar* 126–148; J. WIESE AND D. KULAK, 'Male and female He created them: revisiting gender assignment and treatment in Intersex Children' (2007) 54 *Journal of Halacha and Contemporary Society* 5–29; M. WENIG, 'Male and female, God created them? The intersex, transgender, and transsexual in Jewish tradition and in our lives' (2012) 59(4) *CCAR Journal* 130–142.

In this chapter we wish to portray the ways in which rabbinic literature bridged the gap between a classification system which acknowledges more than two sexes, and a legal system (based on the Biblical law) which only thinks with two sexes and two genders, or rather, does not differentiate between sex and gender. We also wish to point to an historical process by which the recognition of existence of more than two sexes was gradually rejected, as the binary categories of men/women and gender division became more important and constructed.

Rabbinic literature is an interesting *locus* not only of itself, but also in comparison to Roman law and modern law. It addresses gender and sex division in a manner that echoes the ways we tend to think of as modern and born out of the spirit of feminism and deconstruction. Those ancient Jewish texts ask: are there indeed only two sexes? Does the mere recognition that there are indeed more create any implications to the status of such individuals in society? How does a legal system, which is based on a code that only recognises two sexes, incorporate and interpret the natural and discursive reality of more?

What we will show is that while rabbinic literature is able to acknowledge and even categorise different intersex people, the legal system often pushes those people into gender categories as either men or women.

1. A PRELIMINARY TAXONOMY OF THE TANNAITIC SEXES

The Tannaitic texts, i.e. those rabbinic traditions from the first to the third century (and especially the Mishnah, the early rabbinic codex from which any further discussion in Jewish law stems), know of at least four biological sexes: *male*, *female*, *androgynes*[3] and *tumtum*, for humans and animals alike. Male and female, while never properly defined in the Mishnah, are clearly those who are born with either male of female genitals. The *androgynes* is defined as exhibiting both male and female genitalia, in part or in full.[4] It is debated in the texts whether an *androgynes* is able to reproduce.[5] The *tumtum* is a person that lacks

3 As used in legal materials in the rabbinic corpus, the *androgynes* is one born with both male and female genitalia. We intentionally use the Greek loanword used in rabbinic literature אנדרוגינס (*androgynes*, as spelt in good manuscripts of Tannaitic works) and not the English term 'hermaphrodite', which derived from a different concept.

4 Notice the difference between the rabbinic *androgynes* and the Roman hermaphrodite here. If a man has only feminine secondary sex marks (breasts) he is not considered an *androgynes* (Mishan Berkhorot 7:5), but rather a male with a blemish. See I. Rosen-Zvi, 'The Body and the Temple: on the List of Blemishes in the Priestly Body in Mishnah Bekhorort' (2006) *Jewish Studies* 43, 49–87.

5 There seems to be a disagreement on the issue of whether the *androgynes* is sterile or not. Palestinian Talmud Yebamot 2:4 suggests he/she cannot bear children as a man; Mishnah Bikkurinm 4:2 however, argues that he/she is bound to all commandments which men are bound to, which would include procreation.

any visible reproductive organs.[6] There is, however, an assumption that even if such organs cannot be seen they are present in the *tumtum's* body.

To these, some more categories might be added: one mythical, and others real. In the mythic time of creation, there existed a human, much like the one in Plato's Symposium, which was made out of a full male and full female body joined at the back, named in rabbinic literature double-faced – *dupartẓufin*.[7] Unlike in Plato's symposium, in rabbinic literature, this mythical creature has nothing to do with the etiology of desire. Rather it solves the riddle of Genesis 1:27 'So God created man in his own image, in the image of God he created *them*; male *and* female he created *them*.'[8] As this human form is no longer present at the time of the rabbis, and there is no need to make any legal decisions regarding it, and it is seldom discussed. In rabbinic legal reality, however, not only do we know of four sexes, but there also existed categories that blur the lines between sex and reproductive ability, while keeping the category of gender stable. The *saris* and the *aylonit*, the respective man and woman who have not developed normal (either primary or secondary) sex characteristics, are assumed not to be able to reproduce. *Saris* is a term also used to denote men who lost their ability to reproduce due to illness or to damage caused to their penis or testicles. While the terms are gender specific (*aylonit* for a woman and *saris* for a man), their bodies are often described as manifesting traits that the rabbis see as marking the opposite sex. Some of those bodies have much in common with the humans that the Romans named hermaphrodites – bearded ladies or men with a high-pitched voice and no body hair. While the *saris* and the a*ylonit's* genders clearly are recognised, their sex (and with it some aspects of their humanity) are not. Cross-dressing, non-heteronormative sexual practices and sexuality in and of itself do not seem to influence the rabbinic categorisation of a person as male or female, man or woman.[9]

---

6 It is assumed that a piece of skin is covering those organs that do exist within the *tumtum's* body. This skin may accidently be torn and expose the *tumtum* as either male or female, as described in Mishnah Yebamot 8:6, Midrash Tannaim on Deuteronomy, 21:18, Babylonian Talmud Bava Batra 126b.

7 On the relationship between the rabbinic and the Greek myths, see G. Hasan Rokem and I. Yuval, 'Myth, History and Eschatology in a Rabbinic Treatise on Birth', in C.E. Fonrobert, I. Rosen-Zvi, A. Shemesh and M. Vidas (eds.), Talmudic Transgressions: Engaging the Work of Daniel Boyarin, Brill, Leiden 2017, pp. 252–253. See also W. Meeks, 'The Image of the Androgynes: Some Uses of a Symbol in Earliest Christianity' (1974) 13 *History of Religions* 165–208, 185.

8 Since the story is known to the earliest Amoraic midrashim Genesis Rabbah (17:6) and Leviticus Rabbah (15:1) which quote different rabbis telling it, we may assume it was 'common knowledge' by the 4th century. Boyarin sees it as a rabbinic response to Hellenistic culture. See D. Boyarin, *Carnal Israel: Reading Sex in Talmudic Culture*, University of California Press, Berkeley 1993, pp. 35–46. Hasan Rokem and Yuval, following Runnia, suggest that the development of the motif of the *androgynes* from Philo to the rabbis can be formulated as proceeding from the non-sexed to the multisexed being. (Hasan Rokem and Yuval, above n. 7, 254)

9 See Rozen-Zvi above note 4.

2. EARLY v. LATE, ISRAEL v. BABYLON

After this basic mapping of the sexes, we would like to focus on the process by which the Tannaitic deliberations of the first two centuries in the Land of Israel about intersex people, gradually transform into almost a negation of the existence of such humans in the Amoraic period, and specifically in the Babylonian Talmud, a creation of the fourth to sixth centuries.

We can identify two stages in the conceptual development of polarisation of identity.[10] The Tannaitic legal system developed in the Mishnah and the Tosefta generally tend to think in binary oppositions, and define polarised legal categories: there are laws for Jews and laws for non-Jews; laws for minors and laws for adults; laws for men and laws for women and so forth. However, within this dichotomist system, questions arise about those who are 'neither here nor there' and about border-line cases. Tannaitic treatment of both gender and group demarcation (for example) is acknowledging the possibility of the existence of interstitial entities, and the possibility of 'third' categories arises.[11] However, as Fonrobert already noticed, since the legal system is made out of laws that are abiding for men and laws that are abiding for women, the liminal cases where sex and gender do not overlap pose a challenge to the system itself. In the case of intersex persons, the questions are many, but they all revolve around one dilemma: Should the laws regarding the *androgynes* and *tumtum* follow those that apply to men or those that apply to women?[12]

In the second stage, which comes to its fruition in the Babylonian Talmud, a discursive turn can be identified, giving voice to a new and gradually prevailing perspective in which the binary thrust is shifted from the realm of legal categories to an essential understanding of reality, namely of the so-called 'real' nature of the body. Within this framework the world is understood to consist of people who are either male or female, men or women. In this essentialist turn both the

---

10 For the notion of polarisation in the Mishnah in this regard, see S. Fishbane, 'Towards an Understanding of the Methodology of the Mishnah: The Case of Kutim', in *Deviancy in Early Rabbinic Literature*, Brill, Leiden 2007, pp. 121–140.

11 C. Fonrobert, 'Regulating the Human Body: Rabbinic Legal Discourse and the Making of Jewish Gender', in C. Fonrobert and M. Jaffee, (eds.), *The Cambridge Companion to the Talmud and Rabbinic Literature*, Cambridge University Press, New York 2007, pp. 270–294 pointed to the *koi* as one example of this. See also M. Lavee, 'The Samaritan may be included: another look at the Samaritan in Talmudic literature', in M. Mor and F.V. Reiterer (eds.), *Samaritans - Past and Present; Current Studies*, De Gruyter, Berlin 2010, pp. 147–173; M. Lavee, 'No Boundaries to the Demarcation of Boundaries: The Babylonian Talmud's Emphasis on Demarcation of Identity', in T. Ilan and R. Nikolsky (eds.), *Rabbinic Traditions between Palestine and Babylonia*, Brill, Leiden/Boston 2014, pp. 84–116.

12 See Fonrobert, above n. 11; C. Fonrobert, 'The Semiotics of the Sexed Body in Early Halakhic Discourse', in M Kraus (ed.), *Closed and Open: Readings of Rabbinic Texts*, Gorgias Press, New York 2006, pp. 69–96. Note especially her observation that the dual gender system is rooted in the Biblical heritage as understood by the rabbis.

understanding of the physical and the legal world represented in the Tannaitic texts is revised. The problem of the discrepancy in the number of sexes and gender is resolved by negating the existence of more than two sexes, and treating intersex people as cases of doubt.

We will proceed by examining the cases of *androgynes* and *tumtum* studied together, and then the cases in which they are discussed separately. Tosefta Bikkurim 2:3–7, the text which serves as the basis of any further discussion of intersex people in rabbinic literature, engages mostly with the case of *androgynes*, yet, it also refers to the *tumtum*, and to the different categorisation of *androgynes* and *tumtum*. Tosefta Bikkurim 2:3–7 reads:

> The *androgynes* is in some ways like men, and in some ways like women, and in some ways is like both men and women, and in some ways is like neither men nor women.
>
> Ways in which he[13] like men: He is rendered unclean by whiteness [=seminal emission] as men are, he marries but is not taken in marriage [...] does not receive maintenance with the daughter, like men [...]; Ways in which he is like women: He is rendered impure by redness [=menstrual blood] as women are, he may not remain alone with men, like women [...]; Ways by which he is similar to men and women: [...] the ones who kills him intentionally is put to death; unintentionally, is banished to the cities of refuge. His mother [...] should bring a sacrifice on accounts of the birth of [both] a male and female. Ways in which he is similar neither to a man nor a woman: [...] If one said: I will be a Nazirite if this one is not a man and [not] a woman, he is a Nazirite. R. Yose said: an *androgynes* is a kind to itself [sui generis] and the sages could not decide whether it is a man or a woman. But this is not so regarding the *tumum*, who is either a doubtful male or a doubtful female.[14]

As already noted by Fonrobert, this key Tannaitic text concerning the *androgynes* and the *tumtum* defines in which cases the laws regarding them follow those of men, and in which cases the laws follow those of women. We, however, wish to stress the Tosefta's argument that in some cases they should follow both the laws of men and the laws of women. The *androgynes* becomes not only physically but also legally both male and female. This is manifested in the clearest way in the case of the Nazirite, a man who took a vow to abstain from something if his soon-to-be-born child will be of a certain sex. If the child is born *androgynes*, the man's vow is held to be valid, no matter which sex he wished for, as the baby is both male and female. Since no sex can be ruled out regarding the baby the man's vow must also be fulfilled.[15]

---

13 Hebrew does not have a neutrum. It does, however, use the masculine form as a substitute for it in some cases. We preferred 'he' to 'it' in the English translation, in order to avoid objectifying intersex people, and to better reflect the Hebrew source.

14 We refer here to the Tosefta and not the Mishnah as it preserves, in this case, the earlier version of the text.

15 Mishnah Nazir 2:7.

Tumtum, however, is mentioned only in the very last part of the Tosefta, as a being different from *androgynes*. The *tumtum* is a case of a doubt (about his/her sex), as the sex organs, and therefore the sex of the baby cannot be observed.[16]

The sages grasp that the nature of *androgynes* cannot be contained within the existing categories, and hence declare it, in fact, a third sex.

Whereas some Tannaitic midrashim (collections of Biblical exegeses from the early rabbinic period, the time of the Mishnah) seem to be implying the concept of doubt, others seem to go the opposite way and consider both the *tumtum* and the *androgynes* as distinct entities and even distinct legal categories.[17] In such texts we typically find statements considering the Biblical categories of 'male' and 'female' as different from *tumtum* or *androgynes*. One example is found in Sifra Nedava 16:2 14c:

> 'Male of female' (Leviticus 3:6) – [These categories refer to] an absolute [undoubtedly] male and an absolute [undoubtedly] female, but not to a *tumtum* and an *androgynes*.

From reading this source it becomes clear that the *tumtum* and *androgynes* are considered neither male nor female. The same holds true in another Tannaitic source, Mekhilta de-Rabbi Yishmael, Nezikin 11:

> 'If it [a bull] gores a son or a daughter, the owner shall be dealt with according to this same rule' (Exodus 21:31). Why is this said? It had already been said 'it killed a man or a woman' (Exodus, 21:29). Surly the verse refers to adults,[18] but where do we learn it [the law] applies to [the goring] of minors too? It is said 'if it gores a son or a daughter'. We should read 'that is absolutely a son and or absolutely a daughter,' so where do we learn that this law applies also to *androgynes* and *tumtum*? It is said 'It (a bull) gores a son *or* a daughter' (Exodus 21:31).

From this rather strange discussion of what is the liability of a bull's owner in case it gores different people, we learn about rabbinic categories. The owner

---

16 Note the difference between being a case of doubt – which is the status of any given *tumtum* – and being a person the sex of whom the sages could not determine. The concept implied here is that since the sages cannot decide if this person is male or female, it is not considered a sex unto itself.

17 The concept of 4 distinct genders implied in texts like Mekhilta de-Rabbi Yishmael, Parasha Bo, 4, p. 12: 'a male – this excludes *tumtum*, *androgynes* and a female'. Such texts clearly consider both a *tumtum* and an *androgynes* to be separate categories and sexes. Note the treatment of such exegetics in Babylonian Talmud Hagigah 4a, where we see how the Babylonian Talmud actually undermines the concept of 4 different sexes.
It is important to note that a similar discursive pattern is found in a Tannaitic Midrash concerning converts, and it was suppressed in later layers of rabbinic literature (see a survey of these sources in M. Lavee, *A Convert Is like a Newborn Child: The Concept and its Implications in Rabbinic Literature*, Ph.D. Dissertation, Ben-Gurion University of the Negev, Beer-Sheva, 2003 [Hebrew], pp. 81–86.

18 In the category of 'son and daughter' mentioned in the Bible.

of the bull is considered liable for its beast's goring of both *androgynes* and a *tumtum*, since an *androgynes* is considered to be both a son and a daughter, and the *tumtum* either a son or daughter.

Sifra Nega'im 6:1 (65b) follows the same logic:

> Only a man *and* a woman. And how do we learn this applies to *androgynes* and *tumtum*? It was said man *or* woman.

What we see in both the Sifra and the Mekhilta cases stems from the ambivalence of meaning imbedded in the Hebrew grammar where 'and' and 'or' may both be implied by the same prefix ('ve').

Tumtum and *androgynes* are categorised as legally different from both male and female. The wording often used is 'man and woman' to describe both an *androgynes* and a *tumtum*. This is especially interesting because it operates a logic not of 'either/or' but rather of 'this and that'. The intersex person is not considered a flawed male or female, but a normal male-and-also-female human. The questions that all legal sources essentially ask are how can we still follow Biblical law, even if it does not include the category of intersex people? How should we interpret the law, after we added to our legal system classifications of which it was ignorant? The issues are resolved by paying special attention to conjunctions. In cases where the Bible has 'man *and* woman' or 'man *or* woman'[19] the rabbis of the first two centuries interpret these expressions as including intersex people, as they have both male and female traits. Intersex people, and especially *androgynes* are a third sex, and their legal status is read into the Biblical law by means of creative use of grammar.

But the *tumtum* and the *androgynes* are not always categorised together. Often while the *androgynes* is considered a third sex, the *tumtum* is categorised as a case of doubt about one's 'real' sex. Such is the case in Tosefta Megillah 2:7:

> All are obliged to read the megillah [=the Scroll of Esther, during the festival of Purim]: Priests, Levites and Israelites, converts, freed slaves, disqualified priests ... a *saris adam* (eunuch by man's hand) and *saris hammah* (congenital eunuch), those with damaged testicles, those lacking a penis – all of them are liable. All of them have the power to fulfil the obligation on behalf of their community. A *tumtum* and an *androgynes* are obligated but cannot fulfil the obligation of the community. An *androgynes* fulfils the obligation of his own kind and does not have that power over those who are not of his own kind. A *tumtum* does not fulfil the obligation either for his own kind or of those who are not his kind. Women and slaves and minors are exempt and cannot fulfil the obligation of the community.

---

19 Unlike us the Bible and the Mishnah were not very careful with consistently using male and female to denote sex and man and woman to denote gender, but it is not hard to discern what is meant.

Both *androgynes* and *tumtum* are obliged to hear the scroll being read because they have (*androgynes*) or might have (*tumtum*) male sex organs, and men are obliged to hear it. As the *androgynes* is considered a sex to itself, the *androgynes* may act as a representative of this third sex and read the scroll (which is obligated anyway to hear), as his genitalia include a male part. The *tumtum* however cannot represent even 'people of his/her own kind', as in the eyes of the rabbis here, the *tumtum* is not really a 'fourth-gender'. The reason for this is the assumption already mentioned, that the *tumtum* truly does belong to one of the other sexes, and it's only the unobservability of the sex organs that creates a problem of categorisation. The non-observable bodily reality is not considered ambivalent or even potentially unclear. Should a *tumtum* accidently tear and be revealed as female,[20] not only will (she) be exempt from hearing the scroll being read, like all other women, but (she) will not be able to fulfil the obligation on preforming the commandment on behalf of anyone else.[21] Since there is a doubt in the case of the *tumtum*, the Tosefta prefers to prevent a case where the law will not be followed, and treats the *tumtum* as if male for the sake of hearing the scroll, and as a woman for reading it aloud and exempting others. The *tumtum* is treated like a case of doubt. This doubt can be traced even in the earlier legalistic sources we have discussed.

Furthermore, the issue of the sex life of intersex people is of importance to those Jewish sources, as they see homosexual men's intercourse as a punishable sin. For us, this is a good test-case for the rabbinic classification of intersex people. This develops into an even more pressing question when an intersex person wishes to get married.[22] The cases of the *androgynes* and the *tumtum* are different. In the Tannaitic sources, the classification of the *androgynes* as 'a kind to itself', which might be both male and female or either male or female is almost perfectly maintained. Thus, according to Rabbi Eleazar:

> I have heard regarding the *androgynes* that one contracts the death penalty of stoning when having sex with him[23] as in the case of male. To what does this refer? To the

20 The idea that a *tumtum's* flesh may tear and expose a conclusive sex is found already in the Mishnah Yebamoth 8:6. However, one may not tear up a *tumtum's* flesh on purpose in order to find out what s/he is.

21 The halakhic principle is that one cannot act as a public representative in front of God in matters s/he is not obliged to perform. Thus, e.g., a woman cannot lead prayer – because all the men in the crowd would have to pray again in order to fulfil their obligation of prayer.

22 Marriage is one of the fundamentals of Rabbinic culture, as Boyarin showed: D. Boyarin, *Carnal Israel: Reading Sex in Talmudic Culture*, University of California Press, Berkeley/Los Angeles/London 1993. This makes the question of the marriage of intersex people into an essential question of Jewish identity and belonging.

23 All pronouns in Hebrew are gendered; we chose to translate in a way which is consistent with the Hebrew, not necessarily with the person's actual gender/sex.

instance when one has sex with and *androgynes* by way of his maleness. If one does not have sex with him by way of his male genitals, one is exempt from the death penalty (Tosefta Yebamot 10:2).

To quote Fonrobert again 'a man would be exempt from capital punishment for having sex with an *androgynes* if both men restrict themselves to the hermaphrodite's vaginal area'.[24] In other words, both the *androgynes* and the sexual partner can choose whether to consider the *androgynes* a man or a woman. A man may have sex with *androgynes* as long as only the *androgynes*' vagina is involved. A woman may have sexual intercourse with an *androgynes* via his 'maleness'. Sex with an *androgynes* is thus not considered non-normative or forbidden, but while performing it, just like in all other sexual interactions, the laws regulating sex should be observed.

The question of the marriage of intersex people follows somehow the same lines. There is no doubt that women may marry both an *androgynes* and a *tumtum*. According to the rabbinic interpretation of Genesis 1:28 ('be fruitful and multiply') only men, but not women are obligated by the divine precept to procreate. This enables women (but not men) to marry without any hesitation a person who might not able to procreate. Add to this the lack of any specific ban, either Biblical, Tannaitic, and to an extent even Talmudic on sex between women, and the logic becomes clear. However, while the *androgynes* can only marry a woman, a *tumtum* may marry either a man or a woman (Tosefta Yebamoth 11:1).[25] Assuming the *tumtum's* genitals will forever remain hidden, there's no 'danger' of homosexual intercourse with a male, and hence the marriage between a man and a *tumtum* becomes possible. A husband of a *tumtum* may have already fulfilled the obligation to 'be fruitful and multiply' with another woman, or is himself unable to procreate.

Matters start to get more complicated when intersex people divorce or die while married. In those cases, they are treated in a manner that they share with other members of the 'sexually ambivalent' group: the *saris* and the *aylonit*, those who never reach full sexual maturity and are unable to procreate. Let us stress that the special treatment of intersex people here is not on account of their sex, but of their procreative abilities. As Sarra Lev argues, the *saris* and the *aylonit* are mirror categories. They may look like members of the opposite sex or exhibit no secondary sexual characteristics; but they are still binarily gendered. Both the *aylonit* and the *saris* lack pubic hair and some other secondary sex

24 Fonrobert, above n. 11, p. 281. She uses hermaphrodite here as a translation of *androgynes*.

25 The text does leave a place for ambiguity, as it states that when a *tumtum* gets married his marriage is valid. This might imply that the act is not preferable, and this is how it was understood later on.

characteristics (the *aylonit* has 'no breasts' and has thin hair on her head, the *saris* has no beard and no body hair); experience problems during intercourse (pains for her and 'repelling semen' for him); have abnormal primary sex organs (no *mons veneris* for her, a penis that does not form an arch while urinating for him). Both the *aylonit* and the *saris* experience 'voice trouble' (hers is deep while his is thin), and in both 'it is not distinguishable whether (s/he is) a man or a woman' (possibly when dressed).[26] In terms of marriage, both the *saris* and the *aylonit* are allowed to marry. The *aylonit* and the *saris*, even if doubt is expressed about their physical appearance, are not treated as cases of doubt in terms of gender. The *aylonit* is an 'abnormal' woman and the *saris* an 'abnormal' man. They may, therefore, marry men and women respectively. The Mishnah in Yebamot, however, makes things a bit more complicated as it ties the *saris* with intersex people:

> A congenital eunuch [saris] who is a priest, who married an Israelite girl, feeds her of the truma [heave offering, food only designated for consumption by priests and their household]. R. Yose and R. Shimon say: Androgynes who is a priest and married an Israelite girl, feeds her of the truma. R. Judah says a tumtum who was torn and turned out to be a male, needs not preform ḥalitẕa [lit. the removal of a shoe, a ritual performed to release one from the obligation of a levirate marriage], because he is like an eunuch. An androgynes marries but is not taken in marriage. R. Eliezer says: [in the case of] androgynes – those [who have intercourse with him] are liable to stoning on account of him being like a male [namely, as if they had homosexual relations]. (MishnaYebamot 8:6)

This Mishna blurs the neat lines between categories that we have seen so far, and opens up new questions. The first one stems from the last statement, which categorises *androgynes* always as male when acting as a sexual partner of a male, thus contesting the view that allowed him to have vaginal sex with a man. The second is the relationship between a *tumtum* and the eunuch, and the assumption that even if a *tumtum's* genitals would be exposed, we can assume they will be dysfunctional.

To conclude, Tannaitic sources seem to consider favourably the possibility of the existence of more than two sexes and acknowledge specifically *androgynes* as a separate sex. This 'new sex' is still interpreted to be included in the covenant between God and his people, not only as its members are human, but also by means of reading the Biblical verses anew, in a way which interprets exclusive statements (either/or) as inclusive (this and that).

---

[26] Tosefta Yebamot 10:6–7, S. Lev, 'How the 'Aylonit Got her Sex' (2007) *AJS Review* 31:2 297–316; S. Lev, 'They Treat Him as a Man and See Him as a Woman: The Tannaitic Understanding of the Congenital Eunuch' (2010) 17 *Jewish Studies Quarterly* 213–243.

3. THE ESSENTIALIST TURN/THE BABYLONIAN TURN

As opposed to the Tannaitic view that sees in *androgynes* a third sex, we find first in the Palestinian Talmud, and later on with further emphasis in the Babylonian Talmud, a discursive shift. These later sources discuss both *tumtum* and *androgynes* as cases of doubt, not of a third (and/or fourth) sex. This is based on the same Tosefta (Bikkurim 2:3–7) which saw the *androgynes* as a kind to itself, but quoting only its final words, concerning the sages' inability to decide the sex a *tumtum*. The model implied in the phrase 'could not decide' is expanded to include also the *androgynes* and consider him/her a case of doubt.[27] The later sources, from the Amoraic period, seem to favour this view.

The legal revolution is instituted with a myth, referring back to the creation of humankind. It is a mythical moment not only for its content, but also as it marks the Babylonian Talmud's conflation of sex and gender, and its insistence on gender hierarchy. The legend about the creation of man and woman as one creature that was later split into half is discussed in a very specific manner:

> R. Jeremiah said: God created two faces in the first man, as it says, 'Behind and before hast Thou formed me'. [...] which of the two faces went in front? – R. Nahman b. Isaac answered: It is reasonable to suppose that the man's face went in front' (Babylonian Talmud Berakhot 61a).

The Babylonian Talmud here seems to accept the Platonist and Palestinian interpretation of the first creation narrative. But it wants to know more, as it insists on translating the mythical world into the real one. If a double-faced creature ever existed, how did he/she walk? The breach into *realia* marks a breach into the Babylonian social realm. The language of hierarchy, which we did not find at all until this point, comes to life. When the Babylonian rabbis ask who walks at the front, the male side or the female side of this creature, they ask about the hierarchy between the sexes, and rob the mythological creature of its ability to live outside and beyond the boundaries of patriarchy, and the

---

27 See Palestinian Talmud Beiẓa 1:2, 60b; Yerushalmi Niddah 1:1, 48c. Some earlier attestations are found in Tannaitic sources that do not use the word 'doubt', but do use expressions of opposition such as 'undoubted' and 'complete' men and women: Mishnah Arakhin 1:1; Mishnah Zavim 2:1; Mekhita de-Rabbi Yishmael, Nezikin, 11, p. 286: See also Sifra Nedava 16:2, Sifra Beḥukotay 3:1, 112c. However, the opposite of the terms 'undoubted' and 'complete' is not necessarily 'doubted'. They may be seen as similar to the term 'all male' in the Palestinian Talmud Shabbat 19:3 (88a) and the parallels in Palestinian Talmud Yebamoth 8:1, 9a; Hagiga 1:1, 66a. Not being entirely man is not necessarily being a creature of doubtful sex; it might also mean being something which is not entirely male since it contains both feminine and masculine elements. In the parallel in the Babylonian Talmud, Shabbat 135a the term 'all male' is replaced by 'certain foreskin', implying a move towards the language of doubt.

gender divide. The issue of gender and gender hierarchy invades the discussion of the taxonomy of the human sexes. When the Babylonian Talmud discusses a person that may be both male and female it considers the male element as more important, and calls him '*gavra*' which translates as man, but also as strong, mighty, dominant.

The urge to 'masculate' anyone and anything which is not absolutely female is one of the characteristics differentiating Talmudic law from Roman law. The presence of a penis, as Fonrobert argued, becomes decisive for the Talmudic rabbis.[28] The clearest manifestation of this is found when the Talmud discusses intersex animals, rather than people.

> 'These are the ones on account of which they do not slaughter (firstlings) either in the Temple or in the provinces:{...} a beast with scurvy and one with warts [...] an old [beast] and a sick one [...] and a *tumtum* and an *androgynes* ...' (Mishnah Bekhorot 6:12)
>
> [The ruling concerning] the *tumtum* makes sense. In the Temple [it should] not [be slaughtered, since] it might be a female; in the provinces [it should] not [be slaughtered, since] it might be a male who has no blemish [and as such it should be given to the priest for sacrifice]. But [the ruling concerning] the *androgynes* [only] make sense in the case of the Temple [where it may not be slaughtered, since] it might be a female [and thus not subject to the law of the firstborn], but in the provinces, we may say it is a male, and the femaleness [= the vagina] may be considered as a crack [in his body, and hence as a blemish that disqualifies it from being sacrificed, and hence] permits one to slaughter. (Babylonian Talmud Bekhorot 41a)

The Talmud arranges the entire discussion on the topic within the framework of the rabbinic discourse of legal doubt. Biblical law has it that any first-born male animal should be given to the temple (for slaughter). If the animal, however, is somehow physically imperfect, it is still slaughtered, but not at the temple. The Talmud here wishes to explain the Mishnaic ruling that one not may slaughter such a first-born animal neither at the Temple (as a sacrifice) nor in other places. Considering the *androgynes* animal as a case of doubt leads to the following argument: Why should the Mishnah ban the slaughtering of such an animal if outside the Temple? If the *androgynes* is a female, it should not be considered a first-born in any case, since the laws of the first-born only apply to males. However, if the *androgynes* is a male, then it is a male with a blemish, and his vagina is considered a physical blemish of the type of '*ḥariẓ*' – a crack in the body. This means, that although it should have theoretically been sacrificed at the temple (being a male), it was disqualified because it had a blemish, and hence, again, can only be slaughtered (as a male) outside the temple.

28 Fonrobert, above n. 11, p. 282.

The *androgynes* is transformed into a creature whose sex is not known and is either a female or a 'defective' male. The *androgynes* animal is not considered a member of a third sex, and in fact, the possibility of a 'third sex' disappears.[29] Laws concerning doubt are applied to the *androgynes* to resolve the sex/gender ambiguity. Thus, in Babylonian Talmud Bekhorot 77a it says:

> *Tumtum* and *androgynes* should be understood as cases of doubt. R. Simon son of Judah says: (to support) he who thinks this is a case of doubt, the Torah narrowed things down about sacred offerings to an undoubted male and undoubted female.

Now not only are both *tumtum* and *androgynes* dealt with as cases of doubt, they are also kept at a distance from the sphere of the holy. The hermeneutics of doubt makes intersex people, not only animals, and especially *androgynes* into flawed humans, and the discourse distances itself from that of the Mishnah.

The text from Babylonian Talmud Bekhorot, which defines the *androgynes* as a male with a physical blemish in the form of 'a crack' represents again the same issue we marked with the 'mythical text', the aftermath of the separation of the sexes. A separation which is accompanied by, leads to, or represents social hierarchy and discrimination. Indeed, with the Babylonian Talmud's move towards an essentialist understanding of the *androgynes*, comes with a negative portrayal of femininity, and a patriarchal hierarchy. As the Talmud cannot contain the idea of the existence of a physical entity which may be seen as sharing equally both in femininity and masculinity, it prioritises the masculine aspect over the feminine. Thus, at this second stage, the male organs are considered prior to the female organs, which are now understood to be a blemish. The wish for a strong distinction between males and females is immediately developed into a discourse that degrades the feminine aspect and objectifies it. Moreover, femininity itself is interpreted as a flaw.

It is no big surprise, therefore, that the views about sex with an intersex person change in the Babylonian Talmud as well: 'with respect to sex with an *androgynes*, one contracts the death penalty of stoning for [sex by way of] either of the places' (Babylonian Talmud Yebamot 82b). Whereas in the Mishnah this view was attributed to one specific rabbi, Rabbi Elie'zer, who is known to hold marginal and unaccepted views, in the Talmud it is declared as accepted by all. As the ambiguity disappears, the presence of a penis becomes decisive.[30]

Another example is found in the Talmudic discussion concerning the consumption of heave offering by the wife of an *androgynes* priest.[31]

---

[29] As we show below, such a perspective is already hinted at in some Tannaitic sources, clearly in regard to the *tumtum*. However, it is in the Babylonian Talmud that this perspective become the dominant one and is consistently applied to the *androgynes*.

[30] Fonrobert, above n. 11, p. 282.

[31] Babylonian Talmud *Yebamoth* 81a.

The Babylonian Talmud focused on the question of Biblical v. rabbinic authority of related laws, assuming that the core of the question is the doubt as to the 'true' sexual identity of the *androgynes*. The discussion of the theme in the Palestinian Talmud still seems to convey a discourse which is closer to the Tannaitic perspective:

> This situation creates a difficulty. If s/he is a male – no male should disqualify a male; if s/he a female – no female should disqualify a female! The male side (or aspect) of this (person) disqualifies the female side (or aspect) of this (person). (Palestinian Talmud Yebamot 8:6 (50b)).

Though the Palestinian Talmud uses a binary language, and contemplates whether *androgynes* is a male or female, it concludes that *androgynes* has two aspects and the presence of both determines which laws apply for *androgynes*. They are not concerned with 'a true essence'. While it may not see *androgynes* as a sex to itself, it still seems to represent a continuation with the earlier concepts, which were later rejected by the essentialist trend.

It is important to clarify that there are also other voices, and one may also hear echoes of the multiple sexes and genders approach in the Babylonian Talmud.[32] The process we depict here is that of dominantisation[33] in which a certain perspective that appeared in Tannaitic literature becomes dominant in the Babylonian Talmud. A comparative study of parallel discussions provides clear evidence for the rise of the discourse of doubt as dominant in the Babylonian Talmud and lacking or marginal in the Palestinian Talmud.[34] The importance of the discourse of doubt lies in the move from a legal discourse in which the *androgynes* is considered a third sex to that in which he/she is assumed to be either male or female. The dichotomy that characterised the legal categories of Tannaitic literature shifts and becomes the prism through which reality is understood. The reality of multiple sexes is rejected in the Babylonian Talmud conceptualisation and discourse.

---

32 The term 'male side' also appears in the Babylonian Talmud Hagigah 4a in regard to an *androgynes*.

33 For the theoretical framework of the notion of 'dominantisation', see M. Lavee, *The Rabbinic Conversion of Judaism: The Unique Perspective of the Bavli on Conversion and the Construction of Jewish Identity*, Brill, Leiden, 2017, pp. 15–19.

34 Cf. Babylonian Talmud Yebamot 72b with Palestinian Talmud Hagiga 1:1 66a. The Babylonian Talmud quotes Tosefta Parah 5:7 'and R. Judah disqualifies because it is a doubted female', whereas in the Palestinian Talmud the view of Rabbi Yehuda is that 'a bit of him/her is male'. It seems that the Palestinian Talmud was not familiar with the Tosefta, and one may consider the possibility that a Babylonian baraita found its way into the Tosefta in this case. See also the move from 'all male' in the Palestinian Talmud to 'foreskin certainty' in the Babylonian Talmud, above n. 27.

4. CONCLUSION

The cases of the *androgynes* and *tumtum* demonstrate a move from an earlier discursive model of binary legal language to a later essentialist perception. The later perception denies the existence of liminal entities, as well as, in fact, of intersex people. The essentialist discourse makes the legalistic distinction of the former Tannaitic categories into a reality, which intensifies a hierarchy in which one part of binary opposition is considered better than another.

The picture we present here is probably only a part of a wider process of polarisation, in which legal binary oppositions become more and more prominent in the later rabbinic mind. The polarised discourse moves from legal realms to essentialist perceptions of the human sexes and genders, finally becoming an active historical agent. This process is realised through various social mechanisms of separation and distinction, which come, in many cases, with a growing sense of social hierarchy. Similar developments can be observed in discussions of the legal status of Samaritans and converts. While in some early rabbinic sources they are considered to be liminal entities, they are portrayed in the Babylonian Talmud with far less ambiguity. Thus for example, converts are described as 'like an Israelite in every respect' and a 'like a newborn'.[35] Other liminal categories such as 'God-Fearers', people who believe in the Jewish God and follow the law without formally converting, disappear completely from the cultural horizon of the Babylonian Talmud.[36]

An investigation into minor shifts in the rabbinic discourse permits us to glimpse modifications in legal concepts and their reflections in textual developments. These modifications either reflect social and political changes or were important agents in the formation of social and political developments. Moshe Halbertal usefully distinguished between the status of the Talmud as a normative canon, and its status as a formative canon. Halbertal argues that in medieval Europe we see a process by which the Talmud, which was first recognised as a normative canon, namely as an authoritative source to deduce law from, gradually became also a formative canon, i.e., a source that shapes the discursive patterns and the worldview of Jews.[37] Halbertal's observation is important to us for two reasons: firstly, as it helps us to explain the role of

---

35 On the categories of converts and goy/gentile and liminal aspects of those, see I. Rozen-Zvi, 'What if We Got Rid of the Goy? Rereading Ancient Jewish Distinctions' (2016) 47 *Journal of Jewish Studies* 149–182; I. Rosen-Zvi And A. Ophir, 'Goy: Toward a Genealogy' (2016) 28 *Diné Israel*, 69–122; A. Ophir, 'Paul and the Invention of the Gentiles' (2015) 10 *Jewish Quarterly Review* 1–41; L. Schiffman, *Who Was A Jew? Rabbinic and Halakhic Perspectives on the Jewish-Christian Schism*, Hoboken, Ktav 1985.

36 M. Lavee, *The Rabbinic Conversion of Judaism: The Unique Perspective of the Bavli on Conversion and the Construction of Jewish Identity*, Brill, Leiden 2017.

37 M. Halbertal, *People of the Book – Canon, Meaning, and Authority*, Harvard University Press, Cambridge Mass/London 1997.

the Mishna in shaping the thought of the Talmud, and secondly, for thinking of the Talmud's continuous influence. Similar processes to those described by Halbertal in the middle ages occurred in Late Antiquity with regard to Mishnaic law. Through the Talmudic deliberations, the Mishnah shifted from being a normative canon, a text that intended to dictate the law, to being a formative canon. However, this new status is achieved through a process by which Mishnaic legal perspectives and categories gain new weight, and shape rabbinic acts as well as thought, and create a new reality. In a more recent publication Halbertal put forth the idea that the rise of halakhic discourse was a revolution that emerged through the canonisation of the Mishnah.[38] The halakhic revolution includes the wider application of the thick, dense, high-resolution and detailed mode of legal discourse. What we have tried to show here is one stage of this revolution, in which the categories that were used in the Tannaitic legal discourse became prisms through which reality was understood in later sources, and to point to the mechanisms through which legal categories morph into an essential description of reality. In other words, to show how the normative becomes formative.

[38] M. Halbertal, 'The History of Halakha and the emergence of Halakha' (2013) 29 *Dine Israel* 1–23 [Hebrew].

INTERSEX: SOME (LEGAL-)HISTORICAL BACKGROUND

Alain WIJFFELS

Until the eighteenth century, the legal approach to 'hermaphrodites', although it presented distinctive features, was influenced by ancient classical texts and by post-classical literature and scholarship. The latter were in turn more or less informed by the ancient sources, but often also reprocessing those sources for contemporary political or social purposes. Both canon law and secular law were also influenced by Christian religious beliefs and doctrines, which to some extent affected the broader popular culture and attitudes to sexuality and gender issues. As those scholarly and popular approaches sometimes intertwined with legal (in particular, forensic) discussions of intersex cases, a brief introductory reference to some aspects of that broader cultural context may be useful. Another necessary contextualisation (which, however, can only be mentioned peripherally in this introductory contribution) is the interaction between medical science and law on this issue.

1. THE WESTERN CULTURAL TRADITION: THE 'HERMAPHRODITE' AS A *TOPOS* DRAWN AND ADAPTED FROM THE ANCIENT CLASSICAL CULTURE

Among the non-legal sources which have affected legal literature and thinking on transsexuality, intersexuality, sexual orientations, and gender issues in general, the Greek-Roman mythology – as witnessed already by the continuous use of the word 'hermaphrodite' as a term of art in legal authorities until the nineteenth century – has been a powerful factor. It was a cultural reference which contributed to maintaining the notion that intersexuality occurred, even if it was perceived as a challenge to the natural and social order.

In his *Pro populo anglicano defensio* (1651), Milton countered the attacks by the French author Claude Saumaise against the English regicides. In the preface, Milton included a pun on Saumaise's Latinised name (Salmasius), comparing him with the nymph Salmacis, who caused the metamorphosis of Hermaphrodite, and associating his opponent with 'effeminate minds', 'emasculating' generous minds, and reduced by the weakness of this argument to a 'half-man'.[1] Here we have an example of the mythological reference used in a polemical political text, and using the reference to Hermaphrodite in a pejorative, denigrating, sense.

A long and fairly abundant literary tradition from Antiquity to early-modern times documents both empirical and ideational narratives on trans- and intersexuality, in which synchronic or diachronic hermaphrodism is a recurrent theme. That secular literature includes both scientific texts (such as Pliny's accounts) and literary fiction (such as Ovid's *Metamorphoses* based on mythology), where archetypes of hermaphrodite and transsexual figures appear: Hermaphroditus himself (born from Hermes and Aphrodite), but also Caenis/Caeneus (becoming a man after having been raped as a woman by Neptune), or Iphis (transformed into a man by Isis on the eve of her marriage to Ianthe).

Together with classical Antiquity, Christianity has long been one of the pillars on which Western culture rested. Beyond religion and theology, Christianity has for centuries determined the codes of public governance, arts and social norms. In the Christian tradition, gender issues have also been a notoriously vexed topic of debate until the present day. In the Roman Catholic Church, the importance of sexuality and the role of women have mostly been at the same time sublimated and repressed. Even so, it should be remembered that, from the outset, as the Epistle to the Galatians emphasised in vivid terms, the transcendent vision offered by Christ's message implied an emancipation from any discriminatory status by reason of one's race, social status or gender. In the kingdom of heaven, there is 'neither male nor female'.[2]

In the sphere of more popular devotion, the account of the martyrdom of Saint Perpetua is an exceptional document which continues to attract the

---

1 J[OANNIS] MILTON, *Pro populo anglicano defensio Contra Claudii Anonymi, alias Salmasii, Defensionem Regiam* [Editio emendatior, Londini, Typis Du Gardianis, 1651], *Praefatio*, p. 10.

2 Galatians 3:28. An important doctrinal text in the Western Christian tradition was St. Augustine, *De civitate Dei*, XVI.8. In early-modern times, the saying 'The soul has no gender' was sometimes attributed to Queen Christina of Sweden.

attention of early-Christian scholarship.[3] Perpetua, a well-born North-African woman and young mother, became a Christian martyr when she was put to death with five other fellow Christians, including her slave and friend Felicity, who was pregnant, in the amphitheatre at Carthage. Felicity and Perpetua were proclaimed saints and their names were included in the Canon of the Mass, ensuring a lasting fame among Roman-Catholics until modern times. The account of Perpetua's last days, attributed to herself, is a deeply personal record of her anxieties as a mother about her new-born baby, from whom she was separated, and of her subconscious representations featured in a sequence of four dreams. In her fourth and last dream, she is being led to the amphitheatre. Entering the arena, where she expects to confront wild beasts, she is surprised that she will have to fight a different adversary:

> Instead an Egyptian came out as my opponent, hideous to look at, along with his assistants. He was the one who was going to fight me. Some handsome young men came to my side as well, to assist and support me. And I was stripped naked and became masculine, and my assistants started rubbing me down with oil the way they do before an athletic contest ….

A spectacular fight between Perpetua and the Egyptian ensues, from which Perpetua comes out as the winner. Perpetua is given the prize, a branch with golden apples. By then, she must have metamorphosed into a woman again, for when the referee hands over the award, he kisses her and says: 'Peace be with you, daughter'.

This passage has been interpreted in various ways. Perhaps the most convincing line of interpretation, taking into account the text of the passion in its entirety and against the background of classical narratives and culture in general, is to recognise in Perpetua's account a strong self-awareness of her femininity, both physical and social, which, however, does not preclude, in her determination to die for her faith, a capacity to adopt intergender features.

Medieval and Renaissance literature and arts also offer a wide range of philosophical, scientific and literary examples in which trans- and intersexuality themes are more or less explicitly being explored.[4] It was a tradition which has cast a long shadow over the concepts and policies on sexuality in Western history until modern times. Alain de Lille's *Complaint of nature*, for instance, assimilates with hermaphrodism a venereal degeneration of Nature's precepts,

---

3 T.J. Heffernan, *The passion of Perpetua and Felicity*, Oxford University Press, New York 2012; J.N. Bremmer and M. Formisano (eds.), *Perpetua's passions: multidisciplinary approaches to the Passio Perpetuae et Felicitatis*, Oxford University Press, Oxford 2012.

4 Several examples (some of which will be referred to hereafter) are to be found in the essays collected by M. Closson (ed.), *L'Hermaphrodisme de la Renaissance aux Lumières*, Classiques Garnier, Paris 2013.

a discourse aimed primarily at condemning non-reproductive sexual behaviour, in particular male homosexuality.[5] A more positive notion of hermaphrodism can be found in a different tradition, such as the philosophical alchemism of Clovis Hesteau de Nuysement, in his *Visions hermétiques*, poems in defence of alchemy. The author reverts to the concept of the world as a living creature, 'male and female throughout, and joined by mutual love and union of its limbs', a cosmological vision which permeates a great part of his intergender-inspired alchemy.[6] In the visual arts, the intergender theme was occasionally represented by copying artworks from Antiquity, or by imagining fictional representations which often represented more or less 'monstrous' creatures, or representations offering an echo or reinterpretation of ancient mythology.[7] In Jacobean England, hermaphrodites were not only a notion contemporaries were familiar with through legal authorities and testimonies from classical Antiquity. Representations of trans- and intersexuality were also instrumentalised in political polemical writings, such as the famous tracts of 1620 on the 'he-woman' (*hic mulier*) and the 'she-man' (*haec vir*), possibly also a criticism levied against allegations of unconventional sexual behaviour among members of the royal court.[8] In France also, trans- and intersexuality were forms for expressing critical political opinions. In 1605, an anonymous pamphlet (later attributed to Artus Thomas, Lord of Embry) was published under the title (in French) *The Newly Discovered Island of the Hermaphrodites*[9] – which inspired

---

5 D. Rollo, *Kiss my relics – Hermaphroditic fictions of the Middle Ages*, The University of Chicago Press, Chicago and London 2011, pp. 77–142, on Alain de Lille's *De planctu Naturae*.

6 K.P. Long, *Hermaphrodites in Renaissance Europe*, Ashgate, Aldershot 2006, pp. 137–162. Nuysement was a courtier close to the French king Henry III.

7 To quote but one (albeit particularly relevant in art history) work among innumerous examples: Jan Gossaert's *Metamorphosis of Hermaphrodite and the Nymph Salmacis* (1517), H. Caudill 'The Virago, Hermaphrodite, and Jan Gossaert: A Metamorphosis in Netherlandish Art' (2006) *Kaleidoscope*, vol. 5, Article 13.

8 *Three Pamphlets on the Jacobean Antifeminist Controversy – Facsimile Reproductions with an Introduction by Barbara J. Baines*, Scholars' Facsimiles and Reprints, Delmar, New York 1978, including *Hic Mulier: Or, The Man-Woman: Being a Medicine to cure the Coltish Disease of the Staggers in the Masculine-Feminines of our Times* [London, printed for I.T. and are to be sold at Christ Church gate. 1620]; *Haec Vir: Or, The Womanish-Man: Being an Answere to a late Booke intituled* Hic-Mulier. *Exprest in a briefe Dialogue between* Haec-Vir *the Womanish-Man and* Hic-Mulier *the Man-Woman* [London printed for I.T. and are to be sold at Christ Church gate. 1620].

9 Modern edition: *L'isle des Hermaphrodites*, éd. C.-G. Dubois, Droz, Genève 1996. The pamphlet enjoyed more than an ephemeral appeal and was reprinted in the following century – prompting at the time the Roman-Catholic authorities to include it in their index of prohibited works. The 1724 edition reproduced the image already appearing in the 1605 original imprint, showing a figure with male and female characteristics and attributes, but claiming in a few accompanying verses to be neither male nor female – though enjoying the pleasures of both genders. The verses highlight one of the core values attributed to the inhabitants of the island: the purely hedonistic quest for pleasure and self-gratification as the highest goal of all. The subtitle of the book, added in the 1724 edition, gives away that

the following year a polemical pamphlet *L'anti-hermaphrodite*.[10] The Island of the Hermaphrodites is inspired by the format and register of other early-modern political tracts. The story of Europeans being washed up after a shipwreck on the shores of an unknown (and in this case, floating) island with its distinctive people, culture and polity, is of course partly reminiscent of More's *Utopia*. Artus Thomas' pamphlet seems, however, to have targeted a more specific political context, and is usually understood to entail a barely disguised criticism and satire of King Henry III and his court. The fiction of the hermaphrodites in the pamphlet is rather a stylistic and rhetorical device aimed at reinforcing a negative association between the utopian society and the target of the author's criticism, partly by mocking the perceived or alleged effeminate and homosexual tendencies of Henry III's court. Conventional gender roles or gender identities are not being challenged, the caricature of intersexuality implies, on the contrary, an attachment to stereotyped gender definitions.

Mainstream eighteenth-century views did not necessarily converge. This can be illustrated by comparing the entries on 'hermaphrodites' in two general works of reference, the German *Zedler Lexicon* and the French *Encyclopédie*. The German entry (in the 1732 edition)[11] states that the existence of hermaphrodistic features is accepted as a fact by the medical profession ('eine ausgemachte Sache'). Hermaphroditism is also extensively documented in the animal and botanical species. The entry also refers to the legal principles, which, it says, will categorise an individual with hermaphrodistic features according to the prevailing sexual characteristics; if the features are in balance, the individual will make a choice, because (here a moral element creeps in) it would be monstrous to use both sexes; the individual must pledge under oath not to come back on that choice. While still a child, such a person will be deemed to be masculine. When the person intends to marry, a commission of physicians and midwives will have to determine the sex. The entry also considers the vexed issue of a

---

a spoof compilation of the island's legal system is instrumental in articulating a criticism of a certain political establishment and culture. As in other early-modern political essays, this work purports to describe 'the usages, customs and statutes of the inhabitants' of the island. One might expect that hermaphrodites would not be hampered by sex discrimination. However, the island's society remains steeped in the inequalities to be found in other, more conventional societies, and occasionally, a gender-biased note slips into the description of the island's survey, for example when the author lampoons the frivolity of fashion, useful, he says, to converse with *ladies*; or when he describes the discipline in military barracks, which will have to provide for a multitude of *loose women*.

10 As the full title shows, this, too, purported to deal with issues of public governance: *L'anti-hermaphrodite ou le secret, tant désiré de beaucoup, de l'advis proposé au Roy pour reparer par un bel ordre, et legitime moyen aussi facilement, qu'insensiblement, tous les désordres, impiétés, iniustices, abus, meschancetez, & corruptions qui sont en ce Royaume ...* [A Paris, Par Iean Berjon, 1606].

11 *Grosses vollständiges Universal Lexicon Aller Wissenschaften und Künste ...* [Halle und Leipzig, Verlegts Johann Heinrich Zedler, 1732–], T. XII (1735), s.v. Hermaphroditus, col. 1723–1725.

hermaphrodite who after the death of the wife or husband, wants to marry a person of the opposite sex. The author of the entry expresses the opinion that although such a course of action may be warranted by 'natural reason', public policy considerations would prevent it.

By contrast, the principal entry in the *Encyclopédie* states that hermaphrodism does not exist.[12] Ambiguous appearances may have confused popular and unenlightened beliefs, but the author is in no doubt that proper medical inspection of any individual will establish either that such individual may be classified as a woman or a man, either as having neither sex sufficiently developed. It would therefore seem that the concept of hermaphrodism was reduced to an anatomical *utrumque*, not including an individual appearing to be *neutrum*. In a Supplement volume,[13] the same thesis of the non-existence of 'true hermaphrodites' is repeated, but the register of the entry follows entirely a scientific and medical approach (by the standards of the time), including detailed anatomical and clinical observation (when possible by a group of physicians)[14] and when available including the report of a post-mortem dissection. That register is also expressed in some of the illustrations to which the entry refers, and which highlight graphically the progress of anatomical descriptions of the internal side of the reproductive organs.[15]

The detailed scientific graphic depiction of the human body made much progress during the eighteenth century. William Cheselden's work with plates became an important work of reference, reaching a 13th edition by 1792. It included figures on human hermaphroditism, and in particular of an individual from Angola who had been brought to London.[16] The case, illustrated with Cheselden's plates, became a well-known reference in eighteenth-century Europe in discussions on hermaphrodites. Voltaire, for example, expressed his scepticism about the existence of hermaphrodites, without stating an outright

---

12 *Encyclopédie, ou dictionnaire raisonné des sciences, des arts et des métiers* ... [A Paris, Chez Briasson, David, Le Breton, Durand, 1751–], T. 8, s.v. 'Hermaphrodite', pp. 165–167.

13 *Supplément à l'Encyclopédie, ou dictionnaire raisonné des sciences, des arts et métiers* ... [A Amsterdam, Chez M.M. Rey, 1777], T. 3, s.v. Hermaphrodite, pp. 359–365.

14 See below the references to the inquiry in 1802 into the gender of Jacqueline Foroni. An officially sanctioned inquiry was carried out by a commission according to the standards of officialdom and scientific rigour expected by the enlightened agents of the French Republic. The result was that Foroni was a man. Foroni's own wish and expectation to be recognised (as she had always been) as a woman, and even her inclination towards men, was dismissed by the officials as an effect of a misguided education and social patterns. This case may be seen as a strong example of the effects of the same ideology expressed in the *Encyclopédie*, where assertions of intersex were rejected as expressions of non-rational opinions and superstitions.

15 *Suite du recueil de planches, sur les sciences, les arts libéraux, et les arts méchaniques, avec leur explication* [A Paris, Chez Pancoucke, Stoupe, Brunet; A Amsterdam, Chez M.M. Rey, 1777], p. 14 and 3 full-page plates s.v. 'Hermaphrodite' (Histoire naturelle).

16 W[ILLIAM] CHESELDEN, *The Anatomy of the Human Body* [I have used: The VIIth ed., London, Printed for C. Hitch & R. Dodsley 1750], p. 314, Plate 33.

denial. Like many contemporaries, he believed the occurrence might more likely be observed in southern regions. Hence, he referred to the Angolan individual, referring explicitly to Cheselden's work and plates, and also to communications with the author. Voltaire admitted that the existence of full human hermaphrodites was possible. '*Je n'affirme rien. ... Je doute*'.[17]

2. THE WESTERN LEGAL TRADITION: INTERSEX CHALLENGED AND (RE-)AFFIRMED

A handful of fragments from classical Roman jurists which deal explicitly with an issue involving a 'hermaphrodite' (the term of art used in the legal texts) were incorporated in the Digest by Emperor Justinian.[18] From the Second Middle Ages onwards (i.e. from the eleventh to the fifteenth century), the Digest was the main compilation used in the education of students in civil law all over Western Europe until the end of the eighteenth century. The texts of Roman law were also acknowledged and used as legal authorities in legal practice throughout Europe (although in England, only in marginal civil, including ecclesiastical, law courts). For centuries, those fragments therefore ensured that, however peripheral, a notion of intersexuality retained a presence in legal literature.

A complex example of late-medieval doctrine on the subject is a legal opinion (*consilium*) by Baldus de Ubaldis on a question of feudal inheritance. A young person described as a son displayed imperfect genital organs, and his father's will provided that he would not inherit a share of the feudal estate if, by the time he reached the age of 28, his male sexuality had not been ascertained. Baldus' opinion reviews several doctrines, including that of the canonist Henricus de Segusio, according to whom, in the case of doubt, the decision was to be left to the person in question, who, in conscience, was better placed to determine her or his sexuality. Baldus, however, perhaps considering that this was not a case where a doubt was at stake, argued that since the son could not qualify as an heir, he was barred from the feudal inheritance. The argument is nevertheless

17 F[rançois] Raviez, 'Voltaire ou l'hermaphrodite en question(s)', in *L'Hermaphrodisme de la Renaissance aux Lumières*, above, n. 4, pp. 279–303.

18 Perhaps the most comprehensive legal-historical survey on intersexuality remains A. Wacke, 'Vom Hermaphroditen zum Transsexuellen. Zur Stellung von Zwittern in der Rechtsgeschichte', in H. Eyrich, W. Odersky and F.J. Säcker (eds.), *Festschrift für Kurt Rebmann zum 65. Geburtstag*, C.H. Beck, Munich 1989, pp. 861–903. From an historiographical viewpoint, Wacke's remarkably well-documented contribution presents the additional interest that it was written before the rapidly developing scientific, doctrinal, legislative and broader legal changes related to transsexual and intersexual issues of the last quarter-century had taken place: his historical approach therefore still largely reflects the relatively conventional legal-conceptual framework which prevailed until the end of the 20th century.

more complex, for Baldus recites, on the one hand, the line of thinking that the configuration of the sexual organs is decisive, but, on the other, he also presents the argument according to which a person (presumably: whose gender is uncertain) who shows the physical, mental and moral qualities expected from a vassal called to provide military assistance and political counselling (*auxilium et consilium*), should be regarded as a man. The latter argument may be seen to take a (feudal) notion of gender into account rather than an anatomical approach to sex. However, the issue of this case is more complicated because there is strong evidence that the version of Baldus' opinion in that *consilium* (in printed versions, but apparently also in the main manuscript of reference) is truncated or corrupt. Baldus appears to refer to the same case in his lectures on feudal law, where he reports his advice more simply as being in favour of the heir, because it was determined that he was not a woman (and that opinion may have been influenced by the idea that the male sex was deemed to prevail as being stronger). In his lectures on the Code, Baldus also seems to refer to the same case, and provides yet another, somewhat different, argument: if the physical defects of the sexual organs are not commonly visible (which is presumably the case when the person is dressed up) and that person's (physical?) aptitudes are those associated with a man, the defective make-up of the sexual organs will not be decisive. Whatever may have been Baldus' actual opinion in his *consilium*, this case shows the versatility of arguments put forward in late-medieval legal thinking. Although the decision to be reached was necessarily framed in a binary system, which would preclude a stable 'third-gender' categorisation, the reasoning is strongly issue-related, and therefore fact-related, and allows for by-passing the evidence of the genital organs by taking into consideration qualities and inclinations which, in modern terms, come closer to gender identification – both self-identification and social identification. The *consilium* also includes a brief passage which may suggest that Baldus was prepared to accept, if the difficulty was one of imperfectly formed sexual organs, that a surgical intervention might solve the issue.[19]

---

19 I have used the editions: Baldus de Ubaldis, *Consilia*, Venice 1575, vol. 3, Cons. 237, fols. 67v–68r; and Milan 1492–1493, III (no pp. nn. but also Cons. 237); Baldus de Ubaldis, *Lectura super usibus feudorum*, Pavia *ca.* 1474, 1.6 §Mutum, fol. 40rv; Baldus de Ubaldis, *In Sextum Codicis Commentaria*, Venice 1599, ad C. 6.55.12, f. 189rv (with my gratitude to Dr. D. Fedele for providing me with references and print-outs). On the case, its context and its sources, see J. Kirshner and O. Cavallar, 'Da *pudenda* a *prudentia* : il *consilium* di Baldo degli Ubaldi sul caso di Giovanni Malaspina', in A Palazzo (ed.), *Diritto e processo*, Annuario giuridico dell'Università degli Studi di Perugia, Perugia 2010, pp. 97–112; F. Treggiari, *Le ossa di Bartolo. Contributo alla storia della tradizione giuridica perugina*, Dep. Storia Patria Umbria, Perugia 2009, pp. 39–44; A. Wijffels, 'De l'hermaphrodisme à l'intersexualité. Déjuridisation, Médicalisation, Rejuridisation', in F. Lekéal (ed.), *Droit, santé et gouvernance* (forthcoming).

Late-medieval and early-modern legal science was nevertheless mostly influenced by three ancient Roman law texts. A first fragment[20] asks with whom a hermaphrodite should be compared, and the general answer is: one should consider that the hermaphrodite belongs to the sex (or gender? In Latin: *sexus*) which prevails in a particular individual. The answer indicates that the individual will be regarded (in law, or at least for particular legal issues) either as a woman or as a man.

Another text[21] addresses the issue of men who cannot easily procreate (a situation which may arise in very different circumstances, e.g. because of old age and impotence), whether they can institute an heir (in Rome, an important feature of one's social and legal status). Specifically, with regard to the case of a hermaphrodite, paragraph 2 states that if the male capacities prevail in a particular individual, that person has the power to do so.

Finally, a short fragment[22] which says that in order to determine whether a hermaphrodite can witness a testament (a will in Roman law), the determining test is the quality of the sex (again: *sexus* in Latin) which 'lights up'.

These three fragments highlight two features: first, the mention of 'hermaphrodites' in the authoritative Roman legal texts meant that their existence was admitted in law; secondly, they would nevertheless not have a status *sui generis*, but, for specific legal issues, be categorised either as a man or as a woman.

In late-medieval and early-modern legal reasoning, such Roman law texts could be used in various contexts, even entirely outside the sphere of personal status.[23] However, they were generally discussed in their own right in the legal literature of glosses and commentaries. The same texts appear prominently

---

20 D. 1.5.10 [Ulpianus († c. 223 AD) libro 1. ad Sabinum]: 'Quaeritur: hermaphroditum cui comparamus? et magis puto eius sexus aestimandum, qui in eo praevalet'.

21 D. 28.2.6 *pr.* [Ulpianus libro 3. ad Sabinum]: 'Sed est quaesitum, an is, qui generare facile non possit, postumum heredem facere possit. et scribit Cassius et Iavolenus posse: nam et uxorem ducere et adoptare potest, spadonem quoque posse postumum heredem scribere et Labeo et Cassius scribunt; quoniam nec aetas nec sterilitas ei rei impedimento est. §1. Sed si castratus sit, Iulianus Proculi opinionem secutus non putat postumum heredem posse instituere, quo iure utimur. §2. Hermaphroditus plane, si in eo virilia praevalebunt, postumum heredem instituere poterit'.

22 D. 22.5.15.1 [Paulus (2nd/3rd c. AD) libro 3. sententiarum]: 'Hermaphroditus an ad testamentum adhiberi possit, qualitas sexus incandescentis ostendit'.

23 e.g., in a case of 1605 before the High Court of Admiralty in London, where an advocate was using one of the fragments as an authority in order to argue that a Dutch privateer's man-of-war which had been mainly equipped and manned by an English crew had nevertheless to be treated, in spite of the Dutch captain and his commissions, as an English ship and therefore as a venture violating the 1604 Anglo-Spanish peace treaty (A. Wijffels, *Alberico Gentili and Thomas Crompton – An Encounter between an Academic Jurist and a Forensic Practitioner* [*Studia Forensia Historica*, I], Ius Deco Publications, Leiden 1992.

in Barnabé Brisson's sixteenth-century civil law dictionary,[24] which includes a substantial entry on hermaphrodites, referring to both legal and non-legal authorities. In any case, here, too, the hermaphrodite can only be envisaged with reference to 'each of either gender'.

2.1. FRANCE

In commentaries and law reports, cases of transsexuality and intersexuality may not always be differentiated. Brisson's contemporary Le Caron published in 1579 a collection of consultations steeped in French legal practice. Consultation 54 of Book 10 somewhat cryptically refers to 'a remarkable case'.[25] The case is at first sight not particularly remarkable: in an unspecified place, the local feudal custom excluded women from inheriting when there were also male heirs. In the family involved in this case, the deceased had only left two daughters, and the eldest of the two had inherited the entire feudal estate. Six years later, however, the family history took a new twist: 'The younger sister, having reached the age of 14 or 15, when women start menstruating, felt a male organ coming *out* of her, forcefully and violently, changing her from a female into a male individual – upon which her guardian [not so much as a period to introduce this part of the sentence: someone with uncompromising legal reflexes!] immediately notified the elder sister' – and one can only speculate that this became a case of serious sibling rivalry. Le Caron's consultation was in favour of the younger sibling Charles, formerly Charlotte. The lawyer offers two lines of argumentation. In the first, he refers to medical and historical authorities, which supposedly testified that such a change could happen naturally, and that it was not such an uncommon occurrence. The second line of argumentation follows a legal reasoning. In order to refute the argument that in any case, the gender of the heirs at the time the father had died and when his succession had devolved was to be taken into account, Le Caron claims that in fact, it had been the already existing male nature of the younger sibling which had come out with puberty, and the lawyer insists that his new appearance incorporated all the reproductive organs. Once again, even though in such a case the argument is inevitably mixed up with the patrimonial interests at stake, the whole reasoning is directed at categorising the person either as a man or as a woman.

---

24 I used the later edition: B[arnabas] Brissonius, *De verborum quae ad ius civile pertinent significatione opus praestantissimum* ... Halae Magdeburgicae, Impensis Orphanotrophei, 1743, s.v. 'Hermaphroditus', 543–544. The entry also occurs in other legal dictionaries, e.g. (for a much shorter entry) I[acobus] Spiegel, *Lexicon iuris civilis*, Lugduni, Apud Sebastianum Gryphium, 1545, col. 234.

25 L[ouis] Charondas Le Caron, *Responses ou decisions du droict françois* ... A Paris, Chez Pierre Chevalier, au mont S. Hilaire à la Court d'Albret, 1605, fol. 399rv.

A notorious case (also in today's historiography and epistemology)[26] was that of Marine or Marin Le Marcis, in Rouen (Normandy), during the early years of the seventeenth century.[27] According to the printed report on the case by Jacques Duval, a Rouen physician, Le Marcis, had been regarded as a female subject until, around the age of 20, Le Marcis started acting (and dressing) as a man, and made arrangements to marry a widow.[28] In the ensuing litigation,[29] expert witnesses commissioned to examine Le Marcis declared the defendant to be a woman. Le Marcis was accordingly accused of homosexual acts and scandalous behaviour, convicted and sentenced to the death penalty. On appeal, a larger commission of experts was appointed, among whom Duval. Duval argued that through a tactile examination inside the apparent female sex of Le Marcis, he discovered a penis from which sperm ejaculated. That finding, always following Duval's report, saved Le Marcis' life, who was nonetheless ordered to dress henceforth as a woman and to abstain from marriage with either man or woman until the age of 25. Duval's printed report lead Jean Riolan, a King's physician, to publish two years later, in 1614, a counterblast in which he argued that (as the title-page states) contrary to common opinion, there are no true hermaphrodites.[30] Riolan had also been an expert in the case, but argued that Le Marcis' penis was in fact an excrescence, an anatomical deformation which could at least be regarded as a mitigating factor for Le Marcis, who could have bona fide believed that the deformation was a penis. The appellate court's reported decision remains ambiguous, though the conflicting opinions of Duval and Riolan seem nonetheless to suggest that, at least as an interim measure, it classified Le Marcis as a woman.

That decision would not be inconsistent with the apprehension of many lawyers, in the light of shifts in the apparent configuration of sexual organs reported in other cases (such as the one mentioned by Le Caron), to make a

---

26 M. Foucault, *Les Anormaux*, Seuil, Paris 1999, pp. 62–66 on the case here discussed. For a list of historians who have dealt with the case, see the article mentioned below, n. 27, p. 111, note 2.

27 L. Leibacher-Ouvrard, 'Imaginaire anatomique, débordements tribadiques et excisions – Le *Discours sur les hermaphrodits* (1614) de Jean Riolan fils', in *L'Hermaphrodisme de la Renaissance aux Lumières*, above n. 4, pp. 111–124.

28 J[acques] Duval, *Des Hermaphrodits, accouchemens des femmes et traitement qui est requis pour les relever en santé et bien élever leurs enfans*, Rouen, D. Geuffroy, 1612.

29 D. Brancher, 'Le "genre" incertain – De l'hermaphrodisme littéraire et médical', in *L'Hermaphrodisme de la Renaissance aux Lumières*, above n. 4, pp. 307–324. I have not been able to check if any court records on the case are surviving.

30 J[ean] Riolan, *Discours sur les Hermaphrodits – Où il est demonstré contre l'opinion commune, qu'il n'y a point de vrays Hermaphrodits*, A Paris, Chez Pierre Ramier, 1614; to which the first author replied: J[acques] Duval, *Response au discours fait par le sieur Riolan docteur en medicine & Professeur en Chirurgie & Pharmacie à Paris, contre l'Histoire de l'Hermaphrodit de Rouen*. A Rouen, Chez Iulian Courant, demeurant au haut de la ruë S. Croix des Pelletiers s.d. [1614].

final determination of a person's sexuality when faced with conflicting evidence. A hermaphrodite thus existed at least as an unstable, provisional status, for individuals whose uncertain sex had not been definitively determined as male or female by a court.

By the end of the Ancien Régime, relying on medical opinions and referring to several *causes célèbres* from the remote and recent past, the accepted opinion among French lawyers, for which the expertise of physicians was referred to, was that 'real' intersex persons did not exist. Typically, the entry in Guyot's *Répertoire*, echoing in some ways the entry in the *Encyclopédie*, expressed that argument,[31] referring to several cases, and elaborating on the at the time recent case of Anne Grand-Jean[32] – but not, characteristically, to any Roman law texts or civil law scholarship. It should be noted, however, that the received definition of the 'hermaphrodite' was restrictive: it required the test of combining the full physical reproductive apparatus of both sexes. An individual's sense of gender identity was easily set aside, as in the case of Grand-Jean, by considering that the person may have been deceived by her own defective anatomical make-up. Any decision as regards the attribution of the gender, if the sexual identity was in doubt and challenged the apparent status of the person, was therefore a prerogative of forensic determination.

The case of Giacoma Foroni provides a first-hand documented illustration of the resulting administrative practice during the first years of the nineteenth century, when the administrative machinery of the French state intended to operate on rational and scientific grounds. The uncertainty of Foroni's gender (who had since childhood appeared to be a woman) was raised when she wanted to marry a man. A commission of experts, authorised by the government, was charged in 1802 to carry out an investigation in the hamlet where Foroni

31 *Répertoire universel et raisonné de jurisprudence civile, criminelle, canonique et bénéficiale [... publié par M. Guyot ...]*, vol. 8 (A Paris, Chez Visse, 1784), s.v. 'Hermaphrodite', pp. 503–505. The entry was repeated without changes in the edition I have used of Merlin's post-revolutionary *Répertoire universel et raisonné de jurisprudence*, vol. 13, 5th ed., Chez H. Tarlier, Brussels 1826, pp. 325–326.

32 A person who was at first regarded as a woman, but who developed masculine features and attitudes after puberty, and eventually married as an adult. He was convicted in Lyon in the 1760s for having violated the sacrament of marriage, but the Paris Parliament overruled the conviction, apparently accepting that the defendant had acted bona fide. Pamphlets based on the case and proceedings were published at the time, e.g. *Réflexions sur les Hermaphrodites, relativement à Anne Grand-Jean, Qualifiées telle dans un Mémoire de Me Vermeil, Avocat au Parlement* [A Avignon, & se vend à Lyon, Chez Claude Jacquenod fils, 1765]; *Memoire pour Anne Grand Jean, connu sous le nom de Jean-Baptiste Grand Jean, Accusé & Appellant – Contre Monsieur le Procureur General, Accusateur et Intimé. Question. Un hermaphrodite qui a épousé une fille, peut-il être réputé profanateur du Sacrement de marriage, quand la nature qui le trompoit, l'appelloit à l'état de mari? Auquel on joint l'Hermaphrodite, ou Lettre d'Anne Grand Jean à François Lambert sa femme* [A Paris, De l'Imprimerie de Louis Cellot, 1765].

lived. Members of the commission were four physicians and surgeons of the Medical-Surgical Class of the Academy in Mantova, accompanied by a French commissioner and a professional draughtsman. The extensive report of their commission gives a detailed account of their investigation in situ, their interrogation of Foroni's relatives and others, and of the medical and quasi-forensic examination of her body.[33] The report includes several minute drawings of her anatomy, in particular of her genitals. Here again, although Foroni's attitudes and self-conscience as a woman are discussed, the sexual anatomy appears to be the focus of the determination of an individual's gender. The commission concluded that Foroni, in spite of presenting several features of female organs, and although male organs were not fully developed, had to be categorised as a man.[34] The detached scientific approach of the commissioners notwithstanding, the report seems to confirm the underlying opinion that a distinct hermaphrodite category, understood as combining (perfectly) the (physical) features of both sexes, did not exist.

2.2. GERMANY

In the Holy Roman Empire, learned legal literature and the practice of higher courts remained on the whole much more strongly influenced by the academic civil law tradition. A book on 'hermaphrodites' by a non-lawyer, Caspar Bauhin, first published in 1600, includes a compilation of texts from various scholarly works, including (mostly traditional, late-medieval) legal commentaries.[35] From these, the author borrows a list of legal issues which had occupied legal minds.[36] Examples of these issues are: Whether a masculine or feminine name should be given at the child's baptism? Can a hermaphrodite marry? Succeed to a copyhold? Be promoted to holy orders? Be a judge? An arbitrator? An advocate? A VC of a university? How should a hermaphrodite serve in any office? Should such a person stand in judgment as a man or as

---

33 *Jaqueline Foroni rendue à son veritable sexe, ou Rapport, Réflexions et jugement présentés à l'Académie de Mantoue, par la Classe de Médecine, sur le sexe d'un individu vivant, connu sous le nom de Jaqueline Foroni* [A Milan, De l'Imprimerie Française et Italienne à St. Zeno, An X de la République française (1802)].

34 C. Seth, 'Entre *curiosa* et oeuvre scientifique – Le cas Louis Hainaut, Marie Augé et Jacqueline Foroni', in *L'Hermaphrodisme de la Renaissance aux Lumières*, above, n. 4, pp. 125–146.

35 C[aspar] Bauhin, *De hermaphroditorum monstrosorumque partuum natura ex Theologorum, Jureconsultorum, Medicorum, Philosophorum, & Rabbinorum sententia Libri Duo*, [Oppenheimii, Typis Hieronymi Galleri, Aere Johan. Theodori de Bry, 1614; Francofurti, Excudebat Matheus Becker impensis Io. Theo. Io. Israel de Bry, frat., 1620].

36 The list was reproduced in an English translation in a treatise on hermaphrodites published in London one and a half centuries later: J[ames] Parsons, *A Mechanical and Critical Enquiry into the Nature of Hermaphrodites* [London: Printed for J. Walthoe, 1741].

a woman? ... These and other questions reflect gender-related discriminations (but in many ways also other discriminations, e.g. between legitimate and illegitimate children) which influenced a person's legal status and social position in public life and in that person's personal and family relations. It shows that in the late-medieval and early-modern legal scholarship tradition from which Bauhin drew his authorities, the lawyers' approach to persons whose gender was not clearly identified as male or female remained very much (not unlike the approach in the Roman law texts) case- and fact-related, bearing in mind the perceived social interests (i.e. also interests of third parties) at stake.

The learned law tradition in Germany and its reliance on Roman law texts is reflected through several theoretical legal works, such as a treatise published in 1692 by Jacob Möller, in which the author also drew from a wide range of heterogeneous legal and classical sources.[37] Möller's definition of the hermaphrodite is conventionally that of a person who appears to have the sexual make-up of both female and male genders or none of it. However, he adds that the term is also used for persons whose sexual actions are deemed immoral.[38] Möller's treatise still expresses a typically traditional approach consisting in accumulating opinions from various authorities, in his case extensively (but not exclusively) from legal authorities.

The issues he discusses match to a great extent those already advanced in Bauhin's summary a century before, though here they are treated in much greater detail. In some cases, policy considerations appear. For example, when the *topos* of the possibility of a hermaphrodite becoming a university vice-chancellor is raised, the negation in the cases of a person whose male sexuality is not prevalent is explained through a long excursion on the exclusive privilege of masculinity in holding offices of public or corporate governance. In the private sphere, however, such as the baptism name or even marriage, the individual's choice of gender may prevail.

Some eighteenth-century German codifications include provisions on hermaphrodites. This was the case of the Bavarian Civil code of 1756, usually regarded as a conservative codification with respect to the pre-existing state of Bavarian law. A short provision deals with the sex-assignment

---

37 J[ACOBUS] MÖLLERUS, *Discursus duo philologico-juridici, prior De Cornutis, posterior De hermaphroditis, eorumque jure, Uterque Ex Jure Divino, Canonico, Civili, Consuetudinibus Feudorum, variisque Historiarum monumentis, rerumque antiquarum Scriptoribus, private industria, horisotiosis congestus* [Francofurti, Typis Christoph. Andreae Zeitleri, 1692].

38 '... qui sexu sunt indistincti, nimirum, qui vel neutrum, vel utrumque habere videntur; licet etiam Hermaphroditus is dicatur, qui turpiter & facit, et patitur adversus & versus impudicus, uti docet Suidas in voce ἑρμαφρόδιτος' (from the work quoted above, n. 37, in the Berlin 1699 edition, p. 142; the reference at the end of the quote is to the Medieval Byzantine so-called *Suidae Lexicon*).

of hermaphrodites:[39] the main rule is that experts (i.e. physicians)[40] will determine the person's gender. However, if the evidence is that both sexes appear to be equally present, the person herself/himself will make the decision – and have to stand by his or her decision, or be subjected to criminal punishment. The Bavarian statute imposed thus the binary sex-assignment: i.e. that in law, the hermaphrodite would not be recognised as such, but would be identified with a man or woman's legal status.

A few years earlier, in 1749, at an interim stage of the preparations for the Prussian codification, a draft compilation was published, which also included some general provisions on hermaphrodites.[41] The relevant section starts by subdividing human beings in men, women and *Zwitter* (intersex persons). The latter class is defined as persons who have simultaneously the features of both sexes (*utrumque*). The system anticipates that of the Bavarian Code a few years later: the hermaphrodite must be categorised according to the prevailing sex, either as a man, or as a woman. If the two sexes are equally developed, the individual has a choice, but cannot act later contrary to that choice – if the person does, he or she may be convicted and sentenced to corporal punishment. And if the person has married a man, she (as she is then regarded by the law) cannot marry a woman at a later stage. The degree of self-determination remained therefore limited, and, moreover was subordinated to any determination which a previous enquiry might have made.

The Prussian codification of 1794 represents in many ways the non-revolutionary accomplishment of statutory evolutions in Germany (here in particular: Prussia) towards the end of the Ancien Régime. The Prussian Code's system on intersex persons differs from the mid-eighteenth-century project.[42] Again, the lawmaker imposes a choice between male and female gender.

---

39 *Codex Maximilianeus Bavaricus civilis* ... [München, Gedruckt von Johann Vötter, 1756], I.3 §2: '... Hermaphroditen warden 2do dem Geschlecht beygezehlt, welches nach Rath und Meinung deren Verständigen vordringt, falls sich aber die Gleichheit hierin bezeigt, sollen sie selbst eins erwählen, und von dem Erwählten *sub Paena Falsi* nicht abweichen'.

40 During the late 18th century and early 19th century, professional (and academically educated) medics succeeded in barring other professional groups (in particular, midwives) whose expertise on matters of sex determination had traditionally been acknowledged (U. Klöppel, *XXOXY ungelöst – Hermaphroditismus, Sex und Gender in der deutschen Medizin – Eine historische Studie zur Intersexualität*, Transcript Verlag, Bielefeld 2010, pp. 211–215).

41 *Project des Corporis Juris Fridericiani das ist Gr. Königl. Majestät in Preussen in der Vernunft und Landes-Verfassungen gegründete Land-Recht worinn das Römische Recht in eine natürliche Ordnung, und richtiges Systema, nach denen dreyen Objectis Juris gebracht* ... [Halle, In Verlegung des Waysenhauses, 1749], Part I, Book I, Title IV, §3.

42 I have used: *Allgemeines Landrecht für die Preußischen Staaten von 1794. Mit einer Einführung von Dr. Hans Hattenhauer und einer Bibliographie von Dr.Günther Bernert*, Dritte, erweiterte Auflage, Luchterhand Verlag, Berlin 1996, §§19–23, p. 61.

The original choice is left to the parents. Then, once the person has reached the age of 18, he or she can determine his or her gender – which implies the possibility of a different choice from the parents. The individual's own choice is binding for the future. However, when the interests of third parties are at stake, an investigation by experts can be ordered at the request of the latter. The experts' determination prevails over any choice expressed by the parents or the individual. In practice, that system entailed that in any case, a gender determination took place, and that as soon as the gender was relevant in social relations (status, inheritance, marriage, contracts, property, proceedings ...) the case was deferred to experts (probably, increasingly the exclusive preserve of graduated and established medics), whose opinion was decisive.

In the course of the nineteenth century, commentators of the Prussian law paid little attention to the provisions on sex-determination.[43] The binary system of reference[44] became even more important, as, by the second half of the century, commentators would routinely refer to medical opinions denying the

43 While preparing this chapter, I was able to consult a sample of such commentaries, including E.F. Klein, *System des Preußischen Civilrechts ... unter Benutzung der neusten Rechtsquellen und mit Hinverweisung auf das gemeine Recht*, Erster Band, In der Buchhandlung des Waisenhauses, Halle 1830, p. 66; J.F. Thöne, *Fundamental-Lehren des Preußischen Privatrechts, einschließlich der Abfassungsgeschichte des Allgemeinen Landrechts und der Lehre von dem Besitz und der Verjährung*, Erster Band, in der Hahn'schen Verlags-Buchhandlung, Leipzig 1833, p. 283; J.A.L. Fürstenthal, *Das Preußische Civil-Recht nach Anleitung und der Titelfolge des Allgemeinen Landrechts, mit Berücksichtigung der neueren Gesetze, der Doktrin, der Praxis und des Römischen Rechts*, Bei Theodor Theile, Königsberg 1842, p. 34; C.J. Koch, *Lehrbuch des Preußischen gemeinen Privatrechts*, Zweite verbesserte und vermehrte Auflage, I. Band, Verlag von T. Trautwein'schen Buch und Musik-Handlung, Berlin 1851, p. 151; C.C.E. Hiersemenzel, *Vergleichende Uebersicht des heutigen Römischen und Preußischen gemeinen Privatrechts*, Erster Theil, Verlag von Gustav Hempel, Berlin 1852, p. 91; L.E. Heydemann, *Einleitung in das System des Preußischen Civilrechts*, Erster Band. *Allgemeiner Theil*, Verlag von Beit und Comp, Leipzig 1861, p. 132; [C.J. Koch] *Allgemeines Landrecht für die Preußischen Staaten. Unter Andeutung der obsoleten oder aufgehobenen Vorschriften und Einschaltung der jüngeren noch geltenden Bestimmungen, herausgeben mit Kommentar in Anmerkungen von Dr. C.J. Koch.* Erster Band, Sechste Ausgabe, Verlag von J. Guttentag (D. Collin), Berlin 1874, p. 76; J. Schmidt, *Lehrbuch des preußischen Rechts und Prozesses mit Rücksicht auf die Reichsgesetzgebung, das gemeine Recht und den gemeinrechtlichen Prozeß*, Erster Band, Verlag von Maruschke & Berendt, Breslau 1878, p. 68; O. Fischer, *Lehrbuch des preußischen Privatrechts*, Verlag von J. Guttentag (D. Collin), Berlin und Leipzig 1887, p. 50, note 3; H. Dernburg, *Lehrbuch des Preußischen Privatrechts und der Privatrechtsnormen des Reichs – Erster Band: Die Allgemeinen Lehren und das Sachenrecht des Privatrechts Preußens und des Reichs*, Fünfte, neubearbeitete Auflage, Verlag der Buchhandlung des Waisenhauses, Halle a.S. 1894, p. 96, note 8; comp. idem, *Lehrbuch des Preußischen Privatrechts und der Privatrechtsnormen des Reichs – Erster Band*, Zweite, neubearbeitete Auflage, Verlag der Buchhandlung des Waisenhauses, Halle a.S. 1879, p. 93 note 8.

44 See also in that sense the brief statement (referring to Roman-Catholic canon law doctrine) by E. Bartels, *Ehe und Verlöbnis nach gemeinem und partikulärem Rechte in der Provinz Hannover*, Hahn'sche Hofbuchhandlung, Hannover 1871, pp. 94–95.

existence of hermaphrodism.[45] A standard phrase in legal literature was that the paragraphs of the Prussian code on *Zwitter* were 'unpractical'.[46]

That general attitude among legal writers may partly explain why no provisions on hermaphrodites were included in the *Bürgerliches Gesetzbuch* (BGB, the German Civil Code) of 1896. At the risk of simplifying the comparison between France and Germany, it would seem that the medical-scientific approach which tended to deny the existence of intersexuality (largely reduced to the full constitution of reproductive organs) had become, partly for ideological reasons, mainstream thinking among French jurists by the end of the eighteenth century, and from the early nineteenth-century onwards among German legal scholars. However, that perception may have to be qualified or revised in the light of more recent studies of the changing medical approaches in the course of the nineteenth century. Thus, whereas A. Dreger argued that from the later nineteenth century onwards, medical science tended to identify the gonads as the determining organs for identifying the sex of a person and to dismiss on that basis sexual ambivalence and hermaphrodism,[47] U. Klöppel found that the medical literature started focusing on gonads from the early nineteenth century onwards, moved by concerns about demography and eugenics.[48] The relatively early interest for gonads as the test of a person's sexuality, Klöppel suggests, was linked to growing medical concern in establishing a person's procreative capacity. That, in turn, may account for a growing interest – which could in many instances not be satisfied on technical grounds – in examining the internal reproductive organs.

Klöppel's research on the development of medical approaches to intersex (in particular, in German medical literature) throughout the nineteenth century gainsays the German jurists' dismissal of the statutory provisions on hermaphrodites on the grounds that medical science denied their existence. On the contrary, medical scientists sought new criteria for establishing and explaining sexual differentiation, and though the binary distinction between male and female remained the fundamental reference, these two categories were now increasingly situated as the poles of continuous and gradual scales of differentiation between them. Moreover, the medical profession was concerned with both the theoretical coherence of the new criteria put forward, and the

---

45 [C.J. Koch] *Allgemeines Landrecht für die Preußischen Staaten* (above, n 43), p. 76, note 20: '... Die Aerzte behaupten, daß es eine wahre Zwitterbildung nach Theorie und Erfahrung nicht gebe' (with a reference to L.J.C. Mende, *Ausführliches Handbuch der Gerichtlichen Medizins*); see also the quote from Joseph Schmidt's manual, above n. 43.

46 Fischer, above, n. 43, p. 50, note 3: 'Die ganz unpraktischen Bestimmungen über Zwitter'; Schmidt, above n. 43, p. 68: 'Die neuere medicinische Wissenschaft verwirft entschieden die Existenz der Zwitter. Die §§19–23, Tit. I, sind daher unpraktisch geworden'.

47 A. Dreger, *Hermaphrodites and the medical invention of sex*, Harvard University Press, Cambridge (Mass.) 2003.

48 Klöppel, above n. 40, pp. 217–218 and 268–269; the argument mentioned here above is also developed in her article 'The lost innocence of hermaphrodites', in *L'Hermaphrodisme de la Renaissance aux Lumières*, above n. 4, pp. 147–168.

practical relevance of scientific progress. For example, because the reliance on gonads as the decisive test for differentiating male from female could in many instances only be established post-mortem, the test was impractical for physicians who were called to advise the authorities or courts on an individual's sex assignment or determination for birth registration or establishing the person's capacity to marry (or to perform reproductive sexual acts as husband or wife). It seems therefore that such practical necessities may have contributed to convince many practitioners to consider other factors, which in their own way were also referred in scientific debates challenging the exclusive reliance on gonads as the decisive test: other anatomical and physical features than the genitalia, but also mental disposition and even sexual orientation could be taken in consideration alongside or in lieu of gonads. The broadening of the factors and tests in turn revived a debate between the respective role of 'innate' and 'acquired' factors which determined one's sexuality. For scientists, hermaphroditism was sometimes viewed as an observable testimony of their theories. At the same time, the scientific discussion was often intertwined with moral and political issues. In general, attempts at systematisation were prone to be affected by hierarchical representations. Theories which emphasised the developing stages of sexual differentiation from an 'original' cell (which was alternatively presented as sexually indifferent or female) would imply that hermaphroditism was linked to underdeveloped or pathologically developed creatures, and thus inferior to the stage of perfect differentiation, while some nineteenth-century medical theorists would award masculinity a higher position in the 'natural order' than femininity. Early nineteenth century proposals by some lawyers to abolish a separate status for *Zwitter* and to delegate the determination of the sex to medical experts therefore ignored the relevance of hermaphroditism in contemporary medical-scientific debates. Nevertheless, when under imperial rule, an Act was passed (6 February 1875) establishing birth, marriage and death registers, it only provided for the mention of either the male or female sex in the birth register; medical authorities were critical of the suppression of the possibility of leaving the possibility in law to recognise 'real' hermaphrodites, who could either combine essential features of both man and woman, or neither. A practical manual for officials in charge of birth registers included a sample form for cases where the medical experts had not (yet) been able to determine the sex of the child, but this appears to have been a rare acknowledgement of the medical approach in (quasi-)legal literature at the time. However, as the BGB ignored intersex persons, its implementation reinforced the requirement to determine the sex of an individual as male or female – any legal uncertainty could only be temporary and was to be cleared by medical professionals.[49]

---

[49] This paragraph relies on KLÖPPEL, above, n 40, Part I, ch. 3, pp. 235–297 (on specific legal issues in the light of medical developments: pp. 273–276 (19th century and Weimar Republic) and 551–554 (after the Second World War).

3. AN AGE OF CHANGE (LATE TWENTIETH CENTURY AND EARLY TWENTY-FIRST CENTURY)

From the late nineteenth century onwards, and during the twentieth century, the anthropology underpinning Western sciences, humanities, social relations and cultural representations changed fundamentally. Gender identity – and the principle itself of gender identity – was thoroughly challenged. The distinctiveness of intersex issues notwithstanding, the relatively recent tendency towards ensuring a systematic protection of intersex persons against discrimination needs to be seen against the long-term background, during the twentieth century, of women's emancipation, gay rights movements and non-discrimination of transsexuals: all areas in which categories of persons had long been discriminated against, whereby the legal discriminations were based on multi-secular cultural biases against self-determination of gender identity and sexual relationships. A growing number of scientists, not only in the human and social sciences, have contributed in scholarly publications to undermine conventional conceptions about the differentiation between genders, or about the definition of gender identity. Again, their research and publications have received a great deal of press coverage, contributing to a revision of social and cultural attitudes on sexual issues, ranging from sexual orientation to gender identity of inter- and transsexuals. By the beginning of the twenty-first century, at least in Western societies, the traditional gender differentiation has not only been increasingly eroded in mainstream cultural attitudes,[50] in the social sciences and other areas of scholarship, it has also affected areas of the law where gender differentiation seemed at first firmly established. For example, two areas where the law has been challenged on issues which until recently were commonly believed to be beyond the outer limits of legal protection against discrimination are the admission of women to combat units (in regular armies) and the status of transsexuals in sport competitions. (Both issues could be extended with regard to their application to intersex individuals.)

Gender issues of transsexuality and intersexuality have by now largely been recognised as human rights-related issues.[51] Indeed, during the last decades

50 Yet, apparently new artistic expressions of these attitudes have sometimes an ancient analogy: as, e.g., in the film adaptation of David Mitchell's novel *Cloud Atlas*, released in the US in 2012 and early 2013 in Europe. The directors, one of whom was at the time a transgender artist (and her brother has since then, become her sister), have playfully integrated and renewed the old tradition of transsexuality in stage-playing by casting the same actors in different roles representing different genders. The novelty of our age, it seems, is that such devices are now reflecting a much broader popular acceptance and culture in Western societies.

51 That development is now widely perceived among various actors militating in favour of gender-related emancipation and non-discrimination. e.g., the title of the volume *1-0-1 [one 'o one] intersex – Das Zwei-Geschlechter-System als Menschenrechtsverletzung*, Hg. Von der Neuen Gesellschaft für Bildende Kunst, Berlin 2005, includes a variegated

of the twentieth century, the emancipation of women, of gays, lesbians and bisexuals, transsexuals and intersex persons has been fortified by the development of human rights in all walks of life as a form of effective political, social, economic and cultural enfranchising of formerly discriminated categories of persons – because of gender-related issues or otherwise. That development has also provided an opening, especially in Western societies, for developing a non-discriminatory legal protection and status for intergender persons. Human rights, however, should not be seen historically as irreversible. As political populism, religious fundamentalism, and in general discriminatory social attitudes may revive, human rights will be and are already being challenged, and the most vulnerable groups and minorities may be the first to suffer from such reversals. That is, as things now stand, perhaps one of the strongest arguments for pursuing the human rights developments of the past few decades, not least on gender issues.

---

selection of contributions by artists, social scientists, historians ... on current issues of intersexuality (in particular, in the German context), but also includes a legal essay: O. Tolmein, 'Recht und Geschlecht – ein Plädoyer für die Anerkennung von Hermaphoditen', pp. 128–135, with an emphasis on human rights and the issue of consent in medical practices tending to re-categorise young persons displaying intersex characteristics. Human rights also appear prominently in D.C. Ghattas, *Menschenrechte zwischen den Geschlechtern Vorstudie zur Lebenssituation von Inter*Personen*, Schriften der Demokratie Bd. 34, Heinrich-Böll-Stiftung, Berlin 2013.

PART III

TRANSGENDER, TRANSSEXUALITY AND INTERSEX

LESSONS FROM THE LEGAL DEVELOPMENT OF THE LEGAL STATUS OF TRANSSEXUAL AND TRANSGENDER PERSONS

Jens M. SCHERPE

1. AN 'I' IS NOT A 'T'

The voice of intersex persons has been unheard for a long time. Also, often this voice was absorbed into the wider chorus of the voices of the LBGT movement. But an 'I' is not 'T' (and not an 'L', 'G' or 'B' either). Intersex is about experience of body, and trans about experience of gender (and neither are about sexual orientation). It is important to point out right at the outset of this chapter that the legal issues concerning intersex people are different from those of trans individuals and must be dealt with, as a matter of urgency, as a distinct issue and not merely as a part of the debate of other issues, even though they may be or may seem to be related.

However, recently trans individuals have been become much more visible in society,[1] and legal issues surrounding them have received much greater

[1] Examples for this increased visibility are: the novel *The Danish Girl* by DAVID EBERSHOFF (published in 2000 and turned into a film featuring Academy Award winner EDDIE REDMAYNE in 2015; CAITLYN JENNER featuring on the July 2015 cover of *Vanity Fair* and

(and indeed much needed) attention. Significant progress has been made with regard to their rights and recognition in many jurisdictions. The same has yet to happen for intersex persons. While acknowledging the differences between the two groups, this chapter suggests that some lessons can be learned from the paths that were taken to achieve this progress. The chapter by Peter Dunne in this volume will also explore this topic, so this chapter will be based on the findings and recommendations of another research project (which resulted in the publication of the book *The Legal Status of Transsexual and Transgender Persons*)[2] and how they can be made fruitful for the present context.

One of the key things the comparison and analysis for the transgender project brought to light was the importance of continuous and consistent activism, and also the importance of certain individuals in bringing about change. But what was also shown were 'phases' or stages in the development of the law concerning transsexual and transgender persons. It is very likely that we will see (and indeed are seeing) those mirrored for intersex – although it is to be hoped that the development will be much quicker and more efficient.

2. HISTORICAL DEVELOPMENT: THREE PHASES

2.1. FIRST STAGE: THE 'MEDICAL' PHASE

The very first statute which allowed a change of legal gender, the Swedish Act of 1972,[3] was at least partially motivated by intersex issues. As such, it was also meant to address some of the problems intersex person were facing if they were 'wrongly classified'.[4] By today's standards the regulations in that statute are unacceptable and clearly violating the human rights of the people concerned, but at the time the statute was considered ground-breaking.

At this stage, gender identity and difference in sex development were still mainly seen as a 'medical' problem. The main concern was the misguided

talking about her transition; Laverne Cox starring as Sophia Burset and Asia Kate Dillon (who identifies as non-binary) as Brandy Epps in the television series *Orange is the New Black*; Sarah McBride becoming the first openly transgender person to address a major party convention in the United States in July 2016.

2 J.M. Scherpe (ed.), *The Legal Status of Transsexual and Transgender Persons* (2015), and especially the concluding chapter (J.M. Scherpe and P. Dunne, 'The Legal Status of Transsexual and Transgender Persons – Comparative Analysis and Recommendations', pp. 615–663). The research project and international conference (held on 6 and 7 September 2013 in Hong Kong) were funded by the Centre for Medical Ethics and Law (CMEL – see <http://www.cmel.hku.hk/>) of the University of Hong Kong.

3 Lag (1972:119) *om fastställande om könstillhorighet i vissa fall.*

4 On the legal development in Sweden, see J. Garland, 'The Legal Status of Intersex Persons in Sweden', in this volume, and J. Garland, 'The Legal Status of Transsexual and Transgender Persons in Sweden' in Scherpe, above n. 2, pp. 281–311.

perception that there was a need for a 'cure' for the people concerned, and gender recognition was only possible after having undergone full surgery and sterilisation. Subsequent statutes (and court decisions) initially largely followed that approach.[5] The discussion on what the requirements for legal gender recognition (or, to use what arguably is a more appropriate term, the recognition of preferred gender) ought to be generally focused on similar issues:

- age;
- nationality;
- marital status;
- sterility requirements;
- surgery requirements;
- other medical/diagnosis[6] requirements;
- so-called 'real life test'/'living in the other gender' for a specified period of time;
- proof that the 'desire to live in the other gender' was permanent/diagnosis of 'gender dysphoria'.

The medical requirements generally formed the core of any legal recognition regime. They were the most onerous requirements and, in many cases, were insurmountable obstacles. In hindsight it is apparent that many of these 'well-meaning' statutes or administrative/court procedures of the first stage inflicted (and continue to inflict) unnecessary suffering on the persons concerned.

2.2. SECOND STAGE: RIGHTS NOT REMEDIES

Rightly, many of the original stipulations later were found to be human rights violations by national constitutional courts and international courts.[7] The emerging jurisprudence on these issues opened the second stage. In this stage, the question of recognition of preferred gender – slowly – began to detach itself from the medical sphere. We see a 'legalisation' of the issue, particularly through the human rights lens. Increasingly, the issues came to be phrased in terms of rights (rather than mere remedies), and there were a number of legal challenges in national and international fora.

---

5 On this, see the contributions in SCHERPE, above n. 2, and especially the German Gesetz über die Änderung der Vornamen und die Feststellung der Geschlechtszugehörigkeit in besonderen Fällen (Transsexuellengesetz) (TSG) of 1980, BGBl. I 1980, 1654, discussed by A. DUTTA, 'The Legal Status of Transsexual and Transgender Persons in Germany', pp. 207–221.

6 Diagnosis requirements often focused solely on gender dysphoria, and, as a consequence, intersex persons were unable to rely on these gender recognition procedures.

7 For references see Sections 2.2.1 and 2.2.2 below.

2.2.1. National Constitutional Law: The Example of Germany

In the national sphere, the most striking examples of what may be termed as successful 'transadvocacy' can be seen in Germany.[8] Here, almost every single one of the recognition criteria originally contained in the German 'Transsexuals Act' (TSG) was found to violate the German Constitution. The special role the German Constitutional Court (*Bundesverfassungsgericht*) has played in the development of the law in this area can be explained by the quality and persistence of the advocacy,[9] but also by the fact that Germany and the German courts as a reaction to the horrendous atrocities committed in the 1930s and 1940s have a heightened sensitivity towards issues of human rights, and particularly with regard to the social and legal exclusion of those not conforming the views of the majority, and thus the need to protect minorities. The decisions by the German Constitutional Court in many ways can be seen as exemplary for the human rights developments in this area of law and therefore merit some closer examination.[10]

The first of the recognition requirements in the TSG to be declared unconstitutional was the – somewhat arbitrary – age limit of 25.[11] Medical evidence – unsurprisingly – clearly showed that this needed to be determined on an individual basis.[12]

This was followed by the nationality requirement being declared unconstitutional in 2006; given that legal recognition of the preferred gender identity had been established as a fundamental human right, it could not be restricted because of the nationality of the applicant, matters of comity notwithstanding. In the unanimous decision of 18 July 2006 the German Constitutional Court stated that while Germany may not be in a position to issue personal identification documents or birth certificates, etc. to foreign nationals, it could recognise the preferred gender of a person for all intents and purposes

---

8 For an overview of the developments in Europe, see e.g. P. Dunne, 'Transgender sterilisation requirements in Europe' (2017) 25 *Medical Law Review* 554–581.

9 And here particularly Maria Sabine Augstein, who in 2015 was awarded the highest German honour, the Bundesverdienstkreuz (Federal Cross of Merit), by the German President. On Augstein, see I. Gukema-Augstein, *Der intime Blick. Maria Sabine Augstein* (2008).

10 Space precludes an in-depth discussion of the Constitutional Court decisions, but see Dutta, above n. 5, with further references. Of course, the jurisprudence of other courts equally deserves to be noted, e.g. the remarkable decisions of the Columbian Constitutional Court (on which see the chapter by R. Rubio-Marín and S. Osella in this volume).

11 German Constitutional Court decisions of 16.3.1982, *BVerfGE* 60, 123 and of 26.1.1993, *BVerfGE* 88, 87.

12 See e.g. P. Cohen-Kettenis and F. Pfäfflin, *Transgenderism and Intersexuality in Childhood and Adolescence* (2003) with further references, and F. Pfäfflin, 'Transgenderism and Transsexuality: the Medical and Psychological Viewpoints', in Scherpe, above n. 2, pp. 11–23.

(including the right to marry) on German territory.[13] The home state of the person concerned may refuse to recognise the preferred gender/the decision by the German courts, but for the individual in question the recognition in Germany was undoubtedly more important since they had applied for it.

German law also required any applicant for recognition of preferred gender to be unmarried. German law at the time did not recognise same-sex marriages,[14] and this was seen as a necessary provision to maintain that position. In 2008, the Constitutional Court struck down this provision.[15] The institution of marriage is protected by the German Basic Law (the Constitution), and so once a couple is married they are protected. This protection does not cease merely because one of them wants to be recognised in a different legal gender. The Court held that it was unconstitutional to force persons to choose between their constitutionally protected marriage and their constitutionally protected gender identity. For the persons concerned the matter was not a question of choice anyway, as they merely wanted to be recognised by the law as who they really are. Moreover, if the couple wanted to remain married, it would be impossible to fulfil the legal requirements for divorce in Germany, which required irretrievable breakdown of the marriage evidenced by living separately (§1565 German Civil Code, BGB). The Court also emphasised that not requiring a divorce in such cases did not amount to an introduction of same-sex marriage. The law at the time required the two persons who wanted to get married to be of female and male gender, and that remained unchanged by the Constitutional Court decision.

---

13 BVerfGE 116, 243. On this, see also J. Basedow and J.M. Scherpe (eds.), *Transsexualität, Staatsangehörigkeit und internationales Privatrecht* (2004), based on the amicus brief submitted in the proceedings.

14 Since 1 October 2017 marriages in Germany can be entered into by persons of the same or different sex, new §1353 (1) German Civil Code (BGB). The same applies in Denmark, cf §1 *Lov om ægteskabs indgåelse og opløsning*. Similarly, s. 11(c) Matrimonial Causes Act 1973 for England and Wales stipulates that a marriage between 2 persons of the same sex is now legal. Ironically, in all these jurisdictions the legislative aim was that gender should no longer matter for marriage, yet they all saw it as necessary to refer to specific genders in the new provisions. Common sense would have suggested to use a gender-neutral formulation, such as 'two persons', as, e.g., the new Maltese legislation has done; cf. Marriage Act and other Laws (Amendment) Act 2017.

15 BVerfG 27 May 2008, *BVerfGE* 121, 175. Similar decisions were taken in Taiwan by the Ministry of the Interior (on this, see Chih-hsing Ho, 'The Legal Status of Transsexual and Transgender Persons in Taiwan' in Scherpe, above n. 2, pp. 425 et seq.) and in Italy Corte Suprema di Cassazione (Supreme Court of cassation, Cass.), 06.06.2013, No. 14329, (2013) *Corriere giuridico* 1519 (but see Corte costituzionale (Constitutional Court of Italy), 11.06.2014, no. 170). The ECtHR came to a different conclusion in *Hämäläinen v. Finland* [2014] ECHR 787; however, that can be explained by the nature of the ECHR and the role of the Court as a supra-national body. On this, see P. Dunne, '(Trans) Marriage Equality? Challenging Europe's Marital "Dissolution Requirements"' (2016) 28(4) *Child and Family Law Quarterly* 325–346. See also the recent opinion of AG M. Bobek in *MB* (Case C-451/16), 05.12.2017 <http://curia.europa.eu/juris/document/document.jsf?text=&docid=197431&pageIndex=0&doclang=EN&mode=req&dir=&occ=first&part=1&cid=438128> (last accessed 06.02.2018).

Thus, while in the case of one of the spouses legally changing their gender there may be marriages that later changed to become same-sex marriages, one still could not enter into same-sex marriages in Germany.

The line of reasoning that being forced to 'trade' one constitutionally protected right for another was unconstitutional was followed in the next decision on the TSG in 2011, which struck down the surgery and sterility requirements.[16] The Court again held that it was unconstitutional to ask applicants for a legal change of their gender to effectively surrender one constitutional right (here: right to physical integrity) in order to avail themselves of the constitutional right to be recognised in their true gender identity. The applicants were forced to choose one over the other, in a situation where, in reality, there is no choice regarding the gender identity. Therefore, ultimately this may mean forcing unwanted medical and surgical intervention on persons, which was unacceptable. The Court stated clearly that according to all available evidence, physically altering one's sex characteristics to conform to the sex characteristics of the opposite gender was not a valid indicator of a stable and irreversible self-identification with that gender, and thus such requirements a violation of the rights of the person concerned.

As a result of this jurisprudence, only very few of the original legal requirements remain in the TSG, namely that the applicant (1) feels as though they do not belong to their current legal gender but rather to the opposite legal gender; (2) they have felt a 'compulsion' to live according to their perceived gender for at least three years; and (3) there is a high probability that their sense of belonging to the opposite gender will not change in the future. As there is an emerging international consensus that these remaining requirements are not only overly burdensome but lead to an intense intrusion into the private life of the persons concerned, reform debates are ongoing in Germany on these last remaining issues as well.[17]

2.2.2. *International Human Rights Law*

There is a strong, emerging consensus that international human rights law recognises the right of individuals to be legally acknowledged in their preferred gender.

---

[16] BVerfG 11 January 2011, *BVerfGE* 128, 109, and BVerfG 27 October 2011, *Neue Juristische Wochenschrift (NJW)* 2012, 600. For a similar decision in Italy, see Supreme Court of Italy (20 July 2015) and also Court of Roma, 14.04.2011 (2011) Fam. Dir. (Famiglia e Diritto), p. 183. S. also Court of Roma, 18.10.1997 (1998) Dir. Fam. (Diritto della famiglia e delle persone), 1033; Court of Salerno, 05.03.1998 (1998) Dir. fam. Pers. (Diritto della famiglia e delle persone), p. 1057; Court of Siena, 12.06.2013, no. 412, available at <www.dejure.it>. Contra Court Vercelli, 27.11.2014, no. 159, available at www.dejure.it; for Sweden see Stockholm Court of Administrative Appeal, *Socialstyrelsen v. NN* Mål nr 1968–12 (19.12.2012); for Canada, see *XY v. R* [2012] HRTO 726 (Human Rights Tribunal of Ontario); for Argentina, see *PRL*, Criminal and Correction Court No. 4 of Mar del Plata (10 April 2008).

[17] On which, see the chapters by T. Meyer and N. Althoff in this volume.

For Europe, the European Court of Human Rights (ECtHR) decisions in *Goodwin v. United Kingdom* and *I v. United Kingdom* very clearly stand out as the decisive landmark decisions in that respect and firmly entrenched that right for the Contracting States of the European Convention (ECHR).[18] The decisions did not, however, address the requirements or conditions for recognition of the preferred gender. These were the subject of several subsequent decisions, the most important of which so far probably is *A.P., Garçon and Nicot v. France*.[19] Similar to the German decision discussed above, the Court held that making recognition of the true gender identity conditional on submitting to an unwanted sterilising treatment amounted to making the full exercise of one's right to respect for private life conditional on relinquishing full exercise of the right to respect for one's physical integrity; this was a violation of the European Convention. While other medical requirements such as a diagnosis of gender dysphoria and physical medical examination were (still?) deemed to be within the margin of appreciation of the ECHR Contracting States, the case established firmly that sterility requirements are not.

Similarly, the Inter-American Court of Human Rights in a 2017 Advisory Opinion requested by the Republic of Costa Rica emphasised the right to self-determination of legal gender. It expressly held that the procedures for this must not require medical certificates which are unreasonable or imply pathology, and also must not require surgical or hormonal procedures.[20]

As for United nations bodies, the UN Human Rights Committee in 2017 in *G v. Australia* held that:

> 'privacy' under article 17 [of the International Covenant on Civil and Political Rights (ICCPR)] 'refers to the sphere of a person's life in which he or she can freely express his or her identity, be it by entering into relationships with others or alone.' It is the established jurisprudence of the Committee, and undisputed by the parties, that this includes protection of a person's identity, such as their gender identity.[21]

Regarding the requirements for recognition, in previous Concluding Observations, the Committee had encouraged State Parties to remove divorce

---

18 Both decided on 11.07.2002: *Goodwin v. United Kingdom* [2002] ECHR 588 and *I v. United Kingdom* [2002] ECHR 592.

19 *A.P., Garçon and Nicot v. France* (06.04.2017), ECHR 121 (2017). On this, see P. Dunne, 'Legal Gender Recognition in Europe: Sterilisation, Diagnosis and Medical Examination Requirements' (2017) 29 *Journal of Social Welfare and Family Law* 497–500.

20 Inter-American Court of Human Rights, Advisory Opinion (Opinión Consultiva, OC) 24/17 of 24 November 2017, requested by the Republic of Costa Rica, *Opinión consultiva sobre identidad de género, y no discriminación a parejas del mismo sexo*, available at <http://www.corteidh.or.cr/docs/opiniones/seriea_24_esp.pdf> (last accessed 17.01.2018).

21 Communication No. 2172/2012 (CCPR/C/119/D/2172/2012) (UN HRC, 15 June 2017), [7.2]. Available at <http://tbinternet.ohchr.org/Treaties/CCPR/Shared%20Documents/AUS/CCPR_C_119_D_2172_2012_25976_E.pdf> (last accessed 08.02.2018).

requirements from their laws.[22] The case of *G* allowed the Committee to address the point for the first time, and it found that a divorce requirement constituted disproportionate and unnecessary discrimination. In addition, numerous UN human rights actors[23] (including the UN Special Rapporteur on torture and other cruel, inhuman or degrading treatment or punishment)[24] have condemned medical conditions as incompatible with existing human rights norms.

2.2.3. *Focus on the Human Rights Discourse*

So, in this stage, gender identity and the recognition of preferred gender firmly became part of the human rights discourse, and were recognised as such both in jurisprudence and in academic discussion. This often went hand-in-hand with a greater visibility of trans persons (as mentioned above).

While litigation certainly has played a key role in advancing the recognition structures, the changing laws merely reflect a broader movement – at local, regional and international level – for transgender equality without which any legal development would not have been possible. The crucial progress in the second stage was to amend the popular and public discourse so that legal recognition was no longer simply viewed through the lens of medicine but began to be conceived through the language of human rights.

2.3. THIRD STAGE: MOVING AWAY FROM PATHOLOGISATION

In the third stage the human rights discourse became accepted as the core concern, and medicine was first side-lined and then essentially excluded from the legal aspects or transgender. A clear (and continuing) trend away from it being a 'medical issue', away from pathology could and still can be observed. A further sign of this is the revision of the 'International Classification of Diseases' (ICD) of the World Health Organization (WHO) announced on 18 June 2018. This revision will remove the five diagnoses of 'Gender Identity Disorder' from the chapter on 'Mental and Behavioural Disorders'; instead, two 'Gender Incongruence' diagnoses will be added to a new chapter on 'Conditions Related to Sexual Health' for the 11th edition (ICD-11). The move away from

---

22 United Nations Human Rights Committee, 'Concluding observations on the fourth periodic report of Ireland' (19 August 2014) UN Doc No. CCPR/C/IRL/CO/4.

23 United Nations High Commissioner for Human Rights, 'Discrimination and violence against individuals based on their sexual orientation and gender identity' (4 May 2015) UN Doc No. A/HRC/29/23, [79(i)]; United Nations Human Rights Committee, 'Concluding observations on the seventh periodic report of Ukraine' (22 August 2013) UN Doc No. CCPR/C/UKR/CO/7, [10].

24 'Report of the Special Rapporteur on Torture and other cruel, inhuman or degrading treatment or punishment' (5 January 2016) UN Doc No. A/HRC/31/57, [49].

pathologisation and medicalisation is strongly supported by many activists, for example the International Campaign Stop Trans Pathologization.[25]

A further particularly important document in this context are the Yogyakarta Principles.[26] However, the original Principles focused on sexual orientation and gender identity[27] and, thus (as unfortunately was typical for much of the debates at the time) did not address intersex as a distinct and separate issue. This was later remedied in the 'Yogyakarta Principles plus 10' (on which see Section 3 below). Still, some of the original Principles were highly relevant for intersex persons.

For example, Principle 3 states

> Everyone has the right to recognition everywhere as a person before the law. Persons of diverse sexual orientations and gender identities shall enjoy legal capacity in all aspects of life. Each person's self-defined sexual orientation and gender identity is integral to their personality and is one of the most basic aspects of self-determination, dignity and freedom. No one shall be forced to undergo medical procedures, including sex reassignment surgery, sterilisation or hormonal therapy, as a requirement for legal recognition of their gender identity. No status, such as marriage or parenthood, may be invoked as such to prevent the legal recognition of a person's gender identity. No one shall be subjected to pressure to conceal, suppress or deny their sexual orientation or gender identity.

While there is no express mention of intersex and/or sex characteristics, the focus on the right to self-determination with regard to medical issues is of course relevant. Principle 18 is similarly explicit on medical procedures, stating in B. that States shall

> take all necessary legislative, administrative and other measures to ensure that no child's body is irreversibly altered by medical procedures in an attempt to impose a gender identity without the full, free and informed consent of the child in accordance with the age and maturity of the child and guided by the principle that in all actions concerning children, the best interests of the child shall be a primary consideration.

While the reference to the best interest of the child is open to interpretation and does not amount to a ban of medically unnecessary surgery,[28] there at least is an express consent requirement and irreversibility.

---

25 See <http://stp2012.info/old/en> (last accessed 08.02.2018). On this, see also J.T. Theilen, 'Depathologisation of Transgenderism and International Human Rights' (2014) 14(2) *Human Rights Law Review* 327–342.

26 Available at <http://yogyakartaprinciples.org/> (last accessed 08.02.2018).

27 As the full title indicates: *Principles on the application of international human rights law in relation to sexual orientation and gender identity*, available at <http://yogyakartaprinciples.org/wp-content/uploads/2016/08/principles_en.pdf> (last accessed 08.02.2018).

28 Malta has introduced a complete ban; on this, and the difficulties this poses, e.g., with regard to male circumcision for religious purposes, see the contribution by T. Ní Mhuirthile in this volume.

There is an emerging trend, in several cases expressly influenced by the Yogyakarta Principles,[29] to no longer requiring any medical procedures for gender recognition but basing it on self-determination. Since 2004, more and more jurisdictions have enacted gender recognition rules or reformed existing laws and de-medicalised and de-pathologised the law of gender recognition, for example in Sweden, Norway, Spain, Argentina, Colombia, Mexico City, New York City, California, Ontario, Quebec, South Australia, Ireland, Belgium, France, Malta, Taiwan and the Australian Capital Territory.[30] The reasons given for detaching gender recognition and medicalisation also included possible inabilities to undergo treatment due to healthcare complications, insufficient financial resources to obtain treatment, rejection of treatment on religious grounds and personal contentment with existing bodily characteristics. But at the core, the legislative move away from medicalisation and pathologisation is the recognition that a person's legal status should not be based upon their sexed body.

Based on an in-depth comparative study and in line with the developments just described, the concluding analysis and recommendations of the above-mentioned research project upon which this contribution is based,[31] also very strongly emphasise the necessity of de-pathologisation and de-medicalisation, and are based on a self-determination model. These are addressed in particular in Recommendations 6 and 7:[32]

> Recommendation 6: No specific medical treatment or sterility for access recognition of preferred gender
>
> Recognition of preferred gender must not require any specific medical treatment or sterility.

---

29 e.g. in the Netherlands (see W. Pintens, 'The Legal Status of Transsexual and Transgender Persons in Belgium and the Netherlands', in Scherpe, above n. 2, pp. 113 and 119); Denmark (see N.V. Munkholm, 'The Legal Status of Transsexual and Transgender Persons in Denmark', in Scherpe, above n. 2, pp. 157 et seq.), Sweden (see J. Garland, 'The Legal Status of Transsexual and Transgender Persons in Sweden', in Scherpe, above n. 2, p. 290) and New Zealand (see E. McDonald and J. Byrne, 'The Legal Status of Transsexual and Transgender Persons in New Zealand', in Scherpe, above n. 2, pp. 542 and 565).

30 For an overview, see Dunne, above n. 8 and n. 19. On Argentina, see L.M. Giosa, M.V. Schiro and P. Dunne, 'The Legal Status of Transsexual and Transgender Persons in Argentina', in Scherpe, above n. 2, pp. 571 et seq.); on Malta, see the chapter by T. Ní Mhuirthile in this volume; on Ireland, see P. Dunne and L. Black (eds.), *Law and Gender in Ireland: Critique and Reform* (2018); on the Netherlands and Belgium, see Pintens, above n. 29; on Denmark see Munkholm, above n. 29; on Colombia, see the chapter by R. Rubio-Marín and S. Osella in this volume; on Australia, see R. Wallbank, 'The Legal Status of People who Experience Difference in Sexual Formation and Gender Expression in Australia', in Scherpe, above n. 2, pp. 457 et seq; on the United States, see J. Garland, 'The Legal Status of Transsexual and Transgender Persons in the United States', in Scherpe, above n. 2, pp. 585 et seq.

31 Above n. 2.

32 Above n. 2, pp. 651 et seq.

> Recommendation 7: No medical diagnosis requirement
>
> The legal recognition of preferred gender must not require a medical diagnosis but should be effected on the basis of self-determination.

The argument most commonly raised against self-determination is that this may be abused by some people to obtain legal or social benefits or other purposes. However, the fact that legal provisions may be abused by some does not necessarily mean that they should not be enacted. Many legal provisions and institutions can be abused for fraudulent reasons, but the response is not to abolish these but rather to create strong deterrents, including criminal sanctions, for those that do. That of course must be the same for self-determination of legal gender. The – abstract – risk of abuse is insufficient to justify the interference with the right to legal gender recognition. A properly maintained and administered self-determination system is capable of avoiding widespread fraud. In balancing the existing rights and policy arguments in favour of it, self-declaration of gender is the most appropriate, desirable and human rights conscious regime.

3. WHAT LESSONS CAN WE LEARN FROM THIS DEVELOPMENT FOR THE LEGAL STATUS OF INTERSEX PERSONS?

An 'I' is not a 'T'. But some lessons can be learned from the development regarding the legal status of transsexual and transgender persons. The first is that without persistent activism it is unlikely that there is progress. This activism should involve litigation in the right cases, but also engage society as a whole. The very serious problems intersex persons face, socially and legally, must be brought to the attention of the 'mainstream', and become visible. Publications such as 'Standing up for the human rights of intersex people – how can you help' by Dan Christian Ghattas[33] are of immense importance for this, and it is key that such publications are widely spread, read and the issues discussed. People must realise that difference is not disorder.

The second is that the human rights approach is the one most likely to lead to progress, especially since this enables detaching the legal issues from medicalisation and pathologisation. Here activists will be able to build upon the progress achieved, but of course with a focus on the specific issues concerning intersex persons.

[33] First published in December 2015 and available at <https://oiigermany.org/toolkit-standing-up-human-rights-intersex-people/> (last accessed 09.02.2018). Excerpts of this publication can be found in the chapter by D.C. Ghattas in this volume.

As is shown by many of the chapters in this volume,[34] the human rights approach has already started to create results. Importantly, the Yogyakarta Principles have been 'updated' on 10 November 2017 with/to the 'Yogyakarta Principles plus 10', namely with 'additional Principles and state obligations on the application of international human rights law in relation to sexual presentation, gender identity, gender expression and sex characteristics to complement the Yogyakarta Principles'.[35]

> UNDERSTANDING
>
> 'sex characteristics' as each person's physical features relating to sex, including genitalia and other sexual and reproductive anatomy, chromosomes, hormones, and secondary physical features emerging from puberty;
>
> NOTING
>
> that 'sex characteristics' as an explicit ground for protection from violations of human rights has evolved in international jurisprudence, and recognising that the Yogyakarta Principles apply equally to the ground of sex characteristics as to the grounds of sexual orientation, gender identity and gender expression.

So, somewhat belatedly, these important Principles now also apply to intersex. Space precludes an in-depth discussion, but two Principles should be mentioned here. Principle 31 (The right to legal recognition) states:

> Everyone has the right to legal recognition without reference to, or requiring assignment or disclosure of, sex, gender, sexual orientation, gender identity, gender expression or sex characteristics. Everyone has the right to obtain identity documents, including birth certificates, regardless of sexual orientation, gender identity, gender expression or sex characteristics. Everyone has the right to change gendered information in such documents while gendered information is included in them.

Crucially, Principle 32 (The right to bodily and mental integrity) then holds:

> Everyone has the right to bodily and mental integrity, autonomy and self-determination irrespective of sexual orientation, gender identity, gender expression or sex characteristics. Everyone has the right to be free from torture and cruel, inhuman and degrading treatment or punishment on the basis of sexual orientation, gender identity, gender expression and sex characteristics. No one shall be subjected to invasive or

---

34 Particularly those by D.C. Ghattas, M. Carpenter and K. Sandberg, but also those on the developments in India (S. Shah), Malta (T. Ní Mhuirthile), Australia (C. Fenton-Glynn), the USA (J. Greenberg) and Germany (N. Althoff and T. Helms).

35 Available at <http://yogyakartaprinciples.org/wp-content/uploads/2017/11/A5_yogyakarta WEB-2.pdf> (last accessed 09.02.2018).

> irreversible medical procedures that modify sex characteristics without their free, prior and informed consent, unless necessary to avoid serious, urgent and irreparable harm to the concerned person.

This is then elaborated, stating that states shall

> A. Guarantee and protect the rights of everyone, including all children, to bodily and mental integrity, autonomy and self-determination;
>
> B. Ensure that legislation protects everyone, including all children, from all forms of forced, coercive or otherwise involuntary modification of their sex characteristics;
>
> C. Take measures to address stigma, discrimination and stereotypes based on sex and gender, and combat the use of such stereotypes, as well as marriage prospects and other social, religious and cultural rationales, to justify modifications to sex characteristics, including of children;
>
> D. Bearing in mind the child's right to life, non-discrimination, the best interests of the child, and respect for the child's views, ensure that children are fully consulted and informed regarding any modifications to their sex characteristics necessary to avoid or remedy proven, serious physical harm, and ensure that any such modifications are consented to by the child concerned in a manner consistent with the child's evolving capacity;
>
> E. Ensure that the concept of the best interest of the child is not manipulated to justify practices that conflict with the child's right to bodily integrity;
>
> F. Provide adequate, independent counselling and support to victims of violations, their families and communities, to enable victims to exercise and affirm rights to bodily and mental integrity, autonomy and self-determination;
>
> G. Prohibit the use of anal and genital examinations in legal and administrative proceedings and criminal prosecutions unless required by law, as relevant, reasonable, and necessary for a legitimate purpose.

Given the impact the Yogyakarta Principles have had in the past,[36] it is to be hoped that these new Principles will have a similar effect. Indeed, many international bodies and organisations already have expressly condemned 'normalising' surgery.[37] There can be no doubt that 'normalising' surgery is a violation of the human rights of the people concerned and must be prohibited. Malta has introduced legislation to that effect,[38] and hopefully more jurisdictions will follow that example. Moreover, activist can rely on and work judicial precedents such as those described above (2.2.1.) for constitutional protection of bodily integrity and autonomy.

---

36 See above n. 29 for references where the Yogyakarta Principles have influenced legislation.

37 See e.g. those listed in the chapter by D.C. Ghattas in this volume.

38 See the chapter by T. Ni Mhuirthile in this volume.

Futhermore, several court decisions have begun to address legal status issues as well, and in some cases even mandated the end of the binary legal gender order, most notably the decision by the German Constitutional Court of 10 October 2017.[39] Creating a 'third gender' or merely leaving the gender entry of intersex children open at birth can have detrimental rather than beneficial effects, as it may have the effect of 'othering' the persons concerned, to mark them as deviant, and thus increase the pressure on parents to 'normalise' their children.[40] However, a legal gender status beyond the binary which is open to anyone irrespective of their sex characteristics, combined with a gender recognition system based on self-determination undoubtedly would be a massive step forward.[41] A binary legal gender system does not reflect the lived reality of many people, whether intersex or not. However, there must not be a 'mandatory othering' of people at birth merely because of their sex characteristics. Indeed, it can be questioned whether the state should have the right to register a legal gender, whether there even is a need for such a gender registration at all.[42] But as far as children are concerned, it is worth considering postponing the legal gender registration of all children until a certain age when they have developed and are mature enough to decide on their legal gender; until then, the social gender identification could suffice.[43] In any event, issues concerning bodily integrity, gender identity and legal gender must not be taken for other persons, but by the persons themselves. In many jurisdictions this has been achieved for trans persons. Intersex persons deserve no less.

---

39 German Constitutional Court (Bundesverfassungsgericht) 10.10.2017 (1 BvR 2019/16), *FamRZ* 2017, 2046, with a comment by T. Helms at 2054. A press release is available in English at <http://www.bundesverfassungsgericht.de/SharedDocs/Pressemitteilungen/EN/2017/bvg17-095.html> (last accessed 09.02.2018).
On this case and its implications, see especially the contributions by T. Helms, N. Althoff and T. Meyer in this volume.

40 On this, see e.g. M. Carpenter in this volume.

41 See e.g. the proposals discussed in the chapter by N. Althoff in this volume.

42 See e.g. J.M. Scherpe, 'Mehr Freiheit wagen im Familienrecht – Entgeschlechtlichung des Rechts' in A. Dutta and C. Heinze (eds.), *Mehr Freiheit wagen* (forthcoming in 2018). Even the German Constitutional Court in the above mentioned decision (n. 39) suggested that one way of resolving the issues raised in the case concerning the duty of a positive legal gender recognition of an intersex person who does not identify as either male or female was to abolish gender registration altogether.

43 See the suggestions discussed by N. Althoff in this volume.

TOWARDS TRANS AND INTERSEX EQUALITY: CONFLICT OR COMPLEMENTARITY?

Peter Dunne

1. INTRODUCTION

In recent years, the rights and experiences of transgender ('trans') individuals have gained increasing legal, political and social visibility.[1] In the United Kingdom, the landmark Gender Recognition Act 2004 ('the 2004 Act') transformed the relationship between trans identities and the law, and began (what is now) a global movement towards affirming individuals' preferred

[1] K. Steinmetz, 'The Transgender Tipping Point: America's Next Civil Rights Frontier', *Time* 29.05.2014 <http://time.com/135480/transgender-tipping-point/> (last accessed 12.07.2015). See generally J.M. Scherpe (ed.), *The Legal Status of Transsexual and Transgender Persons*, Intersentia, Cambridge 2015; Z. Chan, S. Duffy and M. González Gil (eds.), *Trans Legal Mapping Report*, 2nd ed., ILGA, Geneva 2017.

gender in a more humane and dignified manner.[2] The emergence of high-profile trans personalities, such as Laverne Cox, Caitlyn Jenner and Chelsea Manning, has thrust trans and gender non-conforming identities into the media spotlight. While the ensuing press coverage has sometimes reproduced unwelcome social prejudices, which have long characterised public responses to non-cisgender[3] expression, more often than not social commentators now engage with trans identities in a sensitive and respectful tone.

Despite the advances being made in trans consciousness-raising, however, the lived-realities (and, indeed, the very existence) of those who experience intersex variance remains underexplored, both within legal academia and wider social discourse. While well-publicised 'coming out' stories (such as the personal narrative of model Hanne Gaby Odiele[4]) exist, general public awareness of intersex, and intersex visibility, is significantly lower than compared to knowledge of the trans community. To the extent that, like lesbian, gay and bisexual (LGB) equality, greater legal and social acceptance for trans identities has resulted from increasing social familiarity, populations that experience intersex variance would likely benefit from enhanced protection if both political representatives and the general public better understood intersex realities.

This chapter considers the overlap in modern efforts to secure trans and intersex legal rights. For many scholars, the aims and strategies of these movements appear, at least superficially, as inherently oppositional.[5] Since the 1970s, much trans advocacy has focused on fairer, safer and more affordable access to gender-affirming healthcare. Within global trans communities, there are large numbers of people who seek to affirm their preferred gender through medical transition pathways, aligning their physical bodies with their internalised sense of gender. To the extent that national legal or medical rules have restricted the availability of gender-confirming treatments, a priority for trans activism has been the public provision of appropriate and professional

---

2 P. Dunne, 'Ten Years of Gender Recognition in the United Kingdom: Still a Model for Reform?' (2015) *Public Law* 530; A. Rappole, 'Trans People and Legal Recognition: What the US Federal Government Can Learn From Foreign Nations' (2015) 30 *Maryland Journal of International Law* 191; E. Blincoe, 'Sex Markers on Birth Certificates: Replacing Model with Self-Identification' (2015) 46(1) *Victoria University of Wellington Law Review* 57; K.Y. Wong, 'Taking a Transgender Rights Seriously: A Rights-Based Model of Gender Recognition in Hong Kong' (2015) 45(1) *Hong Kong Law Journal* 109.

3 'Cisgender' refers to persons who self-identify with the gender that was assigned to them at birth. It is derived from the Latin word, 'cis' (meaning 'on this side of').

4 N. Khomadi, 'Model Hanne Gaby Odiele reveals she is intersex', *The Guardian* 24.01.2017, <https://www.theguardian.com/world/2017/jan/24/model-hanne-gaby-odiele-reveals-she-is-intersex> (last accessed 24.02.2017).

5 N. Ben-Asher, 'The Necessity of Sex Change: A Struggle for Intersex and Transsex Liberties' (2006) 29 *Harvard Journal of Law and Gender* 51, 51; J Butler, *Undoing Gender*, Routledge, New York 2004, p. 6.

medical care.[6] On the other hand, in that same period, intersex advocacy has been focused on the reduction of non-therapeutic surgical interventions on infants who experience intersex variance. In the second half of the twentieth century, standard treatment practices provided that, where a child was born with ambiguous sex characteristics, that individual should be 'assigned' to a binary gender through genital 'normalising' procedures.[7] For activists, such medical protocols constituted a violation of bodily integrity and, from the early 1990s, individuals who underwent such interventions began to speak publicly about the resulting trauma and physical/mental discomfort that they had suffered.[8]

Thus viewed, one might assume that trans communities invariably pursue greater access to medical treatment while intersex activism is solely concerned with the de-medicalisation of bodily diversity. Yet, the reality is significantly more complex, and certainly more nuanced. Many persons who experience intersex variance welcome and desire the opportunity to amend their sex characteristics. However, they argue that any medical treatment should not be administered until the person involved can offer informed and meaningful consent. Intersex activism, therefore, may be less about de-medicalisation than *informed* medicalisation.[9] Similarly, since the early 2000s, there has been a concerted, global movement among trans advocates to de-medicalise legal gender recognition procedures. While, as noted, many trans persons strongly desire (even need) appropriate healthcare interventions, trans activism increasingly

---

6 Parliamentary Assembly of the Council of Europe, 'Discrimination against Transgender People in Europe' 22.04.2015, Resolution 2048 (2015); K. Baker and A. Cray, *Ensuring Benefits Parity and Gender Identity Nondiscrimination in Essential Health Benefits*, Center for American Progress 15.11.2012 <https://www.americanprogress.org/issues/lgbt/reports/2012/11/15/44948/ensuring-benefits-parity-and-gender-identity-nondiscrimination-in-essential-health-benefits/> (last accessed 24.02.2017); Open Society Foundation, *Transforming Health: International Rights-Based Advocacy for Trans Health*, OSF February 2013 <http://www.ilga-europe.org/sites/default/files/transforming_health1.pdf> (last accessed 24.02.2017).

7 A. Tamar-Mattis, 'Exceptions to the Rule: Curing the Law's Failure to Protect Intersex Infants' (2006) 21 *Berkeley Journal of Gender, Law & Justice* 59; E. McDonald, 'Intersex People in Aotearoa New Zealand: The Challenges for Law and Social Policy: Part I: Critiquing Gender Normalising Surgery' (2015) 46(3) *Victoria University of Wellington Law Review* 705; A. Kennedy, 'Fixed at Birth: Medical and Legal Erasures of Intersex Variations' (2016) 39(2) *University of New South Wales Law Journal* 813; J. Bird, 'When Sex Means Condition or Impairment: Evaluating the Human Rights of Transgender and Intersex Peoples' (2001) 5 *Southern Cross University Law Review* 1.

8 For a particularly compelling account of intersex personal narratives, see G. Lahood, 'Intersexion', New Zealand 2012 <http://www.intersexionfilm.com/> (last accessed 24.02.2017); T. Jones, M. Carpenter and B. Hart, *Intersex: Stories and Statistics from Australia*, Open Book Publications, Cambridge 2012.

9 'Public Statement of the Third International Intersex Forum' December 2013 <http://ilga-europe.org/what-we-do/our-advocacy-work/trans-and-intersex/intersex/events/3rd-international-intersex-forum> (last accessed 24.02.2017).

argues that medical requirements, including enforced sterilisation and surgery, should not be preconditions for having one's preferred gender acknowledged.[10]

This chapter explores a number of overlapping themes in the struggle for both trans and intersex rights, including bodily integrity, consent, children's rights and living outside the male-female binary. The chapter does not suggest, nor should it be interpreted as arguing, that trans identities and the experience of intersex variance are identical. The chapter acknowledges, and respects, the unique character of trans and intersex realities. Indeed, it is important to affirm that, even within trans and intersex communities, there are a multiplicity of individualised lived-experiences. Many intersex activists voice discomfort with trans narratives which use intersex as a tool to challenge naturalised gender binaries, while insufficiently acknowledging the unique restrictions and obstacles which those binaries impose on those who experience intersex.[11] What this chapter does seek to convey, however, is that, despite important differences, trans and intersex movements affirm common truths which, while fundamental to each individual community, also provide a valuable roadmap towards a more gender-equal and gender-inclusive society.

2. LEGAL GENDER RECOGNITION

In recent years, national and human rights discourse on trans identities has often focused on the right to legal gender recognition.[12] For individuals who experience a preferred gender, which differs from the status assigned to them at birth, obtaining formal affirmation of that preferred gender may be essential to

10 Human Rights Watch, *Controlling Bodies, Denying Identities – Human Rights Violations against Trans People in the Netherlands*, HRW, New York 2011; Commissioner for Human Rights of the Council of Europe, *Human Rights and Gender Identity*, Comm DH/Issue Paper (2009) 2, COE, Strasbourg 2009, pp. 7–9; Transgender Europe (TGEU), *Legal Gender Recognition in Europe*, 2nd ed., TGEU, Berlin 2016, pp. 23–27.

11 M. Davidson, 'Seeking Refuge Under the Umbrella: Inclusion, Exclusion, and Organizing Within the Category Transgender' (2007) 4(4) *Sexuality Research and Social Policy* 60, pp. 68–69.

12 Transgender Europe (TGEU), above n. 10; House of Commons Select Committee on Women and Equalities, *Transgender Equality* (HC 2015–16, 390), The Station Office Limited, London January 2016, pp. 11–23; Human Rights Commission of New Zealand, *To Be who I am: Report of the Inquiry into Discrimination Experienced by Transgender People*, HRC, Auckland 2008, pp. 88–94. For case law, see *Goodwin v. United Kingdom* [2002] 35 EHRR 18; *In re Change of Name and Correction of Family Register* (Supreme Court of South Korea, 22 June 2006); *Foy v. An t-Ard Chlaraitheoir & Ors (No 2)* [2007] IEHC 470; *W v. Register of Marriages* [2013] HKCFA 39 (CFA (HK)); *M v. M* [1991] NZFLR 337. See generally J.M. Scherpe and P. Dunne, 'The Legal Status of Transsexual and Transgender Persons – Comparative Analysis and Recommendations', in J.M. Scherpe (ed.), *The Legal Status of Transsexual and Transgender Persons*, Intersentia, Cambridge 2015, pp. 615–663.

accessing basic rights and services, such as marriage, social security benefits and state-funded education.[13] While a number of jurisdictions worldwide continue to withhold legal gender recognition, there is a growing acceptance (particularly among international and regional rights guarantors) that persons should be affirmed in the gender which is consistent with their lived reality.[14]

When one thinks of legal gender recognition, there is an automatic association with the trans community. This is perhaps unsurprising as gender transition has typically been framed as a trans issue and the vast majority of cases, which affirm the right to recognition, specifically address trans litigants.[15] Yet, as Ghattas notes, persons who experience intersex may also have a need to affirm their preferred gender in law. Where an individual, who experiences intersex variance, does not self-identify with the gender that has been assigned (possibly through surgical intervention) at birth, in the absence of a rectification procedure for incorrect intersex designations, that individual will have to rely upon gender recognition.[16] The fact that the person has an intersex, rather than a trans, identity in no way reduces the hardship that person will experience if no possibility for gender recognition exists.

That gender recognition structures must accommodate intersex, as well as trans, applicants, should be an express consideration when determining the appropriate conditions of recognition that applicants are obligated to fulfil. Like their trans counterparts, so too persons who experience intersex may struggle – for financial, social, medical, age-related, familial and religious reasons – to satisfy entry requirements which force them to undergo sterilisation, submit to invasive surgery or dissolve an existing legal relationship.[17] Persons who experience intersex variance are equally entitled to basic human rights and, just as with trans communities, they should not be subjected to a gender recognition regime which violates core protections.

Yet, intersex identities may also raise additional concerns which must be taken into account when devising rules for legal transitions. Around the world,

---

13 United Nations Development Programme, *Transgender Health and Human Rights*, UNDP, New York 2013, pp. 23–27; L. Mottet, 'Modernizing State Vital Statistics Statutes and Policies to Ensure Accurate Gender Markers on Birth Certificates: A Good Government Approach to Recognizing the Lives of Transgender People' (2012–13) 19 *Michigan Journal of Gender and Law* 373, 392.

14 UNHRC, 'Report of the Office of the United Nations High Commissioner for Human Rights on discrimination and violence against individuals based on their sexual orientation and gender identity' (4 May 2015) UN Doc No. A/HRC/29/23, [17] and [79(h)(i)]. See Scherpe and Dunne, above n. 12, pp. 618–625.

15 *Goodwin v. United Kingdom*, above n. 12; *Van Kück v. Germany* [2003] 37 EHRR 51; *L v. Lithuania* [2008] 46 EHRR 22; *Hämäläinen v. Finland* [2015] 37 BHRC 55.

16 D.C. Ghattas, *Human Rights between the sexes – A preliminary study on the life situations of inter* individuals*, Heinrich-Böll-Stiftung, Berlin 2013, p. 47.

17 D. Spade, 'Documenting Gender' (2009) 8 *Dukeminier Awards Best Sexual Orientation & Gender Law Review* 137, 160.

applicants for gender recognition are typically required to obtain a medical diagnosis related to their preferred gender (e.g. gender dysphoria), either as an express pre-condition set out in statute or as an unavoidable step in accessing medical treatments, which are themselves statutory preconditions.[18] However, some medical officers, particularly those using older diagnosis criteria, may refuse to provide the necessary medical certification if an individual concurrently experiences intersex variance.[19] In such circumstances, intersex persons are indirectly excluded from participating in legal gender recognition processes. Similarly, unlike their trans counterparts, many persons who experience intersex will never undertake an explicit transition, but rather will live their entire lives in their preferred (but non-legal) gender. To the extent that gender recognition rules may require applicants to reproduce the standard trans narratives of 'being-born-in-the-wrong-body' and 'moving-across-the-gender-binary', intersex persons will be less likely to meet those medical expectations. Thus, in seeking to extend legal gender recognition and to create more rights-focused legal structures, advocates must also be conscious to specifically accommodate unique intersex experiences.

The phenomenon of intersex persons, seeking legal gender recognition, highlights the inherent risks in attempting to pre-determine, through surgical intervention, the gendered future of a new-born infant. The simple fact is that, without allowing a child to grow and observing their natural development, medical officers are assigning gendered identities based upon physical characteristics, which may ultimately have little connection to an individual's internal sense of self. For Albritton, the fact that many intersex persons subsequently undertake a legal gender transition is evidence that such gender designations are frequently incorrect.[20] Thus, not only are intersex infants subjected to non-consensual and unnecessary surgical procedures. They are forcibly cornered into an identity from which they may legally and socially have to extricate themselves in later life.

In the early 1990s, the highly influential Intersex Society of North America (ISNA) was established to promote reform in treatment standards for intersex youth. Foremost in ISNA's advocacy strategy were stories from intersex

---

18 In the UK, Spain and Portugal, although applicants for legal gender recognition need not submit to surgical interventions, they must provide a medical diagnosis. In other jurisdictions, such as Turkey and the Czech Republic, a diagnosis is a precondition for obtaining surgical interventions, which must be undertaken before the state will acknowledge an individual's preferred gender. See Scherpe and Dunne, above n. 12, pp. 651–655.

19 The fourth edition of the Diagnostic and Statistical Manual of Mental Disorders specifically defined 'gender identity disorder' as incompatible with a 'concurrent … physical intersex condition' (DSM-IV, Code 302.85).

20 J.C. Albritton, 'Intersexed and Injured: How M C v Aaronson Breaks Federal Ground in Protecting Intersex Children from Unnecessary Genital Normalization Surgeries' (2015) 24 *Tulane Journal of Law and Sexuality* 163.

individuals who had been medically assigned to, and forced to spend their childhood in, a gender with which they did not identify.[21] ISNA's message was both clear and consistent: infant 'normalising' surgeries are so uncertain and speculative that they must be deferred until a child's preferred gender can be reasonably ascertained. Yet, is the possibility of incorrect designations the most compelling argument against surgical intervention on young intersex bodies? Ben-Asher suggests that the inherent uncertainty of assigning gender, while an important consideration, should be secondary to concerns over bodily integrity to which normalising procedures also give rise.[22] Indeed, even if a medical professional was able to reliably predict the future gender identity of an intersex infant, one can still question whether irreparably transforming another person's body, without meaningful knowledge or consent, should be either legally or morally acceptable.[23] As Karen Walsh, a survivor of normalising interventions, argues, the mere coincidence that she now identifies with her assigned gender does not eradicate the violation of bodily integrity to which she was subject.[24]

3. BODILY INTEGRITY

In recent years, national, regional and international actors have increasingly taken steps to defend the bodily integrity of trans and intersex communities.[25] Numerous United Nations Treaty Bodies, including the UN Committee against Torture and the UN Human Rights Committee, have criticised surgical requirements for legal gender recognition and genital-normalising surgeries performed on intersex infants.[26] In 2016, the UN Special Rapporteur on Torture and other Cruel, Inhuman and Degrading Treatment reaffirmed that subjecting 'transgender and intersex persons' to 'forced procedures such as sterilization, "conversion" therapy, hormone therapy and genital-normalizing surgeries' leads to 'severe and life-long physical and mental pain and suffering' and may amount to 'torture and ill-treatment'.[27] In 2015, the Parliamentary Assembly of

---

21 Intersex Society of North America, 'ISNA's Amicus Brief on Intersex Genital Surgery', 07.02.1998 <http://www.isna.org/node/97> (last accessed 24.02.2017).
22 Ben-Asher, above n. 5, 69–70.
23 Ibid.
24 K.A. Walshe, '"Normalizing" Intersex Didn't Feel Normal or Honest to Me' (2015) 5(2) *Narrative Inquiry in Bioethics* 119, 122.
25 Scherpe and Dunne, above n. 12, pp. 643–646.
26 UN Committee Against Torture, Concluding Observations for Germany 12.12.2011, UN Doc No. CAT/C/DEU/CO/5, [20]; UNHRC 'Concluding observations of the United Nations Human Rights Committee on the seventh periodic report of Ukraine' 22.08.2013, UN Doc No. CCPR/C/UKR/CO/7, [10].
27 UNHCR, 'Report of the Special Rapporteur on Torture and other cruel, inhuman or degrading treatment or punishment' (2016) UN Doc No. A/HRC/31/57, [48].

the Council of Europe called upon state parties to 'abolish sterilisation and other compulsory medical treatment as a necessary legal requirement to recognise a person's gender identity in laws'. The same body has also recommended government action so that 'no-one is subjected to unnecessary medical or surgical treatment that is cosmetic rather than vital for health during infancy or childhood'.[28] States parties should 'guarantee bodily integrity, autonomy and self-determination to persons ... and provide families with intersex children with adequate counselling and support'.[29]

The medical interventions to which both trans persons (knowingly) and intersex persons (often unknowingly) are exposed raise important difficulties for the right to bodily integrity. These problems are particularly acute within the specific areas of: (1) consent; and (2) medical necessity.

3.1. CONSENT

A fundamental principle of both medical and human rights law is that individuals should not be subject to physical treatments without their free and informed consent.[30] In general terms, valid medical consent requires that individuals (1) have knowledge about the proposed intervention; (2) are capable of understanding the nature and consequences of that intervention; and (3) undergo intervention of their own free accord.[31]

3.1.1. *Adult Trans Individuals and the 'Voluntariness' of Gender-Confirming Treatment*

For trans persons above the age of majority, there is little doubt that, where an individual agrees to surgery or sterilisation, he or she has the capacity to understand (and does understand) the nature and consequences of the proposed intervention. Save in extreme cases, an adult trans woman who submits to sterilisation knows that she will lose her reproductive capacities. Similarly, adult trans men are aware that mastectomies result in the loss of breasts. The real

28 Parliamentary Assembly of the Council of Europe, 'Children's Right to Physical Integrity' 01.10.2013, Resolution 1952 (2013), [7.5.3].

29 Ibid.

30 UNHCR, 'Report of the Special Rapporteur on Torture and other cruel, inhuman or degrading treatment or punishment' (2013) UN Doc No. A/HRC/22/53, [32]. See also: J Herring, *Medical Law and Ethics*, 4th ed., Oxford University Press, Oxford 2012, p. 149.

31 E. Jackson, *Medical Law: Texts, Cases and Materials*, 3rd ed., Oxford University Press, Oxford 2013, p. 166.

question for mandatory trans medicalisation is whether the treatments, which adult applicants for gender recognition undergo, are undertaken voluntarily?[32]

According to Silver, the environment in which applicants for legal recognition under medical intervention may 'implicate the voluntariness of a decision to undergo … treatment'.[33] Surgery and sterilisation requirements present applicants with an impossible choice between two highly undesirable outcomes. On the one hand, trans individuals can agree to unwanted medical treatments, thereby exposing themselves to painful, unnecessary and possibly unhealthy bodily alterations. On the other hand, applicants may refuse treatment, and 'live with [all] the consequences of a discordant legal identity'.[34] In such circumstances, there is an arguable case that any consent is not voluntary. In *Socialstyrelsen v. NN*,[35] a national court decision which struck down Sweden's sterilisation requirement, the Stockholm Administrative Court of Appeals stated that the notion of coercion should not be restricted to situations where applicants for legal gender recognition are physically incapable of resisting a violation of bodily integrity. Instead, where medical interventions are a 'requirement to enjoy a certain benefit or right' that treatment must 'generally … be seen as forced'.[36] The appeals court held that submission to sterilisation cannot be consensual if it is a prerequisite for gaining basic acknowledgement from the State.

3.1.2. *Trans Minors and Capacity to Consent*

In the context of trans minors, the question of capacity and understanding (as opposed to voluntariness) gains greater relevance. Around the world, most jurisdictions either restrict, or absolutely prohibit, legal gender recognition for persons under the age of majority.[37] The justification for such restrictive policies is two-fold. First, there is a general belief that trans children are incapable of

---

32 *AP, Garcon and Nicot v. France* (Appl. nos. 79885/12, 52471/13 and 52596/13) (06.04.2017), [132]–[135]; P. Dunne, 'Legal Gender Recognition in Europe: Sterilisation, Diagnosis and Medical Examination Requirements' (2017) 39(4) *Journal of Social Welfare and Family Law* 497–500.

33 A.E. Silver, 'An Offer You Can't Refuse: Coercing Consent to Surgery Through the Medicalization of Gender Identity' (2013–14) 26 *Columbia Journal of Gender and Law* 488, 498.

34 L.H. Norton, 'Neutering the Transgendered: Human Rights and Japan's Law No. 111' (2006) 7 *Georgetown Journal of Gender and the Law* 187, 205.

35 *Socialstyrelsen v. NN, Målnr* 1968–12 (2012).

36 Ibid.

37 See generally Scherpe and Dunne, above n. 12, pp. 625–629; Open Society Foundation, *Licence to Be Yourself: Trans Children and Youth*, OSF, New York 2015; Transgender Europe, 'Trans Rights Europe Index 2016', Transgender Europe Website 10.05.2016 <http://tgeu.org/wp-content/uploads/2016/05/trans-map-B-july2016.pdf> (last accessed 14.10.2016).

experiencing (and expressing) a stable gender identity.[38] Trans minors (or their parents) should not be considered competent to affirm a gender identity the full contours of which they are not mature enough to either understand or externalise. Second, even if a trans child could experience and express a consistent gender identity, there are, as yet, no reliable methods to identify those young people and to differentiate them from minors whose trans expression is merely fleeting or temporary.[39] The risks and consequences of misidentification are sufficient to withhold recognition from persons under the age of majority.

As a first point, one might note the inconsistency between legal and medical transition pathways. Around the world, parents increasingly have the right to initiate gender confirming treatments for children as young as ten years old.[40] In many jurisdictions, parents may consent to the administration of hormone blockers, which prevent a child from entering puberty and developing secondary sex characteristics that would be inconsistent with the child's preferred gender. While concerns about gender persistence and misidentification also inform medical discourse, parents are empowered to begin early treatments because the effects of hormone blockers are fully reversible and a child can seamlessly (at least physically) revert to their assigned gender should his or her internal identity subsequently change.[41]

Hormone blockers are not prohibited because, unlike surgery or sterilisation, they do not permanently alter the future life path of a trans young person.[42] In reality, hormone blockers afford trans minors a measure of breathing space – additional time to explore and consider their gender identity, without the risk of either (1) developing natural sex characteristics which might hinder any later definitive transition; or (2) undergoing more substantial cross-sex treatments, which would be difficult to reverse should the trans identity subsequently dissipate. The same reasoning applies equally to legal gender recognition. Unlike physical transitions, recognising a child's preferred gender has no irreversible

---

38 J. Pyne, 'Health and Well-Being Among Gender-Independent Children' in E.J. Meyer and A. Pullen Sansfaçon (eds.), *Supporting Transgender and Gender Creative Youth: Schools, Families and Communities in Action,* Peter Lang, New York 2014, p. 37.

39 M. Forcier and E. Haddad, 'Health Care for Gender Variant or Gender Non-Conforming Children' (2013) April *Rhode Island Medical Journal* 17, 19.

40 World Professional Association of Transgender Health, *Standards of Care for the Health of Transgender, Transsexual and Gender Nonconforming People (Version VII),* WPATH 2012, pp. 10–21; W.C. Hembree et al., 'Endocrine Treatment of Transsexual Persons: An Endocrine Society Clinical Practice Guideline' (2009) 94(9) *The Journal of Clinical Endocrinology and Metabolism* 3132, [2.0]–[2.6].

41 S.R. Vance, D. Ehrensaft and S.M. Rosenthal, 'Psychological and Medical Care of Gender Nonconforming Youth' (2014) 134(6) *Paediatrics* 1184, 1188.

42 H.A. Delamarre-Van de Wall and P.T. Cohen-Kettenis, 'Clinical management of gender identity disorder in adolescents: a protocol on psychological and paediatric endocrinology aspects' (2006) 155 *European Journal of Endocrinology* 131, 136–137.

consequences. Just as a minor's assigned gender can be legally amended, so too could that amended gender be subsequently changed if the trans identification does not persist. As with hormone blockers, legal gender recognition offers time for young people to explore their gender identity in a safe and secure manner, without incongruent identity documents continually revealing their trans history and possibly exposing youth to transphobic bullying and harassment.

Putting the inconsistencies between medical and legal pathways aside, however, the question remains whether trans minors (1) are capable of experiencing a stable and consistent gender identity; and (2) can be reliably identified and differentiated from cisgender youth, whose gender non-conformity does not reflect a persisting trans identification.

There is evidence that minors not only experience, but can also externally express, a stable trans identity well before the age of majority.[43] Hidalgo et al. write that '[r]esearch and … clinical experience suggest that many children develop a strong sense of gender identity at a young age'.[44] The existing medical data suggests that children develop a sense of gender during their second and third years, and that they are able to communicate a firm trans identity by age four or five years.[45] Young people are clear and intelligible in expressing their preferred gender,[46] and can be as consistent and persistent in their self-identification as cisgender peers. To the extent that policymakers or opponents of gender recognition claim that trans children either do not exist or are incapable of reliably experiencing a trans identity, such concerns are not corroborated by existing medical research.

There is, however, much greater uncertainty as to the ability of parents and medical experts to reliably identify those minors who consistently experience their preferred gender and who will actually persist in that preference beyond adolescence. Current data suggests that approximately 75 per cent of all young people, who are identified as trans in childhood, do not identify with their

---

43 H.J. Tobin and J. Levi, 'Securing Equal Access to Sex Segregated Facilities for Transgender Students' (2013) 28 *Wisconsin Journal of Law, Gender and Society* 301, 302; K.A. Stieglitz, 'Development, Risk and Resilience of Transgender Youth' (2010) 21(3) *Journal of the Association of Nurses in Aids Care* 192, 194; WPATH (Version VII), WPATH 2012, p. 12 <https://www.wpath.org/media/cms/Documents/Web%20Transfer/SOC/Standards%20of%20Care%20V7%20-%202011%20WPATH.pdf> (last accessed 26.10.2015).

44 M.A. Hidalgo et al., 'The Gender Affirmative Model: What We Know and What We Aim to Learn' (2013) 56 *Human Development* 285, 286.

45 C. Nicholson and T.M. McGuinness, 'Gender Dysphoria and Children' (2014) 52(8) *Journal of Psychosocial Nursing* 27, 28; F. Lynn, 'To be a Trans* Parent: How Emotion Abuse Statutes Facilitate Parent's Acceptance of their Children's Gender Identity' (2013–14) 7 *John Marshall Law Journal* 89, 112; E.R. Boskey, 'Understanding Transgender Identity Development in Childhood and Adolescence' (2014) 9(4) *American Journal of Sexuality Education* 445, 450; S. Brill and R. Pepper, *The Transgender Child: A Handbook for Families and Professionals*, Cleis Press Inc, San Francisco 2008, p. 61.

46 Hidalgo et al., above n. 44, 286.

former preferred gender as adults.[47] Thus, less than a quarter of supposedly trans children actually progress to living a trans identity in adulthood.[48] Such statistics clearly provide pause for thought in developing trans-affirming policies for young people. If they were reproduced in the operation of an actual regime for gender recognition, the result would be either wholesale de-transitioning or a significant number of individuals living trapped in a now *former* trans identity. To the extent that parents and medical professionals might be incapable of consistently and reliably identifying trans youth, that would be a reasonable justification for limiting legal gender recognition to adults.

The existing research on persistence and desistence is not, however, without critique. The primary (and most important) objection is that the available data is based upon overly inclusive identification criteria. The current 75 per cent statistics rely upon diagnostic guidelines established under the fourth edition of the Diagnostic and Statistical Manual of Mental Disorders (DSM-IV). Under DSM-IV, young people could be marked as experiencing 'gender identity disorder' without ever having expressed a trans identity.[49] A child who merely engaged in gender non-conforming or non-stereotypical behaviour could be identified as trans, and included within the larger set of children whose persistence rates were to be measured. Tannehill criticises the existing data for failing to 'differentiate between children with consistent, persistent and insistent gender dysphoria, kids who socially transitioned, and kids who just acted more masculine or feminine than their birth sex and culture allowed for'.[50] It is perhaps unsurprising that, where children, who never identified as trans or expressed an identity beyond their assigned gender, were arbitrarily included within a trans subset, the desistence rates within that subset became inflated. However, such research does not prove high levels of desistence among trans youth. It merely confirms that minors, who do not identify as trans in childhood, are unlikely to express a trans identity in adulthood.[51]

---

47 P.T. Cohen-Kettenis, H.A. Delamarre-Van de Waal and L.J.G. Gooren, 'The Treatment of Adolescent Transsexuals: Changing Insights' (2008) 5(1) *Journal of Sexual Medicine* 1892, 1893; T.D. Steensma et al., 'The Treatment of Adolescent Transsexuals: Changing Insights' (2010) 16(4) *Clinical Child Psychology and Psychiatry* 499, 500.

48 S. Rosenthal, 'Approach to the Patient: Transgender Youth: Endocrine Considerations' (2014) 99(12) *The Journal of Clinical Endocrinology and Metabolism* 4379, 4384.

49 Ehrbar et al. note that 'it is possible that in children, the criteria for GID as currently delineated (Table 1) can be met through gender role nonconforming behavior, without any indication of gender dysphoria'. R.D. Ehrbar et al., 'Clinician Judgment in the Diagnosis of Gender Identity Disorder in Children' (2008) 34(5) *Journal of Sex & Marital Therapy* 385, 388; see also K. Winters, 'The New York Magazine lies to parents about trans children', *The Trans Advocate* 09.08.2016 <http://transadvocate.com/the-new-york-magazine-lies-to-parents-about-trans-children_n_18875.htm> (last accessed 22.10.2016).

50 B. Tannehill, 'The End of the Desistence Myth', *Huffington Post* 01.01.2016 <http://www.huffingtonpost.com/brynn-tannehill/the-end-of-the-desistance_b_8903690.html> (last accessed 22.10.2016).

51 Winters, above n. 49.

In recent years, medical and psychological researchers have shown that the application of stricter diagnostic criteria significantly decreases false positives for persisting trans youth. There is a growing consensus that, where the trans label is reserved for only those young people who strongly,[52] consistently and persistently assert that they *are* their preferred gender (as opposed to *wishing* they were their preferred gender),[53] there are appreciably higher rates of trans persistence into adulthood.[54] While this research remains largely qualitative and anecdotal, and there is a significant need for greater quantitative analysis, these new stricter approaches suggest that it is possible to construct affirmative policies for trans minors based upon reliable and consistent methodologies.

3.1.3. Consent and Intersex 'Normalising' Surgeries

Consent is also a primary feature of debates over the legitimacy of intersex 'normalising' surgeries. For those who oppose physical interventions, the *de facto* practice of such normalising procedures fails to satisfy the consent requirement in two important respects. First, by delegating consent powers to parents or guardians, who act in consultation with medical officers, it is argued that current medical standards inappropriately disenfranchise intersex individuals in a most intimate and personal aspect of their lives. If invasive surgical alterations are going to take place, advocates recommend that only persons who experience intersex have the capacity to provide meaningful consent. Second, even if one accepts that, in line with standard parental rights in the medical sphere, parents or guardians should be empowered to authorise normalising interventions, these persons typically consent in situations of such comparable ignorance and coercion that their assent should not be considered either informed or free.

While medical law generally requires that individuals personally consent to physical interventions, there are alternative rules within the sphere of childhood treatment.[55] Save for exceptional doctrines, such as '*Gillick* competence'[56] in the United Kingdom and the 'mature minor'[57] principle in the United States,

52 H.J. Bonifacio and S.M. Rosenthal, 'Gender Variance and Dysphoria in Children and Adolescents' (2015) 62 *Paediatric Clinics of North America* 1001, 1004.
53 D. Ehrensaft, 'Found in Transition: Our Littlest Transgender People' (2014) 50(4) *Contemporary Psychoanalysis* 571, 578.
54 K.R. Olson et al.., 'Mental Health of Transgender Children Who Are Supported in Their Identities' (2016) 137(3) *Paediatrics* 2; J. Baum, 'Gender, Safety and Schools: Taking the Road Less Travelled' (2011) 15 *University of California Davis Journal of Law and Policy* 167, 167; C.A. Unger, 'Gynaecologic Care for Transgender Youth' (2014) 26 Current Opinion in Obstetrics and Gynecology 347, 348.
55 Jackson, above n. 31, pp. 256–279.
56 *Gillick v. West Norfolk & Wisbeck Area Health Authority* [1986] AC 112.
57 E. Ikuta, 'Overcoming Parental Veto: How Transgender Adolescents Can Access Puberty-Supressing Treatment in the Absence of Parental Consent under the Mature Minor Doctrine' (2016) 25 *Southern California Interdisciplinary Law Journal* 179, 222.

parents are generally empowered to consent to medical care on behalf of their child. Against that background, it appears consistent that, if a decision regarding genital-normalising for intersex infants arises, parents or guardians should be authorised to provide consent. However, among intersex communities, there is a belief that altering a new-born's sexed body is so fundamental to core identity, and has such a profound impact on one's future life course, that meaningful consent may only be offered by the individual whose body and identity are implicated.[58] As normalising surgeries are typically cosmetic (rather than therapeutically *necessary*) and are a significant invasion of bodily autonomy, there is enhanced justification for postponing treatment until the infant can contribute to the decision-making process.[59] Consistent with guarantees under the UN Convention on the Rights of the Child, parents and medical officers should observe the evolving capacities of intersex youth and only take steps to physically intervene where the child can be, and has been, heard. Arguments over the appropriate individuals in whom to locate consenting authority have been an effective tool in challenging medical responses to bodies which experience intersex.

Even if one concedes that parents have the right to consent to treatment, however, there are questions about the extent to which any consent will be either informed or free. Within the existing medico-legal scholarship, there is significant concern that parents and guardians continue to authorise genital-normalising interventions in circumstances where: (1) they do not fully understand intersex; (2) they are not encouraged or assisted to reflect upon the necessity of surgical alterations; and (3) they are not aware of, nor are they required to consider, the (possibly negative) long term effects of forcibly altering their child's sexed body.

In counselling new parents on the appropriateness of intersex treatments, medical officers too often provide vague or one-sided evidence, which presents intervention as the natural and responsible course of action.[60] Streuli et al. write of a 'framing bias' where ambiguous genitals become a social and medical emergency, and where surgery is key to reducing subsequent emotional and physical trauma.[61] For new parents, who may lack even basic familiarity with

---

58 A. Davidson, 'Beyond the Locker Room: Changing Narratives on Early Surgery for Intersex Children' (2011) 26 *Wisconsin Journal on Law, Gender and Society* 1, 15–16; Tamar-Mattis, above n. 7, 59. Albritton, above n. 20, 175.

59 Albritton, above n. 20, 175.

60 World Health Organisation, *Eliminating forced, coercive and otherwise involuntary sterilization: An interagency statement*, WHO, Geneva 2014, p. 7; H.D. Beh and M. Diamond, 'An Emerging Ethical and Medical Dilemma: Should Physicians Perform Sex Assignment Surgery on Infants with Ambiguous Genitalia?' (2000) 7(1) *Michigan Journal of Law and Gender* 1, 42–50; R. Sparrow, 'Gender Eugenics? The Ethics of PGD for Intersex Conditions' (2013) 13(10) *The American Journal of Bioethics* 29.

61 J.C. Streuli et al., 'Shaping Parents: Impact of Contrasting Professional Counseling on Parents' Decision Making for Children with Disorders of Sex Development' (2013) 10 *Journal of Sexual Medical* 1953, 1958.

bodily diversity and who may be distressed by their child's supposed 'difference', there may be a diminished capacity to question or challenge medical orientation toward intervention. This is particularly so where, in addition to medicalising the language of intersex, doctors present ambiguous genitalia as inconsistent with accepted social conventions.[62] Indeed, Davis and Murphy recall parents who, having initially refused consent to surgery, were subjected by medical officers to implicit and explicit social condemnation.[63] In Germany, where the legislature has sought to remove incentives for early intervention by creating the possibility for a temporary non-specific birth registration option, activists complain that the social opprobrium attached to challenging binary gender norms may in fact increase the pressure on parents to physically alter their new-borns' bodies.[64] In Colombia, where the Constitutional Court has dealt extensively with the relationship between intersex and medicine, parents or guardians must now provide enhanced consent – offered following extensive consultation and information – to ensure that any authorisation, once made, is the product of appropriate and meaningful reflection.[65]

3.2. MEDICAL NECESSITY

An important exception to the 'consent requirement' is the existence of a medical emergency.[66] According to Lewis, '[i]f emergency treatment is required for a patient whose condition prevents him from giving consent, the doctor may give such treatment as is reasonably required'.[67] However, the instances where medical emergencies arise are tightly regulated. In general, courts will only validate non-consensual treatment where the circumstances 'prevent the practitioner from obtaining the appropriate consent', the 'necessary intervention cannot be delayed' and the treatment is carried out 'for the immediate benefit of the individual concerned'.[68]

---

62 Sparrow, above n. 60, 29.

63 G. Davis and E.L. Murphy, 'Intersex Bodies as States of Exception: An Empirical Explanation for Unnecessary Surgical Modification' (2013) 25(2) *Feminist Formations* 129, 144–145.

64 M. Carpenter, 'German proposals for a "third gender" on birth certificates miss the mark', OII Australia 20.08.2013 <https://oii.org.au/23183/germany-third-gender-birth-certificates/> (last accessed 25.02.2017).

65 Sentencia T-551/99, Constitutional Court of Colombia, 02.08.1999; Sentencia SU-337/99, Constitutional Court of Colombia, 12.05.1999.

66 C.J. Lewis, 'Medical treatment in the absence of consent' (1989) *Law Society Gazette* 86 (32) (30.08.1989).

67 Ibid. In *Herczegfalvy v. Austria* ([1992] EHRR 58, [82]), the ECtHR held that a 'measure which is a therapeutic necessity cannot be regarded as inhuman and degrading'.

68 Explanatory Report to the Convention for the Protection of Human Rights and Dignity of the Human Being with Regard to the Application of Biology and Medicine, [56]–[59] <http://conventions.coe.int/Treaty/EN/Reports/Html/164.htm> (last accessed 11.07.2015).

The non-consensual character of trans medical requirements cannot be justified by reference to any medical emergency. Many trans persons who access legal gender recognition have no clinical need for treatment.[69] They enjoy healthy, properly functioning bodies and surgery/sterilisation serves no therapeutic function.[70] Indeed, according to the International Federation of Gynaecology and Obstetrics, 'sterilization for prevention of future pregnancy cannot be ethically justified on grounds of medical emergency'.[71] Medical intervention as part of legal gender recognition pursues social and moral policy goals (e.g. maintain a false 'binary sex paradigm',[72] etc.), rather than the resolution of medical emergencies. They do not fall within the 'medical emergency' exception to free and informed consent.

On the other hand, whether intersex treatments are medically necessary is somewhat more complex. Scholars, such Thorn and Hermer, correctly observe that some physical phenomena which fall within intersex do justify (and mandate) healthcare services, including obstructed urinary tracts and increased risks for cancer.[73] In such circumstances, it is appropriate for medical officers to recommend physical intervention and there is an appreciable benefit for intersex new-borns in receiving the care. However, in many other cases, proposed alterations will respond to merely cosmetic or social preferences,[74] and provide no therapeutic benefit for the child who experiences intersex. The fact that a new-born may have genitalia which differ from standard bodily expectations does not mean that those genitalia require physical alteration. To the extent that intersex surgeries often fail to address a specific medical necessity, in the absence of full, free and informed consent, they cannot be compatible with the principle of bodily integrity.

4. BEST INTERESTS OF THE CHILD

Within both human rights discourse, and national family law structures, the 'best interests of the child' is a vitally important, yet highly controversial,

---

69 *Herczegfalvy v. Austria*, above n. 67.

70 Ibid.

71 International Federation of Gynaecology and Obstetrics, *Ethical Issues in Obstetrics and Gynaecology*, FIGO 2012, pp. 123–124.

72 J.A. Greenberg, 'Defining Male and Female: Intersexuality and the Collision between Law and Biology' (1999) 41 *Arizona Law Review* 265, 275.

73 L.D. Hermer, 'A Moratorium on Intersex Surgeries? Law, Science, Identity and Bioethics at the Crossroads' (2006) 13 *Cardozo Journal of Law and Gender* 255, 258–259; D Thorn, 'Drop the Knife! Instituting Policies of Non-Surgical Intervention for Intersex Infants' (2014) 52(3) *Family Court Review* 610.

74 See generally R. Hupf, 'Allyship to the Intersex Community on Cosmetic, Non-Consensual Genital "Normalizing Surgery"' (2015) 22 *William and Mary Journal of Women and the Law* 73; S. Lloyd, 'Intersex Education, Advocacy and the Law: The Struggle for Recognition and Protection' (2004) 11 *Cardozo Women's Law Journal* 283, 283.

legal standard. Article 3 UN CRC states that '[i]n all actions concerning children', whether they are taken by 'public or private social welfare institutions, courts of law, administrative authorities or legislative bodies', 'the best interests of the child shall be a primary consideration'. A state actor, including a legislator and judge,[75] who engages in conduct, direct or indirect,[76] in relation to children, both individually and collectively,[77] must prioritise the best interests of the child as a primary concern. This general principle is now recognised as *the* global best practice standard for determining the rights of children and adolescents. It has been transposed, either expressly or through equivalent language, into national legal orders across Europe and beyond.[78]

Despite the relative ubiquity of 'best interests' analysis in child-focused decision-making, there has been comparatively little consideration – both judicial and academic – of how trans, intersex and gender-non-conforming young people fit within the principle. It is only recently that both policymakers, and scholars, have turned their attention to the legal and social programmes which would best serve the interests of these groups. To a certain extent, this is not surprising. In a legal and social environment which has systematically erased or supressed minors who transgress accepted bodily and cultural binaries, one would not expect trans and intersex young people to enjoy priority status. Indeed, given the well-documented emotional and physical harm which past reparative and normalising practices have imposed upon trans and intersex youth, it is not difficult to understand why state authorities would have preferred to shield their actions from best interests review.[79]

Yet, with the growing visibility and public awareness of gender-variant child narratives,[80] there is also increasing acceptance that state regulation of, and academic commentary upon, the lives of trans and intersex youth, must apply the same rights lens through which all other cisgender and non-intersex experiences are viewed.[81] In 2012, when Argentina extended the possibility of legal gender recognition to individuals under the age of majority, the controlling statute explicitly required that children's applications be assessed 'taking into

---

75 J. Zermatten, 'The Best Interests of the Child Principle: Literal Analysis and Function' (2010) 18 *International Journal of Children's Rights* 483, 497.

76 J.M. Pobjoy, 'The Best Interests of the Child Principle as an Independent Source of International Protection' 64 *International and Comparative Law Quarterly* 327, 330.

77 UN Committee on the Rights of the Child, General Comment No. 14 on 'The right of the child to have his or her best interests taken as a primary consideration (art. 3, para. 1)' 29.05.2013 UN Doc No. CRC/C/GC/14, [23].

78 See e.g. Children's Act 1989, s. 1 (UK); The Family Law Act, s. 43 (Australia); Guardianship of Minors Ordinance (Cap 13), s. 3 (Hong Kong).

79 P. Burke, *Gender Shock: Exploding the Myths of Male and Female*, Double Day, New York 1997.

80 J. Olson and R. Garofalo, 'The Peripubertal Gender-Dysphoric Child: Puberty Suppression and Treatment Paradigms' (2014) 43(6) *Paediatric Annals* 132, 133.

81 Scherpe and Dunne, above n. 12, pp. 627–629.

account the evolving capacities and *best interests of the child* as expressed in the Convention on the Right of the Child'[82] [emphasis added]. Similarly, under Malta's landmark Gender Identity, Gender Expression and Sex Characteristics Act 2015, the best interests of the child is now the 'paramount consideration' for decisions regarding both legal recognition (section 7(2)(a)) and intersex medical treatment (section 14(5)(a)).

While the movement toward an express, 'best interests', analysis is a positive step, one must be careful to consider how this general standard will operate in the sphere of trans and intersex identities. There is a general presumption that, when acting on behalf of their children, parents will automatically prioritise the latter's best interests.[83] Considering the normal ties of love and affection, as well as the specific knowledge, that parents have for their children, this is perhaps a reasonable assumption to make.[84] Faced with two alternate choices, parents typically will select that option which best promotes child welfare.

Yet, within the specific context of gender diversity and gender non-conformity, there is at least an arguable case that courts and public authorities should more strictly supervise parental choice.[85] There needs to be certainty that, in deciding the social, medical and legal pathways that children must follow, parents and guardians are actually guided by children's interests rather than by other, possibly conflicting concerns. The existing social science and legal scholarship offers ample evidence that parents and guardians overtly disregard the interests of their trans and intersex offspring.[86] Gender prejudice,[87] fear of difference and the desire to avoid social stigmatisation,[88] have led numerous parents to reject, abandon and even physically harm gender non-conforming youth. In its landmark case law on intersex genital surgeries, the Colombian Constitutional Court observed that non-normative gender and sex gives rise to such social and cultural fears among parents that, in many cases, it would be inappropriate to presume that parents can act solely in the interests of their children.[89]

---

82 Act 26.743, Art. 5.

83 S. Shield, 'The Doctor Won't See You Now: Rights of Transgender Adolescents to Sex Reassignment Treatment' (2006–07) 31 *New York University Review of Law and Social Change* 361, 363.

84 *Parham v. J.R* [1979] 442 U.S. 584, 602.

85 G.P. Koocher, 'Competence to Consent: Psychotherapy', in G.B. Melton, G.P. Koocher and M. J. Saks (eds.), *Children's Competence to Consent*, Plenum 1983, p. 112.

86 H. Hussey, *Beyond 4 Walls and a Roof Addressing Homelessness Among Transgender Youth,* Centre of American Progress 2015, p. 1.

87 C. Burgess, 'Internal and External Stress Factors Associated with the Identity Development of Transgendered Youth' (2000) 10(3–4) *Journal of Gay & Lesbian Social Services* 35, 43; F. Susset, 'Between a Rock and a Hard Place' in E.J. Meyer and A. Pullen Sansfaçon (eds.), *Supporting Transgender and Gender Creative Youth: Schools, Families and Communities in Action*, Peter Lang, San Francisco 2014, p. 117.

88 S.L. Johnson and K.E. Benson, '"It's Always the Mother's Fault": Secondary Stigma of Mothering a Transgender Child' (2014) 10(1–2) *Journal of GLBT Family Studies* 124, 138.

89 Sentencia T-551/99, above n. 65; Sentencia SU-337/99, above n. 65.

For trans and intersex youth, there may be disadvantage in extending the ordinary presumptions around parental decision-making.

In medical law, closer scrutiny is exercised over parental decision-making where a parent or guardian consents to treatment which, while offering no therapeutic advantage to the medicalised child, benefits another member of the family.[90] The fear is that the parent may be acting contrary to (or at least with ambivalence towards) the medicalised child in order to serve the interests of another person.[91] Similar concerns arise in the context of trans affirmation and intersex surgery. Save in severe or outlier cases, it should not be legitimate for parents to refuse trans-affirming social, legal and medical recognition because of fears over how the family's reputation will diminish or individual family members will be affected. Parents should not consent to genital-normalising surgeries because they (or members of their family) are unwilling to face possible stigma attached to bodily diversity.[92] Thus, while the movement towards 'best interests' potentially expands human rights protections for trans and intersex children, state authorities must ensure that movement prioritises, rather than subordinates, the welfare of young people.

5. BEYOND THE BINARY

One of the most important and interesting cross-overs for intersex and trans identities is their potential to challenge 'natural' and 'constructed' gender binaries. Around the world, legal, medical and social gender operates as an almost universally dichotomised phenomenon.[93] Reproducing what Greenberg terms the 'binary sex paradigm', individuals are separated into neat 'male' and 'female' boxes and, depending on the prevailing social and cultural mores, they may experience significantly different roles, expectations and opportunities.[94] Intersex and trans identities may disrupt binary gender ideology, challenging its biological bases and highlighting gendered experiences which exist beyond male and female.

Intersex bodies have historically been cited as an obvious, physical challenge to the notions of dichotomised sex and gender. To the extent that man-woman

---

90 Tamar-Mattis, above n. 7, 94.

91 S. Curtis, 'Reproductive Organs and Differences of Sex Development: The Constitutional Issues Created by the Surgical Treatment of Intersex Children' (2010–11) 42 *McGeorge Law Review* 841, 851; F. Bell, 'Children with Gender Dysphoria and the Jurisdiction of the Family Court' (2015) 38(2) *University of New South Wales Law Journal* 426, 447.

92 Sentencia T-551/99, above n. 65; Sentencia SU-337/99, above n. 65.

93 G. Beemyn and S. Rankin, *The Lives of Transgender People*, Columbia University Press, New York 2011, p. 19.

94 J.A. Greenberg, 'Defining Male and Female: Intersexuality and the Collision between Law and Biology' (1999) 41 *Arizona Law Review* 265, 275.

binaries rely upon the inevitability of two (and only two) naturally occurring body types, which are themselves determinative of legal and social gender roles, intersex may explode the myth of a rigid biological binary.[95] While persons whose bodily characteristics do not conform to expected sex configurations often do identify within conventional 'male' and 'female' gender roles, their bodies (irrespective of their gender identity) potentially undermine accepted biological 'truths' and require society to reconsider gendered orthodoxy.[96]

Bodily diversity is not, however, the only way in which trans and intersex identities challenge binary ideology. For many authors, the mere existence of trans identification and expression is an inherently transgressive act.[97] In self-identifying with a gender which has not been assigned to them at birth, trans persons question both the immutability of binary gender and the state's monopoly on enforcing binary rules.[98] Perhaps more significantly, however, many trans and intersex-identified individuals now explicitly express a gender identity which deviates from the male-female orthodoxy. Within global trans communities, especially among younger groups who may feel greater freedom to explore and problematise gender narratives,[99] there is an increasing spectrum of non-binary identifications, including genderqueer, gender fluid and non-gendered.[100]

For lawyers, and those tasked with creating or supervising the law, the question is how to accommodate individuals outside male-female categories. While a full exploration of non-binary legal recognition is beyond the scope of this chapter (and indeed this is an area of law which is emerging and subject to rapid change), a number of observations can be made.

In particular, it is important for trans and intersex advocates to consider the role which biology-based arguments should play in promoting non-binary rights. In many ways, as noted above, it is tempting for advocates to cite intersex bodies as evidence: (1) against rigid binary gender; and (2) in favour of additional categories which extend beyond male and female. To the extent

---

95 P. Currah, 'Expecting Bodies: The Pregnant Man and Transgender Exclusion from the Employment Non-Discrimination Act' (2008) 36(3&4) *Women's Studies Quarterly*, 331; P.-L. Chau and J. Herring, 'Defining, Assigning and Designing Sex' (2002) 16 *Int'l J.L. Pol'y & Fam.* 327, 355; W. O'Brien, 'Can International Human Rights Law Accommodate Bodily Diversity' (2015) 15 *Human Rights Law Review* 1, 5.

96 M.D. Levasseur, 'Gender Identity Defines Sex: Updating the Law to reflect modern medical science is key to Transgender Rights' (2014–15) 39 *Vermont Law Review* 943, 946.

97 Perhaps the most famous example being J. Butler, *Gender Trouble: Feminism and the Subversion of Identity*, Routledge, New York 1990.

98 J. McGrath, 'Are You a Boy or a Girl – Show Me Your REAL ID' (2009) 9 *Nevada Law Journal* 268, 377.

99 Beemyn and Rankin, above n. 93, p. 25; S.E. James et al., *The Report of the 2015 U.S. Transgender Survey*, NCTE, Washington DC 2016, p. 46.

100 K. Bornstein, *Gender Outlaw: On Men, Women and the Rest of Us*, Routledge, New York 1994, pp. 51–52; L.E. Kuper, R. Nussbaum and B. Mustanki, 'Exploring the Diversity of Gender and Sexual Orientation Identities in an Online Sample of Transgender Individuals' (2012) 49(2–3) *The Journal of Sex Research* 244, 249.

that non-traditional sex characteristics undermine binary sex fallacies, they encourage policymakers (and wider society) to move beyond a narrow male-female lens.[101] However, while some intersex persons may also experience an internal gender outside the traditional binary, there are pitfalls in tying legal gender to the presence of certain sex characteristics.

A 'sex-as-gender' approach to law may pressurise state authorities to acknowledge an alternative gender status (or several), but it also re-entrenches biologically essentialist visions of men and women. In opposing surgery as a precondition for legal gender recognition, advocates have endorsed the argument that a person's sexed body is not dispositive of their legal gender. The fact that a man has a vagina or a woman has a penis should not automatically impede formal gender recognition.[102] However, founding a right to non-binary recognition on the existence of intersex bodies directly reconnects legal gender to sex, and implicitly concedes that sex characteristics determine gender. If persons must be able to register a non-male/female gender because they have ambiguous genitalia, must all those persons who identify within the binary reproduce standard male and female anatomy? This approach, while privileging those intersex persons who identify outside the binary, would condemn all other applicants for recognition, trans and binary-identified intersex individuals, to invasive treatments, which are often medically, financially and practically inaccessible.

In addition to concerns regarding biological essentialism, movements towards non-binary gender recognition should also respect individual narratives of gender. While, as noted, scholars have welcomed the inherently transgressive nature of trans and intersex identities, it is important to acknowledge that many trans and intersex individuals do see themselves within (and fully embrace) the gender binary.[103] Although the act of transitioning may be conceptualised as *binary-disruptive*, the reality is that many (if not most) trans persons simply want to be affirmed in their male or female identity. Any efforts to affirm the legal status of non-binary persons must equally acknowledge the right of trans and intersex persons to be affirmed within their preferred binary gender.[104]

---

101 Greenberg, above n. 94; M.V. Carerra, R. Depalma and M. Lameiras, 'Sex/gender identity: Moving beyond fixed and "natural" categories' (2012) 15(8) *Sexualities* 995, 1000.

102 This argument has been accepted by recent legislative reform: Gender Recognition Act 2004 (UK), Gender Recognition Act 2015 (Ireland); Act 3/2007 of March 15 (Spain); Forlag L 182 (Denmark).

103 P. Gagne, R. Tewksbury and D. McGaughey, 'Coming out and Crossing over: Identity Formation and Proclamation in a Transgender Community' (1997) 11(4) *Gender and Sexuality* 478, 501; R. Sanghani, 'Why the UK should ditch male and female toilets for 'gender-neutral' loos', *The Telegraph* 14.12.2015 <http://www.telegraph.co.uk/women/life/why-the-uk-should-ditch-male-and-female-toilets-for-gender-neutr/> (last accessed 25.02.2017).

104 S. Hines, 'What's the Difference? Bringing Particularity to Queer Studies of Transgender' (2006) 15(1) *Journal of Gender Studies* 49, 64.

Put simply: while it is welcome for the law to recognise and accommodate non-orthodox identities, national legal orders must continue to respect trans and intersex persons who identify as male or female. While non-binary activists have rightly identified numerous non-Western societies which make room for individuals outside male-female dichotomies,[105] particularly through the lens of a 'third gender', it remains uncertain whether binary-identified trans individuals must bring themselves within this alternative category, or whether they can achieve formal and social acceptance as either male or female. The law must accommodate persons who genuinely experience their identity outside the binary. However, it must equally embrace those who, while transgressing rules of gender immutability, nevertheless continue to exist within binary norms.

Respecting individual gender narratives must also influence the form(s) which non-male/female recognition takes. A recurring difficulty is formulating a sufficiently wide and inclusive model to include the multiplicity of gendered identities which individuals experience outside traditional binary norms.[106] To a large extent, the goal of introducing alternative gendered frameworks will be defeated if the available additional models merely corner non-binary individuals into new and equally rigid gender categories.[107] In New Zealand[108] and Malta,[109] policymakers have attempted to expand gender recognition categories through the possibility of 'X' gender passports. Persons who experience their identity outside male-female dichotomies can achieve alternative recognition beyond 'M' and 'F' designations. Yet, for individuals who live a fluid gender, or experience no gender whatsoever, the requirement to bring oneself within another rigid marker will be no less oppressive than the existing binary structures. One of the practical hurdles which policymakers, and non-binary communities, have encountered and continue to encounter, is the difficulty of providing categorisation to gendered narratives which are simultaneously fluid and infinite.[110]

Conscious of the difficulty in constructing a gender typology, which sufficiently accounts for the spectrum of gendered lives, one (perhaps) extreme

---

105 B. Boyce, 'Sexuality and Gender Identity Under the Constitution of India' (2015) 18 *Journal of Gender Race & Justice* 1, 21; P.S. Pagadish, 'Mainstreaming Third-Gender Healers: The Changing Perceptions of South Asian Hijras' (2013) 9 *Vanderbilt Undergraduate Research Journal* 1, 1.

106 Davidson, above n. 11, 70.

107 O. Tomchin, 'Bodies and Bureaucracy: Legal Sex Classification and Marriage-Based Immigration for Trans* People' (2013) 101 *California Law Review* 813, 859–860.

108 'Information about Changing Sex/Gender Identity' <https://www.passports.govt.nz/what-you-need-to-renew-or-apply-for-a-passport/information/> (last accessed 25.02.2017).

109 '"X" gender option to be added to passports and ID cards', *Times of Malta* 24.02.2017 <http://www.timesofmalta.com/articles/view/20170224/local/x-gender-option-to-be-added-to-passports-and-id-cards.640544> (last accessed 25.02.2017).

110 S. Marsh, 'The gender-fluid generation: young people on being male, female or non-binary', *The Guardian* 23.03.2016 <http://www.timesofmalta.com/articles/view/20170224/local/x-gender-option-to-be-added-to-passports-and-id-cards.640544> (last accessed 25.02.2017).

solution is to remove gender from the scope of the law. If legal frameworks are incapable of accommodating the nuanced, complex ways in which individuals identify their preferred gender, why require those individuals to bring themselves within an unintelligible regime? For non-binary communities, de-gendering the law is hailed as a meaningful solution to social apprehension and marginalisation.[111] It is also proposed as a strategy to eradicate more general gender and sexual orientation biases, which both explicitly and implicitly rely upon state-sanctioned, oppositional gender roles.[112] To the extent that individuals – cisgender, trans and intersex – can escape the expectations and limitations of binary gender, separating law from gender will promote greater social equality and personal freedom.

Yet, the notion of de-gendering the law is not without critique. While feminist scholars have, for decades, advocated the removal of gender as a legal category, all such efforts have thus far fallen short. Although, since the mid-twentieth century, overtly gendered discrimination has slowly been repealed, and rigid gendered roles have increasingly been relaxed, the idea of two, oppositional legal genders remains a central pillar to which both law and wider society remain unshakably linked. Therefore, in practical terms, proposals to disconnect law from gender may have little real impact upon non-binary and non-gendered lives.[113]

Perhaps more fundamentally, however, a project to fully de-gender the law may elicit strong opposition, both from cisgender communities and from transgender individuals themselves. There are many cisgender persons who enjoy their legally affirmed gender, and who would reject attempts to involuntarily forfeit that status. Even cisgender allies who are sympathetic to non-binary recognition may draw a line at requiring all persons to adopt implied gender neutrality. Similarly, as noted, for many trans people, legal gender recognition is the final stage in a lifelong journey towards gendered affirmation. For these individuals, obtaining formal state acknowledgement validates their sense of self and facilitates greater self-actualisation. Once again, such individuals may support a programme for non-binary recognition, but strongly oppose the loss

---

111 Non-Binary Inclusion Project, *Nonbinary Inclusion Project Right to Recognition: Leaving Nobody Behind Statement of response to the Women & Equalities Committee Transgender Equality Inquiry Report*, p. 7 <http://nonbinary.co.uk/wp-content/uploads/2016/01/NBIP-Statement-on-WEC-Report.pdf> (last accessed 25.02.2017; P. Currah and L.J. Moore, '"We Won't Know Who You Are": Contesting Sex Designations in New York City Birth Certificates' (2009) 24(3) *Hypatia* 113, 123; Act Law Reform Advisory Council, *Beyond the Binary: legal recognition of sex and gender diversity in the ACT*, ACT 2012, p. 30; L. Feinberg, *Transgender Warriors: Making History from Joan of Arc to Dennis Rodman*, Boston Press, Boston 1996, p. 125.

112 M.A. Gilbert, 'Defeating Bigenderism: Changing Gender Assumptions in the Twenty-first Century' (2009) 24(3) *Hypatia* 93, 108.

113 Currah and Moore, above n. 111, 124.

of their own legal status. It is important to remember that, while de-gendering the law may move gender identities outside legal frameworks, it would not eradicate either social gender or gender-related discrimination. While 'law-without-gender' might not reduce gender bias or gender-based prejudices, it would potentially reduce the law's capacity to address and remedy such abuse wherever it arises.[114]

6. CONCLUSION

Trans identities and the experience of intersex variance are not the same phenomena. Trans and intersex communities often share diverging, possibly even oppositional, narratives and their rights-demands frequently differ both in focus and in strategy. In drawing parallels between trans individuals, and those who experience intersex, this chapter does not equate, or seek to fuse, the historical or contemporary reality for both groups. What this chapter has sought to illustrate, however, is that, in working to uphold common core principles – bodily integrity, children's rights, self-determination – trans and intersex advocacy can be complementary, and often speaks to a wider movement toward greater gender and sex equality.

114 C.A. MacKinnon, 'From Practice to Theory, or What is a White Woman Anyway?' (1991) 4(1) *Yale Journal of Law and Feminism* 13, 15; E. Reilly, 'Radical Tweak-Relocating the Power to Assign Sex from Enforcer to Differentiator of Inclusiveness: Revising the Response to Intersexuality' (2005) 12 *Cardozo Journal of Law and Gender* 297, 324.

PART IV

NATIONAL LEGAL DEVELOPMENTS

THE LEGAL STATUS OF INTERSEX PERSONS IN AUSTRALIA

Claire FENTON-GLYNN

1. INTRODUCTION

The legal status of intersex persons of Australia is complicated by the very structure of the Australian legal system. Australia is a federal system, with competence for areas of law divided according to the Constitution. However, the regulation of sex and gender identity falls across several different areas of competence, leaving a patchwork of inconsistent, and at times contradictory, laws.

While states and territories have competence in the area of registration of births – and thus the registration of sex on the birth certificate – the commonwealth holds competency in relation to marriage (and its definition), and the issuance of passports. As such, it is possible for individuals to have two documents used to establish legal identity – the passport and the birth certificate – declaring a different gender. This situation is complicated even further by the fact that different states and territories have established different rules concerning the registration of sex on the birth certificate, as well as how an individual can register a change of gender.

This chapter will attempt to summarise the key features of these various laws, starting with the registration of an intersex child on a birth certificate in different states and territories, then go on to discuss how the birth certificate can be changed at a later date. It will then move to recognition of intersex as a status on a federal level, and the consequences of conflicts between these differing regimes.

It must be recognised that most of the laws in this regard are drafted with transgender individuals in mind, rather than being intended to address the specific context of intersex individuals. Although this is starting to change, with the Australian Capital Territory (ACT) and South Australia leading the way, many states still do not have any legal recognition or protection of intersex individuals. In the absence of more specific and appropriate laws in this regard, the more general transgender mechanisms will be examined to consider whatever imperfect protection can be provided to intersex individuals.

2. REGISTRATION UPON BIRTH

In every jurisdiction, save the ACT and South Australia, the sex of a child must be notified to the Registrar when the birth is registered. The determination of sex at this stage is usually based on a physical inspection of the child's genitals, and only a registration of male or female is possible.

In South Australia, the child's sex must only be registered 'if determined'.[1] However, it is not clear whether such registration must be male or female, or if further categories are permitted. The ACT goes even further, however. While also only requiring the sex of the child to be recorded 'if it is determinable', if the sex is recorded, the child can be registered as: male, female, intersex, indeterminate and 'to be advised'. The amendments also extended the time limit for registering a child to six months, to reduce pressure on parents to make quick decisions concerning the child's sex.[2]

While superficially this change may be seen as a step in the right direction, giving greater recognition to the status of intersex individuals, placing children into an 'other' category can be harmful. As the Organisation Intersex International pointed out:

> Defining intersex as a third classification for infants and children with intersex variations, as is the case in the ACT will places [sic] children at risk. Persons so assigned will have lesser rights, and will face stigma and outing in school environments, and we oppose such classification without the voluntary and informed consent of the person so classified, as a human rights abuse.[3]

---

1 reg 4(c) Births, Deaths and Marriages Registration Regulations 2011 (SA).

2 Births, Deaths and Marriages Registration Act (BDMRA) 1997 (ACT).

3 Submission to the Australian Human Rights Commission national consultation on Sexual Orientation, Gender Identity and Intersex Rights (2015) <https://oii.org.au/wp-content/uploads/2015/01/OII-Australia-SOGII-Submission-2015.pdf> (last accessed 01.07.2017), p. 10.

Likewise, Morgan Carpenter in this volume argues against the 'othering' of intersex populations through the inclusion of this category, while explaining that they fit a narrative about identity recognition that is grounded in the demands of the LGBT movement.

The definition of intersex under ACT law – as a person who has physical, hormonal or genetic features that are (a) not fully female or fully male; or (b) a combination of male or female; or (c) not female or male[4] – conflates intersex characteristics with non-binary gender identities, and the law is predicated on the assumption that a child's 'identity' must match their body. Moreover, it suggests that intersex individuals all fall within a homogenous category, that is, not male or female.[5]

3. CHANGING THE BIRTH CERTIFICATE

Although only one state permits a child to be registered as anything other than male or female, it is possible in other states – potentially all other states – for a person to change the register at a later date to indicate their intersex status. As stated above, these laws have largely been drafted with transgender individuals in mind, leaving the protection they provide imperfect. Nevertheless, they are the only mechanisms currently available under Australian federal and state law.

There are two ways in which a birth certificate can be changed.

1. through administrative correction; or
2. through change of registered sex.

3.1. ADMINISTRATIVE CORRECTION

In all states it is possible for a birth certificate to be amended through administrative correction. The legislation, which on this point is the same in all jurisdictions, allows the Registrar to correct the Register 'to bring an entry about a particular registrable event into conformity with the most reliable information available'.[6]

In Victoria, this has been used to allow an intersex individual to have their sex removed from the birth certificate, and entered as 'not stated'. This was the

---

4 s. 169B Legislation Act 2001 (ACT).

5 On this, see Organisation Intersex International, above n. 2.

6 s. 40(1)(b) BDMRA 1997 (ACT); s. 45(1)(b) BDMRA 1995 (NSW); s. 40(1)(b) BDMRA (NT); s. 42(2)(d) BDMRA 2003 (Qld); s. 42(1)(b) BDMRA 1996 (SA); s. 42(1)(b) BDMRA 1999 (Tas); s. 43(1)(b) BDMRA 1996 (Vic); s. 51(1)(b) BDMRA 1998 (WA).

case for Tony Briffa, a local councillor and Mayor in Victoria, who has publicly spoken about going through this process.[7] There is no evidence of this occurring in other states, although technically it would be similarly possible owing to the same legislative wording.

The NSW Registrar has issued guidance that suggests it would be possible for an intersex individual wrongly assigned male or female at birth to change to the other at a later date through administrative correction, if this were found to be incorrect. However, it was not clear whether this would cover a situation in which the person did not want to change to male or female, but instead wanted recognition that they were intersex.[8]

3.2. CHANGE OF REGISTERED SEX

The other way to change a birth certificate is through mechanisms for the change of registered sex. The ACT and South Australia alone have a specific provision that allows for an individual to change their sex to 'intersex' on the birth certificate.

In the ACT, the Births, Deaths and Marriages Registration Act 1997, section 24(1), provides that

> A person may apply to the registrar-general for alteration of the record of the person's sex in the registration of the person's birth if–
>
> (a) the person is at least 18 years old; and
> (b) the person's birth is registered in the ACT; and
> (c) the person believes their sex to be the sex nominated in the application (the 'altered sex'), and –
>   (i) has received appropriate clinical treatment for alteration of the person's sex; or
>   (ii) is an intersex person.

If the individual in question is a child, a parent or person with parental responsibility can apply on the same grounds, but must also 'believe on reasonable grounds that alteration of the record of the child's sex is in the best interests of the child'.

In 2016, South Australia joined the ACT in liberalising their laws. The amended Births, Deaths and Marriages Registration Act 1996 does not go as far as the ACT, as an application for a change of gender on a birth certificate must

---

7 Organisation Intersex International, <https://oii.org.au/4856/on-birth-registrations/> (last accessed 01.07.2017).

8 Ibid.

still be accompanied by 'a statement by a medical practitioner or psychologist certifying that the person has undertaken a sufficient amount of appropriate clinical treatment in relation to the person's sex or gender identity'.[9] It does not have an equivalent provision that allows for an individual to self-identify as an intersex person and have the register changed on that basis. However, the Act does make improvements in two ways. First, it makes clear that clinical treatment need not involve invasive medical treatment, and may indeed include or be constituted by counselling,[10] which opens the door for intersex individuals to use this route (without having to show surgical or medical intervention). Second, the accompanying regulations allow an individual's gender to be recorded as male, female, non-binary, or indeterminate/intersex/unspecified.[11] In this way, individuals in South Australia are able to identify with a range of different sex and gender identities.

In all other jurisdictions, a change of gender on the birth certificate falls under provisions related to 'gender reassignment', 'sexual reassignment' or 'sex affirmation', all of which require medical or surgical intervention – which does not fit with the reality of the situation of intersex individuals.[12] Moreover, as the provisions were intended for transgender individuals, the focus in these states is changing from male to female or vice versa, rather than to accommodate those wishing to move outside the male/female binary.

Nevertheless, following the High Court case of *Norrie*, it is possible that states may be required to register individuals as 'non-specific'.[13] This case involved a Scottish-Australian individual, Norrie May-Welby. Norrie was born in Scotland with male reproductive organs, and in 1989 underwent a 'sex affirmation procedure'. They considered that the surgery did not resolve their sexual ambiguity, and in 2009 applied for their sex to be registered as 'non-specific' on the birth certificate. The Registrar initially acceded to this request, but later wrote to Norrie again, advising them that the change was invalid.

In the Supreme Court of New South Wales, Acting Chief Justice Beazley recognised 'increasing medical, psychological and social recognition that "sex" or "gender" is not a straightforward notion reflecting only a "male" and "'female" sex', and held that the Registrar had the power to record sex identifications other than male/female. He even suggested alternatives that could be recorded such as 'intersex', 'androgynous' and 'transgender'.[14]

9 s. 29K BDMRA (SA).
10 s. 29H BDRMA (SA).
11 reg 7A, Births, Deaths and Marriages Registration Regulations 2011.
12 s. 32B, 32C BDMRA 1995 (NSW); s. 28B, 28C BDMRA (NT); s. 23(4)(b) BDMRA 2003 (Qld); s. 28A, 28B BDMRA 1999 (Tas); s.30A, 30B BDMRA 1996 (Vic); s. 14(1) Gender Reassignment Act 2000 (WA).
13 [2014] HCA 11.
14 (2013) 84 NSWLR 697.

The Registrar appealed to the High Court, which although it did not support Beazley's line of reasoning as to the scope of other identifications, did order that Norrie's sex be registered as 'non-specific'. The High Court held it was 'unnecessary' to consider whether the Act 'contemplates the existence of specific categories of sex other than male and female … given that the Act recognizes that a person's sex may be neither male nor female'. This case was based on purely on statutory interpretation – when defining 'sex affirmation procedure', the Act stated that it involved:

> a surgical procedure involving an alteration of a person's reproductive organs carried out
>
> (a) for the purpose of assisting a person to be considered to be a member of the opposite sex; or
> (b) to correct or eliminate ambiguities relating to the sex of the person.[15]

In doing so, the Act thus recognised that a person's sex could be indeterminate, and therefore the Registrar must be able to register someone as such.

Of course, it has to be emphasised that this was not a case about an intersex individual, but a transgender individual who did not feel they fitted within the binary allocation of sex under the law. The narrow grounds on which the Court relied on in its decision – statutory interpretation, rather than the much wider recognition in the NSW Supreme Court – means that 'non-specific' can only be used by those who have undergone some kind of surgical treatment. Nevertheless, Norrie does open the door to further litigation on behalf of intersex individuals. If, as the High Court suggests, the legislation explicitly recognises that an individual can be of ambiguous, or non-specific, sex, then it is possible to extend this argument beyond sexual reassignment surgery, to any entry on the birth certificate. In *Norrie*, the High Court emphasised the importance of the accuracy of the register, according to the best available knowledge. It is arguable that, if the Act recognises that a person's sex is ambiguous, then it should be recorded as such – in line with the Victorian approach to administrative correction. However, in doing so, legislators and courts must be aware of the 'othering' of intersex individuals, discussed above. A 'non-specific' identification may be the desire of some, but it is by no means universal.[16]

It must also be noted that the decision in *Norrie* was also based on a NSW statute, which means that it does not automatically give rights to individuals living in other states and territories. Having said this, the same wording is present in the relevant legislation in Northern Territory, Queensland and Tasmania, and it is thus unlikely that there would be a different conclusion in relation to these statutes.

---

15 s. 32A BDMRA 1995 (NSW).

16 On this see especially M. Carpenter, in this volume.

On the other hand, in Western Australia, a 'reassignment procedure' is defined as:

> a medical or surgical procedure (or a combination of such procedures) to alter the genitals and other sexual characteristics of a person, identified by birth certificate as male or female, so that the person will be identified as a person of the opposite sex and includes, in relation to a child, any such procedure (or combination of procedures) to correct or eliminate ambiguities in the child's sexual characteristics.[17]

This is both wider, and narrower, than the legislation in other states. It requires a lesser level of medical intervention, allowing *medical or surgical* procedures, rather than requiring surgical intervention.[18] On the other hand, however, it only recognises procedures to 'correct or eliminate ambiguities' in the case of children (such procedures being problematic in and of themselves), meaning that adults would not be eligible under these grounds.

Finally, we can see that in Victoria, this ruling would not be applicable at all. The Victorian legislation defines a 'sex affirmation surgery' as a surgical procedure involving the alteration of a person's reproductive organs carried out for the purpose of assisting the person to be considered to be a member of the opposite sex. Thus, the legislation does not refer to the possibility of ambiguities, which was so central to the High Court's approach. Neither does Victoria allow minors to apply for a change to the register on these grounds, restricting it to those over 18.[19] However, as discussed above, Victoria is the only state that we are aware of that has used the provisions concerning the correction of the register to allow an individual to register as 'indeterminate' without any medical or surgical procedures. As such, intersex individuals have a different, arguably easier, route to having their identity registered.

It should also be noted that all states also require an individual to be unmarried before changing their sex on the birth certificate.[20] Although the Australian Human Rights Commission has recommended that this should be removed, as it is in breach of Australia's international obligations,[21] only the ACT and SA allow married persons to change their birth certificate as a result of change of sex.

---

17 s. 3 Gender Reassignment Act 2000 (WA).

18 Note that the ACT allows a change of sex to 'intersex' following 'appropriate clinical treatment' (s. 24(1)(c)(i) BDMRA 1997 (ACT)).

19 s. 4 BDMRA 1996 (Vic).

20 s. 32B(1)(c), 32DA(1)(d) BDMRA 1995 (NSW); s. 28B(1)(c) BDMRA (NT); s. 22 BDMRA 2003 (Qld); s. 28A(1)(c) BDMRA 1999 (Tas); s. 30A(1), 30C(3), 30F(6) BDMRA 1996 (Vic); s. 15(3) Gender Reassignment Act 2000 (WA).

21 Australian Human Rights Commission, *The Sex and Gender Diversity Project* (2009) <https://www.humanrights.gov.au/sites/default/files/document/publication/SFR_2009_Web.pdf> (last accessed 01.07.2017), p. 30.

4. RECOGNITION ACROSS STATE BORDERS

The final issue to mention concerning birth certificates is the recognition of change of gender across state borders. In South Australia, the legislation recognises certificates issued under corresponding laws in other states, all of which have been prescribed by the Regulations.[22] Likewise, NSW legislation also recognises certificates issued by other Australian jurisdictions.[23]

On the other hand, while the WA legislation says that a certificate issued under corresponding law is given the same effect as one issued in the state, the only corresponding law prescribed under the Regulations is the – now repealed – South Australian Act, leaving all other jurisdictions in limbo.[24] The Victorian legislation similarly gives effect to an 'interstate recognition certificate', which is defined as a certificate issued in SA, WA or 'any other prescribed law'. No other law has been prescribed.[25]

In the Northern Territory, Queensland and Tasmania, an 'interstate certificate' is recognised, but is defined to include only those who have undergone surgery, rather than a medical procedure which is permitted under WA legislation, or clinical treatment, as under ACT or South Australian legislation.[26] The ACT, actually has no provisions for formal recognition of change of sex in another jurisdiction, which appears to be an oversight.[27]

So, we can see that this creates a very difficult situation – an intersex person is only guaranteed recognition of their status in the ACT or South Australia. In all other states, they would have to go through either medical or surgical intervention before it could be acknowledged that their sex was neither male nor female. Even if they are successful in this, it will not necessarily be recognised in other Australian states or territories, so a person might end up being recognised as 'non-specific' or 'intersex' in one jurisdiction, and male or female in another.

5. PASSPORTS

To add to this confusion, Australian federal law has also weighed in on the issue, in relation to the issuance of passports. In 2003, an Australian named

22 reg 4, Sexual Reassignment Regulations 2015 (SA).

23 s. 32I(2), 32J(2) BDMRA 1995 (NSW); cl. 17 Births, Deaths and Marriages Registration Regulation 2011 (NSW).

24 s. 16(2), Gender Reassignment Act 2000 (WA); reg. 3 Gender Reassignment Regulations 2001 (WA).

25 s. 4 BDMRA 1996 (Vic).

26 s. 28A, 28J BDMRA (NT); s. 24(1), (3) BDMRA 2003 (Qld) s. 24(1), (3); s. 3, 28H BDMRA 1999 (Tas).

27 The previous version of the legislation contained a provision to interstate recognition in s. 29(2), (3), but no equivalent provision was included in the amended version in 2014.

Alex MacFarlane became the first person in Australia to hold a passport with an 'X' in the 'sex' field, recognising their sex as 'indeterminate/intersex/unspecified'. It was not until 2011 that the Federal Government made this an official policy, however, when it issued guidance stating that any intersex person, or person with a non-binary identity, could obtain such a passport.[28]

Unlike change of gender under state law, an application for such recognition on a passport requires only a doctor's letter stating that the individual lives as a person of indeterminate, unknown or non-specified gender. A sample text for the letter, provided by the government, is given as follows:

> I, <medical practitioner/psychologist's full name>, have a clinician/patient relationship with, and have treated, <name of patient> (OR have a clinician/patient relationship with <name of patient> and have reviewed and evaluated their history).
>
> <Name of patient> identifies as the gender of ___________.
>
> ___________________________________
>
> Signature of Medical Practitioner/Psychologist
> Signature block of Medical Practitioner/Psychologist
>
> ___________________________________
>
> Registration number from the Medical Board of Australia or Psychology Board of Australia
> (or equivalent overseas authority)

What this means is that there is no need for the birth certificate to be amended in order to be issued a passport in preferred sex. It is available to all Australian citizens regardless of their place of birth. Furthermore, to the extent that a passport is accepted as a cardinal document, it can operate instead of a birth certificate as a statement of a person's sex and gender identity. However, this adds another layer of difficulty, as it can mean that a person's legal sex is different not only from state to state, but also between state and Commonwealth level.

6. MARRIAGE

In addition to having jurisdiction over the issuance of passports, the Federal Government also has competence over the definition of marriage.

Until December 2017, Australia did not permit same-sex marriage, and the Constitution defined marriage as a union between one man and one woman.

---

[28] See Australian Government Guidelines on the Recognition of Sex and Gender, <https://www.ag.gov.au/Publications/Documents/AustralianGovernmentGuidelinesontheRecognitionofSexandGender/AustralianGovernmentGuidelinesontheRecognitionofSexandGender.PDF> (last accessed 07.06.2018).

This obviously created difficulties for those who are intersex, and indeed in the case of *In the marriage of C and D (falsely called C)*[29] in 1979, the Court found that an intersex person could not legally marry. In this case, the Court considered the validity of a marriage between a woman, and a person born of ambiguous sex who identified and lived as a male. It found that because the 'husband' had been born with ambiguous sex markers, they were 'not in fact … a male but a combination of both male and female'. As such, 'the husband was neither man nor woman but was a combination of both, and a marriage in the true sense of the word … could not have taken place and does not exist'.

This case was heavily criticised by the Full Court of the Family Court of Australia in *Re Kevin*,[30] a 2001 case concerning the marriage of a post-operative transsexual man. The Court in this case stated that the case 'was wrongly decided and should not be regarded as expressing the law in this country'. Instead, the Court endorsed the reasoning of Charles J. in the English case of *W v. W*, that intersex persons can, in effect, choose their sex and marry.[31]

This became more difficult, however, once an individual was registered as intersex, unspecified or indeterminate – either at state or federal level. It was basically implying that the individual had to choose one sex or another, and thus could not be 'non-specific' and married. This was an obvious difficulty arising from the ACT legislation[32] and meant that intersex individuals who did not want to be assigned to either male or female sex had to choose between being recognised as non-binary, or being married.

This position was rectified when the Australian Parliament passed the Marriage Amendment (Definition and Religious Freedoms) Act 2017. This amending Act substituted the words '2 people' in place of the previous definition of marriage between 'a man and a woman' in the Marriage Act 1961. This wide definition is important – unlike the English Marriage (Same Sex Couples) Act 2013, which only says that 'marriage of same sex couples is lawful', the simple wording of '2 people' means that those who are intersex or non-binary can marry a person of any sex.

7. ANTI-DISCRIMINATION LEGISLATION

In 2013, the Federal Government passed legislation that added new grounds of protected status under the Sex Discrimination Act 1984 (Cth).[33] As such, it is

29 (1979) 35 FLR 340.

30 *Attorney-General for the Commonwealth v. Kevin* [2003] FamCA 94.

31 [2001] Fam 111.

32 The South Australian legislation was not in force at this time.

33 The Sex Discrimination Amendment (Sexual Orientation, Gender Identity and Intersex Status) Act 2013 (Cth).

now unlawful under federal law to discriminate against a person on the grounds of their sexual orientation, gender identity, or intersex status. Intersex status is defined for these purposes in the same way as it is in the ACT legislation: as a person who has physical, hormonal or genetic features that are (a) not fully female or fully male; or (b) a combination of male or female; or (c) not female or male. In contrast, no state or territory as yet protects intersex status as a specified ground, leaving a gap in protection in this respect.

8. CONCLUSION

This has been a brief exploration of the legal issues surrounding the status of intersex persons in Australia, but what I hope has become clear is that the situation is far from straightforward. The complex interaction between state and federal laws, not to mention the differences in legislation between states themselves, means that individuals may have their chosen identity recognised in one jurisdiction, in one document, but they may not have it equally recognised in another jurisdiction, in another document or for another purpose. Such a system cannot be desirable, either for the individuals involved, nor the legal system as a whole.

THE LEGAL STATUS OF INTERSEX PERSONS IN SWEDEN

Jameson GARLAND

1. LEGAL FRAMEWORK AND STATISTICS

1.1. OVERVIEW

In many respects, Sweden was once considered a pioneering nation in the regulation of juridical gender. In 1631, Sweden became the first country in the world to establish a population registry for its inhabitants – a registry that reflected acknowledgement over time of the existence of persons who could not be classified simply as 'male' or 'female'.[1] In 1972, Sweden also became the

[1] For a comprehensive overview of this history, see M. BONDESTAM, *Tvåkönad: Studier i den svenska hermaphroditens historia*, Nya Doxa, Nora 2010. For an English summary in a legal context, see also J. GARLAND, *On Science, Law, and Medicine, The case of gender-'normalizing' interventions on children diagnosed as 'different in sex development'*, Uppsala Univ. Press, Uppsala 2016, pp. 51–93.

first country in the world to enact a national scheme for changing one's registered gender, providing gender-affirming medical care in connection with such changes.[2] The Gender Classification Act at the centre of this scheme, however, also appears to have been the first national law to endorse not only sterilisation of transgender persons, but to provide a mechanism for parents to seek changes of registered gender for children born with intersex conditions, as well as gender-conforming surgery on those children, without the children's consent.[3] The Act emerged from the first known governmental investigation in the world to recognise the class of *intersex persons* – a class defined as persons who suffer from social conflict with gender registration.[4] Though the experts that led the investigation concluded that the classes of 'males' and 'females' did not scientifically permit easy categorisation of many individuals, they nevertheless advocated that these classes should be maintained for socio-legal purposes and that all persons should be determined to 'belong' to one of these classes under strict legal controls. This legal scheme is expected to undergo significant transformation in 2018, as the government has announced plans to abolish the Gender Classification Act and to authorise simpler administrative changes of registered gender without any medical preconditions, with at least one such change as a matter of right.[5]

Sweden, however, also shapes and controls juridical gender through a more far-reaching law that medicalises gender identity as binary. The Population Registration Act directs medical personnel to provide data on the gender of an infant as part of the child's juridical registration, despite governmental concessions that no sound definition exists of what constitutes a 'male' or 'female'.[6]

---

2 National Board of Health and Welfare, *Transsexuella och övriga personer med könsidentitetsstörningar: Rättsliga villkor för fastställelse av könstillhörighet samt vård och stöd* (Transsexuals and other persons with gender identity disorders: Legal conditions for approval of sex as well as care and support), 2010, p. 13 (hereafter National Board, *Transsexuella och övriga personer*).

3 This chapter uses the terms 'intersex conditions' and 'divergences in sex development' interchangeably as they are used in Swedish documents. National Board of Health and Welfare, *Care and Treatment of Persons with Intersex Conditions* (*'Vård och behandling av personer med intersexuella tillstånd: Kartläggning av det tidiga omhändertagandet'*), 2017, p. 11–20 (hereafter, National Board, *Care and Treatment of Persons with Intersex Conditions*). A variation on the latter term is the current legal term used in the second section of the Gender Classification Act, see Lag (1972:119) *om fastställande om könstillhorighet i vissa fall* (hereinafter 'KtL'), 2 §. It should also be noted that the word *'kön'* traditionally means 'sex' in the binary male-female sense in many Swedish rules of law though both *'kön'* and *'könstillhorighet'* are often used to represent 'gender' as understood today (in lieu of the scholarly term *'genus'*). Thus, the English phrase 'Gender Classification Act' has been used here, as elsewhere, as shorthand for what the Act does ('to establish in law a "gender belonging" in certain cases').

4 *Intersexuallas könstillhörighet*, SOU 1968:28. For detailed discussion, see below, Section 1.2.2.

5 See below, Sections 2.2 and 2.3.

6 See below, Section 2.1.

Thus, medical opinion for most persons born in Sweden establishes their juridical gender status. In turn, the Gender Classification Act was also grounded on the notion that changes of registered gender should be strictly managed both medically and legally by permitting such changes only after medical review and, in many cases, with medical treatment. Indeed, the National Board of Health and Welfare's Legal Advisory Council, comprised of both medical and legal personnel, still approves all changes of registered gender.[7] Nevertheless, even with a new law replacing the Gender Classification Act, registered gender in Sweden will remain binary as long as the Population Registration Act is not amended. For intersex persons and children born with intersex conditions, the Population Registration Act remains a critical barrier to self-determination because it reinforces a legal presumption that medical personnel will determine which gender is appropriate for children and what medical procedures should be imposed on them to reinforce that gender. Lest there be any doubt as to this effect of the law, the Swedish Government in 2018 reaffirmed its position that non-consensual surgical procedures should be imposed on children with intersex conditions to conform their bodies to their *registered* gender, despite increasing calls from human rights authorities to prohibit those procedures.[8]

This chapter provides a summary of how Sweden's medico-legal system has imposed a cascade of legal disadvantages on persons with intersex conditions and differences of sex development and why this has prompted recent investigations for possible law reform. The need for deeper investigation is reflected only in part by Sweden's population registry, which currently does not contain any data on the existence of its inhabitants who have an intersex or intergender identity or who have sex characteristics that traditionally connote both male and female social classifications. This juridical invisibility is due in no small part to historic medical practices in Sweden that characterise intersex conditions as 'malformations' and a 'disorder', with gender-conforming procedures on infants and young children presumed to be lawful medical care for 'correction' of birth anomalies to reinforce a male or female appearance, in addition to resolving cases of 'unclear gender'.[9] As a result, intersex persons and children with differences

---

7 Förordning (2015:284) med instruktion för Socialstyrelsen, 18 §. On this matter, the council must be staffed by a forensic psychiatrist, 3 physicians, a behavioural scientist, and 1 additional staff member. Prop. 1972:6: *Kungl. Maj:ts proposition med förslag till lag om fastställande av könstillhörighet i vissa fall, m.m.*, p. 31.

8 See below, Sections 2.2 and 2.3.

9 Sweden's leading experts on care for persons with intersex conditions consistently estimate that 5 to 20 children each year are diagnosed with an 'unclear sex' in Sweden relative to a difference of sex development and undergoing possible gender-conforming care relative to that diagnosis. See A. Nordenström et al., 'Pojke eller flicka – gissa aldrig! Diagnostik och behandling av tillstånd med avvikande könsutveckling' (2008) *Läkartidningen* 629–632 (excluding children with hypospadias); *Remissvar: Ändrad könstillhörighet – förslag*

of sex development are excluded from protections for bodily integrity under criminal laws that would protect all other persons in Sweden, even laws that otherwise protect 'normal' children from medical interventions on their genitals and gonads. Persons with intersex conditions or differences of sex development are also largely excluded from protection under Sweden's civil rights laws. While the number of formal governmental investigations continues to mount in Sweden acknowledging ethical and human rights concerns regarding this state of affairs,[10] questions still linger about the rights of persons with intersex conditions and differences of sex development in Sweden, particularly as much about the government's plans to protect them are currently unknown.

1.2. LEGAL BACKGROUND AND EVOLUTION

1.2.1. The History of Binary Gender Status in Sweden

Like many nations, Sweden has long struggled to develop mechanisms to resolve problems associated with having only two classes for registered gender – 'male' or 'female'. Governmental investigations in Sweden from the late 1600s onward reflect an awareness of the difficulties of establishing individuals' legal status and rights when physical 'sex' characteristics do not permit easy classification into one of these categories.[11] Though Sweden began a national population registration system in 1631, no criteria were established to define any gender markers. Instead, for individuals whose gender was contested by others in

---

till ny lag: SOU 2007:16. Stockholm, Karolinska institutet 2007 (same). Both the statistics and the concepts that generate them are suspect. For example, hundreds of boys in Sweden with hypospadias are routinely surgically altered to make their penile appearance and function more 'normal' for boys. L. Örtqvist et al., 'Long-Term Follow-up of Men Born with Hypospadias: Urological and Cosmetic Results' (2015) 193 *Journal or Urology* 975. Conservative estimates place the number of children undergoing these surgeries at 300 or more per year. See Nordenström et al., above, 629. It is also uncertain if children with virilised 'clitorises', for example, whose 'sex' is otherwise deemed 'clear' to clinicians – e.g., a 'female' based on a clinical assessment – are excluded from those numbers but still might be subjected to genital reduction surgery offered to the children's parents as a mode of 'treatment', rather than considering that the children might identify as male and consider the surgery extirpation of their penises. Indeed, the official statistics raise many unanswered questions as the National Board uses the same statistics for those children who have differences of sex development and receive care for having an 'unclear gender'; National Board, *Care and Treatment of Persons with Intersex Conditions*, p. 11 et seq.

10 For the latest review, see SOU 2017:92, *Transpersoner i Sverige: Förslag för stärkt ställning och bättre levnadsvillkor*, which by the government's directive (dir 2016:102), included 'intersex persons' as persons often affected by the same laws and practices in Sweden. See also National Board, *Care and Treatment of Persons with Intersex Conditions*, pp. 36–41; SOU 2014:91, *Juridiskt kön och medicinsk könskorrigering*, pp. 237–258 and 310; Prop. 2011/12:142, *Ändrad könstillhörighet*, pp. 35–39.

11 Bondestam, above n. 1, p. 83 et seq.

marital or property disputes, the legal system's primary response was to deploy medical experts to attempt to determine whether a person was more 'male' or 'female' in order to resolve each controversy as it arose.[12] When such determinations could not be made, the affected persons were determined to be unable to be classified, without the rights associated with a male or female gender, such as the right to inherit property, vote, or marry persons of the 'other' gender, even though some persons were occasionally described as '*hermafrodit*' in legal records without clear consequences. By the eighteenth century, however, forensic specialists in Sweden shifted their concerns to developing a standardised system for assessment of a person's gender – a system highly influenced by the taxonomic theories of Carl Linnaeus, a physician, botanist, and zoologist renowned for revolutionising the scientific classification of living things.[13]

Linnaean taxonomy focused on classifying living entities as a means of better understanding them solely through facts, rather than categorising entities to fit tradition, mythology, and religion. Though this primary organising principle is often forgotten, Linnaeus emphasised that his scheme was not intended to represent a definitive order of nature, but rather a classification that permitted more fact-driven inquiries for objective scientific discourse.[14] His *Systema Naturae*, published in multiple editions throughout the 1700s, reflected a complex classification scheme – most famously for plants – based on the entire morphology of a given entity. His use of the reproductive organs of plants as the basis of categorisation, as well his poetic sexual imagery and gender hierarchies in his taxonomy, have dominated his popular legacy as one drawing upon heterosexuality and binary gender. In actuality, Linnaeus' morphological methodology included categories of 'hermaphroditic' plants as a part of diverse nature – a diversity that Linnaeus acknowledged was likely part of human nature, even though gender classification of humans was not the focus of his taxonomic work.[15] The influence of Linnaeus on taxonomy in Europe, however, is well established, and his methodology is also clearly reflected in the surge of forensic texts that advocated detailed examinations of 'male' or 'female' characteristics in order to develop highly specialised categorisations of humans who were suspected of being 'true' or 'pseudo' 'hermaphrodites'.[16]

---

12 Ibid, pp. 83–210.

13 See Garland, above n. 1, pp. 56–59.

14 See L. Schiebinger, *Nature's Body: Sexual Politics and the Making of Modern Science*, Pandora, New York 1993, p. 17. For a more critical, instrumentalist view of Linnean taxonomy, see P. Fara, *Sex, Botany & Empire*, Icon, Cambridge 2003, pp. 24–38.

15 M. Bondestam, 'When the Plant Kingdom Became Queer: On Hermaphrodites and the Linnaean Language of Nonnormative Sex', in J. Bull and M. Fahlgren (eds.), *Illdisciplined Gender – Engaging Questions of Nature/Culture and Transgressive Encounters*, Springer Intl, Cham, 2016.

16 See Garland, above n. 1, pp. 58–59.

In Sweden, as elsewhere, forensic medicine was often shaped more by socio-legal concerns than by science alone. Thus, forensic examinations often determined an individual's gender status, including how a person could fulfil marital obligations for penile-vaginal intercourse, regardless of one's ability to reproduce, even if medical intervention was required to make penetration possible.[17] By the 1800s, gender classifications in Sweden were also being determined on the basis of whether physical differences were perceived as a means to avert potential violations of legal prohibitions against homosexuality – for example, where a genetic female was deemed to have the capacity to engage in the 'male' role in heterosexual intercourse.[18] In the 1900s, however, Swedish medical experts more broadly incorporated contemporary, emerging theories of gender development into their taxonomies, recognising that a diversity of sex development manifested in humans, whose conditions could, in turn, be classified as *androgyn*, *gynandromorphy* and being two-sexed (*tvåkönad*), signifying a need for clinical expertise to manage the conditions.[19] These approaches flourished throughout Europe and would become highly influential in the medical taxonomies of intersex conditions elsewhere, particularly in the US, where influential medical experts constructed detailed subcategories of children with differences of sex development so that clinicians could determine an 'optimal' gender for each child. In fact, the most renowned advocate for this method in twentieth-century medicine, John Money, described his own method of classifying individuals sexually as 'Linnaean'[20] – even though Linnaeus himself never described his system as anything other than descriptive, and certainly not for the purpose of reconstructing living entities in order to fit social categories.

1.2.2. The Development of the Current Regulatory Scheme

In the first half of the twentieth century, government officials began to question how legal gender classifications were managed, as well as what medical care was provided to transgender persons who sought to change their registered gender. Some transgender persons also sought medical interventions to support them in their gender identity,[21] surgery for which had become more prevalent in the late 1950s. Other persons, including those then classed as '*pseudohermafrodit*' based on differences of sex development, had won *ad hoc* administrative changes to their registered gender.[22] For children with differences of sex development,

---

17 Ibid.

18 Ibid, pp. 61–64.

19 Bondesdam, above n. 1, pp. 200–204.

20 See J. Money, *The Psychologic Study of Man*, Thomas Publ., Springfield 1957, p. v.

21 See J. Wålinder, 'Incidence and Sex Ratio of Transsexualism in Sweden' (1971)119 *British Journal of Psychiatry* 195–196.

22 S. Olsson and A.R. Möller, 'On the Incidence and Sex Ratio of Transsexualism in Sweden' (2003) 32(4) *Archives of Sexual Behavior* 384.

however, by the late 1950s, Swedish clinicians were following protocols developed by US hospitals to eliminate the appearance of intersex conditions and to facilitate each child's functionality in a so-called typical 'male' or 'female' role.[23] While Swedish medical experts defended these latter practices as the correction of physical 'deformities' and consistent with medical science, the legality of surgical assistance for persons considered transgender at the time was considered less clear in Swedish law. In part this was due to transgender patients' perceived lack of physical anomalies relative to their registered gender, as surgery on healthy genital and gonadal tissue generally fell outside the scope of medical law, requiring a medical diagnosis of some sort to justify both medical interventions and changes of juridical gender.[24]

From a legal perspective, these developments soon became difficult for the government to fully assess in the absence of clear rules or complete deference to medical opinion. By 1968, more than 100 adults in Sweden were undergoing treatment of some kind for gender-related distress in a given year, whereas at least 53 individuals – nine of whom were classed as '*pseudohermafrodit*' – had applied to government officials for a change of their name or legal status, with most applications approved administratively but without specific guidelines.[25] Calls for regulatory inquiry had already begun in 1963 when the Central Statistical Office requested legal advice from the Attorney General in such cases as to what specific criteria were used to make gender status determinations as a matter of law. As a result, the Attorney General formally requested a governmental investigation into these matters,[26] with the Justice Department convening a formal committee of medical and legal experts on 30 September 1966 to investigate the issues surrounding requests for a change of registered gender and requests for gender-conforming surgery.[27] The investigation yielded an expert report, *Intersexuals' Gender Belonging*, released on 8 May 1968.

The investigation's primary directive was to determine the conditions under which registered gender could be changed. In their report, the experts framed their inquiry as limited by the presumption that gender status still determined the assignment of rights, privileges, and benefits of individuals in Sweden, even though society was moving away from the notion that gender should determine one's socio-legal fate.[28] Thus, the investigating committee and subsequent government proposal advised that changes to the legal system regarding gender could not be so broad as to create 'conflict with the fundamental values of citizens

23 Garland, above n. 1, p. 84.
24 Ibid, pp. 133–139.
25 See SOU 1968:28, above n. 4, p. 34.
26 Ibid, pp. 12 and 36.
27 SOU 1968:28, above n. 4, pp. 24–25, 45–48 and 52–53.
28 Ibid, pp. 12 and 16–19.

in general'.[29] Instead, they concluded, it would be more efficient to attempt a focused solution for what was perceived as a problem for a small class of persons who suffered from incongruence between their identity and registered gender.[30] All such persons were deemed *intersexuals* – caught 'in between' a male-female assignment and deserving of medical care to support a 'male' or 'female' identity for their health.

Under the new scheme, subcategories of 'intersexes' were sharply constructed, albeit without addressing the lack of definition of the concepts of 'maleness' and 'femaleness' that served as their foundations. Persons who were born with bodies deemed typical for their assigned gender were dubbed *non-somatic intersexuals* ('transsexual'), with the term *somatic intersexuals* used to describe persons with variant sex development.[31] On the specific question of how to define what constitutes one's 'sex', however, the experts concluded that each person's complex feelings of belonging to a gender represent such a personal mix of physiology, psychology, and sexuality that science did not permit a strict formula for establishing categorical definitions that could be applied prospectively to *any* individual, including persons who were not 'somatic intersexuals' but rarely sought to change their registered gender.[32] Instead, the experts concluded, the true gender of *all* persons could only be determined on a case-by-case basis after extensive consultation.[33] Thus, the expert committee and the government recommended that the definition of 'sex' categories should be kept 'vague' as a matter of Swedish law.[34]

Both categories of 'intersexuals' targeted by the Gender Classification Act were presumed to want or need surgery of some kind to support their gender, such that some form of physical conformity, rather than gender identity alone, shaped the resulting rules of law. For *non-somatic intersexuals*, the government Bill emphasised that because such persons had no physical anomalies, careful psychiatric assessment was needed to ensure that (1) any request for a change of gender identity was sincere; (2) that only adults could receive the requested changes; and (3) that any anticipated gender-related medical interventions, particularly surgery, would occur only once.[35] Because adults were involved, the government emphasised that the potential for gendered conflict with traditional notions of familial relations required applicants to be sterile and unmarried (divorced if married to someone of the requested gender). For *somatic intersexuals*, the government considered that most applicants who

29 Ibid, p. 39; see also Prop. 1972:6, above n. 7, p. 17.
30 Prop. 1972:6, above n. 7, p. 18.
31 SOU 1968:28, above n. 4, pp. 13 and 20–48; accord, Prop. 1972:6, above n. 7, pp. 10–16.
32 SOU 1968:28, above n. 4, pp. 20–31 and 38–39.
33 Ibid, p. 39.
34 Ibid, p. 39 and Prop. 1972:6, above n. 7, p. 18.
35 Prop. 1972:6, above n. 7, pp. 15 and 23.

changed gender under this provision would be children,[36] and also presumed (incorrectly) that most children would be sterile or otherwise could be assigned a gender so that they could procreate according to their genetic sex.[37] Following medical consensus at the time that a child's gender development would be impaired by having an atypical gender appearance relative to the assigned sex, the resulting legal scheme endorsed medical interventions on persons with differences of sex development for eliminating physical anomalies, so that gender reclassification could be more rapidly processed if necessary – as long as the body of the person appeared and functioned typically for the chosen gender.[38] Most significantly, because the experts and the government acknowledged that the gender chosen for infants and young children could not be based on an expressed, predictable gender identity at a very young age,[39] the government emphasised a need for a mechanism for a second possible gender reclassification of children who rejected the gender imposed on them, even surgically, with catastrophic effects.[40] The Gender Classification Act based on these requirements became law on 1 July 1972.

1.2.3. Reform Measures Enacted

Sweden's juridical focus on binary gender remained unchallenged for decades following the enactment of the Gender Classification Act. In 2007, after dozens of motions in Parliament called for reform of the Act, the government commissioned an investigation to assess the Act's validity.[41] Notably, the formal committee investigating reform declined to define 'what makes an individual a man in contrast with a woman', concluding instead that a man or a woman is typified by a certain genital appearance, with gonads that enable a person to reproduce in a given sex role.[42] The committee did not seek to extend this definition to the Population Registration Act or address the lack of definition of 'male' or 'female' in Swedish law as a whole, but rather confined the inquiry to the regulation of changes to gender registration. To meet its conceptualisation of gender, the committee proposed that sterilisation was inadequate for changes of registered gender and that the reshaping or removal sexual organs could be compelled.[43] For children with differences of sex development, the committee recommended retaining the possibility for changes of gender as set forth in

36 Ibid, pp. 25 and 58–59.
37 Ibid, pp. 11–14.
38 Ibid, pp. 16 and 19–21.
39 Ibid, p. 24.
40 Ibid, pp. 51 and 57; see also SOU 1968:28, above n. 4, pp. 53–57.
41 SOU 2007:16, *Ändrad könstillhörighet – förslag till ny lag*, p. 79.
42 Ibid, p. 15.
43 Ibid.

the original Act,[44] affirming the view that surgical intervention in infancy was standard care and presuming that the need for changes of registered gender for such children was minimal.[45] The committee recommended, however, that older persons with differences of sex development seeking surgical correction should be treated as 'transsexuals', subject to requirements of proof of gender identity and surgical interventions.[46] After sharp backlash, the proposal was tabled for revision and led to several new inquiries, prompted in part by the Yogyakarta Principles, which were formalised in 2007 as well.

The reform measures that followed prioritised the concerns of transgender persons on the grounds that the concerns of intersex persons were not identical and required special investigation.[47] In 2008, for example, the government established the Discrimination Act to extend protections from discrimination to all persons who changed registered gender as a form of sex discrimination, with additional protections for each person's gender identity and expression, including *intersex* or *intergender* identity.[48] The new law, however, included no protection from discrimination based on intersex conditions or physical differences of sex development – in other words, limiting protection to those whose behaviour or expression conveyed a 'transcendent' gender identity. In 2009, the National Board of Health and Welfare issued a directive for investigation of medico-legal standards affecting intersex and transgender persons.[49] The resulting report, however, proposed changes only for the protection of transgender persons, promising an investigation on intersex matters at a later date.[50] Citing the Yogyakarta Principles and human rights concerns, the Board proposed the abolition of compulsory sterilisation and divorce as prerequisites for changes to the registered gender of transgender adults.[51] Following protracted political debate, the legislature finally adopted the Board's proposals in 2013.[52] In 2018, the government also passed legislation awarding compensation for all transgender persons who had been sterilised to obtain legal recognition of their

---

44 Ibid, pp. 18–19.

45 Ibid, p. 233. The committee also noted that new clinical guidelines were being developed in Sweden. Ibid, p. 44.

46 Ibid, pp. 234–235.

47 National Board, *Transsexuella och övriga personer*, above n. 2, p. 3; SOU 2014:91, above n. 10, p. 310.

48 Diskrimineringslag (2008:567), 1 kap 5 § 1 st & 2 st; See also Prop. 2007/08:95, *Ett starkare skydd mot diskriminering* (2008), pp. 111–117.

49 National Board of Health and Welfare, Dnr 51-9326/2009, *Vård och stöd till transsexuella och intersexuella personer* (18.12.2009).

50 National Board, *Transsexuella och övriga personer*, above n. 2, p. 3.

51 Ibid, pp. 13, 19 and 29.

52 See J. Garland, 'The Legal Status of Transsexual and Transgender Persons in Sweden', in J.M. Scherpe (ed.) *The Legal Status of Transsexual and Transgender Persons*, Intersentia, Cambridge 2015, pp. 287–289.

true gender.[53] The law does not, however, compensate persons with intersex conditions sterilised in childhood without their consent.[54]

To date, the government's only substantive change to Swedish law for persons with intersex conditions and differences of sex development has provided that before registered gender of children is changed, the children should be heard in accordance with their age and maturity.[55] Consent for such changes for children under age 12 is still not formally required. Nevertheless, several investigations have called for reforms of Swedish law in light of ongoing human rights discourse on intersex questions, especially in light of the finally released report of the National Board of Health and Welfare on medico-legal practices affecting persons with intersex conditions, as well as a recent investigation on the quality of life of transgender persons and persons with 'intersex variations'. Both reports, released in 2017, are discussed in greater detail in Section 2.

2. CURRENT RULES FOR ESTABLISHING AND CHANGING LEGAL STATUS

2.1. INITIAL REGISTRATION OF GENDER

Formal registered gender for most individuals in Sweden is established at birth in accordance with the Population Registration Act. The Act permits reporting of only one of two genders to the Swedish Tax Agency – technically, whether one is a 'man' or a 'woman' – as this applies not only to children born in Sweden but also to adults, for example, who move to Sweden.[56] The Tax Agency registers each person's birth with a gender marker in the registry database, as well as in the Swedish *personnummer*, the identification number used by all citizens and long-term residents. In that number, the ninth digit represents the person's juridical gender – an even number for females and an odd number for males.[57] The number must be regenerated if the gender marker is changed, with the resulting new name and number constituting an entirely new identity.[58]

53 Lag (2018:162) om statlig ersättning till personer som har fått ändrad könstillhörighet fastställd i vissa fall.

54 Prop. 2017/18:64, *Statlig ersättning till personer som har fått ändrad könstillhörighet fastställd i vissa fall: Lagrådsremiss* (2017), pp. 13–14.

55 Prop. 2011/12:142, above n. 10, pp. 35–39.

56 Folkbokföringslag (1991:481), 18 §. This applies to children born within Sweden and outside of Sweden to a mother registered in Sweden or a father who is also a custodial parent (2 §). This also applies to children born outside of Sweden whose parenthood is later established (2a § and 14 §) and certain persons with a right to stay in Sweden (3 §).

57 Ibid, 18 §.

58 Under Swedish law, each person's identification number in the registry consists of 2 parts, the first 6 digits indicating the date of birth, and the final 4 digits an informational code,

As a result, gender in the Swedish legal system is literally binary in two senses. First, the numbers available for the gendered digit (0–9) are divided evenly, with 5 digits allocated for females and 5 for males. This division permits no additional gender identities to be registered, nor does it permit a digit to represent a catch-all category for persons who do not want to identify as male or female. Second, the registration system generates a new personal record for the new *personnumer* after change of registered gender, archiving the first, such that both identities remain in the system as matter of present and historic record.[59]

According to the Population Registration Act, medical personnel are primarily responsible for reporting births to the Tax Agency 'as soon as possible', though in cases where this is not possible, the custodian of the child may do so.[60] For most individuals born in Sweden, therefore, the gender marker is reported, if not determined, by medical personnel.[61] Because there is no definition of what constitutes a male or female person in Swedish law, each person's gender determination at birth is based on clinical practice. The clinical determinations required for choosing an initial gender for a child, including medical interventions to make the child appear more typical for a registered gender, are not expressly governed by any legal rules. Thus, an initial decision to assign a female gender to a genetic male child or a child with other intersex conditions in anticipation of 'feminising' medical interventions does not trigger the Gender Classification Act, which only governs changes of registered gender and medical interventions associated with those changes. Surgical and hormonal treatments are governed more generally by the Health and Medical Services Act, which, according to the preparatory works, includes congenital anomalies within the definition of 'illness'.[62] The Children and Parents Code,[63] together with the Patient Act,[64] permits parents to authorise medical interventions on their children unless the child is clinically assessed to have the maturity to consent to treatment alone or to refuse care. No specific age limit is established

in which the third digit is an odd number for male children and an even number for female children. See Folkbokföringslag (1991:481) 18 §. See Prop. 2011/12:142, above n. 10, p. 22 (describing the process required for changing gender).

59 SOU 2017:92, above n. 11, pp. 396–399.; Ds 2018:17 *Ändring av det kön som framgår av folkbokföringen* (2018), pp. 63–64.

60 Ibid, 24 §.

61 Ibid, 26 §.

62 Hälso- och sjukvårdslag (2017:30), 2 kap., 1 §; *See* Prop. 1981/82:97 *om hälso- och sjukvårdslag*, p. 29 (defining the original provision on which the current counterpart provision is based as including birth defects as a form of sickness).

63 Föräldrabalken (1949:381), 6 kap., 11 § (the right and responsibility of parents to make decisions in children's personal matters).

64 Patientlag (2014:821), 1 kap. 8 § (establishing the best interests of the child as the decisive factor in healthcare), 3 kap. 4 § (requiring parents to be informed in healthcare for their children prior to consent) and 4 kap. 3 § (requiring the child's position to be assessed and given weight in accordance with the child's age and maturity).

for when a child may have the maturity to consent to care or refuse it, though clinicians may determine that the child is incapable of consent, with no means of appeal against such determinations provided in the Patient Act.[65] Nevertheless, according to the Patient Safety Act, all medical interventions, including examinations, diagnoses, and treatment, are required to be validated by 'science and carefully tested experience' for their safety and medical benefits[66] – a test that places the legality of gender-conforming procedures in considerable doubt.[67]

No recent government investigation has explained why gender status must be a part of a government-defined identity. In 2008, an investigation on modernising the *personnummer* concluded that rights in Sweden were restricted by gender and, thus, the rationale for a gender-neutral legal identity was not clear at the time.[68] The remaining reason offered for maintaining a gendered *personnummer* was that the number provided a functional code to generate data relevant to gender 'research', as well as to support 'statistical functions'.[69] The report did not acknowledge, however, that the Population Register Database also contains considerable information linked to a personal identity record from which statistical data may be generated – including for family relations, citizenship, and civil status – all of which are maintained for a wide range of governmental purposes but without including the data in one's formal identity or in the *personnummer* itself.[70] Indeed, while the *personnummer* once contained a digit representing each person's place of birth, that digit has since been neutralised, even though the data is maintained in the database and is used to generate statistics.[71] Currently, the gendered digit remains the only personal characteristic apart from the date of birth used to mark the identity of a person in Sweden.

2.2. CHANGES TO REGISTRATION OF GENDER

The Gender Classification Act is structured to provide two separate tracks for changes of juridical gender. The first section (1 §) permits such changes

---

65 Prop. 2013/14:106, *Patientlag*, pp. 41 and 64–67.

66 See Patientsäkerhetslag (2010:659), 6 kap., 1 §, as read through 1 kap., 2 and 4 §§ in relation to prevention, examinations, and treatment of illness or injury under the Health and Medical Services Act. Hälso- och sjukvårds lag (2017:30), 2 kap., 1 § 1 st.

67 Garland, above n. 1, pp. 230–240 and 595–96.

68 SOU 2008:60, *Personnummer och samordningsnummer*, p. 73.

69 Ibid.

70 Lag (2001:182) om behandling av personuppgifter i Skatteverkets folkbokföringsverksamhet, 2 kap. 3 § (registering data including matters such as city of birth and domicile at birth).

71 Through 1991, the *personnummer* indicated the county of a person's birth or whether the person was born outside of Sweden. See Statistiska Centralbyrån, *Personnummer – dess konstruktion och hantering inom Statistiska Centralbyrån*, 2007, p. 9.

based on confirmation of gender identity and is limited to persons over the age of 18, intended primarily for persons today commonly described as transgender adults. Under this section, persons must take steps to confirm their gender identity – namely to 'prove' that they (1) have long identified with the requested gender; (2) have publicly appeared in that gender role for a time; and (3) expect to live in that gender identity for the foreseeable future. The second section (2 §) was intended primarily for children and permits changes of registered gender based on assessments of physical sex development, without an age limit, although consent is required for children aged 12 and older. Thus, for those children whose initial gender registration is later deemed in error, parents are permitted to request changes of registered gender under 2 § if (1) the child has a congenital difference in sex development and (2) the requested change is '*consistent with the development of gender identity*', and '*most consistent with the applicant's physical condition*'. Requests for modification of the genitals or gonads in connection with 1 § and 2 § are also authorised restrictively by the Act.[72] Currently, the National Board of Health and Welfare must approve any changes of registered gender and any surgical interventions to reflect a gender other than that which is first registered for the applicant.[73]

Both of these mechanisms for change of registered gender are applicable, in theory, to persons with intersex conditions or differences of sex development, though, in practice, they were conceived to apply to most such persons in reverse, if at all. Though adults with these conditions can apply for change of registered gender under 2 § without further fulfilling all the requirements in 1 §, the primary purpose of 2 § was to resolve questions about a child's gender status as soon as possible, where it was not clinically resolved prior to gender registration.[74] For both adults and children whose bodies are not deemed to meet the physical requirements in 2 § – or where these persons (or their guardians) refuse gender-conforming surgery – any changes of registered gender are required to proceed under 1 § in adulthood, meeting all of the requirements designed for confirmation of gender identity for transgender persons. Moreover, persons who have been subjected to a change of registered gender under 2 § – either because their bodies in childhood were determined to be consistent with a requested gender or because surgery was utilised to achieve that effect – may seek a second change of registered gender under 1 § if the persons, as adults, determine that the change of gender, without their consent, was made in error in childhood.[75]

72 See Gender Classification Act, 4–4a §§.
73 Ibid, 5 § (requiring Board approval) and 8 § (criminal penalties for surgical modifications without Board approval).
74 Prop. 1972:6, above n. 7, p. 57.
75 Gender Classification Act, 1 §, final clause.

The normative complexities of this scheme derive from the government's position that incongruence between physical sex characteristics and registered gender can be the source of significant stress for an individual and can undermine an individual's mental health. For this reason, transgender adults whose physical sex development is deemed typical for their registered gender are required to take steps to prove their incongruent gender identity, whereas similarly situated transgender minors are required to wait until they are adults to request changes of registered gender as well as any gender-affirming care, all to ensure that these decisions are made once and not in haste or in error. No such safeguard is provided for children with differences of sex development, based on the theory that intersex conditions and any atypical sex characteristics might harm the mental health of the child and interfere with gender development. Thus, because infants, in particular, and children under age three are presumed incapable of clearly articulating their future gender identity, the Act has placed the greatest 'weight' on the appearance on the child for any change of registered gender in childhood, and authorisations for surgery are permitted under 2 § without the children's consent.[76] Though the current version of 2 § of the Act contains updated language designed to de-emphasise a need for surgical modification, 2 § is still written to reflect the presumption that bodily appearance will 'tip' the gender assignment of a child to a male or female one and should be consistent with the anticipated development of gender chosen by clinicians and parents, rather than identity.[77] It is only for older children who have already developed a gender identity that 2 § may serve as some safeguard against imposing a gender on a child that the child rejects (even when consent is not required).

The Gender Classification Act's recognition that children may be assigned the wrong gender – signified by the final clause in 1 § permitting more than one change of registered gender – merits special reflection in light of the clinical practice of surgical modification on infants and young children with differences of sex development, whether performed in anticipation of registered gender or for change of that registration. As noted in Section 1.2.2, Swedish officials understood as early as 1968 that gendered surgical modification on infants offered no guarantees against imposing the wrong gender on children. The legal difficulties that accompany such outcomes, however, because of the Gender Classification Act remain considerable. For those who have been assigned the wrong gender without their consent in childhood – including with genital or gonadal surgery – such persons are not only required to wait until age 18 to seek a change under 1 § to correct the error, but must meet all the conditions applied to transgender persons to prove their gender identity when no respect for that

---

76 SOU 1968:28, above n. 4, pp. 55–56, Prop. 1972:6, above n. 7, p. 25.

77 Prop. 2011/12:142, above n. 10, pp. 37–38.

identity was required when the initial gender assignment was surgically imposed. Though the Act only expressly affirms access to a second change of registered gender for persons whose gender was changed under 2 §, even children whose body modifications were timed with gender registration or carried out to reflect the chosen gender would in most instances formally face the same requirement to proceed under 1 §.[78] All persons remain presumptively ineligible under 2 § for rapid correction of juridical gender whenever their appearance has already been altered under standard clinical practice or deemed to be 'most consistent' with their registered gender.

For persons with differences of sex development aged 12 and older, the harshness of the Gender Classification Act is somewhat abated by the consent requirement, which protects against a gender imposed on an adult or some minors by others, assuming that the minors are not subject to coercion in providing that consent. Notably, however, both the government Bill and the investigation in support of the Act warned that children age three and older who have formed a gender identity would be harmed by attempts to steer their gender development contrary to their identity, even though no delay of any surgical modification or change of registered gender is required to prevent harm to such a child. Rather, the government set the age of consent at 12 solely on the grounds that it was an age at which children could consent to other matters in Swedish law.[79] This age limit was last assessed in a government proposal in 2012, prior to the enactment of the Patient Act's requirement that a child's authority to consent or refuse treatment should be based on the child's maturity without regard to any particular age limit. The conflict between the two laws has not been addressed by the current government, leaving unanswered the question of whether parents may apply for a change of gender (and surgery) under the Act before the age of 12 without the child's consent if the child is deemed mature enough before that age to refuse gender surgery under the Patient Act.

2.3. IMPLICATIONS FOR FUTURE REFORM

While many reforms of Swedish law have historically come at a slow pace,[80] recent reforms of the Gender Classification Act have left persons with intersex conditions and differences of sex development in a particularly vulnerable position. This is especially true for infants, as considerable pressure to register them as a male or female under the Population Registration Act has historically

78 The current Government indeed equates such persons with transgender persons as having a different gender identity relative to gender assignment and bodily classification. Ds 2018:11 *Vissa kirurgiska ingrepp i könsorganen*, (2018), pp. 62–62 and 72–73.

79 Prop. 1972:6, above n. 7, pp. 52 and 59.

80 See GARLAND, 'The Legal Status of Transsexual and Transgender Persons in Sweden', above n. 52, pp. 290–301.

been used as justification for gender-conforming procedures imposed on children in clinical practice. Indeed, these problems persist despite the fact that, in January 2017, the National Board of Health and Welfare released its summary of the standard of care for children with differences of sex development acknowledging that the current scientific evidence is inadequate to confirm these medical interventions as safe and effective and that medical consensus supporting them is lacking.[81] The Board emphasised that further investigation of future law reform was required in order to ensure that care was patient-centred and in accordance with human rights standards.[82] In March 2017, the Swedish National Council on Medical Ethics also formally concluded that irreversible and other 'normalising' gender interventions on a child must be avoided when the consent of the child is lacking.[83] The issuance of these two reports raises significant questions as to how ongoing investigations will adjust any proposed law reforms in light of their findings and recommendations.

The current Swedish Government has confirmed its plans to propose the abolition of the Gender Classification Act in September 2018, with the goal of separating the governance of juridical gender status from regulation of gender-related medical interventions, albeit still providing only male and female gender registration options.[84] The upcoming proposal can be traced back to the government's 2014 investigative committee report, entitled *Juridical Gender and Medical Gender Correction*. That report proposed access to changes of registered gender for all persons aged 15 or older as a matter of right, while retaining provisions for children with differences of sex development to permit their parents to change their gender in accordance with their development and identity, as well as the right for such children to consent at the age of 12.[85] In May 2018, however, the government released a modified proposal for public comment. The new proposed law would require that an initial change of registered gender 'shall' be made at the request of any person aged 18 or older, as well as for minors aged 12 and older, presumptively for whom applications will be made by one or both parents with the child's written consent.[86] For minors who apply for these changes

81 National Board, *Care and Treatment of Persons with Intersexual Conditions*, above n. 3, pp. 7 and 22–25.
82 Ibid, p. 8.
83 Swedish National Council on Medical Ethics, *Smer kommenterar 2017:2 Vården av intersexuella barn – etiska aspekter på tidiga kirurgiska ingrepp* (2017).
84 The preliminary drafts of the new laws have been released in the reports in Ds 2018:11, above n. 78, pp. 7–8 and Ds 2018:17, above n. 59, pp. 11–13. The joint proposal for these two laws was placed on the calendar in the spring of 2018. Regeringskansliet, Propositionsförteckning våren 2018 <https://www.regeringen.se/informationsmaterial/2018/01/propositionsforteckning-varen-2018/> (last accessed 24.05.2018).
85 Ibid, p. 35.
86 Ds 2018:17, above n. 59, p. 11. The parental authority to file applications is not expressly stated in the text of the current draft law, but it is confirmed in the preparatory works, ibid, pp. 89–98.

themselves – as well as for a second change of registered gender by any applicant – all changes will only be made (1) if the person feels that the registered gender is not consistent with the person's gender identity; and (2) it can be assumed that the person will live 'in the same gender identity' in the future.[87] Only minors age 15 or older may apply for themselves, but must also apply to the National Board of Health and Welfare for approval of changes on the bases of these criteria, after a 'needs assessment' from medical personnel or an officer from the local Social Welfare Committee, who purportedly can attest to fulfilment of the criteria.[88] For children with differences of sex development under the age of 12, consent of the child is not required and such changes may be only made if the change is in accordance with the 'development of child's gender identity' and is in the child's best interests.[89] For denials of any changes of registered gender, the law provides for appeals against such denials to administrative courts.[90] The government's new proposal has not detailed how courts will review the decisions of medical personnel or Swedish agencies for error.

For medical interventions formerly approved only in connection with changes of registered gender, both the 2014 investigating committee and the government in 2018 have concurred that a new law is necessary to ensure that gender-affirming genital and gonadal surgeries are permissible, given that such surgeries may not be in accord with 'science and carefully tested experience' as required for healthcare in Sweden.[91] For transgender minors, the proposal is complex and cannot be fully summarised in this chapter. No age limit is proposed for access to surgery, in light of current clinical projections that only older adolescents will be able to undergo such surgery. Though a diagnosis of 'gender dysphoria' is required for surgery, the government has endorsed the view that no particular body modifications should be recommended, but that the patients should freely choose which gender modifications support their gender identity and psychological needs.[92] For children with intersex conditions or differences of sex development, however, the government has now endorsed the continuation of the regulatory scheme designed in 1968, presuming that non-consensual gender-conforming surgeries constitute 'healthcare' under Swedish law, as well as that intersex persons are to be treated as transgender

---

87 Ibid, p. 11.

88 Ibid, pp. 99–105. The proposal does not explain what competence, if any, these varied personnel have to make such determinations. The government does posit in the proposal that medical personnel have experience in diagnosing 'gender dysphoria'. The proposal also notes, however, that such a diagnosis may not be required if the minor can obtain a testimonial from Social Welfare officers. The best reading of the proposal is that medical and social welfare personnel may somehow attest to the sincerity of the claims of the need for change of registered gender.

89 Ibid, p. 12.

90 Ibid, p. 13 and 111–112.

91 Ds 2018:78, above n. 78, pp. 55 and 67–69.

92 Ibid, pp. 59–61.

persons with gender dysphoria when the wrong gender has been assigned to them surgically in childhood.[93] The government's proposal makes no reference whatsoever to international human rights authorities' calls for regulation of these procedures, nor does it make any reference to the National Board of Health and Welfare's recent report conceding that scientific support is lacking to establish these interventions as necessary or beneficial for the children concerned. It also failed to acknowledge that Sweden's leading centre for treatment of children with differences of sex development has published data confirming patient dissatisfaction with surgical results, surgical complications, and, in some cases, impairment to mental health and function as a result of treatment.[94] Inscrutably, the government's explanatory report to the 2018 proposal concluded that no further human rights analysis is required, as the government has claimed that the 2014 investigation adequately surveyed Sweden's international human rights' obligations.[95]

These latest proposals signify the considerable difficulties with which the Swedish Government seems to struggle in coming to terms with the harms imposed by its regulatory scheme. The 2018 government proposal has, of course, acknowledged several problems with registration of binary gender as part of a person's identity, particularly in response to a recent 2017 investigation of the quality of life of transgender and intersex persons in Sweden.[96] That investigation found that the change of registered gender continues to pose severe administrative difficulties on persons who effectively have two different personal identities in records that require significant effort to change them, and that much of Swedish society is still structured around binary gender and is exclusionary and discriminatory.[97] The investigation further noted that for persons with intersex conditions, the science behind non-consensual gender-conforming procedures on children is questionable, while data collected by Sweden's leading hospitals for gender-conforming surgeries confirm that a majority of their own patients who have been surveyed believed that all surgical decisions should be made by the patients themselves.[98] The government's 2018 proposals, however, include no commentary on these latter findings.

---

93 Ibid, pp. 37, 61–66, 66–67 and 72–73.

94 See L. Karlsson et al., 'Cognitive Impairment in adolescents and adults with congenital adrenal hyperplasia' (2017) 87 *Clinical Endocrinology* 651–59; H. Engberg et al., 'Increased psychiatric morbidity in women with complete androgen insensitivity syndrome or complete gonadal dysgenesis' (2017) 101 *Journal of Psychiatric Research* 122–127; A. Strandqvist et al., 'Suboptimal psychosocial outcomes in patients with congenital adrenal hyperplasia: Epidemological studies in a nonbiased national cohort in Sweden' (2014) 99 *Journal of Clinical Endocrinology & Metabolism* 1425–1414; and Örtqvist et al., above n. 9.

95 Ds 2018:78, above n. 78, pp. 57–58 and 90.

96 SOU 2017:92, above n. 10.

97 Ibid, pp. 63–64.

98 Ibid, pp. 786–815.

3. THE CONSEQUENCES OF JURIDICAL GENDER STATUS IN SWEDEN

3.1. LEGAL STATUS AND EQUALITY

Sweden's legal framework and public policies affirm the importance of a commitment to gender equality and protection from discrimination, including protection for sexual and gender minorities.[99] Sweden has thus made most national legislation and regulations virtually gender-neutral, eliminating nearly all of the gender-based distinctions in Swedish law that motivated the original Gender Classification Act, such that one's registration as male or female is largely irrelevant to legal status or rights in almost all circumstances.[100] Thus, most rights, including those related to marriage, are unaffected by a person's actual gender status. The most significant exception in this regard is with regard to parenthood, where until recently, a person's role in procreation would determine a gendered nomenclature for the parenthood registered; for example, a person who gave birth was considered a mother of the born child regardless of the registered gender of the parent. Under current practice, persons who have undergone a change of registered gender are presumptively registered with a parental status consistent with their registered gender, such that a person registered as a male who gives birth is the child's father.[101] In January 2019, the practice will become law, with additional procedural requirements.[102] No official inquiry been made, however, as to whether a parental status could be non-gendered or could reflect the choice of the parent. As the Government's most recent investigation of the quality of life of transgender and intersex persons has extensively documented, the neutralisation of Swedish law has also not obviated the need for the government to take action beyond modifying its own rules – for example, to ensure protection from violence in general and discrimination in schools, access to gender-neutral restrooms and sports, and full recognition in private life according to the corrected gender status. While the latter harm is

---

99 See GARLAND, above n. 1, pp. 462–473.

100 A notable exception is for detainees and single asylum seekers, who are typically housed according to gender, although governing agencies have in practice worked to accommodate gender-variant persons in these circumstances. The National Board has called for regulation in these areas. See NATIONAL BOARD OF HEALTH AND WELFARE, *Administrative problems for persons who change juridical gender* (Dnr. 5.3-51189/2012), 2014, pp. 7–9 and 13.

101 SWEDISH TAX AUTHORITY, *The Population Registry and Change of Registered Gender* (2016) ('*Folkbokföring och ändrad könstillhörighet*'), pp. 13–14.

102 Föräldrabalken (1949:381), 1 kap. 11–14 §§. The new rules will not entitle transgender persons to the marital presumptions that a cisgender man would have when married to the person who gives birth. Instead, the rules will require transgender persons to confirm their parenthood to social welfare officials or courts. Men who give birth will also receive privileges extended to mothers in some cases, ibid 13 §§.

largely fostered by administration of the *personnummer*, redress in other areas still today awaits new government regulation and law enforcement.[103]

In the broader context of discrimination in both the public and private sectors, Sweden's Discrimination Act is often said to prohibit direct and indirect gender discrimination, but the legislation itself is complex.[104] The Act expressly prohibits discrimination on the basis of 'sex' (*kön*) – as the act further defines that term as meaning 'that someone is a woman or a man'.[105] The interpretation of the term 'sex' remains highly limiting and ambiguous because of the lack of definition of what constitutes a 'man' or 'woman' under Swedish law, though transgender persons are included in one of these two classes and protected from 'sex discrimination' if they have changed registered gender or intend to do so.[106] The Discrimination Act also prohibits discrimination on the basis of 'identity and expression transcending sex'.[107] The preparatory works affirm that this broader protection encompasses both identity and expression of 'another sex', including an intersex or intergender identity.[108] Here, too, however, the law depends on how expression is conceptualised relative to the 'sex' of the person concerned – for example, under what conditions a 'transgender' person who identifies as male or female and lives according to that 'sex' may still be perceived as transgender without publicly identifying as such.[109] What is clear, however, is that the Act does not provide any protection from discrimination for a person who identifies as male or female but who is subject to discrimination on the basis of physical sex characteristics. Indeed, in its most recent proposal to strengthen legal protection for transgender persons, the current government has confirmed that persons with intersex conditions who are victims of hate crimes and discrimination will not be covered by the Discrimination Act or the Penal Code unless, in a given case, the harm can be firmly established to be directed at a person on the grounds of a perceived transgender or intersex identity.[110]

---

103 SOU 2017:92, above n. 10, pp. 167–541.

104 The government's human rights internet platform, for example, describes the Swedish Discrimination Act as prohibiting gender discrimination. See 'Mänskliga Rättigheter', <http://www.manskligarattigheter.se/en/human-rights/what-rights-are-there/right-not-to-be-discriminated-against> (last accessed 15.05.2017). The government has made clear to the UN Committee for the Elimination of Discrimination Against Women, however, that its 'sex' discrimination policy is aimed at eliminating discrimination 'between the sexes'. See Eighth and Ninth Periodic Reports of Sweden to the Committee for the Elimination of Discrimination Against Women (2014), paras 3–4.

105 Diskrimineringslag (2008:567), 1 kap., 5 §, st. 1.

106 Ibid, 1 kap.. 5 §, final proviso. This latter provision is required in Sweden as a result of EU law, as well as under the European Convention on Human Rights. SOU 2006:22, *En sammanhållen diskrimineringslagstiftning*, pp. 263–267; Prop. 2007/08:95, above n. 48, pp. 112–113.

107 Diskrimineringslag (2008:567), 1 kap., 5 §, st. 2.

108 Prop. 2007/08:95, above n. 48, pp. 116 and 496.

109 As the Discrimination Act should be interpreted consistently with EU law, such a person would be protected if that person was registered as one sex and changed or intended to change juridical or social gender.

110 Prop. 2017/18:59, *Ett utvidgat straffrättsligt skydd för transpersoner*, pp. 29, 41 and 44.

To define '*sex*', both the government and the investigating committee asserted that its usage in the Act is primarily a juridical one.[111] The government's proposal rejected a recommendation that the term should mean 'biological sex registered at birth, or the sex later established later for her or him'.[112] According to the government, this conceptualisation was neither simple nor clear, as well as that it might not cover all persons in Sweden, especially those not registered in Sweden.[113] The government concluded that it should be sufficient to define 'sex' as meaning that 'someone is male or female', including protection for a person who intends to change or has changed registered gender.[114] Furthermore, the Act narrowly prohibits differential treatment based solely on comparisons of the treatment of persons only in two classes – the class of women versus the class of men – but does not prohibit gender stereotyping of men or women in general.[115]At the time of the passage of the Act in 2008, the investigating committee had concluded that 'sex' determined outcomes in approximately 60 different legislative provisions, including those that declared men and women, as traditionally understood, eligible for sex equality measures.[116] Thus, the government concluded that a broad prohibition on 'sex'-based treatment was not warranted, nor could it be aimed at prohibiting gender stereotyping, but should be 'aimed exclusively at women and men' to promote sex equality and avoid 'uncertainty in the application' of traditional rules regarding prohibitions on differential treatment of women versus men.[117] Notably, under this interpretation, the government proposed that rules that imposed any hardship on both 'male' and 'female' persons in a particular group – such as sterilisation of all transgender persons – would not constitute discrimination if it applied to males and females.[118] Thus, it seems, adverse treatment of the entire class of persons with intersex conditions would also not be covered by the prohibition on 'sex' discrimination.

The Act's seemingly more expansive protection for '*identity or expression transcending sex*' formally includes 'that someone does not identify as male or female, or by their clothing by another manner expresses belonging to *another* sex'.[119] The breadth of the term was intended to protect persons who identify simply as male or female as well as those who express the other 'social sex' through such things as clothing, body language, make-up and hairstyle.[120] Though the

111 Prop. 2007/08:95, above n. 48, p. 113; see also SOU 2006:22, above n. 106, p. 283.
112 Prop. 2007/08:95, above n. 48, p. 113.
113 Ibid.
114 Ibid, pp. 113–114.
115 Diskrimineringslag (2008:567) 1 kap., 5 §, st. 1.
116 SOU 2006:22, above n. 106, pp. 283–284.
117 Prop. 2007/08:95, above n. 48, p. 115.
118 Ibid, p. 261.
119 Ibid, p. 109.
120 Ibid, p. 116.

investigating committee for the law proposed a broad anti-stereotyping category that would protect any 'identity, appearance and behaviour' that 'differs from the norm for men and women',[121] the government curiously rejected that category as too broad because it would protect everyone (presumably, not only gender minorities).[122] Thus, the government concluded that a new category should be designed with narrowing liability in mind, focusing on expression and identity that included 'transcendent' elements that could amount to discrimination if that person (1) identifies by some gender other than male or female; or (2) by their expression – such as dress, make-up, hairstyle and body language – conveys a belonging to 'another sex than what he or she sees as her or his own' – with this latter definition even more narrow than the one in the Act itself and descriptive only of transvestites.[123] The government conceded that this rule reflected 'considerable difficulties' in formulating 'a comprehensive and accurate definition to invoke the ground for discrimination' but ensured that it actually protected those whose gender-non-conforming identity was known to others through identity or expression.[124]

In short, no protection under the Discrimination Act exists from maltreatment or disadvantages imposed on persons for their physical sex characteristics unless the victims can demonstrate that they were treated negatively on the basis of an expressed identity that is neither male nor female or, perhaps, a perceived non-binary identity. This gap in the law, in particular, manifests harshly for children with intersex conditions or differences of sex development, particularly those whose bodies might be seen by others as different, despite their present or forming gender identity as male or female, or who feel unable to express a 'transcendent' identity, but who also might be maltreated by others for their physical differences. Discrimination in schools against such children would not be covered by the Act, for example, where all children may be exposed to the same sex-segregated rules in changing rooms. Of most importance perhaps, even though the Act applies to healthcare, gender-conforming procedures directed at infants with differences of sex development would apparently not be considered discriminatory, as they are perceived to have no gender identity or to be capable of expressing one. As both 'male' and

121 SOU 2006:22, above n. 106, p. 255.

122 Prop. 2007/08:95, above n. 48 p. 116.

123 Ibid, p. 116–117. If this interpretation of the Act were taken literally, this would mean that a person who identifies as female and dresses in a way that she feels accords with that identity would not be intending to dress as the 'other' sex, unless one considered the 'true' sex of that person as male. By that same measure, it still remains unclear whether a person who identifies as neither male nor female and who dresses androgynously would be covered unless the perpetrator of the discriminatory act could be proven to have perceived that identity as something transcending a male or female gender.

124 Ibid, p. 117.

'female' infants with such conditions are targeted for 'normalising' medical interventions, those interventions also cannot be said to impose disadvantages within the meaning of the Discrimination Act on the basis of one 'sex', or 'identity' or 'expression'.

3.2. THE SPECIAL STATUS OF CHILDREN

Sweden's obligations to protect children from harm are well established under national and international law. Under Sweden's Instrument of Government, Swedish law must protect individuals from forced bodily intrusions and must be further consistent with obligations under the European Convention on Human Rights (ECHR).[125] In a recent decision from the Grand Chamber of the European Court of Human Rights (ECtHR), Sweden's obligations were confirmed not only to include the protection of children from known risks of physical and psychological harm, but to recognise that the government has a narrow margin of appreciation in designing such protections wherever an 'important facet of an individual's existence or identity is at stake, or where the activities at stake involve a most intimate aspect of private life'.[126] From this perspective, it would seem clear that Sweden has an obligation to protect children with intersex conditions or differences of sex development from physical and psychological harm and from violations of their identity and intimacy. And yet, even though numerous international human rights organisations have called on individual nations to ban non-consensual gender-conforming procedures on children since 2013, Sweden has taken no such actions.[127] This is all the more perplexing given that Sweden has not only ratified the Convention on the Rights of the Child but plans to begin incorporation of the Convention into Swedish law in 2018.[128] As the UN Committee on the Rights of the Child has increasingly called on several nations to protect children with intersex conditions,[129] significant questions remain as to whether Swedish law is consistent with the Convention and other international human rights instruments.

When viewed through the lens of these positive obligations, the deficiencies in Sweden's protections for children with intersex conditions or differences of sex

---

[125] Kungörelse (1974:152) om beslutad ny regeringsform, 2 kap. 6 § (protection from forced bodily intrusions) and 19 § (conformity with the Instrument of Government).

[126] *Söderman v. Sweden* [GC], Appl. no. 5786/08 (2013), §§ 79–86.

[127] Several organisations from the Council of Europe, European Union and UN have criticised the medico-legal management of children with differences of sex development on these grounds. For a recent summary, see K. Zillén, J. Garland, and S. Slokenberga, *The Rights of Children in Biomedicine: Challenges posed by scientific advances and uncertainties*, Committtee on Bioethics for the Council of Europe, Strasbourg, 2017, p. 44.

[128] SOU 2016:19, *Barnkonvention i svensk lag*.

[129] Garland, above n. 1, pp. 533–536.

development are stark. These deficiencies extend beyond the aforementioned absence of protections in the Discrimination Act. Rather, for protection of children from invasive bodily harm, the disparities are extraordinary. Sweden formally criminalises all cutting on the genitals of female children without qualification, no matter how slight,[130] and has strictly limited sterilisation of persons to adults, with special protections for informed consent.[131] Both of these provisions, however, have never been analysed by a government agency as possibly restricting gender-conforming surgeries on children diagnosed with differences of sex development, even though only the Sterilisation Act has an express exemption, and then only for the treatment of 'bodily disease'.[132] The endorsement of these procedures under the Gender Classification Act, together with the government's presumption that they are covered under the Health and Medical Services Act, effectively puts children at risk of violations of bodily integrity in ways that would be considered unthinkable for children without an intersex status or condition. Similarly, for most persons, a single act of non-consensual genital penetration of a person is a crime in Sweden, including vaginal penetration by a finger or device.[133] For feminised children with intersex conditions or differences of sex development, however, repeated vaginal 'dilatation' of a child (using a finger or device) has long been practised in Sweden, without any question of its legality, to 'maintain' the surgically constructed orifices for these children, often without their consent.[134]

Though the Swedish Government has increasingly invoked human rights perspectives in recommending changes of Swedish law regarding registered gender, its use of such perspectives regarding the protection of children with intersex conditions and differences of sex development has been quite limited until recently. In the context of gender assignment for transgender persons, the government has begun to more thoroughly assess the doctrine of the ECtHR, as well as other soft-law human rights instruments, such as the Yogyakarta Principles, to justify reforms.[135] Recent governmental investigations have also surveyed Sweden's obligations under the Convention on the Rights of the Child toward children with intersex conditions and differences of sex development,

---

130 Lag (1982:316) med förbud mot könsstympning av kvinnor.

131 See Steriliseringslag (1975:580), especially 2–3 §§ and 5 §. See also HSLF-FS 2016:6, *Socialstyrelsens föreskrifter om sterilisering* 3 § and 5 § (requring documentation that adults have received information required for sterilisation).

132 S. Johnsdotter and B. Essén, *Kvinnlig Omskärelse: Könsstympning i Sverige – En kunskaps- och forskningsöversikt*, Nationellt Centrum Kvinnofrid, 2011, pp. 60–64.

133 The Supreme Court interpreted ch. 6, 1 § of the Criminal Code in this manner. NJA 2013 s. 548.

134 A. Nordenström et al., 'Pojke eller flicka – gissa aldrig! Diagnostik och behandling av tillstånd med avvikande könsutveckling' (2008) 105 *Läkartidningen* 629; A Nordenström, 'Commentary to "Secondary Vaginoplasty for Disorders of Sex Development: Is There a Right Time?"' (2013) 9 *Journal of Pediatric Urology* 632.

135 See Garland, above n. 1, p. 152.

but have failed to mention Article 24's prohibition on traditional practices prejudicial to the health of children.[136] Now, as the Parliamentary Assembly for the Council of Europe has promulgated comprehensive recommendations for national law reform to protect children with intersex conditions in light of the requirements of the ECHR,[137] the Swedish Government will face difficulty in maintaining uncertainty as to what will render a legal framework inadequate as protection if the ECtHR were to take up that question. With several governmental investigations underway, the Swedish Government's unwillingness to take a human rights approach to the protection of children with differences of sex development and intersex conditions may soon be openly tested.

4. CONCLUSIONS

When Sweden formally recognised the concept of 'gender belonging' fifty years ago, it remained unclear whether that concept was framed by respect for each individual's own sense of belonging to a particular gender or whether, in the context of gender registration, the final decision as to which gender one 'belongs' would be made by the government. Even more controversially in a modern light, the Swedish concept of 'gender belonging' ('*könstillhörighet*') may be seen as still anchored on the root word 'sex' (*kön*), a word that has, in Swedish law, been dominated by a binary concept of sex and gender. The current Swedish Government has not only boldly declared itself to be not only the world's first feminist government,[138] but one that claims to recognise that the bodies of transgender persons should not be required to conform to any particular gendered body type, as well as that diverse gender identities should be protected from discrimination. For persons with intersex conditions, however, 2018 marks five decades of retrenchment around the notion that such persons should presumably have their bodies altered to match a male or female 'sex' or gender, and that diverse body appearances and non-binary gender identities should not be registered or recognised by law. As Sweden enters its next half-century of regulation, it still remains to be seen whether Sweden will follow international human rights recommendations and respect the diversity of possible futures for children born with intersex conditions – if only to permit them to live without invasive interference by law and medicine.

---

136 The two most recent investigations concerning transgender and intersex youth have done so in only the most general manner. See SOU 2007:16, above n. 41, pp. 143–144 and 267. SOU 2014:91, above n. 10, pp. 86–102, 96–98, and 237–259.

137 Parliamentary Assembly of the Council of Europe, Resolution 2191: Promoting the human rights of and eliminating discrimination against intersex people (2017).

138 Government Offices of Sweden, *A Feminist Government*, <http://www.government.se/government-policy/a-feminist-government/> (last accessed 30.04.2017).

THE LEGAL STATUS OF INTERSEX PERSONS IN INDIA

Smita SHAH*

1. INTRODUCTION

On 15 April 2014, the Supreme Court of India (the Court) handed down judgment in *National Legal Services Authority v. Union of India* (*NALSA*).[1] *NALSA* recognised the identities and rights of Hijra[2] and transgender persons in law, echoing earlier decisions by neighbouring countries, Pakistan and Nepal.[3] By embracing Hijras and transgender persons within its constitutional fold, the judgment in *NALSA* made a promise to them of the promotion and protection of fundamental rights as enshrined within the Constitution of Indian (the Constitution).

* My thanks to the editors for the opportunity to comment upon the *NALSA* case, Jens Scherpe for his guidance, Claire Fenton-Glynn for her support and to Giovanna Gilleri, for her invaluable feedback on this chapter.

1 (2014) 5 SCC 438. The judgment can be found online at <https://indiankanoon.org/doc/193543132/> (last accessed 31.12.2017).

2 For an ethnographic study of 'Hirja', see S. NANDA, *Neither Man nor Woman: The Hijras of India*, 2nd ed., Wadsworth Publishing Company, Belmont 1999.

3 *Sunil Babu Pant & Ors. v. Nepal Government* (Writ Petition No. 917 of 2064 BS) (2007 AD), (Judgment dated 21 December, Supreme Court of Nepal) (translation published in National Judicial Academy Law Journal, 2 NJA Law Journal 2008, pp. 261–286); *Dr. Mohammad Aslam Khaki & Anr. v. Senior Superintendent of Police (Operation) Rawalpindi & Ors.* (Constitution Petition No. 43 of 2009). For a comparative, and by no means exhaustive, approach to intersex, transgender justice and sexual orientation, see the following, which informed this chapter: D. JALAN, 'Trans Gender Justice: Critical Reflections on the Conceptual Limitations of English Law, Implementation of the Law, and the Relationship with Social Progress' (2016)

Upon its arrival, *NALSA* was in turn hailed as 'landmark'[4] and as 'embodying a long tradition of openness by the Court by simultaneously celebrating the universal idea of humanity and values, while emphasising the importance of national and local identities';[5] and derided for vague unenforceable orders and making 'gross generalisations'[6] about Hijra and transgender persons, slipping as it did in and out of 'different notions of transgender identity' pointing to 'an administrative nightmare without further clarification'.[7]

Delineations in law are important; otherwise uncertainty remains as to whom the Court's newly announced recognition applies.[8] For intersex persons this can become an acute problem – intersex persons may be straight, gay, lesbian, bisexual, asexual, and may identify as female, male, both or neither.[9]

---

4 *Legal Issues J.* 43 201; J. Oloka-Onyango, 'Debating love, human rights and identity politics in East Africa: The case of Uganda and Kenya' (2015) 15 *Afr. Hum. Rts. L.J.* 28; and M. Den Brink, P. Reuss and J. Tigchelaar, 'Out of the Box? Domestic and Private International Law Aspects of Gender Registration: A Comparative Analysis of Germany and the Netherlands' (2015) 17 *Eur. J.L. Reform* 282.

4 ICJ, *Briefing Paper: Implementation of NALSA decision*, International Commission of Jurists, 2016 <https://www.icj.org/wp-content/uploads/2016/04/India-QA-NALSA-Advocacy-Analysis-brief-2016-ENG.pdf> (last accessed 10.01.2018). For more preliminary responses, see A. Dutta, 'Thoughts on the Supreme Court Judgement on Transgender Recognition and Rights', Orinam, 19.04.2014 <http://orinam.net/thoughts-supreme-court-judgment-transgender-recognition-rights/> (last accessed 10.1.2018) and R. Kapur 'Beyond Male and Female: The Right to Humanity' *The Hindu*, 19.04.2014 <http://www.thehindu.com/opinion/op-ed/beyond-male-and-female-the-right-to-humanity/article5926142.ece> (last accessed 10.01.2018).

5 B. Boyce, 'Sexuality and Gender Identity Under the Constitution of India' (2015–16) 18 *J. Gender Race & Just.* 1, 59.

6 G.I. Semmalar, 'Gender Outlawed: The Supreme Court Judgement on third gender and its implication' *Round Table India* 19.04.2014 <http://roundtableindia.co.in/index.php?option=com_content&view=article&id=7377:because-we-have-a-voice-too-the-supreme-court-judgment-on-third-gender-and-its-implications&catid=120:gender&Itemid=133> (last accessed 13.02.2017).

7 D. Sheikh, 'National Legal Services Authority versus Union of India – Preliminary Reactions, Law & Other Things', 16.04.2014 <http://lawandotherthings.com/2014/04/national-legal-services-authority/> (last accessed 13.02.2017).

8 J.A. Redding, 'From "She-Males" to "Unix": Transgender Rights and the Productive Paradoxes of Pakistani Policing', in D. Berti and D. Bordia (eds.) *Regimes of Legality: Ethnography of Criminal Cases in South Asia*, Oxford University Press, New Delhi 2015, p. 260; although the author is discussing Pakistan, the point is of universal application.

9 UNFE, *Fact Sheet: Intersex* <https://www.unfe.org/system/unfe-65-Intersex_Factsheet_ENGLISH.pdf> (last accessed 20.02.2017). The definition used by the United Nations Free and Equal campaign for transgender equality, resonated and was adopted in 'Stories of Intersex People from Nepal', an illuminating report of personal testimonies gather in Nepal at the 1st Intersex National Meeting on 8–9.02.2016:

> Intersex people are born with sex characteristics (including genitals, gonads and chromosome patterns) that do not fit typical binary notions of male or female bodies. Intersex is an umbrella terms used to describe a wide range of natural bodily variations rather than a single intersex variation. In some cases, intersex traits are no apparent until puberty. Some chromosomal intersex variations may not be physically apparent at all or may be discovered when trying to conceive or through random chance

This ability to transcend and traverse sexual orientations and gender identities has rendered intersex persons almost invisible and uniquely vulnerable, as if unnecessary of recognition and protection in the law. The lives of individuals with non-conforming sex binary bodies can be a precarious one of fear and violence, attempting to fit into the sex binary.[10]

NALSA appeared to open a space for challenging the gender binary straitjacket by recognising and protecting gender variations in law in India. Recognition in law is the passport to identification documents, which in turn enables access to other fundamental rights, such as housing, welfare benefits, education and healthcare.[11] This chapter asks what does *NALSA* mean for intersex persons in India? Does the promise made to Hijra and transgender persons include or extend to intersex individuals? On one level, the answer will inevitably lie in how *NALSA* is interpreted and applied; *Jackuline Mary v. The Superintendent of Police, Karur*[12] offers a flavour of what this may look like.[13]

(E. Regmi, *Stories of Intersex People from Nepal. Kathmandu* available at <http://orinam.net/content/wp-content/uploads/2016/04/Intersex-Stories-in-Nepal.pdf> (last accessed 10.01.2018) This chapter relies on this definition when using the term intersex.

10 Labia, *Breaking the Gender Binary: Understanding concerns and realities of queer persons assigned gender female at birth across a spectrum of lived gender identities*, April 2013 <https://sites.google.com/site/labiacollective/> (last accessed 10.01.2018), p. 80, in particular the narratives on the lives of Sandya and Divakar, both with intersex variations at pp. 57, 74 and 77 in the NGO report; the report in the Saskia E. Wieringa edition is the more academic of the 2 versions; in S.E. Wieringa (ed.), '*Breaking the Binary Trans/sign: Report of Research Findings*' Riek Stienstra Fonds, 2011, p. 182 available at <http://www.academia.edu/1273065/Breaking_the_binary_Understanding_concerns_and_realities_of_female_assigned_born_persons_across_a_spectrum_of_lived_gender_identities> (last accessed 10.01.2018).

11 S. Narrain, 'Gender Identity, Citizenship and State Recognition' (2012) 8 *Socio-Legal Rev.* 106 and M. Bochenek and K. Knight, 'Establishing Third Gender Category in Nepal: Process ad Prognosis' (2012) 26 *Emory Int'l L. Rev.* 11. See on the importance of sex attribution on birth certificates A.J. Neuman Wipfler, 'Identity Crisis: The limits of Expanding Gender Identity and the Possibility of Genderless Identity Documents' (2016) 39 *Harv. Women's L.J.* 491 and on the impact of third gender on Hindu family law in India, see D. Chowdhury and A. Tripathy, 'Recognising the Right of the Third Gender to marriage and Inheritance under Hindu Personal Law in India' (2016) 3 *BRICS L.J.* 43.

12 [W.P. No.587 of 2014].

13 This chapter is going to focus on *NALSA* with respect to intersex persons; however, for commentary upon jurisprudence seeking to de-criminalise homosexual acts, which informs the history of transgender rights litigation before the Supreme Courts, see A. Kumar, 'All you need to know about the SC's decision to reopen the section 377 debate' First post, 08.02.2017 <http://www.firstpost.com/india/all-you-need-to-know-about-the-scs-decision-to-reopen-the-section-377-debate-2610680.html> (last accessed 10.01.2018); A.S. Vishwajith, 'India's Third Gender and the Kaushal Problem' OxHRH Blog, 25.04.2014 available at <http://ohrh.law.ox.ac.uk/indias-third-gender-and-the-kaushal-problem/> (last accessed 10.01.2018); S. Narrain, 'Crystallising Queer Politcs – The Naz Foundation Case and its Implications for India's Transgender Communities' (2009) 2 *NUJS L. Rev.* 455; and S.M. Akali, 'Learning from *Suresh Kumar Koushal v. Naz Foundation* Through Introspection,

2. *NALSA v. UNION OF INDIA*

A two-judge bench, composed of Supreme Court Justices KS Radhakrishnan and AK Sikri (hereafter Justice Radhakrishnan and Justice Sikri), presided over consolidated public interest litigation petitions filed in or about 2013 by the National Legal Services Authority of India (NALSA), a legal aid provider to marginalised communities, Poojaya Mata Nasib Kaur Ji Women Welfare Society, an NGO, on behalf of the Kinnar Community and the intervener, prominent Hijra activist, Laxmi Narayan Tripathi, represented by the Lawyers Collective, Delhi claiming violations of Articles 14, 15, 16 and 21 of the Constitution of India and seeking legal recognition of a third gender.[14] The case was not contested by either the Central Indian Government[15] or state governments who provided information regarding their efforts to improve the conditions and status of transgender communities.[16]

The Court declared that Hijras are to be treated as third gender, and granted transgender persons the right to self-identify, whether male, female or third gender. Importantly for the Indian context, as per Article 15 of the Constitution, Hijra and transgender individuals are to be classed as socially and educationally backward classes to the extent of the application and benefits of affirmative action measures envisaged within Articles 15 and 16 of the Constitution in education and in public appointments.[17] The Court issued mandatory orders to the Central Indian and state governments to: provide legal recognition of the self-identified

---

Inclusion, and Intersectionality: Suggestions from Within Indian Queer Justice Movements' (2016) 31 *Berkeley J. Gender L. & Just.* 121.

14 I have paraphrased, in the interests of space, the claims made under the Constitution and relief sought by each of the petitioners. To find out more about NALSA, see <http://nalsa.gov.in/about-us> (last accessed 10.01.2018). An interview with Hijra activist Laxmi Narayan Tripathi can be found at: S. Seerva, 'Laxmi Narayan Tripathi: India's Third Gender' *Guernica* 16.03.2015 <https://www.guernicamag.com/indias-third-gender/> (last accessed 10.01.2018). For the origins of public interest litigation in India, see *S.P. Gupta v. President of India And Ors.*, 31.12.1981, AIR 1982 SC 149, 1981 Supp (1) SCC 87, 1982 2 SCR 365 <https://indiankanoon.org/doc/1294854/> (last accessed 10.01.2018).

15 India is a federated union and devolves powers to each state. See Articles 1 and 2 of the Indian Constitution at <https://www.india.gov.in/sites/upload_files/npi/files/coi_part_full.pdf> (accessed on 25.05.2018).

16 *National Legal Services Authority v. Union of India*, (2014) 5 SCC 438, para. 7. p. 7.

17 Govt of India, Ministry of Law and Justice, *The Constitution of India* (as of 9 November 2015) available at <https://www.india.gov.in/my-government/constitution-india/constitution-india-full-text> (last accessed 10.01.2018). Art. 15 of the Indian Constitution states that the state shall not discriminate upon the basis of sex amongst other categories. Art. 15(4) specifically allows for 'special provision for the advancement of any socially and educationally backward classes of citizens or for the Scheduled Castes and the Scheduled Tribes', an attempt to address historical and colonial legislation which discriminated on the basis of affiliation to an indigenous tribe, caste and specified others.

gender of the transgender person; operate separate HIV Sero-surveillance centres; address wider concerns about their well-being; provide for medical care; provide separate public toilets and other facilities; and provide social welfare schemes. The Central Indian and state governments were requested to raise public awareness and take measures to enable transgender persons to 'regain their respect and place in the society which they once enjoyed in our cultural and social life'.[18] Importantly, the Court declared that any insistence for sex reassignment surgery to enable a person to obtain official recognition, through identification documents was immoral and illegal.

After carrying out an extensive survey of the evolution of international and comparative jurisprudence, national and regional legislation and international human rights law on gender identity and sexual orientation,[19] Justice Radhakrishnan concluded that 'the guarantee to equality and non-discrimination' upon the basis of gender identity or expression had gained increasing acceptance in international law and therefore could be applied in India.[20] Continuing in this vein, the Court further reasoned that the absence of domestic provisions to recognise and protect Hijra and transgender persons permitted each of Articles 14 (recognition as person before the law and equal protection of the law), 15 (non-discrimination on grounds of sex and affirmative action measures for socially and educationally backward classes), 16 (non-discrimination based on sex in employment and public office), 19(1)(a) (freedom of expression) and 21 (protection of life and liberty) of the Constitution to be read in harmony with international human rights law, thereby enlarging their content.

This was a remarkable interpretative innovation: Articles 14, 15, 16, 19(1)(a) and 21 were read as gender neutral; freedom from discrimination included both the private and public spheres; freedom of expression included the freedom to express one's chosen gender identity through varied ways of expression, such as speech, mannerism and clothing. Gender identity was at the core of one's personal identity and gender expression, and the state could not prohibit, restrict or interfere with such transgender self-expression.[21] The right to life encompassed all that made it meaningful, including dignity, personal autonomy and privacy; and self-determination of gender fell within the realm of personal liberty.[22]

18 *National Legal Services Authority v. Union of India*, above n. 1, para. 129, pp. 127–129.

19 Ibid, pp. 19–54.

20 Ibid, para. 43, p. 54.

21 *National Legal Services Authority v. Union of India*, above n. 13, para. 69, p. 81. Justice Radhakrishnan is emphatic, 'No restriction was to be placed on one's personal appearance or choice of dressing, subject to the restrictions contained in Article 19(2) of the Constitution' at para. 62, and has been subject to justified criticism as it appears intrinsically contradictory; however, any restrictions, such as a requirement for a particular uniform for particular professions, would need to be prescribed in law, reasonable and for one of the enumerated grounds within Art. 19(2).

22 Ibid, paras. 67 and 69, pp. 79–81.

3. DEFINITIONS AND INTERSEX

As pioneering as *NALSA* was, the learned Justices' opinions were contradictory when considering exactly who the beneficiaries were. The issue became acute where the allocation of state resources to beneficiaries for the provision of affirmative action measures was concerned; in September 2014, six months after the judgment in *NALSA*, the Central Indian Government petitioned the Court to further clarify who exactly fell within the remit of transgender. To date there has been no decision.[23]

The judgment in *NALSA* fluctuated between an expansive definition of transgender as an 'umbrella term' encompassing gender identities such as Hijras, Kothis, Aravanis, Jogappas, Shiv-Shakthis, which may include intersex persons, castrated and non-castrated males; those who undergo sex reassignment surgery and transvestites who cross-dress; to a more restrictive definition based primarily on Hijra and trans women.[24]

A generous explanation, suggested by Redding, would be the 'innocent' judicial fumbling that a legal system may engage in as it confronts peoples and rights with which it is unfamiliar;[25] however, this 'innocent fumbling' had transgender commentators bristling with understandable anger; it led, Semmelar argued, to the marginalisation of trans men and masculine identities.[26] A pragmatic explanation may be that the parties before the Court and the ethnographic literature relied upon predominantly concerned Hijra and trans women, such as Serena Nanda's study and a UNDP report, inevitably framing the parameters.[27]

Justice Radhakrishnan in a lengthy obiter, attempted to engage with the differences between gender identity and sexual orientation and the reasons for any dissonance between sex assigned at birth and gender identity resulting in

23 See A. Dutta 'Contradictory Tendencies: The Supreme Court's NALSA judgment on Transgender Recognition and Rights' (2014) 5 *J. Indian L. & Soc'y* 225, 227. See Narrain, above n. 11, p. 109, looking at early efforts by Karnataka to grapple with putting systems in place to identify the beneficiaries of policies which favoured 'gender minorities'.

24 *National Legal Services Authority v. Union of India*, above n. 13, para. 11, p. 1011 and see Dutta, above n. 23, p. 226.

25 Redding, above n 8, p. 260.

26 See Semmalar, above n 6. and S.I. Anansuya, 'Over Two years after Landmark judgement, Transgender people are still struggling', *The Wire* 15.05.2016 <https://thewire.in/35978/over-two-years-after-landmark-judgment-transgender-people-are-still-struggling/> (last accessed 10.01.2018), a journalistic article which summarises concerns about the judgment by transgender activists.

27 Nanda, above n. 2 and see her preliminary report at S. Nanda 'The Hijras of India: A Preliminary Report' (1984) 3 *Med. & L.* 59 and UNDP INDIA, *Hijras/Transgender Women in India: HIV, Human Rights and Social Exclusion*, UNDP, December 2010 which was relied upon extensively by the Supreme Court Justice.

what Dutta calls biological essentialism and homogenising generalisations;[28] however, when arriving at the ratio, there is inclusiveness:

> Constitution makers, it can be gathered gave emphasis to the fundamental right against sex discrimination so as to prevent the direct or indirect attitudes to treat people differently, for the reason of not being in conformity with stereotypical generalisation of binary gender … gender attributes include one's self image, the deep psychological or emotional sense of sexual identity and character – therefore includes discrimination on gender identity. The use of the word 'sex' is not just limited to biological sex of male or female, but intended to include people who consider themselves to be neither.[29]

It is then troubling how Justice Sikri's judgment sits alongside this. He too indulged in 'innocent' linguistic fumbling but is crystal clear upon whom he has granted legal recognition. While the learned Justice accepted that 'transgender was a wide umbrella term which included, gay, lesbian, bisexual and cross-dressers', they were not of concern for the Court in *NALSA*. The meaning Justice Sikri gave to transgender is Hijra and male to female transgender persons, who after having undergone sex reassignment surgery should face no legal impediment to have their gender identity recognised.[30] The learned Justice concluded that Hijras in India are a distinct and separate category not present in the rest of the world save for neighbouring countries; they are biological males who reject their masculine identities, neither men nor women. Recognition as third gender would enable them to enjoy their human rights.[31]

Staying with Justice Sikri and a restrictive reading, *NALSA* sits as a reflection of *Dr Muhammad Aslam Khaki and others v. Senior Superintendent of Police, Rawalpindi and others*[32] in the Supreme Court of Pakistan, which arose out of a police raid upon a 'suspicious' wedding party in the early morning hours, which recognised only Hijras as a third gender, as citizens of Pakistan and hence subject to constitutional protection.[33] The reasoning in *NALSA* mirrors this, namely that Hijras are socially and culturally unique to the region.

Serena Nanda in her ethnographic survey of a small sample of Hijras, highlighted the story of Salima, an intersex Hijra who joined at the age of 11 to 13 years, suggesting that some Hijras may be intersexed.[34] However as at least one commentator has pointed out some Hijras consider themselves female and it remains unclear whether *NALSA* allows for Hijras to self-identify as female or

---

28 Dutta, above n. 23, p. 230.
29 Para. 59, at page 73–74.
30 *National Legal Services Authority v. Union of India*, above n. 13, para. 106, p. 108.
31 Ibid, para. 109, p. 111.
32 (Writ Petition No. 43 of 2009).
33 Redding, above n. 8.
34 Nanda, above n. 2; Salima, ch. 8 at pp. 77–112.

even as male or whether they are restricted to third gender.[35] For Hijras who are intersex, it is open to them to avail themselves of recognition as third gender in law and full constitutional protection.

Continuing with a narrow reading of *NALSA*, as per Justice Sikri, a transgender individual who is a biological male to female and has undergone sex reassignment surgery can have their self-identified gender recognised. There are a number of difficulties inherent for intersex individuals who would have had to navigate how their sex status was recorded at birth, how they were raised and perceived and finally their own sense of self-identification before fitting into the male to female transgender.

Alternatively, if taking a purposive meaning, as per Justice Radhakrishnan and the expansively construed Articles 19(1)(a) and 21 of the Constitution, an intersexed person who challenges traditional notions of binary gender through non-conformity, should be able to self-identify as male, female or third gender, based on their own 'deep psychological or emotional sense of sexual identity and character'.[36] The orders which follow the judgment state clearly that sex reassignment cannot not be a requirement.

NALSA does not appear to go as far as the Nepal Supreme Court did in *Sunil Babu Pant & Ors. v. Nepal Government*[37] in terms of remit. This was a public interest litigation lead by the Blue Diamond Society, representing sexual and gender minorities, including intersex persons. Hijras were accepted to a degree in Nepal but not other sexual and gender minorities.[38] The Justices accepted that gender identity was to be based upon self-feeling and it was not for other individuals, society, the state or law to decide what type of genitals, sexual partner or the manner in someone engaged in sexual intercourse; these were all matters of self-determination and privacy. Transgender persons, not restricted to Hijras, and including intersex persons, were to be considered third gender, homosexuality was recognised as natural. This can be considered a wider acceptance of diversity, but with a potential 'othering' affect.

For intersexed persons these are all half-measures, swept up with a number of other gender identities which overlap their intersex status, or are simply categorised as third gender. It is not direct recognition that an individual can be born challenging the majoritarian binary sex and gender identities and continue to do so, throughout their lives.

---

35 Semmalar, above n. 6.

36 *National Legal Services Authority v. Union of India*, above n. 13, para. 59, p. 74.

37 (Writ Petition No. 917 of 2064 BS) (2007 AD).

38 M.F. Moscati and H. Phuyal, 'The Third Gender Case' *Decision* of the Supreme Court of Nepal on the Rights of Lesbian, Gay, Bisexual, Transsexual and Intersex People' (2009) 4 *J. Comp. L.* 291, 293.

4. THE PROMISE OF *NALSA*

In 2015, the Central Government of India brought a draft Bill, later revised in 2016, entitled The Transgender Persons (Protection of Rights) Bill.[39] This amended Bill was subject to vociferous criticism from a variety of groups from within the umbrella of transgender and wider human rights community. It galvanised organisations who advocated on behalf of intersex persons to demand specific provisions which address the intersex experience, such as an end to domestic non-consensual cosmetic surgeries upon infants and children and a demand that the birth certificates of intersex infants do not record a sex or gender identity. Their concerns were shared and supported by a broader coalition of transgender civil society organisations. There were wider concerns about the definition of transgender, the process of recognition and the criminalising of certain activities, such as begging, seen by many as a primary form of livelihood for many transgender persons and thereby as criminalisation of poverty.[40] The Bill was sent to a Parliamentary standing committee on social justice and empowerment which made a number of recommendations to bring the Bill into line with *NALSA*. The committee welcomed the Bill, which made provisions for comprehensive access to healthcare but expressed a number of concerns: that the definition of transgender did not meet international norms and violated the right to self-determine identity; it conflated transgender with intersex; intersex persons needed particular provisions; the Bill provided no remedy for discrimination suffered, had omitted establishing provisions under the reservations scheme and recommended a series of amendments.

---

39 This is despite the Tiruchi Siva Bill of 2015 being passed unanimously in the Upper House, Rajya Sabba, and sitting in the in-tray of the Lower House, Lok Sabha. A Bill needs to be passed by both houses to become law. The ICJ has prepared a useful briefing at ICJ, *Briefing Paper India: The Transgender Persons (Protection of Rights) Bill*, International Commission of Jurists, 2016 available at <http://www.icj.org/wp-content/uploads/2016/08/INDIA-TG-BILL-CRITIQUE-Advocacy-Analysis-brief-2016-ENG.pdf> (last accessed 11.01.2018); for a response from an intersex community, see Telanga Hijra Intersex Samiti, 'Telangana Hijra Intersex Transgender Samiti responds to MSJE Transgender Rights bill (2015)' 18.01.2016, available at <http://orinam.net/telangana-samiti-response-msje-trans-rights-bill/> (last accessed 11.01.2018) and Sampoorna, 'Sampoorna response to MSJE Trans Rights Bill' 13.01.2016, available at <http://orinam.net/sampoorna-response-msje-trans-rights-bill/> (last accessed 10.01.2018). For reporting of this see, Anansuya, above n. 26.

40 V.V. Mogli, 'Responses from Trans and Intersex Communities on the Transgender Rights Bill 2016', *Feminism in India* 09.08.2016 <https://feminisminindia.com/2016/08/09/trans-community-response-transgender-rights-bill-2016/#.V_Oky-B97IX%20-> (last accessed 11.1.2018) and Anansuya, above n. 26. See also Roundtable India, 'Transgender person (protection of rights) Bill 2016: responses from the trans and intersex communities' 08.08.2016 <http://roundtableindia.co.in/index.php?option=com_content&view=article&

In 2017, the government indicated that it was seeking to reintroduce for the winter Parliamentary session, the original contentious Bill.[41]

A real test of how *NALSA* has been understood and to whom exactly it applied can be demonstrated in the case of *Jackuline Mary v. The Superintendent of Police, Karur*.[42]

The Honourable Mr. Justice S. Nagamuthu, sitting in the High Court of Madras delivered judgment in *Jackuline Mary v. The Superintendent of Police, Karur* mere days after the *NALSA* decision. The applicant in the matter was raised and self-identified as female, and sought to enter the training programme of the Karur District police force under the women's quota. She was dismissed after an employer-mandated medical examination revealed that she had a male chromosomal study 46XY and Androgen Insensitivity Syndrome, for concealing her 'transgender' status and seeking to inappropriately enter the police force under the women's reservation.[43] The learned judge was entirely sympathetic to the plight of the applicant as having been 'outed' as intersex, the detrimental consequences of this upon her and outraged that notwithstanding that certain posts were reserved for women, there was no law prescribing that women should undergo a medical examination to establish their sexual identity.[44]

The Court found violations of her rights under Article 14, 15, 16, 19(1)(a) and 21 of the Indian Constitution. The Court further found that she was entitled to be declared female as per her self-identified gender and entitled to be considered female for the purpose of property and employment rights amongst others.

The judgment exemplifies some of the confusion caused by *NALSA*. The learned judge relied upon the restrictive definitions in Justice Sikri's opinion,

---

id=8717:the-transgender-persons-protection-of-rights-bill-2016-responses-from-the-trans-intersex-communities&catid=123:policy&Itemid=139> (last accessed 13.02.2017).

41 Lok Sabha Bill No. 210 of 2016, The Transgender Persons (Protection of Rights) Bill, can be found at <http://164.100.47.4/BillsTexts/LSBillTexts/Asintroduced/210_2016_LS_Eng.pdf> (last accessed on 01.01.2018). Standing Committee on Social Justice and Empowerment (2016–2017) 16th Lok Sabha, Transgender Person (Protection of Rights) Bill 2016, 43rd Report, July 2016/Ashadha, 1936 (Saka). Recent reporting: R. Abraham, 'All you Need to Know about Transgender Persons Bill 2016', *The Hindu* 30.11.2017 <http://www.thehindu.com/news/national/all-you-need-to-know-about-the-transgender-persons-bill-2016/article21226710.ece> (last accessed on 01.01.2018); 'Government Set to Re-introduce Transgender Persons' Rights Bill Ignoring Key Recommendations', *The Wire* 20.11.2017 <https://thewire.in/198486/transgender-persons-rights-bill/> (last accessed on 01.01.2018) and A. Narrain, 'How the Centre's Bill to protect the rights of transgender people will actually hurt them', *Scroll India* 01.12.2017 <https://scroll.in/article/859620/how-the-centres-bill-to-protect-the-rights-of-transgender-people-will-actually-hurt-them> (last accessed 01.01.2018).

42 [W.P. No.587 of 2014].

43 Androgen Insensitivity Syndrome is an intersex condition and was mis-labelled as 'transgender' by the medical examiner and was applied by the police; *Jackuline Mary v. The Superintendent of Police, Karur* [W.P. No.587 of 2014], para. 7.

44 Ibid, para. 26.

declaring that *NALSA* only applied to male to female transgender persons and not, as he mistakenly identified the applicant, to female to male transsexuals.[45] The learned judge was of the view that *NALSA* should apply to female to male transgender but that required explicit legislation. The learned judge felt he had no recourse other than to revert back to the traditional legal contortions of fitting the applicant into the gender binary in order to protect their fundamental rights.[46] *NALSA* was argued extensively before the Court in oral argument and in an *amicus curiae* by the Solicitor General of India. The factual convenience for the Court was that the applicant 'fitted' happily within the gender binary; if on the other hand she had decided to embrace her intersex status and wished to be considered third gender or even non-gender specific, as yet there was no space or legal recognition for this.

5. CONCLUSION

Saskia Wieringa, in presenting the case of an intersex individual born with Klinefelter Syndrome in Indonesia, laments the legal lack of space in which to manoeuvre.[47] In this case the individual had been raised as female, whereas infants with Klinefelter syndrome were generally classed as male. Later in life he sought surgery to align his physical appearance with that of his self-identified gender as male. He met and married a woman, and it was this marriage that was legally challenged as fraud. The legal case and media furore became fixated upon ascertaining 'the truth' of his sex, in other words with his biology; if he was a boy then it was a matter of a mistake on his birth certificate and all was well, if female and having undergone sex-reassignment surgery then he was transgender and was required to undergo a protracted and costly legal process to have this recorded which he had not and therefore was liable to a hefty fine or imprisonment for fraud.[48] Like Jackuline Mary, he happily fitted in to the prescribed gender binary and was able to 'prove' the medical mistake. As long as the intersex variation can be compressed into the binary sex identity at birth, there is no oxygen for the intersex aspect of the individual's identity; this lack of oxygen accompanies them through into adulthood. As Semmaler has argued, 'they [the state] want to manage our bodies'.[49] More than any other community, intersex persons are defined by their biology, which is then taken as indicative

45 Ibid, para. 35 and Dutta, above n. 23, p. 229.
46 *Jackuline Mary v. The Superintendent of Police, Karur*, above n. 12, para. 34.
47 S.E. Wieringa, 'Marriage Equality in Indonesia? Unruly Bodies, Subversive Partners and Legal Implications' (2013) 10 *Equal Rights Review* 97.
48 Ibid at 97.
49 Semmalar, above n. 6.

of sex to be assigned at birth and then seen as formulating their baseline gender identity. In other words, an individual must have a fixed sex assigned at birth, and by extension, arguably, a fixed gender and fixed sexual orientation to act as a baseline and only then can they exercise their right to change any of them. The societal and legal construct of humans as existing in binaries being all pervasive; non-conformity causes confusion, concern and suspicion.[50]

Therefore, the starting point for an intersex person, is recognition of intersex as a separate existence in law, medicine and society, and one without stigma or enforced conformity into a binary sex assignment through medical interventions or through having to prove the 'truth' of their biology.

It is unclear whether *NALSA* has transformed the legal and societal reality for intersex persons. However, the Indian Supreme Court is an explicitly political institution, and according to Khaitan 'in NALSA the judges are clear, law must transform social reality'.[51] Or as Sheikh put it, 'an expressive function that the judicial text has, over and above the enumerated text'.[52]

If there has been an impact of the decision, then it is that it has acted as a platform for intersex civil society and the wider transgender movement, supporting their efforts for explicit legislative provisions concerning their specialised needs. In terms of application in lower courts, the results are not entirely promising.

---

50 A good example can be found in this newspaper story about an abandoned intersex infant and the concerns of legal and societal non-conformity; Y.S. Ashwini, 'Does anybody care for this intersex infant?', *Deccan Herald* 14.01.2016 <http://www.deccanherald.com/content/522957/does-anybody-care-intersex-infant.html> (last accessed 10.01.2018).

51 T. Khaitan, 'NALSA v Union of India: What Courts Say, What Courts Do', *U.K. Const. L. Blog* 24.04.2014 <https://ukconstitutionallaw.org/2014/04/24/tarunabh-khaitan-nalsa-v-union-of-india-what-courts-say-what-courts-do/> (last accessed 13.02.2017).

52 D. Sheikh, 'Transgender rights: One year of NALSA', *Daily O* 18.04.2015 <http://www.dailyo.in/politics/transgender-rights-bill-NALSA-tiruchi-siva-section-377/story/1/3236.html> (last accessed 13.02.2017).

THE LEGAL STATUS OF INTERSEX PERSONS IN THE NETHERLANDS

Marjolein VAN DEN BRINK

1. INTRODUCTION

When Katja in her late puberty still had not had her period, her mother sent her to the doctor.[1] This was the start of a two-year medical tour from one expert to the other. Their conclusion was that Katja had no pubic hair and no uterus, but why that was so remained unclear, at least to Katja. Most confusing was that Katja's mother made her promise not to talk to anyone about the 'secrets in her tummy'. It was only when Katja was in her forties that she discovered that she had an XY, thus 'male' chromosomal make-up. Even more shocking was the discovery that her parents and her doctors had known this all along. The decision to keep this knowledge from Katja was based on a medical protocol according to which children with irregular sex characteristics were told as little as possible, to avoid 'gender confusion'. The protocol had been adopted in the Netherlands following the then famous (now infamous) John/Joan case of American doctor John Money, who believed in the possibility to raise children in a specific gender, regardless of their physical characteristics. To ensure the

[1] M. VAN HEESCH recounts and discusses the experiences of 'Katja' (not her real name) and other people with an intersex condition/DSD in her Ph.D. thesis: *Ze wisten niet of ik een jongen of een meisje was: kennis, keuze en geslachtsvariaties. Over het leven met en het kennen van intersekse condities in Nederland* [They didn't know whether I was a boy or a girl: knowledge, choices and sex variations. On living with and knowing about intersex conditions in the Netherlands], Amsterdam University Press, Amsterdam, 2015. ch. VII 'I've got secrets in my stomach', and especially p. 266.

successful gender development of a child as – in this case – female, it was imperative to keep any information from Katja that might raise doubts about her gender. Thus, it made sense not to tell Katja about her chromosomal make-up.

Katja was born in the early 1940s, but her experiences are shared by generations of people after her, since the medical protocol to not disclose information to intersex/DSD individuals[2] that potentially could cause 'gender confusion', was only abandoned around 2003.[3]

The main impetus to change the policy of secrecy regarding sex variations seems to have come from the spread of the World Wide Web: with access to the internet increasing, it became impossible to keep medical facts from the general public. The internet disclosed medical information on intersex conditions that had hitherto been accessible only to the medical profession. This in turn made many individuals with an intersex condition realise they were not in fact unique, as they had been led to believe. And, of course, it is now clear that intersex conditions are far from unique, even though the prevalence can only be determined very roughly. A Dutch study in 2014 concludes that the best possible estimate of the prevalence of intersex conditions, including people who are not even aware of their condition, is about 0.5 per cent or 80,000 individuals.[4] The NNID (Netherlands Network Intersex/DSD) uses a somewhat broader definition, resulting in an estimated 1.7 per cent.[5]

From a present-day, legal perspective the stories of intersex individuals, as recounted by Margriet van Heesch, are quite astonishing because Dutch law actually has been taking the possibility of gender variations at birth into account since 1970, when a new code on personal status and family law was introduced. The code included a provision that made it possible to postpone the attribution of a legal sex (M or F) to the child to a later date. Until that time the entry would state that the child's sex was unknown.[6]As is often the case, law and practice

2 So far there seems to be no consensus on the best way to name individuals with an intersex condition, with a 'disorder of sex development' or a 'difference of sex development' (both DSD). Because 'intersex individual' is short, this text will often use this expression. However, this choice very explicitly is not intended to suggest that intersex conditions give rise to an 'identity', like transgender positions generally are assumed to.

3 Van Heesch, above n. 1, p. 266.

4 J. Van Lisdonk, *Leven met intersekse/DSD; Een verkennend onderzoek naar de leefsituatie van personen met intersekse/DSD* [Living with intersex/DSD; An exploration into the living situation of people with intersex/DSD], SCP, Den Haag, 2014, at pp. 16 and 30 <https://www.scp.nl/Publicaties/Alle_publicaties/Publicaties_2014/Leven_met_intersekse_DSD> (last accessed 02.07.2018).

5 Based on: M. Blackless, A. Charuvastra, A. Derryck, A. Fausto-Sterling, K. Lauzanne and E. Lee, 'How Sexually Dimorphic Are we? Review and Synthesis' (2000) 12(2) *American Journal of Human Biology* 151–166, as cited in Van Lisdonk above n. 4, p. 29.

6 M. van den Brink and J. Tigchelaar, *M/V en verder. Sekseregistratie door de overheid en de juridische positie van transgenders* [M/F and beyond. Sex registration by the government and the legal position of trans genders] Boom Juridische Uitgevers, Den Haag 2014, p. 15.

diverged, and – as will be discussed in more detail below – the option was and still is hardly used in practice. However, on 28 May 2018, the lower court of Limburg applied this provision in an unexpected way, by using it 'in the reverse'. That is, at the request of the Public Prosecutor (*Officier van Justitie*), the Court ordered the registrar of the municipality of Roermond to change someone's gender marker on their birth certificate from female to 'not possible to establish'.[7] This case is discussed in more detail in section 5.

This chapter maps the current legal framework regarding the attribution of legal sex, comparing the position of individuals with an intersex condition/DSD with that of cis and transgender people. It draws upon the results of a study commissioned by the then Deputy Minister of Security and Justice, Fred Teeven, on the possibilities to modify the existing legal framework on legal sex, 'M/F and beyond'.[8] Historical background will be provided where relevant. To conclude some bottlenecks and current developments will be discussed. The Netherlands has no specific legislation regarding surgery on infants with an intersex condition/DSD, and no data on the frequency of such treatment are available. Health law related issues will therefore not be discussed in this contribution.

2. THE DUTCH LEGAL FRAMEWORK ON LEGAL SEX

The practice of keeping official records of the population was introduced in the Netherlands by Napoleon in 1811. Before that time, there was no formal, comprehensive system in place, although clerics did keep records of baptisms and marriages, and caretakers of cemeteries collected information on the dead.[9]

Information on the sex (male/female) of newly-born babies was one of the required entries. Military conscription into Napoleon's armies without a doubt was one of the reasons for the gender marker. Until 1838 parents had to show their child to the registrar, so as to prevent parents fraudulently registering their child as female to save their son from being sent to the army later in life.[10] After 1838 this was no longer obligatory, although the registrar was still entitled to order the parents to show him the child in case of doubt. It is not known what happened in cases where a child's sex was not readily recognisable as male or female.

7 Rechtbank Limburg 28.05.2018, C/03/232248 / FA RK 17-687, ECLI:NL:RBLIM:2018:4931.

8 Ibid. The Deputy Minister commissioned the research because he wanted to know whether it was possible to make the legal framework regarding legal sex more flexible, e.g. by allowing for a 'third box'. The research commission did not encompass the position of intersex/DSD individuals, but it was nevertheless dealt with in the research.

9 J. Kampers, *Inleiding tot de burgerlijke stand* [Introduction to the civil registry], bewerkt door L.J.V. Evers & H. Vat, Kluwer, Alphen aan de Rijn 2010, p. 19.

10 J.N. Elenbaas, *Handboek voor de burgerlijke stand* [Handbook for the civil registry], deel 1, bewerkt door A.J.G.P. Septer and J.C. Schouten, Samsom NV, Alphen aan de Rijn 1952, pp. 320–321.

In 1970, as already mentioned, the legislator decided to introduce an option to postpone decisions on a baby's sex (then Article 1:17(2) *Burgerlijk Wetboek* (BW), the Dutch Civil Code). The public prosecutor (*officier van justitie*) could order the registrar to note on a birth certificate that the baby's sex was unknown. Once its sex had become clear, the entry could be changed (then Article 1:29 BW). However, the 'correction' would remain visible and that was generally considered undesirable.[11] In practice, this often meant that parents, with the consent of the public prosecutor, would postpone the child's registration until its sex could be established, after which the birth of the child would be registered with special authorisation from the public prosecutor. This practice, which strictly speaking was in contravention of the law, was abandoned when in 1995 Article 1:17(2) was replaced by Article 1:19(d) BW. This article, which is still in force today, makes it possible to draw up a provisional birth certificate which, after three months must be replaced by a final document indicating the child's sex as male or female (Article 1:19(d) BW read in conjunction with Article 45(1) *Besluit Burgerlijke Stand* (BBS) 1994). If after three months it still is impossible to determine the child's sex, it is also possible to state that impossibility on the final certificate.

The Dutch Association of Registrars (*Nederlandse Vereniging van Ambtenaren van de Burgerlijke Stand*) had, at the time of drafting, suggested deleting the maximum period and leaving it open. That proposal was rejected because the legislator considered it detrimental to legal certainty. The period of three months was chosen, because practice showed that it is almost always possible to establish the sex of a child within that period.[12]

Owing to Article 1:19(d) BW, the initial uncertainty about a child's sex will only remain visible if the sex entry is to be changed *after* expiry of the three-month period. In that case, a petition can be submitted to the court to ask for the 'correction' of 'mistaken' entries (*misslag*, Article 1:24–24b BW). This article can be relied upon by intersex/DSD individuals (or their parents). For transgender individuals who wish to change their legal sex from male to female or vice versa, there is Article 1:28 BW (since 1986). This article allows for a *change* of legal sex (since 1986), which is considered to be different from the *correction of a mistake*. Dutch law is based on the premise that the wish of transgender individuals to change their sex does not result from a mistake regarding their (biological) sex at birth, but is a conscious *choice*.[13]

---

11 See van den Brink and Tigchelaar, above n. 6, p. 15.

12 *Kamerstukken II*, 1990–1991, 21847, nr. 3, pp. 18–19, as referred to in van den Brink and Tigchelaar, above n. 6, p. 15 in note 13.

13 There are a number of court decisions from the 1970s and early 1980s concerning requests for a change in legal sex, where it is not entirely clear whether the petitioner has an intersex condition/DSD or is a transgender individual. It seems likely that at least in some cases the possibility of 'correction', which is intended to accommodate intersex individuals, was applied to transgender people, because at the time – before 1986 – the law did not yet allow a *change*

In July 2014, the rules regarding legal sex change were modified.[14] Paradoxically, it has now become easier to change one's legal sex than to correct it. To change one's legal sex, a transgender person, if at least 16 years old, can inform the registrar of their conviction that they belong to 'the other sex'. The most important remaining requirement is an expert declaration (Article 1:28a BW). Intersex individuals, on the other hand, need a court order to make the registrar correct their legal sex.

In practice, Article 1:19d BW is rarely used. In answer to a survey, carried out in 2014, only 17 out of 193 responding registrars stated that they had ever applied the provision. Their average number of years of service was 22.5. In only two cases did the registrars report that the child's sex had not been established within three months.[15] A query carried out in December 2013 in the Dutch population register (*Basisregistratie Personen* (BRP)) showed that at that particular moment in time 67 people had been registered in the BRP without information as to their legal sex. Of those 67 people, 20 persons were born in Italy and 24 in Germany. Since Italian and German identity cards do not mention sex, it is highly likely that these people, when registering at the municipality identified themselves with their identity card. That implies that the registrar would not have legal 'proof' of that person's legal sex, and thus is not authorised to fill out the sex entry regarding that person. However, anecdotal evidence suggests that in practice registrars sometimes do note a person's sex despite the lack of legal proof, on the basis of their perception of the individual's appearance. Only one of the 67 persons had been born in the Netherlands and thus may have been an 'Article 1:19d BW baby'.

Another implication of Article 1:19d BW is that, in theory at least, it is possible that someone who has been born in the Netherlands goes through life with 'unknown sex'. Since personal records inform the BRP, which in turn informs other government offices, the person whose sex remains undecided will have an 'unknown sex' for all purposes and will, for example, automatically receive an X (rather than an M or an F) on their passport. At the same time, the system currently in place makes it impossible to obtain an X on one's passport if one's birth certificate cites an M or an F.[16]

---

of legal sex. See e.g. Hof 's-Gravenhage, 23.11.1973, ECLI:NL:GHSGR:1973:AC5378. On this, see e.g. W. Pintens, 'The Legal Status of Transsexual and Transgender Persons in Belgium and the Netherlands', in J.M. Scherpe (ed.), *The Legal Status of Transsexual and Transgender Persons*, Intersentia, Cambridge 2015, pp. 109–123.

14 Act of 18 December 2013, *Staatsblad*, 2014, 1.

15 Survey carried out with the help of the *Nederlandse Vereniging voor Burgerzaken* (NVVB), by van den Brink and Tigchelaar, above n. 6, pp. 25, 31–33 and app. 3.

16 The function of personal records in civil law countries like the Netherlands differs significantly from that in common law countries. Therefore, the introduction of the possibility to obtain a passport with an X, for example, as has happened in Australia and New Zealand, among other countries, would require disconnecting the issuance of passports from the central information system, that is the BRP. See van den Brink and Tigchelaar, above n. 6, pp. 60–61.

3. FLAWS IN THE CURRENT REGISTRATION SYSTEM

The current registration system, although carefully constructed, is not without flaws and gaps. On 11 February 2016, the NNID (Netherlands Network Intersex/DSD) Facebook page proudly announced the victory of Dutch adoption parents over the binary system.[17] The parents suspected that their Chinese adoption baby, who had been identified as male by the Chinese authorities, was actually a girl with an intersex condition. Because they wanted to avoid the hassle of having to change the baby's sex, once attributed, they decided to leave it undecided for a while, and therefore wished to obtain a passport for the baby (who had to travel from China to the Netherlands) with an X. The law does not provide for this kind of situation, nor does it allow the solution arrived at in this case, yet the parents somehow managed to convince the registrar to permit this.

Another gap in the legislative framework came to light in 2004 when the parents of a girl with adrenogenital syndrome asked the Court to order the registrar to draw up a new birth certificate for her.[18] At birth the girl appeared to be a boy because of her external genitalia, and thus her sex was identified as male. However, after just a couple of days it had become clear that she was a girl. The parents wished to avoid reliance on Article 1:24 BW, because that would imply that the correction of the initial mistake would continue to be visible, causing inconveniences throughout the girl's life. On the other hand, Article 1:19(d) BW had not been used, because there had been no doubts about the child's sex at birth. Therefore, it was not just a matter of replacing a provisional certificate with a final one. Article 1:28 BW was also not applicable because 'the girl had been a girl from the start', so no 'change' had taken place. Because the law did not provide for this situation, the registrar originally had denied the request of the parents. However, in court he explicitly waived his right to oppose the parent's request because he felt that the child's best interest was at stake. The Court agreed and ordered the registrar to strike out the girl's birth certificate and draw up a new one.[19]

4. DESPITE EVERYTHING: A BINARY SYSTEM?

Despite Article 1:19d BW, which allows for the possibility that a person's sex which could not be established at birth remains undecided, and despite a

---

17 See 'Eerste Nederlandse paspoort zonder geslachtsregistratie' (*First Dutch passport without gender entry*) 11.02.2016 <https://www.facebook.com/pg/nnid.nl/posts/?ref=page_internal> (last accessed 02.07.2017).

18 Rechtbank's-Gravenhage, 12.07.2004, ECLI:NL:RBSGR:2004:AQ7020.

19 To achieve this result, the Court applied Art. 1:24 and 1:24b BW by analogy. Art. 1:24 allows the striking out of a certificate that has been wrongly drawn up, and Art. 1:24b allows the registrar to draw up a new certificate in case of a missing document.

registration practice that apparently does not always follow the rules that strictly, the Dutch legal framework on legal sex categories is deeply rooted in a binary conception of sex. The study 'M/F and beyond', mentioned in the introduction, shows that Dutch laws and regulations rely heavily on the existence of two distinct sex categories. This study includes an inventory of all legislative provisions mentioning either sex-specific terminology (husband/wife, father/mother) or the word *geslacht* (sex).[20] The impressive number of sex-specific provisions uncovered also makes it quite clear that, even though it is theoretically possible that a person who has been born in the Netherlands never will have an M or an F, this situation has never been seriously considered. To give an example: when marriage was opened up to same-sex couples in 2001, the official marriage forms were adjusted to make room for the situation that the bridal couple would consist of two men or two women, rather than one man and one women. However, the form still mentions 'man' and 'woman', so the possibility that the marriage candidate has another ('unknown') sex clearly was not taken into account. The relevant provision itself (Article 1:30(1) BW) states that marriage is open to two people of 'different or the same sex', again a choice of words that suggests that the possibility of another (or no) sex had not crossed the legislator's mind.

The binary conception of sex speaks also from the fact that it is only possible to correct or change one's legal sex to F or M. This has been confirmed in case law. In 2007 'K' went all the way up to the Dutch High Court (*Hoge Raad*) in an attempt to have their sex entry deleted, rather than having it changed from male to female.[21] K had come to the conclusion they are '*niet geseksueerd*', which may be translated as 'not sexed'. The High Court denied the petition, just like the lower and the appellate court had, because the law does not allow the request, nor does international human rights law require the requested change, at least not as yet.

Five years later, a person identifying as 'hermaphrodite' asked the lower court of Alkmaar permission to change their legal sex from male to female. The petitioner felt both male and female, but overall more female than male. They would have preferred a registration that acknowledged their being a hermaphrodite, but since the law did not allow it, the petitioner felt that female would be second best. The petition invoked both Articles 1:24–24b BW (correction) and 1:28 BW (change). The Court found that Article 1:28 BW was not applicable because the petitioner had both male and female characteristics, a situation which is very different from that of transgender individuals, according to the Court. Article 1:24 BW, however, could be applied: the article does not set a deadline, so even if only much later in life it turns out that the

---

20 van den Brink and Tigchelaar, above n. 6. The inventory is contained in app. 7 to the report. Because of its length this inventory is only available online <https://www.wodc.nl/binaries/2393-bijlage_tcm28-73313.pdf> (last accessed 03.07.2017).

21 Hoge Raad, 30.03.2007, R06/013HR, ECLI:NL:HR:2007:AZ5686.

initially attributed sex was mistaken, the provision allows a correction of the birth certificate.[22]

5. A NOT SO BINARY SYSTEM?

On 28 May 2018, the lower court of Limburg caused quite a stir when it decided that the lack of a gender option other than an M or an F on birth certificates amounted to a violation of the right to self-determination in the case at hand.[23] The Court requested the registrar to draft a new birth certificate indicating that 'the sex could not be determined'.

Remarkably, the Court applied Article 1:19d BW – meant for new-borns with non-conforming sex characteristics – to an adult who had already been attributed a gender marker. The person concerned – referred to in the newspapers as Leonne[24] – was registered as male at birth, decided at some point that they were not and changed their status to female. Now, at 55, the public prosecutor[25] asked the Court to change the F on Leonne's birth certificate to an X, because of Leonne's intersex condition.

In an interim decision of November 2017, the Court in Limburg had ordered the Academic Hospital in Maastricht to examine the person concerned to establish whether they had an intersex condition, as claimed by the public prosecutor.[26] The Court argued that a decision on the request could only be taken if an intersex condition was established and stated that if that turned out to be the case, the decision might not be 'at the free disposal of the parties to the case'. In other words, the judge seemed to argue that the Court would have to grant the request if the intersex condition was established. This would be a remarkable interpretation of the law, and a novelty in Dutch case law on legal sex, as it goes against the letter of the law and overturns the decision of the High Court decision in the case of K, as discussed in the previous section.

The medical expert, however, reported to the Court that an examination of Leonne's chromosomes could not verify whether they were born with an intersex condition. Thereupon, the Court invited a medical expert from another academic hospital (Nijmegen) to explain whether the alleged intersex condition could be established and, if so, how. This expert reported that she did not have sufficient information to establish whether Leonne had been born with a DSD.

22 Rb Alkmaar, 28.03.2012, 134472 – FA RK 12–18, ECLI:NL:RBALK:2012:BW5452.

23 Rechtbank Limburg, 28.05.2018, C/03/232248 / FA RK 17-687, ECLI:NL:RBLIM:2018:4931.

24 See e.g. *De Telegraaf*, 'Leonne (57) mag voortaan genderneutraal zijn: "Ik heb allebei"' ('Leonne (57) allowed to be genderneutral from now on: "I have both"'), 28.05.2018.

25 Article 1:24 BW allows either the person concerned or the public prosecutor to ask the court to order the registrar to correct an incomplete or mistaken entry.

26 Rechtbank Limburg, 06.11.2017, C/03/232248 / FA RK 17-687, ECLI:NL:RBLIM:2017:10713.

She further stated she could not determine whether Leonne was 'intersexual' because that was a question of gender identity rather than DSD.

Remarkably, the Court, despite its initial emphasis on the physical characteristics of the person concerned, decided that it was not necessary to establish a DSD, because, in any event, it would not reveal how gender was experienced by that person. The Court concluded that the attribution of gender should be based on 'gender experience' (*genderbeleving*) rather than physical characteristics. Thus, the Court began with an intersex perspective, and ended by treating it as a transgender issue. Nonetheless, the legal solution applied relates to intersex conditions, rather than (trans)gender identity.

The Court did not grant the public prosecutor's request to change Leonne's F into an X: it argued that the law as it stands does not provide for this solution.[27] However, since Article 1:19d BW does allow the registrar to note that the gender of a new-born cannot be determined, the Court applied this option to Leonne. It ordered the registrar to draw up a new birth certificate, rather than correct the existing certificate, thus effectively dealing with the case as if Leonne were a new-born without an attributed gender. In the Dutch registration system, that implies that the history regarding Leonne's legal gender is wiped out, which is very uncommon.

The legal basis for the decision is equally interesting: the Court argued that Article 8 of the ECHR, in combination with the (non-binding) Yogyakarta Principles, imposes a positive obligation on the Dutch state to ensure a 'fair balance' between individuals' right to self-determination and the public interest that is served with the registration of gender identity.

The Court's decision was not yet final when this chapter was finalised. Individuals with an interest, such as family members, or an (ex-)spouse, might appeal, although that does not seem very likely in this case. Also, the Ministry of Justice and Security might ask for 'cassation in the interest of the law', even if only to seek support for the decision. However, the expectation as expressed by the media seems to be that the Dutch legislator will now have to address the issue. As long as it does not do so, and no new legislation is enacted, other courts are not bound by this decision and may decide differently.

6. WHAT THE FUTURE MAY BRING

Over the past few years several developments have taken place. The legal position of intersex/DSD individuals has quite rapidly conquered the political agenda and policy debates on emancipation and non-discrimination policies for

[27] However, the new birth certificate will result in an X on Leonne's passport.

intersex people are now common.[28] This can be attributed largely to the efforts of the NNID (Netherlands Network Intersex/DSD), which was established as recently as 2013. One of its achievements is the proposal to add a paragraph to the Dutch General Act on Equal Treatment (*Algemene Wet Gelijke Behandeling*) that explicates that the already protected ground of 'sex' does encompass discrimination on the basis of sex characteristics, gender identity and gender expression.[29] In practice the National Institute for Human Rights (*College voor de Rechten van de Mens*, tasked with the adjudication of discrimination claims) already interprets sex as a protected ground this broadly.[30] However, it is considered important to improve the visibility of these issues, and in light of Katja's situation recounted in the introduction, that makes sense.

The government has also announced its intention to become more cautious in asking for and using information on gender. This proposition is a response to the follow-up on the previously mentioned report 'M/F and beyond'.[31] However welcome this may be, especially for gender non-conforming people and individuals who find themselves confronted with the wish or need to change their legal sex, it seems a very modest proposal. The intention to reduce the frequency of questions regarding one's legal sex, seems to consist primarily of linking the databases so that the information on legal sex is available without asking for it. That does not really seem a big step forward, although for some people of course all kinds of identity cards, and railway and library passes without information on their sex will definitely be a relief.

Yet, sex registration is on the agenda, and the government realises that the Dutch reputation as one of the most progressive countries worldwide regarding LGBTI issues is something that does require constant attention and maintenance. Getting rid of the secrecy protocol that impacted Katja's life to such an extent is not enough. In her letter to Parliament in January 2017, the then Minister of Education, Culture and Science, Jet Bussemaker, who was also responsible for emancipation policies, observed that the Netherlands went from sixth to

---

28 See also *Kamerstukken II*, 2016–2017, 20.01.2017, 30 420, no 257, *Emancipatiebeleid*. Letter from the Minister of Education, Culture and Science (Jet Bussemaker) to the president of the Second Chamber of Parliament, The Hague, 20.01.2017. This ministry is also responsible for general emancipation policies.

29 *Kamerstukken II*, 2016–2017, 34 650, no. 2, 16.01.2017, Proposal for an Act by Members of Parliament Bergkamp, Yücel and Van Tongeren to change the General Act on Equal Treatment to elaborate on the prohibition to discriminate on the basis of sex. In Belgium, only gender identity and gender expression were added to the Non-discrimination Act in 2014. Intersex conditions are subsumed in the category 'transgender individuals'. See P. Cannoot, 'Let it be: Het recht op persoonlijke autonomie van personen met intersekse/DSD' (2017) 41(2) *Tijdschrift voor Seksuologie* [special on intersex/DSD].

30 e.g. CRM Oordeel 2014-78, 01.07.2014.

31 Letter of the government to the President of the Second Chamber regarding sex registration, 23.12.2016, no. 2025993.

seventh position in the ILGA annual Rainbow Map.[32] One of the reasons that the Netherlands has been overtaken, according to the former minister, is the lack of legislation regarding the prohibition of medically unnecessary surgery on babies with ambivalent genitalia. Nevertheless, the steps referred to by the minister in her letter to regain the Dutch ranking do not include any plans regarding this issue. But the political climate seems favourable to the advancement of the interests of intersex/DSD individuals. Given the recent decision by the Limburg court, there will undoubtedly be further debate. So, who knows what steps the government may be lobbied or nudged into taking in order to restore its competitive position on the Rainbow Map?

---

32 See *Kamerstukken II*, 2016–2017, Emancipatiebeleid, no. 257, above n. 28, p. 6.

THE LEGAL STATUS OF INTERSEX PERSONS IN FRANCE

Benjamin Moron-Puech*

1. INTRODUCTION

Attention to intersex persons[1] in French legislation and regulation dates back to 1970 when an administrative instruction tried to deal with the issues raised by the birth of an intersex person.[2] Since then, not much has happened, as French politicians either did not perceive this as a problem, or, more recently,

* I would like to thank Geneviève d'Ardailhon Miramon, Marjolein van den Brink and Jens M. Scherpe for the language review and also for the very helpful comments on earlier versions of this text.

1 In this chapter, the terminology 'intersex person' is used in order to denominate the person who biologically does not fit with the male and female biological stereotype. The expression 'intersex person' doesn't say anything about the acceptance of such identity by the person concerned.

2 In this administrative instruction it was decided to allow the parents of an intersex child not to declare any sex for a brief period. For the detail of this instruction, see below. Before that, this question only appeared in very rare case law related either to the change of an intersex civil status from male to female (or its reverse) or else to the validity of marriage, as in the famous judgment rendered by the *Cour de cassation* in 1903: Req. 6 avr. 1903, *DP* 1904, I, 395, concl. Baudouin; *S.*, 1904 p. 273 obs. A. Wahl.

clearly did not want to deal with the issue.[3] However, recently, some ministerial questions were asked[4] and some official reports were published. In February 2017, both the Senate[5] and Human Rights Defender (ombudsman)[6] issued reports on the situation of intersex persons. Public statements were also made by French officials, the most important by the President of the French Republic on 17 March 2017, in which he called for 'a ban on surgeries performed on intersex infants which is increasingly regarded as a mutilation'.[7] So far, these developments have not been not followed by legislative change. When the Senate had the opportunity to deal with the problems that intersex persons encounter regarding their sex marker/civil status, it refused to do so.[8] This apparent lack of political interest led an intersex individual to decide, with the help of lawyers (including the author of this chapter), to turn to the courts in order to ask the judges whether or not it was possible for an intersex person to be registered with a neutral sex in France.[9] The reason for this approach was that unlike politicians, courts have to answer the questions they are asked, even the *Cour de cassation*,[10]

---

3 See e.g. the amendments that had been presented by Senator Rachel Mazuir during the discussion of the Bill *Modernisation of the Justice System for the 21st century*, in order to include intersex persons in the scope of art. 61-5 et seq. of the French Civil Code (dealing with the change of sex marker/civil status). None of these amendments were seriously considered by the other senators. See B. MORON-PUECH, 'Les personnes intersexuées dans le projet de loi sur la justice au XXIe s. ?', *Intersexes et autres thèmes juridiques*, <https://sexandlaw.hypotheses.org/49> (last accessed 20.09.2017).

4 See question n° 48696 asked in the National Assembly by Gwendall Rouillard and questions n°s 1276S and 18533 asked in the Senate by the Senators Maryvonne Blondin and Rachel Mazuir.

5 <http://www.senat.fr/notice-rapport/2016/r16-441-notice.html> (last accessed 24.05.2018).

6 <https://juridique.defenseurdesdroits.fr/doc_num.php?explnum_id=16177> (last accessed 24.05.2018).

7 <https://yagg.com/2017/03/19/une-ceremonie-a-lelysee-en-lhonneur-des-actrices-et-acteurs-lgbt/>, (last accessed 24.05.2018). The relevant part of the speech can be seen at the 12th minute of the video.

8 During the review of the Bill *Modernisation of the Justice System for the 21st century*, 3 amendments related to this topic were debated (Amendements COM-30, -31 and -33; Sénat, Nouvelle lecture, Travaux en commission, session du 21 sept. 2016, <http://www.senat.fr/rap/l15-839/l15-8391.pdf> (last accessed 24.05.2018)). The first one intended to clarify that the new procedure related to the change of sex marker was not only available for trans persons, but also for intersex persons. The second one aimed at prohibiting the disclosure of the sex marker when this was not strictly necessary, so that intersex persons would be protected from discrimination regarding their registered sex. The third one was meant to make clear that the new procedure regarding the modification of the sex marker did not replace the procedure of rectification of sex marker. However, none of these amendments were taken into account. On this, see MORON-PUECH, above n. 3.

9 In this chapter, the word 'sex' and not 'gender' is used when talking about the sex registered in civil status registers. French law uses the word sex and not gender in this situation, even after the *Act of Modernisation of the Justice System for the 21st century*, which in November 2016 regulated the change of the sex registered at birth. Also, by using 'sex' the link to biological characteristics is made clearer.

10 This obligation derives from art. 4 of the French Civil Code.

which is one of the French Supreme Courts.[11] However their hopes were dashed by that court on 4 May 2017.[12] On that day, the *Cour de cassation* held, for the first time ever in France, that no special sex marker could be granted to intersex individuals: 'neutral' (*neutre*) was deemed not to be available as a legal sex marker concerning civil status. Very recently, the same court also issued a judgment where it refused an intersex person the right to access to a criminal court on the basis of the limitation period.[13]

Today in France, intersex persons encounter two types of major problems in their daily life: infringements of the right to bodily integrity (on which see Section 2 below) and infringements of the right to respect for their private life (on which see Section 3 below).

2. RIGHT TO BODILY INTEGRITY

Like many other legal systems, French law protects bodily integrity. Protective provisions have been laid down both in the Constitution and in other laws. Article 16-3 of the Civil Code states that

> There may be no infringement of the integrity of the human body except in case of medical necessity for the person or exceptionally in the therapeutic interest of another.

This prohibition is also guaranteed by the Criminal Code which says it is an offence to infringe the bodily integrity of someone else. Constitutional protection derives especially from a non-written principle, the principle of dignity, which was 'discovered' by the Constitutional Council in 1994.[14]

These legal protections apply to everyone, including intersex persons. Arguably, this right should be understood in such a way that intersex children cannot be subjected to medical acts which only aim at 'normalising intersex bodies' in accordance with medical standards of male and female. Indeed, as I have tried to demonstrate elsewhere,[15] such acts of 'normalisation' do not serve any therapeutic necessity, since intersex conditions as such cannot

---

[11] In France, there is a Supreme Court for private law (the *Cour de cassation*), a Supreme Court for public law (the *Conseil d'État*) and a Supreme Court for constitutional law (the *Conseil constitutionnel*).

[12] <https://www.courdecassation.fr/jurisprudence_2/premiere_chambre_civile_568/531_4_36665.html> (last accessed 24.05.2018).

[13] Cass. crim. 6.04. 2018, n° 17-81.777 <https://www.legifrance.gouv.fr/affichJuriJudi.do?&idTexte=JURITEXT000036718214> (last accessed 24.05.2018).

[14] <www.conseil-constitutionnel.fr/decision/1994/94343_344dc.htm> (last accessed 24.05.2018).

[15] B. Moron-Puech, 'Le droit des personnes intersexuées. Chantiers à venir' *La Revue de Droit de l'Homme* 11/2017, available at <https://revdh.revues.org/2815> (last accessed 20.09.2017).

be necessarily classified as a disorder requiring treatment,[16] and indeed the treatments performed have never proven their efficiency in preventing or diminishing the psychological sufferings of intersex persons.

However, many normalisation operations are performed routinely in France,[17] and this has been replaced by the UN in 2016.[18] Moreover, some policies actually encourage or allow infringement of the bodily integrity of intersex persons. An administrative circular of 2011 encourages parents to perform the appropriate medical treatment on intersex children, in order to determine their sex, which is classified as 'indeterminate' until that time.[19] A ministerial decree of 2006, modified in 2008,[20] created a 'referral centre for rare diseases regarding sexual development' and appointed as head of this centre a doctor, P. Chatelain, who positively advocates for non-therapeutic surgery on intersex children.[21]

The regulation that governs the reimbursement of medical costs allows parents and hospitals to ask for reimbursement of costs made for normalising surgeries from the social security funds. Indeed, the Common Classification of the Medical Act contains a list of all medical procedures that can be reimbursed. Chapter 8.7.1. of this document, entitled 'correction of sexual ambiguities', includes some of the medical treatments performed on intersex persons, most of which lack any medical purpose.

---

16 Admittedly, there are some intersex conditions that require immediate medical treatment, but not because they are intersex conditions but because of the severe health consequences they bring with them.

17 In her response to a question asked by Senator M. Blondin, the Secretary of State for Social Affairs, M. Touraine, acknowledged that approximately 160 intersex children were born in France every year and most of them undergo medical treatments (*JO Sénat*, 10.02.2017, p. 2485, <https://www.senat.fr/questions/base/2015/qSEQ15101276S.html> (last accessed 20.04.2018)). However, those numbers do not include children with hypospadias conditions, who are also often considered as intersex persons and subjected to normalisation surgery. Yet the frequency for hypospadias is now around 1% (*Reproduction et environnement*, INSERM, Expertise collective, p. 11, fig. 1.1.), that is to say 8,000 births per year in France.

18 See the 3 reports by various UN committees: Comité pour l'élimination de la discrimination à l'égard des femmes, 'Observations finales concernant les septième et huitième rapports périodiques de la France', CEDAW/C/FRA/CO/7-8, 22.07.2016, §17, (f); Comité des droits de l'enfant, 'Observations finales concernant le cinquième rapport périodique de la France', CRC/C/FRA/CO/5, 23.02.2016, §47; Comité contre la torture, 'Observations finales concernant le septième rapport périodique de la France', CAT/C/FRA/CO/7, 10.06.2016, §34.

19 §55 of the administratif circular, <http://circulaires.legifrance.gouv.fr/pdf/2011/11/cir_34124.pdf> (last accessed 20.04.2018). Parents are given 1 or 2 years to do so. This implies that this time is not only used to medically determine the sex of the children (through hormonal or genetic tests). It is also used to 'normalise' the body of the child.

20 Arrêté du 29 mai 2008 modifiant l'arrêté du 12 juillet 2006 portant labellisation de centres de référence pour une maladie rare ou un groupe de maladies rares, <https://www.legifrance.gouv.fr/affichTexte.do?cidTexte=JORFTEXT000018934074> (last accessed 20.04.2018).

21 See e.g. M.-F. Callu and P. Chatelain, 'Aspects médico-juridiques des défauts du développement sexuel à la naissance', in *Mélanges en l'honneur de G. Mémeteau*, LEH, Tome 2, 2015, pp. 471–480.

Finally, because these medical interventions nevertheless are seen by the Ministry of Finance as having a therapeutic purpose, hospitals and doctors are exempted from the value added tax for their services, in accordance with Article 132(1)(b) of the 2006 Directive on value added tax.[22]

Recently, however, some French institutions have started to raise concerns about these medical practices. In December 2016, the DILCRAH[23] published a document in which it asked for a ban of the cosmetic surgery performed on intersex persons. The document recalls that

> France has been condemned three times this year [2016] by the UN: in January by the Committee on the Rights of the Child, in May by the Committee Against Torture and in July by the Committee on the Elimination of Discrimination against Women. When they are not justified by medical reasons, those surgeries are mutilations and must stop.[24]

In February 2017, both the Human Rights Defender[25] and the Senate[26] delivered reports in which they more cautiously raised concerns about those medical practices. For instance, the Human Rights Defender recommended improving the information and training of medical practitioners on intersex issues, which implies that this agency believes that these practitioners are nowadays not correctly informed and trained on these issues. The Human Rights Defender also recommended that medical practitioners should review their current medical consensus in order to take into account the 'precautionary principle'. That is another way of saying that currently doctors are not considering sufficiently the risks and consequences faced by children that are subjected to normalising surgery. Also, by promoting the creation of a compensation fund, the Human Rights Defender seems to recognise that intersex persons may have been subjected in the past to wrongful acts.

---

22 Council Directive 2006/112/EC of 28 November 2006 on the common system of value added tax. The ECJ has for instance specified that the notion of 'care', used in Art. 132(1)(b), excluded cosmetic surgery and only applied to therapeutic surgery (ECJ, *Skatterverket v. PFC Clinic AB*, 2013/03/21, nº C-91/12, §29). On this topic see C. Cousin, 'Au cœur de la fiscalité indirecte des actes médicaux : l'enjeu de la définition de la thérapeutique', *Revue de droit sanitaire et social*, janv. 2018, 81–90.

23 DILCRAH stands for 'Délégation interministérielle à la lutte contre le racisme, l'antisémitisme et la haine anti-LGBT'. It is an inter-ministerial agency in charge of, in particular, the discrimination faced by 'LGBT'.

24 DILCRAH, *Plan de mobilisation contre la haine et les discriminations anti-LGBT. La république mobilisée contre la haine et les discriminations anti-LGBT*, 21.12.2016, p. 25.

25 Défenseur des droits, avis nº 17-04, 2017.

26 Délégation aux droits des femmes du Sénat, *Variations du développement sexuel: lever un tabou, lutter contre la stigmatisation et les exclusions*, 2017, http://www.senat.fr/notice-rapport/2016/r16-441-notice.html (last accessed 24.05.2018).

These developments so far have not changed medical practice[27] nor initiated a process of legal reform. Thus, a significant gap continues to exist between the general principle of bodily integrity, applicable to every person including intersex individuals, and the application of this principle in practice. The dogmatic idea prevailing in France that only two sexes exist, leads the institutions involved in the normalising medical treatments performed on intersex children to be blind to the potential infringement of the right to bodily integrity. Hopefully, this can change if the criminal procedure that was started more than a year ago is successful,[28] or if both the French Council of State and the National Consultative Ethics Committee were to advocate for a ban on unnecessary treatments on intersex children, as is expected in the upcoming report they will publish on the current changes in bioethics laws.[29]

3. RIGHT TO RESPECT FOR PRIVATE LIFE

French law protects the right to respect for private life both in its legislation and in its Constitution. Article 9 of the Civil Code has stated since 1970[30] that '[e]veryone has the right to respect for his private life'. Regarding the Constitution, the French Constitutional Court, the *Conseil constitutionnel*, ruled in 1995[31] that the right to respect for private life derives from the right to individual liberty that in turn derives from Article 2 of the Declaration of the Rights of Man and the Citizen of 1789. Recently the *Conseil constitutionnel* clarified that

> the collection, registration, storage, consultation and disclosure of personal data must be justified by a reason of general interest and carried out in a manner which is adequate for and proportional with this objective.[32]

It is argued here that despite this legal protection the right to respect for private life of intersex persons is currently violated in France, since there is no sex

27 See for instance the latest guidelines issued by the French High Autority of Health who still continue to advocate for surgeries on intersex children and an unfair information to their parents. (HAS, *Protocole national de diagnostic et de soins. Insensibilités aux androgènes*, 11 janv. 2018, <https://www.has-sante.fr/portail/upload/docs/application/pdf/2018-01/pnds_ais_version_finale.pdf> (last accessed 24.05.2018)).

28 <http://www.20minutes.fr/societe/2172971-20171126-personne-intersexuee-depose-plainte-contre-medecins-operee-devenir-homme> (last accessed 10.01.2018). This case is different than the one previously mentioned, above n. 13.

29 B. Moron-Puech, 'Les demandes des personnes intersexuées entendues par le CCNE et le Conseil d'État', *Intersexes et autres thèmes (juridiques)*, 2018, <https://sexandlaw.hypotheses.org/375> (last accessed 24.05.2018).

30 Loi n° 70-643 du 17 juillet 1970 tendant à renforcer la garantie des droits individuels des citoyens, Art. 22.

31 CC, n° 94-352 DC, 18 janvier 1995, cons. 3, Rec. p. 170.

32 CC, n° 2012-652 DC, 22 mars 2012, cons. 8, Rec. p. 158.

marker available for intersex to be identified other than in the male and female categories (on which see Section 3.1. below). Furthermore, intersex persons are often compelled to disclose their sex whereas it creates for them a risk of discrimination (on which see Section 3.2 below).

3.1. NON-RECOGNITION OF NON-BINARY SEX MARKERS

On 4 May 2017, the *Cour de cassation* decided that French law does not allow the registration in the civil status of a neutral sex marker. Before that it was at least theoretically possible that a third option was available. The state of the law before this decision will be discussed (Section 3.1.1) and then the law as it stands after this decision (Section 3.1.2).

3.1.1. French Law before the 2017 Decision of the Cour de cassation

There is no provision in the Civil Code that states that male and female are the only sexes that can be registered. Article 57 of the Civil Code merely states that the sex of a child has to be registered. It does not clarify 'sex'. Therefore, the legal question was how Article 57 has to be interpreted, i.e. which sex markers can be used on the civil status registry, especially at birth registration.

To answer this question, one can look at other legal texts. Some provisions (including Article 1 and 3 of the French Constitution) use expressions such as 'both sexes', 'two sexes' or 'man and woman', all of which seems to exclude intersex. Since 1970,[33] an administrative circular has stated that when the sex of the child is 'uncertain', one should avoid entering 'indeterminate sex' on the birth certificate, and rather ask doctors what sex (male or female) should be entered. However,

> if the doctor, in exceptional circumstances, thinks he is not able to give any indication on the foreseeable sex of the child, but if it will be possible in a year or two to definitely determine the sex, the district attorney can authorize that no sex be recorded on the birth certificate.[34]

33 *Instruction du 19 févr. 1970 modifiant l'instruction générale relative à l'état civil*, *JORF*, 28 avr. 1970, art. 228*b* (<https://www.legifrance.gouv.fr/jo_pdf.do?id=JORFTEXT000000701857&pageCourante=03866>, (last accessed 24.05.2018). The new text can be found in the *Circulaire du 28 octobre 2011 relative aux règles particulières à divers actes de l'état civil relatifs à la naissance et à la filiation*, §55 (<http://circulaires.legifrance.gouv.fr/pdf/2011/11/cir_34124.pdf> (last accessed 24.05.2018)).

34 This is apparently used in practice. The author was told by the French National Institute for Statistics and Economic Research that in July 2017, 28 persons were registered in the national directory of natural persons (RNIPP) as 'i' and not 'M' or 'F' ('i' denominating indeterminate), with the oldest child in that group being born in 2013. Between 2013 and February 2017 there were 53 persons born and registered with an 'i' in the RNIPP.

Therefore, one could conclude that French law does not recognise intersex persons since the absence of a sex marker or the specification that sex is 'indeterminate' is only provisional, and that Article 57 of the Civil Code should be understood as allowing only male and female markers.

However, apart from the administrative circular which will be looked at later, none of these provisions is related to civil status as such, and none of them were written with the situation of intersex people in mind. When the Civil Code was written in 1804, lawyers thought, based on the medical knowledge of their time, that 'real hermaphroditism' did not exist. In their view, there were only male and female 'pseudohermaphrodites', who could be considered as male and female. Therefore, it was logical for them not to draft rules for those intersex persons who would have met the standard of 'real hermaphrodism' and to stick to two genders.[35] But today it is scientifically established that 'real hermaphrodism', exists, which implies that if the writer of the Civil Code had to draft these provisions today, they presumably would not ignore intersex persons as they did in the past. Therefore, using an historical and evolutionary method of interpretation instead of a literal one leads to the conclusion that the Civil Code could nowadays be interpreted as allowing a third sex marker for intersex persons.

Applying the method of 'conform interpretation' also supports this conclusion. According to this method, when a text is ambivalent, preference should be given to the meaning that conforms with superior norms. Arguably, the only interpretation consistent with international law is the one that allows a recognition of a neutral sex.[36] Also, more and more international institutions have explicitly acknowledged the right for intersex persons to be identified with a non-binary sex marker. For instance, the Parliamentary Assembly of the Council of Europe, in the Resolution 2048 (2015), calls on Member States to 'consider including a third gender option in identity documents for those who seek it'.[37] In 2017, the same Assembly not only asked Member States to consider such options, but also to 'ensure, wherever gender classifications are in use by public authorities, that a range of options are available for all people, including those intersex people who

Sometimes this 'i' marker in the RNIPP in the birth registration is understood to a positive 'indeterminate' marker, sometimes as a 'no sex' marker. For more data and analysis, see L. Hérault (dir.), *État civil de demain et transidentité*, mai 2018, pp. 243–252, <http://www.gip-recherche-justice.fr/wp-content/uploads/2018/05/15-24-Rapport-final_%C3%89tat-civil-de-demain-et-transidentit%C3%A9_mai-2018.pdf> (last accessed 24.05.2018).

35 E. Wilhelm, 'L'hermaphrodite et le droit', *Revue d'anthropologie criminelle*, 1911, p. 205 et seq., <https://sexandlaw.hypotheses.org/308> (last accessed 24.05.2018).

36 For detailed analysis, see B. Moron-Puech, 'La mention du sexe sur les documents d'identité : Par-delà une binarité obligatoire' *Journées d'étude 'Dimension sexuée de la vie sociale : État civil, genre et identité'*, June 2016, §6-21, <https://hal.archives-ouvertes.fr/hal-01374403> (last accessed 10.01.2018).

37 *Discrimination against transgender people in Europe*, §6.2.4. <http://assembly.coe.int/nw/xml/XRef/Xref-XML2HTML-EN.asp?fileid=21736> (last accessed 24.05.2018). *Adde* the report published by the Council of Europe Commissioner for Human Rights, *Human rights and intersex people*, 2015, <https://rm.coe.int/16806da5d4> (last accessed 24.05.2018).

do not identify as either male or female'.[38] The same goes for the European Union where, in 2015, the Fundamental Right Agency observed that 'Gender markers in identity documents and birth registries should be reviewed to better protect intersex people'.[39] Moreover, the European Court of Human Rights has recently clearly stated, in the case of *A.P., Garçon and Nicot v. France*, that everyone has a right to self-determine their gender identity, on the ground of Article 8 of the European Convention on Human Rights.[40] This decision could be understood to imply that intersex persons who do not fit in the female and male categories should be allowed to be recognised with another sex/gender marker. Arguably, this would otherwise be contrary to the concept of self-determination.[41] That is why the method of 'conform interpretation' potentially could lead to an interpretation of Article 57 of the Civil Code that allows the recognition of sex markers other than male or female. It is by using this method of interpretation that, in the case that led to the decision of the *Cour de cassation* on 4 May 2017 (discussed below), the lower court allowed the plaintiff to use a neutral sexed marker.[42]

That said, such an interpretation of the Civil Code is contrary to the wording of the above-mentioned administrative circular of 1970. However, one should not give too much attention to this circular, as the problem it addresses falls within the exclusive competence of the legislator[43] who is in charge of the Civil Code. Therefore, the rules stated in this administrative circular should not be taken into consideration if they are not in conformity with the interpretation of a legislative text, i.e. Article 57 of the Civil Code.

For all these reasons, it was possible (until the decision handed down by the *Cour de cassation* on 4 May 2017, on which see below) to argue that in France, intersex persons could be recognised in the civil register as neither male nor female. However, apart from a small number of scholars,[44] this view

---

38 Resolution 2191 (2017), *Promoting the human rights of and eliminating discrimination against intersex people*, §6.3.3. <http://assembly.coe.int/nw/xml/XRef/Xref-XML2HTML-en.asp?fileid=24232&lang=en> (last accessed 10.01.2018).

39 *The fundamental rights situation of intersex people*, <http://fra.europa.eu/sites/default/files/fra-2015-focus-04-intersex.pdf> (last accessed 24.05.2018).

40 ECHR, 06.04.2017, <http://hudoc.echr.coe.int/fre?i=001-172556>, §93. The Court uses in French the expression 'identité sexuelle' which, literally translated, means 'sexual identity'. However, if one looks at the translation of this expression in the case *Y.Y. v. Turkey*, the expression was (more appropriately) translated as 'gender identity'.

41 Rappr. B. Moron-Puech, 'Le droit des personnes intersexuées', *Socio*, vol. 9, 2017, pp. 215–237, §12, <http://journals.openedition.org/socio/2983> (last accessed 10.01.2018).

42 TGI Tours, 20 août 2015, <http://www.pitcho.fr/site/wp-content/uploads/2015/10/Cliquez-ici-pour-la-d%C3%A9cision-du-TGI-Tours-20-ao%C3%BBt-2015.pdf>.

43 Art. 34 of the French Constitution: 'Act of Parliaments lay down regulation concerning [...] the status or capacity of natural persons'.

44 See also M.-X. Catto, 'De la neutralité biologique à la masculinité juridique. Note sur la qualification de la Cour d'appel d'Orléans, le 22 mars 2016', (2016) *RDLF*, chron. n° 18, <http://www.revuedlf.com/personnes-famille/de-la-neutralite-biologique-a-la-masculinite-juridique-note-sur-la-qualification-de-la-cour-dappel-dorleans-le-22-mars-2016/> ; 'Intersexualité : binarité des sexes, médecine et droit' (2016) *RDSS*, p. 928 et seq.

did not have much support. For instance, it cannot be found in the reports of the French public authorities who reflected on this subject. The name of the DICLRAH itself does not mention intersex (it only refers to LGBT) and the DILCRAH action plan on the promotion of the right of LGBT persons only calls for a stop of mutilation of intersex children; nothing is said about their legal sex.[45] The reports of the French Senate and Human Rights Defender do not engage with the issue. The Human Rights Defender considered that the recognition of a third sex is a political question, for which he has no jurisdiction,[46] and the Senate, without taking a position on this issue, only said that the acknowledgement of a third sex cannot be established without full and thoughtful consideration of its consequences.[47]

In any event, the decision of the *Cour de cassation* of 4 May 2017 for the time being brought to an end the possibility of interpreting Article 57 of the Civil Code as described in this section.

3.1.2. French Law after the 2017 Decision of the Cour de cassation

On 4 May 2017, for the first time in French legal history, a court decided that 'French law does not allow the inscription, in the civil status record, of a gender marker other than male or female'.[48] It also ruled that this state of law was not contrary to Article 8 of the European Convention on Human Rights (ECHR) since 'the duality of the sex markers in civil status pursues a legitimate aim because it is needed for the social and legal organization of which it constitutes a founding element'. And the Court added that

> the acknowledgment by the judge of a neutral sex would have a profound impact on French legal rules, that were built upon the duality of sexes and it therefore would require many coordination changes of statutory provisions.[49]

---

45 DILCRAH, *Plan de mobilisation contre la haine et les discriminations anti-LGBT. La république mobilisée contre la haine et les discriminations anti-LGBT*, 21.12.2016, p. 25.

46 Défenseur des droits, Avis 17-04, p. 11 : '*Sans se prononcer sur une question qui appartient aux décideurs politiques*, etc. '.

47 Sénat, *Variations du développement sexuel : lever un tabou, lutter contre la stigmatisation et les exclusions*, pp. 86–88.

48 '[L]a loi française ne permet pas de faire figurer, dans les actes de l'état civil, l'indication d'un sexe autre que masculin ou féminin' : Cass., 1re civ., nº 16-17.189, ECLI:FR:CCASS:2017:C100531, <https://www.courdecassation.fr/jurisprudence_2/premiere_chambre_civile_568/531_4_36665.html> (last accessed 24.05.2018).

49 '... la dualité des énonciations relatives au sexe dans les actes de l'état civil poursuit un but légitime en ce qu'elle est nécessaire à l'organisation sociale et juridique, dont elle constitue un élément fondateur ; [...] la reconnaissance par le juge d'un "sexe neutre" aurait des répercussions profondes sur les règles du droit français construites à partir de la binarité des sexes et impliquerait de nombreuses modifications législatives de coordination'.

According to the *Cour de cassation*, all those elements mean that it is not contrary to Article 8 of the ECHR to refuse the applicant the right to use a neutral sex marker.

Regarding the first part of the decision, the refusal of a neutral sex in French law, an explanation of such affirmation may be found in a document exterior to the decision, but published by the Court itself: the press release.[50] Indeed, the press release, which is not written by the judges who wrote the decision, says that 'the duality of sex is mentioned in many statutory provisions evoking "one or other sex" (Article 388 of the Civil Code defining the minority of the child) or "both sexes" (Article L. 131-1 of the Education Code on compulsory education'). The press release also states that the question of 'intersexuality' (*sic*) was not addressed by the Parliament in the above-mentioned Act of Modernisation of the Justice System for the 21st century. This conveys the impression that the Court did not feel that the law allowed a sex marker other than male and female.

However, in the decision itself the judges of the *Cour de cassation* do not give reasons why their conclusion is the right one. This is a very common practice in the French legal system, where judges usually feel they should not explain their decisions as this it might diminish the authority of their judgment.[51]

In the second part of the decision (where the Court reflects on the conformity of French law with international law), the *Cour de cassation* is a bit more explicit on its legal reasoning. As already mentioned above, according to the Court

> the duality of sex markers in civil status have a legitimate purpose since it is necessary for the social and legal organisation, to which it constitutes a fundamental element; the acknowledgment by the judge of a neutral sex would have a profound impact on French legal rules, that were built upon the duality of sexes and it therefore would require many coordination changes of statutory provisions.[52]

Much of this reasoning is open to criticism, not least with regard to the interpretation of Article 8 ECHR. However, since the purpose of this chapter is to explain the current state of French law, it must be sufficient to say that,

---

50 <https://www.courdecassation.fr/IMG///Communiqu%C3%A9%20Sexe%20neutre%20et%20%C3%A9tat%20civil.pdf> (last accessed 10.01.2018).

51 F. Malhière, *La brièveté des décisions de justice*, Dalloz, Nouvelle Bibliothèque de Thèses, 2013.

52 In French: 'si l'identité sexuelle relève de la sphère protégée par l'article 8 de la Convention de sauvegarde des droits de l'homme et des libertés fondamentales, la dualité des énonciations relatives au sexe dans les actes de l'état civil poursuit un but légitime en ce qu'elle est nécessaire à l'organisation sociale et juridique, dont elle constitue un élément fondateur ; que la reconnaissance par le juge d'un "sexe neutre" aurait des répercussions profondes sur les règles du droit français construites à partir de la binarité des sexes et impliquerait de nombreuses modifications législatives de coordination'.

disappointingly, the Court does not even discuss the interests and situation of the plaintiff. The only thing the Court says about the claimant is that they are male according to the appellate court. Nothing is said about the pain and the difficulties they will encounter because of this non-recognition of their gender identity, and the fact that they will have to suffer from the use of an inappropriate sex marker in many situations in daily life, whenever they will be asked to identify themselves.

It is also important to note that the decision of the *Cour de cassation* is only relevant for judicial courts (and thus legal status changes). Administrative courts may hold a different position on this question, especially when dealing with the question of gender markers on identity documents.[53] Indeed, one has to recall that, according to a regulation of the European Union,[54] it is possible to have an 'X' marker on one's passport. Administrative courts could therefore take into account this Regulation and allow other gender options on identity documents other than birth certificates.

3.2. THE OBLIGATION TO DISCLOSE ONE'S LEGAL SEX

Even though gender identity and sex characteristics belong to the private sphere in principle, in practice one is often required to reveal one's legal sex. This happens every time one has to show a passport or ID, since the rules governing those official documents prescribe a sex marker, which has to be the one written on the birth certificate.[55] The same applies, for example, to the electronic card that allows people to benefit from the third-party payment system for healthcare costs (the '*carte VITALE*').[56]

This state of law and practice is arguably not in conformity with the constitutional requirements regarding privacy, according to which

> the collection, registration, storage, consultation and disclosure of personal data must be justified by a reason of general interest and carried out in a manner which is adequate for and proportional with this objective.

---

53 B. Moron-Puech, 'Rejet du sexe neutre : une "mutilation juridique" ?', *Rec. Dalloz*, 2017, pp. 1404–1408.

54 See Council Regulation (EC) No 2252/2004 of 13 December 2004 on standards for security features and biometrics in passports and travel documents issued by Member States, Annex, n° 2, which refers to the Doc. 9303 of ICAO, a document which allows an 'X' marker.

55 Décret n° 2005-1726 du 30 déc. 2005 relatif aux passeports, art. 1 ; Décret n° 80-609 du 31 juill. 1980 portant création d'un système de fabrication des cartes nationales d'identité au ministère de l'intérieur, art. 3.

56 Art. R. 161-31, al. 2, 1° of the Social Security Code which states that this card has to mention a number whose first figure refers to the sex: 1 for male and 2 for female (décret n°82-103 du 22 janvier 1982 relatif au répertoire national d'identification des personnes physiques, art. 4).

Yet very often there is no general interest at stake. For instance, one can hardly see why it is necessary to mention one's sex marker when applying for social housing. Also, even when such a general interest in using legal sex for identification purposes potentially may exist, it is not necessarily the most efficient mechanism for these purposes. For instance, using the sex marker on the ID is not a very efficient way of truly identifying a person, particularly when in this day and age social physical appearance can be altered and thus the appearance may be different from that designated by the sex marker on the identification documents. Biometric data, such as photos, height or fingerprints, may be more reliable than the sex marker. So, arguably, when balancing the right to respect for private life of an intersex person with the general need for having one's legal sex revealed in identification and travel documents, the former should prevail as there are other mechanisms available for identification. Moreover, while most persons may be comfortable with having to reveal their legal sex in those situations (or they simple do not care), this will not apply to all persons, irrespective of whether they are intersex, trans or cis-gender.

4. CONCLUSION

The situation of intersex persons in France clearly is unsatisfactory. Essentially, they are being ignored by the law or, as in the case heard by the *Cour de cassation* outlined above, their rights have to take a backseat compared to fairly abstract general concerns. Moreover, normalising surgery still is being practised, and not enough is being done to deal with these very serious violations of the rights of the persons concerned.

Hopefully, those problems encountered by intersex persons will be dealt in the future. The tools are available for this, especially the possibility of challenging legal norms before the European Court of Human Rights[57] or the *Conseil constitutionnel* that interfere with the rights of intersex persons.

It is to be hoped that reducing the gap between the fundamental rights of intersex persons and its concretisation in France is just a matter of time. It is further to be hoped that legal issues surrounding intersex will be tackled by the new President of the French Republic, so that intersex persons do not have to wait too long for the respect of their right to bodily integrity and to private life.

---

[57] Indeed, the person who was subject of the *Cour de cassation* proceedings above has lodged such a complaint.

BETWEEN RIGHTS AND PRAGMATISM: INTERSEXUALITY BEFORE THE COLOMBIAN CONSTITUTIONAL COURT

Ruth Rubio-Marín and Stefano Osella

1. INTRODUCTION

Often ignored by the law, intersexuality has been the subject of numerous decisions by the Colombian Constitutional Court. For more than 20 years now, this court has discussed the issue of sexual diversity, producing a consistent legal framework for practitioners, activists and intersex people. Such a framework, interestingly, was developed through the interpretation of general constitutional provisions – such as those aimed at protecting dignity (Article 1 *Constitución Política*, henceforth CP), the free development of the personality (Article 16 CP) and the right to equality (Article 13 CP). Moreover, the Constitutional Court has demonstrated a significant will to engage with a difficult area of law from an interdisciplinary angle, relying not only on traditional medical sources, but also on critical theory and activists' insights.

To set the Court's activity in context, we must recall that the model of medicalisation applied to intersexuality, as we know it today and as it has come to be gradually – *de facto* – challenged by the Colombian Constitutional Court, was developed in the mid-1950s in the United States, essentially under the scientific direction of the psychologist Dr. John Money and his team. According to him, what we now call gender identity seemed to be independent from physical characteristics and be the result of different stimuli, including education and social models, which influenced the development of the individual at the early stages of life.[1] Among these stimuli, genitals were given a paramount importance.[2] In Money's understanding, any conflict among the stimuli – primarily, genitalia deviating from established standards of maleness and femaleness (henceforth, non-normative or diverse) – could trigger misalignments with the attributed social gender – what one may call now a 'trans condition' – which was perceived as a risk to psychological health.[3] Normalisation – so to say – of non-normative genitalia was thus prescribed.[4] After the initial gender assignment based on the interpretation of biological markers, came surgical and hormonal therapies, aimed at giving a more usual look to the intersex anatomy.[5] Additionally, practical considerations also played a determinant role in gender assignment – especially with biological males – in consideration of the technical limitations to phallus reconstruction. Boys for whom masculinisation was not a viable option would be reassigned to the feminine gender and subject to consistent treatments.[6] All these therapies were prescribed to take place within the first 18 months at the latest.[7] Further 'confirming' treatments could follow later in life.[8] Parents were advised to keep the initial condition of intersexuality secret, even to the child, who was to be reared in the newly attributed gender.[9]

This practice, which still seems to be applied in many situations today, came to be subject to numerous criticisms. Gender neutrality at birth, and the possibility to artificially shape gender identity through the discipline of the different stimuli lost persuasiveness.[10] Moreover, the prescribed treatments have been reported to cause diminished sexual sensation, sexual dysfunction, psychological distress,

1 The present section heavily relies on: J. Repo, *The Biopolitics of Gender*, Oxford University Press, 2015; K. Karkazis, *Fixing Sex: Intersex, Medical Authority, and Lived Experience*, Duke University Press, 2008.

2 Repo, above n. 1, p. 34.

3 Ibid.

4 We want to specify at the outset that the term 'normalisation' is used in this chapter very critically, to contest the idea of body normality by highlighting the artificiality through which it is achieved.

5 Karkazis, above n. 1, p. 56.

6 Ibid.

7 J. Money, J. Hampson and J. Hampson, 'Hermaphroditism: Recommendations Concerning Assignment of Sex, Change of Sex, and Psychological Management' (1955) 97 *Johns Hopkins Medical Bulletin* 284, 288.

8 A. Domurat Dreger and 'Ambiguous Sex or Ambivalent Medicine? Ethical Issues in the Treatment of Intersexuality' (1998) 22 *The Hastings Center Reports* 24, 28.

9 Repo, above n. 1, p. 40.

10 M. Diamond and H.K. Sigmundson, 'Sex Reassignment at Birth: Long-Term Review and Clinical Implications' (1997) 151 *Archives of Pediatric and Adolescent Medicine* 298.

chronic pain and, often, loss of reproductive potential.[11] The validity of parental consent for treatments to be implemented in early childhood has also been criticised and the cultural stigma against sexual diversity,[12] the atmosphere of medical urgency and pressure to proceed fast to the treatments, the rhetoric of illness/healing attached to intersexuality[13] have been all considered as factors limiting the freedom and genuineness of consent.

Challenges to orthodoxy are largely to be attributed to intersex activism, with its roots in the 1990s and deeply indebted to the figure of Bo Laurent (at the time known as Cheryl Chase), the founder of the Intersex Society of North America. The central aim of intersex activism has been to 'return control of their bodies to people with an intersex condition',[14] by stopping the practice of bodily normalisation. The way in which this objective is to be achieved proved less straightforward, as some have advocated for a complete moratorium on intersex surgeries. Others – settling on a 'middle ground' – have opposed all life-altering and sexual impairing treatment on intersex children, yet also claimed that, sometimes, not administering treatment may be more traumatic than the treatment itself, and thus consider the need to defer to the discretion of parents, on condition that they are fully educated on the pros and cons of the treatments.[15] Less consensus has been gathered around the aspiration to obtain a 'third-gender' legal category recognised in the law. While, undoubtedly, some voices have been raised in that direction, others would rather concentrate on general patterns of discrimination against sexual diversity, without the need to

---

11 See the *Clinical Guidelines for the Management of Disorders of Sex Development in Childhood*, developed by the Consortium on the Management of Disorders of Sex Development in 2006, and the detailed scientific bibliography there provided. Also, see P.A. Lee, A. Nordenström, C.P. Houk, S. Faisal Ahmed, R. Auchus, A. Baratz, K. Baratz Dalke, L.M. Liao, K. Lin-Su, L.H.J. Looijenga III, T. Mazur, H. Meyer-Bahlburg, P. Mouriquand, C. Quigley, D.E. Sandberg, E. Vilain, S. Witchel and the Global DSD Update Consortium, 'Global Disorders of Sex Development: Updated Since 2006: Perceptions, Approach and Care' (2016) 85 *Hormone Research in Paediatrics* 158. Also, S. Osella, '"Harmonic Bodies": Intersex Persons, Corrective Treatments, and Gender Violence in Italian Law. A Research Proposal' in A. Lorenzetti and M.F. Moscati (eds.), *LGBTI Persons and Access to Justice*, Wildy, Simmons and Hill, 2015.

12 Karkazis, above n. 1, p. 180.

13 J.D. Hester, 'Intersex(es) and Informed Consent: How Physicians' Rhetoric Constrains Choice' (2004) 25 *Theoretical Medicine and Bioethics* 21, 39. There are some forms of intersexuality which may present risks to the physical health, and even life, of intersex people, which then require urgent treatment (Consortium on the Management of Sexual Development, Clinical Guidelines for the Management of Disorders of Sex Development in Childhood (2006) 5–7). This chapter is not concerned with them, but only with the treatments intended to deal with the psycho-social aspects of sexual diversity.

14 This very fortunate expression is borrowed from J. Greenberg, 'Health Care Issues Affecting People with an Intersex Condition or DSD: Sex or Disability Discrimination?' (2012) 45 *Loyola of Los Angeles Law Review* 849, 862.

15 J.A. Greenberg, 'International Legal Developments Protecting the Autonomy Rights of Sexual Minorities. Who Should Determine the Appropriate Treatment for an Intersex Infant?', in S. Sytsma, *Ethics and Intersex*, Springer, 2006, pp. 87–90.

have a third-gender legal category assigned. This includes especially those who reject the identitarian ascription to the intersex category.[16]

This, in short, provides the background against which the Constitutional Court of Colombia has been operating. Indeed, responding to a sequence of writs of *amparo*,[17] the Court has been confronted with a wide spectrum of issues starting with the medical reassignment of children which it has banned altogether.[18] As to the normalisation of children's non-normative genitalia – in cases which do not involve gender reassignment – the Court has declared it permissible on the condition of 'qualified, informed, and persistent' parental consent, to address the context of social and cultural hostility against intersexuality.[19] In fact, such treatments, the dangers of which are not ignored, must be even funded by the national healthcare system when parents are not capable of sustaining the cost themselves.[20] Moreover, the time available for substituted consent has been limited to the age when intersex persons reach conscience of their own gender identity and body.[21] Finally, even though the Colombian legal system is still based on the sexual binary (since no alternative to the male and female gender has been introduced), the Constitutional Court has carved a small exception allowing intersex persons to register as neither male nor female[22] and specifically acknowledged the importance of recognising non-binary identities, inviting the legislator to come up with new solutions.

This chapter provides an updated systematisation and analysis of the jurisprudence of the Constitutional Court of Colombia. It places intersex people at the centre of its concerns, and tries to connect the issues of intersex people to the outcomes delivered by the Court itself. The chapter analyses this case law in the following way. Section 2 refers to the prohibition of involuntary sexual reassignment while Section 3 describes the case law about 'qualified, informed, and persistent' parental consent for other forms of normalisation. Section 4 examines the conditions for 'assisted consent' of the minor whereas Section 5 examines the rules on registration of intersex children. The chapter concludes with a summary of the doctrinal elements that have shaped this case law.

---

16 J.A. Greenberg, *Intersexuality and the Law: Why Sex Matters*, New York University Press, 2012, p. 94.

17 The Constitution of Colombia, at Art. 86, grants to each citizen the right to lodge an 'action of *tutela*' (*amparo*) to claim the protection of their fundamental rights.

18 Corte Constitucional, Sala Séptima de Revision, 23.10.1995, sentencia T-477/95, M.P. Martinez Caballero.

19 Corte Constitucional, Sala Plenaria, 12.05.1999, SU-337/1999, M.P. Martinez Caballero.

20 Corte Constitucional, Sala Quarta de Revisión, 20.10.2003, sentencia T-1021/03, M.P. Cordova Trivino.

21 Ibid; also, Corte Constitucional, Sala Quinta de Revisión, 27.11.2002, sentencia T-1025/02, M.P. Escobar Gil.

22 Which the administrative authority narrowly implemented as simply providing for a fast-track for gender reclassification.

2. PROHIBITION OF INVOLUNTARY SEXUAL REASSIGNMENT

The first decision of the Colombian Constitutional Court on intersex treatments dates back to 1995, a time when Money's medical protocols were only beginning to be questioned. A puppy had bitten off the genitalia of his young master: a six-month-old baby. Following standard medical procedures, the boy was assigned to the feminine gender, provided with 'adequate' genitalia, while the parents were instructed to raise the little one in accordance with the new gender. When, later, the boy[23] – who had, in the meantime, been placed in an orphanage – conflicted by the feminine identity ascribed to him, found out what happened, he lodged a writ of *amparo* against the authorities that had taken part in his gender reassignment procedure, asserting that his constitutionally protected human dignity and autonomy had been violated.

In addressing the claim, the Constitutional Court firstly stated that at the time of medical genital reassignment procedure there had been no urgent threat to the life of the child, thus excluding the competence of the doctors to make the decision by themselves.[24] In doing so, the Court challenged the commonly perceived urgency of normalising treatments, taking a first step towards the de-legitimising medical intervention to normalise bodies that do not fit the gender binary.

Although the Court accepted the possibility of parental consent regarding some medical interventions depending on the urgency of the treatment, the seriousness of its effects, and the age of the child,[25] the Court rejected it for gender reassignment. Arguing that children are neither their parents', nor society's, property, the Court referred to sex as a 'non-modifiable feature of the identity of each person, so that only that person is entitled – with full knowledge and after adequate information – to consent to gender reassignment'.[26] For the Court, human beings cannot be the subject to 'de-personalising' experiments, nor can their identity be transformed because one gender is thought to be more appropriate for them. In sum, no external intrusion (be it from doctors, judges or parents) can be allowed in one person's gender identity.[27]

Doctrinally, the Court relied on the right to identity as a manifestation of the dignity of the individual (Article 1 CP), and on the right to autonomy and free development of one's personality (under Article 16 CP). The right to identity,

---

23 We refer to the plaintiff as a boy because – as it emerges from the decision – he identified as such. We refer to the actors throughout this chapter relying – to the best of our knowledge – on gender self-definition.

24 Corte Constitucional, Sala Séptima de Revision, 23.10.1995, sentencia T-477/95, §12.

25 Ibid, §13.

26 Ibid, §13.1.

27 Ibid, §13.1.

said the Court, characterises persons as a self-determining, self-possessing and self-governing being, who are the masters of their own deeds.[28] Moreover, such a right to identity enjoys greater protection when it pertains to a child, to whom the Colombian Constitution grants special protection, as the rights of children are a 'superior legal interest' (Article 44 CP).[29]

The literature denounced some inner tensions running throughout the decision. On the one hand, the decision was said to portray sex as 'natural, essential and non-modifiable', while – on the other hand – it implicitly recognised a right to gender self-reclassification.[30] Also, disregarding feminist or critical theory, the decision lumped together the cultural and biological elements of the categories of sex and gender.[31] In spite of this, the decision bestowed great weight on individual self-definition as pertains to gender identity, implicitly admitting a connection between gender and social rules which can be challenged by self-definition. It also addressed a deeply disconcerting practice, namely the reassignment of children to the female gender essentially for practical purposes, which, especially after the late David Reimer case (generally known as the 'John/Joan' – case), to which the facts of the case at hand were remarkably similar.[32]

All in all, the protection which the Court granted intersexuals by denying parental or medical authority to proceed with gender reassignment of intersex children constitutes a crucial step forward, even if it represents an affirmative – rather than a transformative – form of protection: individual consent and self-definition (related to sexual and gender identify) are brought to the fore, rather than the full acceptance of situations of sexual diversity and gender rebellion.

3. LIMITS TO 'NORMALISING' TREATMENTS: CONDITIONS ON SUBSTITUTED CONSENT

Gender reassignment of intersex children was banned altogether after this decision. Nevertheless, the approach adopted by the Constitutional Court towards other forms of surgical treatment of intersex children has been more nuanced and could be framed as a 'middle ground' approach. Thus, in its decision

28 Ibid §15.1.

29 Ibid §16.

30 L. Céspedes-Báez and J Sarmiento-Forero, 'Como Mira el Estado: Constitucion y Compromisos de Genero del Estado Colombiano' (2011) 13 *Estudios Socio-Juridicos* 389, 406.

31 Ibid.

32 On the history of David Reimer, the child whose penis was negligently cut off and subsequently raised as a girl by his parents, under the advice of Money's team, and subsequently transitioned to the male gender, see Diamond and Sigmundson, above n. 10, and also J. Colapinto, 'The True Story of John/Joan', *Rolling Stone*, 11 December 1997, pp. 54–97.

SU-337 of 1999,[33] the Constitutional Court determined the requirements for a mechanism of what we could call 'reinforced parental consent', a mechanism which was not conceived as a moratorium on intersex normalisation but rather as facilitating information and encouraging reflection and critical thinking, to enable mature, long-term and reasoned decision-making. With this standard, the Constitutional Court struck a balance between the free development of an intersex child and the principle of welfare – which requires doctors to act in the best interest of their patient (in what some have seen as a potentially paternalistic interference with individual autonomy)[34] – in an area, such as intersex surgery, characterised by extreme complexity.[35] Interestingly, this judgment is the first by the Court that acknowledges and problematises the social and cultural elements of gender determination and intersex normalisation explicitly relying on critical gender and intersex theory.

At the root of the problem and the writ of *amparo* leading to the decision was a mother who had unsuccessfully asked doctors to perform feminising surgery on the seven-year-old daughter with virilised genitalia. According to the mother, the girl's right to equality (Article 13 CP), free development of the personality (Article 16 CP), reinforced by the special protection that the Constitution grants to children (Article 44), were all at stake. Without the surgery – the mother argued – the sexual development of her daughter would be abnormal, and this would affect her psychophysical health.[36]

To reach an adequate understanding of the matter, the Court relied on copious expertise, seeking clarification on intersexuality as a physical condition as well as on the complexities of surgeries on non-normative genitalia. Then, the Court's attention shifted to normalising treatments, with a close eye on their justificatory psycho-social rationales, about which the expert testimonies differed considerably. Some of the experts – the majority, as the Court acknowledged[37] – insisted on the importance of early normalising treatments

---

33 Corte Constitucional, SU-337/1999, above n. 19.

34 J. Herring, *Medical Law and Ethics*, 2nd ed., Oxford University Press, 2008, p. 24.

35 On this, the literature is abundant. See D.P. Tovar, 'Desarollo Jurisprudencial de la Intersexualidad: Consentimiento Informado, Infancia, y Derechos' (2013) 47 *Debate Feminista* 76; P. Gonzalez Sanchez, C. Velazquez Acevedo and S.P. Duque Quintero, 'Problemática Juridica de los Statos Intersexuales. El Caso Colombiano' (2010) 23 *Iatreia* 204; G. Maldonado Colmenares and S. Delgado Maldonado, 'Menores con Ambigüedad Genital: Un Análisis del Consentimiento Informado desde el Punto de Vista del Concepto de Corporalidad', in B. Espinosa Pérez (ed.), *Cuerpos y Diversidad Sexual. Aportes Para la Igualdad y el Reconocimiento*, Editorial Pontificia Universidad Javeriana, 2008, p. 96; C. Velásquez Acevedo, P. González Sánchez and I.C. Sarmiento Echeverri, 'Principios y Derechos Involucrados en el Análisis Jurídico de los Estados Intersexuales in Pacientes Menores de Edad en Colombia – El Caso del Hermaphroditismo' (2007) XLIV *Estudios de Derecho* 219.

36 Ibid, §2.

37 Ibid, §II.3.

to allow for the development of a consistent gender identity and to ensure stable psycho-social well-being.[38] Other expertise, solicited by the Court,[39] on the contrary, underscored the lack of conclusive evidence showing the benefits of early medical treatments.[40] In particular, Dr. Alice Domurat-Dreger, historian and leading expert on intersexuality, underscored the high level of uncertainty and disagreement within the medical community while Milton Diamond, Professor of Anatomy at the University of Hawai'i and also a renowned expert on the subject, characterised normalising treatments as 'cosmetic' and supported assigning a gender to the infant without subjecting them to normalising treatments, if not strictly justified by concerns about their physical health.[41] A similar opinion was expressed by Bo Laurent (known then as Cheryl Chase), Executive Director of the Intersex Society of North America, for whom the 'only justification for normalizing treatments [was] the undemonstrated belief that they may contribute to the psychological wellbeing of the individual'.[42] Stressing the irreversibility and potential physical and psychological drawbacks of normalising treatments, Bo Laurent insisted on the need to provide psychological support to the family instead, and petitioned the Constitutional Court not to allow such treatments on children but rather wait for them to become adolescents able to express their own consent.[43] Along similar lines, other experts emphasised that it is the cultural bias, according to which 'newborn babies are either baby boys or girls' which causes negative family and social consequences, also in consideration of the 'masculinist social context' where a new-born intersex baby may be born.[44] In light of this all, they argued, there were good reasons to doubt the genuineness of parental consent, understood as free and informed consent.[45] Finally, still other experts embraced a middle way, recommending the assistance of a multidisciplinary team and a case-by-case analysis, without rejecting the normalising approach altogether.[46]

The Court positioned itself in the middle too, accepting that genital diversity *per se* does not represent a threat to the health or life of individuals, and that it is mostly psycho-social reasons that are at the root of normalisation.[47]

---

38 See e.g. the consultation given by the director of the psychology department of the University of Los Andes (§I.17.1). See also (§I.10.4); and (§I.15.1). For more mature children, a greater weight is to be given to psychological factors, such as self-identification (§II.38).

39 Ibid, §19.

40 Ibid, §17–19.

41 Ibid, §I.19.3.

42 Ibid, §I.19.1.

43 Ibid. We want to mention the seminal article of C. Chase, 'Hermaphrodites with Attitude: Mapping the Emergence of Intersex Political Activism' (1998) 4 *GLQ: A Journal of Gay and Lesbian Studies* 189.

44 Corte Constitucional, SU337/1999, above n. 19, §I.17.3.

45 Ibid, §I.12.

46 Ibid, §I.15.2; and §I.17.2.

47 Ibid, §II.29–36.

For the Court, the ultimate rationale behind intersex treatments is to be found in the 'idea' that only two genders exist, and that parents may find it frustrating, even traumatising, to have a child who does not belong to either.[48] This said, recognising the high level of complexity of the debate and the diverse voices within it, the Court also refused to take clear sides, arguing that this would fall outside of its sphere of competence.[49] Instead, the contested nature of the debate supported a prudent attitude. In so doing, the Court acknowledged the potential risk of provoking serious and irreversible harm;[50] stressed that, beneficial or not, there was no doubt that such treatments are physically invasive and irreversible;[51] and, finally, insisted on their likely effects on the sexual identity of the person, and hence, on the impact on the right to free development of the personality (Article 16 CP) which conceives of the individual as an autonomous and self-governed being.[52]

In view of this, what was the form of consent required? In principle, nothing short of the informed consent of the patient – however young – was necessary:[53] indeed, the prevalence of the principle of beneficence along with parental consent, could not suffice, especially since what 'is best for the patient' is not unproblematic when it comes to intersex normalising treatments, controversial, non-urgent and invasive as they are.[54] In spite of this, the Court was not willing to turn a blind eye to the fact that in real-life scenarios

> postponing the surgeries may entail problems due to the culture of intolerance that informs our relationship to sexual diversity. Persons whose genitals are ambiguous may have to face a hostile social and familiar environment, which could in fact affect [their] psychological development.[55]

In the light of this, the Court underlined that the complete prohibition of surgeries, however justified in theory, could encourage families to look for back-alley treatments to correct what they perceived to be a physical defect, or else, provoke the rejection of the child and the deprivation of parental love.[56]

In building the constitutional architecture of the case, the Court suggested the that the complete ban of surgeries could affect family privacy as a sphere of autonomy (Articles 5 and 42 CP),[57] which could thus said to be in tension with the right to free development of one's personality of the intersex child

48 Ibid, §II.36.
49 Ibid, §II.67.
50 Ibid, §II.69.
51 Ibid.
52 Ibid, §II.39.
53 Ibid, §II.41.
54 Ibid, §II.69.
55 Ibid.
56 Ibid.
57 Ibid, §II.76.

(Article 16 CP) as well as the special protection to be granted to the child.[58] In so doing, the Court accepted the family to be not only the essential cell of society, but also a *locus* of diversity and pluralism, a unit of central weight in the Colombian Constitution.[59] At the same time, the Court held that the trauma caused by the birth of an intersex baby could *per se* be a reason to doubt the parents' capacity of judgement. In their decision, parents could be guided by 'prejudices and fears'[60] which could ultimately affect the right to non-discrimination of the child (Article 13 CP).[61]

In the end, the Court struck a balance by raising the standards of parental consent, requiring it to be not only *informed*, but also *qualified* and *persistent*. For the Court, such a consent must be characterised by a provision of adequate information, which includes an account of the current state of the medical debate and the divisions within it, the complexity of intersexuality and the risks of correcting it. It must also be expressed in a language which is most adequate to the cultural level of parents with doctors making sure that they understand.[62] Parents must not simply receive the objective details about the condition of intersexuality, but also the psychological support they may require handling the emotional shock.[63] The consent is to be given in several steps, and protracted throughout a longer time-frame as well as in writing.[64] Clearly, this does not represent a complete moratorium of surgeries: in spite of the complex procedure to achieve the consent, families are still given the last word, an attitude the legal scholarship has referred to as '*in dubio pro familia*'.[65]

Moreover, the Court was keen on specifying, that the qualified, informed, and persistent consent can be given by parents only until the child reaches the age of five, when – according to the studies relied on by the Court – children usually form a defined gender identity and consciousness of their own bodies. In fact, the child in the specific case was already seven years old, and – hence – over such a critical threshold.[66] Because of this, in the case at hand, the Court could not simply allow the externally imposed normalisation.[67]

---

58 Ibid, §II.77.

59 Arts. 7, 8, and 70 CP.

60 Ibid, §II.79.

61 Ibid.

62 Ibid, §II.82.

63 Ibid.

64 Ibid, §II.90.

65 O.A. Caro Garzón, 'Hermaphroditas en Colombia: Estudio de la Jurisprudencia Constitucional' (2010) 5 *Revista Eletrônica Direito e Política* 218, 235.

66 Because the child had a right to her own say, the Court ordered the creation of an interdisciplinary team – including not only medical practitioners but also a psychologist and a social worker – with the purpose of helping the child and her mother to reach a decision on the debated normalisation. Ibid, §II.88.

67 Ibid, §II.91. The presence of a fixed age-limit was criticised within legal scholarship, which wished for a more flexible approach that could take into consideration the characteristics of

In subsequent case law,[68] the Court has further elaborated upon the requirements of parental informed, qualified and persistent consent. For the Court, the detailed information must include all the elements relevant to understand the choice: for example, the multidisciplinary medical team must inform the parents that a male or a female gender will be assigned in any event, without any necessary treatment; that normalising surgeries and hormonal treatments are just one among several alternatives; that such treatments are not an established routine operation, and that they are in fact an object of increasing debate within the medical community; that there is no convincing evidence that intersex children may benefit from surgery at an early age; that such treatments may cause significant physical and psychological drawbacks; and that often people with non-normative genitalia who were subject to surgery have come to think that they have been sexually mutilated.[69] Moreover, the consent must not only be informed but persistent, which means that it must be reiterated in time, to let parents recover from the emotional shock and take a more mature and reasoned resolution. Interestingly, the family must be given enough time to establish bonds of affection with the child, and only after is deemed prepared for giving the consent. The Court acknowledged that this may be in tension with the urgency typical of the normalising protocols: so, it will be up to the medical community to establish the appropriate time for reflection, in the light of the aforementioned criteria.[70]

Through the doctrine of 'informed, qualified and persistent consent' the Court seemed to find a compromise between the future vision it held for the Colombian society and the present reality it had to confront. The vision is clearly articulated in the SU-337 1999 judgment which literally claims:

> Intersexuality calls on our capacity for tolerance and constitutes a challenge to accept difference. Public authorities, physicians, and citizens, must make room for these persons, until now kept in silence [...]. We must all not only listen to them, and learn to live side by side, but also learn from them.[71]

The reality it had to confront is one in which parents must make choices that can deeply affect their children's destiny. By letting parents have the last word,

each case. See G. Maldonado Colmenares and S. Delgado Maldonado, 'Menores con Ambigüedad Genital: Un Análisis del Consentimiento Informado desde el Punto de Vista del Concepto de Corporalidad', in B. Espinosa Pérez, *Cuerpos y Diversidad Sexual. Aportes Para la Igualdad y el Reconocimiento*, Editorial Pontificia Universidad Javeriana, 2008, p. 133.

68 Corte Constitucional, Sala Séptima de Revisión, 02.08.1999, sentencia T-551/99, M.P. Martinez Caballero.

69 Ibid, §21. In similar terms, see also the decision Corte Constitucional, Sala Cuarta de Revisión, 16.09.1999, sentencia T-692/99, M.P. Gaviria Diaz; and Corte Constitucional, Sala Sexta de Revisión, 12.10.2000, sentencia T-1390/00, M.P. Martinez Caballero.

70 Corte Constitucional, T-551/99, above n. 68, §21.

71 Corte Constitucional, SU-337/99, above n. 19, §II.91.

yet at the same time, ensuring a procedure that helps them overcome ignorance, prejudice around sexual diversity as well as different forms of societal pressure, the Court provided the best protection it could think of to intersex children's free development of their personality and equality.

This decision attracted both praise and criticisms. The Intersex Society of North America praised it for 'significantly restrict[ing] the ability of parents and doctors to resort to the scalpel when children are born with atypical genitals', and highlighted its effort to contextualise the cultural roots of intersex surgeries and the call for the evolution of cultural norms which – back then as, *mutatis mutandis*, today – impose normalisation.[72] Legal scholar and expert on intersexuality Julie Greenberg called it 'a wise decision', in light of the different considerations that had to be weighed against each other.[73] On the other hand, sociologist Morgan Holmes stressed what, in fact, evidently emerges from the decision is that family privacy ultimately is given prevalence over the physical integrity of children, and that the practice of intersex surgery is insufficiently condemned.[74] Finally, it is hard to deny that not all families share the same sensitivity on intersex treatments, thus fragmenting the protection granted by the Court to intersex children.[75] Be that as it may, it seems undeniable that the Constitutional Court engaged in an analysis never carried out before and introduced a deep analysis of intersexuality within the law: a fundamental step towards the protection of intersex children.

4. ASSISTED CONSENT FOR MATURE CHILDREN

An effective protection of individual autonomy and equality requires the attribution of relevance to the lived and felt gender of the individual, especially in a jurisdiction, such as Colombia, which recognises the right to gender identity.[76] It follows that, together with the need to take into account the urgency of the treatment and the impact or the risk of the treatment on the current and future autonomy of the child, the age and maturity of the child also play a role in the case-by-case analysis that determines the sufficiency of parental consent. Thus,

---

72 International Society of North America, Press Release, 25 October 1999, 'Colombia High Court Restricts Intersex Genital Mutilations', available at <http://www.isna.org/search/node/pictures%20of%20intersex?from=74> (last accessed 22.05.2018).

73 Greenberg, above n. 15, 98.

74 M. Holmes, 'Deciding Fate or Protecting a Developing Autonomy? Intersex Children and the Colombian Constitutional Court', in P. Currah, R.M. Juang and S. Price Minter (eds.), *Transgender Rights*, Minnesota University Press, 2006, p. 116.

75 Ibid, p. 117.

76 R. Rubio-Marín, and S. Osella, 'Gender Classification: Between Governance and Fundamental Rights' (forthcoming).

as already put forward in the decision SU-337/99, more mature intersex children are entitled to have a say on their own gender assignment and treatments.

In its judgment T-1025/02, the Court had the opportunity to fine-tune the standard of 'assisted consent' for such children and clarify that the doctrine of the decision SU-337/1999 is not absolute, but must be assessed in view of the specific circumstances of each case.[77] At stake was a five-year-old boy – hence, a boy who, age-wise, was mature enough following the terms established in the SU-337/99 decision, even though he had a slight intellectual disability – in relation to the treatments suggested by the doctors, and which he, with the support of his parents, was willing to undergo. The question concerned his capacity of consent.[78] For the Court, certain conditions applied procedurally. Firstly, as mentioned, a multidisciplinary team must be formed to support and inform the patient and the family. Secondly, any operation of normalisation must be based on a medical consensus about the adequacy of the solution. Thirdly, children – above the five-year threshold – must give their own consent after having been informed in terms that they can understand about the nature of the treatment and the existing alternatives. This must be done by taking into consideration their actual capacity of consenting, to be assessed by the multidisciplinary team. Finally, parents – when their child is mature enough to choose and gives their consent to the treatments in accordance with the medical opinion – have to conform to such opinion.[79]

As systematised in a subsequent decision, essentially a triad of steps will have to be considered: (1) parental consent; (2) the express wish of the child; (3) the view of a multidisciplinary – and not only medical – team, which includes also a social worker and a psychologist.[80] As concretely put by the Constitutional Court, after the multidisciplinary team has adequately psychologically supported and medically informed the family and the child, the latter is to be formally asked about his intentions. If the answer is favourable to the treatments, and coincides with the medical opinion, and the parents have been present throughout the procedure, the treatments can be put in place.[81] Yet, if the decision of the child differs from that of their parents, or the decision of the child and their parents differs from the medical recommendations of the multidisciplinary team, the treatments cannot be carried out.[82] While children's autonomy initially is protected from intrusive treatment, their positive freedom to deal with their own body is also reduced and balanced against the opinion of parents and doctors.

---

77 See Corte Constitucional, sentencia T-1025/02, above n. 21.

78 Ibid, §36.

79 Ibid, §63–67.

80 Corte Constitucional, Sala Tercera de Revisión, 18.09.2008, sentencia T-912/08, M.P. Cordova Trivino, §1.5.

81 Ibid, §2.4.2.

82 Ibid, §2.4.3.

The assistance of a multidisciplinary team with different medical specialists and psychological support becomes thus the key to valid consent. This can also be seen in a more recent case, that of a 12-year-old intersex boy who – having been classified as a female at birth – wanted to obtain medical treatments to confirm his male identification, with the support of his treating doctors and mother.[83] The Court recognised that the requirements of 'qualified, informed, and persistent' consent applied not only to the parents but to the consent expressed by mature children with the assistance of the multidisciplinary team and their parents.[84] In this case, the Court found that the consent expressed was not valid because the psychological support had not been offered and the view of one medical specialist was missing.[85] Needless to say, none of these precautions apply when the person is of age and all that is required is the ordinary informed consent for the correction of atypical genital anatomy.[86]

5. MALE, FEMALE OR NONE OF THE ABOVE? THE LEGAL REGISTRATION OF INTERSEX PERSONS

With the decision T-450A/2013, the Constitutional Court addressed the issue of the mandatory classification of individuals in the civil registries as males or females, and the relevance of this classification for enjoying civil status, and the legal positions connected to it. The case deals with a person whose sexual anatomy was very atypical and, therefore, doctors could not assign them a gender outright. The family, when applying for civil registration, saw the request rejected because the birth certificate did not specify the gender.[87] The rejection had significant consequences for the rights of the child, who was denied admission to healthcare facilities because they were not recorded as a Colombian national.[88] The parents brought the case for *amparo* in front of the

[83] Corte Constitucional, Sala Séptima de Revisión, 28.08.2014, sentencia T-622/14.

[84] Ibid, §2.6.3.2.

[85] Ibid, §2.6.3.3. For a queer-oriented critique of this case, see J.E. García León and D.L. García León, 'Sujetos Intersexuales y Matriz Heterosexual: Los Cuerpos Que Le Importan a la Jurisprudencia Colombiana; Una Lectura Queer' (2017) 52 *Latin American Research Review* 124, where the authors have interestingly discussed the change of language that characterised this decision vis-à-vis the landmark SU-337/99 decision. In particular, the Constitutional Court here recognised the cultural roots of intersex treatments: yet, there was no meaningful criticism of this cultural background, nor a hint at a more permanent change of society.

[86] Corte Constitucional, Sala Primera de Revisión, 30.04.2010, sentencia T-310/10. We must point out that this case is not classified as a form of intersexuality, but simply as a form of unusual genital anatomy.

[87] Corte Constitucional, Sala Secunda de Revisión, 16.07.2003, sentencia T-450A/13, M.P. Gonzalez Cuervo, §1.3.

[88] Ibid, §1.2.5.

Constitutional Court, alleging that the provisions and rights to an adequate living standard, to life in connection to health (Articles 44, 48, 49 and 50 CP), to personal and family privacy (Articles 15 and 42 CP), to social security (Articles 44 and 48 CP), to legal personality (Article 14 CP), as well as the provision on children's rights (Article 44 CP) had been infringed.[89]

In addressing the claim, the Court identified three main questions. The first legal problem to be examined was whether the non-inscription of a child, whose certificate of birth does not specify gender in view of medical disagreement about it, violates the right to be registered as a part of the right to legal personality under Article 14 CP.[90] Secondly, the Court asked itself whether the right to legal personality of the person born without a clearly determined sex is violated by the lack of options other than male and female in the registry.[91] The third question regards the access to healthcare by intersex persons and asks whether the right to health of intersex children is infringed by the omission of health authorities to offer special attention to intersex children who could not be registered in the civil registries.[92]

The Court begins its analysis by considering Article 14 of the CP, which states that all persons – that is, all individuals belonging to the human species, without distinction of sex, family background or condition[93] – have an equal right to the recognition of legal personality.[94] This right, the Court held, does not only entail recognising the individual as a subject of rights and obligations, but also the guarantee of some essential attributes of the personality – such as the name, residence, marital status, nationality and legal capacity – simply because of the very fact of existing.[95] These attributions are inalienable, non-renounceable and imprescriptible, and they last for the whole duration of the life of the individual.[96] Moreover, for the Court, there is a clear connection between the recognition of legal personality and protection of identity, 'legal personality [being] the dynamic version of identity'.[97] The right to identity is conceptually grounded in dignity, because it makes possible the recognition of the individuality of each person in society.[98] Also, the right to legal personality entails the recognition of all individuals as free and equal in that it is a precondition for the recognition of rights and duties.[99]

---

89 Ibid, §1.1.1.
90 Ibid, §2.1.
91 Ibid, §2.2.
92 Ibid, §II.2.
93 Arts. 33 and 74 of the Colombian Civil Code.
94 Corte Constitucional, sentencia T-450A/13, above n. 87, §II.4.1.
95 Ibid, §II.4.1.3.
96 Ibid, §II.4.1.4.
97 Ibid, §II.4.1.5.
98 Ibid.
99 Ibid.

The person's civil status, the Court claimed, has the function to demonstrate the legal capacity of individuals and builds upon facts, acts and elements of life, among which also sex.[100] It determines the individual's legal standing, what one can or cannot do; one's duties, rights and entitlements. A person's civil status as determined by the law is essential to receive benefits and to have a role in the welfare state, as the state must know of the physical existence of individuals, to provide for them.[101] The Court noticed that Colombia recognises only two genders, but also that this is not the only existing option: other countries, such as Australia, Nepal or Pakistan (and now, one could add, India[102] and Germany[103]), have moved beyond the binary and accept registration as 'other than' male-or-female.[104]

To answer the specific legal questions before it, the Court acknowledged the tension between – on the one hand – the interest of the state to identify citizens and register them in order to adequately place them within the state and the family and grant them constitutional rights, and – on the other hand – the right to identity, in general, and sexual identity, in particular.[105] Sex, the Court acknowledged, is a valid criterion of classification, essential for the institution of marriage and for the inclusion and special protection of women and mothers.[106] Nevertheless, the Court granted, there are persons who cannot be classified as men or women and to whom, in spite of this, fundamental rights cannot be denied. For these cases, the legislator is called to provide suitable rules. In the meantime, the Constitutional Court can set some criteria.[107] Sexual diversity, continues the decision, cannot be an obstacle for the determination of legal personality, to which persons are entitled because of their very existence, because of their dignity and equality. There is no justification to exclude children who are neither masculine nor feminine from registration.[108] In the specific case, in order to avoid a deficit of protection of intersex and genitally non-normative persons, endorsing one of the suggestions of Hazel Glenn Beh and Milton Diamond whose international expertise on intersexuality the Court solicited for this case,[109] the Court suggested that children who cannot be identified may be

100 Ibid, §II.4.2.2.

101 Ibid.

102 *National Legal Services Authority v. Union of India*, (2014) 5 S.C.C. 438.

103 BverfG, 1 BvR 2019/16 – Rn. (1–69).

104 Corte Constitucional, sentencia T-450A/13, above n. 87, §II.4.3.3.

105 Ibid, §II.4.5.2.

106 Ibid, §II.4.5.3. It is important to highlight that same-sex marriage was introduced in the Colombian legal system only with a judicial decision in 2016, hence, almost 3 years after this decision.

107 Ibid, §II. 4.5.3.

108 Ibid, §II.4.6.1 and 6.2.

109 H.G. Beh and M. Diamond, 'Individuals with Differences in Sex Development: Consult to Colombia Constitutional Court Regarding Sex and Gender' (2014) 29 *Wisconsin Journal of Law, Gender, and Society* 421, 435.

registered without ticking any of the boxes in the birth certificate and in the civil registry. A separate annotation on a sheet of paper stating the undetermined gender could be allowed but must be destroyed once gender is finally assigned.[110]

Regarding the access of intersex children to medical care, the Court clearly recognised that some intersex children are in need of medical attention, and some may indeed require some special treatment beyond that concerning their genital indeterminacy.[111] For the Court, under no circumstances can children be denied medical care because of irregularity in their identity papers,[112] and this applies, naturally, also to intersex children. The medical treatments which the Constitutional Court specifically spoke about are those intended to preserve the health and the life of intersex persons, as some intersex conditions may be associated with specific health risks.[113]

It is worth mentioning that the subsequent administrative implementation of the decision has not been totally faithful to the dictates of the Constitutional Court. Indeed, the *Registraduria Nacional del Estado Civil* (the office in charge of civil status registration) clarified that, should the birth certificate report the intersexuality condition, this would not be necessarily carried over to birth registries. Instead, parents were free to 'tick the box' (M/F) of their preference.[114] This model of – as one may call it – 'soft assignment' entails the possibility that the sex originally chosen by the parents can then be changed at the request of the person, once maturity is reached, or following a new diagnosis of sex made by interdisciplinary groups of medical specialists.[115]

Hence, a third-gender option has not been introduced in Colombia. The system of sex classification is therefore still binary. In spite of this, there is now a constitutional right for intersex persons not to be registered as males or females, and still be recorded in the civil registries and enjoy the benefits of citizenship. The most recent decision by the Constitutional Court on the matter contains a thorough analysis of alternatives to the gender binary under comparative and international law[116] and, even in the absence of any specific recommendation, highlighted the connection between the provision of legal alternatives to the gender binary in the public registries and the possibility of intersex persons to develop their own sense of identity and understanding of the self without the constraints of a predetermined and not necessarily welcome legal identity.[117] Perhaps an invitation for further solutions which are still to come.

110 Corte Constitucional, sentencia T-450A/13, above n. 87, §II.4.5.5.
111 Ibid, §II.5.3.
112 Ibid, §II.5.3.4.
113 Ibid, §II.5.3.2.
114 Registraduría Nacional del Estado Civil, Circular no. 33 of 24.02.2015, Art. 1.1.
115 Ibid, Art. 2.
116 Corte Constitucional, Sala Séptima de Revisión, 28.08.2014, sentencia T-622/14, M.P. Pretelt Chaljub.
117 Ibid, §2.5.3.

6. CONCLUSION

To summarise, regarding the treatment of intersex persons, the Colombian constitutional system has come a long way, relying for its interpretation on critical gender theory and taking into account the claims articulated by intersex activists. The Constitutional Court has had the leading role in this process confronting the theoretical foundations, the history, the – so often dire – consequences of normalising treatments, and the lack of genuine consent that often underlies the performance of such treatments. In light of these findings, and in a genuine effort to reach out to different voices, the Constitutional Court has subjected a largely dominant medicalised approach to strict conditions and has managed to put in place a mechanism that, albeit still imperfect, represents an important step forward in giving intersex people their bodies back.

A pragmatic attitude is the red thread connecting the Court's various decisions. While involuntary sex reassignment has been altogether banned, no moratorium has been placed on other normalising treatments. One can of course challenge the dogmatic foundation of the decisions that allow parental consent in such cases: is it really acceptable to claim family privacy to authorise what may be dangerous treatments on a child? On the other hand, can one simply ignore real-life scenarios and the reality of family and social rejection, as well as that of back-alley treatments that would undermine the psychological and physical well-being of many intersex children, if legal treatment options were totally denied? Since the dominant cultural bias against sexual diversity is so strong, the Colombian Constitutional Court opted, as a way out of the dilemma, for keeping treatments 'under the sun' and managed by professionals, but *de facto* strongly discouraged through well-specified conditions of qualified, informed and persistent substituted consent. At the same time, the Court has also been careful and pragmatic in spelling out the requirements for the consent of more mature children, who must be assisted so that their wishes but also their concrete capacity for decision-making are duly taken into account in procedures that involve their parents but also qualified and interdisciplinary professional teams. Finally, pragmatism has also been shown also in the solution offered to the challenge of the legal registration of intersex children: even though a third gender has not been introduced, the possibility not to register – at least temporarily – has been granted – so that the early anxiety to 'identify' has been, at least legally, removed. And even if this has been subject to a diverse – less protective, so to say – administrative implementation, and a certain gender is assigned at birth, easy reclassification later on may make the life of intersex persons significantly easier.

It is worth emphasising that in reaching its conclusions, the Constitutional Court of Colombia has paid a significant attention to the needs of intersex children, voiced by activists and academics, and has not limited its reach to the established medical protocols. The Constitutional Court clearly has made an effort to fill the knowledge-gap which way too often surrounds intersexuality. While some of its conclusions can be criticised for not going far enough, the serious engagement of the Constitutional Court has certainly delivered a unique constitutional corpus of decisions and brought a constitutionally grounded system of relief to intersex children. Importantly, the Constitutional Court, while never abandoning its pragmatic attitude, to its credit also has highlighted the cultural roots of intersex medical treatments, problematising approaches which had often been left unproblematised, and dared to express the wish – at least in some of its decisions – of a society where intersexuality is not an embarrassment, but something one may learn from.

APPENDIX

Sexual reassignment treatments at birth

Rule	Constitutional basis
Prohibited.	Right to identity, which finds a constitutional basis in dignity and free development of personality (Article 16 CP).

Normalising treatments (other than sexual reassignment) on children under the age of five

Rule	Constitutional basis
Allowed under the condition of parental qualified, informed and persistent consent: – Detailed and critical information, supported by a multidisciplinary team (including medical professionals, a social worker and a psychologist); – Authorisation given in multiple steps protracted over time; – Written form.	Free development of personality (Article 16 CP) and equality/non-discrimination (Article 13 CP), balanced against family privacy (Article 5 and 41 CP).

Normalising treatments (other than sexual reassignment) on children over the age of five

Rule	Constitutional basis
Allowed with the assisted consent of the child: – Detailed and critical information, supported by the multidisciplinary team (including medical professionals, a social worker and a psychologist); – Assisted by parental consent; – In line with medical prescriptions.	Free development of personality (Article 16 CP).

Legal registration of intersex children

Rule	Constitutional basis
Children who cannot be identified may be registered without ticking any of the boxes on the birth certificate and in the civil registry. A separate annotation on a sheet of paper will be permitted, and must be destroyed once gender is finally assigned.	Right to legal personality (Article 14 CP), and dignity and equality upon which it builds.

THE LEGAL STATUS OF INTERSEX PERSONS IN THE UNITED STATES

Julie A. Greenberg

1. INTRODUCTION

United States citizens typically possess a number of government-issued identity documents that contain a sex indicator. These documents may include a federally issued passport, a state-issued drivers' licence and a birth certificate that may be issued by the state, county or city where the person was born.[1] Each government

1 Some people may have more than these 3 government documents indicating their sex. e.g., students at state-run colleges or universities, government employees, veterans and individuals receiving government benefits may have additional government documents with a sex indicator.

entity issuing these documents operates independently and is governed by different statutes, rules and regulations.[2] Therefore, people who are transgender, intersex, or do not identify as either male (M) or female (F) may possess identity documents with inconsistent gender indicators.

Although transgender people have challenged legal restrictions on their ability to change an M to an F or an F to an M on their identity documents for decades, people who do not identify as either M or F have only recently challenged the rules limiting the gender indicator to the binary classifications of only M and F.[3] In 2016, a few individuals who identify as neither male nor female sought court orders allowing them to be legally recognised as a sex other than male or female. Many of the challenges have been successful, but court recognition of a non-binary sex marker has not led to abandonment of the binary system by state and federal agencies responsible for issuing and amending identity documents.

The current patchwork quilt US system, under which intersex people and people who do not identify within the binary sex classifications may have an M on one official document, an F on another, and an X/I on a third document, will likely remain intact until a court determines that denying someone the right to identify as something other than M or F is unconstitutional.

This chapter discusses the legal challenges that people who identify as neither male nor female have brought and examines the legal limitations on the ability to use a court order affirming someone's sex as non-binary to obtain amended identity documents. It then discusses the constitutional ramifications of denying someone the ability to identify as neither male nor female and concludes that government agencies that deny people the ability to self-identify as a sex other than male or female likely violate the United States Constitution's equal protection and substantive due process guarantees.

2. LEGAL CHALLENGES TO BINARY CLASSIFICATIONS

In 2016, an Oregon court issued an order affirming Jamie Shupe's right to identify as neither male nor female. Shupe, who was identified as male at birth, sought a court order affirming their[4] identity as neither male nor female.

---

2 On this, see J. Garland, 'The Legal Status of Transsexual and Transgender Persons in the United States', in J.M. Scherpe (ed.), *The Legal Status of Transsexual and Transgender Persons* (2015) 585–612, and especially the overview tables at 609–612.

3 Challenges before this time may have been brought, but they have not been publicly reported. According to one article, an intersex person successfully petitioned an Ohio court in 2012 to have their sex on their birth certificate read hermaphrodite. This case has not been publicly reported due to privacy reasons; M. O'Hara, 'Nation's First Known Intersex Birth Certificate Issued in NYC' <http://www.nbcnews.com/feature/nbc-out/nation-s-first-known-intersex-birth-certificate-issued-nyc-n701186> (last accessed 13.07.2017).

4 Throughout this chapter, the pronoun preferred by the person being discussed is used.

On 10 June 2016, the Court issued that order.[5] Despite this affirming court order, Shupe faced barriers to changing their gender marker on some of their identity documents. The US State Department refused to issue Shupe a passport with a non-binary gender marker.[6] The Army has not responded to Shupe's request to have an updated military card issued indicating their sex as non-binary.[7] Shupe received positive responses from the Oregon Department of Motor Vehicles (DMV) and the District of Columbia. The Oregon DMV notified Shupe that it was moving forward with drafting rules and procedures that would allow the DMV to issue drivers' licences and I.D. cards with a gender marker other than M or F[8] and the District of Columbia issued Shupe a new birth certificate that indicates sex is 'unknown'.[9]

Soon after Shupe received their court order recognising their sex as non-binary, a California Superior Court granted a similar order to Sara Kelly Kennan.[10] Kennan was born with an intersex condition that was hidden from her until she was 48-years-old when she discovered the truth through an internet search. When Kennan was born in New York City, her initial hospital records identified her as a male, but the sex marker was switched to female a few weeks later.[11] Kennan lived as a female and underwent surgery at age 16 to remove what doctors told her were her ovaries, but were really her testicles. At age 55, Keenan requested and received a California court order stating that her sex is intersex. After receiving this order, Kennan asked New York City to change the sex marker on her birth certificate to 'intersex'. In December 2016, New York issued her a new birth certificate with intersex as the sex marker.[12]

After the *Kennan* case, California became the first state to adopt legislation allowing people to use a non-binary gender indicator on their official documents.[13] In January 2018, the Washington State Department of Health adopted a rule allowing people who identify as non-binary to change the sex

---

5 M. O'Hara, 'Why Can't the Nation's First Legally Non-Binary Person Get an I.D?' <http://www.dailydot.com/irl/jamie-shupe-dana-zzyym-passport-state-department-gender/> (last accessed 13.07.2017).

6 Ibid.

7 Ibid.

8 M. O'Hara, 'Californian Becomes Second US Citizen Granted 'Non-Binary' Gender Status' <http://www.nbcnews.com/feature/nbc-out/californian-becomes-second-us-citizen-granted-non-binary-gender-status-n654611> (last accessed 27.01.2018).

9 M. O'Hara, 'Movement for Third Gender Option "Exploding" in U.S.' <http://www.nbcnews.com/feature/nbc-out/movement-third-gender-option-exploding-u-s-n696446> (last accessed 27.01.2018).

10 Ibid.

11 S. Levin, 'First U.S. person to have "intersex" on birth certificate: There's power in knowing who you are' <https://www.theguardian.com/world/2017/jan/11/intersex-rights-gender-sara-kelly-keenan-birth-certificate> (last accessed 27.01.2018).

12 Ibid.

13 SB-179: Gender identity: female, male, or nonbinary <https://leginfo.legislature.ca.gov/faces/billCompareClient.xhtml?bill_id=201720180SB179> (last accessed 27.01.2018).

designator on their birth certificates to 'X'.[14] News of Kennan's and Shupe's success led a number of other people who do not identify as male or female to begin the process of obtaining court declarations of their non-binary status.[15]

Dana Zzyym is the only person in the US to challenge the binary sex classification system in a federal court. Zzyym sued the State Department when it refused to issue them a passport because they had written 'intersex' rather than checking the F or M boxes on their passport application.[16] Zzyym was born with an intersex condition and the doctors initially left the sex designation on their Michigan birth certificate blank. After the decision was made to raise Zzyym as a male, M was placed on the birth certificate and Zzyym's intersex condition was hidden from them. Zzyym lived for 36 years as male and served four tours of duty in the US Navy. At age 36, Zzyym accepted that they did not identify as male. Zzyym then tried living as a female, but they were not comfortable living as a female either. Eventually, a urologist confirmed what Zzyym had always suspected; Zzyym was not born with a clear physiological sex. In 2011, Zzyym embraced their intersex identity and was able to have their Michigan birth certificate sex designator as male removed; the current birth certificate does not list any gender.

Later, Zzyym applied to the State Department for a passport and, on the application and supporting documents, indicated that their sex was intersex and that they wanted the sex on the passport to indicate 'X'. The State Department acknowledged that Zzyym qualified for a passport, but maintained that it was unable to issue a passport with a sex marker indicating anything other than M or F. It stated that it was willing to issue Zzyym a passport with an F marker based on Zzyym's Colorado drivers' licence or with an M marker if Zzyym provided a letter from Zzyym's attending physician indicating that Zzyym was male. Zzyym submitted a letter to the Department appealing its ruling and included sworn documents from two US Department of Veterans Affairs physicians who verified that Zzyym's sex is 'intersex'.[17] When the State Department refused to issue Zzyym a passport unless Zzyym was willing to have either M or F as their sex marker, Zzyym filed a lawsuit in the US Federal District Court in Colorado asserting that the Department's refusal to issue a passport with an 'X' gender marker violated the Administrative Procedures Act (APA) and the due process and equal protection guarantees of the Fifth Amendment.[18]

---

14 <https://www.doh.wa.gov/LicensesPermitsandCertificates/BirthDeathMarriageandDivorce/RuleMaking> (last accessed 19.05.2018).

15 See above n. 9.

16 *Zzyym v. Kerry*, 220 F.Supp.3d 1106 (D.CO 2016).

17 Ibid.

18 Ibid.

Under the APA, a court must 'hold unlawful and set aside agency action, findings, and conclusions' that it finds to be, among other things 'arbitrary, capricious, an abuse of discretion, or otherwise not in accordance with law'.[19] The Colorado District Court applied this standard to the State Department's decision-making process that led to its policy of refusing to issue a passport with X as the sex marker. The court found that the agency's process was not rational and the Department did not satisfy the Court that its actions were not arbitrary and capricious.[20] The Court remanded the issue to the State Department for reconsideration with the expectation that the Department would either issue the passport with an X marker or bring additional evidence to the Court that could support the Department's assertion that its decision-making process was rational. The Court issued its ruling in November 2016. In June 2017, the State Department notified Zzyym that it would not issue a passport with the requested gender marker. The Court reopened the case on 27 June 2017.[21]

3. THE PATCHWORK QUILT

People seeking affirmation of their non-binary gender on their official documents face a number of hurdles. Currently federal, and most state and local, laws do not acknowledge that sex is non-binary or mandate that administrative agencies must issue documents with markers other than M or F. Therefore, agencies do not have rules to guide them in the process. In addition, most government agencies do not currently have procedures to accommodate gender markers other than M or F. Therefore, some agencies may simply deny the request because of the lack of controlling law and the administrative burden they may assert it would impose.[22]

In addition, obtaining multiple identity documents can be a complex and cumbersome process. In our increasingly mobile society, people often reside in a state other than the state in which they were born. Therefore, they will need to apply to the state or city where they were born to change their birth certificate, their state of residence to modify their drivers' licence or identity card, and the US State Department to receive a passport.[23]

---

19 Ibid, quoting 5 U.S.C. §706(2)(A), (C).

20 Ibid.

21 M. O'Hara, 'Court Reopens Intersex Passport Lawsuit Against State Department' <https://www.nbcnews.com/feature/nbc-out/state-department-refuses-issue-intersex-passport-n776936> (last accessed 27.01.2018).

22 This was one of the arguments made by the State Department in *Zzyym*. *Zzyym*, above n. 16, at 1113–1114.

23 The laws governing the requirements to change a gender marker from M to F or F to M on birth certificates and drivers' licences vary widely by state. For a state by state summary, see <http://www.lambdalegal.org/know-your-rights/article/trans-changing-birth-certificate-sex-designations> (last accessed 27.01.2018).

Acquiring a court order similar to the ones Kennan and Shupe obtained may not cause a government agency to change the way it indicates sex on an official document. Kennan's court order acknowledged Kennan was intersex and Shupe's court order acknowledged that Shupe's sex was non-binary, but neither order directed an administrative agency to take any specific action. Thus, the effect of the order is unclear. As the Court of Appeals in Maryland stated in *Heilig* when it considered whether to allow a transgender person to change their sex marker from male to female:

> [T]he question may be raised, of what use is a judgment declaring that a person's gender has been changed if we do not specify the effect of such a judgment? The answer is that courts rarely specify the collateral effect of their judgments, unless it is raised as a justiciable issue. The question in a case, ordinarily, is simply whether a party is entitled to the judgment, not what the party may do with it. What effect a judgment has depends on the law governing what the judgment holder seeks to do, and that is true in this regard as well.[24]

The Kennan and Shupe court orders did not specifically address the laws and regulations that control the administrative agencies responsible for issuing identity documents. Although the California and Oregon DMVs will issue new drivers' licences with new gender markers, DMVs in other states may respond differently. A DMV could refuse to modify the sex marker on the drivers' licence after the issuance of an order like those in the Shupe and Kennan cases by noting that the order did not specifically mandate agency action and by citing its controlling rules and regulations that do not recognise a gender other than M or F. If a DMV refuses to modify the gender on the drivers' licence, litigating the validity of these policies could turn a simple petition into a lengthy legal proceeding.[25]

Using a court order to modify the sex on a birth certificate may be a more complex process than amending the sex on a drivers' licence, especially if the birth state is different from the state of the court issuing the order regarding the petitioner's gender. Although New York City voluntarily issued Kennan a new birth certificate indicating her sex was intersex after the California court issued its order, New York was not legally obligated to take any action based on the California decision. Generally, state courts do not have jurisdiction over an administrative agency's actions in another state. An administrative agency in one state is free to ignore the decision of a court in another state, especially if implementing the order would violate the first state's public policy.[26]

---

24 *In re:* Heilig, 186 A.2d 68, 84, n 10 (MD 2003).

25 The arguments in these cases would likely be similar to the arguments raised in *Zzyym*. *Zzyym*, above n. 16.

26 See *In re:* Heilig, above n. 24.

4. CONSTITUTIONAL CONSIDERATIONS

In addition to the APA cause of action, Zzyym asserted that the State Department's failure to issue them a passport with a non-binary gender marker violated their constitutional rights. The Court chose not to address the constitutional claims and limited its decision to the APA issues.[27] Therefore, no court has yet addressed the constitutional issues raised when a government agency refuses to allow a non-binary gender marker on a government document. Government agencies that refuse to recognise someone's sex as non-binary may violate the Equal Protection and Substantive Due Process clauses of the Fifth and Fourteenth Amendments to the Constitution.

4.1. EQUAL PROTECTION

4.1.1. Overview of Equal Protection

The purpose of the Equal Protection Clause is to ensure that the government does not subject its citizens to arbitrary classifications.[28] When the government treats different classes of people disparately, courts scrutinise the treatment under one of three levels of scrutiny, depending on the type of classification at issue.[29]

Under the Equal Protection Clause, courts subject most legislative classifications to the lowest level of scrutiny – rational basis review.[30] Under this minimalist review, a challenger must prove that the government did not have a legitimate governmental objective or that the government failed to use rational means to achieve a legitimate objective. Most government classification systems are upheld under rational basis review.[31]

---

27 Courts typically will rule on a narrower issue if possible rather than issuing a broader constitutional ruling. 'We are not yet at the point where this Court must venture into the constitutional fray.' *Zzyym*, above n. 16, at 1111.

28 *City of Cleburne v. Cleburne Living Ctr.*, 473 U.S. 432, 446 (1985); *Frontiero v. Richardson*, 411 U.S. 677, 683 (1973) (plurality opinion); *Reed v. Reed*, 404 U.S. 71, 71 (1971).

29 The Supreme Court has not specifically accepted a fourth level of review commonly referred to as 'rational basis with bite', but it has applied this type of more searching review to sexual orientation discrimination claims and claims by other groups who historically have suffered discrimination; *Windsor v. U.S.*, 699 F.3d 169, 180 (2nd Cir. 2012). 'The Supreme Court has not expressly sanctioned such modulation in the level of rational basis review; discussion pro and con has largely been confined to concurring and dissenting opinions. We think it is safe to say that there is some doctrinal instability in the area.' (*Windsor v. U.S.* this note, at 180–181).

30 *Mass. Bd. of Retirement v. Murgia*, 427 U.S. 307, 312 (1976).

31 See *Heller v. Doe*, 509 U.S. 312, 319–20 (1993); *FCC v. Beach Commc'ns, Inc.*, 508 U.S. 307, 313–314 (1993); *Williamson v. Lee Optical, 348 U.S.* 483, 488 (1955).

Courts apply the highest level of review, strict scrutiny, when the discrimination involves a suspect classification such as race, national origin and alienage.[32] Under strict scrutiny, the government must establish that it is using narrowly tailored means to further compelling governmental interests.[33] Few governmental actions survive strict scrutiny review.

Sex classifications are subject to an intermediate level of review, falling somewhere between the demanding requirements of strict scrutiny and the permissiveness of rational basis review.[34] Under this intermediate level of review, the government must prove an exceedingly persuasive or important justification for its classification system, and the means it uses to attain its goal must be substantially related to that important government purpose.[35]

4.1.2. *Binary Sex Classification Systems Should be Subjected to Intermediate Scrutiny*

When the government issues an identity document that requires a sex marker and it treats people differently depending on the sex indicator they request, the government is subjecting different groups of people to disparate treatment. In this case, it is allowing people who identify within the binary male-female system to use the identity marker of their choice and receive the desired identity document, while it is refusing that same right to people who do not identify within the binary sex classification system. By imposing this disparate treatment, the government is using a sex-based classification system that must pass intermediate scrutiny because it is treating people differently based on sex.[36]

Although some would argue that rational basis review should apply because the Supreme Court has not declared that people who do not identify within a binary sex classification system are a suspect class,[37] comparing this binary sex classification system to similar racial and religious classifications illustrates

---

32 See *Cleburne*, above n. 28, at 440; *Frontiero*, above n. 28, at 688 (plurality opinion).

33 *Gratz v. Bollinger*, 539 U.S. 244, 270 (2003).

34 *U.S. v. Virginia*, 518 U.S. 515, 523–24 (1996); *Miss. Univ. v. Hogan*, 458 U.S. 718, 723–724 (1982).

35 In *Nguyen v. I.N.S.*, 208 F.3d 528 (2000), the Court accepted that heightened scrutiny applies to sex discrimination claims, but denied an equal protection cause of action and referred to an 'important government interest'. In contrast, in *U.S. v. Virginia*, when the Court ruled that the University of Virginia violated the Equal Protection Clause, it required an 'exceedingly persuasive justification' to justify the university's sex classification. *U.S. v. Virginia*, 518 U.S. at 423–524 (1996).

36 *Whitaker v. Kenosha Unified School District*, 858 F.3d 1034 (7th Cir. 2017).

37 See e.g. *Zzyym v. Kerry* (Defendant's Motion for Judgment on the Administrative Record on Counts One and Two and Motion to Dismiss Counts Three, Four and Five, 2016 WL 1165988 (D.CO 2016).

why this classification system should be considered sex-based and subject to heightened scrutiny.

Imagine a government system that mandated that all people identify as either black or white as a prerequisite to receiving a government benefit. If the system forces multi-racial people or people who identify as neither black nor white to choose one of these two labels or lose the government benefit, it would be obvious that the government classification system is race-based and subject to heightened scrutiny. The Supreme Court rejected an analogous system in *Loving v. Virginia* when Virginia argued that it was not engaging in discrimination against a racial group when it banned interracial marriages because it treated all races the same way.[38]

The same analysis would apply in the context of religious classifications. Although some courts have refused to treat discrimination against transgender people as sex discrimination, in *Schroer v. Billington*,[39] the Court considered an analogous religious discrimination argument when it ruled that discrimination against a transgender person is discrimination because of 'sex'.

> Imagine that an employee is fired because she converts from Christianity to Judaism. Imagine too that her employer testifies that he harbors no bias toward either Christians or Jews but only 'converts.' That would be a clear case of discrimination 'because of religion.' No court would take seriously the notion that 'converts' are not covered by the statute. Discrimination 'because of religion' easily encompasses discrimination because of a *change* of religion. But in cases where the plaintiff has changed her sex, and faces discrimination because of the decision to stop presenting as a man and to start appearing as a woman, courts have traditionally carved such persons out of the statute by concluding that 'transsexuality' is unprotected by Title VII. In other words, courts have allowed their focus on the label 'transsexual' to blind them to the statutory language itself.[40]

The Seventh Circuit Court of Appeals considered a similar issue in *Whitaker v. Kenosha Unified School District*.[41] Whitaker, a transgender high school student, sued the school district when he was denied the right to use the male bathroom at school. The school argued that its policy should be upheld under rational basis review. The Court rejected the school's argument and ruled that heightened scrutiny should apply to Whitaker's request for a preliminary injunction. The Court stated, '[t]he School District's policy cannot be stated without referencing

---

38 *Loving v. Virginia*, 388 U.S.1 (1967).

39 *Schroer v. Billington*, 577 F.Supp.2d 293 (D.D.C 2008).

40 Ibid at 306–307. In *Schroer*, the issue was whether the actions constituted 'sex' discrimination under Title VII. The same considerations would apply in determining whether discrimination against transgender people or people who do not identify within the binary sex classification system assert an Equal Protection claim for 'sex' discrimination.

41 *Whitaker v. Kenosha Unified School District*, 858 F.3d 1034 (7th Cir. 2017).

sex, as the School District decides which bathroom a student may use based on the sex listed on the student's birth certificate. This policy is inherently based upon a sex-classification and heightened review applies'.[42]

Similarly, by requiring all applicants to identify as either male or female or lose the right to a government-issued document, the government has created a sex-based classification system that should be subject to heightened scrutiny. It is irrelevant that intersex people or people who do not identify within the binary sex classifications have not been declared to be a suspect class by the Supreme Court; the focus of the inquiry should be on the nature of the classification system itself and not on the class of people affected.[43]

Thus, the government should have the burden of proving that it has an important or exceedingly persuasive justification for its sex classification system and that the means used are substantially related to the government's goal.

4.1.3. Government Denial of a Non-Binary Gender Marker Fails Intermediate Scrutiny

Because this issue has only been litigated in one case, *Zzyym*, it is difficult to determine all of the arguments that the government may make to support an assertion that it has an exceedingly persuasive justification for its insistence on limiting sex indicators on passports and other government-issued documents to only M and F. In *Zzyym*, the State Department asserted that 'the purpose of sex identification on the passport is to help identify the bearer of the document, and thus ensure that the passport remains a reliable proof of identification'.[44]

Given current concerns about national security, requiring proper verifiable identity documents for people entering the country likely meets the 'exceedingly persuasive justification' test. The government has a valid and important interest in ensuring that identity documents are used only by the people to whom they have been properly issued.

To pass equal protection scrutiny, however, the means that the government uses must be substantially related to the goal of confirming a person's identity. Limiting people to only M or F markers is not substantially related to the goal of confirming a person's identity for a number of reasons. First, the gender marker on the passport may not match the gender presentation of the passport holder for transgender people and others who do not identify within the binary gender classification system. Second, the government's argument that the gender marker is necessary to confirm the person's identity is undercut by the fact that

---

[42] Ibid at 1051.

[43] Ibid.

[44] *Zzyym v. Kerry* (Defendant's Motion for Judgment on the Administrative Record on Counts One and Two and Motion to Dismiss Counts Three, Four and Five, 2016 WL 1165988 at 19 (D.CO 2016).

the government was willing to issue Zzyym a passport with an F gender marker based upon their Colorado drivers' licence or with an M marker if Zzyym provided a physician's statement attesting to Zzyym's gender as male.[45] The fact that the government was willing to issue Zzyym a passport with either an M or an F gender marker indicates that the gender marker does not necessarily confirm a person's identity. In addition, technological advances, including fingerprinting, retinal scans and facial recognition provide far superior methods of confirming a person's identity than a gender marker[46] and are already in use at some airports by the government for security purposes.[47] Finally, the State Department's assertion that an M or F sex marker allows it to coordinate with state and local authorities to determine if a person is a criminal is undermined by the fact that the Federal Government allows transgender people to carry a passport with a sex marker that differs from their state records. Thus, limiting gender markers to only M and F is not substantially related to furthering the government's goal of ensuring reliable identification.

4.2. SUBSTANTIVE DUE PROCESS

4.2.1. Overview of Substantive Due Process

Courts also employ differing levels of review when a person claims that the government has infringed on a right protected under substantive due process. If the law or regulation significantly burdens a fundamental right (for example, the right to interstate travel,[48] marry[49] or vote[50]), the court will subject the law to strict scrutiny and the government must establish that it is using narrowly tailored means to further a compelling governmental interest. Few regulations can meet this exacting standard.

---

[45] *Zzyym*, above n. 16, at 1109. Zzyym provided 2 physician's statements confirming that Zzyym's sex is intersex, but the State Department ignored these documents.

[46] J. McGrath, 'Are you a Boy or a Girl? Show me your real ID' (2009) 9 *Nev. L.J.* 368, 370.

[47] The government already requires fingerprint identification on its Global Entry passes. US Customs and Border Protection Global Entry, <https://www.cbp.gov/travel/trusted-traveler-programs/global-entry> (last accessed 13.07.2017). The government is using eye scans at some airports; J. Bachman, 'Eye Scans are Replacing Airline Boarding Passes' <https://www.bloomberg.com/news/articles/2017-01-25/go-from-airport-curb-to-cabin-in-a-flash-of-your-eye> (last accessed 29.12.2017). The government has started using facial recognition at some airports for some flights; US Customs and Border Protection Deploys Biometric Exit Technology to Washington Dulles International Airport, <https://www.cbp.gov/newsroom/national-media-release/cbp-deploys-biometric-exit-technology-washington-dulles> (last accessed 29.12.2017).

[48] *Shapiro v. Thompson*, 394 U.S. 618, 629–631 (1969).

[49] *Zablocki v. Redhail*, 434 U.S. 374, 384 (1978).

[50] *Reynolds v. Sims*, 377 U.S. 533, 561–564 (1964).

Most other governmental limitations of rights are subject to rational basis review and the government is allowed to infringe on that right as long as it has a legitimate interest in doing so and the means used to accomplish the government's goal are rational. Most government limitations are upheld under rational basis review.

Sometimes, in a substantive due process case, the Court seems to apply a level of scrutiny somewhere between strict scrutiny and rational basis review, often referred to as 'rational basis with bite', but the Supreme Court has never specifically endorsed an intermediate level of review.[51]

4.2.2. Substantive Due Process and the Right to Dignity and Autonomy

No court has considered the level of protection to be accorded to a person's right to governmental recognition of their gender identity. Given the contradictory court opinions on substantive due process,[52] it is difficult to predict how a court will rule when such a case is presented.

Whether the right to gender self-identity will be considered a right subject to heightened scrutiny will depend on how the court chooses to frame the right. In *Glucksburg*, the Supreme Court defined the right narrowly, requiring that specific rights be deeply rooted in our nation's history and traditions and so "'implicit in the concept of ordered liberty,' such that "neither liberty nor justice would exist if they were sacrificed"'.[53] In *Zzyym*, the State Department relied on *Glucksburg* and asked the Court to define the right as the right to have an X marker on a passport,[54] which would not be considered a right deeply rooted in our nation's history.

Zzyym, however, asked the Court to define the right more broadly as a right to dignity and autonomy, which would be consistent with recent Supreme Court cases such as *Lawrence v. Texas* (protecting the right of same-sex couple to engage in intimate sexual acts)[55] and *Obergefell v. Hodges* (protecting the

---

51 e.g. in *Lawrence v. Texas*, 539 U.S. 558 (2003), the Court used rational basis review language, but it struck down the legislation under a more exacting review than it normally applies in rational basis cases.

52 See J. Greenberg and M. Herald, 'You Can't Take it with You: Constitutional Consequences of Interstate Gender-Identity Rulings' (2005) 80 *Wash. L. Rev.*, 819, 874–881; M. Herald, 'A Bedroom of One's Own: Morality and Sexual Privacy After Lawrence v. Texas' (2004) 16 *Yale J.L. & Feminism* 1.

53 *Washington v. Glucksburg*, 521 U.S. 702, 721 (1997) (narrowly defining the right as the right to commit suicide as opposed to broadly defining it as the right of an individual to choose a humane and dignified death).

54 *Zzyym v. Kerry* (Defendant's Motion for Judgment on the Administrative Record on Counts One and Two and Motion to Dismiss counts Three, Four and Five, 2016 WL 1165988 (D.CO 2016).

55 *Lawrence v. Texas*, 539 U.S. 558 (2003) (rejecting a narrow interpretation of the right as the right to engage in sodomy).

right of same sex couples to marry).[56] In these cases, the Court concluded that 'the fundamental right to liberty has been extended to certain personal choices central to individual dignity and autonomy, including intimate choices that define personal identity and beliefs'.[57]

Thus, the question of whether the government's refusal to issue an identity document with a third-gender marker would be subject to more exacting scrutiny as a protected liberty interest depends on how the court decides to frame the issue. If it adopts a *Glucksburg* approach and frames the issue narrowly as the right to a third-gender marker on an identity document, the denial would not affect a fundamental right and thus would be subject to rational basis review. If, however, the right is framed more broadly as a liberty interest based on the right to dignity and self-identity,[58] as the Court framed the issues in *Lawrence* and *Obergefell*, it could be struck down under a more searching review.

4.2.3. Substantive Due Process and the Right to International Travel

The right to international travel has been protected by the Supreme Court since 1958 when it ruled that the State Department was not authorised to deny passports to members of the Communist party.[59] The Court has found that international travel is a liberty interest protected under the Due Process Clause.[60]

In *Zzyym*, the State Department asserted that it was not denying Zzyym the right to international travel because it was willing to issue Zzyym a passport with either an M or an F gender marker, just not an X gender marker.[61] The government's assertion presented Zzyym with a Hobson's choice. Zzyym could tell the truth about their non-binary gender and be denied a passport or Zzyym could lie on the application by swearing that they were either M or F (and thus commit a crime) and receive a passport. Requiring Zzyym to commit a crime

---

56 *Obergefell v. Hodges*, 135 S.Ct. 2584, 2597 (2015).

57 Ibid.

58 This approach would be consistent with the Ninth Circuit's finding that 'sexual orientation and sexual identity ... are so fundamental to one's identity that a person should not be required to abandon them'. *Hernandez-Montiel v. INS*, 225 F.3d 1084, 1093 (9th Cir. 2000) (*overruled in part on other grounds* by *Thomas v. Gonzales*, 409 F.3d 1177 (9th Cir. 2005) (holding that requiring a person to abandon her gender identity is untenable).

59 *Kent v. Dulles*, 357 U.S. 116 (1958).

60 *Aptheker v. Sec. of State*, 278 U.S. 500, 505–508 (1964); *Haig v. Agee*, 453 U.S. 280, 307 (1981). For an argument that the right to international travel should be analysed as a right of citizenship subject to a higher level of scrutiny, see J. Kahn, 'International Travel and the Constitution' (2008) 58 *UCLA L. Rev*. 271.

61 *Zzyym v. Kerry* (Defendant's Motion for Judgment on the Administrative Record on Counts One and Two and Motion to Dismiss counts Three, Four and Five, 2016 WL 1165988 at 14 (D.CO 2016). The State Department asserted that 'Plaintiff was merely denied the "right" to be issued a passport containing particular information – an "X" in the sex field', and was not denied the right to travel (*Zzyym v. Kerry*, this note).

and lie on their application to obtain a passport limits their ability to travel internationally and the State Department's rules must be analysed to determine if they impermissibly infringe on Zzyym's substantive due process rights.

As discussed in Section 4.1.3, the government has a valid interest in ensuring that the identity of a passport holder entering the United States is accurate. Rules limiting the ability of US citizens to use only an M or an F gender marker on their passport, however, do not reasonably further that purpose for three reasons.

First, allowing X markers on passports is consistent with international security standards. The International Civil Aviation Organization (ICAO) is the international body responsible for establishing global standards for international travel documents and the US works through the ICAO to improve aviation security internationally.[62] The ICAO has approved F, M and X sex markers for international travel documents and has confirmed that using a non-binary system does not impose a security risk.[63]

Second, the US government allows people with foreign passports with an 'X' marker to enter the country.[64] Therefore, the State Department has implicitly accepted the ICAO determination that acceptance of an 'X' marker from non-citizens does not impose a security risk. The State Department cannot establish a reason that US citizens with 'X' sex markers pose more of a security risk than non-citizens entering the country with 'X' sex markers.

Finally, as discussed above, the State Department does not necessarily rely on the sex marker to confirm someone's identity. The State Department would have allowed Zzyym to travel with a passport with either an F or an M marker. A rule denying someone a passport who cannot honestly check an M or an F box on the passport application does not further the government's interest in national security.

4.3. RATIONAL BASIS REVIEW

Even if a court were to adopt the position that rational basis review applies to the equal protection claim because the classification is not sex-based and also applies to the substantive due process claims because the rights asserted are not fundamental or entitled to heightened scrutiny, a government agency's

---

62 22 U.S.C. §5501.

63 Machine Readable Travel Documents, ICAO Document 9303, 7th ed., 2015, Part IV at 14 <http://www.icao.int/publications/Documents/9303_p4_cons_en.pdf> (last accessed 13.07.2017).

64 *Zzyym v. Kerry* (Plaintiff Zzyym's Opening Brief in Support of Declaratory, Injunctive, and Other Relief and Opposition to Defendants' Motion for Judgment on the Administrative Record and Motion to Dismiss, 2016 WL 1660095 at 16 (D.CO 2016).

insistence on a binary sex system may fail to pass even rational basis review.[65] Although the Zzyym court did not analyse the constitutional issues, it did examine the government actions to determine whether they were rational under the APA and it concluded that the policies were arbitrary and capricious.

In *Zzyym*, the government asserted that its binary system is rational for a number of reasons. First, the government claimed that the binary sex requirement was required because all other federal, state and local government regulations rely on a binary system. Therefore, it argued that a binary system is needed to be consistent with these other government agencies.[66] As the Court found, however, the government did not uniformly rely on these other binary systems because it issues transgender applicants passports with a sex marker that is different from the sex marker on other identity documents if the applicant provides a physician's statement confirming their gender. Therefore, the Court found that the consistency argument was not rational.[67]

The government also asserted that it needed to limit the sex marker to M or F because that is the data that is encoded on the chip embedded in the passport.[68] The government did not advance a reason to explain why the chip could not be recoded to include additional gender markers and the Court rejected this argument as not having a rational basis.[69]

The State Department also stressed the importance of synchronising its database with law enforcement databases throughout the country that rely on binary gender systems.[70] The government admitted, however, that not all law enforcement systems include a sex marker. In addition, the government's argument is difficult to square with the State Department's willingness to issue Zzyym a passport with a sex designator that is inconsistent with Zzyym's other government documents. The State Department would give Zzyym an F document based on the drivers' licence or an M document based on a physician's letter, regardless of the sex indicator on the state documents.[71]

Finally, the government argued that although the ICAO allows a third-gender marker on international documents, allowing US citizens to have such

---

65 Rational basis review is extremely deferential to the government. Most cases applying rational basis review uphold the government action. A small but significant number of cases have struck down government action under this low standard, but these cases 'follow no obvious pattern. The Court's analysis differs from case to case. None of these cases has had a significant precedential impact on subsequent cases'; R. Farrell, 'Successful Rational Basis Claims in the Supreme Court from the 1971 Term Through Romer v. Evans' (1999) 32 *Ind. L. Rev.* 357, 357–358.

66 *Zzyym*, above n. 16, at 1113.

67 Ibid.

68 Ibid.

69 Ibid.

70 Ibid.

71 Ibid at 1114.

a marker on their passport may lead to inconvenience and uncertainty when US citizens try to enter a country that does not recognise a third-gender marker. The Court found this argument unpersuasive because it appeared to be based on speculation and if it actually becomes a problem for a traveller, it would be the problem of the applicant who made the choice to have a non-binary gender marker.[72]

The Zzyym court considered all the reasons the government advanced to justify its binary sex classification system and found that the State Department's decision-making process that led to the binary sex classification system policy was not rational. It concluded that the government had not advanced sufficient reasons to support a finding that the government's policy was not arbitrary and capricious.[73] For the same reasons that the Court found the government policy to be arbitrary and capricious under the APA, it is likely to find that the policy does not meet the rational basis test in a constitutional challenge.[74]

5. CONCLUSION

Some jurisdictions, like Oregon, California, Washington D.C.[75] and Maine[76] have adopted or are moving to adopt legislation and regulations that will allow people who do not identify within the binary sex classification system to have their identity documents reflect their sex as something other than M or F. The same is not true in a majority of US jurisdictions and it is unlikely to become the reality in most states given the current political make-up of state legislatures and the Federal Government.[77]

---

72 Ibid.

73 Ibid.

74 'Review of an equal protection claim in the context of agency action is similar to that under the APA. That is, an agency's decision must be upheld if under the Equal Protection Clause, it can show a "rational basis" for its decision'; *Nazareth Hospital v. Sec. U.S. Dept. of HHS*, 747 F.3d 172, 180 (2014).

75 E. Grinberg, 'You Can Now Get a Gender Neutral Driver's License in D.C.' <https://www.cnn.com/2017/06/27/health/washington-gender-neutral-drivers-license/index.html> (last accessed 23.06.2018).

76 C. Capatides, 'Maine to Offer Third, Non-binary gender Option on Driver's Licenses, Ids' <https://www.cbsnews.com/news/maine-to-offer-non-binary-gender-option-on-licenses-ids/> (last accessed 23.06.2018).

77 Many states are considering legislation to restrict the rights of sexual minorities to marry, use the bathroom that matches their gender identity and demand service on an equal footing with non-LGBT people. 23 U.S. States Advancing Anti-Gay Bills <https://www.yahoo.com/news/23-us-states-advancing-anti-gay-bills-rights-222313147.html> (last accessed 27.01.2018). The Federal Government is also pulling back on LGBT protections put in place during the Obama administration; D. Trotta, 'Trump Revokes Obama Guidelines on Transgender Bathrooms' <http://www.reuters.com/article/us-usa-trump-lgbt-idUSKBN161243> (last accessed 27.01.2018).

Given the increasing social acceptance of non-binary gender markers,[78] challenges to government refusals to recognise a person's non-binary sex are likely to increase. Before a government agency refuses to issue an identity document with a non-binary sex indicator, it should carefully consider whether such a refusal is based on a sound analysis. In the absence of a rational reason for such a denial, the government may violate equal protection and substantive due process guarantees.

78 See e.g. R. Goldman, 'Here's a List of 58 Gender Options for Facebook Users' <https://abcnews.go.com/News/heres-a-list-of-58-gender-options-for-facebook-users/blogEntry?id=22504704/> (last accessed 19.05.2018).

THE LEGAL STATUS OF INTERSEX PERSONS IN MALTA

Tanya Ní Mhuirthile

The Maltese Gender Identity, Gender Expression and Sex Characteristics Act, 2015 (the 2015 Act) has been described as 'the most expansive, ground-breaking and comprehensive bill of its kind'.[1] This chapter will analyse this Act to assess how it has impacted upon the status of intersex people in Malta.

Over the past few decades discourse about intersex has been divided into two types of discussions: deliberations aimed at achieving recognition of intersex identity which may differ from that recorded at birth, and debates about medical management. While these may seem to be two disparate aims at their core, they concern questions of dignity, respect and the realisation of human rights. It is by addressing simultaneously both sides of the discussions that the 2015 Act earns its praise.

---

1 A.J. Neuman Wipfler, 'Identity Crisis: The Limitations of Expanding Government Recognition of Gender Identity and the Possibility of Genderless Identity Documents' (2016) 39 *Harvard Journal of Law and Gender* 491, 511.

1. THE PROVISIONS IN THE LEGISLATION

The 2015 Act is ambitious in its aim. It unequivocally states that it will enable both the recognition of a person's gender identity and protect the bodily integrity of people.

1.1. THE RIGHT TO GENDER IDENTITY

The 2015 Act states unambiguously that all people have a right to gender identity. This is defined in Article 2 as

> each person's internal and individual experience of gender, which may or may not correspond with the sex assigned at birth, including the personal sense of the body (which may involve, if freely chosen, modification of bodily appearance and/or functions by medical, surgical or other means) and other expressions of gender, including name, dress, speech and mannerism.

In Article 3 the legislation outlines the four component elements of this right:

- the recognition of people's gender identity;
- the free development of their person according to their gender identity;
- the right to be treated according to their gender identity, and in particular to be identified that way in identity documents; and
- the right to bodily integrity and physical autonomy.

Article 3 further notes that the right requires that the gender identity of the person be respected at all times. Finally, it clarifies that a person shall not be required to provide any independent evidence in order to establish a right to exercise the right to gender identity. Article 3(4) explicitly states that

> [t]he person shall not be required to provide proof of surgical procedure for total or partial genital reassignment, hormonal therapies or any other psychiatric, psychological or medical treatment to make use of the right to gender identity.

1.2. THE GENDER RECOGNITION PROCESS

Having outlined the details of the right, the 2015 Act then notes in Article 4 that it is a right of citizens to request that their name and recorded gender be changed 'if the person so wishes' in order to reflect their 'self determined gender identity'. This is a simple process. A person who wishes to change their legal gender completes a declaratory public deed, which must include:

- a copy of their birth certificate;
- a clear, unequivocal and informed declaration that their gender identity does not match that assigned at birth;
- a specification of the gender particulars; and
- the first name by which they wish to be registered.

These requirements do not necessitate any proof beyond the statement of identity of the applicant. The 2015 Act confirms that the applicant is the ultimate arbitrator of their gender identity and reiterates that there are no further gatekeepers which may prevent access to the exercise of the right. Indeed, the Act strengthens this commitment in Article 5(2) where it specifies that the notary shall not request 'any psychiatric, psychological or medical documents' in order to draw up the deed and further entrenches this policy in Article 4(3) where it states that neither shall the Director for Public Registry require any evidence beyond that contained in the declaratory public deed as published.

The 2015 Act also includes provision for minors. Under Article 7, parents or the tutor of a minor may make an application to the Civil Court (Voluntary Jurisdiction Section) requesting that the recorded gender and first name of a minor be changed. The article requires that in determining whether to order such a change the court must be guided by the best interests of the child and any views that the minor may express on the matter must be given due weight having regard to their age and maturity. Thus, the key principles underpinning the rights of the child as espoused in the UN Convention on the Rights of the Child are incorporated in the legislative scheme as foundational principles.

Article 18 of the 2015 Act amends Article 278 in the Acts of Birth section of the Civil Code, which lists the required particulars of the birth that must be declared to the state, to enable a delay in declaring the sex of a child 'until the gender identity of the minor is determined'. Where a declaration of gender has not been made at birth, Article 7(4) of the 2015 Act enables parents or tutors of the minor to file an application declaring the gender and first name of the minor can be made. Such an application must be made with the express consent of the minor in light of their maturity and best interests.

Once an amendment has been made under the 2015 Act within 15 days from the effective date of recognition of gender identity, the person must request an amended identity card and other identification documents reflecting the amended gender and first name by which they wish to be known. Article 6(3) enables a person to request that other official documentation and certificates be reissued in the preferred gender and with the preferred name from other competent authorities such as government departments and employers as well as educational or other institutions.

1.3. ENHANCED PROTECTION FOR RELATED RIGHTS

The legislation also includes measure to protect and respect the privacy of people who make amendments to their birth records under this Act. Article 11 introduces an offence of knowing exposure of a person who has availed of the provisions of the Act. Anyone convicted of this offence shall be liable to a fine of between €1,000 and €5,000. Subsection 2 of that article enhances the protections available under the hate crime law through the specific inclusion of gender expression and sex characteristics as motivations which attract the increased penalties under Article 83B of the Criminal Code for offences which are racially aggravated or motivated by xenophobia or homophobia. Article 12 ensures that officials who acquire information in the course of carrying out their duties under the Act are restrained from disclosing that information in accordance with both the Professional Secrecy and Data Protections Acts.

The 2015 Act explicitly extends the protection for anti-discrimination and promotion of equality to the right to gender identity in Article 13. Thus, it requires that norms, regulations and procedures are interpreted and enforced in a manner that favours access to and exercise of the right to gender identity. Subsection 2 of this article imposes an obligation on the public service to eliminate unlawful discrimination and harassment on the basis of gender identity, gender expression and sex characteristics. Simultaneously it mandates that equality of opportunity must be promoted by the public service regardless of sexual orientation, gender identity, gender expression and sex characteristics. Finally, Article 13(3) extends these obligations beyond the public service to include private sector departments, agencies and all competent authorities that maintain personal records and/ or collect gender information. The article gives to all relevant agencies three years from the date of entry into force of the Act to modify their forms, records and information to reflect these new standards.

1.4. EXPLICIT GUARANTEE OF RIGHT TO BODILY INTEGRITY AND PHYSICAL AUTONOMY

Perhaps the most innovative aspect of the 2015 Act is the right to bodily integrity and physical autonomy guaranteed under Article 14. This deals very specifically with the question of medical and/or surgical treatment of intersex minors. It starts from the position that any sex assignment treatment or surgical intervention on the sex characteristics of a minor will be unlawful if those treatments or interventions could be postponed until the person treated can provide informed consent. However, the 2015 Act does enable such treatment and interventions to be carried out on a minor who gives informed consent through their parent or tutor.[2] In administering such treatment the medical professionals are charged with ensuring that the best interests of the child are the paramount consideration and that weight is given to the views of the minor in accordance with their age and maturity.[3] Under Article 14(2) treatment is permissible in 'exceptional circumstances' when agreement is reached by the interdisciplinary treatment team and the parents or tutor where the minor is unable to provide consent and such treatment would ordinarily contravene the provisions of the legislation.

An interesting question arises when this newly recognised right to bodily integrity and physical autonomy meets other more traditional rights such as the right to religious freedom, in particular, the issue of male circumcision for members of the Jewish faith. For many within the Jewish community circumcision shortly after birth is a central prerequisite to membership of the religious community.[4] The wording of Article 14(1) of the legislation is such that it might be read such as to prohibit circumcision of neo-natal males. As of yet this is not an issue that has drawn official attention within Malta. A case which did consider the question of circumcision and the right to bodily integrity, but in England, was *Re J (Child's Religious Upbringing and Circumcision)* (2000).[5] The case came to judicial attention as there was a disagreement between the parents as to whether their son should be circumcised. J's parents, his English non-practising Christian mother and his Turkish non-practising Muslim father, had raised him in a secular environment. Having relocated back to his native Turkey, J's father wished to ensure that his now five-year-old son would be brought up according to some Muslim traditions: to be circumcised and not to eat pork. In support of his position he advanced an argument under Article 9 of the European Convention on Human Rights that circumcision would help his son identify with the father and establish himself within the Muslim community. The mother did not want her son circumcised. There was no medical reason compelling the circumcision. The Court found that undergoing the procedure

2 Art. 14(1) of the Gender Identity, Gender Expression and Sex Characteristics Act 2015.
3 Art. 14(5) of the Gender Identity, Gender Expression and Sex Characteristics Act 2015.
4 The circumcision of young boys is not practised by all Jews and has been the subject of debate within the community. See L. Hoffman, *Covenant of Blood: Circumcision and Gender in Rabbinic Judaism*, University of Chicago Press, Chicago 1996. This reflect a growth in the 'intactness' movement of those who argue that the circumcision of neo-natal males is a gender-specific offence similar to female gender mutilation and ought to be expressly outlawed. See further L.M. Sardi, 'The Male Neonatal Circumcision Debate: Social Movements, Sexual Citizenship, and Human Rights' (2011) 6(3) *Societies Without Borders* 304; R. Dardy and S. Savboda, 'A Rose by Any Other Name: Rethinking the Similarities and Differences Between Male and female Genital Cutting' (2007) 21(3) *Medical Anthropology Quarterly* 301.
5 *Re J (Child's Religious Upbringing and Circumcision)* [2000] 1 FCR 307.

was not in J's best interests as he was essentially experiencing a secular upbringing in England, the procedure was not medically indicated, it would cause pain and distress and was irreversible. As Dame Butler-Sloss stated:

> There is, in my view, a small group of important decisions made on behalf of a child which, in the absence of agreement of those with parental responsibility, ought not to be carried out or arranged by a one-parent carer although she has parental responsibility under section 2(7) of the Children Act 1989. Such a decision ought not to be made without the specific approval of the court. Sterilisation is one example. The change of a child's surname is another.[6]

Thus, the Court was willing to limit the autonomy of a parent to consent to the circumcision of his child on the basis that the immediate harm to the child outweighed the speculative future benefits should he identify as Muslim in later life.

This would seem to support a reading that in balancing the right to religious freedom on one hand and the right to bodily integrity and physical autonomy on the other, the latter would win out. However, it is important to remember that *Re J* concerned a disagreement between parents as to what was in the child's best interests in a context where the child had thus far been raised, and would primarily continue to be raised, in a secular fashion. Where parents are in agreement and fully intend to raise their son in a religious community that requires circumcision as a prerequisite to membership the balancing may weigh differently. It remains to be seen how this balancing will be achieved in Malta should such a case come to official attention.

The 2015 Act provides in Article 15 that all people who may seek psycho-social counselling, support or medical intervention relating to sex or gender should be given expert sensitive and individually tailored support by psychologists and medical practitioners or peer counselling. There are no limits on the access to this support and it is available from the moment of diagnosis or self-referral for 'as long as necessary'.

In a related vein, Article 16 requires the establishment of a working group to review the current medical treatment protocols in line with current best medical practices and human rights standards and to issue a report with recommendations for revision of the current medical treatment protocols. This working group would be appointed by the minister with responsibility for equality following consultation with the minister for health. It shall consist of a chairperson, who shall be a medical doctor with at least 12 years' experience and nine other members. These nine members shall include three experts in human rights issues, three psychosocial professionals and three medical experts. As of the date of publication, this working group has not yet been established.

---

6 Above n. 5, at para. 31.

2. ANALYSIS OF THE 2015 ACT AS IT RELATES TO INTERSEX PEOPLE

As stated in the introduction, the strength of the 2015 Act lies in how it responds to both the potential need to amend the gender of legal recognition and to protect people with intersex variations from unwanted interventions on their bodies.

2.1. GENDER RECOGNITION

In order to come *sui juris* and to avail of the protection and rights contained in law one must be able to be recognisable by the law. Records are available for births in Malta since 1863, the year that the Registration of Births, Deaths and Marriages Act introduced the first system of civil registration in England and Wales. The Public Registry, the office responsible for maintaining such records, was established on 3 August 1889.[7] The information required for a record of birth has since then included a requirement that the sex of the child be declared. Malta has a binary understanding of gender; thus, one must be declared as either male or female in order to be legally recognisable.

Until the introduction of the 2015 Act there was no mechanism by which to dispute the gender assigned at birth. A particular difficulty arises for intersex people in this context. When access to registration is predicated on a binary understanding of sex as either male or female, this can have the effect of excluding intersex people whose bodies may be configured such that they fall outside these classifications. The mid/late twentieth century saw a growth in the prevalence for 'corrective' or 'normalisation' procedures on the genitalia of children with intersex variations to reconstruct them along more apparently male or female lines.[8] As has been well documented, the majority of such re/assignments were to the female sex.[9] Tellingly, former US Surgeon General Joycelyn Elders was quoted in the *New Yorker* magazine 'I always teach my students you can't make a good male but you can make a pretty good female. Just take everything out and make a pouch.'[10] Thus if the gender as which an intersex person identified did not correspond with the sex noted in the birth record it was impossible for that person to be legally recognised in their identified gender.

---

7 See further <www.identitymalta.com/public-registry> (last accessed 8 January 2018).

8 See further G. Davis, *Contesting Intersex: The Dubious Diagnosis*, New York University Press, London 2015; S.E. Preves, *Intersex and Identity: The Contested Self*, Rutgers University Press, London 2005; A. Fausto-Sterling, *Sexing the Body: Gender Politics and the Construction of Sexuality* Basic Books, New York 2000 and S.J. Kessler, *Lessons from the Intersexed*, Rutgers University Press, New Brunswick 1998.

9 Fausto-Sterling, above n. 8.

10 N. Atkins, 'Dr Elders' Medical History' (1994) 26 September *New Yorker* 45–46.

As Neuman Wipfler noted, there is an emerging crisis about the role of gender in establishing legal identity. The presumption that a sex designation is necessary on identity documents has harmed those who do not conform to normative binary understandings of sex/gender.[11] As an appreciation of the fluidity of gender, gender identity and gender expression increases and governments become more aware, there has been a growth in legislation and other measures that relax and expand the ways in which gender is classified. Attempts to account for greater gender variation has caused tensions to emerge both in terms of how best to acknowledge variance within gender markers to enable access to gender identity rights and how best to challenge the presumptive need for such markers in the first place as a significant aspect of the self that underpin legal identification documents.

In response to these challenges, the 2015 Act has opted to create a scheme for legal recognition that enables movement between the genders. While not entirely abandoning the need of gender markers, the Maltese legislation, in permitting delayed declaration of gender for minors under Article 18, does acknowledge that such markers are not absolutely essential in navigating legal existence. This openness towards thinking beyond the binary gender paradigm is reflected in the Maltese approach to consideration of foreign gender recognition determinations. Article 9(2) states that a gender marker other than male or female, or the absence of a marker, that is recognised by the relevant competent foreign authority will be recognised by Malta. Notwithstanding this acceptance of non-binary or absence of markers in these limited circumstances, in general the Maltese approach requires that all adults over the age of 18 years declare a gender of legal recognition and that must be male or female.

The exercise of the recognition rights in 2015 Act is not dependent on any preliminary diagnosis or determination by anyone other than the person making the declaration and amendment to their birth record. This is a welcome feature of the 2015 Act. Thus the rights in the Act are available to all. Other recognition systems, such as that under the Gender Recognition Act 2004 in the United Kingdom require certification by multiple medical professionals and subsequent determination on the authenticity of the application by a panel, thus introducing many gatekeepers which can prevent access to the rights.[12] Where recognition is dependent on a particular diagnostic label, such as 'gender dysphoria' under

---

11 Neuman Wipfler, above n. 1.

12 Gender Recognition Act 2004 (England and Wales), ss. 2 and 3. For critiques of the gatekeeping functions of medical professionals, see L. Fishbayn, 'Not Quite One Gender or the Other: Marriage Law and the Containment of Gender Trouble in the United Kingdom' (2006) 15 *American University Journal of Gender, Social Policy and the Law* 413; A.N. Sharpe, 'A Critique of the Gender Recognition Act 2004' (2007) 4 *Bioethical Inquiry* 33; S. Cowan, '"Gender is No Substitute for Sex": A Comparative Human Rights Analysis of the Legal Regulation of Sexual Identity' (2005) 13 *Feminist Legal Studies* 67.

the scheme in the UK, it inherently excludes those, like people with intersex variations, who might otherwise wish to avail of the scheme. By adopting a de-pathologised approach to recognition, the Maltese 2015 Act ensures that all people, including intersex people, can exercise the rights contained therein.

A further important aspect of the de-pathologised approach contained in the 2015 Act is the implication that it may reduce the social pressure on parents to consent to irreversible interventions on their intersex children that may not be mandated by urgent medical concerns. This is particularly so when the declaration of sex can be delayed until the gender identity of the minor emerges as the child grows. Indeed, aside from questions of gender recognition, the primary strength of the 2015 Act, from the perspective of those concerned with realising rights for intersex people, are those aspects of the Act that address the question of the medical management of intersex.

2.2. MEDICAL MANAGEMENT OF INTERSEX

For the majority of the twentieth century the discussion around intersex concerned the medical management of intersex conditions. Discourse centred on the technicalities of intervention rather than whether intervention should take place.[13] While the medical profession has ceased to officially classify intersex as a 'social emergency'[14] nonetheless these interventions continue. The 2015 Act is innovative in its efforts to protect against irreversible interventions that have not been consented to by the person upon whom they have been carried out.

This is achieved in a number of ways. First, the act eschews a definition of intersex. In a context where language surrounding intersex is contested avoiding a definition removes any latent sense of stigmatising or pejorative language.[15] Rather the 2015 Act focuses on the substance of the protection it enshrines. Article 2 defines 'sex characteristics' as referring

> to the chromosomal, gonadal and anatomical features of a person which include primary characteristics such as reproductive organs and genitalia and/or in chromosomal structures and hormones; and secondary characteristics such as muscle mass, hair distribution, breasts and/or structure.

This is a broad definition that cover all bodies without distinction and thus it encompasses intersex variations without isolating them.

---

13 See references in n. 8 above and A.D. Dreger, *Hermaphrodites and the Medical Invention of Sex*, Harvard University Press, Cambridge (Massachusetts) 1998.

14 American Academy of Pediatrics, 'Evaluation of the Newborn With Developmental Anomalies of the External Genitalia' (2000) 106 *Pediatrics* 138.

15 See Davis, above n. 8.

The past few years have seen an increase in statements from human rights organisations identifying the need to protect intersex bodies from interventions to which they have not expressly consented. The first explicit such statement was contained in Article 18 of the Yogyakarta Principles which exhorted states to

> ensure that no child's body is irreversibly altered by medical procedures in an attempt to impose a gender identity without the full, free and informed consent of the child in accordance with the age and maturity of the child and guided by the principle that in all actions concerning children, the best interests of the child shall be a primary consideration.[16]

This was supported by the report from the UN High Commissioner for Human Rights in 2011.[17] The following year the Special Rapporteur on Torture published a report on violence in medical settings which included specific mention of intersex issues.[18] This trend continues to be evident in the recent resolution of the Parliamentary Assembly of the Council of Europe on Promoting the human rights of and eliminating discrimination against intersex people adopted in October 2017 which called on states to prohibit medically unnecessary sex-normalising surgery, sterilisation and other treatments practised on intersex children without their informed consent.[19]

The 2015 Act explicitly vindicates the rights of people with intersex variations through the inclusion of Article 14. In doing this it aims to strike a balance between various actors while keeping the child at the centre of the focus. As stated above, the default position adopted by the Act is that any intervention on the sex characteristics of a minor that has not been consented to by the minor is unlawful. Yet the prohibition is not complete.[20] The article allows for minors with the capacity to do so to consent to interventions through their parents or guardians. In placing both the best interests of the child and respect for the evolving maturity at the centre of this exception, the 2015 Act succeeds in

---

16 The Yogyakarta Principles <http://yogyakartaprinciples.org> (last accessed 08.02.2018).

17 UN High Commissioner for Human Rights, *Discriminatory laws and practices and acts of violence against individuals based on their sexual orientation and gender identity* UN Doc. A/HRC/19/41 available at <http://www.ohchr.org/_layouts/15/WopiFrame.aspx?sourcedoc=/Documents/Issues/Discrimination/A.HRC.19.41_English.pdf&action=default&DefaultItemOpen=1> (last accessed 08.02.2018).

18 J.E. Mendez, *Report of the Special Rapporteur on torture and other cruel, inhuman or degrading treatment or punishment*, UN Doc A/HRC/22/53 available at <http://www.ohchr.org/Documents/HRBodies/HRCouncil/Regularsession/Session22/A.HRC.22.53_English.pdf> (last accessed 08.02.2018).

19 Parliamentary Assembly of the Council of Europe, *Resolution on Promoting the Human Rights of and Eliminating Discrimination Against Intersex People*, Resolution 2191 (2017) available at <http://assembly.coe.int/nw/xml/XRef/Xref-XML2HTML-en.asp?fileid=24232&lang=en> (last accessed 08.02.2018).

20 See the discussion above regarding neo-natal male circumcision as part of the Jewish faith.

vindicating the rights of children in a meaningful way. The second exception to the prohibition contained is in Article 14(2) and permits intervention in 'exceptional circumstances' where the interdisciplinary team and parents are in agreement. Thus, urgent medical need can be attended to without risk of violating the protections offered by the Act.

In a similar vein the provisions in Article 15 guaranteeing access to healthcare for so long as it is required are important in the context of addressing the health needs of those who may have been subjected to interventions prior to the introduction of the Act.

3. CONCLUSION

The scheme introduced in the 2015 Act is comprehensive. It facilitates intersex people to change the gender by which they are legally recognised while simultaneously offering comprehensive protection from unwanted medical interventions. Thus, the Act successfully meets the challenge of responding to both aspects of the discourse centred on intersex rights. In achieving this, it manages to respect the dignity and human rights of intersex people in Malta.

THE 2013 GERMAN LAW: ANALYSIS AND CRITICISM

Tobias HELMS*

This chapter discusses the 2013 German civil status law regarding intersex. After a quick look back on the law before the reform in 2013, the first focus will be on the interpretation of the 2013 law and its consequences for German family law as a whole. Then the ground-breaking decision of the Federal Constitutional Court of 10 October 2017 will be looked at. In this decision, the Federal Constitutional Court ruled that the reform of 2013 (which explicitly allowed leaving the gender entry blank when an intersex child is born) had not gone far enough and that German civil status law must allow a third 'positive' gender option. Finally, this chapter will ask whether we can do without gender as a legal category completely.

---

* I would like to thank Jeremy Fenner for the translation of this chapter.

1. THE BINARY SOCIAL (GENDER) ORDER

The categorisation of human beings as part of either the female or the male sex is seen as natural and self-evident in everyday life. When relatives or friends inform us that they are expecting offspring, one of the first questions is always: 'A boy or a girl?' When we meet someone for the first time we automatically assign that person to one of the gender categories, even before learning their name or having spoken to them. Should we not immediately succeed with this gender categorisation, we become irritated to the extent that we are literally rendered speechless. After all, the German language has no personal form of address that does not use the words '*Frau*' or '*Herr*'. We essentially cannot imagine life without gender categorisation.

The binary gender system is deeply rooted in the history of civilisation and of mankind. As Verse 27 of the Book of Genesis famously states: 'God created man in His own image, ... male and female He created them.' The attraction between the sexes is the basis for the propagation of the human species. It shapes our mating conduct and social behaviour and – to a certain extent – continues to determine the power structures of human society. Nonetheless, throughout history there has always been a certain level of awareness of the fact that there are humans that do not fall into the usual sex categories. A classic example of this awareness is Hermaphroditus, a figure of Greek mythology, who was created by merging a water nymph (Salmacis) with the son of Hermes and Aphrodite.[1]

2. THE FORMER POSITION OF GERMAN LAW

In view of the binary social (gender) order of everyday social life, the legal treatment of intersex is inevitably fraught with difficulties. In order to be able to properly understand the 2013 German civil status law, it is necessary to briefly describe the previous civil status law practice in dealing with intersex persons.

Under German law, the birth of a child must be registered at the registry office (*Standesamt*) within one week. Recording the child's sex in the register of births was mandatory (§21(1) No. 3 German Civil Status Act – *Personenstandsgesetz* (PStG)) before the latest reform. Under the old civil status law practice a certificate provided by a doctor or midwife had to be submitted where the child's sex was in doubt. This certificate was primarily issued on the basis of the child's predominant predisposition towards either the male or the female sex,[2]

---

1 Cf. A. Wacke, 'Vom Hermaphroditen zum Transsexuellen. Zur Stellung von Zwittern in der Rechtsgeschichte', in H. Eyrich, W. Odersky and F.J. Säcker (eds.), *Festschrift für Kurt Rebmann zum 65. Geburtstag*, CH Beck Verlag, 1989, pp. 874–875.

2 OLG Naumburg 14.12.2000, *Das Standesamt (StAZ)* 2002, 169, 170; KG 11.1.1965, *Neue Juristische Wochenschrift (NJW)* 1965, 1084.

though – owing to a lack of prescribed criteria for gender assignment – parents and their doctors were ultimately given a wide discretion in that assessment.

Registration of the sex of a child – like all entries in the civil status register – only has a declaratory effect. Where the child's later development showed that its gender had been assessed incorrectly, German civil status law provided for the correction of the register on request by way of a court order.[3] In doing so the courts recognised that the 'psychological proclivities' of intersex persons were of 'particular importance' where gender assignment was concerned.[4]

3. INTERSEX UNDER THE 2013 CIVIL STATUS LAW

3.1. THE REFORM OF THE CIVIL STATUS ACT

For a long period of time, intersex had hardly been given any attention in German family law. This issue has only raised increased public attention since the German Ethics Council (*Deutscher Ethikrat*) published a position statement on this topic on 14 February 2012 and therein recommended a rather far-reaching reform of German civil status and family law.[5] This position statement was a reaction to a report of the UN Committee on the Elimination of Discrimination against Women which admonished the German Government in 2009 that Germany had not entered into a dialogue with some organisations which represent intersex citizens. The law came into effect on 1 November 2013.[6]

The 2013 §22(3) PStG reads: 'Where the child cannot be assigned to either the female or the male sex, its civil status is to be recorded in the register of births without such declaration.' In that case, the person's sex is to be specified as 'X' in their travel passport; identity cards in Germany do not show the sex of the person concerned anyway.

3.2. INTERPRETATION OF THE 2013 §22(3) PStG

The 2013 provision has made it possible to leave the gender entry for an intersex child blank when registering its birth. This decision was primarily motivated by

3 OLG Zweibrücken 15.1.2003, *StAZ* 2003, 171, 172.

4 OLG Naumburg 14.12.2000, *StAZ* 2002, 169, 170; KG 11.1.1965, *NJW* 1965, 1084; AG Freiburg 2.2.1982, *StAZ* 1983, 16–17; AG Hannover 15.9.1978, *StAZ* 1981, 240.

5 Statement by the German Ethics Council regarding intersex (Stellungnahme des Deutschen Ethikrates zum Thema Intersexualität), Bundestagsdrucksache (BT-Drucks) 17/9088 of 14.2.2012.

6 Art. 10(2) Gesetz zur Änderung personenstandsrechtlicher Vorschriften of 7.5.2013 (Bundesgesetzblatt [BGBl.] Teil I, p. 1122) <http://dipbt.bundestag.de/extrakt/ba/WP17/451/45180.html> (last accessed 07.12.2017).

the desire to ease the burden of the parents having to assign a gender to intersex children as quickly as possible.[7] At the same time, it was intended as a signal to parents and their doctors that both the legal system and society accept the existence of intersex, that there is no need for hasty decision-making and that the child can also find its identity and social role 'between the sexes'.

§22(3) PStG is applicable to all children born intersex. Where the provision speaks of the impossibility of assigning the child to either the female or the male sex, it is referring to those cases where such assignment is not 'unequivocally' possible.[8] From the perspective of the registrar in charge, the deciding factor in that regard is whether or not the birth announcement contains a reference to the child's sex (No. 22.2 *Verwaltungsvorschrift zum Personenstandsgesetz* – PStG-VwV). §22(3) PStG enables a person to live their entire life without having their gender determined under civil status law. This represented a paradigm shift: the law implicitly accepted that association with either the female or the male sex may be permanently impossible.

The 2013 provision has been criticised for allegedly making it mandatory to leave the gender entry for intersex children blank, thereby automatically revealing their intersex nature. This has been said to even increase the pressure on their parents to subject them to gender reassignment surgery.[9] However, this interpretation of the provision is based on a misconception: according to the intent and purpose of the provision, as well as the will of the legislature,[10] §22(3) PStG merely provides the *option* of leaving the gender entry blank when an intersex child is born – it does not make it mandatory in any way. This means that at the birth of an intersex child there is a right to choose whether to make use of §22(3) PStG or to register its 'predominant' gender (as had previously been the practice).[11]

Where no gender has been declared at birth registration, the parents can submit this information at any later date by making a declaration to the registry office. §27(3) No. 4 PStG provides for the subsequent declaration of a child's

7 Member of the German Parliament (Mitglied des Deutschen Bundestages – MdB) U. Jelpke, Deutscher Bundestag, Plenarprotokoll 17/219 of 31.1.2013, p. 27220 (C); R. Bockstette, 'Das Personenstandsrechts-Änderungsgesetz' [2013] *StAZ* 169, 172–173.

8 Recommendation and report of the Committee for the Interior (Beschlussempfehlung und Bericht des Innenausschusses) of 30.1.2013, BT-Drucks 17/12192, p. 11.

9 Cf. W. Sieberichs, 'Das unbestimmte Geschlecht' [2013] Zeitschrift für das gesamte Familienrecht (*FamRZ*) 1180, 1184.

10 Member of the German Parliament (Mitglied des Deutschen Bundestages – MdB) P. Tauber, Deutscher Bundestag, Plenarprotokoll 17/219 of 31.1.2013, p. 27222 (C).

11 T. Helms, 'Personenstandsrechtliche und familienrechtliche Aspekte der Intersexualität vor dem Hintergrund des neuen §22 Abs. 3 PStG', in I. Götz, K. Seelmann, I. Schwenzer, J. Taupitz and I. Rakete-Dombek (eds.), *Festschrift für Gerd Brudermüller zum 65. Geburtstag*, CH Beck Verlag, 2014, 301, pp. 304–305; W. Sieberichs, 'Das unbestimmte Geschlecht' [2013] *FamRZ* 1180, 1184.

gender to be entered in the birth register (*Folgebeurkundung*). This entry is conditional on the presentation of a doctor's certificate;[12] a court order is not required. §27(3) No. 4 PStG obviously also is applicable where a now adult child wishes to declare their previously undetermined gender to the registry office.

The law thus explicitly regulates two situations. §22(3) PStG addresses the situation at childbirth: if no declaration of sex is made in a birth announcement, no entry in this regard is recorded in the register. §27(3) No. 4 PStG ties in with that provision and provides for a subsequent declaration of the sex of a person whose gender entry was left blank at their birth.

However, what about cases where unambiguous adherence to one of the genders was assumed at birth and the child's intersex only came to light as it grew up? This is certainly not uncommon in medical practice, as is shown by the chapter by Hughes in this volume on the different variants of intersex. Furthermore, it is unclear what rights intersex persons possess where they were born before the 2013 provision came into force. The Act contains no specific provision for these cases, meaning that the general principles of civil status law must be applied. The correction of a gender entry can only be effected by way of a correcting amendment (*Personenstandsberichtigung*). The question that now poses itself is whether an amendment can retroactively make the register's gender entry blank. In my opinion there is no reason why that should not be possible: had the registrar already known at the time of their birth that the person in question could not be assigned to either the female or the male sex, no gender would have been recorded. Furthermore, allowing only some intersex persons to register a blank gender entry while barring others from doing so would violate the fundamental principle of equality. The German Federal Court (*Bundesgerichtshof* – BGH) in a decision of 22 June 2016 took the same stance.[13]

3.3. PRACTICAL RELEVANCE

The Federal Ministry of the Interior (*Bundesinnenministerium*) conducted a survey to determine how many persons have made use of the 2013 option in the first two years since the enactment of the law: according to the results, there were only 12 cases of a child's sex not being reported in its birth announcement.[14] In roughly half of those 12 cases, the child's gender entry was submitted within the next few months after birth. Furthermore, among the 12 cases there were apparently a few applications for retroactive correction from persons who

[12] R. Bockstette, 'Das Personenstandsrechts-Änderungsgesetz' [2013] *StAZ* 169, 172.
[13] BGH 22.6.2016, *FamRZ* 2016, 1580, 1581.
[14] BT-Drucks 18/7310, p. 3. For further details see the chapter by Meyer in this volume.

already had an unambiguous gender entry in the register, of which all but one succeeded.

Given that there were only a few cases, one might be tempted to ask whether the legislator ought not to have listened to the advice of classical Roman lawyers: 'Quod raro fit, non observant legislatores' ('What is rarely done is not observed by legislators').[15] When passing judgement it must, however, be borne in mind that this initial statistic does not reveal how many intersex persons actually live in Germany. During the reform process of 2013 the estimate was that there might be around 150 to 340 births of intersex children per year in Germany. This estimate is not contradicted by the numbers that are available thus far. Even doctors that are critical of existing treatment recommendations nonetheless advise parents to choose a gender for their child 'as a working assumption' in order to facilitate their integration into our society's binary gender order.[16] However, at present the leaving blank of gender entries is being recommended in some cases. A recent article in the professional journal *Kinder- und Jugendarzt* (which refers specifically to the 2013 §22(3) PStG in this context) reads:

> In exceptional cases in which assignment to the male or female sex cannot be made definitely at all, the possibility of leaving this matter undecided and observing the child's later development should be considered. This path requires a very high standard of information and support for the parents, but may be better than having to correct a bad decision at a later date.[17]

The first reports from parents that had already left their child's gender undetermined in social life before the reform of the PStG have become available and are positive.[18] A process of discussion among doctors and the parents concerned has been initiated in this matter, the outcome of which is not yet foreseeable. There is reason to believe that the number of parents deciding to make use of the option provided by §22(3) PStG will increase in future, but it is to be suspected that the rise will be slow and that of all families concerned still only a few will choose this option.

---

15 Cf. WACKE, above n. 1, p. 869.

16 G. SINNECKER, 'Wenn das Geschlecht nicht eindeutig ist …' [2014] *Kinder- und Jugendarzt* 24, 35: 'als Arbeitshypothese'.

17 Ibid: 'In Einzelfällen, in denen eine Zuordnung zum männlichen oder weiblichen Geschlecht überhaupt nicht sicher möglich ist, sollte die Möglichkeit bedacht werden, diese Entscheidung offenzulassen und die tatsächliche weitere Entwicklung des Kindes zu beobachten. Dieser Weg bedarf einer sehr guten Aufklärung und Unterstützung der Eltern, kann aber besser sein, als eine Fehlentscheidung später korrigieren zu müssen'.

18 Statement by J.M. KRIEGLER, representative of the XY-women's group of parents for the hearing in the German Parliament on 25 June 2012 on the subject of intersex, Ausschuss für Familie, Senioren, Frauen und Jugend, Ausschussdrucksache 17 (13), pp. 181–182.

3.4. CONSEQUENCES: THE FAMILY LAW STATUS OF PERSONS WITH A BLANK GENDER ENTRY

Even though the number of cases has been rather low thus far, §22(3) PStG has considerable potential to disrupt the current legal system and certainly calls for a critical reconsideration of the existing gender-specific distinctions made by the law. This is even more true since the Federal Constitutional Court in its decision of 10 October 2017 has ruled that the reform has not gone far enough and a 'positive' third-gender option must be introduced (see in more detail below at Section 4).

3.4.1. *Marriage*

On 1 October 2017, a new law introducing the right to marry for same-sex couples (*Gesetz zur Einführung des Rechts auf Eheschließung für Personen gleichen Geschlechts*)[19] came into force in Germany. At the same time the institution of registered partnership (*eingetragene Lebenspartnerschaft*) was abolished. The new §1353(1) *Bürgerliches Gesetzbuch* (BGB) reads: 'Marriage is entered into by two persons of different or same sex' ('Die Ehe wird von zwei Personen verschiedenen oder gleichen Geschlechts … geschlossen.'). It is quite astonishing that the new law speaks of two persons of either different or the same sex, thus leaving out those persons who have made use of the option of the 2013 §22(3) PStG to leave their gender entry blank.[20] One reason for this shortcoming is that the new law was passed under extreme time pressure since Chancellor Angela Merkel only signalled at the very end of the legislature that – although she personally, was not in favour of allowing same-sex marriages – she would not stand in the way of such a reform.[21] It would have been easy and much better if the wording of the new law had defined marriage as an institution entered into by 'two persons'. But to me it is quite clear that this result can be reached by way of interpretation. The main thrust of the new law was to clarify that the institution of marriage is no longer restricted to two persons of a different sex. Intersex persons clearly were not taken into consideration. In the light of the strong constitutional protection of marriage (Article 6 basic law – *Grundgesetz* (GG)) the new law can be only interpreted in allowing any two persons to marry – regardless of their sex.

---

19 BGBl. 2017 part I, p. 2787.

20 D. Schwab, 'Eheschließung für Personen gleichen Geschlechts' [2017] *FamRZ* 1284, 1286–1287.

21 Angela Merkel made this statement in an interview by the women's magazine *Brigitte* on 26 June 2017. The Bill (which had already been introduced into Parliament as a political signal but initially never seemed to have any chance of being passed) was voted on in Parliament 4 days later on 30 June 2017, the last day of the Parliamentary session in this legislature.

3.4.2. *The Law of Filiation*

The question as to whether gender adherence can be completely ignored in the context of the law of filiation is more difficult to answer.

That said, maternity does not appear overly problematic. Although §1591 BGB reads: 'The mother of a child is the woman who gave birth to it', there are no difficulties in applying this provision by way of teleological interpretation to a person whose gender assignment is undecided. If an intersex person gave birth to a child §1591 BGB would certainly be applied even under the current state of the law.[22]

Paternity, on the other hand, poses more difficult questions. A child's legal father is not necessarily its biological father. Instead, a child is first and foremost assigned the 'man' as its legal father 'who is married to the mother ... at the date of the birth' (§1592 No. 1 BGB). This rule was not extended to same-sex married couples when same-sex marriage was introduced on 1 October 2017. If the mother of the child is not married, the father is principally the 'man' 'who has acknowledged paternity' (§1592 No. 2 BGB). While the law assumes in both cases that the legal and biological father are usually one and the same person, it accepts that there are constellations where that is not so. If none of the above-mentioned criteria for assigning paternity are applicable, the courts will determine paternity on the basis of the child's genetic ancestry (§1592 No. 3 BGB).

The rules of the German law of descent represent a compromise between biological and social criteria. When posing the question as to whether the law of descent now in force can ignore the gender of the 'father', cases where an intersex person is the child's biological father can be considered unproblematic. There are no difficulties in, for example, overriding the wording of §1592 No. 3 BGB by way of interpretation and thereby allowing for a determination of paternity on behalf of or against an intersex biological father by way of a court order. However, it seems debatable whether an intersex person without an assigned gender under current German law has the right of acknowledging paternity in regard to a child that is not descended from them. It must be borne in mind that the law also does not currently allow an 'acknowledgement of parenthood' by a female partner of the child's mother. In fact, in Germany joint parenthood is only available to same-sex couples by way of adoption, and this is always conditional on the other biological parent's consent (§1749(1) BGB). Currently, intersex persons without a gender entry will most likely also have to be referred to (stepchild) adoption.

---

[22] Cf. the case of a trans man giving birth to a child who was considered to be – in legal terms – the mother of the child: BGH 6.9.2017, *FamRZ* 2017, 1855.

Nonetheless, the debate has also been moving forward in relation to this issue: some of the European jurisdictions that provide for same-sex marriage or registered same-sex partnership now also allow – under certain conditions – same-sex parenthood without prior adoption. In these legal systems co-motherhood is automatically established either owing to the existence of a same-sex marriage or registered partnership (comparable to §1592(1) BGB), or as a result of the female partner's unilateral declaration (comparable to an acknowledgement of paternity). Ultimately, the gender of the other parent besides the birth mother has thereby become irrelevant. However, most of the aforementioned jurisdictions restrict these 'gender-neutral' rules for establishing parenthood to cases involving artificial insemination by way of sperm donation. As the sperm donor is unavailable to fill the role of legal parent it seems obvious to automatically assign the child a second parent without requiring an adoption. But the Belgian and Dutch law, for example, has already gone beyond such constellations, and has extended the rules on co-motherhood to cases involving natural conception.

In Germany a reform of the law of descent is on the agenda;[23] how far it will go is not yet foreseeable. However, one thing that seems certain to me is that gender of a parent will become less important under the law of descent in the future.

4. A REFORM THAT HAS NOT GONE FAR ENOUGH? THE DECISION OF THE FEDERAL CONSTITUTIONAL COURT OF 10 OCTOBER 2017

In July 2014, shortly after the 2013 civil status law had come into force, an intersex person named Vanja applied to have their female sex entry in their birth registration deleted and replaced with 'inter/diverse'. The applicant claimed that they had a right to have their entry in the civil status register reflect their true gender identity. Leaving their gender entry blank would not conform to their self-perception. The registry office's rejection of their application was confirmed by the Federal Supreme Court (*Bundesgerichtshof* – BGH) on 22 June 2016.[24] The applicant challenged this decision before the Federal Constitutional Court (*Bundesverfassungsgericht* – BVerfG).

---

23 Federal Ministry of Justice and Consumer Protection (Bundesministerium für Justiz und Verbraucherschutz) (ed.), *Arbeitskreis Abstammungsrecht: Abschlussbericht*, Bundesanzeiger Verlag, 2017, pp. 68–70; T. Helms, *Rechtliche, biologische und soziale Elternschaft – Herausforderungen durch neue Familienformen, Gutachten F zum 71. Deutschen Juristentag Essen*, CH Beck Verlag, 2016, pp. F 37–38.

24 BGH 22.6.2016, *FamRZ* 2016, 1580.

On 10 October 2017, the Federal Constitutional Court overturned the decision of the Federal Supreme Court and declared that German civil status law must allow a 'positive' third-gender option (so go beyond the already existing option of leaving the gender entry blank).[25] It based its decision both on the general right of personality (Article 2(1) GG in conjunction with Article 1(1) GG) and the constitutional requirement of non-discrimination and equal treatment (Article 3(3) GG). The Court held that the possibility to choose leaving the entry blank did not reflect that, since the person in question did not see themselves as a genderless person, but rather perceives themselves as having a gender beyond male and female. The Federal Constitutional Court ordered the legislature to enact new provisions by 31 December 2018.

Personally, I do not find the conclusion of the German Federal Constitutional Court that the Basic Law compels the German legislator (although German law already allowed the gender entry to be left blank) to introduce a third 'positive' gender option very convincing. The reasoning of the German Federal Constitutional Court does not reflect the purposes and functions of civil status register entries. §1(1) PStG defines civil status and reads: 'Civil status within the meaning of this Act is a person's status within the legal system as determined by the criteria of family law.' ('*Personenstand im Sinne dieses Gesetzes ist die sich aus den Merkmalen des Familienrechts ergebende Stellung einer Person innerhalb der Rechtsordnung*'). First and foremost, this definition demonstrates that civil status register entries have a subservient function: they contain particulars that, according to the rules of substantive family law, are of fundamental importance for a person's legal status. It therefore follows that as long as substantive family law does not contain any specific rules for the 'intersex/diverse' gender, there is no point in recording such an entry in the civil status register.

Furthermore, civil status register entries are not mere statements of fact, but rather normative in character. For example, the question of who is to be registered as a child's father in the birth register does not depend on genetic descent, but on the rules of §1592 BGB.

Moreover, the effects of civil status register entries on an individual's public self-expression are limited: nobody is under a general legal obligation to identify themselves with their civil status register entry in social or commercial situations. As a result, the Federal Constitutional Court had previously emphasised the fact that anyone is generally free, for example, to present themselves under a name they have chosen, unless the law prescribes an obligation to use their formally registered name when dealing with the authorities as an exception.[26]

---

25 BVerfG 10.10.2017, *FamRZ* 2017, 2046, with a comment by T. Helms – *StAZ* 2018, 21 with a comment by S. Wiggerich – *NJW* 2017, 3643 with a comment by S.L. Gössl.

26 BVerfG 8.3.1988, *BVerfGE* 78, 38, 51–52.

The claim for having a third gender recorded in the civil status register heavily relied on the Federal Constitutional Court's older case law with regard to the legal status of transgender persons.[27] But in my opinion the situation in question is not the same.[28] The difference between transgender and intersex in this regard is not merely that 'male' and 'female' are categories in substantive family law, but rather that there are also social role models for the female and male genders. The Federal Supreme Court's decisions on transgender were at least partially a result of the desire to acknowledge and strengthen the transgender person's sense of belonging to the respective social group by enabling their full legal transition to their self-perceived gender. The problem faced by intersex persons, however, is that there are, as yet, no widely accepted role models present in social reality, and the acceptance of a self-attribution to an 'intersex/diverse' gender is hardly going to make a difference in helping to solve the issues that arise from having to live in a binary social gender society.

Although the German Federal Constitutional Court has stressed that (apart from retaining the option of leaving the gender entry permanently blank) only one more 'positive' category has to be introduced into German civil status law, it is difficult to see how this can be achieved. Once the link between substantive family law and civil status law (as explained above) is abandoned, gender declarations will ultimately have to be freed of any and all legal requirements and left to the free choice of the individual. In a survey of intersex persons conducted by the German Ethics Council in regard to the desired designation of their gender identity, 50 per cent chose female and 10 per cent chose male; the remainder chose a different designation: 10 per cent chose intersex, 6 per cent preferred to have no designation and small numbers voted for one of the following: '*Zwitter*', hermaphrodite, human being, transgender human being etc.[29] Hence the gender categories that lie between the two poles 'unequivocally female' and 'unequivocally male' appear not to be clearly delineated. I therefore found it justified that the German legislator had restricted itself to allowing gender entries to be left blank in order to take into account the special situation of intersex persons.

---

27 BVerfG 11.10.1978, *BVerfGE* 49, 286, 298; cf. also BVerfG 27.5.2008, *BVerfGE* 121, 175, 190–191; BVerfG 11.01.2011, *StAZ* 2011, 141, 144. On this and other seminal decisions by German courts, see A. Dutta, 'The Legal Status of Transsexual and Transgender persons in Germany', in J.M. Scherpe (ed.), *The Legal Status of Transsexual and Transgender Persons*, Intersentia 2015, pp. 207–221.

28 Other authors are of a different opinion, cf. e.g. J.T. Theilen, 'Intersexualität bleibt unsichtbar: Kritische Anmerkungen zum Beschluss des Bundesgerichtshofs zu nicht-binären Eintragungen im Personenstandsrecht' [2016] *StAZ* 295, 300 and S.L. Gössl, 'Intersexuelle Menschen und ihre personenstandsrechtliche Erfassung' [2016] *Neue Zeitschrift für Familienrecht* (*NZFam*) 1122.

29 BT-Drucks 17/9088, p. 26.

5. PROSPECTS OF A CIVIL STATUS REGISTER WITHOUT GENDER ENTRY?

In its decision, the Federal Constitutional Court also hinted several times at the option to abolish the assignment of gender in the civil status register. At first glance, this seems to be a plausible option After all, what rules will remain that are necessarily dependent on adherence to a particular gender? Compulsory military service – which applies only to men under Article 12a GG – has been abolished, and it hardly seems essential to register a person's sex in the birth register because there are different points systems for boys and girls when they engage in sport competitions at school. Indeed, the German Ethics Council's position statement of 14 February 2012 asked the German legislator to consider whether entering a person's gender in the civil status register is even still necessary.[30] Scholars are also already debating the vision of a gender-neutral family law under the catchphrase 'sexless family law'.[31]

However, what must not be overlooked in this regard is that civil status issues are of international character. Even if the German legal system were to successfully refrain from any and all differentiation based on sex, it would nevertheless – in light of the current state of international developments in (family) law – not be advisable to completely forgo a gender entry in the civil status register: there are currently roughly seven million (exclusively) foreign nationals residing in Germany whose civil status in many respects is determined – in accordance with German private international law – by the national law of their (foreign) homeland (cf. e.g. Articles 10, 13(1), 19(1), 22(1) Introductory Act to the German Civil Code (*Einführungsgesetz zum Bürgerlichen Gesetzbuch* – EGBGB)).[32] So even if German (family) law were framed in gender-neutral terms, the German authorities and courts would still have to apply foreign law under which legal sex will continue to come into play for the foreseeable future; for this reason alone it seems sensible to continue to include a gender entry in the civil status register. Most importantly, though, the mobility of German citizens is increasing continuously; if a German is required to verify their gender abroad – in connection with, e.g., marriage, adoption or acknowledgement of paternity – under the rules that apply there, they are reliant on being able to easily do so by providing an excerpt from the German civil status register.

30 BT-Drucks 17/9088, p. 59 (Empfehlung No. 4 zum Personenstandsrecht).

31 Cf. e.g. A. Büchler and M. Cottier, 'Intersexualität, Transsexualität und das Recht' (2005) 17 *Freiburger FrauenStudien* 115, 127 and 131–132.

32 The gender of a person is also determined according to their national law, OLG Frankfurt 12.11.2004, *StAZ* 2005, 73, 74; OLG Karlsruhe 28.1.2003, *StAZ* 2003, 139; S.L. Gössl, 'Intersexuelle Menschen im Internationalen Privatrecht' [2013] *StAZ* 301, 302–303.

These private international law considerations therefore arguably preclude the general abolishment of gender entries in German civil status registers – regardless of the way in which the German legal system will develop.

6. CONCLUSIONS

§22(3) of the German civil status law had, from a legal perspective, not introduced a third gender into German law. However, the German Federal Constitutional Court has now ruled that German civil status law has to go one step further and introduce a 'positive' third-gender option. How the legislator will react is still unclear.

The key challenge facing family law is not the creation of a special status for a third gender. What is actually needed is a critical examination in order to determine whether the few gender-dependent provisions that remain are still required. In this regard it has been shown that the current trend is towards abolishing family law differentiations based on sex in any event. However, this does not mean necessarily that the gender of a person should not be recorded in the civil status register at all.

THE GERMAN INTER-MINISTERIAL WORKING GROUP ON INTER- AND TRANSSEXUALITY

Thomas MEYER

This chapter is intended to give a short overview of the situation of transsexual and intersex persons in Germany, and particularly on how the German Government currently approaches the topic.

1. LEGAL SITUATION IN GERMANY

1.1. INTERSEX PERSONS

German law currently only differentiates between two legal genders/sexes: male and female. The official rationale for the Civil Code of 1896 states: 'Today's science does not recognise intersex persons.' Therefore, every child had to be registered as male or female. The possibility of leaving the legal designation of sex open in a child's birth certificate only came into existence at the end of 2013, when section 22(3) of the Act on Civil Status (*Personenstandsgesetz*) was amended. The child in question then does not have a sex in the legal sense. Adults also have the possibility of correcting their sex designation to 'no information on sex'. Registrars may carry out this correction; but, as a rule, it is done by the court. Only a certificate from a doctor is required. Assigning a sex-neutral first name in the same procedure is not possible. However, at the end of 2017, the Federal Constitutional Court held that these provisions were in violation of the Basic Law (the German Constitution).[1] The gist of the decision is that that there must be a positive recognition of a legal gender which is not 'female' or 'male', and not recording any information on the legal gender is insufficient. The Court suggested that, alternatively, civil status registers could stop recording the legal gender of any person. As a result of this decision, the legislature must enact new provisions by 31 December 2018 at the latest.

Some figures may be of interest here: it is estimated that there are approximately 8,000 to 10,000 people in Germany (82.2 million inhabitants as of 31 December 2015) with variations in their sexual characteristics. Despite this, from 2013 to January 2016, the possibility of leaving the sex registration open on the birth certificate was made use of just 12 times.

1.2. GERMAN ACT ON TRANSSEXUALS

There is a German Act on Transsexuals (*Gesetz über die Änderung der Vornamen und die Feststellung der Geschlechtszugehörigkeit in besonderen Fällen – Transsexuellengesetz* – TSG, of 10 September 1980). There are two options available under that law:

First, the court changes the male first name or names of a transsexual individual to a first name corresponding to their perceived sex of male or female (section 1 TSG). For this, the court must procure two expert opinions from specialists for transsexuality which confirm that the applicant is transsexual (section 4(3) TSG).

Second, the court may also adjust the first name *and* legal sex entered into the civil status register to the perceived sex of the transsexual person (section 8 TSG). As such, it may change the sex entered into the civil status

1 BVerfG 10.10.2017 (1 BvR 2019/16), FamRZ 2017, 2046, with a comment by T. Helms at 2054. A press release is available in English at <http://www.bundesverfassungsgericht.de/SharedDocs/Pressemitteilungen/EN/2017/bvg17-095.html> (last accessed 16.01.2018).

register from male to female or the other way around. Previously, there were other conditions which applied in addition to the two expert opinions:

- The applicant was required to be unmarried (section 8(1) number 2 TSG).
- The applicant was required to be infertile (section 8(1) number 3 TSG).
- The applicant was required to have had sex reassignment surgery (section 8(1) number 4 TSG).

But the Federal Constitutional Court has declared those preconditions, which were contained in the original statute from 1980, to be in violation of the German Constitution and therefore as null and void.[2] This means that now conditions for a mere name change are the same as those as for a full change of sex. Obviously, this does not really make much sense, and legislation should provide for clarity in this regard.

In 2016 in Germany 1,868 cases were initiated pursuant to the Act on Transsexuals. In 1995 only 400 cases were initiated.

This legal situation is inconsistent. Changing one's sex from male to female or the other way around with a corresponding change of the first name requires two expert opinions from specialists. But a doctor's certification is sufficient to delete an entry as to an individual's registered sex (on which see above). However, following the Constitutional Court's decision of 10 October 2017[3] reform of these provisions can be expected before the end of 2018.

1.3. MARRIAGE FOR INTER- AND TRANSSEXUAL PERSONS

Until 1 October 2017 only two individuals of different legal gender could enter into marriage in Germany, but two persons of the same sex could form a registered life partnership pursuant to the Act on Registered Life Partnerships. Therefore, an individual whose civil status is neither male nor female cannot marry or enter into a life partnership. The opinion on 'Intersexuality' published by the German Ethics Council on 23 February 2012 stated that persons whose sex is recorded as 'other' should be able to enter this into a registered civil partnership.[4] Some Council members also took the view that intersex persons should also be permitted to marry any other person.[5]

---

2 On this, see further A. Dutta, 'The Legal Status of Transsexual and Transgender Persons in Germany', in J.M. Scherpe (ed.), The Legal Status of Transsexual and Transgender Persons, Intersentia, Cambridge 2015, pp. 207–221.

3 Above n. 1.

4 See <http://www.ethikrat.org/themen/medizin-und-pflege/intersexualitaet> (last accessed 20.07.2017). The texts are available in English and French.

5 Ibid, Recommendation 9.2.3 'On the civil status law', p. 167.

Opening up marriage for all people did not seem a viable political option at that time, and the opinion has to be understood accordingly. However, this changed somewhat surprisingly during the last Parliamentary session before the general election in September 2017. Hence, since 1 October 2017 two persons of different sexes and two persons of the same sex have been able to enter into marriage. Section 1353, 'Conjugal community' of the German Civil Code reads: '(1) Marriage is entered into for life by two persons of different or same sexes.'[6] Registered life partnership cannot be entered into any more, but existing life partnerships may be continued, or converted into marriages. Individuals whose legal gender is neither male nor female are not mentioned in the law;[7] therefore, it is unclear whether they can marry.

2. MEASURES BY THE GOVERNMENT

For the legislative term running until September 2017, the Conservatives and the Social Democrats had specified in their coalition agreement that they would evaluate the improvements attained for intersex persons since section 22(3) of the Act on Civil Status was amended in 2013. It was agreed that, if appropriate, more improvements would be made with a focus on the special situation of trans and intersex persons.

Within the Federal Government, the Ministry of Family Affairs, Senior Citizens, Women and Youth has taken on primary responsibility for the issue. Also involved, however, are the Ministry of the Interior (being responsible for civil status law), the Ministry of Justice and Consumer Protection (being responsible for family and criminal law) and the Ministry of Health (being responsible for healthcare issues).

In 2014, the Ministry of Family Affairs, Senior Citizens, Women and Youth established an inter-ministerial working group on 'Inter- and Transsexuality' with the above-mentioned ministries. The working group has established the goal of identifying the many potential problems by exchanging experiences with experts and interest groups, discussing recommendations for potential solutions at the legislative level, and publishing the results in a report in mid-2017 at the end of the legislative term.

The working group addressed the following issues:

- Block I – Medical treatment for persons with congenital variations in their sexual characteristics (DSD – disorders or differences of sex development), protection from medically unnecessary operations.

6 Text available in English <https://www.gesetze-im-internet.de/bgb/> (last accessed 16.01.2018).

7 *Gesetz zur Einführung des Rechts auf Eheschließung für Personen gleichen Geschlechts* of 20 July 2017, BGBl. 2017, p. 2787.

- Block II – Expansion and enhancement of counselling, educational and prevention structures.
- Block III – Evaluation of required statutory changes

These had been discussed in turn.

3. BLOCK I: MEDICAL INTERVENTION/IS THERE A NEED FOR REGULATION?

The Federal Government wants to prevent unnecessary medical interventions on intersex persons at a very young age. Protecting children's best interests and ensuring that people take autonomous and informed decisions concerning their own body are the major issues addressed in the debate. There is a group of Parliamentarians who want to pass a law on this as a matter of urgency. Some interest groups are pushing for quick legislative action as well.

A 2015 opinion[8] submitted by the German Medical Association, the organisation representing German doctors, states that especially irreversible operations and treatments that are not medically necessary, but rather serve to enable a visual attribution as female or male., should generally require that the child has the capacity to consent. This means that such operations should not be carried out before the child is about 14 or 15 years old. However, the opinion by the German Medical Association advocates allowing exceptions to this requirement because we do not know how children whose sex is open will develop. In such cases, the parents, as the representatives of their children, would continue to have to consent to any operation. But this subject is controversial. Another problem is children with congenital adrenal hyperplasia (CAH). There is disagreement as to whether they or their parents must consent to medical intervention; therefore, the medical committee tasked with developing guidelines addresses the issue in a footnote. The July 2016 guideline (S2k guideline 174/000 of the AWMF – Association of the Scientific Medical Societies in Germany)[9] concerning variations in sexual development was ratified by the various medical societies and provides advice to doctors.

One current demand is that only the person affected by DSD should be allowed to consent to an operation, and thus would prohibit parents from consenting to medical interventions as representatives of their children.

---

8 <http://www.bundesaerztekammer.de/aerzte/medizin-ethik/wissenschaftlicher-beirat/veroeffentlichungen/weitere-themen/dsd/> (last accessed 16.01.2018).

9 <http://www.awmf.org/leitlinien/detail/ll/174-001.html> (last accessed 16.01.2018).

In such cases, there will be difficulties in establishing statutory boundaries for determining the permissibility of medical interventions. For example, at what stage is the risk of cancer so high that an early operation is indicated and can be approved by parents? Others demand that parental consent should be possible only with court approval. Yet another opinion holds that medical counselling for parents in advance of the operation should be mandatory.

Reflections of the inter-ministerial working group on 'Inter- and Transsexuality' stated that mandatory counselling for parents and children is necessary. This should be directed toward enabling the parents to support the child in their own development, to accept them, and in the final analysis allowing them to independently decide with which gender identity and with what form of gender characteristics they wish to live. It is primarily the parents rather than the children who need support and information about the fact that there are people whose sex is not clearly male or female, and about the fact that it is of great significance for the development of children to allow them self-determination in terms of their sexual identity when they are old enough to make that decision on their own. After all, as this topic affects the core of an individual's personality, parents must be given to understand that only the best interests of the child must be at the centre of their decision. Mandatory counselling could be connected with obligations to provide documentation, and possibly also with a waiting period, before a medical measure is carried out.

By contrast, the working group did not consider an express prohibition of all surgery to be appropriate. A statutory prohibition would serve neither the child nor the parents, and could lead to circumventions of the law (justification of surgery by way of other diagnoses, moving to another hospital, carrying out surgery abroad, etc.).

Likewise, in the opinion of the working group, introducing an obligation to obtain approval from the family court would not effectively improve the protection of children. The court would have to procure an expert opinion on the medical necessity of the surgery, which would not lend itself to a binding legal definition for the individual case, especially given the large number of varieties/variations of sex development.

Furthermore, protection under the criminal law already exists owing to the criminal offences of bodily injury and genital mutilation (sections 223 et seq. *Strafgesetzbuch*) if an intervention not medically necessary is undertaken on a child who has not provided personal consent. Accompanying mandatory psycho-social counselling by qualified experts and peer counselling by participating in already-existing counselling structures would be desirable.

It would also be desirable to use Federal Government pilot projects for the structural promotion of psycho-social counselling and peer counselling to develop counselling guidelines for various stakeholders and to establish methods of cooperation with medical competence centres consistent with the recommendations of the current S2k Guideline 174/001[10] on variations in sexual development.

Nevertheless, the Conservatives and the Social Democrats have specified in their new coalition agreement for the legislative term running until September 2021, that sex assignment medical treatment of children should only be lawful to avoid danger of death.

4. BLOCK II: COUNSELLING AND SUPPORT STRUCTURES

The working group also addressed the question of the necessity and appropriateness of measures to improve the structure of counselling for trans- and intersex children and teenagers, for their parents and guardians, and for adults as well. Special psycho-social counselling offers for persons with congenital variations in physical sex characteristics, transsexual persons and their families that do not focus on medical issues exist in only a few locations in Germany, or are usually done on a volunteer basis by interest groups of affected persons.

4.1. FOR PEOPLE WITH CONGENITAL VARIATIONS IN PHYSICAL SEX CHARACTERISTICS

In order to ascertain the status quo and the need for counselling, educational and preventive activities, people with different variations in their physical sex development, their parents and interest groups, including peer counsellors and experts in various professions, were asked about their own experiences with counselling, their need for counselling and further training, as well as possibilities and conditions for the development of counselling structures that do justice to existing needs.

Based on the results, the Federal Government will develop and fund a pilot project with the goal of building up and strengthening offers of peer counselling.

4.2. FOR TRANSSEXUAL, TRANSGENDER AND TRANS IDENTITY PERSONS

An expert meeting on counselling structures took place in June 2016 and was attended by 59 members from a total of 33 associations, initiatives and groups. The results are currently being evaluated.

---

10 Ibid.

4.3. IMPARTING KNOWLEDGE/POLICY OF ACCEPTANCE/ 'INTER-TRANS-MAINSTREAMING'

The Family Ministry has funded a flyer titled 'Girl? Boy? My intersex child',[11] as well as the publication of a set of guidelines for counselling centres on counselling intersex persons and their families. This has been available since early March 2016 and can be obtained in pregnancy, sex, partnership and family planning counselling centres. These materials are designed to provide medical and psychological experts and members of other professions, such as midwives, educators and family counsellors, with encouragement for treatment and counselling of trans and intersex persons and their families in a manner that is founded in the recognition of their human rights. Assuming that the necessary budget funds are allocated, plans are to fund another flyer for parents of transsexual children.

5. BLOCK III: CHANGES IN THE LAW

5.1. SEX 'AVOIDABLE' AS A LEGAL CATEGORY – 'ANOTHER SEX'?

The Family Ministry has commissioned an expert report on the topic of 'Sex and Law: Status Quo and Development of Regulatory Models to Recognise and Protect Sexual Identity'.[12] The report also includes a synoptic list of those legal rules in which the German legal system uses the characteristic of sex, as well as an analysis as to whether that use is necessary or can be abandoned. Concrete language of substantiated regulatory proposals for the recognition and protection of sexual identity will be developed. The proposals for legislation will take into account the results of a comparative law study on legislation on the topic, e.g. from Malta and Argentina, with regard to the rules on civil status and to the protection, recognition and support with regard to sex.

5.2. CIVIL STATUS – CHANGE OF FIRST NAME/CIVIL STATUS – REFORM OF THE ACT ON TRANSSEXUALS

In 2016 and 2017, the working group also focused specifically on the situation and concerns of transsexual individuals.

---

[11] <https://www.bmfsfj.de/bmfsfj/service/publikationen/weiblich--maennlich----ihr-intergeschlechtliches-kind-/83714> (last accessed 16.01.2018).

[12] On this, see the chapter by N. Althoff in this volume.

In 2015, the Family Ministry commissioned another expert study which will evaluate in legal terms the procedure pursuant to the Act on Transsexuals with regard to compliance with human rights and international law standards. The study will also examine the processes and barriers encountered in practice by persons who wish to change their civil status. This will include a comparative law analysis of the rules in other countries. The expert opinion was delivered in autumn 2016.[13] The results will serve to supply the inter-ministerial working group with indications for necessary changes in the law, as well as proposals as to how these can be designed.

6. FINAL REMARKS

The inter-ministerial working group could not agree on a joint final report. Therefore, the Family Ministry issued a report,[14] which shows only the opinion of this ministry, but not necessarily the views of the other ministries. However, because of the decision of the Constitutional Court concerning intersexual persons[15] the legislature will have to act quickly. The Federal Ministry of the Interior has prepared a draft, which will be sent to Parliament soon.

13 <https://www.bmfsfj.de/bmfsfj/service/publikationen/regelungs--und-reformbedarf-fuer-transgeschlechtliche-menschen/114070> (last accessed 16.01.2018).

14 <https://www.bmfsfj.de/bmfsfj/service/publikationen/zusammenfassung-forschungsergebnisse-und-erkenntnisse-des-bundesministeriums-fuer-familie--senioren--frauen-und-jugend-aus-der-begleitarbeit-zu-der-interministeriellen-arbeitsgruppe--inter--und-transsexualitaet---imag-/120646> (last accessed 16.01.2018).

15 See n. 1 above.

GENDER DIVERSITY IN LAW: THE GERMAN PERSPECTIVE

Nina ALTHOFF*

The right to legal recognition of sex and gender identity is recognised as a fundamental and human right in Germany, as is protection against discrimination and violence based on gender identity and gender diversity in the context of the principle of non-discrimination. Against this background, the German Institute for Human Rights was commissioned by the Federal Ministry for Family Affairs,

* This contribution is based on a report commissioned by the German Bundesministerium für Familie, Senioren, Frauen und Jugend (BMFSFJ). The report and the translation of this chapter (in a previous version) were commissioned and funded by the BMFSFJ and can be found at the following links: <https://www.bmfsfj.de/blob/114066/8a02a557eab695bf7179ff2e92d0ab28/imag-band-8-geschlechtervielfalt-im-recht-data.pdf> and <https://www.bmfsfj.de/blob/116952/2f2af83b324af52cbb1d0efbfda212e2/geschlechtervielfalt-im-recht---englisch---gender-diversity-in-law-data.pdf> (last accessed 29.05.2018).

Senior Citizens, Women and Youth (BMFSFJ)[1] to prepare a report on gender diversity in law, which was published in February 2017.[2]

The report entitled 'Gender Diversity in Law – Status Quo and Development of Regulatory Models for the Recognition and Protection of Gender Diversity' examines how the legal recognition and protection of the diversity of physical sex development, gender identities and gender expression in Germany against the background of fundamental and human rights can and must be improved. The authors conclude that the current legal rules, in particular with regard to the situation of intersex persons[3] and trans/transsexual persons[4], are inadequate. The report is an in-depth analysis of the current law, and uses a comparative[5] as well as a socio-scientific assessment of the civil status regulation for the blank gender entry of intersex new-borns (§22 para. 3 Civil Status Act – *Personenstandsgesetz* – PStG). Several types of regulatory models for the recognition and protection of sex and gender identities have been developed (Part 1 and Annex of the report). Ultimately, the report recommends the drafting of a comprehensive legal framework on the recognition and protection of gender diversity (Part 2 of the report).

The development of regulatory alternatives was carried out in consultation with intersex and trans/transsexual persons, their parents, associations, counsellors and academics, and the initial draft of the Bill sent to an extended

---

1 The report was prepared on behalf of the BMFSFJ to advise the work of the Inter-ministerial Working Group on Inter- and Transsexuality in the 18th legislature. The Federal Government has used it to illuminate questions and problems by exchanges with experts and interests, to discuss proposals for possible legislative solutions and to submit a final paper (see the position paper by the BMFSFJ, *Schutz und Akzeptanz von geschlechtlicher Vielfalt*, Berlin 2017, available at <https://www.bmfsfj.de/blob/119686/619f9892b9f7d198c205dbdc82bcad56/positionspapier-schutz-anerkennung-inter-trans-data.pdf> (last accessed 16.03.2018).

2 N. Althoff, G. Schabram and P. Follmar-Otto, *Geschlechtervielfalt im Recht: Status Quo und Entwicklung von Regelungsmodellen zur Anerkennung und zum Schutz von Geschlechtervielfalt*, BMFSFJ (ed.), Berlin 2017, available in German at <https://www.bmfsfj.de/blob/114066/8a02a557eab695bf7179ff2e92d0ab28/imag-band-8-geschlechtervielfalt-im-recht-data.pdf> (last accessed 29.05.2018).

3 The term 'intersex' refers to persons (inter*, intersexual, intersex persons) whose physical-biological gender and sex characteristics do not fit into the medical and social norms of male and female bodies. This may be due to the appearance of the chromosomes, the germinal glands or the anatomical development of primary or secondary sexual characteristics. The term thus refers to congenital variations of the sexual characteristics.

4 The term 'trans/transsexuality' refers to persons (trans*, transgendered, transsexual, transident persons) who do not identify themselves (only) with the gender assigned to them at birth or who belong to another gender. The term thus refers to the multitude of sexualities and gender identities.

5 Malta, Argentina, Denmark, Ireland and Australia were compared with regard to recognition and protection of gender diversity. In addition to the legal materials, reports of personal experiences and assessments (as far as they were available) were also considered. The results are presented in short table form as well as in detailed country overviews, cf. Althoff, Schabram and Follmar-Otto, above n. 2, Annex 2 (Synoptic legal comparison).

circle of independent organisations with a perspective on inter and trans/transsexuality as well as by scientists and practitioners for comments.

1. SOCIAL-SCIENTIFIC ASSESSMENT OF §22 PARA. 3 OF THE CIVIL STATUS ACT

The focus of the social-scientific assessment was the amendment of the Civil Status Act (PStG), which came into effect on 1 November 2013 and according to which children who 'cannot be attributed to the female or the male gender' (...) are to be entered without a gender specification in the register of births (§22 para. 3 PStG).[6] This statute had been adopted by the legislature to partially address the previous proposals by the German Ethics Council on intersexuality.[7, 8]

The number of applications relying on §§22 para. 3 and 27 para. 3 no. 4 of the PStG was recorded in the period from November 2013 to November 2015 by means of a survey among the states by the State Ministries of the Interior. The application practice was assessed by qualitative and quantitative surveys. For this purpose, semi-structured guideline interviews were conducted with relevant professional groups (from the civil registry office, obstetrics units and counselling centres) as well as those affected and their parents. In addition, the professional groups were also involved through quantitative online surveys.

The assessment shows that §22 para. 3 PStG has so far hardly ever been applied in practice at all. Based on information provided by the Ministries of the Interior, it is estimated that only about 4 per cent of intersex children born by medical assessment after its entry into force have been registered with blank gender entry.[9] The reasons for this include a lack of knowledge of the new regulations for medical professional groups, a lack of implementation in forms and IT systems (birth announcements), and also uncertainty as to when the medical conditions for a blank gender entry are met. Moreover, there appears to be the tendency of medical personnel, parents and registrars to assign a supposedly predominant binary gender. Intersex persons and parents of intersex children criticise the risk of stigmatisation of children by leaving their gender registration entry blank, that the medical profession in practice still

---

6 Personenstandsrechts-Änderungsgesetz of 07.05.2013, Bundesgesetzblatt (BGBl.) 2013 Teil I, p. 1122.

7 Stellungnahme des Deutschen Ethikrates zum Thema Intersexualität (Statement by the German Ethics Council regarding intersex) Bundestagsdrucksache (BT-Drucks) 17/9088 of 14.02.2012.

8 Beschlussempfehlung und Bericht des Innenausschusses (Recommendation and report of the Committee for the Interior), BT-Drucks. 17/12192 of 30.01.2013.

9 See ALTHOFF, SCHABRAM AND FOLLMAR-OTTO, above n. 2, ch. 4.1.

seems to prefer to classify according to a 'predominant' gender, and the lack of an independent positive gender category other than male and female.[10]

2. THE CURRENT LAW AND REFORM PROPOSALS

When canvassing the current law, the German federal law was sifted through by means of a full-text search in legal databases for statutory provisions conceptually linked directly or indirectly to sex/gender.[11] This showed that gender was used in a large number of provisions across a wide range of legal areas, which directly or indirectly differentiate according to gender, or according to which gender-related data are registered or transmitted. In doing so, the law is predominantly based on a binary gender rule. This therefore excludes persons who do not correspond to the typical binary understanding of gender, and particularly intersex and some trans/transsexual persons. If a person does not meet the gender-specific characteristic of the legal rule in question, it simply does not apply to them.

Legal rules differentiating according to gender, which presuppose having a specific legal gender are not – at least not directly – applicable to persons without a gender entry according to §22 para. 3 PStG. Although applicability can to some extent be established by means of analogy because of the existence of an unintended regulatory gap, legal uncertainties remain. As will be shown, application questions cannot always be resolved by means of analogies or may be considered appropriate in the light of the fundamental and human rights of intersex and trans/transsexual persons.

In some cases, however, the rules also use binary language without necessarily using this to treat people differently according to their legal gender. This usually is done with the aim of linguistic equality between women and men. Arguably, there is no immediate need for change in this case group. These provisions can be interpreted according to fundamental and human rights law in such a way that they apply to all persons irrespective of their legal gender – and thus, for example, persons with a blank gender entry according to §22 para. 3 PStG. However, in the long term these provisions should also be changed to use gender-inclusive language.

For other provisions which actually differentiate according to legal gender or according to which gender-related data are registered or processed, groups were identified for which model proposals for solutions were developed within

10 Althoff, Schabram and Follmar-Otto, above n. 2, ch. 4.1.3.

11 All legal provisions identified were transferred into 2 Excel tables, which are available on the Institute's website (in German): <http://www.institut-fuer-menschenrechte.de/themen/diskriminierungsschutz/sexuelle-selbstbestimmung-und-geschlechtsidentitaet/geschlechtervielfalt-im-recht/> (last accessed 25.01.2018).

the context of the proposed draft Bill. In the following, selected results and proposals for the civil status rules governing the registration on gender, the rules on parenthood in family law and the rules on the protection of the physical integrity of intersex infants and young children will be presented.

2.1. THE GENDER MARKER IN CIVIL STATUS RULES

First steps towards the recognition of the rights of intersex and trans/transsexual persons in Germany were made by the transsexual law (*Transsexuellengesetz* – TSG), first introduced in 1980 and subsequently amended. This was followed in 2013 by the above-mentioned introduction of §22 para. 3 PStG which allowed leaving the gender entry for intersex children blank. More extensive reform requirements were mandated by the Federal Constitutional Court (*Bundesverfassungsgericht*) decisions with regard to transsexual persons,[12] in 2017 also with regard to intersex persons[13] and also by the German Ethics Council and the *Bundesrat* with regard to intersex persons.[14] Nevertheless, interest groups representing intersex and trans/transsexual persons, state anti-discrimination agencies, science and practice continue to report discrimination and threats against the persons concerned.[15]

2.1.1. Functions of the Civil Status Register and the Importance of the Right to Legal Recognition of Gender

The collection of civil status data is intended to assist with the identification of individuals as well as the assignment of specific rights and obligations.

12 Federal Constitutional Court (*Bundesverfassungsgericht* – BVerfG), *BVerfGE* 60, 123; 88, 87; 115, 1; 116, 243; 121, 175; 128, 109.

13 BVerfG 10.10.2017, *Zeitschrift für das gesamte Familienrecht (FamRZ)* 2017, 2046, with a comment by T. Helms at 2054. Excerpts of the decisions are available in English at <http://www.bundesverfassungsgericht.de/SharedDocs/Entscheidungen/EN/2017/10/rs20171010_1bvr201916en.html> (last accessed 16.03.2018). A press release is available in English at <http://www.bundesverfassungsgericht.de/SharedDocs/Pressemitteilungen/EN/2017/bvg17-095.html> (last accessed 25.01.2018).

14 Deutscher Ethikrat (German Ethics Council), above n. 7; Bundesrat, Beschluss, *Bundesrats-Drucksache* 29/14 of 14.03.2014, pp. 12 et seq.

15 Cf. BMFSFJ, *Situation von trans- und intersexuellen Menschen im Fokus. Sachstandsinformation*, BMFSFJ (ed.), Berlin 2016, pp. 9 et seq.; Antidiskriminierungsstelle des Bundes – ADS, *Gleiche Rechte – gegen Diskriminierung aufgrund des Geschlechts. Bericht der unabhängigen Expert_innenkommission der ADS*, ADS (ed.), Berlin 2015; K. Plett, *Diskriminierungspotentiale gegenüber trans- und intergeschlechtlichen Menschen im deutschen Recht*, Landesstelle für Gleichbehandlung – gegen Diskriminierung (ed.), Berlin 2015; D.C. Ghattas, *Menschenrechte zwischen den Geschlechtern*, Heinrich-Böll-Stiftung (ed.), Rheinheim, 2013; W. Fuchs, D.C. Ghattas, D. Reinert and C. Widmann, *Studie zur Lebenssituation von Transsexuellen in Nordrhein-Westfalen*, Lesben- und Schwulenverband in Deutschland (ed.), Cologne 2012.

Certification or registration in the civil status is not constitutive, but has a presumptive effect according to §54 PStG (presumption of correctness).[16] The entries thus have a special evidential function. The civil status resulting from substantive law (§1 para. 1 PStG) must be clear. In this way, the state interest in the permanence and uniqueness of the civil status is protected. The register entry is meant to reflect the truth and ensure that there are no misconceptions about the legal status of a person, thus allowing reliance on this entry.[17] The task of the civil status register is, therefore, to provide clear information about identity and personal status, such as affiliations and partnerships between persons. After an entry or change of a gender registration, the civil status registers have certain notification duties; this also applies to certain other authorities (particularly registry offices). These duties are governed by various laws and regulations.[18]

The regulations on gender entry in the civil status register are a central element of the legal recognition of sex and gender identity, as required by fundamental and human rights. While the formal, 'operational' function of registration law is in the foreground and merely reflects legal decisions,[19] by virtue of the documents based on the register entry, such as birth certificates and passports, the registered gender is presented externally and thus directly affects the persons concerned. This has also been recognised in the case law of the Federal Constitutional Court and the European Court of Human Rights on the right to self-determination of gender identity and protection of the intimate sphere and private life.[20]

The courts emphasise two different components of the right to the recognition of gender identity in terms of the universal personality right and the right to private life: on the one hand, the right to self-determination of individual identity and its external representation (protection of identity) and thereby protection against a wrongly perceived misattribution of gender; on the other hand, the protection of the intimate sphere (protection of integrity) from unintentional disclosure and thus also against a need for justification of this identity to society and the authorities.[21]

---

16 A. Dutta, 'Die Zuordnung zu einem Geschlecht nach deutschem Recht' in R. Hepting and A. Dutta (eds.), *Familie und Personenstand. Ein Handbuch zum deutschen und internationalen Privatrecht*, 2nd ed., Verlag für Standesamtswesen, Frankfurt am Main 2015, para. I-10.

17 S.L. Gössl, 'Materiellprivatrechtliche Angleichung der personenstandsrechtlichen Eintragung bei hinkenden Statusverhältnissen' (2015) *Praxis des Internationalen Privat- und Verfahrensrechts (IPRax)* 273, 276.

18 See §68 PStG, §57 para. 4 PStV, et al. §34 Bundesmeldegesetz.

19 Bundesgerichtshof (BGH) 22.06.2016, FamRZ 2016, 1580, para. 15; T. Helms, *Brauchen wir ein drittes Geschlecht?*, De Gruyter, Berlin 2015, p. 26.

20 See Althoff, Schabram and Follmar-Otto, above n. 2, ch. 3.1.

21 See European Court of Human Rights, *Y.Y./Turkey*, 10.03.2015, Appl. no. 295/07, para. 56 et seq.; BVerfG 11.01.2011, *BVerfGE* 128, 109, para. 51. The BVerfG in its historic decision of 10.10.2017 confirmed and emphasised: 'Der Zuordnung zu einem Geschlecht kommt für die individuelle Identität unter den gegebenen Bedingungen herausragende

Recognition must be non-discriminatory; the diversity of the sexes/gender in terms of physical development, identity and expression is one of the bases of the prohibition of discrimination. The prohibition of discrimination based on gender in Article 3 para. 3 of the Basic Law (*Grundgesetz* – GG) increasingly is considered to include intersex and trans/transsexual persons in Germany.[22] And it is already enshrined in the European Union's prohibition of gender discrimination.[23]

2.1.2. Gender Registration in the Civil Status Register

Against this background, the current civil status regulations on gender entry are problematic. The legal allocation of a person to a gender takes place at the time of birth by registration of gender in the register of births (§21 para. 1 no. 3 PStG). There are no statutory provisions on the registration of gender, but practice, case law, literature and secondary legislation specify an entry of 'male' or 'female.[24] In addition, 2013 §22 para. 3 PStG states that the gender specification in the birth entry can remain blank when a 'child cannot be attributed to either the female or the male gender'.[25] According to the wording of §22 para. 3 of the PStG, the blank gender entry for intersex children is compulsory and is limited in its application to persons who physically are intersex.[26] In those cases the gender entry can

---

Bedeutung zu.' ('Under the given circumstances, the assignment of the gender is of paramount importance for individual identity') (see n. 13, para. 39).

22 In its latest decision, the BVerfG ruled that Art. 3 para. 3 also protects persons who do not permanently identify as male or female against discrimination based on gender (see above n. 13, para. 56). See also C. Langenfeld, 'Kommentierung Art. 3 GG', in T. Maunz and G. Dürig (eds.), *GG-Kommentar*, Munich 2016, 78th supplementary delivery, para. 42, with further references; L. Adamietz, *Geschlecht als Erwartung*, Nomos, Baden-Baden 2011.

23 See, e.g. Court of Justice of the European Union, *P. v. S.*, judgment of 30.04.1996, Case C-13/94 [1996] ECR I-2143 (on transsexual persons); on this, see S. Agius and C. Tobler, *Trans- und intersexuelle Menschen*, Europäische Gemeinschaften, Luxembourg 2011; F. Welti, 'Kommentierung §1 AGG', in D. Schiek (ed.), *Allgemeines Gleichbehandlungsgesetz. Ein Kommentar aus europäischer Perspektive*, Sellier, Munich 2007, paras. 27, 32; European Commission, *Report on the application of Directive 2014/113/EC*, COM (2015) 190 final, p. 5.

24 No. 21.4.3 Allgemeine Verwaltungsvorschrift zum Personenstandsgesetz (PStG-VwV); B. Gaaz, 'Kommentierung §21 PStG', in B. Gaaz and H. Bornhofen (eds.), *Personenstandsgesetz, Handkommentar*, 3rd ed., Verlag für Standesamt, Frankfurt am Main 2014, para. 30; Dutta, above n. 16, para. IV-224.

25 Introduction with reference to the recommendations of the German Ethics Council, above n. 7, with the Personenstandsrechts-Änderungsgesetz of 07.05.2013, BT-Drucks.17/10489.

26 Dutta, above n. 16, para. IV-224; L. Lettrari and M. Willer, 'Aktuelle Aspekte der Rechtslage für intersexuelle Menschen', in *Inter* und Trans*identitäten*, Psychosozial-Verlag, Gießen 2016, p. 260; Ghattas, above n. 15, p. 36; K. Plett, 'Trans* und Inter* im Recht: Alte und neue Widersprüche', in *Inter* und Trans*identitäten, Ethische, soziale und juristische Aspekte*, Psychosozial-Verlag, Gießen 2016, pp. 215, 224; R. Bockstette, 'Das Personenstandsrechts-Änderungsgesetz' (2013) *Zeitschrift für Standesamtswesen (StAZ)* 2013, 169, 172; see also Helms, above n. 19, p. 10 with regard to the limitations of §22 para. 3 PStG to intersex persons.

be left open indefinitely, and a male or female gender entry after birth can also be deleted retrospectively in the case of persons who physically are intersex.[27] According to the case law, however, there is no legal recognition of another gender alongside male and female in the regulation. While the Supreme Court had ruled that the registration of 'inter/other' was not possible,[28] the Federal Constitutional Court decided that a positive recognition of a legal gender status other than male or female was mandated by the German Constitution, and also suggested that the requirement of an entry of a legal gender could be abolished altogether.[29]

2.1.2.1. Registration Options

Taking into account fundamental and human rights, in particular the right to recognition of sex and gender identity in connection with the principle of non-discrimination,[30] it indeed is unacceptable, as confirmed by the Federal Constitutional Court, to allow a blank entry without making possible the positive registration of gender categories beyond the binary system.[31] In Australian law such non-binary categories have been made possible by legislation, and in other countries this has been recognised by Supreme Court rulings.[32] The medical assessment of intersexuality has also changed: intersex is no longer viewed as a disorder or disease, but as a recognisable variation of gender.[33] Importantly, in interviews of trans persons in Germany, a large portion (one-quarter to one-third) indicated a non-binary gender identification.[34]

---

27 BGH 22.06.2016, FamRZ 2016, 1580; see also Oberlandesgericht Celle 21.01.2015, StAZ 2015, 107.

28 BGH 22.06.2016, FamRZ 2016, 1580, para. 12; Constitutional complaint <www.dritte-option.de> (last accessed 08.08.2017); for a different view, see S.L. Gössl, 'Intersexuelle Menschen und ihre personenstandsrechtliche Erfassung' (2016) *Neue Zeitschrift für Familienrecht (NZFam)*, 1122; already S.L. Gössl, 'Die Eintragung im Geburtenregister als "inter" oder "divers"' (2015) *StAZ* 171; see the criticism by J. Theilen, 'Intersexualität bleibt unsichtbar: Der Beschluss des Bundesgerichtshofs zu Intersexualität im Personenstandsrecht', *Junge Wissenschaft im öffentlichen Recht*, 09.08.2016, <juwiss.de> (last accessed 08.08.2017).

29 See above n. 13.

30 On this, see Althoff, Schabram and Follmar-Otto, above n. 2, ch. 3.1.

31 However, Helms, above n. 19, p. 26.

32 See for Australia: Althoff, Schabram and Follmar-Otto, above n. 2, Annex 2; Example of Nepal: Supreme Court of Nepal, Sunil Babu Pant and Others, Nepal Government and Others, decision of 21.12.2007 ('third gender'); India: Supreme Court of India, Write Petition (Civil) No. 400 of 2012, decision of 15.04.2014 ('third gender'); Pakistan: Supreme Court of Pakistan, Khaki by Rawalpindi, decision of 12.12.2009 ('hirja').

33 Bundesärztekammer (German Medical Association), *Stellungnahme zur Versorgung von Kindern, Jugendlichen und Erwachsenen mit Varianten/ Störungen der Geschlechtsentwicklung*, 30.01.2015; Arbeitsgemeinschaft der Wissenschaftlichen Medizinischen Fachgesellschaften e.V. (Working Group Scientific Medical Specialists), *S2k–Leitlinie Varianten der Geschlechtsentwicklung*, 07.2016.

34 A. Bora, *Zur Situation intersexueller Menschen. Bericht über die Online-Umfrage des Deutschen Ethikrates*, Deutscher Ethikrat (ed.), Berlin 2012, p. 32; L. Adamietz and

Equal recognition of their sex and gender with regard to body and identity is denied to intersex persons by simply leaving the gender entry blank. The blank entry is not positive recognition of a gender, but merely negates an assignment to the binary categories male and female. Protection of the fundamental right to recognition of sex/gender for persons who are outside the binary gender categories must be secured. From a legal point of view this is not necessarily a question of the creation of gender(s) through legislation, but rather question of legal recognition of sex and gender on the basis of an individual person's psychological and physical self-perception.[35] According to the Federal Constitutional Court, the fundamental rights of persons who do not permanently identify as male or female are violated if the civil status law requires that the gender is registered but does not allow for a positive entry other than male or female.[36] The Court stipulated that 'under the given circumstances, the recognition of gender under civil status law has an identity-building and expressive effect' and that 'civil status is not a marginal issue'.[37] It is also problematic that in case of physical intersex the current legal provision stipulates that the gender entry must be left blank, and that it is not regulated sufficiently whether and how physically intersex persons with a male or female gender identity can achieve a corresponding gender entry.[38]

2.1.2.2. Registration Time

Irrespective of whether the gender entry is left blank for intersex children as in the applicable law or a positive third category is registered, this concerns the protection of gender intimacy from unintentional disclosure as part of the protection of the general personality right. In the assessment of §22 para. 3 PStG, the inevitable forced 'outing' of the minority of intersex children was seen as very problematic.[39] Even if the legal gender entry is only one element of the binary order, not a few respondents considered that a legal gender assignment for all children instead of a special arrangement for intersex children would represent a sensible reduction in the pressure on parents and medical personnel.

In addition, the Federal Constitutional Court bases its case law on the transsexual law (TSG) on the scientific finding that 'the affiliation of a person to a gender cannot be determined solely by external sex characteristics at the time

K. Bager, *Regelungs- und Reformbedarf für transgeschlechtliche Menschen*, BMFSFJ (ed.), Berlin 2017.

35 But see BGH 22.06.2016, FamRZ 2016, 1580; on this, see Althoff, Schabram and Follmar-Otto, above n. 2, ch. 6.

36 See above n. 13.

37 See above n. 13, para 45.

38 See Althoff, Schabram and Follmar-Otto, above n. 2, ch. 5.3.1.2.

39 See Althoff, Schabram and Follmar-Otto, above n. 2, ch. 4.1.

of his/her birth, but also essentially depends on his/her psychical constitution and self-perceived gender'.[40] In its ruling regarding §22 para. 3 PStG, the Court explicitly refers to gender identity as an important element of gender.[41] If, therefore, gender affiliation only becomes apparent later in life for everyone, the question arises whether the entry and thus determination of a legal gender immediately at birth actually is necessary or even meaningful, given that it by necessity is undertaken by someone other than the person concerned. For children and adolescents who develop or have a trans/transsexual identity, legal attribution to a gender at birth as a result of the sex characteristics becomes a burden and is an interference with their right to recognition of their sex and gender identity and the protection of their intimate sphere.

Postponement of a gender entry at birth is also not precluded by overarching state interests, such as the function of gender assignment for legal obligations and rights and family allocation. Indeed, the right of affiliation and partnership is irrelevant at least for the period of childhood before puberty.[42] Moreover, the need for a family law amendment already arises from the current law so that the respective allocation function may be omitted altogether.[43] With regard to military and civil service obligations (as there may be), the issue only is relevant at/after the age of 18. As regards freedom of travel, not having a gender entry would be unproblematic, since the gender could be registered in travel documents for all persons with the marker 'X'.[44]

That said, a complete abolition of a gender entry in the civil status register at present does not appear to be a viable alternative. In a society characterised by the binary gender system with a multitude of areas which are structured by gender, it can be important for the implementation of the right to the recognition of gender identity to be positively recognised in a legal gender. This is particularly true for persons who differ in their appearance or self-perception from the gender categories assigned by society.[45] Abolition of the gender entry may also be problematic with regard to family and inheritance law constellations with foreign nationals, since without a binary gender entry a person may not be able to marry abroad, be recognised as a parent of a child or for inheritance purposes.[46]

---

40 BVerfG 06.12.2005, *BVerfGE* 115, 1, 15; BVerfG 11.01.2011, BVerfGE 128, 109, para. 51.

41 See above n. 13.

42 B. Tönsmeyer, *Die Grenzen der elterlichen Sorge bei intersexuell geborenen Kindern*, Nomos, Baden-Baden 2012, p. 68.

43 See below Section 2.2. Filiation; on this, see Althoff, Schabram and Follmar-Otto, above n. 2, ch. 5.2.

44 Regulation (EC) 2252/2004 in conjunction with Document No. 9303 of the International Civil Aviation organisation – ICAO.

45 On the TSG, see Adamietz and Bager, above n. 34.

46 Helms, above n. 19, p. 23, with reference to the 'Internationalität von personenstandsrechtlichen Statusfragen'; cf. also S.L. Gössl, 'From the question of the question of law to the question

The Draft Bill

Against this background, the draft Bill provides for the possibility to choose a third-gender entry or to renounce a gender entry indefinitely. The proposed Gender Diversity Act (*Gesetz zur Anerkennung und zum Schutz der Geschlechtervielfalt – Geschlechtervielfaltsgesetz* – GVielfG-E) provides for four entry options: the categories 'male', 'female', 'other gender options' and 'not specified' (§2 para. 2 GVielfG-E). From a legal point of view, there is a legitimate interest in the fact that the number and designation of possible gender categories is fixed. Therefore, an umbrella concept was chosen for the third category. To respect the right to self-determination, the possibility of adding a separate gender designation in the registry entry is suggested, which on request could also be indicated in the birth certificate. The 'not specified' category is independent of the physical development of the sex/gender of each person and is intended to be an express, positive entry instead of a non-entry. This was chosen because of the difficulties that have arisen with the practical implementation of leaving the entry blank.

In addition, a gender entry is proposed to be postponed for all children after birth, and instead 'not specified' (§21 para. 1 p. 1 PStG-E) is supposed to be entered into the register for all children. At the same time, an intrinsic right to determine the gender entry for the register of births would be introduced (§2 para. 1 GVielfG-E).

2.1.3. *Procedure for Changing the Gender Marker*

There currently is no statutory regulation according to which the gender of a child is determined, or according to which the assignment of legal gender has to take place. However, in practice the gender classification of a person at the time of birth is usually determined according to the external physical condition, in particular according to the external sex characteristics.[47] Any change of gender entry is also based on medical evaluation. Although the blank entry can be replaced by an entry as male or female, by virtue of §27 para. 3 no. 4 PStG, the secondary regulations still provide for a change of the blank gender entry only in the event that the affiliation to one of the binary sexes is medically proven.[48] Similarly, proof of intersexuality is required for a deletion of a gender entry.[49]

---

of private international law: the question whether a person is male, female, or … ?' (2016) 2 *Journal of Private International Law* 261–262.

47 J. Ellenberger, 'Kommentierung §§1–6 BGB' in O. Palandt, *Bürgerliches Gesetzbuch: BGB*, 76th ed., Beck, Munich 2017, para. 10. Confirmed in 2011 by BVerfG 11.01.2011, BVerfGE 128, 109.

48 No. 27.8 of the PStG-VwV.

49 By way of a judicial correction under §§48 para. 1, 47 para. 2 no. 1 in conjunction with §22 para. 3 PStG, Helms, above n. 19, pp. 12, 13 with further references.

However, the jurisprudence of the Federal Constitutional Court does not support the determination of legal gender according to purely external sex characteristics. Instead the Court in a number of decisions has attached importance to the 'psychic constitution and self-perceived gender'[50] and referred to gender identity in its latest ruling.[51] The TSG provides for the amendment of the gender entry on request for persons who do not regard themselves as belonging to the 'gender specified in their birth entry, but to the other gender'.[52] This obviously perpetuates the binary gender regime and not only disregards intersex persons but also anyone who does not identify as male or female. In addition, the prescriptive and cost-intensive court procedure requires, in particular, two assessments according to which a 'feeling of belonging to the other gender, which has existed for at least three years and is highly probable to be permanent', has to be proved.[53]

These psychiatric diagnosis procedures according to the TSG impose a considerable limitation on the principle of self-determination. They constitute a considerable psychological hurdle, are time-intensive and are perceived as a heavy burden by trans/transsexual persons. Moreover, they arguably are unnecessary as the results very rarely deviate from the self-definition of the person in question.[54] With respect to intersex persons, the assessment carried out within the context of the report also highlighted problems when procedures necessitated medical records and assessments.[55] In their statutes, Malta, Argentina, Denmark and Ireland[56] only require self-declaration and no form of medical proof. The resolution of the Parliamentary Assembly of the Council of Europe of 2015 also calls on states to develop rapid, transparent and accessible procedures for changing name and gender in personal documents based on the principle of self-determination.[57] Likewise, the Yogyakarta principles stipulate

---

50 BVerfG 11.01.2011, BVerfGE 128, 109, para. 51; see also BVerfG 06.12.2005, BVerfGE 115, 1, para. 50.

51 See above n. 13.

52 §1 para. 1. no. 1 TSG; on the TSG, see A. Dutta, 'The Legal Status of Transsexual and Transgender Persons in Germany', in J.M. Scherpe (ed.), *The Legal Status of Transsexual and Transgender Persons*, Intersentia, Cambridge 2015, pp. 207 et seq.

53 On this, see Adamietz and Bager, above n. 34, with further references.

54 The assessment of 670 expert opinions from 2005 to 2014 showed that in less than 1% of the cases the court's rejection of the application is recommended; see B. Meyenburg, K. Renter-Schmidt and G. Schmidt, 'Begutachtung nach dem Transsexuellengesetz. Auswertung von Gutachten dreier Sachverständiger 2005–2014' (2015) 28 *Zeitschrift für Sexualforschung* 107–120.

55 See Althoff, Schabram and Follmar-Otto, above n. 2, ch. 4.2.2.

56 Only for adults; for 16–18 year olds, a medical certificate of maturity and transition is required.

57 Parliamentary Assembly Resolution 2048, Discrimination against transgender persons in Europe, 2015.

that the procedures must be efficient, fair and non-discriminatory, and must respect the right to privacy.[58]

The Draft Bill

The procedure for later registration of the gender should be easily accessible and should not require much time and effort. The draft Bill provides for a standard registry procedure for the determination of the gender entry, which is based solely on the self-declaration of the person (§2 para. 1 GVielfG-E). No further verification and official inspection obligations exist. At the same time, it is proposed that the possibility of changing the gender entry should be similarly facilitated (§3 GVielfG-E).

Multiple changes of gender would be possible, since gender identity can be fluid and may change several times during the lifetime of a person. In order to prevent fraudulent changes of legal gender, a minimum waiting period of 12 months since the last application for a change of legal gender is proposed.[59] It is worth noting that Denmark takes a different approach here, namely a six-month 'reflection period' *after* the application is made. Once the six months have passed, the applicant needs to confirm their application. Unlike this approach, the proposal would not, in principle, restrict access to the procedure and does not require a waiting period once an application has been made. The Danish legislation takes insufficient account of the fact that the decision to change legal gender entry often is made for a concrete reason, such as an imminent journey or a change of employment, which necessitates changes in personnel documents in order to prevent discrimination or to protect the intimate sphere. However, there needs to be a mechanism with which cases where persons fraudulently seek to use legal changes of gender for personal gain can be dealt with, and the waiting period between two applications is an effective means of doing that.

Applications by children who have not yet reached 14 years of age are proposed to be subject to the consent of their parents or legal representatives. Children over 14 years of age should be allowed to apply without the need for consent by their parents or legal representatives, see §2 para. 3 GVielfG-E. This is in accordance with the German provisions on the right to religious self-determination (§5 Act on Religious Child Education). Even if the age of 14 has not yet been reached, gender identity should be recognised and a corresponding determination of the gender entry should be allowed, especially since this is not

58 Yogyakarta Principles, Principles on the application of international human rights law in relation to sexual orientation and gender identity, available at <http://yogyakartaprinciples.org/> (last accessed 25.01.2018).

59 Even though abuse and/or multiple changes of gender have not occurred in jurisdictions that have already implemented such laws.

irrevocable but can be changed again. Should the parent or legal representative refuse consent, the Family Court according to the proposal may replace it and allow the application. This decision must be based on the child's best interest and can only be refused if the welfare of the child is likely to be adversely affected through the application.

Non-German nationals who are habitually resident in Germany can also make applications under the Gender Diversity Act (GVielfG-E). Furthermore, it is proposed that under certain conditions persons with parental responsibility/legal guardianship can opt for to defer the gender entry at birth; cf. proposal for an added Article 13a of the Introductory Act to the Civil Code (*Einführungsgesetz zum Bürgerlichen Gesetzbuch* – EGBGB-E) and §§2 para. 4, 3 para. 1 no. 2 GVielfG-E.

2.2. FILIATION

For the legal recognition of gender diversity, adjustments are necessary not only in civil status law, but also and particularly in family law. For example, there are various legal uncertainties in particular in relation to the right to affiliation, which involves gender-specific conditions and designations; such as in the core regulation on maternity in §1591 Civil Code (*Bürgerliches Gesetzbuch* – BGB), according to which the mother of a child is the woman who gave birth. §1592 no. 1 BGB allocates paternity to the father who is married to the mother (§1592 no. 1 BGB), or recognises his paternity with the consent of the mother (§§1592 no. 2, 1595 BGB), or if his paternity is established through the court (§1592 no. 3 BGB).

Thus, parenthood of persons who are outside the binary system is not recognised, as the current provisions are based on binary gender categories (mother and father, man and woman). Therefore, it is unclear whether persons with a blank gender entry according to §22 para. 3 PStG can establish parenthood at all. This obvious legal lacuna could, of course, be filled by applying the relevant provisions by analogy. However, while this may be straightforward for maternity according to §1591 BGB, it is not for paternity according to §1592 BGB.[60] While ultimately it is to be expected that paternity would be determined according to this provision, some authors argue that this approach would be limited to the judicial paternity test based on genetic origin under no. 3 and that the other options would not be open.[61] Hence it may be that paternity would have to be established by a court in some cases.

---

60 W. Sieberichs, 'Das Unbestimmte Geschlecht' (2013) *FamRZ* 1180, 1181–1182; Helms, above n. 19, pp. 19 et seq.; Lettrari and Willer, above n. 26, pp. 257, 269 et seq.

61 Helms, above n. 19; see also Sieberichs, above n. 60; Affirmative Lettrari and Willer, above n. 26, p. 270; Plett, above n. 15, p. 56.

In addition, trans/transsexual persons are also not adequately covered by the current legislation. After the sterilisation requirement was declared unconstitutional,[62] a legal man can now give birth to a child and a legal woman 'father' a child. Yet according to two recent decisions by the Federal Court (*Bundesgerichtshof*), the 'biological' gender should prevail and thus a legal man giving birth must be registered as the mother of the child (and, even more controversially, under their previous female name), and vice versa in case of the legal woman whose sperm created the child.[63] According to this jurisprudence, they are denied the recognition of parenthood according to their gender identity or their registered gender. This inevitably leads to the parent being revealed as having changed their legal gender whenever official documents concerning the child need to be shown, violating the rights to non-disclosure by the parents.[64] This could be prevented by legislation such as in Malta or Australia, where a gender-neutral designation of the parents is given on the children's birth certificate.

The basic right of the child to know their origin, including their genetic origin under Article 2 para. 1 in conjunction with Article 1 para. 1 of the Basic Law (GG),[65] cannot justify the retention of gender-specific names and conditions. Admittedly, it might be an interference with the personality rights of affected children if the possibilities for clarifying genetic origin were limited by family law and birth registration.[66] But linking parenthood to reproduction rather than gender would also make knowing one's origin possible, as the person who gave birth to the child and the genetic affiliation would still to be identified. Furthermore, if the personal status right of the child would be extended beyond the genetic lineage to the knowledge of which of the parents has actually given birth, this could also be done, for example, by means of references to the 'birth parent' and the 'other parent' in the civil status register, without any gender-specific assignment or disclosure of gender in the birth certificate.

The Draft Bill

The proposed umbrella law would change the current central provisions on affiliation. The purpose of these changes is the legal protection of the parent and

62 BVerfG 11.01.2011, BVerfGE 128, 109.

63 BGH 06.09.2017, *FamRZ* 2017, 1855 and BGH 29.11.2017, FamRZ 2018, 290. On this, see J. Theile, *Transsexualität im Familienrecht*, S. Roderer Verlag, Regensburg 2013, pp. 267 et seq; and J. Remus, 'Rechte von trans- und intergeschlechtlichen Eltern' (2014) 3 *Neue Juristische Wochenschrift-aktuell* 14.

64 On the prohibition of disclosure, see e.g. the decision by the Amtsgericht Münster 04.01.2016, FamRZ 2017, 1862, referred to in the decision by BGH 06.09.2017, *FamRZ* 2017, 1855.

65 See also Art. 7 para. 1 of the UN Convention on the Rights of the Child, which lays down the right of the child to know his or her parents.

66 U. di Fabio, 'Kommentierung Art. 2 Abs. 1 GG' in Maunz-Dürig (eds.), *GG-Kommentar*, Munich 2016, 78th supplementary delivery, para. 212.

parenthood, without reference to gender-specific terms.[67] Instead, parenthood is linked to reproductive function and partnership, and gender-neutral terms are used.[68] According to the proposed regulation in §1591 BGB-E, under the title 'Parenthood', parental status is independent of the gender entry of the person giving birth; the same applies to the person who either already is married to (or in registered partnership with) the birth parent, or who has legally recognised parenthood, or for whom parenthood is judicially determined. §1592 BGB on paternity would be repealed.

The basic rules on affiliation law thus would be adapted to be gender-inclusive and be able to reflect the many possibilities for parenthood and new family forms, as well as gender diversity.[69]

2.3. PROTECTION OF PHYSICAL INTEGRITY: SURGERY AND OTHER MEDICAL TREATMENT OF INTERSEX INFANTS AND CHILDREN

Intersex infants and children are still undergoing operations and medical treatments that are not medically necessary in Germany, with the aim of reconciling their physical appearance and function in line with the medical perceptions of the 'normal' binary gender.[70] These procedures usually are irreversible and can cause severe long-term physical and mental suffering.[71] Human rights bodies have repeatedly pointed out that medically unnecessary interventions in intersex infants and children without their explicit and informed consent constitute inhumane treatment and harmful practices that must be prohibited. States are required to ensure the principle of informed consent to medical and surgical interventions in intersex persons as well as effective investigations and compensation in the event of violations of this principle.[72]

---

67 Cf. Helms, above n. 19, p. 22 and Remus, above n. 63, p. 14.

68 This is already the case, e.g., in the Australian Capital Territory (ACT) where the terms 'birth parent' and 'other parent' are used; in addition, parents can choose freely how they would be designated on the birth certificate; see the legal comparison in Annex 2 of the report Althoff, Schabram and Follmar-Otto, above n. 2.

69 Consequently, a large number of other provisions would have to be amended in line with the proposed changes. Extensive reform discussions on the law of descent are currently taking place among the experts of a working group, organised by the Federal Ministry of Justice and Consumer Protection.

70 A. Krämer, K. Sabisch and J. Woweries, 'Varianten der Geschlechtsentwicklung – die Vielfalt der Natur', (2016) 5 *Kinder- und Jugendarzt*, pp. 2248 et seq.; U. Klöppel, *Zur Aktualität kosmetischer Operationen "uneindeutiger" Genitalien im Kindesalter*, Zentrum für transdisziplinäre Geschlechterstudien der Humboldt-Universität zu Berlin, Berlin 2016.

71 German Ethics Council, above n. 7, pp. 26–27.

72 Last addressed to Germany: UN Women's Rights Committee, *Concluding remarks Germany 2017*, para. 24d-e. (CEDAW/C/DEU/CO/7-8); see also UN Children's Rights Committee, *Concluding remarks Ireland*, paras. 39–40. (CRC/IRL/CO/3-4); *Concluding*

In German law, consent by parents/legal representatives according to §§1626, 1629 Civil Code (BGB) is prohibited in cases on medically unnecessary treatments, as consent in these cases is deeply personal in nature (in German: *höchstpersönlich*) it cannot be substituted by the consent of other persons. Thus, interventions which are nevertheless carried out constitute a criminal offence. But neither criminal sanction nor the gradual revision of medical treatment guidelines since 2005[73] have so far resulted in a reduction in the number of medical interventions carried out. This has been confirmed most recently in a study of December 2016, which found that the relative frequency of interventions between 2004 and 2014 essentially remained unchanged.[74] The medical recommendations and guidelines are non-binding and obviously do not provide adequate protection in individual cases. States therefore are required under human rights law to take further, effective measures to prevent unauthorised interventions, and various options are being discussed.[75]

In view of the continuing high number of medical interventions, clearly an express clarification of the law is necessary. This could be done in the criminal law (as for example was done in the case of female genital mutilation in §226a of the German Criminal Code) or in the law of parental responsibility custody (as is currently the case with regard to sterilisation of children in §1631c Civil Code – BGB). The advantage of the placing the relevant provisions in the Civil Code is that it could be combined with a family court authorisation procedure for those cases where medical intervention is absolutely necessary to avoid risk to life or the danger of serious health impairment.[76]

---

remarks Switzerland, paras. 42–43 (CRC/C/CHE/CO/2-4); *Concluding remarks France*, paras. 47–48 (CRC/C/FRA/CO/5); UN Anti-Torture Committee, *Concluding remarks Switzerland* 2015, para. 20 (CAT/C/CHE/CO/7); *Final remarks Germany*, para. 20 (CAT/C/DEU/CO/5); UN Disability Committee, *Final remarks Germany*, paras. 37–38 (CRPD/C/DEU/CO/1).

73 German Medical Association, above n. 33; Working Group Scientific Medical Specialists e.V., above n. 33.

74 Klöppel, above n. 70.

75 German Ethics Council, above n. 7, pp. 55 et seq.; see also Tönsmeyer, above n. 42; cf. also B. Schmidt am Busch, 'Intersexualität und staatliche Schutzpflichten bei geschlechtszuweisenden Operationen' (2012) 137 *Archiv des öffentlichen Rechts* 441, 454 et seq.; J. Woweries, 'Intersexualität. Medizinische Eingriffe und Beteiligung von Kindern an medizinischen Entscheidungen' (2014) 17 *Frühe Kindheit* 40, 45 et seq.; A. Kolbe, *Intersexualität, Zweigeschlechtlichkeit und Verfassungsrecht,* Nomos, Frankfurt 2009, in particular pp. 200 et seq.
Of the countries studied, only Malta has introduced an explicit ban on any non-urgent operation of intersexual minors before they can consent effectively. In exceptional cases, which may not be based on social factors, an intervention can take place if representatives of the authorities and a specially established interdisciplinary team agree on it. See Althoff, Schabram and Follmar-Otto, above n. 2, Annex 2.

76 See also Tönsmeyer, above n. 42.

The Draft Bill

Consequently, for the protection of self-determination and the physical integrity of intersex children in the law of parental responsibility/custody the draft Bill contains a clarifying prohibition on the consent of persons entitled to custody in a gender-altering or gender-adjusting medical intervention on the genitalia or gonad glands in cases of children not yet capable of understanding the severity and consequences of these interventions (§1631e para. 1 BGB-E with the title 'Medical interventions on the genitals or gonads'). It would introduce a family court authorisation procedure for medically necessary interventions to prevent risk to life or serious health impairment; this would also strengthen the enforcement of the prohibition and ensure adequate protection in individual cases (§1631e para. 2 BGB-E).

3. SUMMARY

In summary, it can be stated that:

- the rule on leaving open the gender entry for intersex children (§22 para. 3 PStG), introduced in 2013, is hardly applied in practice;
- the introduction of a non-binary gender category is necessary in respect of fundamental and human rights and can be expected in Germany before the end of 2018;
- a gender entry in the birth registry right after childbirth in principle is not necessary for all children;
- procedures to allocate and change the gender entry must be based on the right to self-determination;
- the provisions of the TSG and §22 para. 3 PStG must be abolished or revised accordingly;
- the state has a duty under the protection of human rights to prevent medically unnecessary interventions on intersex children;
- gender-inclusive legislation is mandated, not limited to personal status law, but for all areas of law; and
- a comprehensive legislative approach to the recognition and protection of gender diversity is to be recommended and, as shown by the draft Bill, is feasible.

Against this background, a draft Bill for an umbrella Act was developed in consultation with intersex and trans/transsexual persons, their parents, associations and counselling centres as well as academia and legal and medical practitioners. The draft Bill recommends that the requirement to have a gender entry immediately after birth is dropped, and at the same time the right of every person to self-determine the gender entry in the register of births is stipulated and given effect. The procedure for this certification of the gender entry must be easily accessible, and based on a self-declaration, without further evidence, to the registry office. It is expressly suggested to make this procedure available to children as well. In addition, it is proposed that there should be the opportunity to choose a third, non-binary gender entry or to dispense with a gender entry indefinitely. The draft Bill also suggests facilitating the possibility of changing the gender entry with registration authorities, the possibility of changing the first given names, and also extending the possibilities for gender entries in passports.

At the centre of the proposed umbrella Act is a new Act on the recognition and protection of gender (Gender Diversity Law – *Geschlechtervielfaltsgesetz* – GVielfG). Changes in the law of civil status (PStG and personal status regulation), the Introductory Act to the Civil Code (EGBGB), the amendment of the Act on right to change names (NamÄndG) and the Passport Act (PaßG) are proposed. Importantly, specific counselling requirements on the law of gender diversity for parents and children have been added in the Eighth Book of the Social Code – Children and Youth Welfare (SGB VIII).

All of the above-mentioned provisions are meant to apply to everyone irrespective of gender. This means that the specific rules for transsexual and transgender persons in the TSG as well as the special rules for intersex persons in §22 para. 3 PStG no longer are necessary and could be repealed. According to the decision of the Federal Constitutional Court the legislator must enact provisions that are compatible with the Constitution by 31 December 2018. In implementing the decision, the legislator should not solely provide for an isolated amendment in civil status law but improve the legal recognition and protection of gender diversity with a comprehensive gender diversity law.[77]

Thus, core provisions for a gender-inclusive legal system are suggested to be amended in other legal areas. These include, in particular, the provisions laid down in family law on affiliation. Gender-specific requirements and terms within the context of legal parenthood should be abolished. Clarifications and additions are also proposed for the General Equal Treatment Act (AGG) and the Federal Equalisation Act (BGleiG). A clarification of the range of beneficiaries is suggested for the Maternity Protection Act (MuSchG). Amended provisions on search and accommodation under the Prison Act (StVollzG) and the Federal Police Act (BPolG) are meant to take the special situation and needs of intersex and trans/transsexual persons into account. The allocation of personal

[77] Also see the statement by an advocacy group supporting the complaint ('Dritte Option, available at <http://dritte-option.de/historic-ruling-of-the-german-federal-constitutional-court-bye-bye-binary/>) and the joint statement by Oii Europe, Ivim-Oii Germany, TGEU and the German Trans* Association, available at <https://tgeu.org/joint-statement-civil-society-welcomes-ground-breaking-german-constitutional-court-demand-for-a-new-regulation-of-sex-registration/> (both accessed 16.03.2018).

identification numbers in accordance with the Sixth Book of the Social Code – Statutory Pension Insurance – (SGB VI) and the corresponding implementing regulation is proposed to be amended in such a way that there is no longer any reference to gender. In the context of child and youth welfare, access to counselling for parents, children and adolescents under the Eighth Book of the Social Code (SGB VIII) are to be broadened to specifically include the needs of including intersex and trans/transsexual children and their parents. The draft Bill also contains proposals for further amendments necessary in the light of the above-mentioned changes and new provisions, and also suggests repealing outdated gendered provisions.

As a core rule for the protection of intersex and trans/transsexual persons, the draft Bill further contains proposals for protection of physical integrity and against discrimination.

Structurally, the report summarises the results of the stocktaking, evaluation and assessment of the existing German law in Part 1; Part 2 contains the draft Bill with general and special explanatory notes. Further materials can be found in the extensive annexes to the report as well as in materials available on the website of the German Institute for Human Rights.[78]

[78] <www.institut-fuer-menschenrechte.de> (last accessed 26.01.2018).

PART V

PRIVATE INTERNATIONAL LAW ASPECTS OF INTERSEX

PRIVATE INTERNATIONAL LAW ASPECTS OF INTERSEX

Anatol DUTTA and Walter PINTENS

The first question we have to deal with is – at least at first sight – rather simple: which law shall decide on the legal gender of an intersex person and the consequences of that gender in cross-border cases, if that person has links to more than one jurisdiction? This question is, of course, crucial: while all jurisdictions of the world agree that natural persons can be legally male or female, there is no such agreement on the question whether intersex persons can acquire a special gender status, for example, a third category of legal gender (however this is named). Currently only a few jurisdictions offer such a specific gender status for intersex persons. In order to answer this seemingly easy question, several issues need to be distinguished and dealt with separately. First, is gender for private international law purposes a matter of fact or a matter of law (on which see Section 1 below)? If the latter, we then have to decide on the applicable law (on which see Section 2 below). However, the problem can also arise as a preliminary question (on which see Section 3 below). Finally, every jurisdiction will have to deal with the recognition of an intersex status acquired abroad (on which see Section 4 below).

1. WHAT IS THE NATURE OF THE QUESTION?

When addressing private international law issues of intersex, one first has to clarify whether the attribution of a legal gender to a certain person is a legal question and, if so, whether it is a question of substance or procedure.

It is, of course, rather obvious that the legal gender of a person is a question of law and not of mere facts,[1] and therefore the issue of the applicable law arises.[2] The gender of a natural person is different from merely factual personal criteria, for example, the colour of the person's eyes, the birth weight, or the religion of a person – all criteria, which might be registered in some jurisdictions in the civil status registers or identity documents. The fact that many jurisdictions contain provisions on the recognition of the preferred gender identity for transsexual and transgender persons makes clear that the gender of a natural person has to be a legal question. If the gender of a natural person was only a question of facts, there would be no need for a legal gender recognition. Gender is therefore not just a personal matter, at least as long as the law distinguishes between different genders and attaches legal consequences to that distinction, as it still does in many jurisdictions (unlike, for example, regarding the colour of one's eyes).

However, the conclusion that gender (and, hence, a specific gender status for intersex persons) is a legal concept, does not answer the question whether this concept is part of substantial or procedural law.

Why is this characterisation relevant in private international law? If the legal attribution of a gender has to be characterised as a question of procedure, the *lex fori* principle would apply. Consequently, when registering the birth of the child the civil status registrar could apply the rules of the *lex fori* for the attribution of a gender. It is widely recognised that judicial or administrative bodies in principle apply their own procedural law.[3] Procedural law is public law and states are, in principle, reluctant to apply foreign public law. The true reason behind the *lex fori* principle, however, is that applying foreign procedural law would cause difficulties because procedural law is often intertwined with a certain organisation of the competent judicial or administrative authority. Hence, if the assignment of a legal gender is a procedural question and subject to the *lex fori*, the provisions which determine the jurisdiction of a certain state for the registration of a person's birth would, at the same, define the international scope of that state's provisions on the gender of that person. In many jurisdictions such a *lex fori* approach would, in effect, create a hidden freedom of choice of law, at least to some extent: most states are rather generous as to the registration of a person's birth. Under the German *Personenstandsgesetz* (PStG), the German Civil Status Act, the German civil status authorities are competent to register a person's birth if the person is born in Germany (irrespective of nationality or

1 See e.g. D. Coester-Waltjen, 'Geschlecht? Kein Thema mehr für das Recht?' (2010) *JZ* 852.

2 S.L. Gössl, 'From question of fact to question of law to question of private international law: the question whether a person is male, female, or … ?' (2016) 12 *JPIL* 261, 262 et seq.

3 See G. Panagopoulos, 'Substance and Procedure in Private International Law' (2005) 1 *JPIL* 69 et seq.; E. Spiro, 'Forum Regit Processum' (1969) 18 *ICLQ* 949 et seq.

habitual residence) or if the person is born abroad but has German nationality or – in case the person is stateless or a refugee – habitually resides in Germany (cf. §36(1) PStG).

But the answer would be different if the legal gender of a person was a matter of substantive law. Issues of substantive law are traditionally subject to private international law, at least in systems which, for issues of substantive law, do not follow the *lex fori* principle as well. However, a general *lex fori* approach in private international law is an exception, even in a system like England and Wales, where the *lex fori* is only applied in certain areas of family law, for example, divorce and its financial consequences. In those fields the courts in England and Wales have wide discretion and should, therefore, if they have jurisdiction, always apply the *lex fori*, although they can take foreign elements of the case into account.[4]

Therefore, we must answer the question whether rules on the legal gender are of substantive or procedural nature. At first sight, one could get the impression that the legal gender of a person is an issue of procedure. For example, in German law the legal gender of a child is not addressed by the *Bürgerliche Gesetzbuch* (BGB), the German Civil Code, unlike the other questions relevant for the civil status of a person (for example, maternity and paternity, validity of a marriage or a person's name). Rather the legal gender of a person is only regulated in the Civil Status Act, which deals with the procedure of the German civil status authorities. Once a child is born, the civil status registrar is required by the Civil Status Act to certify in the birth register, not only the child's name, place, day, hour and minute of birth and the parents' names, but also the gender of the child (see §21(1) No. 3 PStG). The gender to be registered – which until recently could only be either female or male[5] despite the wording of the Civil Status Act actually being silent on that point[6] – is solely determined by the biological characteristics of the child and whether those characteristics conform to either the female or male legal sex. Also, the special gender status for intersex persons can be found amongst those procedural provisions. Since the end of 2013, a new provision again in the Civil Status Act (the new §22(3) PStG) permits the civil status registrars to refrain from certifying a child's legal gender in the birth register if the child cannot be assigned a male or female legal gender at the time of birth. In the meantime, the *Bundesverfassungsgericht*, the German

---

4 A.V. Dicey, J.H.C Morris and L.A. Collins, *The Conflict of Laws*, vol. 2, 15th ed., Sweet & Maxwell, London 2012, p. 108, approved by *Radmacher (formerly Granatino) v. Granatino* [2010] UKSC 42, para. 103 et seq.

5 See No. 21.4.3 of the *Allgemeine Verwaltungsvorschrift zum Personenstandsgesetz*, General Administrative Regulations for the German Civil Status Act, which states: '*Das Geschlecht des Kindes ist mit "weiblich" oder "männlich" einzutragen*'.

6 See, however, the principle of equality regarding sex enshrined in Art. 3(2) *Grundgesetz*, German Constitution, which suggests that there is only a male and a female sex.

Constitutional Court, has ruled that the German legislator must grant a positively defined special gender status for intersex persons.[7]

While this may seem to lead to the conclusion that determination of legal gender is a procedural matter, at closer inspection it is quite clear that the gender of a natural person is a question of substantive law, even though admittedly it still is categorised as a question of procedural law in some jurisdictions. In most jurisdictions gender is a matter of civil status, although there is a tendency to consider it as an instrument of mere identification.[8] But status means the standing of a person in law, as, for example, the German Civil Status Act expressly puts in its §1(1):

> Personenstand im Sinne dieses Gesetzes ist die sich aus den Merkmalen des Familienrechts ergebende Stellung einer Person innerhalb der Rechtsordnung (...).

This standing is determined by a person's attributions and conditions to which the law attaches consequences.[9] Even in those jurisdictions where the gender is of lesser importance since there is nominal equality of men and women in law and marriage has been opened up to same-sex couples, the law still attaches consequences to the legal gender. For example, the rules on maternal and paternal affiliation normally are different; compulsory military service, where that still exists, is mostly obligatory only for male persons; in certain public or administrative bodies as well as company boards, etc. a minimal representation of female persons is sometimes required. But even more importantly, a person's gender identity constitutes a decisive feature of his or her personality.[10] On an international level the concept of sex and the broader concept of gender are seen as matters of private life. The European Court of Human Rights has repeatedly stated that the right to gender identity is a fundamental and most intimate aspect of private life and therefore falls within the ambit of Article 8 of the European Convention on Human Rights (ECHR).[11] Protection is to be given to the personal sphere of each individual. This includes the rights to establish details of his or her identity as an individual human being.[12] The right to a legal gender in accordance with the individual's gender identity is seen as a personality right and a human right.[13]

---

7 See BVerfG 10.10.2017, *FamRZ* 2017, 2046 with a (critical) note by T. Helms.

8 F. Swennen, *Het personen- en familierecht*, 5th ed., Intersentia, Antwerp 2017, p. 104.

9 J. Heaton, *The South African Law of Persons*, 4th ed., LexisNexis, Durban 2012, p. 35.

10 Recommendation 1117 (1989) of the European Parliament of 29.09.1989 on the condition of transsexuals, recital 3.

11 *Goodwin v. United Kingdom* Appl. no. 28957/95, §77, ECHR 2002-VI; *Van Kück v. Germany* Appl. no. 35968/97, §75, ECHR 2003-VII; *Schlumpf v. Switzerland* Appl. no 29002/06, §104.

12 *Goodwin v. United Kingdom*, above n. 11, §90; *Van Kück v. Germany*, above n. 11, §69.

13 See O. Todts, 'Le droit à l'orientation sexuelle et à l'identité de genre: un droit fondamental?' (2013) *Annales de droit de Louvain* 133 et seq.

The gender of a person is therefore a matter of substantive law. The factual establishment of a gender might be a procedural issue, but not the question how a gender is defined. Here again the provisions on gender identity of transsexual and transgender persons demonstrate that the legal gender of a person is a normative concept and governed by substantive rules.[14] Whether the gender is defined by biological characteristics only, or whether any personal identification is irrelevant or determinative is a question of a substantive nature.

Therefore, the attribution of a legal gender is governed by private international law. This unfortunately in many ways is bad news, because in most jurisdictions private international law is silent on the law governing the legal gender of a person. As far as we can see there are no explicit conflict of law rules for the legal gender. Even in jurisdictions which provide for special provisions on the legal gender of intersex persons, rules of private international law are missing. This applies to systems where a special gender status for intersex persons was introduced by courts and not by legislation, as for example in India.[15] But even where there is legislation on a special gender status of intersex persons, private international law issues are not addressed. This is, for example, the case in Germany where an 'indeterminate' gender was introduced without explicitly clarifying the private international law rules. Hence, it is a task for conflict lawyers to create suitable private international law rules.

2. A PLEA FOR A SPECIFIC GENDER CONFLICT RULE

The question of the applicable law first arises when in a cross-border case the birth of an intersex person is registered.

As far as the jurisdiction in which registration takes place has a general conflict rule for the personal status of natural persons, at first sight that provision could also cover the legal gender of a person. In particular, on the continent the idea of a general regime governing personal status as a '*statut personnel*' or '*Personalstatut*' – a general personal status regime – is still prevalent. For example, the Spanish and Portuguese *Código civil* still define a law governing personal status generally.[16] Similarly, the French *Code civil* provides in its

---

14 Belgium: Art. 62bis *Code civil*; France: Art. 61–5 *Code civil*.

15 *National Legal Services Authority v. Union of India & Others*, AIR 2014 SC 1863. On this, see M.K. Sahu, 'Case Comment' (2016) 3 *BRICS Law Journal* 164 et seq. and the chapter by S. Shah in this volume.

16 See Art. 9(1) Spanish *Código civil*: '*La ley personal correspondiente a las personas físicas es la determinada por su nacionalidad. Dicha ley regirá la capacidad y el estado civil, los derechos y deberes de familia y la sucesión por causa de muerte*'; Art. 25 Portuguese *Código civil*: '*O estado dos indivíduos, a capacidade das pessoas, as relações de família e as sucessões por morte são regulados pela lei pessoal dos respectivos sujeitos (...)*'.

famous Article 3(3) a bilateral rule stating that the civil status and the capacity of natural persons (*l'état et la capacité des personnes*) is governed by the law of the person's nationality. The idea of a general personal status regime can to a certain extent also be found in more recent private international law codifications. For example, the Austrian *Gesetz über das Internationale Privatrecht* (IPRG), the Private International Law Act, in its §9 defines a general personal status regime (*Personalstatut*) to which the conflict rules for legal personality and capacity, names, marriage and filiation refer (see §§12 et seq., §16(2), §17(1), §§21 et seq. IPRG). In jurisdictions with such general personal status conflict rule it could be rather easy to characterise the gender of a person as an element of the personal status and, hence, subject to this general conflict rule.

However, the notion of a general law governing the personal status of natural persons is eroding, even in continental systems. In many systems, the private international law legislators have realised that questions of personal status require differentiated conflict rules rather than a 'one-size-fits-all' approach. It is therefore no surprise that in most jurisdictions names, filiation, parental responsibility, marriage and partnership, at the least, are subject to specific choice of law rules. Often only the legal personality and capacity as core areas of personal status are still subject to a general personal status category.[17] In such jurisdictions with differentiated conflict rules on personal status legal gender in the absence of a specific rule therefore needs to be dealt with following the rules for one of the personal status categories. The legal gender of a person is closely related to the category 'legal personality and capacity'. Hence, for example, some German courts and authors subject the legal gender to the conflict rule for legal personality and capacity, at least applied by analogy.[18] The same approach is advocated by some Dutch scholars.[19] This categorisation leads to nationality as a connecting factor.

The traditional approach of applying the existing conflict rules on personal status to legal gender issues is probably currently the only solution available in

---

17 See e.g. Art. 34 Belgian *Code de droit international privé*, Private International Law Code; Art. 7 German *Einführungsgesetz zum Bürgerlichen Gesetzbuche*, Introductory Act to the Civil Code; Arts. 5 et seq. Greek *Astikos kōdikas*, Civil Code; Arts. 20 et seq. Italian *Legge di riforma del sistema italiano di diritto internazionale privato*, Private International Law Act; Arts. 11 et seq. Polish *Prawo prywatne międzynarodowe*, Private International Law Act; Art. 33(1) Swiss *Bundesgesetz über das Internationale Privatrecht*, Private International Law Act.

18 S.L. Gössl, 'Intersexuelle Menschen im Internationalen Privatrecht' (2013) *StAZ* 301, 303; R. Hepting and A. Dutta, *Familie und Personenstand*, 2nd ed., Verlag für Standesamtswesen, Frankfurt a.M., Berlin 2015, p. 400; V. Lipp, 'Art. 7 EGBGB', in F.J. Säcker, R. Rixecker and H. Oetker (eds.), *Münchener Kommentar zum BGB Band 10*, 6th ed., Verlag C.H. Beck, Munich 2015, paras. 27 et seq.; Cf. H. Tigchelaar, P. Reuss and M. van den Brink, 'Out of the Box? Domestic and Private International Law Aspects of Gender Registration' (2015) 17 *European Journal of Law Reform* 283, 289.

19 Tigchelaar, Reuss and van den Brink, above n. 18, 290. Although in cases of transsexuality the *lex fori* law is applied (Art. 1:28 *Burgerlijk Wetboek*; see below).

most jurisdictions. However, it is not the most convincing solution. Firstly, the personal status approach is only an option if there are general conflict rules on personal status at all or at least concerning the core area of the personal status, i.e. legal personality and capacity. This is, for example, not the case in the common law jurisdictions, where a general notion of a law governing personal status has never existed. In those jurisdictions capacity is generally not seen as a personal status issue, but rather a special issue subject to the choice of law rules for the field of law in which the issue of capacity arises. This leads, for example, to the applicability of the choice of law rules on marriage, succession or contract.[20] However, there is a second weighty argument against the application of the general conflict rules to personal status issues. At least in continental jurisdictions, nationality will be the pertinent connecting factor. But is it appropriate to apply to a person's legal gender the law of the state whose nationality that person has? The only advantage of this solution is that the law of the state of origin always applies and that this state is also in charge of the personal identity documents. Hence, it is guaranteed that those documents are in conformity with the civil status records of the state of origin. However, a nationality-based approach would mean that in jurisdictions having a specific gender status for intersex persons those rules would be restricted to nationals of that country. This would, for example, mean that such a special gender status could not be awarded to a child born in that country but having a foreign nationality of a state not providing for a special gender status. Given that the introduction of special gender status rules was usually introduced for the protection of individuals and their human rights, such a differentiation cannot be acceptable.

What would be the optimal or at least a better solution? The problem of defining jurisdiction and applicable law in cross-border gender cases is not new. A rather similar problem arises regarding the gender identity of foreign transgender or transsexual persons. Here some jurisdictions have introduced specific legislation establishing rules on jurisdiction and applicable law. Belgium, for example, did not restrict the 2007 reform to substantive law but introduced conflict of law rules. The Belgian civil status registrars are competent to receive a declaration of gender reassignment not only from Belgian nationals residing in Belgium or abroad but also from foreigners being registered in the Belgian population register or the alien register as having their principal residence in Belgium (Article 35bis(1) *Code de droit international privé*, Belgian Private International Law Code). Article 35ter of the Code refers to the general conflict rule concerning status and capacity. The law of the state, whose nationality the applicant has, is applicable. If the national law of the applicant does not exclude

---

20 See e.g. A.V. Dicey, J.H.C Morris and L.A. Collins, above n. 4, Rules 74, 151, 228.

the registration of a new gender identity, but has no specific provisions, Belgian law applies to the substantial and procedural requirements. If specific provisions exist, substantial requirements, such as age and consent, are governed by the national law of the applicant, but procedural requirements, such as the medical doctor's attestation, are governed by Belgian law.[21] Provisions of the applicant's national law excluding gender reassignment are not applicable because they are contrary to public policy and Belgian law applies (Article 35ter(2) of the Belgian Private International Law Code).[22] Another example for specific legislation on the international scope of specific gender regimes based on nationality is the German *Transsexuellengesetz* (TSG), Transsexuals Act. This Act requires, in principle, the German nationality of the applicant (§1(1) No. 3 lit. a TSG).[23] However, foreign nationals can also make applications under the Transsexuals Act if the law of their state of origin does not contain provisions comparable to the German Transsexuals Act and if the foreign national has legal status under German immigration law.[24] This means that while German private international law still follows the nationality principle, it allows foreigners a kind of *forum necessitatis* in Germany. German law applies only where the applicant's state of origin does not permit him or her to obtain gender recognition and in cases where the applicant is strongly connected with Germany. This *forum necessitatis*, like many other important developments in the area of gender recognition in Germany, was not introduced by the German legislator, but rather by the Constitutional Court. In a 2006 decision the Court held that the equality principle, enshrined in Article 3(1) *Grundgesetz* (GG), German Constitution, would be violated if Germany refused to recognise the preferred gender of foreigners whose national law does not provide for the recognition of the preferred gender.[25]

By contrast, Dutch law follows a rather different approach. Foreign nationals may file a request for legal gender recognition if they have a valid residence permit and have been domiciled in the Netherlands for at least one year (Article 1:28(3) *Burgerlijk Wetboek* (BW), Dutch Civil Code). The court does not apply the national law of the applicant but Dutch law since the applicant must meet all the requirements of the *lex fori* (Article 1:28(3) BW).[26] English law

21 W. Pintens, 'The legal status of transsexual and transgender persons in Belgium and the Netherlands', in J.M. Scherpe (ed.), *The Legal Status of Transsexual and Transgender Persons*, Intersentia, Cambridge 2015, p. 117.

22 S. Cap, 'La loi du 10 mai 2007 relative à la transsexualité' (2009) *Revue trimestrielle de droit familial* 59, 76 et seq.; Pintens, above n. 21, p. 117.

23 Including a stateless or displaced person having his or her habitual residence in Germany (§1(1) No. 3 lit. b TSG), a person who is entitled to a grant of asylum and a foreign refugee domiciled in Germany (§1(1) No. 3 lit. c TSG).

24 In such cases, the foreign national must either have an unlimited right of residence in Germany or a renewable residence title, and he or she must reside permanently and lawfully in Germany (§1(1) No. 3 lit. d TSG).

25 BVerfG 18.07.2006, *BVerfGE* 116, 243.

26 Gericht 's Gravenhage 19.11.2009, ECLI:NL:RBSGR:2007:BB8201.

is even more generous, as there are no specific nationality or residency requirements in the Gender Recognition Act 2004.

The legislation on transgender persons should not necessarily be a starting point for a specific gender status for intersex persons. But with specific legislation for transgender persons the legislator has expressed its view that gender and sex should not automatically fall under the category 'status and capacity' but merits a specific conflict rule. This specific rule should apply to all matters of gender without any distinction between transgender and intersex persons. Another source of inspiration can be found in a proposal of the German Institute for Human Rights.[27] The proposal sees gender as a specific category distinct from status and capacity and applies nationality as the connecting factor. Private autonomy is underlined by allowing a *professio iuris*. A foreign national with habitual residence in Germany or a minor having a parent with habitual residence in Germany according to the proposal could opt for German law.

3. LEGAL GENDER AS A PRELIMINARY ISSUE IN A 'GENDER-SENSITIVE' OR 'BINARY' *LEX CAUSAE*

Another set of private international law questions arises if the legal gender is a preliminary issue in other areas of law. In many jurisdictions particularly family law is still 'gender-sensitive' or 'binary'[28] and presupposes that every natural person has a legal gender of male or female. For example, under German law, the mother of a child can only be a woman who has given birth to the child (§1591 BGB). Similarly, the father of a child can only be a man who meets the conditions for his legal fatherhood (§1592 BGB).

Comparable questions arise in jurisdictions where marriage is restricted to heterosexual couples. But even in systems having opened marriage to same-sex persons the question of the marriage of an intersex person can arise. For example, in Germany new §1353(1) BGB states that marriage can be concluded by two persons of the opposite or the same gender, leaving open the question whether persons with an indeterminate gender can marry.[29] What happens if

---

27 German Institute for Human Rights, 'Gender diversity in law: the status quo and the development of regulatory models for recognizing and protecting gender diversity' (2017) <https://www.bmfsfj.de/blob/116952/2f2af83b324af52cbb1d0efbfda212e2/geschlechtervielfalt-im-recht----englisch---gender-diversity-in-law-data.pdf> (last accessed 27.12.2017), on which see the contribution by N. Althoff in this volume. See also S.L. Gössl, 'Art. 10a EGBGB-Vorschlag: Kollisionsrechtliche Ergänzung des Vorschlags zum Geschlechtervielfaltsgesetz (GVielfG)' (2017) *IPRax* 339.

28 The latter term is used, e.g., by Tigchelaar, Reuss and van den Brink, above n. 18, 288.

29 See D. Schwab, 'Eheschließung für Personen gleichen Geschlechts' (2017) *FamRZ* 1284, 1286 et seq.; D. Kaiser, 'Gleichgeschlechtliche Ehe – nicht ganz gleich und nicht für alle' (2017) *FamRZ* 1889, 1897 et seq.

such a gender-sensitive family law applies as the *lex causae* but one of the parties has a special gender status as an intersex person acquired under another law?

In our view, in answering this question two scenarios have to be distinguished. In the first scenario the *lex causae* also offers a specific gender status for intersex persons. In that case – for purposes of applying the *lex causae* – the foreign status has to be transposed into the special gender status available for intersex persons in the *lex causae*.[30]

In the second scenario the *lex causae* does not provide a special gender status for intersex persons: In this scenario difficult questions of what conflict lawyers call substitution and adaption arise.[31] Does the foreign gender status substitute a male or female gender under the *lex causae* or has the *lex causae* to be adapted to the special gender status of intersex persons? That will, for example, be the case if an intersex person gives birth to a child and the applicable *lex causae* restricts – as German law does – motherhood to the woman who has given birth. In such a case, a person with a foreign gender status can be treated as a female person for purposes of the gender-sensitive *lex causae*.[32]

However, to complicate the matter further, in some jurisdictions both scenarios will merge. For example, in German law there is a special gender status for intersex persons but German family law nevertheless is – as already described above – still gender sensitive in some areas. Therefore, questions of substitution actually also arise in purely internal cases. The answers developed for internal cases – for example, as to the question whether a person with indeterminate gender can be the mother or the father or a child or can marry – should then apply for cross-border cases as well.

4. THE RECOGNITION OF A SPECIAL GENDER STATUS FOR INTERSEX PERSONS ACQUIRED ABROAD

Private international law is not only relevant when the legal gender of a person is registered for the first time and a specific gender status is acquired. Also later in life the legal gender of a person can be relevant and the question of private international law then will have to be answered. Problems will arise, in particular, if an intersex person was registered in the birth registry with a specific intersex gender status and the gender of that person becomes relevant in another jurisdiction which does not provide for a comparable status.

A general conflict rule – for example, using nationality as a connecting factor – would not be a convincing solution. As already seen, there can be cases where,

30 Gössl, above n. 18, 304.
31 See Gössl, above n. 2, 278 et seq.
32 Cf. Tigchelaar, Reuss and van den Brink, above n. 18, 291; Gössl, above n. 2, 277 et seq.

upon birth of that person, an intersex gender status is acquired although the intersex person is not a national of that country. The only practicable solution is the introduction of a duty to recognise the foreign gender status once registered in a foreign birth register. This approach was recently adopted by Maltese law, the only jurisdiction which, so far, specifically deals with the recognition of a special gender status acquired abroad. Article 9(2) of the Maltese Gender Identity, Gender Expression and Sex Characteristics Act 2015 provides that a special gender status 'other than male or female' will be recognised in Malta if 'recognised by a competent foreign court or responsible authority acting in accordance with the law of that country'.

Such a recognition approach would, of course, be another step in the direction of a general recognition principle, which is controversial is some jurisdictions. However, at least within the European Union such a duty to recognise could be established on the basis of the fundamental freedoms. An example can be found in the law of names. In the *Grunkin and Paul* decision, the Court of Justice of the European Union (ECJ) has held that a name registered in a Member State where the bearer has habitual residence has to be recognised in all other Member States.[33] Otherwise the freedom of movement and residence, enshrined in Article 21 of the Treaty on the Functioning of the European Union would be violated. The legal gender of a person must have the same relevance as the name of that person. It therefore is not inconceivable (and indeed to be expected) that the ECJ would establish a duty to recognise a specific gender status for an intersex person granted by another Member State.[34]

The recognition principle could even be clothed in a conflict rule, which provides that the legal gender of a person registered by a competent authority is governed by the law of the state of registration. Similar conflict rules can also be found in other areas of family law, for example, as to registered partnerships. Here, the new European Property Regulation for registered partners[35] follows the register principle: Article 26(1) of that Regulation subjects the property consequences to 'the law of the State under whose law the registered partnership was created'.

The recognition principles are universally limited by a public policy exception. This exception has, of course, to be applied restrictively. A specific gender status for intersex persons will probably not be regarded as a violation of

33 Case C-353/06, *Grunkin and Paul*, ECLI:EU:C:2008:559. See also Case C-541/15, *Freitag*, ECLI:EU:C:2017:432.
34 Gössl, above n. 2, 266 et seq. is more cautious in that respect.
35 Council Regulation (EU) 2016/1104 of 24 June 2016 implementing enhanced cooperation in the area of jurisdiction, applicable law and the recognition and enforcement of decisions in matters of the property consequences of registered partnerships [2016] OJ L 183/30.

public policy, at least in most European jurisdictions,[36] especially if one keeps in mind the human rights dimension.[37]

5. CONCLUSION

This short contribution proposes a twofold approach. First, the acquisition of an intersex legal gender status should be subject to the same conflict rules which govern the recognition of the preferred gender for transsexual or transgender persons. Transferring the basic idea of those conflict rules to intersex leads to the applicability of the law of nationality. However, domestic law should be applicable if a specific gender status for intersex persons is not available in the state of origin. Second, the recognition of an intersex gender status acquired abroad should be governed by the law of the state in which this status was first registered.

While it may seem rather premature to discuss intricate questions of private international law before introducing special substantive provisions for intersex persons, experience shows that quickly after a new regime is introduced, cross-border cases will arise within the area of personal status. The legislator should therefore always keep the private international law dimension in mind.

36 Gössl, above n. 18, 303; Tigchelaar, Reuss and van den Brink, above n. 18, 288 et seq.

37 See Gössl, above n. 2, 271 et seq. Cf. above section 1.

PART VI

INTERSEX AND HUMAN RIGHTS

STANDING UP FOR THE HUMAN RIGHTS OF INTERSEX PEOPLE

Dan Christian GHATTAS*

1. WHO ARE INTERSEX PEOPLE?

Intersex individuals are born with sex characteristics (such as chromosomes, genitals and/or hormonal structure) that do not belong strictly to male or female categories, or that belong to both at the same time.

* This contribution consists mostly of excerpts from D.C. GHATTAS, *Standing up for the human rights of intersex people – how you can help* (2015), edited by and reprinted here with the kind permission of ILGA Europe and OII Europe.

'Intersex' stands for the spectrum of variations of sex characteristics that naturally occur within the human species. It also stands for the acceptance of the physical fact that sex is a spectrum and that people with variations of sex characteristics other than male or female do exist.

Historically, the term 'intersex' was used as if it was as a disorder that needed medical intervention to 'fix it'. In the past two decades, the term has been reframed and established by intersex human rights defenders and their organisations as the human rights-based umbrella term.

Our sex characteristics are set out from birth, whether we are intersex or not. However, the fact that someone has an intersex body can become apparent at different times in their life: at birth, during childhood, in puberty or even in adulthood. Depending on the specific life circumstances and the degree of taboo in their environment, a person might learn that they have an intersex body at a very early age or later in life. Some intersex people never find out at all.

People with an intersex body can have as many gender identities (and sexual orientations for that matter) as people with a non-intersex body. Some intersex people have an intersex gender identity.

Intersex people are still very much invisible in our society. People who do not have an intersex body and want to use 'intersex' to describe their gender identity, should be aware of the fact that, unfortunately, they are actually making intersex human rights violations less visible.

Being intersex does not mean that the sex of the person is unspecified/unclear/unknown. It is only the current practice of recognising only two sexes, male and female, that leads to categorising intersex as 'unspecific'. Equating intersex with an unclear or unknown sex is disrespectful and deprives intersex people of the rightfulness of their body. This false judgement also leads to the fact that their right to bodily integrity is often violated by unconsented medical treatments.

Doctors often advise parents to perform surgical and other medical interventions on intersex new-borns and children, to make their body (seemingly) conform to male or female characteristics. In most cases, such interventions are not medically necessary and can have extremely negative consequences on intersex children as they grow older.

2. WHAT ARE THE IMPORTANT DIFFERENCES AND COMMONALITIES BETWEEN INTERSEX AND TRANS PEOPLE?

The most important differences are:

- Intersex is about the body: being intersex means to be born with sex characteristics that do not conform to the medical and societal norms of

so-called male and female bodies. Trans is about gender identity: being trans means to have a gender identity that is other than the gender/sex assigned at birth. Most people who are trans were born with a body that matches with the medical and societal norms of so-called male and female bodies.
- Intersex people are subjected to invasive, irreversibly treatment without their consent. Trans people often seek medical interventions to adjust their body to their gender identity but face problems getting the medical care they need.

However, it is important to note that intersex individuals may have a gender identity that does not match the sex that was enforced on them at birth. As a result, they may decide to use the legal mechanisms available in their country to adjust their name, gender marker and/or body to their personal comfort zone. Very often the only mechanisms available are those available to trans people. In practice though, some intersex people can be prevented from accessing those mechanisms, depending on legal or other requirements for each of those steps in their country.

The most important commonalities between intersex and trans people are:

- Both lack recognition of their fundamental right to self-determination. Intersex people because they are subjected to invasive medical treatment without their consent; trans people because they often face massive hurdles in obtaining the medical care they need as well as the recognition of their gender.
- Both are still considered to have a 'disorder' according to medical guidelines, protocols and classifications (although trans people have to deal with a 'psychological disorder' whereas intersex persons are attested to have a 'physical disorder').
- Both suffer from discrimination and human rights violations in a society where the dichotomy of male and female prevails, e.g. in school, at the workplace or when practising sport.

3. WHAT ARE THE MAIN PROBLEMS AND HUMAN RIGHTS VIOLATIONS FACED BY INTERSEX PEOPLE IN EUROPE TODAY?

In a world where the overwhelming majority of people and governments only know and accept two sexes ('male' and 'female') the existence of intersex people and their bodies is not recognised. Instead, healthy intersex bodies are considered to be a 'medical problem' and a 'psycho-social emergency'[1] that needs to be fixed by surgical, hormonal, other medical and sometimes psychological means.

---

1 J.V. Ladee-Levy, 'Ambiguous genitalia as a psychosocial emergency' (1984) 39 *Z Kinderchir* 178–181.

According to a ground-breaking 2015 European Union Agency for Fundamental Rights' focus paper on the fundamental rights situation of intersex people in the European Union, 'normalising' surgery is carried out on intersex children in at least 21 Member States.[2] This situation is mirrored all over the world.[3]

3.1. PATHOLOGISATION AND RESULTING HUMAN RIGHTS VIOLATIONS

All over Europe, intersex people face pathologisation and extreme violations of their human rights. Because being intersex is seen, in itself, as a disorder, when pre-implantation diagnosis or pre-natal screening show a risk of variation of sex characteristics in embryos and foetuses, the latter may be prevented from further developing. In other cases, prenatal treatment with high-risk off-label use medication (dexamethasone) is prescribed.

After birth, as children, adolescents and adults, intersex people face violations of their physical integrity, including medical interventions without personal, prior, persistent and fully informed consent. This can cause psychological trauma as well as severe physical impairments, ranging from painful scar-tissue or lack of sensation to osteoporosis and urethral issues. Intersex children face the risk of a disturbed family life due to taboo and medicalisation. They are also at risk of dropping out of school, owing to the effects of medical treatments and bullying.

Intersex adults may have difficulty finding a job owing to lack of education, physical impairments or a lack of self-esteem caused by social stigma. There is a reported higher risk of poverty due to lack of education as a result of pathologisation and related trauma. At every age, intersex people can face stigma, structural and verbal discrimination, harassment, lack of adequate medical care, lack of access to needed medication, lack of legal recognition, and the invisibility of their bodies in our society.

When growing older, just like anyone else, intersex people need to rely on the health sector much more. However, because they had to undergo traumatising treatments in the past, becoming dependent on health services is very challenging for them. In addition, there is very little information on how their health may be affected by the treatments they took for most of their lives.

---

2 In 8 Member States, a legal representative can even consent to sex 'normalising' medical interventions if the minor is old enough to decide. On this, see European Union Agency for Fundamental Rights, *FRA Focus Paper. The Fundamental Rights Situation of Intersex People* (2015), available at <http://fra.europa.eu/en/publication/2015/fundamental-rights-situation-intersex-people> (last accessed 27.01.2018).

3 D.C. Ghattas, *Human Rights between the sexes. A preliminary study on the life situations of inter* individuals* (2013), ed. by Heinrich Böll Foundation, available at <https://www.boell.de/en/2013/10/21/human-rights-between-sexes> (last accessed 27.01.2018).

3.2. ACCESS TO HEALTHCARE AND VIOLENCE IN MEDICAL SETTINGS

Access to general healthcare is often impaired by prejudices of healthcare professionals and the refund policies of health insurance companies. This is particularly true where accessibility to particular services (e.g. availability of preventive check-ups for certain conditions or general health services) is related to the sex/gender of the individual seeking the service or where the medical history of a person matters (e.g. life insurance, private health insurance, own-occupation disability insurance).

Disbelief, prejudices and disgust expressed by healthcare personnel can lead intersex people to avoid seeking healthcare. They can also lead health professionals to deny intersex people access to health services. Such incidents have been reported to OII Europe and its member organisations from all over Europe. Contrary to what medical advice often suggests, having sex-altering surgery does not help intersex people to avoid these barriers to health services in later life: incidents have been reported both by intersex individuals who have had surgery and by those who have not.

Intersex individuals have repeatedly reported physical and psychological abuse by medical staff (e.g. unconsented examination, rough use of examination tools or blaming intersex people for deliberately not cooperating when their bodies did not allow the traditional examination to take place).

Other common issues faced by intersex people in Europe are a lack of access to hormone substitution (after the surgical removal of a hormone-producing tissue) or a hormone substitution which does not fit the real needs of the person's body (and instead aims to enforce the assigned sex of female or male).

3.3. EDUCATION

Problems can exist for intersex people in educational settings from the very outset. To start with, intersex people are not constructively included in any educational curriculum.[4] Most often, they do not appear at all. If they are mentioned, they find themselves treated as an imaginative product of mythology (hermaphrodite), as an example of abnormity or viewed in a pathological way (in biology texts, medical handbooks or encyclopaedias).

In addition, sex education does not refer to their existence or their bodily experience. Instead, it tends to perpetuate the notion that only two sexes exist.

---

4 With the exception of the Maltese 'Trans, gender-variant and intersex students in schools policy' and the Icelandic queer education program that is brought to schools with the long-term goal of implementing it in the regular curriculum.

These experiences increase the feeling of shame, secrecy, not existing at all or being a fraud at a vulnerable age.

Moreover, intersex students may face direct discrimination at school and in further education if their gender expression, stature or other parts of their appearance do not conform with the female or male norm. Intersex individuals have reported bullying at school on those grounds (e.g. use of derogatory language, psychological and physical violence). Places where the body becomes visible to others, such as toilets and changing rooms, are common areas of anxiety and reported harassment, regardless of whether the intersex person has had a so-called 'normalising' surgery performed on them or not.

On an even more alarming level, intersex individuals also face educational impairments directly linked to the violation of their bodily integrity. Most surgeries, which are performed at an early age, lead to several follow-up operations over the years. These are often performed during the school holidays, at the expense of the child's need to relax and have fun. Some children drop out of school as a result of this long-term recovery process. Unwanted hormonal treatment, in childhood or puberty, with the aim of altering the body towards the assigned sex has also been reported to coincide with a decrease in school grades.

This physical and psychological strain often prevents intersex people from developing their full potential and leads to under-achievement at school. As a result, these children and young adults face significant difficulties in obtaining a higher education degree and are at risk of poverty when growing older.[5]

Intersex people who manage to achieve higher education still struggle with the combined impact of the human rights violations they experienced and the discrimination they still face in adulthood.

3.4. EMPLOYMENT

Challenges faced by intersex people in school often continue into their working life, perpetuating taboo, secrecy and shame. They can be victims of direct or

---

[5] An Australian study gathering data on 272 intersex individuals, aged 16–85+, showed that only a quarter of participants rated their overall experience at school positively. The overwhelming majority of participants (92%) did not attend a school with inclusive puberty/sex education. Overall, 18% of people with variations of sex characteristics had primary school education only (compared to 2% of the general Australian population). Many participants (66%) had experienced discrimination ranging from indirect to direct verbal, physical or other discriminatory abuse. Well-being risks were reportedly high. Source: UNESCO, *From Insult to Inclusion. Asia-Pacific report on school bullying, violence and discrimination on the basis of sexual orientation and gender identity* (2015), p. 38, available at <http://unesdoc.unesco.org/images/0023/002354/235414e.pdf> (last accessed 27.01.2018).

indirect discrimination and harassment because of their physical appearance or gender expression.[6]

When applying for a job, intersex people might need to explain gaps in their education or employment history, resulting from times where they were hospitalised or when they were not able to work owing to depression or trauma. Past and ongoing treatments have an impact on the physical and psychological well-being of the person and directly reduce their ability to work.

Employee medical checks can be extremely difficult for intersex people; especially when the medical practitioner in charge is not educated about the existence of intersex individuals at all or considers intersex people to have a disorder of sex development. When applying to join some professions (e.g. police force, fire fighters), intersex people have reportedly been rejected on the grounds of their DSD diagnosis and/or the surgeries they had been subjected to without their consent.

Once they secure employment, intersex people have reported intrusive curiosity about their body from co-workers.[7] Some intersex people who dared to open up about their intersex body have reported disbelief and rejection by colleagues and superiors.[8] Just as in education, the strain of discrimination and stigmatisation leads to higher absence rates, increasing the risk of intersex people losing their job.

Some intersex people have obtained a disability status due to the physical impairments they have as a result of unconsented surgery. Depending on the country, this status can offer some protection, but it can also come at the cost of additional discrimination and stigma as a disabled person.[9]

3.5. DISCRIMINATION IN OTHER AREAS

Intersex people are at risk of discrimination when their gender appearance does not fit within social norms of so-called male and female bodies. As a

6 Unpublished interviews conducted by the project 'Antidiskriminierungsarbeit und Empowerment für Inter*' with intersex people living in Germany. A summary of the results can be found at <https://interprojekt.files.wordpress.com/2015/09/interprojekt_konzept.pdf> (last accessed 27.01.2018).

7 OII Australia/Pride in Diversity, *Employers' Guide to Intersex Inclusion* (2014). p. 17. Available at <https://oii.org.au/wp-content/uploads/key/Employer-Guide-Intersex-Inclusion.pdf> (last accessed 27.02.2018).

8 J. van Lisdonk, *Living with intersex/DSD. An exploratory study of the social situation of persons with intersex/DSD* (2014), p. 56.

9 OII Europe, Statement of OII Europe on Intersex, Disability and the UN Convention on the Rights of People with Disabilities (2015): <http://oiieurope.org/wp-content/uploads/2015/05/CRPD_2015_Statement_OII_Europe.pdf> (last accessed 27.01.2018).

result, they may face harassment or discriminatory practices in all areas of life, including when accessing goods (e.g. medicine, clothes, cosmetics) and services (e.g. fitness club, hotels rooms, flight tickets).

4. RECOGNISING THE HUMAN RIGHTS OF INTERSEX PEOPLE

4.1. LEGAL RECOGNITION

While growing up, intersex individuals may find that the sex they were assigned at birth through official registration (and often after medical treatments) does not fit their own gender identity. The process that individuals have to go through to access gender recognition varies greatly between European countries. If legal gender recognition is available at all, the procedure often requires intersex people to declare themselves as trans in order to change their gender marker. In some countries, the requirements for legal gender recognition may prevent people with an intersex-related medical diagnosis from using those legal procedures, most often leaving them in legal limbo.

4.2. WHAT DO INTERSEX PEOPLE WANT?

The unanimous demands of the international intersex human rights movement were laid out in the Declaration of Malta at the 3rd International Intersex Forum in 2013.[10] The Declaration demands that an end is put to mutilating and 'normalising' practices such as genital surgeries, psychological and other medical treatments. Instead, intersex people must be empowered to make their own decisions about issues that affect their bodily integrity, physical autonomy and self-determination.

Practices like infanticide and killings of intersex people are happening in some parts of the world. In Europe, the fact that the pathologisation of intersex increasingly leads to pre-implantation genetic diagnosis, pre-natal screening and treatment, and selective abortion of intersex foetuses is concerning. These abuses result directly from the notion that intersex bodies are disordered. The Declaration therefore calls for de-pathologising variations in sex characteristics

---

10 Reprinted in this volume at p. 7 and available at <https://oiieurope.org/malta-declaration/> (last accessed 27.01.2018). See also the Darlington Statement and the Vienna statement, reprinted at pp. 11 and 19 in this volume.

in medical guidelines, protocols and classifications, such as the World Health Organization's International Classification of Diseases (ICD).[11]

The Malta Declaration also emphasises that creating and facilitating supportive, safe and celebratory environments for intersex people, their families and surroundings is key. This includes enacting anti-discrimination legislation protecting the ground of sex characteristics and ensuring that intersex people are protected against intersectional discrimination. It also means ensuring the provision of all human rights and citizenship rights to intersex people, including the right to marry and form a family and the right to have documents that reflect the person's gender identity. In relation to the injustice and suffering caused to intersex people in the past, the Declaration calls for providing adequate redress, reparation, access to justice and the right to truth. This means that intersex people must have the right to full information and access to their own medical records and history.

Medicalisation and stigmatisation of intersex people results in significant trauma and mental health concerns. It is important to ensure that non-pathologising psycho-social and peer support should be available to intersex people as required throughout their life, as well as to parents and/or care providers.

4.3. INTERNATIONAL HUMAN RIGHTS BODIES' REFERENCES TO INTERSEX

In the past ten years, more than 15 international human rights bodies have issued very clear recommendations that call on governments to end non-consensual medical interventions on intersex individuals.

- In 2011, the UN High Commissioner for Human Rights Navi Pillay, in a submission to the Human Rights Council, highlighted that intersex children are subject to discrimination and medically unnecessary surgery performed without their consent or that of their parents.
- In that same year, the UN Committee on the Elimination of Discrimination against Women expressed concern about intersex women as 'victims of abuses and mistreatment by health service providers'[12] in Costa Rica.

[11] See also the report *Intersex Issues in the ICD* (2014), available at <https://globaltransaction.wordpress.com/intersex-issues-in-the-icd/> (last accessed 27.01.2018). The submission addresses specific concerns related to intersex issues in the ICD reform process.

[12] CEDAW/C/CRI/CO/5-6, para. 40.

- Also in 2011, the UN Committee against Torture called, in its review on Germany, to ensure the application of 'best practices of granting informed consent to medical and surgical treatment of intersex people, including full information, orally and in writing, on the suggested treatment, its justification and alternatives' and to properly inform intersex individuals and their parents about consequences of unnecessary surgical and other medical treatment. The Committee further asked to investigate incidents that lacked informed consent and to provide redress and adequate compensation. Finally, the Committee urged Germany to provide adequate training for medical and psychological professionals on the range of sexual and related biological and physical diversity.[13]
- The UN Special Rapporteur on torture and other cruel, inhuman or degrading treatment or punishment Juan Mendez reaffirmed (in 2013) the Committee's against Torture recommendations by calling upon all states to repeal laws permitting intrusive and irreversible treatments, 'including forced genital-normalizing surgery [and] involuntary sterilization [...] when enforced or administered without the free and informed consent of the person concerned' and to provide special protection to individuals who are part of marginalised groups.[14]
- In 2014, the UN High Commissioner for Human Rights Navi Pillay again stressed that 'irreversible surgeries and sterilisations continue to be performed on intersex children without their informed consent, causing lifelong harm'.[15]
- The UN Committee on the Rights of Child in its 2014 review of Switzerland urged the country to protect intersex children's rights to bodily integrity, autonomy and self-determination, to prevent unnecessary medical or surgical treatment, and provide families of intersex children with adequate counselling and support.[16]
- In 2014, the Commissioner for Human Rights of the Council of Europe, Nils Muižnieks, published his human rights comment, *A boy or a girl or a person – intersex people lack recognition in Europe*. In this document the Commissioner affirmed that 'early "normalising" treatments do not respect intersex persons' rights to self-determination and physical integrity' and that 'proxy consent given by parents may not be free and fully informed and can hardly take into account the best interests of the child in the long-run'.[17]

---

13 CAT/C/DEU/CO/5, para. 20.

14 A/HRC/19/41, para. 56.

15 <http://www.ohchr.org/en/NewsEvents/Pages/DisplayNews.aspx?NewsID=14654&LangID=E> (last accessed 27.01.2018).

16 CRC/C/CHE/CO/2-4 (26.02.2015).

17 <https://www.coe.int/en/web/commissioner/-/a-boy-or-a-girl-or-a-person-intersex-people-lack-recognition-in-euro-1> (last accessed 27.01.2018).

- That same year, seven UN bodies, some of which had not previously spoken out on intersex issues, released an interagency statement describing non-consensual, cosmetic and other non-medically necessary surgery on intersex infants as human rights violations.[18]
- In 2015 alone, three UN bodies called on seven states parties, four of which in Europe, to protect the physical integrity, bodily autonomy and right to self-determination of intersex individuals. The recommendation included a call to take the 'necessary legislative, administrative and other measures to guarantee the respect for the physical integrity and autonomy of intersex persons and to ensure that no one is subjected during infancy or childhood to non-urgent medical or surgical procedures intended to decide the sex of the child'.[19]
- Also in 2015, the UN High Commissioner for Human Rights, Zeid Ra'ad Al Hussein, addressed the human rights violations faced by intersex people in his opening speech for the 30th Human Rights Council, emphasising that intersex children and adults are 'frequently subjected to forced sterilization and other unnecessary and irreversible surgery, and suffer discrimination in schools, workplaces and other settings' because their bodies do not comply with typical definitions of male or female.[20]
- Earlier that year, the Office of the High Commissioner for Human Rights had already published a Fact Sheet on Intersex as part of the UN Free & Equal Campaign, which included an extensive list of action points, addressing states, the media and the general public.[21]
- In 2015, the Commissioner for Human Rights of the Council of Europe, Nils Muižnieks, published his issue paper, *Human Rights and Intersex People*, which calls on member states to 'end medically unnecessary "normalising" treatment of intersex persons when it is enforced or administered without the free and fully informed consent of the person concerned' and provides ways forward in terms of protection against discrimination of intersex people, adequate

18 OCHR/UN WOMEN/UNAIDS/UNDP/UNFPA/UNICEF/WHO, *Eliminating forced, coercive and otherwise involuntary sterilization. An interagency statement* (2014), available at <http://www.who.int/reproductivehealth/publications/gender_rights/eliminating-forced-sterilization/en/> (last accessed 27.01.2018).

19 Committee on the Rights of the Child Concluding Observations on Switzerland (CRC/C/CHE/CO/2-4); Committee on the Rights of People with Disabilities Concluding Observations on Germany (CRPD/C/DEU/CO/1); Committee Against Torture Concluding Observations on Austria (CAT/C/AUT/CO/6), Denmark (CAT/C/DNK/CO/6-7) and Switzerland (CAT/C/CHE/CO/7).

20 <http://www.ohchr.org/EN/NewsEvents/Pages/DisplayNews.aspx?NewsID=16414&LangID=E#sthash> (last accessed 27.01.2018).

21 Available at <https://unfe.org/system/unfe-65-Intersex_Factsheet_ENGLISH.pdf> (last accessed 27.01.2018).

recognition of their sex on official documents and access to justice (a summary of the Commissioner's recommendations is given below at 5.).[22]

- The European Union Agency for Fundamental Rights (FRA) joined the Commissioner's recommendations by publishing its own focus paper, *The Fundamental Rights Situation of Intersex People*. The findings of the FRA confirmed the concerns expressed by intersex human rights NGOs, stating that in 'at least 21 Member States sex "normalising" surgery is carried out on intersex children' and that in '8 Member States a legal representative can consent to sex "normalising" medical interventions independently of the child's ability to decide'. The FRA concluded that legal and medical professionals lacked knowledge about the fundamental rights of intersex people, particularly children and emphasised that 'Member States should avoid non-consensual "sex-normalising" medical treatments on intersex people'. The paper also pointed out that intersex concerns sex characteristics and therefore was better to be covered under the ground of 'sex' rather than on the basis of sexual orientation and/or gender identity. In regard to sex/gender markers in official documents, the FRA recommended to review the current laws and practices to better protect intersex people.[23]
- In 2017 Parliamentary Assembly of the Council of Europe adopted the first intersex-specific resolution of its kind from a European intergovernmental institution.[24] The resolution was unanimously approved by the Committee on Equality and Non-Discrimination. The resolution is a clear message to policymakers across Europe that they must take action to install legislative protections for intersex people and highlights the steps that need to be taken to protect the fundamental rights of intersex people. The resolution confirms intersex people's right to bodily autonomy and physical integrity as it calls for prohibition of 'medically unnecessary sex-"normalising" surgery, sterilisation and other treatments practised on intersex children without their informed consent'. In the adopted recommendations it calls on the Committee of Ministers to bring the resolution to the attention of their governments and highlights the need to bring about rapid change within Council of Europe Member States.

---

22 Council of Europe, *Human Rights and Intersex People* (2015), available at <https://rm.coe.int/16806da5d4 > (last accessed 28.05.2018).

23 European Union Agency for Fundamental Rights, above n. 2.

24 Parliamentary Assembly of the Council of Europe, Resolution 2191 (2017), *Promoting the human rights of and eliminating discrimination against intersex people*, reprinted below and available at <http://assembly.coe.int/nw/xml/XRef/Xref-XML2HTML-en.asp?fileid=24232&lang=en> (last accessed 26.02.2018).

4.4. SUMMARY OF THE RECOMMENDATIONS OF THE COMMISSIONER FOR HUMAN RIGHTS OF THE COUNCIL OF EUROPE[25]

- Stop unnecessary medical treatment and surgery of intersex people without their consent.
- Respect intersex persons' right not to undergo sex assignment treatment.
- Review medical classifications which pathologise intersex people.
- Improve law and policy to facilitate the legal recognition of intersex individuals on official documents, respecting their right to self-determination.
- Ensure that national equal treatment and hate crime legislation protects intersex people.
- Give intersex people full access to their medical records.
- More in-depth research needed to adequately address discrimination and other violations of intersex people's human rights.
- Raise public awareness and improve professional training about the problems encountered by intersex people.
- Involve intersex people in the development of measures to address these problems.
- Improve counselling of intersex children and their parents.
- Facilitate intersex people's access to justice and investigate and acknowledge past human rights violations.

4.5. PARLIAMENTARY ASSEMBLY OF THE COUNCIL OF EUROPE RESOLUTION 2191 (2017): PROMOTING THE HUMAN RIGHTS OF AND ELIMINATING DISCRIMINATION AGAINST INTERSEX PEOPLE

1. Intersex people are born with biological sex characteristics that do not fit societal norms or medical definitions of what makes a person male or female. Sometimes a person's intersex status is detected at birth; sometimes it only becomes apparent later in life, notably during puberty. Despite the wide variety of situations concerned, the majority of intersex people are physically healthy. Only a few suffer from medical conditions that put their health at risk. Yet the situation of intersex people has for a long time been treated as an essentially medical issue. The prevailing medical view has been that intersex children's bodies can and should be made to conform to either

25 See <https://rm.coe.int/CoERMPublicCommonSearchServices/DisplayDCTMContent?documentId=09000016806daa0a> (last accessed 28.05.2018).

a male or a female paradigm, often through surgical and/or hormonal intervention; that this should be done as early as possible; and that the children should then be raised in the gender corresponding to the sex assigned to their body.

2. The Parliamentary Assembly considers that this approach involves serious breaches of physical integrity, in many cases concerning very young children or infants who are unable to give consent and whose gender identity is unknown. This is done despite the fact that there is no evidence to support the long-term success of such treatments, no immediate danger to health and no genuine therapeutic purpose for the treatment, which is intended to avoid or minimise (perceived) social problems rather than medical ones. It is often followed by lifelong hormonal treatments and medical complications, compounded by shame and secrecy.

3. Parents are often under pressure to make urgent, life-changing decisions on behalf of their child, without having a full and genuine understanding of the long-term consequences for the child of the decisions made about their body during their infancy and early childhood.

4. Understanding of these issues is gradually increasing, but concerted efforts are still needed to raise public awareness as to the situation and rights of intersex people so as to ensure that they are fully accepted in society, without stigmatisation or discrimination.

5. The Assembly emphasises that it is crucial to ensure that the law does not create or perpetuate barriers to equality for intersex people. This includes ensuring that intersex people who do not identify as male or female have access to legal recognition of their gender identity, and that where their gender has not been correctly recorded at birth, the procedure for rectifying this is simple and based on self-identification only, as set out in Assembly Resolution 2048 (2015) on discrimination against transgender people in Europe. Anti-discrimination laws may also need to be amended to ensure that the situation of intersex people is effectively covered.

6. The Assembly considers that the above may raise important issues under a number of provisions of the European Convention on Human Rights (ETS No. 5), notably Articles 3 and 8.

7. In the light of the above, and bearing in mind the provisions of the Convention for the Protection of Human Rights and Dignity of the Human Being with regard to the Application of Biology and Medicine: Convention on Human Rights and Biomedicine (ETS No. 164, 'Oviedo Convention') and the relevant recommendations made in its Resolution 1952 (2013) on children's right to physical integrity, as well as those by the Council of Europe Commissioner for Human Rights and numerous treaty bodies of the United Nations, the Assembly calls on Council of Europe member States to:

- 7.1. with regard to effectively protecting children's right to physical integrity and bodily autonomy and to empowering intersex people as regards these rights:
  - 7.1.1. prohibit medically unnecessary sex-'normalising' surgery, sterilisation and other treatments practised on intersex children without their informed consent;

- 7.1.2. ensure that, except in cases where the life of the child is at immediate risk, any treatment that seeks to alter the sex characteristics of the child, including their gonads, genitals or internal sex organs, is deferred until such time as the child is able to participate in the decision, based on the right to self-determination and on the principle of free and informed consent;
- 7.1.3. provide all intersex people with health care offered by a specialised, multidisciplinary team taking a holistic and patient-centred approach and comprising not only medical professionals but also other relevant professionals such as psychologists, social workers and ethicists, and based on guidelines developed together by intersex organisations and the professionals concerned;
- 7.1.4. ensure that intersex people have effective access to health care throughout their lives;
- 7.1.5. ensure that intersex people have full access to their medical records;
- 7.1.6. provide comprehensive and up-to-date training on these matters to all medical, psychological and other professionals concerned, including conveying a clear message that intersex bodies are the result of natural variations in sex development and do not as such need to be modified;

7.2. with a view to assisting intersex people, their parents and the people around them in dealing with the challenges posed, *inter alia*, by social attitudes towards variations in sex characteristics:

- 7.2.1. ensure that adequate psychosocial support mechanisms are available for intersex people and their families throughout their lives;
- 7.2.2. support civil society organisations working to break the silence around the situation of intersex people and to create an environment in which intersex people feel safe to speak openly about their experiences;

7.3. with regard to civil status and legal gender recognition:

- 7.3.1. ensure that laws and practices governing the registration of births, in particular as regards the recording of a newborn's sex, duly respect the right to private life by allowing sufficient flexibility to deal with the situation of intersex children without forcing parents or medical professionals to reveal a child's intersex status unnecessarily;
- 7.3.2. simplify legal gender recognition procedures in line with the recommendations adopted by the Assembly in Resolution 2048 (2015) and ensure in particular that these procedures are quick, transparent and accessible to all and based on self-determination;
- 7.3.3. ensure, wherever gender classifications are in use by public authorities, that a range of options are available for all people, including those intersex people who do not identify as either male or female;
- 7.3.4. consider making the registration of sex on birth certificates and other identity documents optional for everyone;
- 7.3.5. ensure that, in accordance with the right to respect for private life, intersex people are not prevented from entering into a civil partnership or marriage or from remaining in such a partnership or marriage as a result of the legal recognition of their gender;

7.4. with regard to combating discrimination against intersex people, ensure that anti-discrimination legislation effectively applies to and protects intersex people, either by inserting sex characteristics as a specific prohibited ground in all anti-discrimination legislation, and/or by raising awareness among lawyers, police, prosecutors, judges and all other relevant professionals, as well as intersex people, of the possibility of dealing with discrimination against them under the prohibited ground of sex, or as an 'other' (unspecified) ground where the list of prohibited grounds in relevant national anti-discrimination provisions is non-exhaustive;

7.5. collect more data and carry out further research into the situation and rights of intersex people, including into the long-term impact of sex-'normalising' surgery, sterilisation and other treatments practised on intersex people without their free and informed consent, and in this context:

7.5.1. conduct an inquiry into the harm caused by past invasive and/or irreversible sex-'normalising' treatments practised on individuals without their consent and consider granting compensation, possibly through a specific fund, to individuals having suffered as a result of such treatment carried out on them;

7.5.2. in order to build a complete picture of current practice, keep a record of all interventions carried out on children's sex characteristics;

7.6. carry out campaigns to raise awareness among the professionals concerned and among the general public as regards the situation and rights of intersex people.

8. Finally, the Assembly invites national parliaments to work actively, with the participation of intersex people and their representative organisations, to raise public awareness about the situation of intersex people in their country and to give effect to the recommendations made above.

THE 'NORMALISATION' OF INTERSEX BODIES AND 'OTHERING' OF INTERSEX IDENTITIES

Morgan CARPENTER*

1. INTRODUCTION

In 2015, a UN factsheet named Australia and Malta as countries that have made demonstrable progress in recognising the human rights of intersex people. Australia had held the first Parliamentary inquiry on involuntary or coerced medical interventions, and also added an attribute of 'intersex status' to federal anti-discrimination law.[1] Australia also implemented a federal

* This chapter was first drafted in partial completion of a Master of Bioethics program at Sydney Health Ethics, at the University of Sydney. I would like to thank Christopher Jordens, my research supervisor at Sydney Health Ethics. I also thank Mauro Cabral Grinspan, Steph Lum, Bonnie Hart, Tony Briffa and all the other people with whom I have discussed the concepts and issues detailed in this chapter.

1 OFFICE OF THE HIGH COMMISSIONER FOR HUMAN RIGHTS, *Free & Equal Campaign Fact Sheet: Intersex*, 2015 <https://unfe.org/system/unfe-65-Intersex_Factsheet_ENGLISH.pdf> (last accessed 20.07.2017).

third-sex classification,[2] and laid claim in 2017 to 'some of the most advanced laws in the world, including on intersex status'.[3] Yet the report of the Parliamentary inquiry has not been implemented and so-called medical 'normalisation' of intersex bodies continues with the imprimatur of the Family Court of Australia.[4] In contrast, Malta had enacted legal protections for the bodily autonomy of infants and children.[5]

The coexistence in Australia of both legal inclusion and surgical 'normalisation' indicates a disjunction between what is said and what is done; between a rhetoric of inclusion and the reality of human rights violations. The situation also indicates a lack of connection between policies and practices designed to protect people with non-normative identities, and policies and practices affecting the treatment of people born with non-normative bodies.[6]

A series of epistemic claims underpin these disjunctions. Policies and practices affecting people born with non-normative bodies are grounded in a medical discourse about abnormality and, in the context of non-normative sex characteristics, a medical discourse of 'disorders of sex development'. In response to challenges to medical jurisdiction, clinicians have made claims about consensus regarding treatment; attempted to marginalise and discredit critics; and made claims about change or improvements to clinical practices.

Policies and practices affecting people with non-normative identities are reflected in legal and social discourse associated with lesbian, gay, bisexual and transgender (LGBT) populations. This discourse directly and indirectly frames intersex people as being members of a third sex. This is associated with claims about solutions for the human rights concerns regarding forced medical interventions; claims of deception that promote medical authority over intersex bodies; and claims of sex diversity that are deployed to justify the demands of other populations.

This chapter outlines and discusses these claims and counter-arguments, drawing upon international developments and events in Australia. It will show

---

2 Attorney General's Department, *Australian Government Guidelines on the Recognition of Sex and Gender*, 2013 <http://www.ag.gov.au/Publications/Pages/AustralianGovernmentGuidelinesontheRecognitionofSexandGender.aspx> (last accessed 01.07.2013).

3 Department of Foreign Affairs and Trade, *Australia's candidacy for the United Nations Human Rights Council 2018–2020*, 2017 <http://dfat.gov.au/international-relations/international-organisations/pages/australias-candidacy-for-the-unhrc-2018-2020.aspx> (last accessed 13.09.2017).

4 *Re: Carla (Medical procedure)* [2016] FamCA 7 (20 January 2016) <http://www.austlii.edu.au/cgi-bin/sinodisp/au/cases/cth/FamCA/2016/7.html> (last accessed 20.07.2017).

5 Malta. Gender Identity, Gender Expression and Sex Characteristics Act: Final version (2015).

6 M. Carpenter, 'The human rights of intersex people: addressing harmful practices and rhetoric of change' (2016) 24(47) *Reproductive Health Matters* 74–84.

that the two dominant discourses – medical normalisation and socio-legal othering – reflect radically different understandings about who intersex people are, with profound ethical, human rights and health consequences arising from their resulting policies and practices. The two discourses interact, sometimes with only incidental consideration, or even knowledge, of the other, but this is not well recognised or understood. Similarly, the two dominant discourses are themselves sometimes inconsistent or even contradictory.

This chapter will show that the two approaches and their disjunctions have harmful consequences. The chapter will show that neither model is based around principles of self-determination, that is, around the principles of autonomy, choice and informed personal consent. Disjunctions, paradoxes and popular misconceptions also have consequences for the exercise of self-determination, including access to information, and to peers. These disjunctions have led to policy developments that fail to take full account of the human rights and health needs of affected individuals and their families. The effect is that intersex bodies remain 'normalised' or eliminated by medicine, while society and the law 'others' intersex identities. That is, medicine constructs intersex bodies as either female or male, while law and society construct intersex identities as neither female nor male. Indeed, medicalisation is posed as a solution to stigma and othering, while legal othering is posed as a solution to medicalisation. Neither approach is grounded firmly in evidence.

In response to incommensurate medical and third-sex models, an emerging human rights model seeks to address these harms, disjunctions and paradoxes, focusing on the rights to bodily integrity and truth, and the principle of self-determination.

2. HISTORICAL BACKGROUND

Since 2006, a medical model has constructed 'congenital conditions in which development of chromosomal, gonadal or anatomical sex is atypical' as 'disorders of sex development'.[7] This medical model regards intersex variations as physical malformations that can be 'corrected' to ensure the healthy physical and psychological development of intersex persons as either female or male; to ameliorate stigma and mitigate parental and societal antipathy. In contrast, a 'third-sex' model constructs intersex people as neither female nor male but, instead, people who should be marked as having a non-standard sex.

---

7 I.A. Hughes, C. Houk, S.F. Ahmed, P.A. Lee and LWPES/ESPE Consensus Group, 'Consensus statement on management of intersex disorders' (2006) 91 *Archives of Disease in Childhood* 554–563, 554.

For example, Noël Wise, a judge in the California Superior Court, stated in *Time Magazine* in 2017 that female or male birth certificates of such persons are 'inaccurate':

> Many individuals are born with sex chromosome, endocrine or hormonal irregularities, and their birth certificates are inaccurate because in the United States birth records are not designed to allow doctors to designate an ambiguous sex.[8]

Both models share the same assumptions on the fundamental biological characteristics of intersex people, though there are uncertainties (and some clinical disagreement) about whether or not particular diagnoses qualify as intersex or disorders of sex development. Indeed, the medicalisation of intersex bodies has been accompanied by a repetitive cycle whereby clinical nomenclature has been adopted, claimed to be pejorative, and replaced.[9] Underlying this there may be deeper truths about the impact of stigma, and the role and impact of medicalisation. In contrast, and despite the precision of Wise's statement, the third-sex model is generally less concerned with drawing lines around diagnoses as it is with drawing lines within boxes, on forms and documents.

Both medical and third-sex models are to some extent ahistorical, reflecting the availability of new technologies and new social constructions. At least in the West, intersex people, 'hermaphrodites', have been regarded in canon (church) law and early common law as either male or female, depending on predominant characteristics.[10] For example, the *Decretum Gratiani*, compiled in the twelfth century, states: 'Hermafroditus an ad testamentum adhiberi possit, qualitas sexus incalescentis ostendit'.[11] This has been translated by Christof Rolker as: 'Whether an hermaphrodite may witness a testament, depends on which sex prevails.'[12]

Julie Greenberg cites Bracton, a contemporaneous source on English law and custom, who classified mankind as 'male, female, or hermaphrodite', where a 'hermaphrodite [wa]s classed with male or female according to the predominance of the sexual organs'.[13] Greenberg cites a similar approach

8 N. Wise, 'Judge: Gender Laws Are at Odds with Science', *Time* (08.03.2017) <http://time.com/4679726/judge-biological-sex-laws-marriage-bathrooms/> (last accessed 20.07.2017).

9 Carpenter, above n. 6, 74.

10 J. Greenberg, 'Defining Male and Female: Intersexuality and the Collision Between Law and Biology' (1999) 41 *Arizona Law Review* 277.

11 *Decretum Gratiani*, C. 4, q. 2 et 3, c. 3. <http://geschichte.digitale-sammlungen.de/decretum-gratiani/kapitel/dc_chapter_1_1585> (last accessed 20.07.2017) p. 32.

12 C. Rolker, 'Double sex, double pleasure? Hermaphrodites and the medieval laws' presented at the IMC Leeds, 2013, Leeds, England <https://www.academia.edu/4101811/Double_sex_double_pleasure_Hermaphrodites_and_the_medieval_laws> (last accessed 20.07.2017).

13 Greenberg, above n. 10, 277.

taken by Edward Coke in the sixteenth century, in his *Institutes of the Laws of England*:

> Every heire is either a male, or female, or an hermaphrodite, that is both male and female. And an hermaphrodite (which is also called Androgynus) shall be heire, either as male or female, according to that kind of the sexe which doth prevaile.[14]

In the centuries after Coke wrote the *Institutes*, doctors sought to determine whether or not hermaphrodites existed. As part of the same process, hermaphroditism became defined in narrower, more precise terms, to describe organisms able to perform 'sexual functions of both sexes'.[15] If human hermaphrodites, capable of such functions did not exist, then doctors sought to determine how best to determine the 'true' sex of their patients,[16] perhaps to determine which sex might prevail.

In addition to the term hermaphrodite, Elizabeth Reis has documented the labels 'hybrid', 'impostor' and 'monstrosity',[17] and clinical preoccupations with themes – or perhaps fears – of sexual and racial transformation, and the preservation of structures of power.[18] She says, 'themes of dishonesty and sexual promiscuity lurk in what are otherwise dispassionate and clinical medical cases'.[19] These themes and preoccupations persist today.

Peter Conrad describes how medicalisation is 'a process by which non-medical problems become defined and treated as medical problems',[20] proposing that rationales for medicalisation might include 'discovery of new etiologies, availability and profitability of treatments … and the presence of individuals or groups who promote or challenge medical definitions'.[21] He observes that 'medical ideologies, interventions, and therapies have reset and controlled the borders of acceptable behaviour, bodies, and states of being'.[22] Irving Zola argues that medicine is a form of social control, critiquing the notion that 'medical involvement in social problems leads to their removal from religious and legal scrutiny and thus from moral and punitive consequences'.[23] The treatment of individuals with intersex variations provides an example.

14 Ibid, 277–278.
15 E. Reis, 'From Monsters to Deceivers in the Early Nineteenth Century', in *Bodies in Doubt: An American History of Intersex*, Johns Hopkins University Press, Baltimore 2012, p. 42.
16 Ibid, p. 29.
17 Ibid, p. 24.
18 Ibid, p. 37 and p. 40.
19 Ibid, p. 30.
20 P. Conrad, 'Medicalization: Context, Characteristics and Changes', in *The Medicalization of Society: On the Transformation of Human Conditions into Treatable Disorders*, Johns Hopkins University Press, Baltimore 2007, pp. 3–19, at p. 4.
21 Ibid, p. 7.
22 Ibid, p. 12.
23 I.K. Zola, 'Medicine as an Institution of Social Control' (1972) 20(4) *The Sociological Review* 487–504, 489.

The medicalisation of intersex bodies took place as a product of a medicalisation of homosexuality, of a disproportionate medicalisation of non-normatively male bodies (what Conrad describes as the disproportionate medicalisation of women),[24] and of the construction of clinical norms, classifications and standards. This is exemplified in Reis' description of how:

> Physicians in the 1880s and 1890s wanted their patients to understand their hermaphroditic conditions as deformities and not as a physical license to commit sexual immorality.[25]

An example was provided by JW Long, in 1896:

> I believe that we owe it to these poor unfortunates to impress upon them, as well as upon others, that they are *not* part man and part woman ... The peculiarities which make them appear mixed, are only deformities like hair-lip or club-foot.[26]

In this moment, a nascent medical model is juxtaposed against an abject otherness, with medicalisation posed as an alternative to criminality and immorality.

3. THE MEDICAL MODEL

The early surgical assignment of sex became institutionalised in the 1950s and 1960s, through the work of John Money, his investigations of the lives of intersex people and, notably, the case of David Reimer. Nevertheless, Money's doctorate research on 250 children who received no genital surgeries showed that, as reported by Mike O'Connor: 'Ironically ... the vast majority grew into well-adjusted adults'.[27]

The David Reimer case epitomised Money's 'optimal gender' policy of surgical and social assignment. Reimer was a twin boy whose penis was ablated during circumcision and who was subsequently raised as a girl. Milton Diamond and Keith Sigmundson report that: 'Orchiectomy and preliminary surgery to fashion a vagina followed within the year to facilitate feminization'; this was followed by

24 Conrad, above n. 20, p. 10.

25 E. Reis, 'The Conflation of Hermaphrodites and Sexual Perverts at the Turn of the Century', in *Bodies in doubt: an American History of Intersex*, Johns Hopkins University Press, Baltimore 2012, pp. 55–81, at p. 68.

26 J.W. Long, 'Hermaphrodism So-Called, with an Illustrative Case' (1896) 9(8) *International Journal of Surgery* 243–4, 244.

27 M. O'Connor, 'The treatment of intersex and the problem of delay: The Australian Senate inquiry into intersex surgery and conflicting human rights for children' (2016) 23(3) *Journal of Law and Medicine* 531–543, 536.

regular monitoring, and reports of successful gender assignment. Reporting on the case, Money and Tucker stated that:

> her record to date offers convincing evidence that the gender identity gate is open at birth for a normal child no less than for one born with unfinished sex organs or one who was prenataly [sic] over-or underexposed to androgen, and that it stays open at least for something over a year after birth.[28]

The post-surgical reality for David Reimer was different from that reported, with a difficult childhood. Following disclosure by his parents, he switched back to his originally-assigned male gender. This reality was published by Diamond and Sigmundson in 1997, and views on Money's work came to be regarded far more critically.[29] Core elements of his medical model nevertheless persist.

The institutionalisation of early surgical assignment has led to radical clinical interventions, on the basis of flawed and inadequate evidence. Surgical assignment and 'unambiguous sex of rearing was considered pivotal' for success, and this was accompanied by a deliberate 'policy of concealment', of non-disclosure of a diagnosis to an affected person.[30] By 1969, the UK clinicians Christopher Dewhurst and Ronald Gordon reported that the alternative to medicalisation had to be imagined, and that imagined alternative could be 'remedied' through surgery:

> To visualize individuals who properly belong neither to one sex nor to the other is to imagine freaks, misfits, curiosities, rejected by society and condemned to a solitary existence of neglect and frustration … The tragedy of their lives is the greater since it may be remediable[31]

The medical model has since become dominant globally, practised everywhere that Western medicine is accessible. In a 1996 position statement, the American Academy of Pediatrics said:

> The Academy is deeply concerned about the emotional, cognitive, and body image development of intersexuals, and believes that successful early genital surgery minimizes these issues.[32]

---

28 As quoted in M. Diamond and K. Sigmundson, 'Sex Reassignment at Birth: A Long Term Review and Clinical Implications' (1977) 151(3) *Archives of Pediatrics and Adolescent Medicine* 298–304.

29 L. Downing, I. Morland and N. Sullivan, *Fuckology: Critical Essays on John Money's Diagnostic Concepts*, University of Chicago Press, Chicago 2014.

30 F. D'Alberton, 'Disclosing Disorders of Sex Development and Opening the Doors' (2010) 4(4–5) *Sexual Development* 304–309, 305.

31 C.J. Dewhurst and R.R. Gordon, Preface, in *The intersexual disorders*. Baillière, Tindall & Cassell, London 1969, pp. vii–viii, at p. vii.

32 American Academy of Pediatrics. American Academy of Pediatrics Position on Intersexuality. Intersex Day, 2010, <http://intersexday.org/en/aap-position-1996/> (last accessed 20.07.2017).

These rationales indicate a belief that early interventions pre-empt suffering, stigma and discrimination. Other issues are also at play. In the 1970s, John Money and Anke Ehrhardt described how 'one may begin with the same clay and fashion a god or a goddess'.[33] In 1993, Melissa Hendricks interviewed clinicians at Johns Hopkins, including Gary Berkowitz:

> Today, a child need not grow up with the genitalia he or she was born with. 'The way we explain it to parents is that the genitalia aren't finished,' says Berkowitz. 'Nature hasn't finished the job.'[34]

When diagnosed at or close to birth, decisions about sex of rearing – and the choice of feminising or masculinising surgeries – depended upon tests and examinations, including an examination of a family history, by a multidisciplinary 'team of endocrinologists, urologists and paediatricians' and, sometimes, religious ministers or a social worker. 'The parents have the final say',[35] but another interviewee, John Gearhart explained how parents are educated by clinicians. He:

> freely admits that recommending what a child's sex should be is like playing God … 'That is why we spend hours educating these parents,' who ultimately have the final say in the child's gender … In truth, the choice of gender still often comes down to what the external genitals look like.[36]

Decisions about sex of rearing were made based on technical aspects of surgery and heteronormative function. Hendricks reported in 1993:

> Doctors who work with children with ambiguous genitalia sometimes put it this way: 'You can make a hole but you can't build a pole.'[37]

Concerns about post-surgical loss of sexual function and sensation were dismissed. Writing in the same year about clitorectomies associated with congenital adrenal hyperplasia, Milton Edgerton remarked that no patients had complained:

> Not one has complained of a loss of sensation, even when the entire clitoris had been removed.[38]

---

33 J. Money and A.A. Ehrhardt, *Man and woman, boy and girl: Differentiation and dimorphism of gender identity from conception to maturity*, Johns Hopkins University Press, Baltimore 1972, p. 152.

34 M Hendricks, 'Is it a Boy or a Girl?' (1993) 45(6) *Johns Hopkins Magazine* 10–16, 15.

35 Ibid, 11.

36 Ibid, 15.

37 Ibid.

38 M.T. Edgerton, 'Discussion: Clitoroplasty for Clitoromegaly Due to Adrenogenital Syndrome Without Loss of Sensitivity' (1993) 91(5) *Plastic & Reconstructive Surgery* 956, 956.

1993 was also the year that the first intersex advocacy organisation was formed, with an announcement by Bo Laurent (writing as Cheryl Chase) in a letter to *The Sciences* of the establishment of the Intersex Society of North America:

> I find myself forced to wonder whether a concept of sexual normalcy that defines the sex organs of up to 4% of newborn infants as 'defective' is not itself defective.[39]

Throughout the 1990s and early 2000s, a medical model of early intervention was challenged, leading to a clinical 'Consensus' meeting in Chicago in 2005. This was an event that Georgiann Davis states enabled 'medical professionals to reinforce medical jurisdiction', in a context where 'the medicalization of intersexuality was successfully being contested by intersex activists who were framing intersexuality as a social rather than biological problem'.[40]

Pressure for the meeting may also have built from the first known public report where an intersex person secured a birth certificate and passport with a non-binary sex marker. Reported in early 2003, Alex MacFarlane had obtained both a birth certificate marked 'indeterminate – also known as intersex' from the state of Victoria in Australia, and an Australian passport with an 'X' marker.[41] The following year, Heino Meyer-Bahlburg and others cited the report in a survey of people with XY intersex variations that included a question about survey participants' agreement with a third gender for 'children born with unfinished sex organs'.[42]

3.1. CLAIMS OF CLINICAL CONSENSUS

Present claims of clinical consensus regarding the treatment of infants and children with intersex variations derive from an eponymous clinical gathering in Chicago in 2005. An invite-only 'Intersex Consensus Meeting' organised by Ieuan Hughes and Peter Lee established a new term for intersex traits, 'disorders of sex development', and attempted to achieve consensus about clinical treatment.[43] As Robert Aronowitz has observed, expert 'consensus' panels are

39 C. Chase, 'Intersexual Rights' (1993) 33(4) *The Sciences* 3.

40 G. Davis, '"DSD is a Perfectly Fine Term": Reasserting Medical Authority through a Shift in Intersex Terminology', in P. McGann and D.J. Hutson (eds.), *Advances in Medical Sociology* Emerald Group Publishing, Bingley 2011, pp. 155–182, at p. 158.

41 J. Butler, 'X Marks the Spot for Intersex Alex', *Western Australian* (11.01.2003).

42 H.F.L. Meyer-Bahlburg, C.J. Migeon, G.D. Berkovitz, J.P. Gearhart, C. Dolezal and A.B. Wisniewski, 'Attitudes of Adult 46,XY Intersex Persons to Clinical Management Policies' (2004) 171(4) *The Journal of Urology* 1615–1619.

43 I. Hughes and P. Lee, 'Intersex Consensus Meeting', 2005, <http://www.aissg.org/PDFs/Chicago-Agenda-Oct-05.pdf> (last accessed 20.07.2017).

a means of legitimating poorly understood symptom-based diagnoses that ultimately derive from social influences.[44]

It was anticipated that the new nomenclature would retire the pejorative term 'pseudo-hermaphroditism';[45] however, the meeting participants also replaced the word intersex in clinical settings. This was stated to ensure a focus on biological realities, rather than what Barbara Thomas, a community group representative at the meeting, describes as 'the person as a whole, as a social being or about identity'.[46] Amongst the decisions on treatment were proposals to empower multidisciplinary teams and specialist centres.

The meeting failed to include dissenting clinical voices. For example, a London clinical team involving Sarah Creighton and others was absent, following publication of a series of journal articles earlier that decade critiquing early surgical interventions.[47] Also absent were Diamond and Sigmundson, the practitioners who uncovered the truth of the David Reimer case.[48]

Two community group representatives were invited alongside around 50 clinical invitees. Barbara Thomas, one of the community participants, remarked in her report on the event that the two were marginalised and outnumbered at the meeting,[49] yet their participation is often employed to validate the new nomenclature and other outcomes of the meeting.[50] As an illustration, Mike O'Connor describes the 2005 meeting as 'the Chicago Consensus Conference of medical experts and patient advocacy representatives in 2006',[51] while Heino Mayer-Bahlburg stated in a 2017 editorial in *LGBT Health* that 'two leading intersex activists participated' in 'the International Consensus Conference on Intersex' that introduced a new term.[52] Notably, it is the nomenclature that Meyer-Bahlburg recalls as an outcome of the meeting; his editorial raises an

---

44 R.A. Aronowitz, 'When do symptoms become a disease?', in A. Caplan, J.J. McCartney and D.A. Sisti (eds.), *Health, disease, and illness: Concepts in medicine* Georgetown University Press, Washington, DC 2004, pp. 65–72, at p. 70.

45 A.D. Dreger, C. Chase, A. Sousa, P.A. Gruppuso and J. Frader, 'Changing the Nomenclature/Taxonomy for Intersex: A Scientific and Clinical Rationale' (2005) 18(8) *Journal of Pediatric Endocrinology and Metabolism*, 729.

46 B. Thomas, 'Report to AISSG on Chicago Consensus Conference October 2005', 06.2006, <http://www.aissg.org/PDFs/Barbara-Chicago-Rpt.pdf> (last accessed 20.07.2017) p. 2.

47 e.g. S. Creighton and L.-M. Liao, 'Changing attitudes to sex assignment in intersex' (2004) 93 *BJU International* 659–664.

48 See also a response to the 'Consensus' Statement: M. Diamond, 'Human Intersexuality: Difference or Disorder?' (2009) 38(2) *Archives of Sexual Behavior* 172.

49 Thomas, above n. 46, p. 5.

50 I.A. Hughes, 'Disorders of sex development: a new definition and classification' (2008) 22(1)46 *Best Practice & Research Clinical Endocrinology & Metabolism* 119–134, 120.

51 O'Connor, above n. 27, 533.

52 H.F.L. Meyer-Bahlburg, Intersex Care Development: Current Priorities (2017) 4(2) *LGBT Health* 77–80.

issue of more than 20 years, 'genital surgery for other than strictly medical indications' as, still, a 'current' topic.[53]

A 'Consensus Statement on management of intersex disorders' was published out of the consensus meeting in the following year. The statement has been foundational to subsequent clinical practices. Its validity as such a tool should be questioned.

The document outlines the available evidence on cancer risks, albeit in many cases based on few studies and small sample sizes, and recommends actions considered appropriate, including gonadectomies or monitoring. However, regarding cosmetic 'normalising' practices, the statement is notable for its use of terms like 'felt' and 'belief'; necessary given a lack of evidence to underpin clinical practices:

> It is generally felt that surgery that is carried out for cosmetic reasons in the first year of life relieves parental distress and improves attachment between the child and the parents. The systematic evidence for this belief is lacking.[54]

This position reflects the earlier stance of the American Academy of Pediatrics, and claims that interventions would reduce anticipated suffering and stigmatisation. The model remains still evident in draft codes for the forthcoming version of the International Classification of Diseases (ICD) that require a surgically-assigned sex based on perceived technical outcomes. For example, the draft ICD 11 beta code for 17-beta-hydroxysteroid dehydrogenase 3 deficiency states that genital surgery is stipulated, whichever gender is assigned, while removal of gonads is gender-dependent:

> gender assignment must be discussed, depending on the expected results of masculinizing genitoplasty. If female assignment is selected, feminizing genitoplasty and gonadectomy must be performed.[55]

Indeed, this is also supported by the 2006 'Consensus Statement'. A summary version of the statement suggests that 'appearance-altering surgery is not urgent' but, at the same time, rationales for early 'reconstruction' of genitals include the

---

53 Ibid.

54 Hughes, Houk, Ahmed, Lee and LWPES/ESPE Consensus Group, above n. 7, 557.

55 World Health Organization, '46,XY disorder of sex development due to 17-beta-hydroxysteroid dehydrogenase 3 deficiency', in *ICD-11 Beta Draft (Foundation)*, 2017, <https://icd.who.int/dev11/f/en#http%3a%2f%2fid.who.int%2ficd%2fentity%2f887793448> (last accessed 18.12.2017); M. Carpenter and M. Cabral Grinspan, Submission by GATE to the World Health Organization: Intersex codes in the International Classification of Diseases (ICD) 11 Beta Draft. (06.2017) <https://transactivists.org/wp-content/uploads/2017/06/GATE-ICD-intersex-submission.pdf> (last accessed 20.07.2017).

relational and cultural goals of 'minimizing family concern and distress, and mitigating the risks of stigmatization and gender-identity confusion of atypical genital appearance'.[56]

This means that the Consensus Statement does not *rule out* 'normalising' interventions. Its authoritativeness lies not in comprehensive clinician input, nor meaningful community engagement, but instead in its utility as an expert 'Consensus Statement', and to *rule in* any 'normalising' medical interventions felt or believed appropriate by multidisciplinary teams. Further, the manifest goal appears to have been to provide rationales for medical intervention, but not to question or substantiate their underlying principles, so the Consensus Statement did not lead to systematic collection of evidence, nor longitudinal or comparative research on outcomes.

Within the Australian context, the global statement was given effect by a set of decision-making principles presented by Lynn Gillam, Jacqueline Hewitt and Garry Warne in 2010. These principles are superficially appealing but abstract, inviting attention to (in order) physical risks to a child, psycho-social risks, fertility preservation, capacity for sexual relations, future options and parental wishes. Despite claims that the 2006 'Consensus Statement' would separate biological factors from relational or social roles and identities, the principles outline 'psycho-social risks' that can be minimised through medical interventions as including impaired parental bonding and 'reduced opportunities for marriage'.[57] Until December 2017, marriage in Australia remained a heterosexual institution.[58]

By 2013, the principles had been widely disseminated across Australia and incorporated into Victorian government principles on decision-making,[59] and pressure brought to bear on policymakers by intersex and disability advocates at Intersex Human Rights Australia and People with Disability Australia led to the broadening of a Senate inquiry on the involuntary or coerced sterilisation of people with disabilities to also encompass people with intersex variations.

---

56 C.P. Houk, I.A. Hughes, S.F. Ahmed, P.A. Lee and Writing Committee for the International Intersex Consensus Conference Participants, 'Summary of Consensus Statement on Intersex Disorders and Their Management' (2006) 118(2) *PEDIATRICS* 753–757, 755.

57 L.H. Gillam, J.K. Hewitt and G.L. Warne, 'Ethical Principles for the Management of Infants with Disorders of Sex Development' (2010) 74(6) *Hormone Research in Paediatrics*' 412–418, 415.

58 P. Gerber, 'Australia Has Finally Achieved Marriage Equality, but There's a Lot More to Be Done on LGBTI Rights', *The Conversation* (07.12.2017) <http://theconversation.com/australia-has-finally-achieved-marriage-equality-but-theres-a-lot-more-to-be-done-on-lgbti-rights-88488> (last accessed 18.12.2017).

59 Department of Health, Victoria, 'Decision-Making Principles for the Care of Infants, Children and Adolescents with Intersex Conditions', 02.2013, <https://www.aph.gov.au/DocumentStore.ashx?id=a6118bba-01b1-4402-902e-32a31ab519b4> (last accessed 20.07.2017).

A public submission to that inquiry by Jacqueline Hewitt, Garry Warne and others for the Australasian Paediatric Endocrine Group (APEG) claimed that 'consensus statements ... describe recommended indications for genital and gonadal surgery'.[60] APEG enumerated cases where, despite 'particular concern' regarding post-surgical 'sexual function and sensation',[61] surgery is indicated not only for sterilisation but also:

> for the purpose of appearance ... for functional reasons such as to allow a male individual to urinate while standing, and for psychosocial reasons such as to allow the child to develop without the psychosocial stigma or distress which is associated with having genitalia incongruous with the sex of rearing.[62]

Reviewing the evidence from both public and private submissions, Senators in that inquiry reported that 'there is no medical consensus around the conduct of normalising surgery'.[63] Indeed, this statement is reflected in literature[64] and personal communications with clinicians who are able to make claims about their work and that of their own teams, but who otherwise acknowledge great variation in practices within hospitals, between hospitals, and between jurisdictions, often determined by the beliefs of the clinician with whom parents have first contact.[65]

Nevertheless, the variability of practices supported by a claimed clinical 'consensus' is not evident to policymakers in those jurisdictions. In a letter to me about the Senate inquiry report in 2014, Katy Gallagher, the then Chief and Health Minister of the Australian Capital Territory (ACT), stated that infants with 'disorders of sex development' were treated in line with 'a standard investigation and management practice that is consistent with a national approach from APEG and international consensus statements from key disciplines such as paediatric endocrinology, surgery' with surgeries 'performed in centres of excellence' in Melbourne and Sydney.[66]

---

60 Australasian Paediatric Endocrine Group, J. Hewitt, G. Warne, P. Hofman and A. Cotterill, Submission of the Australasian Paediatric Endocrine Group to the Senate Inquiry into the Involuntary or Coerced Sterilization of People with Disabilities in Australia: Regarding the Management of Children with Disorders of Sex Development (updated), 27.06.2013, <http://www.aph.gov.au/DocumentStore.ashx?id=aafe43f3-c6a2-4525-ad16-15e4210ee0ac&subId=16191> (last accessed 20.07.2017) p. 2.

61 Ibid, p. 4.

62 Ibid, p. 4.

63 Community Affairs References Committee, Senate of Australia, 'Involuntary or coerced sterilisation of intersex people in Australia. Canberra', 10.2013, <http://www.aph.gov.au/Parliamentary_Business/Committees/Senate/Community_Affairs/Involuntary_Sterilisation/Sec_Report/index> (last accessed 20.07.2017) p. 68.

64 D. Klein, 'Gender X: The Battle over Boy or Girl' (2011) *Stanford Medicine Magazine* <http://stanmed.stanford.edu/2011spring/article4.html> (last accessed 20.07.2017).

65 Ibid.

66 Letter by K. Gallagher, dated 21.04.2014, on file with the author.

A 2015 position statement on sexual and reproductive healthcare for young people by the Royal Australasian College of Physicians details how international human rights institutions and local organisations have advocated for deferral of early cosmetic and psycho-social interventions, but similarly also recommends the use of 'expert multidisciplinary management teams' employing rationales identified by Lynn Gillam, Garry Warne and Jacqueline Hewitt, including 'minimising physical and psycho-social risk'.[67]

The lack of evidence to support early interventions was examined at an event in Annecy, France, in March 2012, nine years after the 2005 Intersex Consensus Meeting. Kavot Zillén, Jameson Garland and Santa Slokenberga, writing for the Committee on Bioethics of the Council of Europe sum up the event's conclusions:

> (1) 'quality of life' studies on patients into adulthood are lacking and are 'poorly researched', (2) the overall impact on the sexual function on children surgically altered is 'impaired' and (3) the claim that gender development requires surgery is a 'belief' unsubstantiated by data.[68]

The lack of clinical consensus identified by Australian Senators in 2013 has since also been summarised succinctly by a 2016 global update to the earlier clinical 'Consensus Statement'. The 'Global Disorders of Sex Development Update since 2006' stated:

> There is still no consensual attitude regarding indications, timing, procedure and evaluation of outcome of DSD surgery. The levels of evidence of responses given by the experts are low … Timing, choice of the individual and irreversibility of surgical procedures are sources of concerns. There is no evidence regarding the impact of surgically treated or non-treated DSDs during childhood for the individual, the parents, society or the risk of stigmatization.[69]

Thus, claims that medical interventions mitigate anticipated future stigma and suffering lack evidence. Claims or assumptions that there exists any clinical

---

67 Royal Australasian College of Physicians, Sexual and Reproductive Health Care for Young People Position Statement, 2015, <https://www.racp.edu.au/docs/default-source/advocacy-library/pa-ps-sexual-and-reproductive-health-care-for-young-people.pdf> (last accessed 20.07.2017) p. 29.

68 K. Zillén, J. Garland and S. Slokenberga, *The Rights of Children in Biomedicine: Challenges posed by scientific advances and uncertainties*, Committee on Bioethics of the Council of Europe, 2017, p. 43.

69 P.A. Lee, A. Nordenström, C.P. Houk, S.F. Ahmed, R. Auchus, A. Baratz, K. Baratz Dalke, L.-M. Liao, K. Lin-Su, L.H.J. Looijenga, T. Mazur, H.F.L. Meyer-Bahlburg, P. Mouriquand, C.A. Quigley, D.E. Sandberg, E. Vilain, S. Witchel and Global DSD Update Consortium, 'Global Disorders of Sex Development Update since 2006: Perceptions, Approach and Care' (2016) 85(3) *Hormone Research in Paediatrics* 158–180, 176.

'consensus' about the medical treatment of intersex variations, including necessity and timing, are themselves unreliable, and should be viewed with scepticism. Nevertheless, they persist as pervasive claims that underpin current clinical practices.

3.2. CLINICAL RESPONSES TO CRITICISM

In 2017, Kavot Zillén, Jameson Garland and Santa Slokenburga remarked that 'clinicians have not responded well to charges of torture',[70] referring to a 2013 report by a United Nations Special Rapporteur. However, clinicians have never 'responded well' to criticisms made by intersex advocates. Juxtaposed against claims of clinical consensus, the claims of clinicians in response to intersex activists are particularly striking.

While vague and evaluative clinical beliefs are typically portrayed as facts, the views of intersex-led advocacy and peer support organisations are more often portrayed as unsupported beliefs. These contrasting perspectives on intersex organisations are evident, for example, in a 2013 Australian Senate report and a 2016 statement by the Victorian State Department of Health and Human Services. The Senate report on involuntary or coerced sterilisation of intersex people called for protocols and guidelines consistent with recommendations by Intersex Human Rights Australia.[71] Nevertheless, three years after that report, the Victorian State Department of Health and Human Services outlined the perspectives of intersex advocacy organisations in a way that, while technically correct, presented them as an isolated 'belief', omitting evidence of third party support:

> Intersex advocacy groups believe intersex children should be raised as either male or female, but that surgeries to remove physical ambiguities should not occur until the child can provide informed consent.[72]

This is an example of what Miranda Fricker describes as testimonial injustice: the credibility of intersex voices is diminished, even where they speak about personal lived experience, and even though contrary perspectives lack evidence.[73]

---

70 Zillén, Garland and Slokenberga, above n. 68, p. 79.

71 Intersex Human Rights Australia was formerly known as OII Australia. See Community Affairs References Committee, Senate of Australia, above n. 63, p. 74.

72 Department of Health and Human Services, Victoria, 'Health of intersex people', 06.2016, <https://www2.health.vic.gov.au/about/populations/lgbti-health/rainbow-equality/lgbti%20populations/health-of-intersex-people> (last accessed 20.07.2017).

73 M. Fricker, *Epistemic Injustice: Power and the Ethics of Knowing*, Oxford University Press, Oxford 2007.

In addition to attacks on the credibility of critics, responses to criticism have included outright denial, and unsubstantiated claims of changed practices.

There is a history to this injustice. Milton Edgerton wrote in 1993 that no patients had complained 'even when the entire clitoris had been removed'.[74] A mere three years later, following the establishment of the Intersex Society of North America, some clinicians 'dismissed its members' and 'refused to discuss the organization'; Natalie Angier, reporting in the *New York Times* in 1996, reported that intersex advocates were described by John Gearhart as 'zealots':[75]

> It is the unhappy ones, the disgruntled ones, doctors say, who have joined the intersex movement.[76]

Face-to-face dialogue between advocates and clinicians will often reflect views expressed in 2006 and 2016 statements; that is, claims are made expressing the importance of support and advocacy groups, and the importance of early contact between parents, individuals and peers – but this does not translate into referrals. At times, direct attacks on credibility are published, showing the reason for that lack of referrals; that advocacy groups are partisan or, more subtly, that such organisations contest clinical practices, presenting patients with a different perspective. For example, APEG said to the Australian Senate in 2013:

> Some individuals are unhappy with their childhood treatment and have formed advocacy groups or pursued litigation. Other patients report satisfaction with early surgery.[77]

This statement distinguishes critics who can be discredited from individuals who express satisfaction. However, these claims of satisfaction were not supported by evidence. Considering also Milton Edgerton's earlier report that no patients complained even after loss of an entire clitoris, it is more likely that stigma, shame and isolation are reasons for lack of complaint. Ron Amundson cites 'abundant social evidence' that atypical characteristics and 'modes of function

---

74 Edgerton, above n. 38.

75 N. Angier, 'Intersexual Healing: An Anomaly Finds a Group', *The New York Times*, 04.02.1996, <http://www.nytimes.com/1996/02/04/weekinreview/ideas-trends-intersexual-healing-an-anomaly-finds-a-group.html> (last accessed 20.07.2017).

76 Ibid.

77 Australasian Paediatric Endocrine Group, Hewitt, Warne, Hofman and Cotterill, above n. 60, p. 4.

are stigmatized',[78] to make the apposite point that such characteristics are hidden where possible, because of prejudice.

Patients instead disengage when they are able; loss of patients to follow-up and lack of engagement with adult services are well established consequences of early medical intervention.[79] Indeed, the 2016 global 'consensus' follow-up report states that such disengagement is frequent:

> The practice of withholding medical history details, along with the possibility of negative medical experiences, likely contributes to patients with DSDs frequently being 'lost to follow-up.'[80]

This also indicates that that many individuals may have no clear idea about their medical history, or why they have undergone medical interventions. Clinical practices have even relatively recently involved deliberate obfuscation and omission of diagnostic information, in the belief that disclosure was harmful for 'normal' development.[81] A recent UK press report described how information on diagnosis and treatment, including the nature of an orchidectomy at age 16, was withheld from a woman with androgen insensitivity syndrome until her chance discovery at age 50; an omission that denied her the ability to properly understand and manage her health and sexuality.[82] Similar cases are known to intersex advocacy and support organisations in Australia, including situations where individuals lack access to childhood medical records. A 2018 post by the New Zealand Office of the Privacy Commissioner identifies variable progress in changes to this clinical paradigm.[83]

---

78 R. Amundson, 'Against normal function' (2003) 31(1) *Studies in History and Philosophy of Science Part C: Studies in History and Philosophy of Biological and Biomedical Sciences* 33–53, 48.

79 T. Jones, B. Hart, M. Carpenter, G. Ansara, W. Leonard and J. Lucke, *Intersex: Stories and Statistics from Australia*, Open Book Publishers, Cambridge 2016, p. 110; G. Conway, 'The practical management of an adult at risk of gonadal tumourigenesis', Proceedings of the 4th International Symposium on Disorders of Sex Development, University of Glasgow, Glasgow 2013, <http://www.gla.ac.uk/media/media_279274_en.pdf> (last accessed 01.07.2013) p. 21.

80 Lee et al., above n. 69, 170.

81 D'Alberton, above n. 27; J. Conn, L. Gillam and G. Conway, 'Revealing the diagnosis of androgen insensitivity syndrome in adulthood' (2005) 331(7517) *British Medical Journal* 628–630.

82 F. Kirkland, 'Intersex patients "routinely lied to by doctors"', *BBC News* (22.05.2017) <http://www.bbc.com/news/health-39979186> (last accessed 20.07.2017).

83 Office of the Privacy Commissioner (New Zealand), 'Handling Health Information of Intersex Individuals', 2018, <https://www.privacy.org.nz/blog/handling-health-information-of-intersex-individuals/> (last accessed 07.03.2018).

Even so, it is plausible that some individuals might report satisfaction; this is also true of female genital mutilation and other harmful practices, but this does not make those interventions acceptable. The credibility of claims of satisfaction should be questioned. Clinical convenience samples will inherently suffer from frequent lack of engagement; individuals who choose to disengage may well share similar characteristics and differ from individuals who continue to engage. Furthermore, satisfaction can be based on uninformed or partial data, or misreported, with the available evidence tainted or cherry-picked.

The limited available clinical research asserting degrees of satisfaction typically lacks the rigour of independence, being conducted by the institutions and researchers directly involved in medical interventions themselves, and framed around clinical preoccupations with cosmetic appearance and consequential claimed necessity of repeat surgeries, heterosexuality and gender conformity. For example, a Hong Kong study published in 2014 evaluated outcomes of early genital surgeries on 23 individuals, scored by clinicians on 'appearance of the clitoris, labia and vagina, plus requirement for revision surgery', also remarking on pregnancy numbers (a proxy for heterosexuality) and persistence 'with the female gender assigned at birth'.[84]

In a review of literature purporting to demonstrate satisfaction with early interventions, Arlene Baratz and Ellen Feder identify methodological issues including low response rates, reported outcomes not being supported by the data, and leading questions. In a cited study by Heino Meyer-Bahlburg and others, leading questions included a failure to give respondents the option of 'not having surgery at all'; another asked 'do you agree?' to a statement on a perceived need for 'unfinished sex organs' to be 'corrected'.[85]

In a response to Baratz and Feder, Meyer-Bahlburg cited[86] a small, 2011 questionnaire study by Riitta Fagerholm and others of 45 of their former patients, with responses by '24 females who had undergone genitoplasty in childhood'.[87] The 53 per cent response rate was disclosed but not discussed by the report authors, however, the data are notable – to Meyer-Bahlburg as well as the study authors – as three respondents felt that cosmetic genital surgery was 'too late'.

---

84 C. Houben, S. Tsui, J. Mou, K. Chan, Y. Tam and K. Lee, 'Reconstructive surgery for females with congenital adrenal hyperplasia due to 21-hydroxylase deficiency: a review from the Prince of Wales Hospital' (2014) 20(6) *Hong Kong Medical Journal* 481–485, 482.

85 A.B. Baratz and E.K. Feder, 'Misrepresentation of Evidence Favoring Early Normalizing Surgery for Atypical Sex Anatomies' (2015) 44(7) *Archives of Sexual Behavior* 1761–1763, 1762. Meyer-Bahlburg et al., above n. 42, 1617.

86 H.F.L. Meyer-Bahlburg, 'Misrepresentation of Evidence Favoring Early Normalizing Surgery for Atypical Sex Anatomies: Response to Baratz and Feder (2015)' (2015) 44(7) *Archives of Sexual Behavior* 1765–1768, 1766.

87 R. Fagerholm, P. Santtila, P.J. Miettinen, A. Mattila, R. Rintala and S. Taskinen, 'Sexual Function and Attitudes Toward Surgery After Feminizing Genitoplasty' (2011) 185(5) *The Journal of Urology* 1900–1904, 1900.

Less notable to Meyer-Bahlburg were that three respondents reported poor or 'very poor' clitoral sensation, while five (23 per cent) reported dissatisfaction with 'genital function', and two regretted surgery.[88]

Rationales for responses that surgery was 'too late' were not asked or explored beyond a separate, potentially leading, question about 'what kind of memories are associated with the operation?'[89] The respondents' surgeries took place at ages 9, 14 and 17, with the latter two ages indicating that the individuals should have been able to participate in decision-making, but why might any cosmetic genital surgery be considered to be too late? Cosmetic surgery, by its very nature, is not urgent, and claims that it is somehow time-sensitive need to be critically examined. The reasons might, perhaps, be technical concerns about surgery timing or outcomes, or relational or social issues.

The researchers surmised that 'early introitoplasty patients avoided an unpleasant primary operation for the urogenital sinus at the difficult age when starting menstruation',[90] based on responses to a specific question on memories associated with surgery, but it is not appropriate to extrapolate from that a justification for interventions before children can comprehend treatment and participate in decision-making.

A larger 2013 Chinese hospital study by Heng Zhang and others, also cited uncritically by Meyer-Bahlburg, was explicit about this, stating:

> Some [rural] patients are unwilling to see a doctor due to economic and cultural concerns. Thus, the diagnosis of DSD in these patients is usually done at late stage. Under this condition, DSD treatment is difficult.[91]

This study, with a convenience sample of hospital patients, reported that adolescent respondents had a median age at surgery of 14.2 years, while adults had a median age at surgery of 23.2 years.[92] Most adolescent and adult respondents in this study also stated that they would have preferred earlier interventions but, like the study by Fagerholm and others, this is dubious. Despite a lack of clinical consensus on timing, clinicians at this hospital and their patients favoured early surgeries, suggesting that patient responses have been shaped by clinician beliefs. Further, the patients at this hospital were old enough to consent to their late surgery. Patient responses may indicate disappointment with actual surgical outcomes and a desire for different outcomes. For example,

---

88 Ibid, 1902.
89 Ibid, 1901.
90 Ibid, 1904.
91 H. Zhang, J. Pan, H. Ji, Y. Wang, W. Shen, L. Liu, G. Lu and Z. Shou, 'Long-Term Evaluation of Patients Undergoing Genitoplasty due to Disorders of Sex Development: Results from a 14-Year Follow-Up' (2013) *The Scientific World Journal*, 1–7, 6.
92 Ibid, 4.

and in comparison to individuals subjected to early surgeries, those subjected to later surgeries may be better able to distinguish pre- and post-surgical loss of sensation and function.

In contrast, Meyer-Bahlburg has expressed strong criticism of sociological research. For example, stating in relation to a US study by Sharon Preves that constructed a convenience sample by building upon a pool of visible intersex people: 'does she really believe that participants' self-statements can be taken as absolute fact, particularly when given in the context of a political activist movement?'[93] By the same token, personal recollections of surgeries reported in research by Fagerholm and others are not reliable. This indicates a situation where clinicians fail to acknowledge that their own samples are convenience samples, and where personal testimony is cherry-picked: accepted when it can justify clinical practices and rejected as politically motivated when it does not.

It is possible that relational or social issues might be evident in clinical research that describes cosmetic genital surgeries as 'too late', with individuals responding to experience of stigma or discrimination, or an education or self-understanding as abnormal. Nevertheless, fear of discrimination is proffered as a rationale for medical interventions; many clinical rationales anticipate or imagine future suffering. Mike O'Connor, for example, states that the human right to self-determination 'may actually threaten other human rights of the child such as the right to be free from discrimination'.[94] However, as with the lack of evidence or consensus on surgical timing and other technical issues, the 2016 global statement indicates that there is no evidence that surgery and other forms of medicalisation mitigate risks of stigmatisation;[95] this is imagined, as a way in which medicalisation can solve stigma and othering.

Further, such claims are not accepted by intersex-led organisations, nor human rights institutions. The Asia Pacific Forum of National Human Rights Institutions, for example, states that: 'Fear of discriminatory attitudes can never justify human rights abuses, including forced medical treatment and violations of an intersex person's right to physical integrity'.[96] In General Comment 14 on

---

93 H. Meyer-Bahlburg, 'Intersex: Fact or Fiction? Intersex and Identity. The Contested Self by Sharon E Preves' (2005) 42(2) *The Journal of Sex Research* 177–80, 179.

94 O'Connor, above n. 27, 541–542.

95 Lee et al., above n. 69, 176.

96 Asia Pacific Forum of National Human Rights Institutions, *Promoting and Protecting Human Rights in relation to Sexual Orientation, Gender Identity and Sex Characteristics*. Sydney, Australia: Asia Pacific Forum of National Human Rights Institutions, 2016 <http://www.asiapacificforum.net/resources/manual-sogi-and-sex-charactersitics/> (last accessed 20.07.2017) p. 73.

the application of the 'best interests' test, the United Nations Committee on the Rights of the Child cautioned that the test is open to manipulation and should not be abused to justify discriminatory policies,[97] while the Committee's General Comment 13 states that 'interpretation of a child's best interests … cannot be used to justify practices … which conflict with the child's human dignity and right to physical integrity'.[98] Nor are fears of discrimination accepted by the 2013 Senate report, which instead identifies stereotypes and stigma as sources of unnecessary medical interventions.[99]

> There is frequent reference to 'psychosocial' reasons to conduct normalising surgery. To the extent that this refers to facilitating parental acceptance and bonding, the child's avoidance of harassment or teasing, and the child's body self-image, there is great danger of this being a circular argument that avoids the central issues.[100]

Certainly, the onus is placed on the child to conform to social expectations, rather than on those who may engage in harassment or teasing. A self-understanding as abnormal is perhaps the most likely outcome of an experience of medicalisation that regards innate physical characteristics as abnormal. Adrienne Asch comments that 'routine surgery may exacerbate the societal values that make them propose changing the child's body in the first place', and undertaking surgery before children can themselves participate in decision-making:

> can unwittingly undermine the child's confidence that she is lovable and loved. It is confidence in that love and lovableness that provides the foundation for dealing with what life brings.[101]

Fears about normality and 'fitting in' are known to heighten in puberty, and peer support groups endeavour to provide the kinds of social connections that can tackle negative self-perceptions. On the other hand, clinicians also internalise subjective views about genital normality or abnormality. Research by Welmoed Reitsma and others on clinical attitudes towards women's genitalia

---

97 Committee on the Rights of the Child, General Comment No. 14 (2013) on the right of the child to have his or her best interests taken as a primary consideration (Art. 3, para. 1). 2013 May. Report No.: CRC/C/GC/14, para. 34.

98 Committee on the Rights of the Child, General Comment 13: Article 19: The right of the child to freedom from all forms of violence. 2011 Feb. Report No.: CRC/C/GC/13, para. 54.

99 Community Affairs References Committee, Senate of Australia, above n. 63, p. 69 and p. 74.

100 Ibid.

101 A. Asch, 'Appearance-Altering Surgery, Children's Sense of Self, and Parental Love', in E. Parens, *Surgically Shaping Children: Technology, Ethics, and the Pursuit of Normality*, Johns Hopkins University Press, Baltimore 2008, p. 686.

has shown that both gender and clinical specialty are related to attitudes towards surgical solutions, with male physicians and plastic surgeons more likely than other physicians to suggest surgical procedures when asked to evaluate images of vulvas.[102] Clinical ethicists such as Merle Spriggs are also known to consider as a surgical justification 'the possibility of psychological harm' or even 'humiliation' arising from a parent's negative attitude towards a child's body.[103]

Infants, children and adolescents with intersex variations, and their parents, are vulnerable populations, with limited access to information mediated by medical professionals. The information received by parents and caregivers has a significant impact on attitudes towards medical interventions,[104] yet the necessity of medical interventions is typically not questioned by clinical teams, and nor are relational aspects of autonomy questioned beyond the role that a child is expected to play in the lives of their parents.

This material highlights several issues. Firstly, no research to date, including clinical research, may have captured a representative, informed population. Indeed, this may be impractical given a legacy of clinical secrecy and dismissal of dissent. Secondly, clinicians are comfortable positioning themselves as Donna Haraway's modest witnesses, possessing an objective, credible and 'self-invisible' epistemological agency by virtue of social location,[105] but are not reflective about their own role in reinforcing or promoting subjective social norms. Susan Sherwin argues that clinicians, hospitals and societies determine the choices and opportunities that are 'made available and desirable',[106] and that 'we must think not only about how to change the individual patient but ... how to change society'.[107]

Thirdly, whenever people are unable to provide free and informed consent to such interventions they remain coercive, including through a coercive social

---

102 W. Reitsma, M.J.E. Mourits, M. Koning, A. Pascal and B. van der Lei, 'No (Wo)Man Is an Island-The Influence of Physicians' Personal Predisposition to Labia Minora Appearance on Their Clinical Decision Making: A Cross-Sectional Survey: Labia Minora Reductions: Physicians' View' (2011) 8(8) *The Journal of Sexual Medicine* 2377–2385.

103 M. Spriggs, 'Parent-led request for female genital cosmetic surgery in an adolescent', in *When Doctors and Parents Disagree Ethics, Paediatrics and the Zone of Parental Discretion*, Federation Press Annandale, NSW 2016, pp. 227–43, at pp. 235–238.

104 J.C. Streuli, E. Vayena, Y. Cavicchia-Balmer and J. Huber, 'Shaping Parents: Impact of Contrasting Professional Counseling on Parents' Decision Making for Children with Disorders of Sex Development: Parent Decision in Disorders of Sex Development' (2013) 10(8) *The Journal of Sexual Medicine* 1953.

105 D.J. Haraway, 'Modest–Witness@Second–Millennium', in *Modest–Witness@Second–MillenniumFemaleMan–Meets–OncoMouse: Feminism and Technoscience*, Routledge, New York 1997, pp. 23–39, at pp. 32–33.

106 S. Sherwin, 'Whither Bioethics? How Feminism Can Help Reorient Bioethics. *IJFAB: International Journal of Feminist Approaches to Bioethics*' (2008) 1(1) 7–27, 14.

107 Ibid, 13.

or clinical environment, limited information disclosure, and justifications for interventions based on clinical beliefs. These result in what Miranda Fricker describes as a 'hermeneutical injustice', where a marginalised individual is unable to make sense of their experience due to prevailing social norms:

> the lived experience of being unfairly disadvantaged in rendering one's social experiences intelligible, to others and possibly even to oneself.[108]

In this context, even the formation of communities that offer 'resources for resistance' in the face of testimonial injustice 'is itself a social achievement and not a social given'.[109]

3.3. CLAIMS ABOUT CHANGE TO CLINICAL PRACTICES

Rather than promote reflection on the necessity of early medical interventions, or the human rights of individuals affected, clinicians have tended to deflect criticism of medical practices and authority by claiming improved clinical practices. These include both claims of improved techniques, and claims of fewer medical interventions. While these might imply an acceptance of the necessity for changed clinical practices, there is little evidence to support this. Instead claims of change tend to reflect a broader narrative of scientific progress.

Claims of improved techniques have been made at least since 1987, when Thom Lobe and others remarked that 'factors [contributing to] improved results since 1975 are the earlier timing of diagnosis and operative intervention, and newer improved operative techniques'.[110] Melissa Hendricks reports similar claims at Johns Hopkins in 1993.[111] David Sandberg made similar claims to those of Lobe and others in a 1995 call for long-term clinical research published by the Intersex Society of North America, stating that 'although the result of surgeries performed decades ago may have been very poor, that is no longer the case'.[112]

---

108 Fricker, above n. 73. p. 70.
109 Ibid, p. 54.
110 T.E. Lobe, D.L. Woodall, G.E. Richards, A. Cavallo and W.J. Meyer, 'The complications of surgery for intersex: Changing patterns over two decades' (1987) 22(7) *Journal of Pediatric Surgery* 651–652, 652.
111 Hendricks, above n. 34, 14.
112 D. Sandberg, 'A Call for Clinical Research' in Intersex Society of North America, *Hermaphrodites with Attitude*, Fall/Winter 1995–96, <http://www.isna.org/files/hwa/winter1996.pdf> (last accessed 20.07.2017), p. 8.

Media reports appear to show how clinicians feel, rather than the evidence available to them, thus a 2013 press article in *The Age* by Andrew Bock reported gynaecologist Sonia Grover's claim of 'good' outcomes from early surgeries – including what were described as 'genital enhancement operations' – and no pressure to change practices.[113] However, her hospital differed. In a submission that same year to the Australian Senate, the Royal Children's Hospital Melbourne formally cited 'increased medical knowledge and better surgical techniques', while advising that '... we acknowledge that outcomes related to current approaches remain to be established'.[114]

Such claims assert clinical authority but also express a narrative of continuous scientific improvement. Their effect is that adults who speak out against human rights violations on their own bodies during childhood are dismissed as making claims about obsolete medical practices. To be clear, infants subjected to practices under the paradigm described by Edgerton may still only be in their early and mid-twenties. However, claims of surgical improvement do not address concerns regarding the necessity of treatment, nor the human rights of those affected, and medical journals have given these issues little attention. The Committee on Bioethics of the Council of Europe has summarised those instances where medical intervention is indicated:

> On the scientific question of whether intervention is necessary, only three medical procedures have been identified as meeting that criteria in some infants: (1) administration of endocrine treatment to prevent fatal salt-loss in some infants, (2) early removal of streak gonads in children with gonadal dysgenesis, and (3) surgery in rare cases to allow exstrophic conditions in which organs protrude from the abdominal wall or impair excretion.[115]

There is limited transparency in relation to numbers of surgeries. From the perspective of intersex advocates and peer support volunteers, claims that interventions are increasingly rare and carefully considered by multidisciplinary teams have been deployed to dismiss human rights concerns, and dismiss as anecdotal the experiences shared (often confidentially) by parents and individuals.

Australian governments, including the Australian Capital Territory and Queensland governments, have nevertheless made claims of changed

---

113 A. Bock, 'It takes more than two' *The Age*, 20.06.2013 <http://www.theage.com.au/national/it-takes-more-than-two-20130619-2oj8v.html> (last accessed 20.07.2017).

114 Royal Children's Hospital Melbourne, Submission of the Royal Children's Hospital Melbourne to the Senate Inquiry into the Involuntary or Coerced Sterilization of People with Disabilities in Australia: Regarding the Management of Children with Disorders of Sex Development, 10.07.2013, <http://www.aph.gov.au/DocumentStore.ashx?id=84e279b0-e824-4d4a-9aba-080b11077117&subId=16195> (last accessed 20.07.2017) p. 7.

115 Zillén, Garland and Slokenberga, above n. 68, p. 43.

practices. For example, the Queensland Department of Communities stated in 2012:

> Previously it was an accepted practice to assign the external genitalia of a child during their childhood, often through surgical intervention, to determine the sex of the child early in their life. Research and investigation now advises against any irreversible or long-term procedures being performed on intersex children, unless a condition poses a serious risk to their health.[116]

However, there is little evidence of such change to clinical practices. In the UK, increasing numbers of clitoral surgeries in under-14s may reflect higher rates of diagnosis or simply higher numbers of interventions, according to a paper published in 2014.[117] German data published in 2016 shows no decline in numbers in the period from 2005 to 2014, but a shift in diagnostic classifications from specific to more general classifications.[118]

In Australia, Sonia Grover reported to Andrew Bock in 2013 that '10 to 15 genital reconstruction operations a year often on girls under the age of two' with 'genital surgery conducted mostly on infants with female chromosomes and congenital adrenal hyperplasia' (CAH) at the Royal Children's Hospital Melbourne.[119] Additionally, Mike O'Connor has reported that the two Sydney children's hospitals have a multidisciplinary team that, in 2014/15, reviewed 13 referrals. These mostly related to gonadectomies, but also to questions of genital surgical timing that imply a predetermined consensus about necessity: 'Severely virilised females with CAH are also reviewed with regard to early versus late clitoral reduction and vaginoplasty'.[120]

---

116 Department of Communities. *Engaging Queenslanders: A guide to working with Lesbian, Gay, Bisexual, Transgender and Intersex (LGBTI) communities* (01.2012) Report No.: 2896–11 FEB12, p. 14.

117 S.M. Creighton, L. Michala, I. Mushtaq and M. Yaron, 'Childhood surgery for ambiguous genitalia: glimpses of practice changes or more of the same?' (2014) 5(1) *Psychology and Sexuality* 1–10, 5; Zwischengeschlecht.org, Intersex UK, OII-UK and The UK Intersex Association, *Intersex Genital Mutilations Human Rights Violations of Children with Variations of Sex Anatomy*: NGO Report to the 5th Periodic Report of the United Kingdom on the Convention on the Rights of the Child (CRC) (Zurich 2016) <http://intersex.shadowreport.org/public/2016-CRC-UK-NGO-Zwischengeschlecht-Intersex-IGM_v2.pdf> (last accessed 25.05.2016).

118 U. Klöppel, 'Zur Aktualität kosmetischer Operationen "uneindeutiger" Genitalien im Kindesalter' (2016) 42 *Gender Bulletin* <https://www.gender.hu-berlin.de/de/publikationen/gender-bulletins/bulletin-texte/texte-42/kloeppel-2016_zur-aktualitaet-kosmetischer-genitaloperationen/view> (last accessed 17.05.2018); OII Germany, CEDAW Shadow Report. With reference to the combined Seventh and Eighth Periodic Report from the Federal Republic of Germany on the Convention on the Elimination of All Forms of Discrimination against Women (CEDAW), 2017.

119 Bock, above n. 113.

120 O'Connor, above n. 27, 538.

The Australian Institute of Health and Welfare (AIHW) publishes Australian hospital data from the National Hospital Morbidity Database,[121] recording procedures by Medicare Benefit Schedule item code. These data are sorted by age cohort[122] but are associated with numerous limitations. In particular, the data are not associated with diagnostic codes, nor linked to claims of surgical indications. Additionally, these data are inadequate to ascertain whether or not interventions have changed in character or classification, involved a shift from early to later interventions, or a displacement from specific or contested procedure codes to other, less contested or more generic, procedure codes.

Acknowledging these limitations, a subset of relevant feminising and masculinising genital surgical procedures follows. This subset is also indicative-only as it excludes a range of potentially relevant item codes, including other genital surgery codes, gonadectomies, hormonal interventions, prenatal treatments and prenatal selection. These data nevertheless provide an indication of surgery numbers and trends during a period of purported changes to clinical practices.

In relation to feminising interventions, low numbers for most procedure codes make it difficult to distinguish random fluctuations from trends in clinical practices. With the exception of procedure codes categorised as 'procedures for anomalies of genitalia' it is not possible to determine precisely which procedure codes may be relevant to persons with intersex variations in any period. Further, sub-classifications of 'procedures for anomalies of genitalia' have changed in different editions of the Database, but it remains possible to aggregate all such procedures in each year. These item codes are not available for the periods 2000–02 and before, so these years are excluded from analysis.

In age groups 0 to 19, numbers of such procedures have fluctuated between 2002/03 and 2014/15, with a peak of 33 in 2005/06 and a low of 6. The average in the period 2002/03 to 2004/05 was 17, and the average from 2006/07 to 2014/15 was 10.7. The peak in 2005/06, the period where the 'Consensus Statement' was devised and published, is striking. It is potentially consistent with expectations of the introduction of subsequent restrictions or oversight of procedures. Assuming a stable population and rate of diagnosis, and flexibility about surgical timing, a peak is also consistent with a lower subsequent number of pre-operative children and so fewer procedures. However, the data on genital reconstructions at the Royal Children's Hospital in 2013,[123] and O'Connor's report on multidisciplinary team referrals at two centres in Sydney in 2014/15 are a poor fit with the AIHW data for 'procedures for anomalies of genitalia'. Other item codes can also be expected to be relevant, including 'vulvoplasties'.

---

121 Australian Institute of Health and Welfare, 'Procedures data cubes', 2002–17, <https://www.aihw.gov.au/reports/hospitals/procedures-data-cubes/contents/data-cubes> (last accessed 17.05.2018).

122 Relevant specified cohorts are <1, 1–4, 5–9, 10–14 and 15–19 years.

123 Bock, above n. 113.

In a 2014 review of vulvoplasties, the federal Department of Health defines the vulva as the 'the external genital organs of the female mammal', including the clitoris, vulval vestibule and vaginal opening, as well as labia majora and labia minora. A vulvoplasty is defined as 'any surgery performed on the outside female genital structures' including labioplasties.[124] In age groups 0 to 19 years, numbers of vulvoplasties have increased from 101 in 2002/03 to 258 in 2014/15. Vulvoplasties in under-15s have averaged 71.15 in the period 2002/03 to 2014/15, with a range from 57 to 95 procedures per year.

Some diagnostic information is available in the 2014 departmental review of vulvoplasties regarding the period from 2007/08 to 2011/12. This shows that overall numbers of vulvoplasties for 'congenital malformation' diagnoses appear to have averaged 74.2 per year over the report's five-year period (based on a figure where n = 371), with no trend evident.[125] These include 'fusion of labia or other congenital malformation of the vulva' (ICD 10 codes Q52–Q529), enumerated as adrenogenital syndrome (congenital adrenal hyperplasia), vaginal agenesis and hermaphroditism. This annual number of diagnoses slightly exceeds the annual average number of vulvoplasty procedures in under-15s over the longer period from 2002/03 to 2014/15. This would be consistent with an association between vulvoplasties in young age groups and 'congenital malformations' but, while plausible, this association cannot be proven from the available published data.

Numbers of vulvoplasties reported for other diagnoses – including cosmetic, hypertrophy and non-inflammatory disorder diagnoses – increased over the same period, and some of these may also be relevant diagnoses. The review reported that there 'are no Australian clinical practice guidelines on vulvoplasty or labioplasty surgery'.[126] It also stated that 'there is very little literature' on 'congenital malformation',[127] and no reference was made to APEG or to paediatric guidelines or principles.

Some data are available for two residual codes for 'other procedures' on vulva and clitoris in persons aged under 20, also included in the following table for comparison purposes, though this should not be regarded as an exhaustive list of relevant codes.

In relation to numbers of masculinising surgeries, the Australian Institute of Health and Welfare hospital procedures data include classifications that provide a proxy for 'complex' or 'serious' forms of hypospadias, including proximal hypospadias surgeries, multi-stage surgeries and repeat surgeries for iatrogenic fistulae. Data for these procedures show neither a downward nor an upward trend in the period 2002/03 to 2014/15. The Institute reports 200 repeat surgeries

---

124 Department of Health, *MBS Reviews Vulvoplasty Report*, 04.2014, <http://www.health.gov.au/internet/main/publishing.nsf/content/E393B5FFC5978400CA257EB9001EEC59/$File/Vulvoplasty_Review_Report.pdf> (last accessed 30.09.2017) p. 9.

125 Ibid, p. 29.

126 Ibid, p. 46.

127 Ibid, p. 47.

Table 1. Numbers of selected feminising surgeries in persons aged under 20, in the period 2002/03 to 2014/15

Year	02/03	03/04	04/05	05/06*	06/07	07/08	08/09	09/10	10/11	11/12	12/13	13/14	14/15
1298 Procedures for anomalies of genitalia	19	15	17	33	18	15	9	9	12	6	13	6	8
35533-00 Vulvoplasty	101	171	170	199	192	203	212	214	219	254	261	237	258
– under 15s	95	95	71	72	79	68	59	64	58	81	68	57	58
90441-00 Other procedures on vulva	25	30	19	20	18	11	14	20	16	11	12	13	17
90441-01 Other procedures on clitoris	2	3	3	0	2	1	3	7	4	4	5	3	1

Notes: '02/03' refers to the period July 2002 to June 2003; other periods follow the same rule. *2005/06 was the year of the clinical 'Consensus' meeting and statement. All data except the under 15s row are for 0–19 year age groups.

Source: Compiled by the author using data from the Australian Institute of Health and Welfare.[128]

Table 2. Numbers of selected masculinising surgeries on persons aged under 20, in the period 2002/03 to 2014/15

Year	02/03	03/04	04/05	05/06*	06/07	07/08	08/09	09/10	10/11	11/12	12/13	13/14	14/15
37824-00 Proximal hypospadias, single stage repair	70	73	73	59	74	70	100	83	76	66	81	76	93
337827-00 Hypospadias, staged repair, first stage	92	90	88	99	86	84	84	78	85	77	94	98	100
337830-00 Hypospadias, staged repair, second stage	115	111	99	81	83	57	76	90	76	107	97	104	90
337833-00 Hypospadias, repair of postoperative urethral fistula	185	148	141	173	162	168	185	198	190	151	182	200	173

Notes: '02/03' refers to the period July 2002 to June 2003; other periods follow the same rule. *2005/06 was the year of the clinical 'Consensus' meeting and statement. All data are for 0–19 year age groups.

Source: Compiled by the author using data from the Australian Institute of Health and Welfare.[129]

128 Australian Institute of Health and Welfare, above n. 121.
129 Ibid.

on persons aged under 20 for 'repair of postoperative urethral fistula' in 2013/14, including 125 such repeat procedures in children aged one to four years.[130]

A range of other procedures, including meatotomy and hemicircumcision for hypospadias, glanuloplasty for hypospadias, and surgery for distal hypospadias were excluded, along with various procedures relating to the chordee. This exclusion is imperfect but intended to be broadly consistent with clinical definitions of 'disorders of sex development', which exclude 'simple' forms of hypospadias such as distal hypospadias, despite a familiar contentious, perceived need for 'normalising' surgery, an absence of evidence of necessity, and evidence of adverse consequences.[131]

The following chart shows the number of all selected procedures in the period from 2002/03 to 2014/15.

Figure 1. Selected procedures in persons aged under 20, 2002/03 to 2014/15

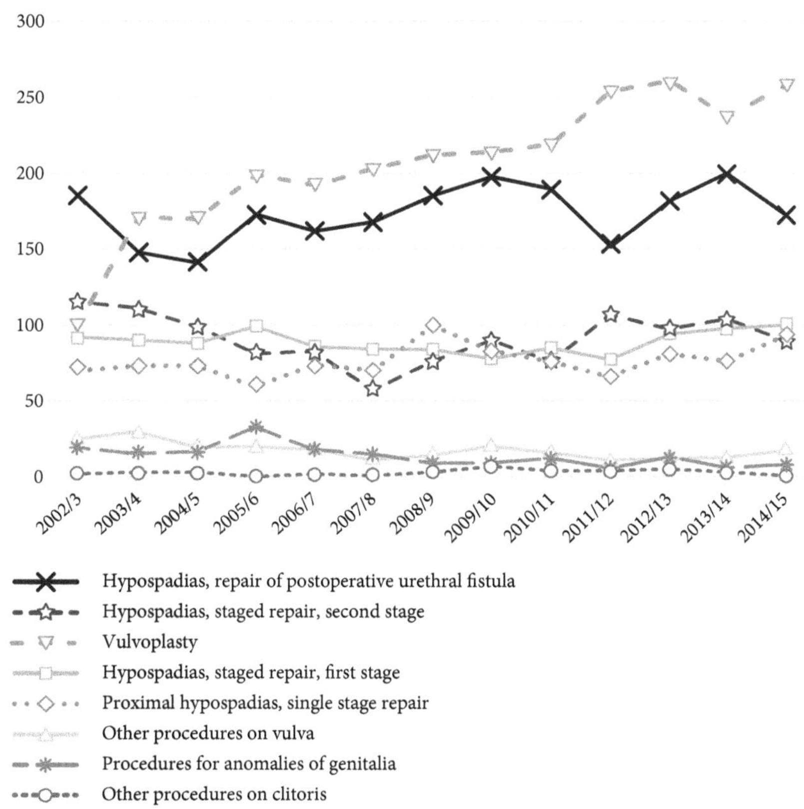

Note: Data are for 0–19 year age groups.

Source: Produced by the author using data from the Australian Institute of Health and Welfare.[132]

130 Ibid.

131 A. Carmack, L. Notini and B. Earp, 'Should Surgery for Hypospadias be Performed before an Age of Consent?' (2015) 53(8) *Journal of Sex Research* 1047–1058.

132 Australian Institute of Health and Welfare, above n. 121.

In summary, these data indicate possibilities of delay to vulvoplasties, and a marginal reduction or displacement to other codes of 'procedures for anomalies of genitalia', but they do not support claims of clear or systemic change to clinical practices in Australia.

Adding to the limited numerical data, details of clinical and legal rationales for medical interventions are evident through cases put to Australia's Family Court system. Some few intersex-related cases have been put before the Family Court, predominantly those with an uncertain case for sterilisation or those with a need for court approval for treatment for gender dysphoria. The decisions and incidental disclosure of invasive and irreversible medical interventions in these cases provide published, real world examples of current medical practices, including their nature and the rationales given for them, within the context of the international clinical 'Consensus' Statement, and Australian ethical principles regarding the treatment of children with intersex variations. The cases thus provide evidence of how those statements and principles are implemented, and how clinical practices may or may not have changed. These include the case of *Re: Carla (Medical procedure)* in 2016,[133] and *Re: Kaitlin* in 2017.[134]

The case of *Re: Carla (Medical procedure)* was taken to the Family Court by the parents of a child pseudonymously named Carla. An anonymous government department in the state of Queensland participated as a friend of the Court.

Born in 2010, Carla was aged five and about to start school at the time her case was adjudicated. She was said to have 'a sexual development disorder, described, in more particular medical terms, as 17 beta hydroxysteroid dehydrogenase 3 deficiency',[135] with XY sex chromosomes, testes, and predominantly female genitalia. The adjudicating Justice Forrest stated that 'the proposed surgery for Carla involving the bilateral removal of her gonads ('gonadectomy') … may be authorised by either of Carla's parents' without requiring court approval.[136]

Justice Forrest argued that the gonadectomy (sterilisation) was justifiable based on a potential cancer risk, stating that 'the Consensus Statement for Management of Disorders of Sexual Development puts the risk of germ cell malignancy at 28% … said to be an intermediate level of risk of malignancy',[137] and it was '… virtually impossible to regularly monitor them for the presence of tumours'.[138]

However, the 'Consensus Statement' referenced in the judgment was the 2006 'Consensus Statement on management of intersex disorders', misquoted perhaps

133 *Re: Carla (Medical procedure)*, above n. 4
134 *Re: Kaitlin* [2017] FamCA 83 (22 February 2017).
135 *Re: Carla (Medical procedure)*, above n. 4, at [1].
136 Ibid at [3].
137 Ibid at [19].
138 Ibid at [20].

to avoid mentioning the word intersex. The statement outlines a gonadal tumour risk of 28 per cent associated with 17-beta-hydroxysteroid dehydrogenase 3 deficiency, but also states that clinicians should 'monitor' gonads in children.[139]

A more recent clinical review published in 2010 (well before the case) reduces risk levels to 17 per cent,[140] while a representative of a German multidisciplinary team advised Amnesty International in 2017 that, 'cancer risk even for the high-risk groups is not so high. We can monitor with ultrasound and for tumour markers'.[141]

In *Re: Carla*, the predominant clinical narratives of consensus and improved techniques and practices appear to have broken down. If the 2006 'Consensus Statement' is to be taken seriously as a consensus, and according to subsequent clinical literature, the retention and monitoring of gonads should have been unambiguously supported and this case should not have been brought.

Gender stereotyping appears to substantively comprise the rationale for sterilisation. As Carla is not yet an independent agent, this was mostly based on parental reporting and affidavits from the child's multidisciplinary team:

a. Her parents were able to describe a clear, consistent development of a female gender identity;
b. Her parents supplied photos and other evidence that demonstrated that Carla identifies as a female;
c. She spoke in an age appropriate manner, and described a range of interests/toys and colours, all of which were stereotypically female, for example, having pink curtains, a Barbie bedspread and campervan, necklaces, lip gloss and 'fairy stations';
d. She happily wore a floral skirt and shirt with glittery sandals and Minnie Mouse underwear and had her long blond hair tied in braids; and
e. Her parents told Dr S that Carla never tries to stand while urinating, never wants to be called by or referred to in the male pronoun, prefers female toys, clothes and activities over male toys, clothes and activities, all of which are typically seen in natal boys and natal girls who identify as boys.[142]

The depth and breadth of this explication is quite extraordinary, and this may be indicative of its weight in the judge's reasoning. Given the absence of clear medical evidence in support of Carla's sterilisation, her current gender presentation and future gender identity should be irrelevant. However, these

139 Hughes, Houk, Ahmed, Lee and LWPES/ESPE Consensus Group, above n. 7, 558.

140 J. Pleskacova, R. Hersmus, J.W. Oosterhuis, B.A. Setyawati, S.M. Faradz, M. Cools, K.P. Wolffenbuttel, J. Lebl, S.L. Drop and L.H. Looijenga, 'Tumor Risk in Disorders of Sex Development' (2010) 4(4–5) *Sexual Development* 259–269.

141 Amnesty International, *First, Do No Harm* (No. EUR 01/6086/2017) Amnesty International, London 2017, p. 28.

142 *Re: Carla (Medical procedure)*, above n. 4, at [15].

become relevant given the gender stereotyping evident in the judgment, and Australian clinical literature, published in 2009, which states:

> As is well known, spontaneous change of gender identity from female to male occurs after the onset of puberty in 46,XY children with … 17β-hydroxysteroid dehydrogenase deficiency.[143]

A 2005 clinical review puts the rate of such changes as between 39–64 per cent,[144] unusually high in comparison to most other intersex variations.[145] Further, Justice Forrest suggested that sterilisation should *deliberately* proceed early, stating that it would be:

> less psychologically traumatic for Carla if it is performed before she is able to understand the nature of the procedure[146]

The implications are that surgery was not urgent, but that Carla needed saving from herself. Despite this justification, disturbing as it is in constraining Carla's legal capacity,[147] Justice Forrest made no such claim about trauma arising from a possible future medical intervention to enable a particular heterosexual role:

> Carla may also require other surgery in the future to enable her vaginal cavity to have adequate capacity for sexual intercourse.[148]

Finally, Carla's medical history was also put before the Family Court:

> Surgery already performed on Carla has enhanced the appearance of her female genitalia.[149]
>
> In 2014, Carla underwent … a 'clitoral' recession and labioplasty.[150]

---

143 J. Hewitt and G. Warne, 'Management of Disorders of Sex Development' (2009) 3(1) *Pediatric Health*, 51–65, 60.

144 P.T. Cohen-Kettenis, 'Gender Change in 46,XY Persons with 5α-Reductase-2 Deficiency and 17β-Hydroxysteroid Dehydrogenase-3 Deficiency' (2005) 34(4) *Archives of Sexual Behavior* 399–410, 399.

145 P.S. Furtado, F. Moraes, R. Lago, L.O. Barros, M.B. Toralles and U. Barroso, 'Gender dysphoria associated with disorders of sex development' (2012) 9 *Nature Reviews Urology*, 620–627, 620.

146 *Re: Carla (Medical procedure)*, above n. 4, at [30].

147 Committee on the Rights of Persons with Disabilities, General Comment No. 3 (2016) on women and girls with disabilities (No. CRPD/C/GC/3), p. 11.

148 *Re: Carla (Medical procedure)*, above n. 4, at [18].

149 Ibid at [2].

150 Ibid at [16].

The incidental disclosure of these irreversible, non-therapeutic and, frankly, abhorrent, interventions highlights that such practices take place in Australia without any requirement for independent oversight, whether from the Family Court or other avenues.

Ian Kerridge, Michael Lowe and Cameron Stewart state that, if an Australian common law distinction arising from *Marion's Case*[151] between purportedly 'therapeutic' and 'non-therapeutic' interventions is to be respected, then such interventions are permissible as 'treatments for "malformations"',[152] or 'cosmetic deformity'[153] but such claims have nothing to say about timing, indications or sexual function outcomes, let alone the future identity and preferences of the child. When the clitoris and penis are homologues, that is, they are fundamentally the same genital structures that have developed in different ways, the nature of a claim of a 'malformation' in *Re: Carla* is uncertain; a 'malformation' or 'deformity' of what, and on what basis? Claims of surgical necessity reflect social norms and stigma, and not medical urgency.

Zillén, Garland and Slokenberga, writing for the Council of Europe Committee on Bioethics, remark that a right to freedom from experimentation is adversely impacted, as 'children continue to undergo unproven treatments without proof of their therapeutic character'.[154] Practices must change as no clinically accepted standard of care 'has emerged to explain, as a matter of science, how infant surgery will be certain to coincide with the child's actual identity, sexual interests, and desires for bodily appearance'.[155]

The description by the Court of a clitorectomy and labioplasty on a young child with a 'sexual development disorder' as an 'enhancement' is thus disturbing (though unexceptional, given earlier media reporting),[156] and it suggests that children with intersex variations lack access to justice. Bernadette Richards states that the case lacked 'any voice in the alternative',[157] and the decision regarding sterilisation stretched the boundaries of parental responsibility at an age when the child's wishes are difficult to ascertain.[158] Aileen Kennedy describes 'complicity between the medical and the legal construction of variations of sex development as pathological disorders in urgent need of correction' where

[151] *Department of Health and Community Services v. JWB and SMB (Marion's Case)* [1992] HCA 15; (1992) 175 CLR 218 (6 May 1992).

[152] I. Kerridge, M. Lowe and C. Stewart, 'Children', in *Ethics and law for the health professions*, 4th ed., The Federation Press, Annandale, NSW 2013, p. 582–604, at p. 592.

[153] *Re: Kelvin* [2017] FamCAFC 258 (30 November 2017) at [139].

[154] Zillén, Garland and Slokenberga, above n. 68, p. 44.

[155] Ibid, p. 42.

[156] Bock, above n. 113.

[157] B. Richards and T.M. Pope, 'Stretching the Boundaries of Parental Responsibility and New Legal Guidelines for Determination of Brain Death' *Journal of Bioethical Inquiry* (16.08.2017) 1.

[158] Ibid.

a 'tension between the medical and judicial responses to variations of sex development has disappeared'.[159]

The analysis presented in the case is also profoundly subjective. The judge problematised an unmodified puberty including risks of 'virilisation', and an alternative possibility where the child's testosterone production may require supplementation to virilise.[160] Justice Forrest also problematised puberty suppression, including a consequential need for regular examinations but also 'detrimental physical effects'.[161] However, he failed to similarly acknowledge the oversight required for a puberty and life dependent on hormone replacement, and he failed to acknowledge even the most immediate physical consequences of the early unnecessary genital surgeries, including repeat examinations, possible 'sensitivity' testing and the potential for follow-up surgeries as the child grows into adulthood.

While it is always challenging to outline in hindsight what should have happened, Carla's family do not appear to have had contact with a peer support or advocacy organisation, and so they lacked role models and peers who could have helped them to make better informed decisions. Carla should not have been subjected to early surgeries that set a path predicating further interventions; she should have had access to age-appropriate information to help prepare her for the potentialities inherent to her genetic heritage, and to exercise her right to make her own decisions in her own time.

Surgical interventions are not the sole cause for concern. In 2017, the Family Court saw the case of *Re: Kaitlin*, also in Queensland, of an adolescent born with a pituitary impairment and unable to commence or undergo puberty without hormone treatment. Until the Family Court case of *Re: Kelvin*, adjudicated in November 2017, transgender adolescents required Family Court approval to commence hormone treatment on the basis that it would be irreversible.[162] The Family Court had chosen to apply section 67ZC of the Family Law Act, which permits the Court 'to make orders relating to the welfare of children'.[163] However, this did not apply to children and adolescents with intersex variations – at least where the chosen hormones were considered to be in line with their assigned sex.

---

159 A. Kennedy, 'Fixed at Birth: Medical and Legal Erasures of Intersex Variations' (2016) 39(2) *UNSW Law Journal* 813–842, 834.

160 *Re: Carla (Medical procedure)*, above n. 4, at [22].

161 Ibid at [24].

162 *Re: Kelvin*, above n. 153.

163 Australia. Family Law Act 1975 (Cth); S. Strickland, 'To Treat or Not to Treat: Legal Responses to Transgender Young People Revisited' Association of Family and Conciliation Courts Australian Chapter Conference, 14.08.2015, <http://www.familycourt.gov.au/wps/wcm/connect/fcoaweb/reports-and-publications/speeches-conference-papers/2015/> (last accessed 18.05.2018) p. 7.

For Kaitlin, this meant that: 'At about age 12 or 13 she was prescribed testosterone in order to commence puberty',[164] but Kaitlin also 'identified as female from a very early age. She has always resented being characterised as male'.[165] When Kaitlin became aware of the nature of her treatment she became non-compliant. Her family had to seek court approval for 'cross sex' hormone treatment.

In an analysis justifying court oversight of hormone treatment for gender dysphoria (i.e. for transgender children), Justice Strickland remarked that, based on *Marion's Case*, Family Court authorisation is required for medical interventions on children and adolescents unable to consent:

- when the treatment is invasive, permanent and irreversible;
- when the treatment is not for the purpose of curing a malfunction or disease;
- where there is a significant risk of making a wrong decision; and
- where the consequences of a wrong decision would be particularly grave.[166]

Yet, as with Carla, these rules have not been applied consistently to Kaitlin. The judge in *Re: Kaitlin* recognised this, to an extent, in approving access to estrogen. Justice Tree commented:

> It would seem fanciful to suggest that court authorisation was required before Kaitlin could be prescribed testosterone by Dr W in 2014. And yet the effect of that testosterone would have been to irreversibly see her develop as a pubescent male. Precisely why court authorisation for the administration of estrogen is then said to be required by Re Jamie is difficult to explain. True it is that the effects of its administration will be irreversible over time, but not in any conceptually different way to the irreversible effects of the administration of testosterone.[167]

To this extent, the prescribing of testosterone was barely questioned, regarded as an historical fact rather than something to be justified. Instead, the question that exercised the mind of the judge was not the inappropriate hormone treatment, but the need for him to approve an appropriate treatment; the implication might be that neither require oversight, but how then could or should children be protected from appropriate interventions?

Testosterone treatment was not only inappropriate it was permanent and irreversible; from a human rights perspective, it comprised a forced treatment, with the potential (had she been compliant with that treatment) to result in unwanted and irreversible physical development without her informed consent.

---

164 *Re: Kaitlin* [2017] FamCA 83 (22 February 2017) <http://www.austlii.edu.au/au/cases/cth/FamCA/2017/83.html> (last accessed 20.07.2017) at [6].
165 Ibid at [5].
166 Strickland, above n. 163, p. 8.
167 *Re: Kaitlin*, above n. 164, at [19].

Unlike other hormone treatments, necessary for her health, in this case Kaitlin should have had a choice. It would have been better to continue without hormone treatment until Kaitlin could express her own wishes about such irreversible treatment, a policy now afforded to non-intersex transgender children.

Between the two local Family Court cases of *Re: Carla* and *Re: Kaitlin*, the Queensland Government published a new sexual health strategy that represents a more emboldened justification for clinical practices. The strategy details how intersex children may be subject to 'normalisation and gender affirmation' where:

> Medical treatment is sometimes necessary to help development proceed as normally as possible and for some conditions, surgical treatment may be recommended.[168]

In practice, medical interventions take place in pursuit of an arbitrary 'normality' that Ron Amundson might describe as deriving from social judgement rather than biology: 'Cosmetic normality wins over functional performance.'[169]

In practice, medical interventions in *Re: Carla* include experimental treatments without adequate evidence; treatments deliberately proceeding prior to a child's ability to consent; and treatments that, as in *Re: Kaitlin*, may be described as 'gender affirmation', but that take place without adequate or appropriate consultation with the affected child. Further, *Re: Carla* takes decision-making in similar cases out of the judicial system, owing to a decision that parents could authorise treatment, while judicial oversight in cases of adolescent gender dysphoria like *Re: Kaitlin* is no longer required owing to the subsequent judgment of the full Family Court in *Re: Kelvin*.[170]

In press reporting, advocates in *Re: Kelvin* proposed that hormone treatment is not 'sufficiently grave' or 'sufficiently medical or … surgical' to warrant Court supervision.[171] The full Family Court itself took the position that it only be *required* by *Marion's Case* to consider 'non-therapeutic sterilization of a child' who is not competent and who will never be able to exercise capacity for consent,[172] and that decisions should take account of, inter alia, 'evolving medical science'[173] and standards.[174] Counsel and advocates appear to focus solely on access to treatment, without consideration of harms or protections from inappropriate medical treatment.

---

168 Queensland Health, *Queensland Sexual Health Strategy* (Text No. QH845 11/16), 2016, p. 33 and p. 50.

169 Amundson, above n. 78, 33.

170 *Re: Kelvin*, above n. 153.

171 N. Berkovic, 'Judges to decide court's role in hormone therapy for children', *The Australian* (21.09.2017) <http://www.theaustralian.com.au/news/judges-to-decide-courts-role-in-hormone-therapy-for-children/news-story/49a09eb00cb19cf370d75623ec028acd> (last accessed 24.09.2017).

172 *Re: Kelvin*, above n. 153, at [126] and [137].

173 Ibid at [139] and [152].

174 Ibid at [159].

While the 2006 'Consensus Statement' promoted the concept of multidisciplinary teams, Sarah Creighton has pointed out that their existence is no guarantee of changed clinical practices when they may be led by, and for, surgeons committed to early intervention and no credible non-surgical pathways yet exist.[175] Psychological support for families and individuals remains marginalised with patchy availability.[176]

The genital 'enhancements' in *Re: Carla* were made by a multidisciplinary team, and the Court cited statements by three of its members. Those genital 'enhancements' are supported by the 2006 'Consensus Statement', subsequent ethical principles, and, despite contrary statements in a World Health Organization report on sexual health and the law,[177] by the draft ICD 11 beta code for 17-beta-hydroxysteroid dehydrogenase 3 deficiency.[178]

In summary, practitioners employing the medical model still seek to construct 'normal' female or male bodies. They do so in the absence of meaningful clinical consensus, necessity, timing and outcomes, and despite a nascent human rights consensus calling for informed consent by the recipients of medical interventions.

Medicalisation has had some clear benefits in that more children with intersex variations, such as salt-wasting forms of congenital adrenal hyperplasia, have survived, but this does not account for genital surgeries associated with congenital adrenal hyperplasia, and nor does it account for cases like *Re: Carla* and *Re: Kaitlin*.[179] Claims of improved or changed clinical practices must be properly substantiated, or else disregarded as anecdotal. Lack of transparency, and a lack of oversight for contentious interventions, may instead explain why such interventions are perceived or claimed to be rare or no longer practiced.

Current practices, documented incontrovertibly through Family Court cases, demonstrate failures of clinical 'consensus' and self-regulation. The Senate inquiry report called in 2013 for more oversight, for 'all proposed intersex medical interventions for children and adults without the capacity to consent

---

175 S. Creighton, 'Surgical Management of DSD: New Insights' in 55th Annual Meeting of the European Society for Paediatric Endocrinology (ESPE) (Paris, France 10–12 September 2016): Abstracts (2016) 86 (suppl. 1) *Hormone Research in Paediatrics* 1–556, 14.

176 L.-M. Liao and M. Simmonds, 'A values-driven and evidence-based health care psychology for diverse sex development' (2013) 5(1) *Psychology & Sexuality* 83–101.

177 World Health Organization, *Sexual health, human rights and the law*, World Health Organization, Geneva 2015, p. 27.

178 World Health Organization, above n. 55.

179 The two cases are not unique. The circumstances and decision in *Re: Carla (Medical procedure)* are substantively like the case *Re Lesley (Special Medical Procedure)* [2008] FamCA 1226 (12 December 2008). Other notable and relevant cases include *Welfare of A Child A* [1993] FamCA 68; (1993) FLC 92-402 16 Fam Lr 715 Children (30 June 1993) and *Re: Sally (Special Medical Procedure)* [2010] FamCA 237. The case of *Re: Dylan* [2014] FamCA 969 (5 November 2014) provides a (still medicalised) contrasting example where an adolescent was able to participate in decision-making.

require authorisation from a civil and administrative tribunal or the Family Court'.[180] The Family Court of Australia does not appear capable or willing to effectively provide that role.

4. THE THIRD-SEX MODEL

Historically, canon and early common law regarded intersex people, or 'hermaphrodites', as either male or female, depending on predominant characteristics,[181] but that traditional model has broken in the modern period not only due to deconstruction and redefinition of hermaphroditism in narrow biological terms, and the surgical construction of 'normalised' female and male bodies, but also the development of concepts of gender, and of non-binary and third genders.

In recent decades, anthropologists such as Gilbert Herdt have described intersex individuals, such as men with 5 alpha reductase deficiency in a region of Papua New Guinea where the trait is more common, in order to present a vision of societies with recognised third-gender roles.[182] In doing so, they rejected earlier anthropological work, often by what Morgan Holmes describes as 'theologically minded anthropologists, unable to think beyond their own cultural frameworks'.[183]

In a review of anthropological studies on non-Western third sexes and genders, Holmes argues that much of that recent work portrays 'simplistic visions in which societies with more than two sex/gender categories are cast as superior to those that divide the world into just two', without comprehending how the various groupings are valued. In doing so, recent anthropological work may express the same historical fallacy, through the application of their own, new cultural frameworks, reflecting a broader cultural shift in the West, based in part of the work of John Money.

Nikki Sullivan has described how John Money was a 'quintessential social constructionist', with a 'purported theory of gender as an effect of nurture' that made him a guru of second wave feminism, as well as a key proponent of the medical model.[184] Unafraid of self-promotion, Money himself claimed

---

180 Community Affairs References Committee, Senate of Australia, above n. 63, p. xiii.

181 Greenberg, above n. 10, 277.

182 G.H. Herdt and J. Davidson, 'The Sambia "turnim-man": sociocultural and clinical aspects of gender formation in male pseudohermaphrodites with 5-alpha-reductase deficiency in Papua New Guinea' (Feb 1988) 17(1) *Archives of Sexual Behaviour* 33–56.

183 M. Holmes, 'Locating Third Sexes' (2004) 8 *Transformations* <http://www.transformationsjournal.org/wp-content/uploads/2017/01/Holmes_Transformations08.pdf> (last accessed 20.07.2017) p. 1.

184 Downing, Morland and Sullivan, above n. 29, p. 44.

to first use the term 'gender' as something other than a grammatical term,[185] and he is cited by Sullivan stating that: 'The social history of our era cannot be written without naming gender, gender role, and gender identity as organizing principles.' Sullivan writes: 'gender identity is the experience one has of oneself as a man or a woman – "the kingpin of your identity" as he and Patricia Tucker describe it.'[186] Iain Morland follows Foucault, to argue 'that gender names one of many ways in which power – including medical power – grips bodies to produce individuals who are at once constrained and enabled by norms', and that the norms expressed through gender relate to 'behaviors, attributes, and sensations' rather than 'a descriptive claim about one's genitalia'.[187] That is, gender has de-centred the social organising role of sex.

The reimagining of (mostly lost) societies within new organising frameworks may have facilitated a reimagining of intersex people. This, in turn, can be described as a product of absence; facilitated by the deployment of surgery, diagnostic secrecy, the existence of stigma and social taboos and the banishment of intersex bodies to the imagination.[188]

Herculine Barbin, possibly the first intersex person with a memoir available in print, provides an example. Following a convent affair with another girl, she underwent medical examinations as part of a court investigation and was reassigned male, as that was determined to be the dominant sex. While this legal case conformed to an historical Western norm, it has been interpreted in very different ways. Barbin's memoirs were published by Michel Foucault in the 1970s, accompanied by a commentary. Morgan Holmes describes how Foucault saw Barbin as an example of the 'other'. Barbin was described, after the court case, as:

> still without a definite sex, but she was deprived of the delights she experienced in not having one ... what she evokes in her past is the happy limbo of a non-identity.[189]

Holmes nevertheless writes that, 'it is clear in Barbin's own text that although she saw herself in many ways as an *exceptional* female, she did not perceive herself as necessarily beyond the boundaries of the female'.[190]

Coined as a result of Money's work with Reimer and intersex individuals, Sullivan describes how 'gender identity' and 'gender role' were presented as ways of encapsulating sometimes discordant aspects of the embodied self into a

---

185 Ibid, p. 49.
186 Ibid, p. 51.
187 I. Morland, 'Intersex' (2014) 1(1–2) *TSQ: Transgender Studies Quarterly* 111–115, 112.
188 Dewhurst and Gordon, above n. 31.
189 M. Foucault, *Herculine Barbin*, Knopf Doubleday Publishing Group, New York 2013, p. 17–18.
190 Holmes, above n. 183, p. 6

masculine or feminine whole.[191] While enabling the construction of a whole self, the separation of sex and gender was also a separation of bodies and identities, reflecting a deeper and more enduring Cartesian duality, enabling Money to understand the identities of intersex people, and for feminists and lesbians, gay men, bisexual and transgender (LGBT) people to distinguish cultural gender-specific roles and norms from biology. Gender – and the existence of intersex people – have thus been utilised to support human rights demands by marginalised populations.

4.1. CLAIMS ABOUT SOLUTIONS TO HUMAN RIGHTS CONCERNS

All too often, solutions proposed to address human rights violations against intersex people are reductive and unrealistic. In recent decades, moves towards legal recognition of queer, transgender, third and non-binary sex and gender categories have grown, and these are increasingly seen as both progressive and of benefit to intersex people. However, a choice between accepting either a disordering or the replacement of an existing sexuality and gender identity with a third or non-binary gender identity is, for many people, no choice at all. To illustrate the problem, Tatiana Kondratenko has claimed that:

> Some countries, like Germany, Malta, Australia and New Zealand, added the third box corresponded to gender on the birth certificates. It gives parents of intersex infants the right to choose the third option: marking the sex category 'X' or 'other'. By doing so, parents and doctors are not forced to put intersex babies through surgeries that would turn them into male or female. Thus, as intersex children grow up, they have the right to realise their identity by themselves.[192]

The Australian Government has introduced and expanded the availability of a third-sex marker since the first Australian passport with an 'X' sex marker was issued, likely in late 2002, to Alex MacFarlane, a person with XXY sex chromosomes.[193] However, an assumed consequential relationship between the existence of third-sex classifications and an end to 'normalising' medical intervention is a non-sequitur. Kondratenko's analysis assumes a narrowness to female and male categories, and a precise relationship between genetic and phenotypic ('biological') sex and legal sex classifications. Further, she

---

191 Downing, Morland and Sullivan, above n. 29, p. 50.

192 T. Kondratenko, 'Born intersex in Russia: the right to be recognised', *Prospekt Magazine* (21.12.2016) <http://www.prospektmag.com/2016/12/intersex/> (last accessed 20.07.2017).

193 Butler, above n. 41; I. Holme, 'Hearing People's Own Stories' (2008) 17(3) *Science as Culture*' 341–344.

assumes that the presence of a third box will necessarily obviate forced medical interventions; a pious hope that the mere existence of a new classification changes practices by parents, clinicians and society. Instead, this analysis homogenises and naturalises intersex bodies as 'others'; assuming that a natural and singular identity realised by intersex people is necessarily non-binary.

Kondratenko's argumentation is illustrative of many similar approaches, including those of policymakers. In her analysis of the flaws in US birth registrations, unable to provide a specific classification for individuals 'born with sex chromosome, endocrine or hormonal irregularities', Justice Noël Wise used the existence of intersex variations to undermine US laws that demarcate who has access to gender-segregated public sanitation facilities. In stating that 'their birth certificates are inaccurate',[194] Wise claimed that all intersex people have inaccurate birth certificates, regardless of assignment at birth, age of diagnosis, socialisation, identification or self-determination.

A few months after the Chief and Health Minister of the Australian Capital Territory wrote to me in 2014 explaining national, consistent, 'consensus' standards on the investigation, surgical and other treatment of infants with disorders of sex development,[195] she wrote to me regarding proposed reforms to birth certificates. These are a state and territory issue in Australia, and the ACT Government proposed – and later implemented – new classifications for all citizens, including for infants and children. These included a classification of 'intersex' that, she argued, would address parental rights by providing them with flexibility, and address certain 'risks':

> The availability of the third marker for children will also reduce the risk that parents will force their child to conform to a particular gender or subject them to gender assignment surgery or other medical procedure to match the child's physical characteristics to the chosen sex.[196]

Another pious wish, this framing of the same practices as both 'standard', 'consistent', 'consensus' practices and as a 'risk' is disconcerting. Both risks and standard practices take place in publicly-funded hospitals in, or at the behest of, her government.

Intersex-led organisations in Australia have opposed the creation of new classifications for children in part, then, because the governments proposing them do not have a coherent understanding of the population affected by them.[197] Opposition is also based on fears that they achieve the opposite result,

194 Wise, above n. 8.
195 Letter by K. Gallagher, above n. 66.
196 Letter by K. Gallagher, dated 15.04.2014, on file with the author.
197 Representatives of Intersex Human Rights Australia and the Androgen Insensitivity Syndrome Support Group met with the then Attorney General of the Australian Capital Territory, Simon Corbell, in February 2014.

that parents of a child marked as 'other' would fear repeated disclosure and stigma, and their children would have lesser rights in a still strongly gendered society.[198] A 2015 Council of Europe issue paper expressed the same argument, stating that:

> The availability of a third sex classification at birth, and fear of a poorly-understood identity category, may promote sex assigning treatments to avoid uncertainty for a family and child.[199]

In early 2018, four years after implementation of the new ACT law, the government confirmed that no children have been assigned to a new sex classification; this means that, from both ministerial and opposing perspectives, children remain at risk.[200]

Intersex-led organisations also opposed the Australian Capital Territory legislation, and the 'othering' of intersex populations, because intersex people are more diverse than the legislation assumes. To date, limited data on the gender identities of people with intersex variations have been published for a jurisdiction with an available non-binary gender classification, and clinical reviews otherwise show that a minority of intersex people experience gender dysphoria, though at higher levels than non-intersex people.[201]

A 2015 Australian sociological study by a researcher at the University of New England generated a convenience sample of 272 people born with atypical sex characteristics. It found that 19 per cent of respondents favoured X or other non-binary sex classifications, while 75 per cent chose binary sex classifications.[202] Around half of respondents self-described as non-heterosexual, and 60 per cent used the term intersex to describe themselves.[203] This 60 per cent figure includes people who 'are' intersex, and people who 'have' an intersex variation or condition. These data mean that intersex cannot be assumed to be an identity label. The numbers who 'are' intersex far exceed the numbers with non-normative gender identities, so it cannot be assumed that people describing themselves as being intersex are describing a gender identity. On the contrary, intersex as identity may more typically affirm or celebrate a stigmatised embodiment.

Despite this, the inclusion of 'intersex status' as an attribute relating to physical features in Australian anti-discrimination law has typically been

---

198 e.g., marriage in Australia remains between a man and woman at time of writing; school sports and sanitation are strongly gendered.

199 Commissioner for Human Rights of the Council of Europe, *Human rights and intersex people, Issue Paper*, 2015, <https://wcd.coe.int/ViewDoc.jsp?Ref=CommDH/IssuePaper(2015)1&Language=lanEnglish&Ver=original> (last accessed 12.05.2015) p. 38.

200 Personal communication, June 2017.

201 Furtado et al., above n. 145, 620.

202 Jones, et al., above n. 79, p. 70.

203 Ibid, p. 96.

imputed as protecting the rights of a third sex,[204] even though this was explicitly not sought or intended by either government or community advocates.[205] This has been reinforced by poorly drafted guidelines on recognition of sex and gender, derived from 2003 Australian Capital Territory legislation,[206] via the Australian Institute for Health and Welfare National Health Data Dictionary,[207] and passport guidelines introduced in 2011.[208] The guidelines simultaneously frame intersex as part of the definition of 'X', a non-binary classification, and also recognise, at least, that intersex people may identify as female, male or neither.[209] In 2015, a consortium of community organisations requested that the definition of 'X' be changed to 'non-binary', in order to end a collateral impact on intersex men and women.[210] Changes to Australian Standards during 2017 appear to be moving towards this position.[211]

Arguably the ACT origins and the evolution of federal Australian guidelines show that it is governments that have a need to categorise or classify people using biological labels that purportedly describe a sex. US developments add weight to this argument. In December 2016, Sara Kelly Keenan became the first person in the US to receive a birth certificate stating their sex as 'intersex'. Keenan had sought legal recognition as 'non-binary'; such a classification that could be

---

204 M. Yoosuf, 'Recognition and protection for intersex persons' (2015) 89(4) *Law Institute Journal*, 52–56; S. O'Dwyer, '"Treatment" of Intersex Children as a Special Medical Procedure' (2017) 24 *Journal of Law and Medicine* 870–885.

205 House of Representatives, Explanatory memorandum, Sex Discrimination Amendment (Sexual Orientation, Gender Identity and Intersex Status) Bill 2013, 2013 <http://www.aph.gov.au/Parliamentary_Business/Bills_Legislation/Bills_Search_Results/Result?bId=r5026> (last accessed 08.11.2014) p. 12; M. Carpenter and Organisation Intersex International Australia, *Submission on the proposed federal Human Rights and Anti-Discrimination Bill*. Sydney 08.12.2012, <http://ihra.org.au/21433/submission-human-rights-anti-discrimination/> (last accessed 20.07.2017) p. 1.

206 Australian Institute of Health and Welfare. *National Health Data Dictionary 2012 version 16* (2012) <https://www.aihw.gov.au/getmedia/a90ff140-8abf-4e30-8861-da2ebf368d35/14306.pdf.aspx?inline=true> (last accessed 11.09.2017) pp. 1942–1943.

207 Ibid.

208 S. Dingle, 'Passport gender choice made easier', *ABC News* (15.09.2011) <http://www.abc.net.au/news/2011-09-15/passport-gender-choice-made-easier/2899928> (last accessed 11.09.2017); Department of Foreign Affairs and Trade, Australia, *Sex and Gender Diverse Passport Applicants, Revised Policy*; Department of Foreign Affairs and Trade <https://web.archive.org/web/20111019035814/https:/www.passports.gov.au/web/sexgenderapplicants.aspx> (last accessed 22.05.2018); K. Rudd and R. McClelland, 'Getting a passport made easier for sex and gender diverse people', 2011, <http://foreignminister.gov.au/releases/Pages/2011/kr_mr_110914b.aspx?ministerid=2> (last accessed 11.09.2017).

209 Attorney General's Department, Australia, above n. 2, para. 12 and pp. 19–21.

210 Sex and Gender Advisory Group, RE: Commonwealth Attorney-General's Department Review of the Australian Government Guidelines on the Recognition of Sex and Gender, 2015, <http://lgbtihealth.org.au/resources/submission-review-agd-guidelines/> (last accessed 20.07.2017).

211 Letter by L. Wallace, 12.12.2017, on file with the author.

available to diverse intersex and non-intersex people who identify in ways other than female or male,[212] but the chosen label was a government requirement. In reports to NBC, a spokesperson for New York City's Department of Health and Mental Hygiene stated that the Department preferred a biological definition for a third-gender marker, supported by certification from a US doctor.[213]

In response to the New York City's Department of Health and Mental Hygiene issuing an 'intersex' sex marker on a birth certificate and stating that the Department preferred a biological definition for such a marker, geneticist and 'Consensus Statement' signatory Eric Vilain made a contrary set of claims:

> 'Intersex' is an identity. So there is no definition of 'intersex.' ... Among doctors and clinicians, it is referred to as Disorders/Differences of Sex Development, or DSD.[214]

It is not clear what interest Vilain would have in commenting if intersex were merely an identity and, if intersex were an identity term, it would not preclude the possibility or existence of a definition. In fact, a definition published in a United Nations fact sheet in 2015 is widely cited internationally and it frames intersex instead as an umbrella term for bodies born with non-normative sex characteristics.[215] Eric Vilain's comments suggest that framing, or dismissing, intersex as an identity issue is a deflection, helping to maintain clinical authority over disordered female and male bodies: where 'disorders of sex development' are identified as separate entities under clinical jurisdiction.

Certainly, the construction of intersex as a third sex has resulted in a consequential loss of comprehension of human rights issues relating to bodily autonomy, and a focus on issues of identity, honorifics and gender markers.[216] Counter-arguments that intersex people already have diverse sex classifications and gender identities have been interpreted as a form of biologically deterministic identity-policing. For example, the 2014 case of Norrie before the High Court of Australia saw an individual who was assigned male at birth and who underwent

---

212 M.E. O'Hara, Nation's First Known Intersex Birth Certificate Issued in NYC, *NBC News* (29.12.2016) <http://www.nbcnews.com/feature/nbc-out/nation-s-first-known-intersex-birth-certificate-issued-nyc-n701186> (last accessed 20.07.2017); H. Agerholm, 'First intersex birth certificate issued in the US', *The Independent* (30.12.2016) <http://www.independent.co.uk/news/world/americas/first-intersex-certificate-issued-us-55-year-old-trans-lgbtqi-sara-kelly-keenan-a7501501.html> (last accessed 20.07.2017).

213 O'Hara, above n. 212.

214 S. Scutti, 'NYC issues nation's first "intersex" birth certificate', *CNN* (30.12.2016) <http://www.cnn.com/2016/12/30/health/intersex-birth-certificate/index.html> (last accessed 31.12.2016).

215 Office of the High Commissioner For Human Rights, above n. 1.

216 Yoosuf, above n. 202; K. Le Lievre, 'Canberra Hospital now offers support for transgender children', *The Canberra Times* (15.08.2015) <http://www.canberratimes.com.au/act-news/canberra-hospital-now-offers-support-for-transgender-children-20150814-gizch3> (last accessed 20.07.2017).

'failed' female gender affirmation, seek legal classification as intersex because they did not identify as either female or male;[217] Norrie won classification as having 'non-specific' sex. In the *New York Times*, Julia Baird wrote on the case that:

> Members of the intersex community had argued that Norrie should not be able to call herself 'intersex' because she had not technically been born so.[218]

The framing of intersex as a third sex has been naturalised to the extent that, for example, Tamara Browne, in a 2017 bioethical analysis of gender essentialism underpinning sex selection, presented intersex as a distinct and arbitrary sex available to parents and children alongside female and male sexes.[219] This incidental naturalisation of intersex as a third sex is challenging not only because intersex children do not comprise an arbitrarily distinct sex, but because, despite the very real impact of gender essentialism and stereotyping on intersex children, this construction ignores the existence and impacts of the medical model on both parents and children.

In the context of Australian policy frameworks around assisted reproductive technologies, intersex traits are regarded not as sex nor subject to policy prohibiting most forms of sex selection, but instead as potentially serious genetic conditions that may be de-selected where they might 'severely limit the quality of life of the person who would be born'.[220] In the context of the child in the Family Court case *Re: Carla* with 17-beta hydroxysteroid dehydrogenase 3, the World Health Organization's draft International Classification of Diseases version 11 beta supports this, stating that: 'Prenatal diagnosis is available for the kindred of affected patients if causal mutations have been characterized.'[221]

This failure to comprehend the actual processes and impacts of medicalisation is the most significant cost of the third-sex model. Far from providing a solution to the medical model, third-sex models of intersex assume much, and fail to explain how the existence of third sexes interacts with or changes medical practices.

---

217 DLA Piper Australia, 'NSW Registrar of Births, Deaths and Marriages v. Norrie: Respondent's Submissions', 16.01.2014, <http://www.hcourt.gov.au/assets/cases/s273-2013/Norrie_Res.pdf> (last accessed 20.07.2017) at [39] and [40].

218 J. Baird, 'Neither Female Nor Male', *The New York Times*, 06.04.2014, <http://www.nytimes.com/2014/04/07/opinion/neither-female-nor-male.html> (last accessed 20.07.2017).

219 T.K. Browne, 'How Sex Selection Undermines Reproductive Autonomy', *Bioethical Inquiry* 15.03.2017, 1–10, 9.

220 National Health and Medical Research Council, Ethical guidelines on the use of assisted reproductive technology in clinical practice and research. National Health and Medical Research Council, 2017, p. 73.

221 World Health Organization, above n. 55.

Almost all individuals with intersex variations, and families, first experience an intersex variation as a medical disorder. My personal experience provides an example. When I was diagnosed by my doctor as intersex, I was not told I was intersex; I was told I had a set of medical conditions, and that these warranted treatment. Diagnosis triggered treatment with testosterone, and then, a year later, I had one 'normalising' surgery that became multiple surgeries within a single four-month period, immediately followed by a subsequent diagnosis with depression. These traumatic, life-changing events took place without peer support, and it took me years to comprehend what I had been through. I sought support and it was my then clinical psychotherapist who told me that I was intersex. That information later helped me to find an intersex community online. Finding that community, finding peers, was life-changing.

A coming to knowledge of intersex people is made challenging, not only by what Irving Zola describes as 'certain processes which will prevent the public from ever knowing what has taken place and thus from doing something about it'.[222] The end of institutionalised secrecy-based models of care for persons with intersex variations came only some few short years before the language of intersex was replaced by 'disorders of sex development'. The effect has been that, as with the previous model of secrecy, medicine has retained control over the narrative presented to patients and their parents and, because the new language was deeply contested, this has reinforced the isolation of individuals from their peers.

A coming to knowledge is made more complex by the dominance of non-medicalised legal and social narratives that fail their needs. Access to community and peers requires good and accurate information provision, including accurate information on what it means (and does not mean) to be intersex.

Miranda Fricker suggests that stereotypes construct and distort 'who the subject really is', and persistent epistemic injustices 'inhibit the very formation of self'.[223] Thus, stereotypes and misrepresentations of intersex as a third sex are as damaging as a medical model based on the pre-emptive 'normalisation' of sex characteristics to suit societal preferences. Both approaches are socially constructed, reflecting ideals of normality and the abject other; neither approach is based on sound evidence that it meets intended goals. Neither meets the needs of people who instead need self-determination, access to choice about their own pathways and affirmative ways of understanding themselves.

Third-sex models of intersex erect barriers to self-understanding and self-determination. This suits the interests of institutions resisting human rights claims seeking protection of children's bodily autonomy as it maintains

222 Zola, above n. 23, 501.
223 Fricker, above n. 73, p. 55.

a boundary between medical jurisdiction over bodies and socio-political influences over classifications of identities.[224]

4.2. INSTRUMENTALISATION FOR THE BENEFIT OF OTHER POPULATIONS

It is troubling that third-sex approaches to intersex, such as those of Tatiana Kondratenko,[225] Katy Gallagher[226] and Tamara Browne,[227] rely on imagination and beliefs about intersex people. This may be because such approaches to intersex primarily serve other purposes; of direct perceived benefit to other populations, where the impact on people born with intersex variations is considered to be of little or no intrinsic significance.

Emi Koyama and Lisa Weasel stated that in a 2001 study of how intersex issues were taught in women's studies, 'nearly all respondents stated that one of the main purposes was to deconstruct one or more conventional understandings of human sexes, genders, and sexualities'.[228] They found that intersex is presented as means to illustrate the social constructions of gender and heterosexuality. In this deconstruction, a previously unrecognised 'other' is created, often in pursuit of the recognition of non-binary gender itself. Arguably however, using 'non-binary' bodies to illustrate non-binary gender identity is less social constructivist and more deterministic because it reifies the role of non-normative bodies in deconstructing gender and explicitly associates non-binary bodies with non-binary gender. That is, it relies upon Money's idea that sex characteristics determine gender identity.

This is an increasingly widespread phenomenon,[229] exemplified by the Norrie High Court case,[230] where the legal team acting for Norrie in a successful claim for recognition of non-specific gender made unsuccessful appeals claiming the term 'intersex', based not on any realities of intersex people but instead on an appeal to Greek mythology.[231]

224 Scutti, above n. 214.
225 Kondratenko, above n. 192.
226 Letter by K Gallagher, above n. 196.
227 Browne, above n. 219.
228 E. Koyama and L. Weasel, 'From Social Construction to Social Justice: Transforming How We Teach about Intersexuality' (2002) 30(3/4) *Women's Studies Quarterly* 169–178, 171.
229 J.P. McCormick, In one perfect post this person shut down 'scientific' arguments that trans women 'aren't women', *The Pink Paper* (03.03.2017) <http://www.pinknews.co.uk/2017/03/03/in-one-perfect-post-this-person-shut-down-scientific-arguments-that-trans-women-arent-women/> (last accessed 20.07.2017).
230 Baird, above n. 218.
231 DLA Piper Australia, above n. 217, at [39].
High Court of Australia, NSW Registrar of Births, Deaths and Marriages v. Norrie: Transcript of hearing. Canberra: AustLII, 04.03.2014, <http://www.austlii.edu.au/au/other/HCATrans/2014/36.html> (last accessed 20.03.2014).

The instrumentalisation of intersex has nothing to say about the disordering of intersex variations, to the extent that claims about the diversity of sex, and its proof of diversity of gender, may refer uncritically to 'disorders of sex development'. Such claims are often built on exaggerated, misleading and stigmatising beliefs to support claims that justify the rights of other populations. Jeremy Colangelo, published at *SBS Sexuality*, for example, exaggerates, pathologises and instrumentalises intersex bodies in support of a claim for recognition of the rights of queer and transgender people, and without acknowledging what happens to intersex bodies:

> High schools all teach the same narrative in sex-ed: Chromosomes determine genitals, which determine sex, which determines gender. Women are XX, and men are XY. One has a penis, the other a vagina. It's science. Right? But what about people born with congenital adrenal hyperplasia (CAH), a disorder of sexual development (DSD) in which a person with two X chromosomes is born with a functioning penis?
>
> … Schools need to update their biology curriculums to reflect the current state of the research, and they need to explicitly address the needs of their queer students through non-discriminatory sex-ed classes. To do anything less is not only unscientific – it is also unjust.[232]

By 2006, a growing use of intersex as a queer identity label led Emi Koyama to surrender, at least temporarily, the word 'intersex' itself. She questioned the media's gender lens, and the way that she saw intersex activism at that time attract people who saw intersex as an identity, and a justification for being born queer or transgender. To Koyama, a disassociation between a gender lens on intersex and the interests of most intersex people justified the introduction of 'disorders of sex development'. The word intersex 'simply didn't work' and DSD would, she argued, result in intersex

> once again retreat[ing] into the shadows of public consciousness, leaving behind activists and intersex individuals who also happen to be trans or genderqueer as the only people who still refer to DSD as 'intersex.'[233]

Koyama was wrong in that assertion. For example, while some intersex people use the term DSD, there was little evidence of this in the 2015 Australian sociological study, where 3 per cent of respondents used 'disorders of sex development' to describe their characteristics out of choice, but 21 per cent used

---

232 J. Colangelo, 'The myth that gender is binary is perpetuated by a flawed education system', 04.07.2017, <http://www.sbs.com.au/topics/sexuality/agenda/article/2017/07/04/myth-gender-binary-perpetuated-flawed-education-system> (last accessed 20.07.2017).

233 E. Koyama, 'From "Intersex" to "DSD": Toward a Queer Disability Politics of Gender. Translating Identity', University of Vermont, 02.2006, <http://www.intersexinitiative.org/articles/intersextodsd.html> (last accessed 20.07.2017).

the term when accessing medical services.[234] Specific diagnostic terms were also widely used. In a study by a Chicago hospital and a US peer support group published in 2017, 'intersex' was the most popular term for use in research (67.4 per cent of respondents were comfortable or very comfortable with the term), with specific diagnostic terms such as androgen insensitivity syndrome (80.9 per cent) and intersex (60.8 per cent) the most popular terms 'to describe myself/my child'.[235] The research found that affected persons' views of disorders of sex development terminology appears to 'negatively impact healthcare utilization, and decrease participation in research',[236] and this was consistent with previous research findings.

Nevertheless, the tensions evident to Koyama in 2006 remain just as evident (and unresolved) today. Cary Gabriel Costello suggests that a medical framework is common in the US amongst people who understand themselves as conforming to the gender binary, and also that a 'disorder framework' is the majority perspective, with a minority of intersex people using a social justice ('identity') framework. Costello contrasts this with a similar but smaller medicalised/larger non-medicalised distinction in the US transgender population.[237] Costello's reasoning includes 'the necessity of solidifying a trans* identity in order to take personal steps to self-actualize',[238] but that reasoning may also indicate a tacit acceptance of occasional clinical claims of a silent and invisible majority of happy former patients. These dichotomies between happy and unhappy, and between medicalised and non-medicalised former patients may, however, be just as simplistic and speculative as clinical attitudes towards their patients and the intersex movement, given the hermeneutical injustices that limit or skew self-understanding by intersex people.

Even so, Costello is correct to identify the existence of a population of transgender people who employ a medicalised framework, and this includes a population who claim that transsexualism is a form of intersex of the brain. Indeed, as indicated by Koyama, the existence of transgender people who self-identify as intersex is a stated rationale for the 2006 shift in clinical terminology,[239] and Barbara Thomas noted 'dissatisfaction' at the Intersex Consensus Meeting in 2005 about 'confusion' with transsexualism.[240]

---

234 Jones et al., above n. 79, p. 95.

235 E.K. Johnson, I. Rosoklija, C. Finlayson, D. Chen, E.B. Yerkes, M.B. Madonna, J.L. Holl, A.B. Baratz, G. Davis and E.Y. Cheng, 'Attitudes towards "disorders of sex development" nomenclature among affected individuals' *Journal of Pediatric Urology*, 05.2017. In press, 1.e4-5.

236 Ibid, 1.e7.

237 C.G. Costello, 'Intersex and Trans* Communities: Commonalities and Tensions', in S. Horlacher (ed.). *Transgender and Intersex: Theoretical, Practical, and Artistic Perspectives*, New York, Palgrave Macmillan US, 2016, pp. 83–113, at p. 102.

238 Ibid, p. 100.

239 Koyama, above n. 233.

240 Thomas, above n. 46, p. 2.

The concept that transsexual people have an intersex brain is sometimes termed 'Harry Benjamin Syndrome', a contested condition based on contested science as it is predicated on the existence of significant differences between female and male brains that are not due to brain plasticity, lived experience, gender roles or research methodology,[241] and an implicit but significant difference between transsexual and other LGBT people. This approach is evident amongst numerous trans activists in Australia, including those involved in early legal reform,[242] such as the enactment of provisions to change sex classification,[243] anti-discrimination protection on transgender grounds in NSW[244] and litigation.[245]

This contested phenomenon was found to be a biological 'fact' in the Family Court case of *Re Kevin* in 2001 that recognised the marriage of a transgender man to his wife.[246] The case, according to Karen Gurney, established that 'transsexualism is, indeed, an intersex condition and established that people with transsexualism should not be treated differently to others with intersexed conditions'.[247] A key proponent of this ideology, Rachel Wallbank, was a solicitor acting for the respondents in the case of *Re: Kevin*. She is also a founding member of the clinician-led Australian and New Zealand Professional Association for Transgender Health,[248] and a member of the Legal Issues Committee of the World Professional Association for Transgender Health,[249] the international body that produces standards of care for the treatment of transgender people. Wallbank has written for the National Foundation for Australian Women and the University of Melbourne:

> Transsexualism [is] a naturally occurring form of diversity in human sexual formation and a form of intersexual disorder of sexual development with a clearly therapeutic medical treatment protocol and not a mental disorder or a psychological phenomenon.[250]

---

241 G. Rippon, R. Jordan-Young, A. Kaiser and C. Fine, 'Recommendations for sex/gender neuroimaging research: key principles and implications for research design, analysis, and interpretation' *Frontiers in Human Neuroscience*. 28.08.2014, 8.

242 T. Bennett, 'No Man's Land: Non-Binary Sex Identification in Australian Law and Policy' (2014) 37 *University of New South Wales Law Journal* 847, 853.

243 K. Gurney, 'Twisting the Knife – Discrimination in the Law' (2004) 9 *Deakin Law Review* 339, 341.

244 New South Wales. Transgender (Anti-Discrimination and Other Acts Amendment) Act 1996, No. 22 of 1996.

245 R. Wallbank, 'Re Kevin in Perspective' (2004) 8 *Deakin Law Review* 461.

246 Gurney, above n. 243, 341.

247 Ibid, 347.

248 National Foundation for Australian Women and The University of Melbourne, 'Wallbank, Rachael – Woman – The Australian Women's Register', 2016, <http://www.womenaustralia.info/biogs/AWE5634b.htm> (last accessed 11.09.2017).

249 World Professional Association for Transgender Health. Legal Issues Committee Members, 2017 <http://www.wpath.org/site_committees_members.cfm> (last accessed 11.09.2017).

250 National Foundation for Australian Women and The University of Melbourne, above n. 248.

An unalterable sense of internal self-identification is taken to indicate a biochemical origin for gender identity, relieving stigma arising from being perceived to have a mental disorder. This condition is thus a case where Peter Conrad describes patients as 'active collaborators in the medicalization of their problems or downright eager for medicalization'.[251] In addition to relieving the stigma associated with mental disorders, such claims are also based on a perceived 'ease' of access to medical intervention, by which intersex children are 'fixed'. Medicalisation of what Wallbank describes as 'a form of intersexual disorder of sexual development' justifies medical interventions to align an individual's embodiment with their brain;[252] with treatment that, as Gurney says, should be no different 'to others with intersexed conditions'.[253]

Cary Gabriel Costello remarks that such use of intersex to provide a biological justification for transgender identification causes significant conflict between intersex and transgender populations, 'acting in opposition to the goals of the intersex community':

> Trans* people who position themselves as suffering from an intersex disorder are basing their claim to medical treatment on an argument that supports the perpetuation of binary-normalizing infant genital surgery.[254]

Costello also describes fanciful stories, and an expectation that gender issues and transition are inherent to having an intersex variation.

The continued use of such rationales reflects the medicalisation of this transgender population that favours medicalisation. Wallbank's utilisation of 'disorders of sexual development' terminology shows that the 2006 change in clinical terminology has been co-opted into the narrative of a medicalised transgender population. To this extent, the new terminology may have met the goals of clinical proponents, but it has not succeeded in distinguishing issues of embodiment from issues of identity and gender role, and so it has not succeeded in meeting the goals of early intersex supporters of new terminology.

Trans people who claim that to be transgender is to be intersex also obscure a fundamental human rights issue, that of an injustice in the surgical and hormonal imposition of the wrong gender on intersex children who later experience gender dysphoria. In a 2012 clinical review, Paulo Furtado and others put the percentage of people with intersex variations who experience gender dysphoria at between 8.5 per cent and 20 per cent, depending on diagnosis, with higher rates associated with a small number of variations.[255] This suggests that

---

251 Conrad, above n. 20, p. 9.
252 National Foundation for Australian Women and The University of Melbourne, above n. 248.
253 Gurney, above n. 246, 347.
254 Costello, above n. 237, p. 105.
255 Furtado et al., above n. 145, 620.

birth sex assignments are correct for people with most intersex variations in the majority of cases. The claim that to be transgender is to be intersex ignores the majority of cisgender (non-transgender) intersex people, but it also renders unintelligible the injustice faced by the child in the Family Court case *Re: Kaitlin*, who was prescribed testosterone despite identifying as a girl, as well as rendering incomprehensible the broader human rights agenda of the intersex movement. Fundamentally, claims that transgender identification is an intersex disorder use the existence of intersex variations to benefit the health, or promote the rights, of a different, albeit intersecting, population.

More broadly, claims that third classifications are necessarily progressive and that they solve problems of medicalisation fit a narrative about identity recognition that is grounded in the demands of the LGBT movement. The Australian LGBT movement has become a claimed intersex-inclusive LGBTI movement for sexuality and gender diverse people, but this shift is largely rhetorical, and it likely reflects not so much an understanding of the demands of the intersex movement as a means of differentiating Australian discourse on LGBTI issues from an otherwise indistinguishable US 'LGBTQ' discourse and UK 'LGBT+' discourse.

Rhetorical inclusion may meet the objectives of communications teams who favour simple, standardised messaging, and institutional backers who prefer to deepen existing funding relationships and aggregate sexual and gender minorities together, but it has harmful consequences.

As illustrations, a former AIDS health promotion organisation ACON claims that: 'Since 2000, ACON has taken an active role in promoting the health and well-being of lesbian, gay, bisexual, transgender and intersex (LGBTI) people throughout their life';[256] yet the organisation failed to participate in the 2013 Senate inquiry on involuntary or coerced sterilisation, and it lacks competence or relevance on issues affecting infants and children, and heterosexual, cisgender intersex people (that is, neither same-sex attracted nor gender diverse).[257]

A 2017 report by ReachOut, the Black Dog Institute, Headspace and the University of Sydney Brain and Mind Centre framed as dichotomous an LGBTIQ population and a heterosexual population.[258] The population of 'young

---

[256] J. Kolstee and M. Hopwood, 'The Impacts of Marriage Equality and Marriage Denial on the Health of Lesbian, Gay and Bisexual People: Evidence Review & Annotated Bibliography' Centre for Social Research in Health UNSW and ACON, 2016, <http://www.acon.org.au/wp-content/uploads/2016/09/Marriage-Equality-Evidence-Review_web.pdf> (last accessed 20.07.2017) p. 2.

[257] ACON, Intersex People | ACON – Here for Health, 2016, <https://web.archive.org/web/20180320032742/https://www.acon.org.au/who-we-are-here-for/intersex-people/> (last accessed 16.07.2018).

[258] ReachOut, 'Extract ReachOut Cohort Study: Suicide Ideation Questionnaire (SIQ) analysis across sexuality', 2017, <http://about.au.reachout.com/wp-content/uploads/2017/09/Extract-Data-ReachOut-SIQ.pdf> (last accessed 05.10.2017).

people identifying as LGBTIQ' were an 'incredibly vulnerable group' at risk of poor mental health outcomes,[259] but this framing can only be more harmful to those people born with intersex variations who are both heterosexual and cisgender. Recalling the circumstances surrounding the nineteenth-century medicalisation of intersex bodies, this rhetoric has become another form of hermeneutical injustice where intersex people are coercively represented as queer and transgender, regardless of our diverse personal experiences, and so represented by queer institutions.

An equally challenging scenario, a series of Australian 'LGBTI' events have been (and may continue to be) sponsored by clinics offering assisted reproductive technology services that eliminate genetic intersex variations.[260]

Claims of representation within an LGBTI community perpetuate misconceptions about identity, and policy disjunctions. They fail to address profound gaps in resourcing for intersex-led advocacy and peer support organisations. However, to argue, as happens in clinical discussions and discussions with parent groups, that an association with 'LGBT' or 'LGBTI' is alienating to parents of young or potential children with intersex variations is to risk treating such stigmatisation of LGBT people as acceptable and justified, to risk reinforcing heteronormative rationales for medical intervention,[261] and to instil a misplaced sense of certainty about children's future identities, rather than an open-mindedness and a focus on a child's happiness. To dismiss a genuine connection between the LGBT and intersex movements is to deny the history of stigmatisation identified by Elizabeth Reis,[262] a more recent history of clinical research on intersex individuals aimed at eliminating homosexuality,[263] and the use of prenatal hormone interventions claimed to reduce 'behavioral masculinization' in infants with congenital adrenal hyperplasia raised as girls.[264]

Nevertheless, claims of representation, and claims that utilise the existence of intersex variations to justify the rights of other populations, do not meet the needs of infants, children and adolescents with intersex traits. As discussed

---

259 ReachOut, '#mindthefacts – new research confirms LGBTIQ young people at higher risk | About ReachOut Australia', 2017, <https://about.au.reachout.com/mindthefacts-new-research-confirms-lgbtiq-young-people-at-higher-risk/> (last accessed 05.10.2017).

260 M. Carpenter, 'LGBTI sponsorship and the elimination of intersex traits', 10.07.2016, <https://ihra.org.au/30555/sponsorship-elimination-intersex-traits/> (last accessed 20.07.2017).

261 K. Knight, 'If a Doctor Tells a Parent That Surgery Could Prevent Their Child's Suicide, It's Not True' Human Rights Watch, 2017, <https://www.hrw.org/news/2017/09/10/if-doctor-tells-parent-surgery-could-prevent-their-childs-suicide-its-not-true> (last accessed 10.09.2017).

262 Reis, above n. 25.

263 H.F.L. Meyer-Bahlburg, 'Will Prenatal Hormone Treatment Prevent Homosexuality? *Journal of Child and Adolescent Psychopharmacology*, 01.1990 1(4): 279–283.

264 S. Nimkarn and M.I. New, 'Congenital adrenal hyperplasia due to 21-hydroxylase deficiency' *Annals of the New York Academy of Sciences*. 01.04.2010 1192(1): 5–11, 9.

by Emi Koyama and Lisa Weasel, such claims start 'from a wrong place with a wrong set of priorities'.[265]

4.3. CLAIMS OF DECEPTION

Claims that intersex is a third sex risk framing binary (female and male) sex assignments and identification in intersex people as deceptive or transgressive. They also tend to reinforce expectations or claims that medical intervention is necessary for binary sex identification.

'Normalising' interventions of the kind performed early in the case of *Re: Carla* are facilitated not only by selective appeals to a dubious clinical consensus, but also by an exemption in federal policy frameworks on female genital mutilation that permits sexual 'reassignment' in 'a person whose sex is ambivalent [sic]'.[266] The same perspective is evident in clinical papers. For example, Mike O'Connor stated in 2016 that feminising surgery was a 'reassignment' in 'a true hermaphrodite':

> In 2013, a United States Federal Court held that non-consensual genital and gonadal surgery may violate the constitutional rights of affected children. The claim concerned MC, a 16-month-old male infant born in South Carolina in 2004. The boy was a true hermaphrodite, possessing an ovotestis and was subjected to reassignment surgery (a feminising genitoplasty) involving amputation of the penis and removal of testicular tissue.[267]

In addition to federal guidelines on gender recognition that simultaneously recognise the diversity of *identities* of intersex people and include intersex as part of a third-sex classification,[268] the Australian Bureau of Statistics implemented new statistical standards for both sex and gender in 2016, both containing an 'other' category. It is not clear whether most respondents to statistical surveys will understand any difference between the two measures. Nevertheless, the sex standard contains an 'other' category, deemed applicable to intersex people.[269]

---

265 E. Koyama and L. Weasel, 'Teaching Intersex Issues', 2001, <http://isna.org/pdf/teaching-intersex-web.pdf> (last accessed 20.07.2017) p. 7.

266 Attorney General's Department, *Review of Australia's Female Genital Mutilation Legal Framework – Final Report*, 2013, <http://www.ag.gov.au/Publications/Pages/ReviewofAustraliasFemaleGenitalMutilationlegalframework-FinalReportPublicationandforms.aspx> (last accessed 25.05.2013) p. 8.

267 O'Connor, above n. 27, 541.

268 Attorney General's Department, Australia, above n. 2, p. 6.

269 Australian Bureau of Statistics, 1200.0.55.012 – Standard for Sex and Gender Variables, 2016 – Underlying Concepts, 02.02.2016, <http://www.abs.gov.au/ausstats/abs@.nsf/Latestproducts/1200.0.55.012Main%20Features192016?opendocument&tabname=Summary&prodno=1200.0.55.012&issue=2016&num=&view=> (last accessed 20.07.2017).

But if 'normalising' interventions are claimed to create a 'normal' subject, what 'accurate' sex should be recorded and reported for the children in *Re: Carla* or *Re: Kaitlin*?

A 1979 Family Court of Australia case, *In the Marriage of C and D (falsely called C)*, adopted an approach similar to that of Justice Wise. The Family Court's Justice Bell found that an intersex man, assigned male at birth, who was raised and who identified as male, and who had undergone medical interventions to reinforce his male characteristics, was not a man. Lack of consummation is no longer a rationale for annulment but, at the time, this and his diagnosis as a 'true hermaphrodite' annulled his marriage:

> Marriage as understood in Christendom is the voluntary union of one man and one woman to the exclusion of all others for life, and since the respondent was a combination of both, a marriage in the true sense of the word could not have taken place and did not exist[270]

The subsequent case of *Re: Kevin* in 2001 instrumentalised intersex to justify the identity and marriage of a man who experiences transsexualism,[271] making it unlikely that heterosexual intersex people can be excluded from access to marriage under current Australian law.[272] However, this case raises a different issue. The judge states of his then putative wife:

> The wife's consent to the marriage was not a true consent because she was mistaken as to the identity of the husband at the time of the marriage. She believed that she was marrying a male whereas in fact she was marrying a combination of both male and female.[273]

The case is based on a presumption of deception without disclosure, but the available evidence in the case suggests that the man identified as a man, and that he had lived his entire life as a man, albeit one with a medical condition; what should have been disclosed? A third-sex category or identity was not available in 1979, and a claim based on identity conflates identity with embodiment, but also ignores a lifetime of experience and identification.

These cases, exemptions and classifications establish claims that intersex men and intersex women are not really men or women, and that such identification is questionable and inaccurate.

---

270 *In the marriage of C and D (falsely called C)* (1979) FLC 90-636, p. 524 at [v].

271 The Attorney-General for the Commonwealth & 'Kevin and Jennifer' & Human Rights and Equal Opportunity Commission [2003] FamCA 94 (21.02.2003), <http://www.austlii.edu.au/au/cases/cth/family_ct/2003/94.html> (last accessed 20.07.2017) at [53]–[56] and [188].

272 Ibid, at [205] and [231].

273 *In the marriage of C and D (falsely called C)*, above n. 270, at [iv].

There are significant risks associated with the naturalisation of any third sex category for intersex people based on biological characteristics, beyond failing to recognise an individual's birth or chosen classification. In multiple recent UK and Israeli convictions of rape by deception involving transgender men and cisgender (non-transgender) women were based on a charge that 'consent was obtained by deception regarding the perpetrator's identity'.[274] The cases have been criticised on numerous grounds, including by Aeyal Gross, who suggests that the case with most detailed legal discussion demonstrated 'a conception that holds biological sex to be determinative regarding a person's true identity and accords gender identity secondary status'.[275]

Claims of deception are also evident in sport, where women athletes with perceived or actual intersex variations are perceived as dominating competitors, and even a threat to women's sport warranting 'forced treatment', despite a familiar inadequacy of evidence or necessity.[276]

Rebecca Jordan-Young, Peter Sonksen and Katrina Karkazis cite International Olympic Committee policy mandating that national organisations 'actively investigate any perceived deviation in sex characteristics'.[277] Claims of dominance and of a threat to women's sport coexist uncomfortably with claims that intersex variations are malformations or defects, perhaps sharing common ground only in a monstering of people with non-normative bodies. Adrian Dobbs, for example, states that 'if these women really have a medical problem that they want to ignore because it gives them an advantage on the playing field, then in many ways they should be treated'; those health issues being identified as 'such as infertility, cardiovascular disease and insulin resistance'.[278]

Patrick Fénichel and others claimed in 2013 that: 'The world of sports has struggled with the issue of gender abnormalities since the Olympic Games of Berlin in 1936.'[279] This report revealed that four elite women athletes from

---

274 A. Gross, 'Rape by Deception and the Policing of Gender and Nationality Borders' (2015) 24 *Tulane Journal of Law & Sexuality* 1–33, 1.

275 Ibid, 4.

276 M. Kelner and J. Rudd, 'Caster Semenya could be forced to undertake hormone therapy for future Olympics', *The Guardian* (04.07.2017) <https://www.theguardian.com/sport/2017/jul/03/caster-semenya-could-be-forced-to-undertake-hormone-therapy-for-future-olympics> (last accessed 20.07.2017).
K. Karkazis, 'The ignorance aimed at Caster Semenya flies in the face of the Olympic spirit', *The Guardian* (23.08.2016) <https://www.theguardian.com/commentisfree/2016/aug/23/caster-semenya-olympic-spirit-iaaf-athletes-women> (last accessed 20.07.2017).

277 R.M. Jordan-Young, P.H. Sonksen and K. Karkazis, 'Sex, health, and athletes', *BMJ*, 28.04.2014 348(apr28 9):g2926–g2926, 1.

278 C. Caruso, 'Track authorities move to again bar women with naturally high testosterone', *STAT* (2017) <https://www.statnews.com/2017/08/07/track-women-testosterone/> (last accessed 08.08.2017).

279 P. Fénichel F. Paris, P. Philibert, S. Hiéronimus, L. Gaspari, J.-Y. Kurzenne, P. Chevallier, S. Bermon, N. Chevalier and C. Sultan, 'Molecular Diagnosis of

'rural or mountainous regions of developing countries'[280] had undergone partial clitoridectomies and sterilisation as part of a process to 'allow them to continue elite sport in the female category'.[281] As with other clinical research, Nathan Ha and others point out that the report's authors were researchers, 'treating physicians and policy enforcers'.[282] Under such circumstances, athletes are vulnerable, informed consent is questionable, and the athletes may have limited access to the lifetime of hormone replacement subsequently required.[283]

South African 800 metres athlete Caster Semenya has become a *cause célèbre*, following sex verification testing in 2009 that occurred because her appearance failed to meet gender stereotypes. The results, including claims of high testosterone levels ('hyperandrogenism'), were claimed to be leaked, but their details have not been verified and it is not certain that she has an intersex variation. Nevertheless, Semenya is the object of intense scrutiny that has at once been proclaimed, in *The Guardian* on 29 July 2016, as both a 'sensitive and complicated issue',[284] and a 'ticking timebomb'.[285] In August 2017, the same newspaper suggested in an article headline that she 'could be forced to undertake' medical interventions to compete in future Olympic games,[286] while the religious news site *TruNews* describes how she is evidence of 'Transgenders to Compete in 2018 Winter Olympics'.[287] These claims were made due to a legal challenge in 2015 that suspended (potentially permanently) sports policies on hyperandrogenism, itself due to a lack of scientific evidence.[288]

In an article entitled 'Is it fair for Caster Semenya to compete against women at the Rio Olympics?' Tim Layden in *Sports Illustrated* interviewed Eric Vilain,

5α-Reductase Deficiency in 4 Elite Young Female Athletes Through Hormonal Screening for Hyperandrogenism' *The Journal of Clinical Endocrinology & Metabolism*, 06.2013 98(6):E1055–9, E1.

280 Ibid, E2.

281 Ibid, E4.

282 N.Q. Ha, S.L. Dworkin, M.J. Martínez-Patiño, A.D. Rogol, V. Rosario, F.J. Sánchez, A. Wrynn and E. Vilain, 'Hurdling Over Sex? Sport, Science, and Equity' *Archives of Sexual Behavior*, 08.2014 43(6):1035–42, p. 1039.

283 Jordan-Young, Sonksen and Karkazis, above n. 277, 2–3.

284 Guardian sport. 'What is an intersex athlete? Explaining the case of Caster Semenya', *The Guardian* (29.07.2016) <https://www.theguardian.com/sport/2016/jul/29/what-is-an-intersex-athlete-explaining-the-case-of-caster-semenya> (last accessed 20.07.2016).

285 D. McRae, 'The return of Caster Semenya: Olympic favourite and ticking timebomb', *The Guardian* (29.07/2016) <https://www.theguardian.com/sport/2016/jul/29/the-return-of-caster-semenya-olympic-favourite-and-ticking-timebomb> (last accessed 20.07.2016).

286 Kelner and Rudd, above, n. 276.

287 TruNews, 'Transgenders to Compete in 2018 Winter Olympics', TRUNEWS (2017) <http://www.trunews.com/article/transgenders-to-compete-in-2018-winter-olympics> (last accessed 13.09.2017).

288 Court of Arbitration in Sport. CAS 2014/A/3759 *Dutee Chand v. Athletics Federation of India (AFI) & The International Association of Athletics Federations (IAAF)*.

who argued for restoration of the suspended sports policies, and posed the possibility of 'a third category' of gender described in the article as intersex, or:

> A more likely possibility, given societal trends: 'You put everybody in the same bag, just compete by gender identity,' says Vilain. ' … And that would be a disaster for women's sports.'[289]

In what appears to be a minority perspective amongst clinicians linked to international sporting authorities, Myron Genel, Joe Simpson and Albert de la Chapelle argued in 2016 that:

> with the passage of time and the recurring public spectacle of young women … having their underlying biology indiscriminately scrutinized in the world media, it has become evident that the hyperandrogenism policies are no more salutary than earlier attempts to define sharp sex boundaries.[290]

Until the International Association of Athletics Federations (IAAF) introduced new regulations on women with 'differences in sex development' in 2018, it was not entirely clear if the point of 'forced' interventions has been to remove the spectacle, reassert expectations of 'normality', or both. Those new regulations, however, offer a situation where elite women athletes who have a specified subset of intersex variations can choose between medicalisation, or legal othering, or quitting sport; between medically reducing their testosterone levels or competing in a male or intersex category.[291] Explicitly, this proffers a third sex category as a form of public othering for those that refuse unnecessary medical intervention.

Claims favouring surgical 'normalisation' and forced treatment suggest narrower definitions of sex, greater specification and more medical management of boundaries between them, not less. Mauro Cabral Grinspan states that the normative sex categories become stronger, or even purified, through the creation of new categories available only to persons with specific personal characteristics:

> People tend to identify a third sex with freedom from the gender binary, but that is not necessarily the case. If only trans and/or intersex people can access that third category, or if they are compulsively assigned to a third sex, then the gender binary gets stronger, not weaker.[292]

---

289 T. Layden, 'Is it fair for Caster Semenya to compete against women at the Rio Olympics?', *Sports Illustrated* (11.08.2016) <http://www.si.com/olympics/2016/08/11/caster-semenya-2016-rio-olympics-track-and-field> (last accessed 20.07.2017).

290 M. Genel, J. Simpson and A. de la Chapelle, 'The Olympic Games and Athletic Sex Assignment' *JAMA* (04.08.2016); in press, p. E1.

291 International Association of Athletics Federations, 'Eligibility Regulations for Female Classification (Athletes with Differences of Sexual Development)' (23.04.2018).

292 J. Byrne, 'License to Be Yourself Laws and Advocacy for Legal Gender Recognition of Trans People', New York, Open Society Foundations, 2014, <http://www.opensocietyfoundations.org/reports/license-be-yourself> (last accessed 26.10.2014) p. 21.

When new classifications focus on issues of identity, they encourage familiar assignments and increase 'risks' of coercive practices, or simply fail to have any relevance to the circumstances of children. Georgiann Davis states that clinician experts on intersex have a binary-focused 'gender essentialist' approach:

> Medical professionals rely on their gender essentialist views to justify the medicalization of intersexuality, and more specifically, the validity of the disorder of sex development diagnosis itself. Fundamental to a gender essentialist view is that gender is and should be neatly correlated with sex, and sexuality, and each is binary. If one deviates from the pattern, modification is needed in order for normalcy to be achieved.[293]

Davis also quotes a clinician who argues, 'In my experience, intersex people are so raised to conform to a gender role that they do.'[294] These statements demonstrate the continued application of John Money's thesis, and the perceived power of clinical authority in determining how people born with intersex variations understand ourselves.

Yet, at the same time, arguments are made in medicine that intersex people are not a (compulsory) normative binary sex until after 'normalising' interventions. Mike O'Connor's description of the reassigned 'true hermaphrodite' fits this narrative.[295] Similar argumentation is evident in governmental policy frameworks governing the right to freedom from ill-treatment through female genital mutilation. Morgan Holmes remarked in 2008 that clinicians shape the views of parents, and:

> without the clinical encounter we would likely still see intersex in terms of difference but not necessarily of monstrosity that forecloses on the child's species membership as a human.[296]

Alice Dreger and Ellen Feder refer in 2016 to a 'monster approach' to ethics by George Annas,[297] to state the same point made by Holmes: that only after surgery may intersex children 'be regarded as entitled to the sexual and medical rights and protections guaranteed to everyone else by current ethical guidelines and laws'.[298]

The risk, then, is that the creation of new sex categories, particularly those termed or made available specifically for intersex people, and in the absence of

---

293 Davis, above n. 40, p. 168.
294 Ibid, p. 169.
295 O'Connor, above n. 27, 541.
296 M.M. Holmes, 'Mind the Gaps: Intersex and (Re-productive) Spaces in Disability Studies and Bioethics' (2008) 5(2–3) *Journal of Bioethical Inquiry* 169–81, 170.
297 G.J. Annas, 'At Law: Siamese Twins: Killing One to Save the Other' (1987) 17(2) *The Hastings Center Report* 27–29, 28.
298 E.K. Feder and A. Dreger. 'Still ignoring human rights in intersex care' *Journal of Pediatric Urology* 05.2016 12(6): 436–4377, 436.

legal safeguards to protect bodily integrity, will not only coexist with a medical model of intersex, but reinforce it. Further, so-called 'normalising' interventions may reassure parents and create an impression of future certainty about a child's future gender identity and role in society, but this too may be disregarded through claims of deception. It is not only individuals who escape 'normalisation' who risk being portrayed as deceptive, but all individuals with sex characteristics that defy the narrow set of accepted norms, or that can be so classified by association.

Third classifications thus risk becoming a form of gender cleansing. They fail to relieve pressure to assign sex, promote medical boundary policing and so may increase 'risks' of coercive interventions, and they promote the misgendering of intersex women and men.

Legal frameworks are typically loose or vague in how they distinguish between sex and gender, if at all, and few frameworks yet distinguish between legal sex classifications and sex characteristics. Theodore Bennett suggests that 'a person's sex identification', which appears to designate a legal sex classification rather than a person's identity, dictates the sex of marriage partners, school attendance and access to a range of other social services, whether voluntary or involuntary.[299] In a clinical setting, sex characteristics have consequences for health. However, a person's sex classification has always had a somewhat loose relationship with sex characteristics in the case of people born with intersex variations. The existence of an intersex population and a growing, visible, transgender population increasingly imposes demands on segregated services to make accommodations.

The general approach of progressive commentators to legal reform has been to regard the creation of new classifications as beneficial. For example, Bennett suggests that the passing of federal anti-discrimination legislation and the publication of guidelines on gender recognition could be critiqued:

> for extending legal protections to sex and gender diverse people on the basis of their biological realities and personal experiences whilst simultaneously disavowing that these constitute a meaningful identity by denying them full legal recognition.[300]

However, such analysis fails to consider whether or not the affected populations wish to receive such 'full legal recognition' as anti-discrimination legislation was not 'intended to create a third sex in any sense',[301] and it fails to consider the consequences, for example, for intersex women and men who are quite happy with pre-existing legal classifications and who do not wish their legal status or identities to be questioned, overruled or subject to forced treatment. The affected

299 Bennett, above n. 242, 864.
300 Ibid, 870.
301 House of Representatives, above n. 205, p. 12.

populations are far from homogeneous, and so this analysis fails to respect any principle of self-determination.

It is important to recognise that some intersex people will prefer third or alternative sex classifications in any system that requires legal sex classifications, as too will some non-intersex people. Perceived requirements to conform, physically and psychologically, to binary classifications are frequently understood to cause harm.

Equally, it is important to recognise that new classifications have deleterious consequences for people unable to personally consent to them, or who are included in them by association. While institutions and governments create classifications and access requirements based on poorly-framed associations between biology and identity, they will have damaging side effects. To achieve this balance, intersex as identity must be additive, not supplanting nor subtractive of other identities.

For these reasons, as with the human rights issues associated with other erstwhile legal categories of ethnicity and religion, intersex community statements, including both the international Malta Declaration of 2013[302] and the Australian-Aotearoa/New Zealand Darlington Statement of 2017,[303] call for a more universal solution to problems of classification and categorisation through an end to legal classification of sex and gender. In doing so, these statements are compatible with international human rights obligations. For example, Article 24 of the International Covenant on Civil and Political Rights recognises a right to freedom from discrimination on grounds of, inter alia, sex, race, religion and birth, but requires only that:

> 2. Every child shall be registered immediately after birth and shall have a name.
>
> 3. Every child has the right to acquire a nationality.[304]

Elsewhere in this book, the ending of legal classifications by sex or gender has been challenged due to the international acceptability of new identity documentation – but such a difficulty is also presented by blank or third classifications, and these may be mandatory for some children. If that difficulty

---

302 Various, *Public statement by the third international intersex forum (Malta Declaration)*. Floriana, Malta, 12.2013, <http://intersexday.org/en/third-international-intersex-forum/> (last accessed 20.07.2017).

303 Androgen Insensitivity Syndrome Support Group Australia, Intersex Trust Aotearoa New Zealand, Organisation Intersex International Australia, E. Black, K. Bond, T. Briffa, M. Carpenter, C. Cody, A. David, B. Driver, C. Hannaford, E. Harlow, B. Hart, P. Hart, D. Leckey, S. Lum, M.B. Mitchell, E. Nyhuis, B. O'Callaghan, S. Perrin, C. Smith, T. Williams, I. Yang and G. Yovanovic, *Darlington Statement*. Sydney, NSW, 03.2017, <https://ihra.org.au/darlington-statement/> (last accessed 20.07.2017).

304 Office of the High Commissioner for Human Rights. International Covenant on Civil and Political Rights, 1966, Art. 24.

can be disregarded, a just solution might be to assign all citizens to a blank or third category in official documentation.

Australian federal guidelines have already sought to de-emphasise the importance of sex or gender classifications, calling for their use in federal documentation only where necessary but the situation that has resulted from federal legislation and regulation promotes inconsistencies and lacks attention to broader consequences. For example, Bennett acclaims:

> Whilst sex and gender diverse people are freed from identifying a binary sex on government documents, they are simultaneously explicitly protected from any discrimination they may suffer from living a non-binary sex/gender within society.[305]

The forms of any discrimination are never examined or enumerated in Bennett's analysis of 'non-binary sex identification in Australian law and policy',[306] and Bennett's analysis also takes as self-evident the concept that a freedom to identify is necessarily associated with consenting adults. Like other material acclaiming the creation of third-sex categories, Bennett's expresses a pious hope. In contrast, in *Re: Carla*, the Family Court may have detached any consideration in the case of federal discrimination protections on grounds of 'intersex status' simply by citing the title of the 2006 clinical 'Consensus' Statement, but removing the word 'intersex'.[307]

Intersex people have the potential to be profoundly affected by the third-sex model, including through the unintended consequences and side effects of policy developments focused on matters of identification. Claims that intersex is a third sex risk framing female and male sex assignments and identification in intersex people as deceptive or transgressive. They risk reasserting an intrinsic connection between intersex bodies and sexual abjection. They also risk reinforcing expectations or claims that medical intervention is necessary for binary sex assignment or identification.

5. HUMAN RIGHTS AND A THIRD WAY

Today, competing claims about medical 'consensus', changing clinical practices, and lack of transparency and effective oversight, give rise to what Melinda Jones describes as 'the culpability of health systems and the medical profession' and a 'failure of the state to protect the rights' of children with intersex variations.[308] This has resulted in reported possible outcomes including loss of sexual function

305 Bennett, above n. 242, 871.
306 Ibid.
307 *Re: Carla (Medical procedure)* above, n. 4 at [19].
308 M. Jones, 'Children's Health Rights and Gender Issues', in *Children's Rights in Health Care* Brill, Leiden (forthcoming), p. 2.

and sensation, a need for repeat surgeries, incorrect legal sex assignment, infertility and life-long need for hormone replacement, genital examinations, loss of bodily integrity, and trauma.

At the same time, the naturalisation of a third-sex category promotes false expectations of solutions to human rights concerns; and the existence of intersex people is instrumentalised for the benefit of other, overlapping, populations. This reinforces historical and pervasive misconceptions that intersex people are necessarily queer or transgender, yet these forms of biological essentialism also underpin 'normalising' medical interventions and create risks associated with claims of deception.

The medical model seeks to make intersex bodies either female or male, while an incommensurate third-sex model seeks to classify intersex persons as neither female nor male. This creates complex, challenging circumstances for a population that is impacted simultaneously by both models.

An intersex rights movement has existed since the early 1990s, both internationally and in Australia. Groups such as Intersex Human Rights Australia and the Androgen Insensitivity Syndrome Support Group Australia have coexisted with (predominantly parent-led) diagnosis-specific groups, AIDS councils and other LGBT/LGBTI organisations, and also transgender legal activists such as Norrie and Rachael Wallbank whose primary focus is access to services and not protection from forced and coercive interventions.

Advocates from volunteer-run groups in Australia have participated in legal reform work since at least the early 2000s, and have engaged in discussion with clinical professionals and policymakers for more than 20 years. Comprehension of intersex human rights issues has fluctuated during that time, and attitudes towards clinical practices have shifted. In 2009, a report on intersex surgeries by the Human Rights Commission merely noted the existence of interventions in cases of 'medical emergency or to treat a malfunction or disease (therapeutic surgery), and/or to make the body appear more male or female'.[309] In 2013, significant developments included the Senate inquiry into involuntary or coerced sterilisation, representing an institutional challenge to those practices. That year also saw the passing of federal anti-discrimination protection on grounds of 'intersex status', and federal recognition of a third gender category.

Legislative and regulatory developments have not been without flaws or concerns about implementation, exemplified by Family Court cases like *Re: Carla (Medical procedure)*, and complexities associated with third sex or gender classifications. In response to those issues, advocates and peer support workers from Australian and New Zealand groups constructed a joint Consensus Statement in March 2017. The Darlington Statement called for the legislative and policy

309 Australian Human Rights Commission. Surgery on intersex infants and human rights, 2009, <https://www.humanrights.gov.au/surgery-intersex-infants-and-human-rights-2009> (last accessed 20.07.2017) p. 6.

changes to reflect rights to bodily integrity and self-determination. Amongst other proposals, it called for the prohibition of modifications to children's sex characteristics without personal consent, participatory development of human rights-affirming standards of care, access to independent and resourced peer support and an end to the legal classification of sex and gender.[310] The statement also recognised that people born with intersex variations are entitled to use other language. Self-determination presupposes that, if used as an identity label, the term intersex must be additive, not supplanting nor subtractive of other identities.

The Darlington Statement follows the international Malta Declaration, an earlier statement in 2013,[311] that made similar demands and which arguably represents the beginnings of a consensus about the demands of a poorly resourced and previously fragmented movement.

Both intersex community declarations are succeeded by a 2017 supplement to the Yogyakarta Principles on the application of international human rights law in relation to sexual orientation, gender identity, gender expression and sex characteristics.[312] This expert statement outlines a right to bodily integrity, autonomy and self-determination; freedom from torture, ill-treatment and experimentation, irrespective of sex characteristics; and a right to truth about human rights violations, unrestricted by statutes of limitations. The supplement also calls for an end to sex and gender registration as part of individuals' legal personality, in line with the provisions of UN treaties on civil and political rights,[313] and the rights of the child.[314] It also calls on states to address discrimination in prenatal treatments, genetic selection and emerging genetic modification technologies.

These developments represent the emergence of a new and alternative model, grounded in concepts of human rights, bodily integrity and self-determination. On the one hand, the new model challenges the unnecessary and forced interventions central to the medical model of disorders of sex development. On the other, it also attempts to balance the desire of many intersex and non-intersex

---

310 Androgen Insensitivity Syndrome Support Group Australia, Intersex Trust Aotearoa New Zealand, Organisation Intersex International Australia, Black, Bond, Briffa, Carpenter, Cody, David, Driver, Hannaford, Harlow, Hart, Hart, Leckey, Lum, Mitchell, Nyhuis, O'Callaghan, Perrin, Smith, Williams, Yang and Yovanovic, above n. 303 para. 8.

311 Various, above n. 302.

312 The Yogyakarta Principles Plus 10: Additional Principles and State Obligations on the Application of International Human Rights Law in Relation to Sexual Orientation, Gender Identity, Gender Expression and Sex Characteristics, to Complement the Yogyakarta Principles, 2017, <http://www.yogyakartaprinciples.org/principles-en/yp10/> (last accessed 12.12.2017).

313 e.g. Office of the High Commissioner for Human Rights, above n. 304.

314 United Nations, *Convention on the Rights of the Child* Geneva, United Nations <http://www.ohchr.org/Documents/ProfessionalInterest/crc.pdf> (last accessed 12.12.2017) Art. 7.

people to opt out of binary sex and gender classification while acknowledging the limitations of the third-sex model. While it is also important to acknowledge uneven progress in these tasks, the new human rights model does this by applying principles of personal consent and self-determination to each situation.

A human rights consensus has also emerged in response to this movement and the application of international human rights law. International human rights actions are grounded in treaties on civil and political rights, freedom from torture and ill-treatment, the rights of the child, and the rights of women, and persons with disabilities. Of particular relevance, the Human Rights Committee identifies Article 9 of the International Covenant on Civil Political Rights on liberty and security of the person as 'the first substantive right protected by the Universal Declaration', where security of the person 'concerns freedom from injury to the body and the mind, or bodily and mental integrity'.[315] Medical procedures that lack proof of therapeutic character violate a right to freedom from experimentation.[316] The Committee on the Rights of the Child has issued guidance on interpretation of 'best interests' tests that state it cannot be used to justify violence, or 'practices that conflict with the right to physical integrity'.[317]

Attention to intersex human rights issues can be traced through an early 2005 San Francisco Human Rights Commission report,[318] the 2007 Yogyakarta Principles,[319] a 2012 Swiss report by the National Advisory Commission on Biomedical Ethics,[320] and a first statement by a UN expert in 2013 by Juan Méndez, the UN Special Rapporteur on torture and other cruel, inhuman or degrading treatment or punishment.[321] Méndez remarked that:

> Children who are born with atypical sex characteristics are often subject to irreversible sex assignment, involuntary sterilization, involuntary genital normalizing surgery, performed without their informed consent, or that of their parents, 'in an attempt to fix their sex', leaving them with permanent, irreversible infertility and causing severe mental suffering.[322]

---

315 Committee on Civil and Political Rights, General Comment No. 35: Article 9 (Liberty and security of person) 2014 Dec. Report No.: CCPR/C/GC/35, p. 1.

316 Zillén, Garland and Slokenberga, above n. 68, p. 44.

317 Committee on the Rights of the Child, General Comment No. 13: Article 19 (The right of the child to freedom from all forms of violence) 2011 Feb. Report No.: CRC/C/GC/13, p. 23.

318 Human Rights Commission of the City and County of San Francisco, 'A Human Rights Investigation Into the Medical "Normalization" Of Intersex People', San Francisco 2005.

319 The Yogyakarta Principles. Principles on the application of international human rights law in relation to sexual orientation and gender identity, 2007.

320 National Advisory Commission on Biomedical Ethics NEK-CNE, *On the management of differences of sex development. Ethical issues relating to 'intersexuality'. Opinion No. 20/2012*, Berne, Switzerland 2012.

321 J. Méndez, Special Rapporteur on torture and other cruel, inhuman or degrading treatment or punishment, *Report of the Special Rapporteur on torture and other cruel, inhuman or degrading treatment or punishment.* 02.2013, Report No.: A.HRC.22.53.

322 Ibid, pp. 18–19.

He recommended the repeal of laws permitting 'forced genital-normalizing surgery, involuntary sterilization, unethical experimentation, medical display, "reparative therapies" or "conversion therapies", when enforced or administered without the free and informed consent of the person concerned', and the prohibition of forced sterilisation in all instances.[323]

A rapid succession of statements, reports and investigations have followed since, by UN bodies, regional human rights institutions, intersex and mainstream human rights organisations. UN Treaty Bodies have now received reports from intersex-led groups across six continents, issuing relevant recommendations more than 25 occasions to more than 15 UN member states.[324] In 2016, the Committee on the Rights of Persons with Disabilities specifically identified forced or coercive surgery or treatment performed on intersex children without their informed consent as a form of 'cruel or inhuman treatment',[325] and identified restrictions or removal of legal capacity to facilitate such interventions as a violation of Article 12 on the right to equal recognition before the law.[326]

In parallel, litigation has been successful in Germany and Chile,[327] with an out-of-court settlement of a case in the United States.[328] Christiane Völling in Germany was the first person to win damages, in 2008, for what the International Commission of Jurists describe as a lack of appropriate disclosure prior to surgical intervention, and so a lack of informed consent.[329]

To date, few jurisdictions have responded to these developments with legislative change to protect the rights of infants, children and adolescents and promote self-determination. Only Malta has implemented coherent protections, through a new legal attribute of 'sex characteristics'. This attribute is universal, providing some (albeit not fully examined) measure of protection from discrimination and human rights violations in medical settings.[330]

---

323 Ibid, p. 23.

324 Zwischengeschlecht.org, 'IAD 2016 > Now 23 UN Reprimands for Intersex Genital Mutilations!' 2016 <http://stop.genitalmutilation.org/post/IAD-2016-Soon-20-UN-Reprimands-for-Intersex-Genital-Mutilations> (last accessed 20.07.2017).

325 Committee on the Rights of Persons with Disabilities, General Comment No. 3 (2016) on women and girls with disabilities (No. CRPD/C/GC/3), p. 9.

326 Ibid, p. 11.

327 Centro de Derechos Humanos UDP, C Godoy Peña, Informe Anual sobre Derechos Humanos en Chile 2016. Ediciones Universidad Diego Portales, 2016 <http://www.derechoshumanos.udp.cl/derechoshumanos/images/InformeAnual/2016/Godoy_ddhhpersonasintersex.pdf> (last accessed 20.07.2017) p. 346.

328 A. Ghorayshi, 'A Landmark Lawsuit about an Intersex Baby's Genital Surgery Just Settled for $440,000', *BuzzFeed* (2017) <https://www.buzzfeed.com/azeenghorayshi/intersex-surgery-lawsuit-settles> (last accessed 27.07.2017).

329 International Commission of Jurists, *In re Völling*, Regional Court Cologne, Germany (6 February 2008) | ICJ <http://www.icj.org/sogicasebook/in-re-volling-regional-court-cologne-germany-6-february-2008/> (last accessed 20.07.2017).

330 M. Carpenter, 'Submission on the Yogyakarta Principles, 10 year review', 2017, <http://morgancarpenter.com/submission-yogyakarta-principles/> (last accessed 20.07.2017) p. 8.

The latter goal is achieved by a requirement to defer non-urgent modifications to sex characteristics to a time when the person concerned can provide informed consent. In contrast to the Australian anti-discrimination attribute of 'intersex status', which has arguably been gamed in situations like the case of *Re: Carla*, the attribute of 'sex characteristics' is universal and clearly relates to embodiment.

For Intersex Awareness Day in October 2016, multiple UN Treaty Bodies, Special Rapporteurs on health, torture, and violence against women, and the Office of the High Commissioner for Human Rights, African Commission on Human and Peoples' Rights, the Council of Europe Commissioner for Human Rights, and Inter-American Commission on Human Rights issued a joint statement condemning human rights violations, stating:

> In countries around the world, intersex infants, children and adolescents are subjected to medically unnecessary surgeries, hormonal treatments and other procedures in an attempt to forcibly change their appearance to be in line with societal expectations about female and male bodies. When, as is frequently the case, these procedures are performed without the full, free and informed consent of the person concerned, they amount to violations of fundamental human rights.
>
> Parents of children with intersex traits often face pressure to agree to such surgeries or treatments on their children. They are rarely informed about alternatives or about the potential negative consequences of the procedures, which are routinely performed despite a lack of medical indication, necessity or urgency. The rationale for these is frequently based on social prejudice, stigma associated with intersex bodies and administrative requirements to assign sex at the moment of birth registration.[331]

The joint statement called for the tackling of 'root causes of these violations such as harmful stereotypes, stigma and pathologisation', the holding of perpetrators to account, and 'integration of these human rights principles in standards

---

[331] Committee against Torture, Committee on the Rights of the Child, Committee on the Rights of People with Disabilities, Subcommittee on Prevention of Torture and other Cruel, Inhuman or Degrading Treatment or Punishment, Juan Méndez, Special Rapporteur on torture and other cruel, inhuman, or degrading treatment or punishment, Dainius Puras, Special Rapporteur on the right of everyone to the enjoyment of the highest attainable standard of physical and mental health, Dubravka Šimonoviæ, Special Rapporteur on violence against women, its causes and consequences, Special Representative of the UN Secretary-General on Violence against Children Marta Santos Pais, African Commission on Human and Peoples' Rights: Commissioner Lawrence Murugu Mute, Chairperson of the Committee for the Prevention of Torture in Africa, Nils Muižnieks, Commissioner for Human Rights of the Council of Europe, and Inter-American Commission on Human Rights, 'Intersex Awareness Day – Wednesday 26 October. End violence and harmful medical practices on intersex children and adults, UN and regional experts urge', Office of the High Commissioner for Human Rights, (24.10.2016), <http://www.ohchr.org/EN/NewsEvents/Pages/DisplayNews.aspx?NewsID=20739&LangID=E> (last accessed 20.07.2017).

and protocols issued by regulatory and professional bodies'. Such actions and declarations represent significant steps toward inclusion, recognition and a reappraisal of the impact of pathologisation or medicalisation.

Peter Conrad argues that, for demedicalisation to occur, 'the problem must no longer be defined in medical terms, and medical treatments can no longer be deemed appropriate interventions'.[332] Indeed, intersex is now framed in ways that identify normative expectations for female or male bodies as the problem, rather than something intrinsic about intersex variations themselves. In addition to their comments on the appropriateness of medical interventions, UN and regional experts stated in 2016:

> Intersex people are born with physical or biological sex characteristics (such as sexual anatomy, reproductive organs, hormonal patterns and/or chromosomal patterns) that do not fit the typical definitions for male or female bodies.[333]

In doing so, this model reflects an argument, concisely summarised by Eric Parens, according to which construction of 'normal human variations as pathological' is understood as a category error: 'To treat human problems as medical problems … is to make a mistake about the nature of the world':[334]

> insofar as medicine focuses on changing individuals' bodies to reduce suffering, its increasing influence steals attention and resources away from changing the social structures and expectations that can produce such suffering in the first place.[335]

The emergent human rights model does not deny that people with intersex variations may have medical issues. It instead calls for those structural issues to be effectively addressed, and for medical interventions to be underpinned by evidence of necessity, of rigorous evaluation of long-term clinical outcomes, and accompanied by the freely-given informed consent of the individuals undergoing them.

Similarly, the new human rights language around the concept of 'sex characteristics' can be understood as avoiding a different category error: one that constructs intersex as a distinct and arbitrary sex. This new language offers greater precision, in that it relates specifically to bodily characteristics, while also avoiding conflation with sex classifications, identities and their attendant risks.

It is too early to determine whether or not this new human rights model can disentangle the contradictions, paradoxes and failings of the medical and

---

332 Conrad, above n. 20, p. 7.

333 Committee against Torture et al., above n. 331.

334 E. Parens, 'On Good and Bad Forms of Medicalization' (2013) 27(1) *Bioethics* 28–35, 29.

335 Ibid, 30.

third-sex models. Nevertheless, this new approach provides a firm ethical basis for policies and practices that avoid both the violence of medical 'normalisation' and the symbolic violence of social and legal 'othering'.

6. CONCLUSIONS

Elizabeth Reis' work on the nineteenth-century history of intersex portrayed a future where intersex people could be rescued from an assumed criminality and perversion through medicalisation. This co-opted an historical Western conception of hermaphroditism into a hegemonic and global medical model that 'normalises' intersex bodies, leaving a vacuum that has been filled by new concepts of gender. Those concepts also have an origin in medicine.

The medical construction of intersex bodies as disordered has justified so-called 'normalising' interventions to make intersex bodies more typically female or male. Opposition to such interventions by intersex advocates has been met by attempts to marginalise and discredit critics, and reassert clinical authority over the bodies of women and men with 'disorders of sex development'. However, claims of clinical consensus have been selectively constructed and applied, including through biased research and authoritarian epistemology. These practices have been employed to support clinical beliefs that lack evidence, and they have perpetuated the isolation of affected families and individuals. Limited transparency and lack of access to justice have helped to perpetuate forced and coercive clinical practices. There is no clear evidence of change to clinical practices; disturbing genital 'enhancements' and other 'normalising' practices persist.

The new twentieth-century concept of gender has facilitated new understandings of identity and diverse forms of self-identification, but the discourse used to justify these concepts remain wedded to pre-existing, often abstracted, concepts of biology and embodiment, such that non-normative bodies justify the possibility of non-normative identities. The construction of intersex as a third legal sex category has been accompanied by pious hopes and unfounded expectations of the consequences. However, the existence of such classifications does not equate with the valuing of intersex bodies, nor recognition of the diversity of intersex identities and experiences – including the seeming majority of intersex persons who identify with sex assigned at birth or a different binary sex. Intersex has often simply been instrumentalised for the benefit of other, intersecting, populations. The creation of third categories associated with intersex bodies has created profound risks, including the paradoxical reinforcement of a narrowed and normative gender binary.

These developments combine to have the effect that intersex bodies are 'normalised' by medicine while society and the law simultaneously 'other' intersex identities. This has created an untenable situation where medicine constructs intersex bodies as either female or male, while law and society construct intersex as neither female nor male. Neither approach provides individuals born with non-normative sex characteristics the same rights to bodily integrity and self-determination that other populations generally take for granted. Further, claims that medicalisation tackles stigma, discrimination and othering are mirrored in claims that legal othering tackles medicalisation; neither claim is supported by evidence.

Legal and regulatory reform and Parliamentary inquiries in Australia have failed to protect the rights of intersex children to bodily integrity, including in medical settings funded and nominally under the aegis of Australian governments. Attempts at reforms to recognise the rights of intersex people have either failed to adequately comprehend the population affected or lacked adequate implementation. To a significant extent, this is because such actions have frequently addressed matters of identity without consideration of matters relating to embodiment. However, it also would appear that clinicians and medicine interact with third-sex models, at times exhibiting similar essentialist concepts around sex and gender, while also benefiting from misconceptions, including consequences that limit public comprehension and scrutiny of so-called 'normalising' practices.

Underlying this tangled web of disjunctions and paradoxes are issues of knowing, truth and justice; about what it means to have an intersex variation and the personal and societal consequences that arise from that understanding. In many ways, these questions have been made more complex by the creation of a new language of 'disorders of sex development', and the co-option of intersex into 'LGBTI' constructs centred on matters of identity. Nevertheless, these twin concepts of medicalisation and sexual othering can each be regarded as new formulations of older concepts. Now, as then, biological essentialism and ideas of sexual abjection underpin 'normalising' medical interventions and create risks associated with claims of deception. Disentangling these complexities and paradoxes necessitates the shedding of more light on both medical and third-sex models, critical analysis and different perspectives.

An emerging advocacy and human rights consensus focuses on simple common demands, for self-determination and the rights to bodily integrity and truth, demanding an end to forced and coercive medical interventions, social prejudice, stigma and abjection.

Policymakers should act to end forced and coercive medical interventions and ensure the development of human rights-affirming standards of care. States should also interrogate their need to legally register citizens by sex or gender. As long as legal classification is required, access to binary and neutrally-termed 'non-binary' sex/gender markers should be available for any person (intersex or not) preferring such options on the basis of self-determination.

INTERSEX CHILDREN AND THE UN CONVENTION ON THE RIGHTS OF THE CHILD

Kirsten Sandberg

1. INTRODUCTION

The term 'intersex children' is often used as a short term for children born with ambiguous sex characteristics, or put differently, diagnosed as having special medical conditions associated with differences in sex development.[1] In fact there are a number of varieties, but the common feature is that it is difficult to determine whether the child is a girl or a boy. A major question is whether the child should be assigned a sex at birth or in early infancy and go

[1] J. Garland (2016), *On science law and medicine: The case of gender-'normalizing' interventions on children who are diagnosed as different in sex development*, Uppsala universitet (dissertation), preface.

through surgery and other forms of treatment to obtain that sex. For decades such medical interventions have been performed in the belief that they were necessary. However, doubt has been cast on whether it is possible to successfully assign a gender to an infant.[2] Not only is it questionable whether the treatment is beneficial to the person concerned, but it has also gradually become known that the treatment in many instances has had various harmful effects on the children (and later adults) concerned, both physically and mentally.[3] Consequently, over the last 10 to 15 years increasing attention has been paid to the person's human rights in this regard.

Children have rights under the UN Convention on the Rights of the Child (CRC) as well as under all other human rights conventions. This chapter mainly deals with the CRC, which focuses specifically on children and whose provisions are adapted to their special situation and needs, but other conventions will be mentioned where they are relevant. The chapter seeks to interpret and apply the CRC in the context of intersex children, in order to answer the question of whether a child may and should be assigned a sex in the early stages of life. The aim is also to outline the more specific obligations of the state under the Convention in this respect.

Almost all states in the world have ratified the CRC, making it a globally recognised instrument.[4] The implementation of the CRC in the various countries is monitored by the UN Committee on the Rights of the Child, which is a body comprised of 18 members from around the world, so-called independent experts.

---

2 Ibid, pp. 108–118.

3 L. Brinkmann, K. Schuetzmann and H. Richter-Appelt, 'Gender Assignment and Medical History of Individuals with Different Forms of Intersexuality: Evaluation of Medical Records and the Patients' Perspective' (2007) 4(4) *J of Sexual Med* 964–980; UN Special Rapporteur on the right of everyone to the enjoyment of the highest attainable standard of physical and mental health, Report to the General Assembly (on informed consent and right to health) 2009, A/64/272, para. 49; Swiss National Advisory Commission on Biomedical Ethics NEK-CNE, On the Management of Differences of Sex Development: Ethical Issues Relating to 'Intersexuality' (Berne, 2012) 8 and 13; WHO, 'Sexual Health, Human Rights and the Law' (2015) at <http://www.who.int/gender-equity-rights/knowledge/sexual-health-human-rights-and-the-law/en/>, 26, para. 3.4.9 (last accessed 27.05.2018); Council of Europe, 'Human Rights and Intersex People', Issue paper published by the Council of Europe Commissioner for Human Rights (2015) at <https://wcd.coe.int/ViewDoc.jsp?p=&Ref=CommDH/Issue Paper(2015)1&Language=lanEnglish&direct=true> (last accessed 17.02.2018); UNFE, 'Free and Equal, United Nations for LGBT Equality, Fact Sheet Intersex' (undated) at <https://www.unfe.org/system/unfe-65-Intersex_Factsheet_ENGLISH.pdf> (last accessed 17.02.2018); Swiss NGO Report 2014: Intersex Genital Mutilations. Human Rights Violations of Children with Variations of Sex Anatomy, compiled by: Zwischengeschlecht.org (Human Rights NGO), Intersex.ch (Peer Support Group) and Verein SI Selbsthilfe Intersexualität (Parents Peer Support Group), submitted as a shadow report to the CRC in 2014; and K. Karkazis and W.C. Rossi, 'Ethics for the Pediatrician: Disorders of Sex Development: Optimizing Care' (2010) 31 *Pediatr. Rev* e82–e85, e84, 1st column.

4 All states in the world except the US.

The ratifying states are obliged to submit reports to the Committee every five years on their efforts to implement the Convention, although there are no sanctions if they are late. Based on the state's own report and additional information from various sources, the Committee holds a dialogue with a delegation from the state and afterwards issues 'concluding observations' with recommendations to the state on how to improve the implementation of the Convention. In addition, the Committee has issued 23 general comments providing guidance to states on the interpretation and implementation of certain rights or in certain contexts. None of the general comments have gender identity or difference in sex development as its main topic, but it is touched upon in a few of them. General comments and concluding observations will be referred to below.

Children's rights are indivisible, and the Convention should be interpreted in a holistic way, meaning that the rights should not be seen separately or in isolation from each other. Four of its articles have been termed 'general principles' by the Committee, which implies that they are cross-cutting and should be used in the interpretation and application of all the other articles. These are Article 2 on the right to non-discrimination, Article 3 no. 1 on the best interests of the child, Article 6 on the right to life, survival and development and Article 12 on the right to be heard.[5] The right not to be discriminated against because of an intersex condition is a different issue from the question of whether or not a child should undergo surgery and other forms of treatment for its intersex condition.

Other relevant CRC provisions are Article 24 on the right to health, Article 8 on the right to identity, Article 16 on the right to private life, Article 19 on protection from all forms of violence, and Article 24(3) on harmful practices. The implications for intersex children of the general principles and the just-mentioned provisions will be discussed below.

2. NON-DISCRIMINATION

2.1. OVERVIEW

The right not to be discriminated against because of an intersex condition mainly relates to situations in the child's life other than the question of whether or not the child should undergo surgery and other forms of treatment for its intersex condition. However, there might be a discrimination issue in determining who

[5] COMMITTEE ON THE RIGHTS OF THE CHILD, Treaty-specific guidelines regarding the form and content of periodic reports to be submitted by States parties under article 44, para. 1(b), of the Convention on the Rights of the Child (rev 2015), 03.03.2015, UN Doc CRC/C/58/Rev.3, paras. 23–27.

should receive treatment and who should not. The whole notion of assigning a sex to a child could be termed discriminatory as it is based on the stereotyping of persons as being either men or women and does not accept the child as it is, with unclear sex characteristics. It does not take into account the 'fluidity of gender'.[6] The Joint General Recommendation No. 31(CEDAW)/General Comment No. 18 (CRC) on harmful practices explains that harmful practices are 'strongly connected to and reinforce socially constructed gender roles … and sometimes reflect negative perceptions or discriminatory beliefs towards certain disadvantaged groups of women and children' (para. 8).[7] Although the Joint General Comment refers to systems of patriarchal power relations and has a particular focus on girls, it recognises that boys are also victims of harmful practices (para. 3). It does not mention children who do not fit into any of these categories, but the negative perceptions and society's wish to construct gender roles are just as pressing for this group, if not more. I will return to this issue in Sections 3.4 and 3.5 below.

CRC Article 2 holds that states shall respect and ensure the rights in the Convention without discrimination of any kind, irrespective of the child's or his or her parents' or legal guardian's race, colour, sex, language, religion, political or other opinion, national, ethnic or social origin, property, disability, birth or other status.

A basic requirement for considering an action or a practice with regard to intersex children to be discriminatory would be that intersex is covered by Article 2 as one of the grounds on which discrimination is prohibited. The issue of whether it is covered will be discussed in the following, based on the Committee's general comments. Then I will briefly touch upon the issues of whether a differential treatment may still be justifiable owing to it having a legitimate aim and being proportionate. Finally, I will look at some concluding observations from the Committee and other treaty bodies.

2.2. INTERSEX AS A GROUND FOR DISCRIMINATION

Gender identity is not explicitly mentioned in Article 2, but the term 'other status' makes it possible to include other grounds than those mentioned. The Committee on the Rights of the Child has interpreted the expression to

6 J. Viau-Colindres, M. Axelrad and L.P. Karaviti, 'Bringing back the term "intersex"' (2017) 5 *Pediatrics* 1405.

7 Joint General Comment No. 18 (2014) Joint General Recommendation/General Comment No. 31 of the Committee on the Elimination of Discrimination against Women and No. 18 of the Committee on the Rights of the Child on harmful practices, 04.11.2014, CEDAW/C/GC/31-CRC/C/GC/18.

include sexual orientation and gender identity, the latter being the most relevant in our context. Sexual orientation was mentioned in two of the Committee's early General Comments, no. 3 on HIV/AIDS and no. 4 on adolescent health and development, both from 2003.[8] Gender identity was first touched upon in General Comment No. 13 (2011) on the right of the child to freedom from all forms of violence, where transgender and transsexual children were included among potentially vulnerable or marginalised groups of children who should be protected from discrimination.[9] However, intersex children were not expressly covered.

General Comment No. 15 (2013) on the child's right to health was the first one to include gender identity in general under discrimination grounds,[10] which includes intersex, whereas No. 14 (2013) on best interests does not list any discrimination grounds. Sexual orientation is mentioned in another context, but gender identity is not.[11] Joint General Comment No. 18 on harmful practices (2014), issued jointly with the CEDAW Committee, simply lists 'sex, gender, age and other grounds' as prohibited categories for discrimination.[12]

The first time the situation and rights of intersex children were explicitly acknowledged in a General Comment by the Committee was in 2016, in General Comment No. 20 on the rights of the child during adolescence. In the chapter 'Adolescents requiring particular attention' there is a separate subsection on 'Lesbian, gay, bisexual, transgender and intersex adolescents'. This group of children is described as 'commonly fac[ing] persecution, including abuse and violence, stigmatization, discrimination, bullying, exclusion from education and training, as well as a lack of family and social support, or access to sexual and reproductive health services and information'.[13] The General Comment links

---

8 General Comment No. 3 (2003) HIV/AIDS and the rights of the child, 17.03.2003, CRC/GC/2003/3, para. 8, and General Comment No. 4 (2003) Adolescent health and development in the context of the Convention on the Rights of the Child, 01.07.2003, CRC/GC/2003/4, para. 6.

9 General Comment No. 13 (2011) The right of the child to freedom from all forms of violence, 18.04.2011, CRC/C/GC/13, paras. 60 and 72 (g). See K. Sandberg, 'The Rights of LGBTI Children under the Convention on the Rights of the Child' (2015) 33(4) *Nordic Journal of Human Rights* 337–352.

10 General Comment No. 15 (2013) on the right of the child to the enjoyment of the highest attainable standard of health (Art. 24), 17.04.2013, CRC/C/GC/15, para. 8.

11 General Comment No. 14 (2013) on the right of the child to have his or her best interests taken as a primary consideration (Art. 3, para. 1), 29.05.2013, CRC/C/GC/14, para. 55.

12 Joint General Comment No. 18, above n. 7, paras. 6, 14.

13 General Comment No. 20 (2016) on the implementation of the rights of the child during adolescence, 06.12.2016, CRC/C/GC/20, para. 33, with reference to Statement dated 13 May 2015 by the Committee of the Rights of the Child and other United Nations and regional human rights mechanisms, available from <www.ohchr.org/EN/NewsEvents/Pages/DisplayNews.aspx?NewsID=15941&LangID=E> (last accessed 06.09.2017).

these rather dramatic experiences 'to low self-esteem, higher rates of depression, suicide and homelessness'.[14]

Specifically regarding discrimination, the General Comment states:

> 34. The Committee … urges States to … repeal all laws criminalizing or otherwise discriminating against individuals on the basis of their sexual orientation, gender identity or intersex status and adopt laws prohibiting discrimination on those grounds. States should also take effective action to protect all lesbian, gay, bisexual, transgender and intersex adolescents from all forms of violence, discrimination or bullying by raising public awareness and implementing safety and support measures.[15]

The word 'urges' indicates that it is a strong recommendation. Discriminatory legislation against persons with intersex is unacceptable and should be repealed, and instead legislation should contain a prohibition against discrimination on the grounds mentioned. As we can see, intersex status is mentioned expressly in addition to the more general term 'gender identity', making it more visible. Besides legislation, the states have an obligation to take effective measures to change attitudes in order to prevent discrimination and violence against this group. More direct safety and support measures to protect them are also needed.

In General Comment No. 21 (2017) on children in street situations, sexual orientation and gender identity/expression are listed among the diverse characteristics of children in such situations.[16] Under systemic discrimination the same characteristics are mentioned as a basis for multiple and intersecting forms of discrimination.[17] Intersex children also appear explicitly in this General Comment, among the causes for children being in such situations. They are grouped together with LGBT children in this way:

> children cast out from families as a result of questioning their sexuality or identifying as lesbian, gay, bisexual, transgender, intersex or asexual …[18]

2.3. LEGITIMATE AND PROPORTIONATE?

Based on the general comments referred to above, there is no doubt that intersex status is covered as a prohibited ground for discrimination. Still, a differential treatment – or equal treatment of unequal cases – may be legal if it has a legitimate aim and is proportionate. For instance, making all children

14 Ibid.
15 Ibid, para. 34.
16 General Comment No. 21 (2017) on children in street situations, 21.06.2017, CRC/C/GC/21, para. 6.
17 Ibid, para. 26.
18 Ibid, para. 8.

have a shower after physical exercise lessons at school may have the legitimate aim of hygiene. However, if an intersex child feels strongly about not appearing naked in front of the other pupils, it may be disproportionate to require the child to do so.

It is hard to think of examples where it would be legitimate to treat the intersex child differently in a negative way. On the other hand, positive discrimination of intersex children in the form of measures aimed at redressing a situation of real inequality, would have a legitimate aim and would often be acceptable and even desirable. For instance, with regard to sexual and reproductive health services, General Comment No. 20 states that

> particular efforts need to be made to overcome barriers of stigma and fear experienced by, for example, adolescent girls, girls with disabilities and lesbian, gay, bisexual, transgender and intersex adolescents, in gaining access to such services.[19]

Thus, if no extra effort is made to reach intersex children, it may be an example of wrongful equal treatment where their needs should have been specifically accommodated.

The CRC and the Committee's jurisprudence do not deal with the issue and it will not be pursued further in this chapter.

2.4. TREATY BODIES' RECOMMENDATIONS TO STATES

In its concluding observations,[20] the Committee on the Rights of the Child in 2015 started including intersex children among the groups exposed to discrimination. However, other treaty bodies had already pointed to the discrimination against intersex persons before that. The CEDAW Committee in 2011 to Costa Rica expressed its concern about 'discrimination in the access to education, employment and health-care services against lesbian, bisexuals, transgender and intersex women in the State party'.[21] As early as 2009 that same Committee requested Germany to 'enter into dialogue with non-governmental organizations of intersexual and transsexual people in order to better understand their claims and to take effective action to protect their human rights', without mentioning non-discrimination explicitly at that time.

The UN Economic and Social Council in 2011 noted with concern that

> transsexual and inter-sexed persons are often assimilated to persons with mental illness and that the State party's policies, legislative or otherwise, have led to discrimination

[19] General Comment No. 20, above n, 13, para. 60.
[20] Explained in the introduction to this chapter.
[21] CEDAW/C/CRI/CO/5-6, Concluding Observations Costa Rica (2011), para. 40.

> against these persons as well as to violations of their sexual and reproductive health rights (arts. 12, 2.2).[22]

The practice of aligning intersex persons with persons with mental illnesses led to discrimination, as they were thus ascribed some features that they did not have. Furthermore, they were not provided with the services they should have received based on their own needs.

Out of the 16 states reviewed under the CRC in 2014, discrimination against LGBTI children was raised with six: Hungary, the Holy See, Russia, Kyrgyzstan, Portugal and Venezuela.[23] To Russia the wording was quite strong, the Committee expressing its concern at:

> the recent legislation of the State party prohibiting 'propaganda of unconventional sexual relationships', ... which encourages the stigmatization of and discrimination against lesbian, gay, bisexual, transgender and intersex (LGBTI) persons, including children, and children from LGBTI families.[24]

Discrimination was linked to violence as the vague definition of propaganda led to persecution of the LGBTI community, 'including through abuse and violence, in particular against underage LGBTI rights activists'.[25]

Russia was recommended to repeal the law, as it is seen as unacceptable for a state to have legislation prohibiting so-called unconventional sexual relationships. It gives the opposite signal of that which a government is supposed to send to its people to avoid discrimination. However, abolishing the Act was not deemed to be sufficient, attitudes also needed to be changed. Thus, Russia was recommended to ensure that LGBTI children and children from LGBTI families are not subjected to any forms of discrimination, by raising the public awareness of equality and non-discrimination on the basis of sexual orientation and gender identity.

---

22 E/C.12/DEU/CO/5, Concluding observations Germany (2011), para. 26.

23 Based on the author's own examination of the concluding observations. Concluding observations on the combined third, fourth and fifth periodic reports of Hungary, 14.10.2014, CRC/C/HUN/ CO/3–5, paras. 19–20; Concluding observations on the second periodic report of the Holy See, 25.02.2014, CRC/C/VAT/ CO/2, paras. 25–26; Concluding observations on the combined fourth and fifth periodic reports of the Russian Federation, 25.02.2014, CRC/C/RUS/CO/4–5, paras. 24–25; Concluding observations on the combined third and fourth periodic report of Kyrgyzstan, 07.07.2014, CRC/C/KGZ/CO/3–4, paras. 18–19; Concluding observations on the combined third and fourth periodic report of Portugal, 25.02.2014, CRC/C/PRT/CO/3–4, paras. 25–26(a); and Concluding observations on the combined third to fifth periodic reports of the Bolivarian Republic of Venezuela, 13.10.2014, CRC/C/VEN/CO/3–5, paras. 27–28(c).

24 Concluding observations to Russia, above n. 23, para. 24.

25 Ibid.

Examining the concluding observations in 2017, it appears that the Committee's practice still varies with regard to the issue of discrimination against intersex children. To 11 out of 20 countries, LGBTI children were not mentioned at all.[26] To the Democratic Republic of Congo, Mongolia and Serbia, discrimination against lesbian, gay, bisexual and transgender children were included in the part on discrimination, whereas intersex children were not.[27]

The reason may be that there simply was no information before the Committee about intersex children in those countries. Another possibility is that the Committee has started having doubts about whether intersex children should be grouped together with LGBT children. Such doubts may be valid as it is not self-evident that they face the same discrimination issues. Having an intersex condition is not visible in the same way as the others can be since it does not manifest itself in practices in relation to partners, nor in the expression of gender identity.

However, the concluding observations to several states did mention intersex children in the section on discrimination. Ecuador was requested to

> Adopt a strategy, specific legal provisions and clear guidelines for public authorities aimed at upholding non-discrimination against children on any grounds and combating stigma against … lesbian, bisexual, gay, transgender and intersex children.[28]

---

26 Antigua and Barbuda, Barbados, Central African Republic, DPR Korea, Estonia, Georgia, Malawi, Qatar, Saint Vincent and the Grenadines, Tajikistan, Vanuatu. See Concluding observations on the combined second to fourth periodic reports of Antigua and Barbuda, 30.06.2017, CRC/C/ATG/CO/2-4; Concluding observations on the second periodic report of Barbados, 03.02.2017, CRC/C/BRB/CO/2; Concluding observations on the second periodic report of Central African Republic, 03.02.2017, CRC/C/CAF/CO/2; Concluding observations on the fifth periodic report of the Democratic People's Republic of Korea, 23.10.2017, CRC/C/PRK/CO/5; Concluding observations on the combined second to fourth periodic reports of Estonia, 08.03.2017, CRC/C/EST/CO/2-4; Concluding observations on the fourth periodic report of Georgia, 09.03.2017, CRC/C/GEO/CO/4; Concluding observations on the combined third to fifth periodic reports of Malawi, 06.03.2017, CRC/C/MWI/CO/3-5; Concluding observations on the combined third and fourth periodic reports of Qatar, 22.06.2017, CRC/C/QAT/CO/3-4; Concluding observations on the combined second and third periodic reports of Saint Vincent and the Grenadines, 13.03.2017, CRC/C/VCT/CO/2-3; Concluding observations on the combined third to fifth periodic reports of Tajikistan, 29.09.2017, CRC/C/TJK/CO/3-5 (advance unedited version); Concluding observations on the second to fourth periodic reports of Vanuatu, 29.09.2017, CRC/C/VUT/CO/2-4 (advance unedited version).

27 Concluding observations to the Democratic Republic of the Congo, 28.02.017, CRC/C/COD/CO/3-5, para. 15; Concluding observations on the fifth periodic report of Mongolia, 12.07.2017, CRC/C/MNG/CO/5, para. 15 (the same 4 groups mentioned in para. 18(c) on respect for the child's views); Concluding observations on the combined second and third periodic reports of Serbia, 07.03.2017, CRC/C/SRB/CO/2-3, paras. 22–23.

28 CRC/C/ECU/CO/5-6, Concluding observations on the combined fifth and sixth periodic reports of Ecuador, 26.10.2017, para. 16(c). In the Concluding observations to Moldova, LGBTI children were also included in the section on non-discrimination, Concluding observations on the combined fourth and fifth periodic report of the Republic of Moldova, 29.09.2017 (advance unedited version), CRC/C/MDA/4-5.

To Cameroon, the Committee expressed concern that the delegation during the dialogue rejected the identity of lesbian, gay, bisexual, transgender and intersex children. Rejecting their identity means closing one's eyes to their existence, which paves the way to stigma and discrimination. The Committee urged Cameroon to recognise their identity and protect them against discrimination, as well as conduct awareness-raising and educational programmes.[29]

To Romania, intersex children were among those that the Committee was deeply concerned about with regard to discrimination in access to education, healthcare, employment and a decent standard of living, and the state was urged to ensure full implementation of relevant existing laws prohibiting discrimination, including by enforcing monitoring and complaints mechanisms and strengthening public education campaigns.[30]

For Bhutan, the issue was included under violence, where the Committee was concerned about the 'occurrence of peer violence and sexual harassment in schools, also affecting lesbian, gay, bisexual, transsexual and intersex children' and recommended that initiatives to combat such acts, including bullying, were developed. The recommendation was also to 'train teachers and students to resolve conflicts peacefully, to create an environment of tolerance and respect'.[31] This is in line with Article 29 on the aims of education, one of the aims being '(d) The preparation of the child for responsible life in a free society, in the spirit of understanding, peace, tolerance, equality of sexes …', which is crucial for improving the situation of children in these situations.

Interestingly, recommendations are also made with regard to political participation of children with differences in gender identity or sex development. To Lebanon, the matter was included under respect for the views of the child and, in particular, regarding participation in the Lebanese National Youth Parliament. The recommendation was to promote inclusive participation in that Parliament by ensuring that, among others, lesbian, gay, bisexual, transgender and intersex children are able to participate fully.[32] On a similar note, to Ecuador the same groups of children were included under cooperation with civil society, in a recommendation to

> [s]ystematically and meaningfully involve non-governmental organizations working in the field of children's rights, including … organizations representing … lesbian,

---

29 Concluding observations on the combined third to fifth periodic reports of Cameroon, CRC/C/CMR/CO/3-5, 06.07.2017, paras. 14–15.

30 Concluding observations on the fifth periodic report of Romania, CRC/C/ROU/CO/5, 13.07.2017, paras. 16–17.

31 Concluding observations on the combined third to fifth periodic reports of Bhutan, CRC/C/BTN/CO/3-5, 05.07.2017, paras. 38–39.

32 Concluding observations on the combined fourth and fifth periodic report of Lebanon, CRC/C/LBN/CO/4-5, 22.06.2017, para. 16(e).

> gay, bisexual, transgender and intersex children, in the development, implementation, monitoring and evaluation of laws, policies and programmes relating to children's rights.[33]

Although such recommendations are not made under the heading of discrimination, they concern the inclusion of children who may otherwise be left out.

Thus, it is worth noticing that discrimination of various groups is not only dealt with as a general matter of discrimination, but also in more specific sections on violence, participation or cooperation with civil society. By being more targeted, these recommendations may be easier for the states to implement – and for civil society and the groups in question to follow up on whether the state is actually doing what it is supposed to.

To the question of whether it is right to group intersex children together with LGBT children, it must primarily depend on what the children themselves would prefer. However, opinions on this may differ, and in the absence of information on an agreed view to the contrary, I would say it is better to include them than to leave them out. In the above-mentioned examples from the concluding observations it seems justifiable to include them. Even if their situation is somewhat different, some of the children may experience discrimination in various ways and then need this support.

3. MEDICAL INTERVENTIONS AND THE CRC

3.1. THE RIGHT TO IDENTITY

The right of the child to identity follows from Article 8(1) CRC:

> States Parties undertake to respect the right of the child to preserve his or her identity, including nationality, name and family relations as recognized by law without unlawful interference.

While nationality, name and family relations are explicitly mentioned, and the background of creation of the provision was the disappearances of children in Argentina in the 1970s and 1980s,[34] the article is not formulated in such a way as to limit the scope to those three aspects. The word 'including' indicates that the list is not exclusive. The identity of a person is commonly understood

---

33 Concluding observations to Ecuador, above n. 28, para. 14(b).

34 R Hodgkin and P. Newell (2007), *Implementation Handbook for the Convention on the Rights of the Child*, UNICEF, p. 113.

in a broader sense as everything constituting the person's feeling of self and distinguishing the person from others.

In General Comment No. 14 on the best interests of the child, identity is mentioned as one of the elements to be taken into account in assessing the child's best interests under Article 3. It is interpreted broadly to encompass 'characteristics such as sex, sexual orientation, national origin, religion and beliefs, cultural identity, personality'.[35] Although sexual orientation is mentioned, and gender identity is not, there is no reason why the latter should not be considered as an aspect of the child's identity in line with the others mentioned.[36]

The obligation of the state under Article 8 is to respect the right of the child to 'preserve' his or her identity. When a child is born with an intersex condition, it is part of the child's identity at that time, and preserving it would mean that it should not be changed. This is especially so since any surgical sex assignment is an irreversible process where the child cannot at a later stage decide to return to its original intersex identity or choose the other sex.

The provision holds open the possibility that an interference with this right could be lawful. Probably this will be the case if it is necessary for the best interests of the child.[37] A medical intervention on an intersex infant may in certain instances be medically necessary and thus justifiable even if it would mean assigning a sex to the child. However, 'medically necessary' is a term which creates uncertainty. In light of the far-reaching consequences for the child, it should be interpreted strictly and probably limited to cases where the child's vital bodily functions otherwise would not work. Even then the intervention should be limited and carried out without assigning a sex unless it is an unavoidable part of the process. Since all decisions concerning a child have to be made according to the best interests of the child, the medical issues cannot be seen in isolation. An overall assessment needs to be made, taking all aspects into account.

Another question is whether parents can consent to an interference with the child's identity. This concerns the issue of the child's autonomy which will be dealt with in Section 3.3.

3.2. THE RIGHT TO INTEGRITY AND PRIVATE LIFE

Under Article 19 CRC the child has the right to be protected from all forms of violence. The concept of violence in the provision is broad, encompassing among others all violations of the child's physical integrity, however small. Surgery on a

35 General Comment No. 14, above n. 11, para. 55.
36 This is supported by Hodgkin and Newell, above n. 34, p. 116.
37 Ibid.

child is an interference with its physical integrity, as is medication, when the child cannot consent him- or herself. Still, it is accepted that medical interventions may be performed on small children, but only if they are medically necessary and in the best interests of the child under Article 3(1). If an intervention is not necessary for life-saving purposes, the need for the intervention at any stage should be balanced against the harm that may be caused and not least the possibilities to postpone the decision. The issue of consent will be discussed below.

The child's right to private life is regulated in Article 16 CRC, stating that the child should not be subjected to arbitrary or unlawful interference with his or her privacy. The medical process of sex assignment does not only include surgery and medication but extensive and repeated examinations of intimate parts of the body as well. Again, this may be necessary as part of a medical process which may all in all be in the best interests of the child, but only within strict limits.

3.3. AUTONOMY

As mentioned, surgery and other medical interventions are often performed on infants and young children. Obviously, infants cannot form a view on whether to undergo the interventions. Somewhat older children may have views on whether surgery is scary or painful, but will still not be able to assess the whole situation in order to make up their minds in any meaningful way as to whether to undergo the treatment. Hence the question is whether it is acceptable to perform the interventions with the consent of the parents.

The parents normally represent their children in decision-making, at least up to the point where children are considered to be competent to make decisions for themselves. Under the CRC children have no explicit right to self-determination. What they do have is the right under Article 12 to participate in all matters affecting themselves, as soon as they are capable of forming their own views. Participation means the right to express their views freely and that their views should be given due weight in accordance with the age and maturity of the child (Article 12(1)). Before decisions are made by the authorities, including doctors in the healthcare system, the decision-making body has the obligation to actively provide the child with the opportunity to be heard (Article 12(2)).

The Committee has stated that children are able to express views from a very early age and they need to be involved even if they do not understand the full implications of a decision.[38] Consequently, hearing a small child on a sex

[38] General Comment No. 7, Implementing child rights in early childhood, 20.09.2006, CRC/C/GC/7/Rev.1, para. 14, and General Comment No. 12 (2009) The right of the child to be heard, 20.07.2009, CRC/C/GC/12, para. 21.

assignment issue would be in line with Article 12 if the information given and the situation of the hearing are adapted to the child and its age. However, even though hearing a small child in decisions on sex assignment may be necessary, it does not protect its autonomy.

The autonomy of the child is a central underlying value of the CRC. Although the Convention does not explicitly give the child a right to self-determination, the right to identity and the right to privacy both imply a certain autonomy for the child. Furthermore, Article 12 clearly emphasises the value of respect for the child's own views. Making decisions with far-reaching consequences for the child before the child is able to make up its mind on the issue itself is not reconcilable with the concept of autonomy and respect for the child's views as expressed in the CRC, provided the decisions can be postponed. For most intersex children, the decision concerning potential medical intervention may be postponed until the child is of a sufficient age and maturity to have a well-reasoned position on whether or not to have treatment, and on what kinds of treatment they are willing to undergo.[39] Indeed, the decision of assigning a sex to the child is so crucial for the child's identity, integrity and future life that treatment should not be carried out without the child's consent, which is a stronger requirement than just listening to the child's view, if it is at all possible to wait.

Consequently, if an intervention is performed with parental consent at an earlier stage without being strictly medically necessary for vital bodily functions, or going further than needed, this is a violation of the child's right to identity under Article 8 and the right to integrity under Article 19, and will be contrary to the best interests of the child under Article 3.

Under Article 18(1) CRC parents have the primary responsibility for the upbringing and development of their children, including for making decisions on behalf of the child. However, their competence is limited by the child's right to identity, integrity and participation. A further limitation follows from the same provision, stating that the best interests of the child 'will be their basic concern'. Consequently, where a treatment can be postponed until the child can at least form a well-reasoned view or even decide for itself, the parents cannot validly consent to such treatment.

3.4. HARMFUL PRACTICES

Another approach to the medical interventions on intersex children is to view it as a harmful practice. According to Article 24(3) states shall 'take all effective and appropriate measures with a view to abolishing traditional practices prejudicial

39 Swiss National Advisory Commission, above n. 3, p. 14. See further references above n. 3.

to the health of children'. The practices no longer need to be 'traditional', as new practices may be just as harmful as the traditional ones.[40] Harmful practices are often based on discrimination of the group which is exposed to the practice, and female genital mutilation is one of the harmful practices that states shall seek to abolish. The practices 'often involve violence and cause physical and/or psychological harm or suffering'.[41] As mentioned in Section 2.1 on discrimination above, Joint General Comment No. 18 on harmful practices does not mention persons without a clear gender. However, depending on the circumstances, the medical interventions performed on intersex children may fall within its definition of harmful practices and have been termed 'intersex genital mutilation'. In any event, they certainly concern surgical manipulation of the genitals. Whether this can be considered a mutilation depends on the medical necessity.

3.5. BEST INTERESTS OF THE CHILD

Some would argue that it is in the best interests of the child to have a sex assigned at an early age even if it is not medically necessary, taking into account the psycho-social aspects of being neither a girl nor a boy. Indeed, this has been the justification for performing such surgery on infants for decades, and it is true that a best interests assessment should cover all relevant aspects (see General Comment No. 14). However, the parents and doctors would have to make that decision on behalf of the child. As Garland indicates, it is debatable how fit the parents are to make decisions in the best interests of their child in such a situation, where their child 'may be a gender variant minority in their own family'.[42] The parents may be in a state of shock and confusion, where their own interest in having a 'normal' child may influence what they think is in their child's best interests.[43] Nor is the physician in a position to judge the full implications of one or the other solution for the child and the child's future life and thus make a well-informed and impartial consideration of its best interests, which are to be seen, as far as possible, from the child's perspective. Actually, it is questionable if anybody else than the child itself is able to make an informed assessment of its best interests in this respect, both regarding the decision of whether or not to assign a sex, and not least, regarding what that sex should be.[44] Consequently,

---

40 See Joint General Comment No. 18, above n. 7.

41 Joint General Comment No. 18, above n. 7, para. 14.

42 Garland, above n. 1, p. 124. On parents' confusion, see also T.M. Jenkins and S.E. Short, 'Negotiating intersex: A case for revisiting the theory of social diagnosis' (2017) 175 *Social Science & Medicine* 91–98, pp. 94–95.

43 A. Wilcox, I. Côté and G. Pagé, L'enfant intersexué: dysphorie entre le modèle médical et l'intérêt supérieur de l'enfant (2015) 142 *Intervention* 65–77.

44 Garland, above n. 1, p. 93.

even if one were to accept the assumption that the decision should be based on the best interests of the child, the decision would have to be postponed.

However, regardless of whether or not anybody is able to carry out a best interests assessment at such an early stage, the best interests of the child cannot override other rights under the CRC. As argued above, a decision to assign a sex to a child when it is not medically necessary constitutes a violation of the child's right to identity, physical integrity and the right to be heard. Adults' assessment that surgery is in the best interests of a child may not be used to set aside these other rights. Additionally, the other rights of the CRC should inform the best interests consideration, implying that the result of the best interests assessment at an early age, if correctly done, would be that the intervention should not be made until the child can have a say.

Another matter is that under CRC Article 3(3), a best interests consideration should be undertaken even if the treatment is considered medically necessary. There may be some cases, though probably not many, where for some reason a medical intervention might not be in the best interests of the child even if it is considered necessary.

4. MEDICAL INTERVENTIONS – TREATY BODIES' RECOMMENDATIONS TO STATES

The first UN treaty body to raise the routine surgical alterations in intersex children with a state was the Committee against Torture (CAT) in its review of Germany in 2011. The Committee noted that the Ethical Council in Germany would review the practices, but was concerned about

> cases where gonads have been removed and cosmetic surgeries on reproductive organs have been performed that entail lifelong hormonal medication, without effective, informed consent of the concerned individuals or their legal guardians, where neither investigation, nor measures of redress have been introduced.[45]

Some rather detailed recommendations were made:

> (a) Ensure the effective application of legal and medical standards following the best practices of granting informed consent to medical and surgical treatment of intersex people, including full information, orally and in writing, on the suggested treatment, its justification and alternatives;
> (b) Undertake investigation of incidents of surgical and other medical treatment of intersex people without effective consent and adopt legal provisions in

[45] Concluding observations of the Committee against Torture, Germany, 12 December 2011, CAT/C/DEU/CO/5, para. 20.

order to provide redress to the victims of such treatment, including adequate compensation;

(c) Educate and train medical and psychological professionals on the range of sexual, and related biological and physical, diversity; and

(d) Properly inform patients and their parents of the consequences of unnecessary surgical and other medical interventions for intersex people.[46]

The Committee did not explicitly request Germany to end the practice but to ensure informed consent and to investigate cases where effective consent might be lacking. However, the recommendations of training professionals and informing parents in (c) and (d) are more far-reaching, in that they may contribute to a greater acceptance of sexual diversity and an increased awareness that these interventions may not be necessary, thus reducing the perceived need to undertake such interventions.

When the Committee on the Rights of the Child for the first time in its review of a state report dealt with sex assignment to intersex children, it chose the angle of harmful practices. Under that heading the Committee in 2015 to Switzerland expressed its deep concern at:

> Cases of medically unnecessary surgical and other procedures on intersex children, without their informed consent, which often entail irreversible consequences and can cause severe physical and psychological suffering, and the lack of redress and compensation in such cases.[47]

Switzerland received this recommendation:

> In line with the recommendations of the National Advisory Commission on Biomedical Ethics on ethical issues relating to intersexuality, ensure that no one is subjected to unnecessary medical or surgical treatment during infancy or childhood, guarantee bodily integrity, autonomy and self-determination to the children concerned, and provide families with intersex children with adequate counselling and support.[48]

As appears from the concern, the surgery was still being practised by some doctors on infants and small children. The Swiss National Advisory Commission on Biomedical Ethics previously had made timely and apt recommendations in 2012 which regrettably the Swiss Government did not comply with. What parents of a new-born intersex child need in the first place is adequate counselling and support, in order to make them understand that a child can live well with that condition until it is able to take decisions itself. The parents

46 Ibid.

47 Concluding observations on the combined second to fourth periodic reports of Switzerland, CRC/C/CHE/CO/2–4, 26 February 2015, para. 42(b).

48 Ibid, para. 43(b).

need this understanding to be able to accept the child as it is and support the child in leading a normal life. The child then needs medical and other forms of counselling and support all the way through childhood as well as when a possible decision is to be taken when it is older.

Crucially, compared with the concluding observations of the Committee against Torture, those of the CRC Committee focus on children more specifically. They also emphasise more clearly the 'bodily integrity, autonomy and self-determination' of the children concerned.

All the same, the Committee against Torture recommendations have served as an inspiration for the CRC Committee.[49] When dealing with Ireland in February 2016 the CRC Committee expanded its recommendations to include investigation, redress and training of professionals,[50] and much the same was done for the UK, in June 2016.[51] The concern and recommendation to Switzerland were repeated to these countries, but with an important change of wording in the concern. The statement included now was 'before they are able to provide their informed consent'[52] which is more to the point than 'without their informed consent', particularly considering the age of the children concerned.

In the recommendation to France in 2016, the autonomy of the child was emphasised somewhat differently:

> Develop and implement a rights-based health-care protocol for intersex children, ensuring that children and their parents are appropriately informed of all options; that children are involved, to the greatest extent possible, in decision-making about their treatment and care; and that no child is subjected to unnecessary surgery or treatment.[53]

The most elaborate recommendations were given to New Zealand in October 2016:

> (b)[54] Develop and implement a child rights-based health care protocol for intersex children, setting the procedures and steps to be followed by health teams, ensuring that no one is subjected to unnecessary medical or surgical treatment during infancy or childhood, guaranteeing the rights of children to bodily integrity, autonomy and self-determination, and provide families with intersex children with adequate counselling and support;

---

49 As foreseen in Sandberg 2015, above n. 9, p. 350.

50 Concluding observations on the combined third and fourth periodic reports of Ireland, 01.03.2016, CRC/C/IRL/CO/3-4, para. 40.

51 Concluding observations on the fifth periodic report of the United Kingdom of Great Britain and Northern Ireland, 12.07.2016, CRC/C/GBR/CO/5, paras. 46–47.

52 Concluding observations to Ireland, above n. 50, and the UK, above n. 51, paras. 39 and 46, respectively.

53 Concluding observations on the fifth periodic report of France, 23.02.2016, CRC/C/FRA/CO/5, para. 48(b)

54 Letter (a) did not concern intersex but early marriage.

> (c) Promptly investigate incidents of surgical and other medical treatment of intersex children without informed consent and adopt legal provisions to provide redress to victims of such treatment, including adequate compensation;
>
> (d) Educate and train medical and psychological professionals on the range of biological and physical sexual diversity and on the consequences of unnecessary surgical and other medical interventions on intersex children;
>
> (e) Extend free access to surgical interventions and medical treatment related to their intersex condition to intersex children between the age of 16 and 18.[55]

Regrettably, the Committee here used the term 'without informed consent' which is not sufficiently clear about whose consent is needed. However, both (b) and (e) represent further steps compared to earlier recommendations. Particularly the development of a protocol would be a great improvement. It should not only provide guidance on procedures but also on the threshold for undertaking medical interventions, preventing the decisions from being fully left to the doctors' discretion. Where practice has been too lenient, it could hopefully be the starting point for a more restrictive practice. As for free access to surgery and other medical interventions to children all the way up to the age of 18, this recommendation is necessary in countries where children above 16 years are considered to be 'adults' in the healthcare system, thus losing the protection they should have under the Convention.

In 2017, similar recommendations were made to Denmark, except the last one (e) which was more country-specific. Additionally, the issue of developing a protocol was separated from the issue of unnecessary medical or surgical treatment, making both of these recommendations stand out more clearly.[56] No other concluding observations to states from the CRC Committee in 2017 mentioned medical interventions on intersex children. Only the discrimination issue was raised (as presented above). The reason may be that the Committee did not have information on the issue of unnecessary medical interventions in the countries in question, making it impossible to state a concern and recommendation in this regard.

5. CONCLUSION

As demonstrated above, the rights of the child to identity, integrity and privacy are central to the treatment of children with differences in sex development.

---

55 Concluding observations on the fifth periodic report of New Zealand, 21.10.2016, CRC/C/NZL/CO/5, para. 25.

56 Concluding observations on the fifth periodic report of Denmark, 26.10.2017, CRC/C/DNK/CO/5, para. 24.

They all support the idea of a certain autonomy for the child in relation to decisions to undergo surgery or other medical treatment. In addition, the right of the child to participate in decisions affecting itself is a strong right and a general principle. Although it does not give the child a right to self-determination, it arguably implies that decisions with far-reaching consequences for the child should not, if at all possible, be made before the child has the maturity to make up its mind in a meaningful way.

Not all decisions regarding a child's health can be postponed; thus, it may be medically necessary to make certain irreversible interventions before the child is able to consent. However, medical necessity should be the only justification for making an irreversible medical decision on behalf of a child at this early age. If this requirement is not met, the intervention will constitute a violation of the child's right to identity, physical integrity, privacy and the right to be heard. As the line of argument is related to the autonomy of the child, parental consent does not change this conclusion, and they cannot validly consent to such treatment.

What is medically necessary is not clear-cut. It needs to be strictly interpreted in order not to lose its restrictive effect. In this chapter it has been limited to the issue of making vital bodily functions work; psycho-social aspects of not being clearly a girl or a boy during childhood should not be included in the understanding of medical necessity. Where it is necessary to perform surgery on an infant or a small child to make its vital bodily functions work, such intervention should be done without assigning a sex, unless it is unavoidable.

Placing the issue under the heading of harmful practices does not mean these medical interventions are not recognised as interferences with identity, integrity etc. Rather, the reason is that they are not stand-alone incidents, but part of a common practice which the state has a responsibility to prevent and seek to eliminate.[57] Like other harmful practices this practice violates several rights.

Some may invoke the best interests of the child as a reason for doing a sex assignment to an infant or a small child even if it is not linked to medically necessary surgery. However, neither the parents, the physician nor anybody else is able to make a well-reasoned best interests consideration in this respect, with such far-reaching implications for the child itself. Even more importantly, the child's best interests may not be used as a justification for violating other rights of the child. Thus, the decision should be postponed until the child is able to make a well-reasoned choice about the procedures.

Consequently, medically unnecessary surgery and other interventions, with irreversible implications, on children who are unable to consent should be regarded as a violation of the UN Convention on the Rights of the Child.

Over the last few years, attention to the issue of persons with differences in sex development has increased rapidly in the international community and many

---

57 General Comment No. 18, above n. 7, para. 9.

initiatives have been taken in the UN system.[58] Among the UN bodies engaging in this area, the Committee on the Rights of the Child has a unique position in dealing only with children and taking a holistic child rights approach to the issue.[59] This makes it all the more important that the Committee keeps raising the situation of intersex children, not only in relation to discrimination but also concerning the harmful practice of unnecessary surgery on small children. In order to do this in a meaningful way the Committee needs information. Like in most areas, the Committee's work is dependent on an exchange with National Human Rights Institutions and civil society, including NGOs and academics. For the Committee to continue issuing concrete and relevant recommendations to states in this area, it is essential that these actors continue to provide it with information about the situation on the ground.

---

58 See e.g. Opening Statement by UN High Commissioner for Human Rights Zeid Ra'ad Al Hussein at the 30th session of the Human Rights Council, <http://www.ohchr.org/EN/NewsEvents/Pages/DisplayNews.aspx?NewsID=16414> (last accessed 17.02.2018); Free & Equal, United Nations for LGBT equality, <https://www.unfe.org/system/unfe-65-Intersex_Factsheet_ENGLISH.pdf> (last accessed 17.02.2018); Expert meeting organised by OHCHR Sept. 2015, <http://www.ohchr.org/EN/NewsEvents/Pages/Astepforwardforintersexvisibility.aspx> (last accessed 17.02.2018); UN Human Rights Council, Report of the Special Rapporteur on torture and other cruel, inhuman or degrading treatment or punishment, 5 January 2016, A/HRC/31/57, <http://www.refworld.org/docid/56c435714.html> (last accessed 27.05.2018), Joint statement by United Nations and regional human rights experts for Intersex Awareness Day 2016, <http://www.ohchr.org/EN/NewsEvents/Pages/DisplayNews.aspx?NewsID=20739&LangID=E> (last accessed 17.02.2018).

59 On a child rights approach, see General Comment No. 21, above n. 16, paras. 10–11.

www.ingramcontent.com/pod-product-compliance
Ingram Content Group UK Ltd.
Pitfield, Milton Keynes, MK11 3LW, UK
UKHW051918100926
8556IPUK00021B/1239

9 781780 684758